Orpheus
in the New World

The Symphony Orchestra as
an American Cultural Institution

by PHILIP HART

W · W · NORTON & COMPANY · INC · NEW YORK ·

125129

Copyright © 1973 by W. W. Norton & Company, Inc.

FIRST EDITION

Library of Congress Cataloging in Publication Data
Hart, Philip, 1914–
 Orpheus in the New World.
 Includes bibliographical references.
 1. Symphony orchestras—United States. I. Title.
ML1211.H3   785'.06'610973   73–3151
ISBN 0–393–02169–6

1 2 3 4 5 6 7 8 9 0

To the memory of
FRITZ REINER

Contents

PART TWO · SIX ORCHESTRAS IN TIME OF CRISIS

PART THREE · THE INCOME GAP

Tables and Graphs

Preface

This book concerns an institution devoted to perpetuating an important segment of our cultural heritage—music composed mainly during the past two hundred years for the symphony orchestra. This musical heritage and the continuing creative efforts of composers of our own time require realization in actual performance which is possible only through the collective efforts of a diverse company of artists, administrators, and patrons. Their collaboration for the common purpose of performing great orchestral music, their pursuit of this goal in their individual ways, and the manner in which they meet, clash, and blend with one another, all create the fabric of the American symphony orchestra as a cultural institution. Since it requires a high degree of professionalism and skill both in performance and in the logistics of production, the symphony orchestra has become a highly specialized and expensive operation. Though often attacked as irrelevant to contemporary life or as serving only the interests of a limited elite, the orchestra may claim as ultimate justification the continually renewed communication of a great art to those who respond to its creative message.

The United States today enjoys an unrivaled quality and quantity of orchestral performance. Though our orchestras have borrowed important aspects of their functions from abroad—most notably in such artistic matters as repertory and distribution of performing forces—their institutional structure, artistic and business direction, and the manner in which they both serve and represent the communities in which they perform are uniquely American. Other nations may surpass ours in the quantity and quality of their drama, opera, or museums, but none enjoys the variety, scope, and impact of the American symphony orchestra. Not only is virtually every metropolitan center in our nation served with high professional expertise, but the American symphony is also represented in literally hundreds of colleges, universities, and amateur groups.

In studying this institution, I have set certain limits that, although implied by my subtitle, require more precise definition here. At the risk of offending our neighbors to the north, I have applied the term *American* to the orchestras of the United States. To have included those of Canada would have involved exploration of developments that, increasingly, combine elements borrowed both from Europe and the United States. I have further limited myself to some one hundred orchestras in this nation that, by one standard or another, can be called *professional,* a term that embraces not only payment for services rendered but also a special sense of responsibility on the part of all concerned. Within this group of orchestras, I am more interested in the vast majority that plays reasonably extensive seasons of concerts and enjoys broad community support than I am in those few which exist for special limited purposes, generally in areas already served by the more community-oriented efforts. This does not mean that I am unmindful of the importance of the educational and amateur symphonic activities that have proliferated across this country; but it must be pointed out that these latter are in fact ancillary to and often dependent upon the central professional sector.

Within these limits, I shall first trace the background of our orchestras—not by a comprehensive historical review but rather through the careers of a few important people who played major roles in shaping them. Then, to illustrate the current symphonic picture in its variety of quality and scope, I have chosen six orchestras for more intensive study. Though my choice may seem arbitrary, and certainly is very much my own, I have selected orchestras that provide a representative sample from the standpoints of geography, size, and operational aspects; in combination they should give a notion of the total institution. In the third and fourth sections, I shall describe the national symphonic field in terms of economics and artistic service. Though many general evaluations are anticipated in specific contexts, here and in the final summary I shall deal with the problems and challenges that our orchestras will face in the coming decades.

Unless specifically stated otherwise, I shall describe the symphonic scene as it existed during the 1970–71 season, especially regarding economic and statistical data. Though it may seem strange to base my account on information predating this publication by two years, the time lag in assembling data makes the use of later comprehensive figures impossible; important subsequent information will be clearly identified as such.

In this study of the orchestra as a cultural institution, I shall describe the various elements that combine to make it—the conductors, musicians, managers, boards of directors, and audiences—and to show how they work together to produce symphonic music. Wherever possible, in my discussions of specific orchestras as well as of the national scene, I shall present quantitative data, both financial and statistical; and, when these data have limited scope or reliability, I shall qualify them accordingly. However, neither a description of the institutional structure nor mere figures can depict the total picture of the American orchestra without some account of the people—artists and laymen—who have dedicated so much of their lives to it. In the last analysis, the orchestra exists for the art of music, and its progress toward its goals is advanced only by the collective efforts of talented and dedicated men and women.

Inevitably because of the scale of my subject, I have made major and regrettable omissions. I deplore the fact that my scheme did not allow me to give proper recognition, for instance, to the achievements and ideas of George Szell. Shortly before his death, he expressed great interest in my study and we had planned to meet after his Far East tour in 1970 for a more intensive discussion that might have developed significant material for this book. Circumstances beyond my control prevented dealing with Leopold Stokowski, certainly one of the towering figures on the American musical scene, as fully as he deserves. There are other conductors and other orchestras that have played major roles, and other individuals who might have been discussed in greater detail. But the length of this book already places a heavy burden on the reader and choices had to be made: I have made those that I believe most effectively illumine the symphonic picture as I see it.

Although previous studies have been made of my subject, they are now out-of-date, nor did they attempt to cover the institutional relationships that are my concern here. In 1940 Margaret Grant and Herman S. Hechinger studied the orchestras under a grant from the Carnegie Endowment, an excellent but uncritical study of conditions at that time. A decade later, John H. Mueller published his *The American Symphony Orchestra: A Social History of Musical Taste*. As his subtitle indicates, Mueller's field of interest was somewhat specialized, though he assembled a great deal of important information. Dr. Mueller's painstaking survey of the symphonic repertory has been continued by his widow, Dr. Kate Hevner Mueller, providing me with indispensable information for my own discussion of this topic. More recently, in 1967, Henry Swoboda edited a collection of talks on the American symphony scene by some twenty-one commentators for broadcast by the Voice of America; these tend toward diverse subjective views without a central thrust.

Both in specifics and in its largest implications, my book deals with an institution now subjected to pervasive, rapid, and crucial change. Not only do devastating financial problems face most of our orchestras, but their basic rationale and future viability have been widely questioned. At the same time that economic pressures have brought the orchestras to the government for substantial funding, the traditional policy direction and artistic objectives of our orchestras have been challenged from a variety of sources. Under these circumstances, many within and without the symphony world have asked not only whether the orchestras of America *can* survive but whether, despite their inherently limited appeal, they *should* survive, given that their increasing demands for private and public money and community support compete with the pressures of other modern urban social needs. No matter how deeply one may be committed to the symphony orchestra, he must maintain a salutary perspective by realizing that this enterprise involves a very small, and possibly static, proportion of the national population. Yet this institution, dedicated to perpetuating a repertory that is an important part of both the cultural heritage of Western civilization and the on-going creativity of our time, has become the focus of the professional musical life in most American communities, not only providing personnel for wider nonsymphonic activity but setting and maintaining standards for music education. In my involvement here with the specific minutiae of symphonic life, I have tried to keep these concerns in balanced perspective.

On many pages of this book I have resisted the impulse to belabor the crisis condition of our orchestras or the shortcomings of the institution. Without evading my critical responsibilities, I have sought to present pertinent factual information for an informed appraisal of the role and viability of symphonies. No one acquainted with the complexity and diversity of the subject can produce ready answers to the simple, and often justified, questions raised today about the orchestra, but I have suggested, especially in my final section, some lines of future development that would, in my opinion, assure perpetuation and enrichment of the service of our orchestras.

Unlike some other recent studies of the performance arts and cultural activities, by foundations and public agencies, mine is a distinctly personal approach, drawing on my experience of more than three decades in arts management and education administration and supported by nearly three years of intensive research throughout the country. Though I owe a great debt to orchestras, foundations, arts organizations, and government agencies for providing information, I have undertaken this study without support from or obligation to any of them, beyond the information they gave and my gratitude for it. My choice of information from the wealth of data made available to me is my own—as are the conclusions I draw.

In the notes that follow my text I have recorded specific acknowledgment to the individuals and organizations who have given me factual data; to all of them I here offer my deepest thanks. It has been a source of great personal satisfaction to me, and is worthy of note for the record, that virtually everyone I approached responded with information freely and frankly, expressing enthusiastic interest in this book. I must, in addition, acknowledge indebtedness to several whose counsel and help has been of a more general nature than could be specified in the notes: John S. Edwards, Donald L. Engle, Joseph P. Farrell, Gary Graffman, Sheldon Gold, Jacob Lateiner, Martin Mayer, Carlos Moseley, Mark Schubart, William Schuman, Rudolf Serkin, Isaac Stern, and Thomas Willis. Though I shall cite the specific help of the American Symphony Orchestra League in appropriate places later, its staff has rendered valuable aid and encouragement in innumerable ways: I must especially thank Helen M. Thompson (later manager of the New York Philharmonic), Richard H. Wangerin, William F. Nelms, Ralph Rizzolo (later with the National Endowment for the Arts), and Benjamin S. Dunham. At the Associated Councils of the Arts, Suzanne Fogelson gave me much help. The staff of the National Endowment for the Arts has been especially cooperative and I am indebted to Dr. Walter Anderson and Douglas Richards there. Later specific acknowledgments will mention by name the managers, conductors, directors, and staffs of the six intensively studied orchestras, but, without their collective and individual cooperation my task would have been impossible.

To these acknowledgments I must add several very personal expressions of thanks. My editor David Hamilton not only guided me through the intricacies of producing this book with patience and efficiency but has been a warm friend and valued counselor as well. Ninka Hainer labored long and concientiously on my manuscript and sundry other duties, and Linda Hall prepared the graphs. In my dedication I have sought posthumously to express my special debt to Fritz Reiner, both for his friendship and for contributing uniquely to my experience of the beauties of symphonic music and to my understanding of the artistic life. Many years ago Edna Whitman Chittick began my musical studies with an infectious enthusiasm and intellectual integrity that have placed me in her debt ever since. Finally, my wife Margaret and our four sons, Philip, Henry, James, and Paul, have by their patience, understanding, and support, endured the changes in our way of life entailed by writing this book and created the circumstances that allowed me to work effectively.

Sante Fe, New Mexico
October 1972

PART ONE

The Past

"Americans of all ages, all conditions, and all dispositions constantly form associations. They have not only commercial and
manufacturing companies, in which all take part, but associations
of a thousand other kinds, religious, moral, serious, futile, general
or restricted, enormous or diminutive. . . . If it is proposed to
inculcate some truth or foster some feeling by the encouragement
of a great example, they form a society. . . . Nothing, in my
opinion, is more deserving of our attention than the intellectual
and moral associations of America."

ALEXIS DE TOCQUEVILLE
Democracy in America, 1835–40

Though based on European models and performing an essentially
European repertory, the symphony orchestra in this country developed in a uniquely American fashion; with roots extending
back to Europe and to the emerging musical life in the young
republic, it assumed its characteristic identity only after the Civil
War. As the first major American conductor, Theodore Thomas
made an extraordinary contribution both to musical standards
here and to laying the foundation for the maintenance of the orchestra on a permanent basis. In Boston, Henry Lee Higginson
not only founded the Boston Symphony Orchestra but established
a tradition of private patronage and support for music that has
been an essential element ever since. In Arthur Judson, the symphonic institution found its first comprehensive professional manager. But essential as a conductor, a sponsor, and a manager are

to the symphonic institution, it could not exist without a body of professional musicians: their stake in the American symphony, and the particular role they play, has been shaped in many respects by their union and dramatized by such a leader as James C. Petrillo. The proliferation of orchestras across the nation, especially in the last generation, has created a cultural institution here without parallel elsewhere; this phenomemon has found its most concrete manifestation in the American Symphony Orchestra League under the leadership of Helen M. Thompson. Though these five individuals and the organizations they created by no means encompass the whole history of the symphony orchestra in America, their contributions to it are essential to an understanding of how this institution came into existence and assumed so important a place in our national culture.

CHAPTER I

Before Thomas

Horticulturists refer to the "hybrid vigor" of certain plants, in which selective breeding has not only brought out the best characteristics of their lineage but has also produced offspring with a vitality exceeding that of either parent. The symphony orchestra in America has displayed something akin to this hybrid vigor: its outward aspects—the performers and the music they play—inherited from European ancestry, its institutional structure and place in the national culture distinctly American. It may seem strange to refer to the vitality of the symphony orchestra in this country in the face of the widely publicized vicissitudes it has suffered and continues to suffer, but it has survived and will continue to survive these and other challenges in large part because of an inherent strength arising from its hybrid nature.

Except for the orchestras of state radio and television or such occasional, recently organized groups as the Orchestre de Paris, inspired in part by the American model, most of the symphony orchestras of Continental Europe are adjuncts of the opera theater, a phenomenon with deep historical roots.* In England there is a tradition of orchestral independence similar in some respects to the United States, but these orchestras are generally musicians' cooperatives receiving, in recent years, substantial government subsidy. The permanent resident orchestra, with musicians devoting the major portion of their efforts to symphonic music, with artistic direction vested in one conductor, and supported and controlled by laymen, is a specifically American phenomenon which has developed in the past one hundred years. If the Continental European pattern may be described as the periodic emergence of the orchestra from the theater pit to the concert stage, in many cities of this country the home base of the orchestra has been the concert stage, with occasional descent into the opera pit. The symphony is the center of the players' artistic life, and their other professional activities are ancillary to it.

Thus, when an orchestra here goes into the opera theater, it is reversing the historical process begun in Europe in the 18th century, when the or-

---

* Howard Taubman, *The Symphony Orchestra Abroad,* is a good though incomplete account of European orchestras in 1970.

chestras in the court theaters began to play nondramatic music, not just as an accompaniment for social occasions, but as performances in themselves.* Though the structure of these orchestras was decided to a large degree by the requirements of opera, its final makeup was determined by the compositions written for it by the three great Viennese masters, Haydn, Mozart, and Beethoven, whose music is still the foundation of the symphonic repertory. Later composers expanded and modified the orchestra, adding their own personal expression to the repertory, but, until recently at least, the Austro-German concept has persisted. The creative achievements of the Viennese masters and their followers became the *raison d'être* of the symphony orchestra, the magnet that drew performing musicians out of the theater pit onto the concert stage, and the inspiration for the development of the American concept of the permanent orchestra.

In early colonial and federal times, America possessed neither the professional talents nor sufficient population to support public concerts on a regular basis. Much musical activity was centered in religious services, and such large-scale public concerts as took place involved choruses singing religious music or such religiously inspired works as those of Bach, Handel, and Haydn. In fact, the oldest surviving music organization in this nation, the Handel and Haydn Society of Boston, was founded in 1815 for just this purpose. Instrumental music had its devotees among amateurs, singly or in small groups: Thomas Jefferson, for example, was a dedicated violinist. But apart from such groups as the Handel and Haydn Society in Boston and the Musical Fund Society in Philadelphia, organized instrumental music performance developed only gradually in the early republic,† and then with musicians imported or emigrating from Europe. The great Spanish tenor, teacher, and imprèsario Manuel del Pópolo Vicente García came to New York in 1825 with his opera company—consisting largely of relatives, including his daughter, Maria Malibran—and opened his season with Rossini's *Barber of Seville*. There he found, teaching Italian at King's College (later Columbia University), Lorenzo da Ponte,‡ who had come to America in 1805. At da Ponte's urging, and with his advice, García presented the first American performance of a Mozart opera, *Don Giovanni*.[1] From then on, opera developed great popularity in New York, as well as in Boston, Philadelphia, and New Orleans, mostly with European singers in the Italian repertory presented by a variety of impresarios of European origin. These enterprises, which thrived and failed with extraordinary irregularity, also found warm welcome in such Latin-American centers as Havana and Mexico City.

Though many of these opera ventures brought a few orchestra players

---

* Adam Carse, in *The Orchestra in the XVIIIth Century* and *The Orchestra from Beethoven to Berlioz*, gives an exhaustive account of the early history of the orchestra. For a more popular account, see Paul Bekker, *The Orchestra* (originally published as *The Story of the Orchestra*), which also deals with repertory and covers developments to the present.

† John Tasker Howard and George Kent Bellows, *A Short History of Music in America*, covers these early developments.

‡ Lorenzo da Ponte (b. near Venice, 1749; d. New York, 1838) was the incomparable librettist of Mozart's *Le Nozze di Figaro*, *Don Giovanni*, and *Così fan Tutte*. He arrived in the United States from England in 1805, engaging in a number of disastrous business ventures in Pennsylvania and eventually settling in New York.

over from Europe, they relied more and more on resident musicians. In New York, which enjoyed the greatest concentration of such performers, there were sporadic efforts during the 1830s to organize orchestral concerts independent of the opera theaters. Eventually, in 1842, these New York musicians succeeded in founding the first sustained symphonic enterprise in this country, the Philharmonic Society of New York, a cooperative venture undertaken less for financial gain than for the pleasure of playing great symphonic music.[2]

The Philharmonic Society of New York

Early personnel lists indicate that the founders of the Philharmonic Society were a mixture of native or immigrant Anglo-Saxons and Germans. Imbued by an idealistic desire to perform, for their own satisfaction as much as for the benefit of an audience, the new orchestral repertory of Beethoven, his predecessors, and his still emerging successors, the Society's members considered their election a great professional honor. Including the best musicians of the city, they governed the affairs of the Society by democratic procedures, passed on the election of new members, and received as compensation for rehearsals and concerts a modest share of the "takings" after the payment of expenses.* After 1848, the Society became more and more dominated by newly arrived German musicians and remained a basically German group for the next seven decades. From its inception, it elected its conductors—frequently several during a season of four concerts—from its own membership: during the 1850s the choice alternated between two Germans, Theodor Eisfeld and Carl Bergmann, the former a more conservative "classicist," the latter an exponent of the "Music of the Future" of Wagner and Liszt, who had come to this country as cellist in the Germania Society and served on occasion as one of its conductors.

Though the Society at first relied primarily on ticket sales for its income, it soon instituted a system of associate membership for those who neither played nor voted, but who were entitled to attend all concerts and many rehearsals. This laid the foundation both for the contribution and subscription systems and for the open rehearsals, which eventually became the afternoon concerts still a fixture of several of our orchestras. In 1847, the Society received an application for associate membership that was to have momentous implications in the future of the American orchestra. The story was told in a letter to the *New York Post* in 1892:

> When I came to New York in 1847 I went to the last Philharmonic concert of the season, and saw on the programme notice to the effect that "Persons wishing to become Associate Members of the Philharmonic Society, with the privilege of attending the rehearsals, should call on Scharfenberg and Luis in October and give their names." In October I called, saw Mr. Scharfenberg, and told him I wished to become an Associate Member of the Philharmonic Society in order

* Appendix B lists a summary of Philharmonic finances from 1842 to 1890.

to attend the rehearsals. He looked at me with some surprise and said, "Ladies do not go to the rehearsals." I said, "Why not?" . . . "Are you willing to have your name proposed at the next meeting of the Society?" I said, "Yes, unless you know of some reason why I should not." And so it was settled, and in a few days I received a printed form, stating that I had been admitted as an Associate Member of the Philharmonic Society, with the privilege of attending the twelve rehearsals and four concerts, and for the modest sum of five dollars. On the afternoon of the first rehearsal I went, with some trepidation, to the Apollo Hall; the only persons present besides myself were a man and a small boy. I soon smelled cigar smoke, and the conductor arose and said: "Gentlemen, I presume, now that we have agreed to admit ladies as Associate Members, you will agree with me that we should throw away our cigars." I wanted very much to call out and tell them not to, but I kept still, and there was no more cigar smoke. At the next week's rehearsal there were twenty or thirty ladies, and at the third at least one or two hundred.[3]

In the fall of 1855, John Dwight's *Journal of Music* reported that the Philharmonic Society was forced to employ ushers to keep order among the associate members at rehearsals and passed the following resolution:

That the most efficient measures be taken for preventing the disgraceful habit of talking aloud at the rehearsals while the performance is going on; which, to say nothing of such gross breach of manners, has of late become a source of annoyance, that it has provoked serious and just complaints, the more so, as this unwarrantable conduct seems to emanate from but a *few* of those present, who —to the detriment of the *many* true lovers of music—would seem to be more attracted and charmed by the sounds of their own voices, than by the inspiring, solemn, majestic tones of BEETHOVEN or MENDELSSOHN.[4]

An indication of the slow acceptance of the Philharmonic may be seen in its protracted efforts to secure from the General Assembly in Albany an Act of Incorporation. Starting in 1844, the bill lost by a small majority in the upper house, the representatives of the Society reporting to the membership that "everyone to whom they spoke of the subject agreed at once to the harmlessness, and at the same time to the great utility to the Society, of the Act, but they had difficulty in getting members of that body to consider the subject as so much business was before them."[5] However, the necessary legislation was finally passed in 1853. This report has a familiar ring today in our orchestras' efforts to enlist government interest in the arts.

The Philharmonic Society at this time fell far short of being a well-disciplined orchestra. Its members had only a small financial stake in it, with annual shares per player ranging during the 1850s from thirty-five to a hundred and forty-three dollars for a season of four or five concerts. Since they were dependent upon other work, teaching or in theaters, the players were irregular in attendance at rehearsals and even at concerts. Critics of the time, while granting the superior size of the Philharmonic, compared it unfavorably with the orchestra of the Germania Musical Society, which arrived in this country from Berlin in 1848 and for the next six years played a significant part in the early symphonic history of the nation.

The Germania Musical Society

A part of the massive emigration of Germans following the political up-heavals in that country in 1848, the Germania Musical Society,[6] though it seldom numbered more than twenty-five musicians, was the first full-time orchestra in this country to devote itself exclusively to serious symphonic music. Originally composed of twenty-five young Berlin musicians, imbued with the mission of bringing the music of the great symphonic masters to America, the Germania Society arrived in this country in 1848 and continued to tour throughout its settled portion for six years. During this period they played some nine hundred concerts (seven hundred orchestral programs, one hundred additional matinees or soirées, and another hundred performances with local choral societies and other organizations); it has been estimated that their audiences totaled nearly one million listeners. Barnum engaged them for portions of Jenny Lind's American visit, and they also toured with the violinist Ole Bull and the singer Adelina Patti. Traveling as far afield as New Orleans, St. Louis, and Montreal, they virtually introduced the basic symphonic literature to America, playing all of the Beethoven symphonies (the Ninth usually without its choral Finale), the symphonies of Haydn, Mozart, and Schubert, and also the new music of Mendelssohn, Schumann, and Wagner. They had less impact in New York, with its Philharmonic Society of over sixty players, than in Boston, Philadelphia, Baltimore, St. Louis, and Chicago. They made frequent appearances in Boston, climaxed in 1854 by a complete performance of the Beethoven *Choral Symphony* with the Handel and Haydn Society.

After six seasons of such touring, interrupted by summers of playing light music in Newport, Rhode Island, the Germania Society disbanded, its members settling in a number of cities where they played an important role in early efforts to organize local orchestras and choral societies. After the Germania group disbanded in 1854, many American cities heard no symphonic music until Theodore Thomas began touring in 1869.

Louis-Antoine Jullien

The next major orchestral event in America was the arrival in 1854 of Louis-Antoine Jullien, the flamboyant conductor whom Thomas later described as "the musical charlatan of all ages." [7] Despite Thomas's strictures, as well as the contempt bestowed on him by Berlioz * and Joachim, Jullien was a gen-

---

* Jullien, though not specifically named, figures as the London impresario in the ninth of Hector Berlioz's *Evenings with the Orchestra,* and his employment of that composer as conductor of the Grand English Opera in 1847 is reported in Berlioz's *Memoirs.* Max Maratzek, who was also involved in that venture, reports on it, too. Adam Carse and Harold C. Schonberg have also given accounts of Jullien's career.[8]

uine master conductor with a serious sense of mission in bringing great music
to the public. But he did so with an element of showmanship that often
obscured the loftiness of his intentions. He revered Beethoven above all
composers, expressing that reverence by wearing white gloves when he conducted Beethoven's music and using a special jeweled baton handed to him
by a servant on a silver tray. He believed that he could attract the public to
his concerts only by presenting popular dances, waltzes, and quadrilles, which
he interspersed with movements, often truncated, from the symphonies of
Beethoven. In his manner on the podium and in the glamorous life he was
widely reported to lead, he was the first of the virtuoso charismatic conductors. For him, a devastating impact on the audience was all-important: one
of his most spectacular presentations was a *Fireman's Quadrille,* complete
with fireworks and a simulated conflagration so realistic that women screamed
hysterically and fainted.

Upon his return to Europe, he suffered a series of financial reverses, eventually landing in debtors' prison, and died at Paris in 1860, penniless and
insane. In his last years he succumbed to paranoia to such an extent that he
proposed to set the Lord's Prayer to music, with a title page reading:[9]

The Lord's Prayer
Words by
JESUS CHRIST
Music by
JULLIEN

Nevertheless, Jullien made a serious impact on the American symphonic
scene in 1854. He brought with him some twenty-five of the foremost instrumentalists of Paris and London, to whom he added the best orchestral
players available in the American cities he visited. These European musicians, including some extraordinary woodwind and brass players, left an
indelible impression on such American musicians as Theodore Thomas and
set standards of performance to which they aspired in years to come. Moreover, the almost hysterical response of the public to Jullien's productions
aroused an interest in purely orchestral music comparable to the excitement
generated by the great singers of that time.

Except for Jullien, such singers as Jenny Lind, Grisi, Sontag, and Patti
aroused the greatest musical sensation among the American musical public
of the 1850s, either in concerts with orchestra accompaniment or in the
opera theaters. As various impresarios, Barnum included, vied with one another in exploiting these singers, the public was treated to a succession of
vocal and operatic sensations.[10] These ventures provided musical employment for a considerable number of orchestra musicians, many of them recent
immigrants from Germany, Bohemia, and Austria, and eventually some former players from the Germania Society. Such was the emphasis on the singers that one seldom knows who conducted the orchestras that accompanied

them.* But this activity laid the basis for subsequent independent orchestra concerts by providing musicians with ample opportunity to work professionally, and the musical environment in which Thomas eventually developed his orchestral enterprises, the first truly "permanent" symphonic activity in this country, or, for that matter, elsewhere.

* As we shall have occasion to note later, it is impossible for this reason even to know the precise date of Theodore Thomas's conducting debut.

CHAPTER II

Theodore Thomas—Conductor

Lying on his deathbed in January, 1905, Theodore Thomas, in one of his last conscious moments, uttered what his widow reported as his last words: "I have seen a vision—a beautiful vision." [1] Mrs. Thomas surmised that he was thinking of their summer home in the White Mountains of New Hampshire, but we may be pardoned if we recall these words as the epitaph of his career.

Thomas's career was more than a vision; it was the triumphant realization of a dream—the establishment of the American symphony orchestra as the vehicle for the dissemination of great musical art. For Thomas the symphony orchestra was not an end in itself, but the medium for communicating to the audience the uplifting moral message of great music. His concern with technical precision and orchestral discipline was more than mere professionalism: only a fine instrument could serve the art of music. Thomas's conception of the moral force of music was no metaphor; he regarded that art as the highest achievement of man and his own gift as a calling to a sacred duty. In the pursuit of his vision, Thomas engaged in an incredible variety of musical projects: chamber music, opera, education, solo recitals, touring, and the direction of three orchestras in New York. In over forty years he conducted nearly seven thousand concerts and opera performances in more than two hundred American cities, [2] providing the inspiration and setting the standards for many of the orchestras that were eventually established in America. His impact on public taste and the appetite he created for symphonic music were incalculable. Learning from arduous experience the limitations of a touring orchestra, he dreamed of establishing a permanent orchestra in New York. Frustrated in this, he finally found in Chicago the support he required.

Short in stature, stern in countenance and personal relationships, Thomas was a strict disciplinarian in his management of the orchestra. He expressed his tenacity to his ideals with a lack of compromise and social grace that often alienated both press and potential supporters. But from contemporary comment, pro and con, there emerges an impression of an artist who belonged to the school of literal interpretation and fidelity to the composer's score in conducting, as opposed to the more flamboyant personalization of music exemplified by Richard Wagner and Arthur Nikisch. Internationally known artists like Nicholas Rubinstein, Lilli Lehmann, and Richard Strauss testified enthusiastically to the quality of Thomas's orchestra and to his musical leadership. In their opinion, there was no better orchestra in Europe or America during the three decades of Thomas's greatest activity. Thomas was admirably equipped by temperament and talent to respond to the musical environment about him and to shape the resources at hand. Though born in Germany, he came to this country early enough to develop in a characteristically American manner, while retaining a commitment to European culture. Except for early musical training by his father, he was almost completely self-taught both in music and in general education, but no musician, however renowned, questioned his authority, and his command of literature and history was worthy of a college graduate.

His sense of mission and moral recititude was implanted in Thomas from a pietistic background in his native northern Germany. One of his most vivid childhood memories was of his grandmother: on returning from the funeral of one of his playmates, she found that young Theodore had misbehaved in her absence and berated him, declaring that it should have been his funeral and not his companion's.[3] Throughout his life, Thomas retained an ethical austerity that was both a spiritual resource and often the root of his alienation from potential friends and supporters.

To these musical and moral traits this austere man brought a phenomenal bodily energy and acute business instinct. For years, he survived the physical strain of performing night after night, often in a new city each night, conducting in some years as many as two hundred fifty concerts. He organized his own orchestra, supervised the management of its touring and promotion, and risked his own limited financial resources on its success, all the while studying and learning a fantastically large repertory of music.

The Young Musician in New York

Born in 1835 at Esens, in North Germany, Thomas was the son of a town horn player, from whom he received his only instruction on the violin. Such was the precocity of young Theodore that when he played at the age of seven for the king of Hannover, the monarch offered to underwrite the boy's education. Declining this offer, the Thomas family emigrated to America in 1845, settling in New York. Apparently the elder Thomas found it difficult to make a living there and young Theodore very early began to supplement the family income by playing the violin at dancing schools, saloons, and parties. Before he was fourteen, he was playing in the pits of the English and German theaters, where he first encountered the literature of Shakespeare, Goethe, and Schiller; this was to remain regular reading throughout his life. At a performance of Shakespeare's *Coriolanus,* he played in Beethoven's Overture to Heinrich von Collin's play on the same subject, an occasion which he recalled as his first professional encounter with that composer's orchestral music.[4]

When he was fourteen, Thomas and his father enlisted in the navy as horn players on the U.S.S. *Pennsylvania,* stationed at Portsmouth, Virginia. After a year there, he received his discharge and set out alone by stagecoach and horseback to tour the South as a boy-prodigy violinist. Returning to New York in 1850, Thomas found a considerable change in the musical life of that city. Whereas the profession had been dominated earlier by native Yankees and Englishmen, there was now a great influx of musicians from Germany and Central Europe. A new musical climate was being created in America with the exploitation of sensational attractions from Europe, among them Barnum's promotion of the American tour of Jenny Lind between September, 1850, and May, 1852. Thomas played in the orchestra which accompanied the Swedish Nightingale's Castle Garden concerts in New York and in later years recalled how indelibly she had impressed upon him the beauties of vocal artistry and lyric phrasing. Lind was but the first of several great singers whom Thomas heard from his place in the violin section of the orchestra during the 1850s, either in concert or in opera; the husband-and-wife team of Mario, Cavaliere di Candia, and Giulia Grisi, the soprano Henriette Sontag, and the youthful Adelina Patti were luminaries of the age of *bel canto* who made a lasting impression on young Thomas.

Henriette Sontag was of special importance to Thomas, for, unlike the Italian singers, she represented a German tradition to which he was more responsive. She had created the leading role in the premiere of Weber's *Euryanthe* and had sung under Beethoven's supervision in a revival of *Fidelio* and in the premieres of the Ninth Symphony and *Missa solemnis.* Sontag brought with her Karl Eckert, who later distinguished himself in the opera theaters of Vienna and Berlin. Eckert was the first real conductor Thomas had encountered, and the young musician long after acknowledged a deep debt to him, describing him as "the only really fully equipped and satisfactory conductor who visited this country during that period. All the rest were more or less 'time beaters.' "[5] Thomas had a low opinion of opera conductors in general; their role, he said, was usually "to pound on the piano with singers until they knew their parts well enough to go to an orchestra rehearsal."[6] But Eckert was more than a musical model for young Thomas, for he recognized the organizational ability of the young man and initiated him into the fundamentals of orchestra discipline and management. At the Italian opera, Eckert promoted Thomas, then aged nineteen, to the position of leader of the second violins and gave him broad responsibilities managing the personnel of the orchestra in matters of contracts, salaries, and scheduling. After Eckert left, his successor, Luigi Arditi, appointed Thomas as leader—or, in modern terminology, concertmaster—of the orchestra. From an early age, therefore, Thomas was in touch with most of the best musicians in New York and with those that arrived in that city as immigrants.

New York during the 1850s was the center of a great deal of operatic activity, promoted by a number of rival impresarios. At times there were as many as four companies performing in various theaters, of which the most notable were the Astor Place Opera, built in 1847, and the considerably larger Academy of Music on Fourteenth Street, which opened in 1854; Thomas played in all of these theaters, usually as concertmaster and orchestra contractor, for more than fifteen years, and eventually began to conduct opera performances as well.

As one of the New York musicians with whom Jullien augmented his twenty-five imported Europeans, Thomas had a good opportunity to study the French conductor. Despite his condemnation of Jullien as a charlatan, Thomas came to share his wish to elevate popular taste and later in his career successfully combined lighter music with serious classics to educate the public, finding more musically honest and less sensational ways to advance his educational mission. Moreover, despite his misgivings, Thomas respected Jullien's technical mastery of the orchestra and gained a lasting impression of the potentialities of fine orchestral playing from the superb musicians Jullien brought with him.

Thomas was nineteen years old when he was elected to membership in the Philharmonic Society of New York, an indication of how firmly he was established in the music profession of the city. Though he remained a playing member until 1868, appearing several times as violin soloist, it was not a major opportunity for him and he used to recall later his dislike for the sloppy and old-fashioned habits of the Philharmonic. To a large extent his experience as a player merely intensified his conviction that a full-time orchestra was necessary.

An enterprise of exceptional musical importance to Thomas was his association with the American pianist William Mason in an annual series of chamber-music concerts in New York and other cities. Mason, a member of an old New England family long distinguished in music, had returned from studies in Germany, with Liszt and other teachers, to New York; here he organized an ensemble combining his own piano playing with a string quartet of outstanding players, members of the Philharmonic. From 1855 until 1870, Thomas not only played first violin in this ensemble but soon assumed responsibility for planning its programs, usually six a season in New York. In these Mason-Thomas concerts, as they soon came to be known, Thomas included virtually all of the major ensemble music then in the repertory, from Bach, Haydn, and Mozart through Beethoven and Schubert to Schumann and the young Brahms.* He campaigned ardently for the late quartets of Beethoven, when this music was still viewed by many as the creation of a senile madman, and fully explored the ensemble counterpart of the symphonic repertory which he was eventually to master, gaining a strictly musical experience that few other conductors matched. Devoting three mornings a week to rehearsal in preparing six concerts a year, the Mason-Thomas group set an unprecedentedly high standard of repertory and performance, offering programs every bit as exacting as those one may hear today at the Library of Congress.

Long after the Mason-Thomas ensemble ceased to play, Thomas continued

---

* This ensemble's very first program included the world premiere of Brahms's Trio in B major. The second volume of Upton's original edition of Thomas's autobiography includes a listing of all of the Mason-Thomas programs.

to place a high value on chamber music: it was an important part of the educational program at the Cincinnati College of Music, and he actively encouraged the Orchestral Association in Chicago to present ensemble concerts by members of the Chicago Symphony. He remained a close friend of William Mason, frequently inviting him to play with his orchestra. Mason was, in fact, one of the very few people who addressed Thomas by his first name.

Thomas engaged in an extraordinarily varied and intensive musical career as a young man in New York. He traveled at least twice to the West, as far as Chicago and St. Louis, as a member of orchestras accompanying tours of Ole Bull and Henriette Sontag; at the concerts of the latter, he played as a featured violin soloist. He was highly regarded as a solo violinist by his colleagues and the critics, but never captured popular fancy: his musicianship and reserved style of playing offered little competition to the now forgotten child prodigies or the colorful Bull, to whom the public flocked at this time. During these years, too, Thomas supplemented his practical musical experience with theoretical study, some of it by himself and some privately with local teachers. By the time he conducted his first orchestral concert, he was an extraordinarily complete musician.

Thomas as Conductor

In his *Musical Memories*, written after Thomas's death, Mason has a highly circumstantial account of Thomas's debut as an opera conductor, a tale cast in the traditional mold: the young orchestra violinist rescues the performance by mounting the podium when the regular conductor fails to appear.* Mason placed this event in December, 1860, but there is evidence that Thomas was conducting opera at the Academy of Music earlier. Thomas's own *Autobiography* is silent on this matter, because he no doubt placed little musical importance on his role in opera at this time. So far as he was concerned, his real debut as a conductor took place only in 1862, when he first organized his own orchestral concert. This concert, in Irving Hall on May 12, 1862, employed the supporting services of William Mason in Liszt's arrangement of Schubert's *Wanderer Fantasy*, the Teutonic Choral Society in a sacred hymn; a violin soloist, Bruno Mollenhaupt; and an operatic soprano, Mme. de Lussan, in arias by Rossini and Meyerbeer. Among the orchestral selections was the first performance in this country of the Overture to Wagner's *Flying Dutchman*.[8]

As a result of this concert, Thomas undertook, in the following autumn, a series of concerts in New York that laid the foundation of his career as a conductor. On October 24 he gave the first of ten weekly matinee programs

---

* Mason's account [7] was accepted by both Mrs. Thomas and Charles Edward Russell in their books on Thomas, but Upton notes that Thomas was conducting for Ullman's opera company during the previous spring, and there are indications in Odell's *Annals of the New York Theater* that even these were not Thomas's first performances as a conductor.

in Irving Hall. Whereas his debut in May was something of a hodgepodge repertory, this Irving Hall series featured major symphonic works. Each program included a complete symphony, a practice that even the Philharmonic had not consistently established. Among the soloists were the American pianist Louis Moreau Gottschalk and singers from the various opera theaters. The programs of this first season included three symphonies (the First, Second, and Fifth) and two overtures by Beethoven, two symphonies by Mozart, and one each by Haydn and Niels Gade. Two movements from Berlioz's *Harold in Italy* and the Prelude to Act III of Wagner's *Lohengrin* were played for the first time in America.

Thomas continued to organize orchestral concerts in and around New York during the following years, and also continued to conduct opera. In addition to the Irving Hall concerts, he organized a series of lighter concerts in Lyric Hall. For all of these ventures, he hired his players at a fixed scale of pay for rehearsals and concerts and took the financial risks himself, though during this period he may have begun to enjoy some financial assistance from the Steinway piano makers: he played many of his concerts in Steinway Hall, after it opened in 1866, and had space in the Steinway building for his office and for the storage of his growing library of performance materials.*

Though the Mason-Thomas concerts ceased in New York in the spring of 1868, no doubt on account of Thomas's increasing activities as conductor, they continued at Miss Porter's School in Farmington, Massachusetts, for two more seasons. There was on the faculty of this school a German musician, Karl Klauser, a friend of Mason and Thomas, who arranged regular appearances of the ensemble at the school every year from 1856 through 1870. There Thomas met Miss Minna Rhodes, daughter of a moderately prominent New York family, whom he married in 1864. After their marriage, Mrs. Thomas so completely devoted her life to the care of her husband and children that virtually nothing is known of her; when Thomas's second wife wrote her *Memoirs* in 1910, she was unable even to locate a portrait of the first Mrs. Thomas. Speaking of his wife, Thomas once commented, "I do not care for so-called pretty women. What I admire is character and intelligence. If a woman has these, she does not need beauty, but I will confess that if a woman of character and intellect has beauty in addition, it is like a lamp shining through an alabaster vase. But that is a rare combination." [9] Minna Rhodes Thomas proved to be an admirable wife: not only did she maintain a home to which Thomas could return from long tours, but she provided an atmosphere of intellectual activity that bolstered his career.

---

* William Steinway undoubtedly played an important role in Thomas's career, both as a friend and in business matters. As will be seen shortly, Thomas's orchestra joined Anton Rubinstein and Henri Wieniawski in a Steinway-sponsored tour. In addition to supplying Thomas with space for his office and orchestra library, Steinway probably also loaned him money; the archives of the Steinway firm at Astoria on Long Island include a promissory note from Thomas for $1,000, but there is no record of its repayment. The various lists of patrons sponsoring special Thomas enterprises usually included the name of William Steinway, and there was a long-standing general impression in New York music circles that he aided Thomas financially on more than one occasion.

Thomas was conscious of the deficiencies of his formal education, and from his youth in the English and German theaters was an avid reader, retaining much in his remarkable memory; his wife's formal education supplemented and guided his continuing quest for knowledge and broader culture. She also made a special effort to follow her children's education closely, even to the point of keeping up with her sons' studies at Yale and Columbia.

Between 1862 and 1869, Thomas gradually widened his orchestral activities, employing an increasingly stable group of players whose services he could command, if not full-time as yet, at least on an expanding basis. In 1862, he began a long association with the Brooklyn Philharmonic Society, which differed from that of New York in being a group of sponsors of concerts rather than players. At first Thomas shared the direction of these concerts with Eisfeld, but from 1866 until 1891 he was their regular conductor, presenting at least six concerts a year in Brooklyn with personnel of his own selection. He received an annual stipend of twenty-five hundred dollars for his own services and the Society paid the players; once he had established his own orchestra, its personnel played these Brooklyn concerts.

In 1864, Thomas began presenting series of summer concerts, at first in New York and later in Chicago, St. Louis, Cincinnati, Milwaukee, and Philadelphia. Thomas defined the musical rationale of the concerts in these terms: "What our overworked business and professional men most need in America is an elevating recreation which is not amusement." [10] Though these programs were generally lighter than his winter symphonic concerts, Thomas gradually added more substantial fare, at first by the inclusion of separate movements from symphonies and eventually by playing some of the more popular symphonies complete. He developed the idea of programs built around a theme—a composer, a historical series, or a nationality. Some notion of the development and variety of this summer repertory can be gained from these typical programs, chosen from the thousands he devised:

June 4, 1865—Belvedere Lion Park, New York
FAHRBACH: *Festival March*
ROSSINI: Overture, *La Gazza Ladra*
GUNGL: Waltz, *Hydropathen*
WAGNER: Fantasia from *Tannhäuser*
WEBER: Overture, *Oberon*
ROSSINI: *Cujus animam,* from *Stabat Mater*
STRAUSS: Polka, *Aurora Ball*
HETSCH: *Potpourri*
AUBER: Overture, *Le domino noir*
DONIZETTI: Selections from *Don Sebastian*
HAMM: Galop, *Gun Cotton*
STRAUSS: Quadrille, *Artists*

July 10, 1877—Exposition Building, Chicago
    BEETHOVEN PROGRAM

Overture, *Leonore No. 2*
Choral Fantasy, Op. 80
Symphony No. 7, A major, Op. 92

Septet, E-flat, Op. 20
Overture, *Fidelio*

These programs show the degree to which Thomas's conception of popular programming, starting at a point considerably beyond that of Jullien, progressed in seriousness. From that point of view, Thomas looked upon this repertory as a way of introducing his audience to more serious music. With rare exceptions, these series of as many as a hundred and thirty-five programs a summer attracted large crowds, who enjoyed their informality and the opportunity to relax on a warm evening.*

In the spring of 1867, Thomas made his first trip to Europe since leaving there as a ten-year-old boy, visiting London, Paris, Munich, Vienna, Dresden, Berlin, and Hannover, hearing a great deal of music and comparing performances there with his experience in New York. In Paris he called upon the ailing Berlioz, whose music he played, some of it for the first time in America. In appreciation of these efforts, Berlioz gave him an inscribed copy of his Requiem. He heard a great deal of opera, but really admired only the performances in London (*Faust* at Covent Garden) and Paris (Verdi's *Don Carlo*). He was favorably impressed by the violin playing of Joachim and delighted by the conducting of Johann Strauss; from Vienna he brought back as much Strauss music as he could afford, anticipating its success at his own concerts. By and large, Thomas's principal impression of European music was that it was no better than what he was doing in New York; he returned to America confirmed in his belief that he was on the right track musically.[12]

The Thomas Orchestra on Tour

The first tour of the Theodore Thomas orchestra began in the fall of 1869 and covered the Middle Atlantic states and New England; its success prompted a more extensive trip to Chicago and St. Louis in the spring of 1870. For several seasons these tours precluded wintertime appearances in New York. In the years that followed, these concerts, frequently one-night stands, were played in virtually every city or town east of the Mississippi that contained a suitable hall or possible audience.† Thus was established the "Thomas highway" that first reached the South in 1872 and the Pacific Coast in 1883, and continued even after 1891, when the Chicago Symphony replaced the Thomas orchestra on tour. In certain cities—notably Boston, Chicago, Philadelphia, Cleveland, Detroit, St. Louis, and Cincinnati—Thomas gave one or two series of concerts a season, scheduling appearances in nearby towns between the

* At first Thomas's orchestra numbered forty players, then fifty, and finally sixty. "It may be doubted whether in any other audience outside Germany one could have heard in this period such a wealth and variety of important orchestral music." In a typical summer during the 1860s, Thomas presented more concerts than the Philarmonic Society had offered in its entire history.[11]

† During one of these tours, on April 19, 1875, the Thomas orchestra played the dedicatory concert of the Troy Music Hall, an auditorium still so renowned for its acoustics [13] that the Philadelphia Orchestra has hopes of using it for recordings.

programs in the major city. His orchestra performed six or seven times a week, traveling on the railroad by day, sleeping in local hotels.

Though Thomas's papers in the Newberry Library of Chicago include scrapbooks containing virtually every program that he ever conducted, they are singularly lacking in any documentation of the finances or logistics of these tours. Despite the implication that Thomas himself took on the financial risk and business management, many of the printed programs list the names of various managers, who also served as orchestra librarian and Thomas's secretary on tours. Moreover, it is likely that these tours were booked through one or more of the theatrical booking agencies in New York that represented local theaters at this time. However, except for his annual fee from the Brooklyn Philharmonic, Thomas had no guaranteed income from conducting and had to count for his living on some profit from touring, which involved considerable contractual commitment on his part for musicians' wages, railroad fares, and other expenses. Thomas signed contracts with the players individually and in his own name personally: he regarded these contracts as one of his most sacred obligations. Though the Musicians' Protective Association and other early unions were formed at this time, there is no indication that Thomas had any difficulties with either his players or their union; in this he was unlike many theatrical promoters who thought nothing of abandoning their performers hundreds of miles from home if they suffered financial reverses, a practice that gave much impetus to unionization in its early days. Thomas, with his conscientious and paternalisitic attitude toward his "Kinder," was undoubtedly not only a model employer but also the source of steady employment and unique artistic standards at this time.

Just as we know nothing of the salaries paid by Thomas, we know little of his financial returns. When ticket prices are indicated in the printed programs, they generally range from twenty-five cents to one dollar, and from the prevailing size of the theaters at this time, we must assume that the total income ranged between a thousand and fifteen hundred dollars a concert, before deduction of local expenses and hall rental; Thomas probably did not receive more than sixty or seventy percent of ticket sales. We do not know how much risk Thomas took personally or how much money he may have been guaranteed by local managers, nor do we know precisely whether others shared Thomas's financial risks. It was, in any event, a perilous enterprise and Thomas had good reason for becoming increasingly concerned with establishing his orchestra on a full-time basis in New York.

On these tours, Thomas regularly engaged one or more soloists to appear at virtually every concert; their fees varied between fifty and a hundred dollars per concert. Certain members of the orchestra—the concertmaster, the first trumpeter, or cellist—also appeared frequently as soloists.[14] The tour programs which Thomas offered in the spring of 1870 in Boston, a city always responsive to this conductor, are typical of his tour. Anna Mehlig was the piano soloist in four of these concerts, as she was throughout several of Thomas's tours, and the conductor joined her on this occasion as violinist in the sonata on the final Beethoven program. The first program of the series is typical of those played in the one-night stands of the orchestra on tour and was probably offered to stimulate attendance at the first concert and to build the audience for those that followed. The other three programs are representative of those that Thomas offered in the larger, more "cultured" cities.

October 4
WEBER: Overture, *Euryanthe*
SCHUMANN: Piano Concerto, A minor, Op. 54
WAGNER: Prelude, *Lohengrin*
BEETHOVEN: *Egmont Overture*
BURGEL: *Schlummerlied*
STRAUSS: Waltz, *Königskinder*
DAVID: Concerto for Trombone
STRAUSS: *Pizzicato Polka*
THOMAS: Overture, *Mignon*

October 5
BEETHOVEN: Symphony No. 6, F major, Op. 68
LISZT: Piano Concerto
WAGNER: *A Faust Overture*
BERLIOZ: *March of the Pilgrims* from *Harold in Italy*
GLINKA: *Kamarinskaya*
SCHUMANN: Overture, *Genoveva*

October 7
 BEETHOVEN PROGRAM
Symphony No. 3, E-flat major, Op. 55 (*Eroica*)
Piano Concerto No. 4, G major, Op. 58
Coriolanus Overture
Septet, E-flat, Op. 20
Choral Fantasy, C major, Op. 80

October 14
WAGNER: Overture, *The Flying Dutchman*
WEBER: *Konzertstück,* F minor
LISZT: *Gretchen* from *Faust Symphony*
MENDELSSOHN: Overture, *Ruy Blas*
BEETHOVEN: *Andante and Variations* from String Quartet No. 5, A major, Op.
  18, No. 3
STRAUSS: Waltz, *Bürgersinn*
STRAUSS: *Pizzicato Polka*
SCHUBERT: *Reiter Marsch*

October 15
 BEETHOVEN PROGRAM
Symphony No. 8, F major, Op. 93
Piano Concerto No. 5, E-flat major, Op. 73
Overture, *King Stephen*
Sonata No. 9 for Violin and Piano, A major, Op. 47 (*Kreutzer*)
Overture, *Leonore No. 3*

Though the emphasis here on Beethoven was occasioned by the centenary of that composer's birth, his music was the very center of Thomas's repertory. Otherwise these programs and their musical standard indicate the kind of repertory that Thomas presented from the very outset of his conducting career.

Boston became a favorite with Thomas, as he was with its audience, and he enjoyed great success there until 1881, when Higginson established the Boston Symphony. In all, he conducted over two hundred performances in Boston alone. In 1876, he presented as soloist the young American pianist Amy Fay in her American debut after several years of European study, thus beginning an association with her family that was to have important consequences.[15]

In the summer of 1872, the operatic impresarios Jacob and Maurice Grau signed a contract with Anton Rubinstein to tour the United States under the auspices of the Steinway piano firm, which was basing the promotion of its product on the endorsement of renowned virtuosos. Rubinstein was guaranteed a fee of forty thousand dollars for a tour of two hundred concerts, and the violinist Henri Wieniawski was engaged, at a lower fee, to "assist" on the tour, which opened in September with a New York Philharmonic concert. The first tour presented Rubinstein, Wieniawski, an assortment of singers, and a small instrumental ensemble. It was not a success, artistically or economically, and William Steinway and Maurice Grau conceived the idea of combining Rubinstein and Wieniawski with Theodore Thomas and "his Unrivalled Orchestra." (Rubinstein eventually persuaded his sponsors to permit him to play a series of solo "historical" recitals that also proved to be successful.) [16]

The joint tour of Thomas with these soloists, in which the orchestra received equal billing, was an artistic triumph, and a financial one also. The soloists played a variety of standard concertos, Rubinstein played his own compositions, and both he and Thomas conducted the orchestra in Rubinstein's music. It is an indication of the hold of Thomas's orchestra on the American public, four years after he started touring, that his participation could play such an important part in the success of this venture. The association with Rubinstein also called forth this comment from the pianist to William Steinway at the end of the tour:

> I shall take away with me from America one unexpected reminiscence. Little did I dream to find here the greatest and finest orchestra in the wide world. . . . Never in my life have I found an orchestra and a conductor so in sympathy with one another, or who followed me as the most gifted accompanist can follow a singer on the piano. . . . There exists but one orchestra of sixty or eighty men which plays so perfectly, and which is known as the Imperial Orchestra of Paris. . . . They play as perfectly as the Thomas Orchestra, but, unfortunately, they have no Theodore Thomas to conduct them.[17]

Despite their success, Thomas came to view his tours as an onerous task which he undertook only to improve American musical taste and to keep his orchestra together. In combination with his summer seasons, they made it possible for him to maintain a full-time professional orchestra for appearances in New York, Chicago, Boston, Philadelphia, and Cincinnati, and to develop such major events as the biennial Cincinnati Festivals after 1873. Gradually Thomas cut down on visiting smaller towns, concentrating his activities in the larger cities and, beginning in 1883, traveling as far west as San Francisco. He also intensified his activity in cities near New York—Newark, Orange, and Jersey City, in addition to the Brooklyn Philharmonic—which could be played without extensive travel.

Thomas's ability to secure through regular employment a firm economic hold on good musicians was essential to his development of the orchestral discipline necessary for good performance. He was, from all accounts, a stern taskmaster, but his men respected him for his unquestioned musical authority and loved him for his fairness and concern with their welfare. Most of these players were Germans, like their conductor, and they shared his dedication to German symphonic music. They referred to Thomas as "Der Alte" or, borrowing American terminology, "the boss." Though he later received honorary doctoral degrees, which he valued highly, he firmly refused to be addressed, in the German manner, as "Doctor" or "Herr Professor." He treated his players with invariable courtesy, even when correcting their mistakes in rehearsal, though he remained aloof from them in personal contacts. He addressed individual players as "Mr." and no one, even close friends or professional associates, apart from William Mason, ever thought of calling him by his first name. His use of the German *Du* was paternal and authoritative, not an indication of intimacy.

The diversity of Thomas's concert activity was reflected in the variety of his programming. Unlike Jullien, who played all of his concerts as a crowd-pleasing mixture of popular and popularized serious repertory, Thomas strictly distinguished the various types of programs he offered, recognizing that there was not just one symphonic audience but a variety of them. In his serious programming, Beethoven was for him the very center of the musical universe. In this he was a man of his time: in the 19th century, before the scrupulous research of A. W. Thayer had shown his human frailty, Beethoven was worshiped, not only as a great musician but at an almost divine embodiment of moral virtue. Though Thomas did not borrow Jullien's device of conducting Beethoven with white gloves and jeweled baton, he approached that composer with a truly religious attitude accorded to no other. Beethoven's predecessors —Bach, Handel, Mozart, and Haydn—were viewed in their relation to Beethoven, and the then modern composers—Schumann, Brahms, Mendelssohn, and Wagner—were seen as his successors, with Beethoven occupying the lofty summit at the center of this musical cosmos.

Otis recalls an occasion during Thomas's last years in Chicago when the conductor was asked, at a late evening supper, whether he expected Wagner to replace Mozart and Beethoven in the orchestral repertory. For half an hour Thomas held the floor, pacing up and down and expounding his views in English and German. "Bach, Handel, Mozart, and Beethoven were the sons of God! Wagner was an egoist! All sensuousness! Beethoven worked for humanity. There are three great epochs in the history of art: (1) the Greek; (2) the period which produced Shakespeare; (3) the period which gave the world Beethoven." [18]

Thomas approached his musical mission with a stern, religious morality. Throughout his career he strictly forbade anyone to tell a risqué story or to speak vulgarly in his presence, and he refused to attend plays or read books that he considered "trashy." "I avoid trashy stuff," he said. "Otherwise, when I come before the public to interpret masterworks, and my soul should be inspired with noble and impressive emotions, these evil thoughts run around my mind like squirrels and spoil it all. A musician must keep his heart pure and his mind clean if he wishes to elevate, instead of debasing, his art." [19]

To the composers of his own time—German and other nationalities—he was extremely open-minded. He played all of the new music, and did so with a dedication as firm as it was impartial. Some of his evaluations may seem strange to us, such as his considering Berlioz inferior to Saint-Saëns and his fondness for now forgotten composers like Raff and Gade. He gave the first American performances of many important compositions of Wagner, Brahms, Liszt, Bruckner, Berlioz, and Saint-Saëns. Even before it was played in Europe, he performed music by the young Richard Strauss, to whom he had been introduced in Munich by the composer's father, then one of the leading horn players, and continued to play Strauss's music as fast as it was composed. Toward Wagner, Thomas entertained an ambivalent attitude. In his youth he was known as one of the young radicals in the deliberations of the Philharmonic Society on account of his advocacy of the "Music of the Future," and he gave the premiere in this country of many excerpts from Wagner's music dramas, often securing the orchestral material through unofficial sources. However, he was repelled by Wagner's notoriously immoral behavior and, as we shall see in the episode of the March for the Philadelphia Centennial, was the victim of Wagner's shady business dealings. Nevertheless, he faithfully played Wagner's music and was a major force in establishing the popularity of that composer in this country. He was the first president of the Wagner Verein in New York, conducting concerts for the benefit of the Bayreuth construction fund. But he was never as ardent a Wagnerite, in programming or conducting style, as the Damrosches or Anton Seidl. Many American composers of his time were friends and he played a great deal of their music. Such musicians as John Knowles Paine, Frederick Converse, Silas Pratt, and Henry Chadwick are now little more than names in our musical encyclopedias, but Thomas played their music enthusiastically and frequently.

Thomas's preeminence as a conductor and impresario during the 1870s and 1880s brought him offers to engage in special activities that, in at least three cases, resulted in personal humiliation and financial hardship. In 1876, his participation in the Philadelphia Centennial had disastrous financial consequences and profound embarrassment at the hands of Richard Wagner. From 1878 to 1880 he organized and directed the Cincinnati College of Music, an educational project very close to his heart, but in the end was forced to leave the college because of sharp conflict with its backers. From 1885 to 1887, he was musical director, and later president, of the American Opera Company for two seasons. The story of these ventures has been set forth elsewhere in depressing detail: though they were not strictly a part of his symphonic activity, they did have a crucial impact on his career.

Three Setbacks

In Cincinnati, Thomas had a strong following, not only among the German population there but also in the highest social circles. Here he first organized the mammoth festival productions that played an important part in his career, and it was natural that a group of prominent citizens would turn to him when they decided to organize a music conservatory. Thomas assumed that his financial backers would provide the funds for the school, leaving him in full artistic control; no one, least of all Thomas, realized that his kind of artistic standards could cost more money than his sponsors expected, or that their financial limitations could impede his educational objectives. When his backers wanted to augment income by accepting all applicants, Thomas insisted on admitting only the best qualified who were willing to take a full course of music study. The Cincinnati businessmen found his attitude unreasonable and his expression of it insubordinate. Though Thomas did not lose money on this enterprise, he suffered personal humiliation and the interruption of his other activities. Nor did his conflict with the college backers interfere with the continuation of the Music Festivals in Cincinnati, which he continued to plan and direct until the year before his death.*

In 1876, Thomas accepted the invitation of the Philadelphia Centennial Women's Commission to bring his orchestra there for an entire summer of concerts; they assured him of a good location for these concerts, but he assumed all of the financial risks. Through Thomas the group also commissioned a special composition from Richard Wagner, who not only sent a meretricious march—although it was accompanied by a flowery dedication—but also charged the Commission an outrageous fee of $5000 and broke virtually every provision of the contract, to the acute embarrassment of Thomas. The location for the concerts turned out to be unsuitable, and Thomas was left with huge debts, some of them covered by sheriff's auction sale of the orchestra's assets.† These latter included his entire working library, which was purchased by a New York friend, Dr. Franz Zinzer, who promptly turned it over to Mrs. Thomas with the admonition to make sure that her husband never risk it again.

The American Opera Company, sponsored by Mrs. Jeannette Thurber,‡ was not the first operatic project that Thomas had considered: when Henry Abbey was planning the first season for the new Metropolitan Opera House in 1883, he held extensive consultations with Thomas that almost resulted in his being

* As will be noted later, the Music Hall in Cincinnati was built to house Thomas's May Festivals and a larger than lifesize bronze statue of him still stands in its lobby.
† Thomas partly recouped this failure with a successful concert series the following fall in the Academy of Music, sponsored by the same Mrs. E. D. Gillespie who had headed the Centennial Women's Commission. However, she did not succeed in an effort to organize a permanent orchestra in Philadelphia under Thomas's direction, though the conductor continued to bring his orchestra there regularly until 1891.
‡ The wife of a prominent New York merchant, Mrs. Thurber also organized the National Conservatory in New York, where Antonín Dvořák was director from 1892 to 1895.

the Metropolian's first musical director. However, in the Byzantine maneuverings of opera in New York, Thomas's ideas came to nothing. When Mrs. Thurber approached him in 1885, there were already two opera companies in New York: one at the old Academy of Music, as well as the Metropolitan. Mrs. Thurber's American Opera Company envisaged a quite different national touring company, all operas * to be sung in English by native American singers, and the eventual establishment of a conservatory to train American musicians. To achieve these ends, she not only engaged Thomas as music director but organized a prestigious board of directors, headed by Andrew Carnegie; she chose some of these directors from other cities—Higginson in Boston, for instance—in the hope of securing nationwide backing for this company.

Thomas put his orchestra at the disposal of the opera company, translated the librettos into English, and assembled and trained a company that made two tours of this country, as far west as San Francisco. Such a project lay close to his heart: the emphasis on American singers, performance in a language intelligible to the audience, the nationwide scope of the venture, and the long-range educational aims. But the entire affair was inadequately financed: Mr. Carnegie and his fellow-backers were appalled by the deficit and many withdrew during the first season. An unscrupulous adviser suggested reincorporating the company in New Jersey, where laws were less stringent, and Thomas signed these new papers as president. For the first and only time in his career, Thomas was forced to leave his company stranded on the road: it could not get beyond Buffalo on its return eastward. Thomas discovered that under New Jersey law he was personally liable for the debts of the company. For years afterward, he reported, he could not hear the doorbell ring without cringing for fear of a visit from a creditor, though eventually the courts ruled that he was not personally liable in this case.

Through all these vicissitudes, Thomas by no means abandoned his symphonic activities. Elected, as we shall see shortly, conductor of the Philharmonic Society of New York in 1877, he withdrew for his first year in Cincinnati, but returned in 1879 while he was still officially in Cincinnati. He never relinquished his Brooklyn post, returning there for the necessary concerts. His orchestra not only served on the faculty of the Cincinnati College of Music but also toured the Midwest under Thomas's direction and played summer concerts in Cincinnati, Chicago, and other cities. Throughout the two years of the American Opera Company, the Thomas Orchestra played for its performances and also made separate orchestral tours.

In these experiences in Philadelphia and Cincinnati and with the American Opera Company. Thomas betrayed a naïve miscalculation of the ways of the backers with whom he was working. He assumed that they had entered these ventures in full knowledge of the financial risks, and that they were as dedicated as he was to their artistic ends. They, in turn, found him under pressure

---

* During its two seasons, the American Opera Company presented the following operas: *The Taming of the Shrew* by Goetz; *Orpheus and Euridice* by Gluck; *Lohengrin* and *The Flying Dutchman* by Wagner; *The Magic Flute* by Mozart; *The Merry Wives of Windsor* by Nicolai; *Lakmé* by Delibes; *Faust* by Gounod; *Aïda* by Verdi; *Martha* by Flotow; *Nero* by Rubinstein; and *The Marriage of Jeannette* and *Galatée* by Victor Massée. Two Delibes ballets, *Sylvia* and *Coppélia,* were also presented.

to be an impractical idealist and rather unreasonable in business matters. Devastating as these experiences were to Thomas, they taught him lessons that he would apply later in Chicago.

In 1880, Thomas made a second trip to Europe. In London he received an invitation to become conductor of the London Philharmonic Orchestra; although he was tempted to accept, his experience in Cincinnati being still fresh in his mind, he decided that his work must be pursued in America. During this trip Thomas visited many composers and musicians, as well as hearing many operatic and symphonic performances. In her memoirs, Mrs. Thomas quotes extensively the acute comments on music in Europe which he recorded in his diary.[20] A long-anticipated visit with Liszt had been scheduled to coincide with Wagner's presence in Weimar, but he failed to appear, and Thomas thus missed his only opportunity to meet that artist, toward whom he entertained such mixed feelings. In Berlin, he heard *Tristan und Isolde, Die Meistersinger,* and the *Nibelungen Ring* for the first time in full productions; he was disappointed in *Tristan und Isolde:* "I do not believe this music will ever be popular." In Berlin he also visited Joachim, heard his quartet play, and studied with him the manuscripts of Schumann's string quartets.

Conductor of the Philharmonic

Symphonic concerts in New York were Thomas's central interest throughout the 1870s and 1880s, though he also became involved in organizing choral groups and festivals. As early as 1872, when he had omitted New York from his winter tours for three years, a group of music lovers had petitioned him to resume a season of symphonic concerts there. Whether this invitation carried with it any assurance of financial guarantee cannot be determined now, but it is quite possible that the support of such men as William Steinway, Julius Hallgarten, and Henry de Coppet may have been more than verbal. In 1873, Thomas drew up a comprehensive proposal for the construction of a new music hall in New York that would not only house winter and summer concerts but would also include a school for training musicians. Though this scheme was sufficiently hopeful for Thomas to announce his 1873–74 season as the "farewell tour" of the Thomas Orchestra, nothing came of it.

More than a decade later, early in 1885, Thomas received a letter from Mayor William R. Grace of New York, signed by some three thousand citizens, appealing to him to organize a full season of weekly lighter symphonic concerts in New York. To this letter, Thomas replied, saying in part:

> The benefits of a permanent orchestra and frequent performances are of great value. We shall thus be enabled to give, in a finished manner, a class of musical works which now have little opportunity to be heard. The Philharmonic Society, with its high standard, and few concerts, can only give standard works of the highest character. It cannot give experimental music. My idea of the concerts which you propose, would be to give the lighter symphonies and all the best novelties. The second part of the program would always be devoted to lighter

music, or music of a popular character. The concerts would be, in fact, educational, leading public taste up to the Philharmonic standard. In short, the programs would be similar to those given years ago in the Central Park Garden Concerts. For the matinees it might be well to have the programmes of the alternate concerts especially arranged for young people like the present series of that name.

The assurance of support given me by the three thousand signatures appended to your letter, including as they do, so many of our leading citizens, seems to guarantee the entire success of the project.[21]

Both Mayor Grace's letter and Thomas's reply indicate that they summarized, rather than initiated, extensive discussions of this topic, which was undoubtedly stimulated by the success of the Boston Symphony Orchestra. This project did not materialize, partly because Steinway Hall was too small and the Academy and Metropolitan too large for such concerts, partly because support was never organized, and partly because Thomas soon became involved in the American Opera Company.

Therefore, despite his misgivings about its discipline and organization, the Philharmonic Society remained an important factor in Thomas's career from 1877 until he moved to Chicago in 1891. As noted earlier, his association with the Philharmonic went back to his nineteenth year, when he was elected to its membership. However, as he began to organize his own orchestra after 1862, he came more and more into direct competition with the Philharmonic; the impact of that competition on the Society's financial fortunes is reflected in the sharp drop in per-player income after Thomas resumed winter symphony concerts in New York in 1872–73.* Under these circumstances, it is not surprising that when the Society began to consider replacing Carl Bergmann † as its conductor in the mid-1870s, the members thought of Thomas. Bergmann had conducted the Philharmonic with only moderate distinction; Thomas thought he was lazy, not sufficiently serious about his calling (though he denied later reports that he had learned conducting from Bergmann, Thomas defended him when he was under attack after his release by the Philharmonic). By the mid-1870s, Bergmann was beginning to show symptoms of a physical and mental breakdown. He was unable to complete the 1876 season, and there is reason to believe that the Society informally approached Thomas at this time. However, when Thomas was unwilling to grant its requirement that he give up his own orchestra's concerts in New York, the Philharmonic elected Dr. Leopold Damrosch as its conductor.

Damrosch was a distinguished orchestral and choral conductor, well trained in Germany, where he was closely associated with the circle of Wagner, von Bülow, and Liszt. Though he later achieved notable success with his own or-

---

* Appendix B summarizes the Philharmonic Society finances at this period and shows how the rise and fall of its fortunes reflected first the competition of Thomas and then his acceptance of its direction.

† Carl Bergmann (b. Saxony, 1821; d. New York, 1876) emigrated to this country in 1850 to join the Germania Society as cellist and conductor; he was briefly a member of the Mason-Thomas ensemble. After sharing the conducting of the Philharmonic with Theodor Eisfeld from 1855 to 1865, he became its sole conductor. During his tenure he introduced a great deal of new music, especially that of Wagner, Liszt, and their followers.

chestra, the New York Symphony, and with German opera at the Metropolitan, his one season with the Philharmonic was disastrous financially: the players' annual share, which had fallen under Bergmann from a high of $203 in 1870–71 to $30 in 1875–76, dropped to $18 per man under Damrosch. In these straits the Society now turned officially to Thomas in the spring of 1877. Though still in debt from the Philadelphia Centennial fiasco, Thomas held fast to his terms. Writing to a Mr. Wait that summer, Thomas promised to repay a loan of two hundred dollars and reports the offer from the Philharmonic. "I have accepted the position only conditionally, but am afraid it will not come to anything. All they wish is that I should give up my symphony concerts, gain theirs and step down to their comfortable muddy ways. There being no opposition, the public would have to go to their concerts or have no music. I wonder they did not know me better. They find out now." [22] Apparently the Philharmonic did, in fact, accept Thomas's terms, for he not only conducted that orchestra but continued his winter series of six concerts in Steinway Hall with his own orchestra.

As director of both organizations, Thomas planned their respective activities to avoid the earlier conflicts in rehearsal schedules and presentation of concerts in close succession. Though the printed programs of Thomas's concerts never listed his personnel, as did those of the Philharmonic, there is considerable evidence that by 1877 an appreciable number of the Society's members were also employed in Thomas's orchestra. The Steinway Hall program at the beginning of the 1877–78 season notes, in a column of music news, that the Philharmonic personnel is to be changed substantially with the replacement of players. Thus, Thomas not only had voting support among the Society's members, but his employment of many of them in his own orchestra gave him a measure of musical discipline enjoyed by no other Philharmonic conductor up to this time. The conductor of the Philharmonic was paid by assigning to him additional cooperative shares in the Society's profits. In 1877, Thomas received ten shares, with a guaranteed minimum income of fifteen hundred dollars for the season; this was substantially less than he was receiving in Brooklyn. When he returned from Cincinnati in 1879, the Philharmonic agreed to double his shares and to guarantee him twenty-five hundred dollars a season. Actually, the affairs of the Society so prospered under Thomas that the proceeds of his twenty shares exceeded the guarantee, but he conscientiously returned the excess to the treasury.

Except for Thomas's first year in Cincinnati, he remained conductor of the Philharmonic until 1891. His fourteen seasons were the most prosperous so far in the Society's history, despite the competition of the New York Symphony Orchestra, which Leopold Damrosch had organized to fill the vacuum left by Thomas's departure for Cincinnati in 1878–79. It was worth noting that during this one season without Thomas, the Philharmonic Society under Adolf Neuendorff * saw its players' annual share drop from $82 in Thomas's

---

* Adolf Neuendorff (b. Hamburg, 1843; d. New York, 1897) was the first conductor of the Music Hall Promenade Concerts, later the Boston "Pops"; he is not mentioned in the official history of the Boston Symphony Orchestra, but Slonimsky includes him in *Baker's Biographical Dictionary of Musicians*.

first season to $25, only to recover to $123 when Thomas returned the following year. Under Thomas's direction the Philharmonic Society also gained a stature and renown to which it had long aspired. In addition, it provided Thomas with a stable New York outlet for his conducting career through the vicissitudes he suffered during these fifteen years. From this firm base in the Philharmonic Societies of New York and Brooklyn, he continued to offer his own concerts in New York and vicinity and on tour to Chicago and the West Coast, May Festivals in Cincinnati, and summer concerts in Chicago, but his tours now skipped the smaller cities and concentrated on the larger ones.

In New York, Thomas's principal rivals for public acclaim and support were Leopold Damrosch and, after his death in 1885, his son Walter,* who succeeded his father both as conductor of German opera at the Metropolitan and as director of the New York Symphony Orchestra. The Damrosches were generally more successful than Thomas in enlisting financial support of New York society for their musical enterprises, and young Walter made an exceptionally advantageous marriage to the daughter of the politically powerful James G. Blaine. The rivalry between the Damrosches and Thomas was intense on every level, and was felt mutually. Walter Damrosch, in his autobiography, gives almost grudging credit to Thomas's achievements, and reports an early encounter in Schubert's music store between Thomas and Leopold when the former stated, "I hear, Dr. Damrosch, that you are a very fine musician, but I want to tell you one thing: whoever crosses my path I crush."

Despite his failure to organize a full-time permanent orchestra in New York, Thomas continued to enjoy great success there. Following the example of Leopold Damrosch's lavish music festival in 1881, Thomas organized an even more elaborate one in 1882, giving seven concerts with an orchestra of three hundred and a chorus of three thousand in the Seventh Regiment Armory. For this he assembled a group of renowned opera singers and brought in choral societies from other cities, including the Handel and Haydn Society of Boston and choruses from Philadelphia, Reading, Worcester, and Baltimore. The repertory included an all-Beethoven program (the Fifth Symphony and *Missa solemnis*), an all-Wagner program with excerpts from the four *Ring* operas, and a complete presentation of Handel's *Israel in Egypt*. The financial statement of this festival shows that the total orchestra payroll was substantially less than the soloists received, the player's average pay being a little over sixty dollars for the seven concerts and their rehearsals. Though the festival guarantors had been prepared to lose as much as fifty thousand dollars on the affair, the loss was actually less than the thirty thousand dollars actually advanced. The financial summary of this festival is interesting as an example of performance arts operations at that time.[23]

* Walter Damrosch (b. Breslau, 1862; d. New York, 1950) served as conductor of the New York Symphony from 1885 until its merger with the Philharmonic Society in 1927. He also conducted the Philharmonic in 1902–03, and the Metropolitan Opera from 1885 to 1891 and again in 1900–02. He and his brother Frank played important roles in New York musical life, and Walter became a household musical figure nationally with his music-appreciation broadcasts for NBC from 1927 to 1947. For further details on him and the New York Symphony, see Chapter IV. He wrote an autobiography, *My Musical Life*, in 1923.

RECEIPTS

Guarantee Fund	$ 30,000.00
Subscriptions	53,325.00
Single ticket sale	48,044.00
Auction premiums *	8,081.50
Interest	455.40
	$139,465.90

DISBURSEMENTS

Rent and fitting of halls	$ 29,875.07
Soloists	26,654.62
Orchestra	19,205.20
Chorus transportation, Board, etc.	17,083.95
Advertising, printing, etc.	11,637.68
Conductor and assistants	9,984.91
Music and organ	5,485.39
Business manager	2,500.00
Cables, telegrams, postage	1,143.00
	$123,569.90
Returned to guarantors	15,896.00
	$139,465.90

Such was the success of this festival that its directors presented Thomas with a gold-mounted ivory baton inscribed with the opening theme of Beethoven's Fifth Symphony.† Following the New York festival, many of the same soloists joined Thomas's orchestra in similar festivals, with local choruses, in Chicago and Cincinnati.

In 1884, to educate a wider audience for symphonic music, Thomas offered his first Young People's Concert and a Workingmen's Concert.

YOUNG PEOPLE'S CONCERT—Steinway Hall, February 2, 1884
   WEBER: Overture, *Jubilee*
   HAYDN: Andante from Symphony No. 94
   MOZART: *Batti, Batti* from *Don Giovanni*
   SAINT-SAËNS: *Le Rouet d'Omphale*
   GRIEG: *Humoresque*
   MOSKOWSKI: Minuet
   ROSSINI: *O bel raggio* from *Semiramide*
   BOCCHERINI: Minuet
   NICOLAI: Overture, *The Merry Wives of Windsor*

WORKINGMEN'S CONCERT—Steinway Hall, February 24, 1884
   BACH-ABERT: Prelude, Chorale and Fugue

---

* Auction premiums represent additional income from the sale of especially desirable seats by auction, a device used by Barnum in promoting the Jenny Lind concerts and retained for many seasons by the Boston Symphony Orchestra.
† When Mrs. Thomas distributed her husband's memorabilia to various Chicago institutions after his death, this baton was among the items given the Art Institute, which in 1906 disposed of them as unworthy of their collection. The baton and other mementos are now in the custody of the Orchestral Association.[24]

SCHUBERT-THOMAS: *Am Meer*
BEETHOVEN: Symphony No. 5, C minor, Op. 67
MENDELSSOHN: Overture to *A Midsummer Night's Dream*
SCHUMANN: *The Two Grenadiers*
WEBER-BERLIOZ: *Invitation to the Dance*
WAGNER: Overture, *Rienzi*

Concerning such programs, Thomas took a rather patronizing attitude:

Symphonic music is the highest flower of art. Only the most cultivated persons are able to understand it. How, then, can we expect the ignorant or immature mind to grasp its subtleties? The kind of music suitable for them is that which has very clearly defined melody and well-marked rhythms, such, for instance, as is played by the best bands. The orchestra, with its unlimited palette, whereby the modern composer paints every shade and gradation of tone color, as well as the complexities of symphonic form, are far beyond the grasp of beginners. There should be, it is true, concerts for these classes, which would prepare them for a higher grade of musical performances. But it is a waste of time for a great symphony orchestra to do this work, which could be equally well accomplished by smaller and less costly organizations. In my judgment an orchestra, such as mine, can be of more service to the community by selling a certain number of twenty-five-cent tickets to all its concerts, for the benefit of students and music-lovers of small means, than by giving an occasional free concert to people who can only enjoy it to a limited degree.[25]

Thomas suffered his first unsuccessful orchestral tour in 1888, thanks to a combination of unfavorable circumstances. The public had become too accustomed to his appearances, and the opera fiasco undoubtedly tarnished his glamour. He was now sharing the national spotlight with Walter Damrosch and with Arthur Nikisch and the Boston Symphony, both of whom were covering the "Thomas highway." Moreover, the increasing government regulation of railroads prohibited making special rates for favored customers, and Thomas was faced with substantial increases in tour expense. The Boston Symphony Orchestra especially was cutting into Thomas's lucrative eastern tours, for it could afford, under Major Higginson's subsidy, to absorb its losses to a degree that Thomas could not. Thomas had ample reason to look longingly at Boston, where Higginson had established the kind of orchestra of which Thomas had long dreamed, but he firmly refused the efforts of some dissident Bostonians in 1882 to engage him to head an orchestra there as a rival to Higginson's.[26]

In his failure to attract similar support in New York, Thomas was undoubtedly paying the personal price for his independence and uncompromising attitude toward the public, press, and potential backers. We have already noted the difficulties caused by his unbending posture toward public taste and toward wealthy patrons. Among the press he had many friends and many enemies: some of the latter would have opposed any serious symphonic ventures, but there was a faction that favored the more flamboyant school of Wagner. Though Thomas conducted much of Wagner's music, he was less and less identified as an apostle of that composer, especially when compared to Damrosch and Anton Seidl. However, not all of the pro-Wagner press was opposed to Thomas: the influential Henry Finck, for instance, was a great admirer of Thomas's throughout this period. Part of the problem with the press arose from what we would today call bad public relations: Thomas was capable of responding to questions and criticisms with abrupt discourtesy and, on occasion, ordered unfriendly reporters to be removed from his presence.[27]

The years 1888 and 1889 were further clouded for Thomas by the lingering illness of his beloved wife Minna. Through all the vicissitudes and triumphs of his career, through all his interminable touring, she had maintained his New York home and raised his children, staying completely in the background of his public life. But Thomas was extremely dependent upon her, and her illness and death in April, 1889, shattered him. This extraordinarily energetic and ambitious man, faced with failure and frustration in his career and suffering a personal tragedy at home, for the first time prepared to admit defeat. He even contemplated giving up conducting altogether to accept a comfortable teaching position.

It is one of the happy miracles of Thomas's career that at the depths of this depression he at last found the opportunity to realize his life's ambition to form a resident orchestra. But it is quite possible that he would never have adjusted himself to the problems that developed in Chicago had he not been realistically prepared for them in the years before moving there. The Theodore Thomas who rewarded his loyal Chicago supporters with equally loyal dedication to their cause, who was able to accommodate himself to the shortcomings of his new home, was a quite different man from the one who had treated his Cincinnati backers imperiously or who had naïvely accepted at face value the financial backing of Mrs. Thurber's sponsors.

The Chicago Symphony Orchestra

Thomas's roots in Chicago went back to his youth as a member of traveling orchestras accompanying Henriette Sontag and Ole Bull, and that city soon became an important stop on his touring schedules after 1870—except in 1871, when Thomas and his orchestra arrived there the morning after the disastrous fire. From 1877 on, Thomas gave many of his summer series in the old Exposition Building, which stood where the Art Institute now is. These extended summer visits not only created a large and admiring audience for Thomas but they also gave him an opportunity to make friends there among musicians and business leaders interested in promoting Chicago's cultural life. One of these was Charles Norman Fay, a prominent business executive who had come to Chicago during the railroad strike of 1877.[28]

Fay was the son of the Reverend Dr. Charles Fay, a native New Englander and graduate of Harvard. After serving in Louisiana, where his children were born, Dr. Fay sought a transfer to New England; he felt that the cultural opportunities there would be more advantageous for bringing up his children. His wife, the daughter of an Episcopal bishop in Vermont, was a self-taught pianist who encouraged the study of music among all of her children. One of them, Amy, progressed so well that she was sent to Germany to study piano with Liszt and other notable pedagogues. Another daughter, Rose, was also an ardent musician, but did not pursue her interest professionally. Though brought up in Vermont, Charles Norman Fay eventually moved to Milwaukee, where he was in the railroad business, and then to Chicago, where he played an important part in developing the streetcar system and electric utilities. His sister Rose followed him there, and Amy joined them after her American orchestral debut in 1876 with Thomas's orchestra in Boston. Through this appearance Thomas became acquainted with the Fay family in Chicago, a friendship that was sufficiently close, by 1883, for him to ask Rose Fay for her help in finding him a suitable boarding house for the summer.

In the spring of 1889, shortly before the death of Minna, Fay encountered Thomas on Fifth Avenue in New York and the two retired to Delmonico's for lunch. Fay found Thomas desperately depressed, feeling that he had, at the age of fifty-four, reached the end of his career.

> "Is there no one," Fay asked Thomas, "no rich and generous man, to do here in New York as Major Higginson has done in Boston—keep your orchestra going, and pay the deficit?"
>
> "No one," Thomas replied. "I have often told them, those who say they are my friends, that for good work there must be a permanent orchestra, which will not pay, there must be a subsidy. My work is known. I am old now, and have no axe to grind. But they do not care. They think I have always kept body and soul together somehow, and that I always will—that I have nowhere else to go. They treat me as a music merchant, a commercial proposition, subject to the laws of supply and demand."
>
> Fay then asked, "Would you come to Chicago if we could give you a permanent orchestra?"
>
> "I would go to hell if they gave me a permanent orchestra." [29]

Fay returned to Chicago to propose to other business leaders his scheme of organizing an orchestral association that would not be dependent upon the support of any one man or offer its backers any prospect of profit.[30] He first planned to secure from ten men pledges of annual contributions of five thousand dollars each for three years to underwrite the losses of starting the Chicago Symphony Orchestra; at the suggestion of Marshall Field, one of the first to subscribe five thousand dollars a year, Fay eventually sought and obtained a larger number of thousand-dollar pledges. In December, 1890, the Chicago Orchestra Association (later renamed the Orchestral Association) was incorporated, and a contract was drawn up with Thomas to take effect in the fall of 1891.

This contract specifically stated, to Thomas's great satisfaction, "the intention of the Association being to lodge in the hands of the Director the power and responsibility for the attainment of the highest standard of artistic excellence in all performances given by the Association." The Association could hire out the orchestra for opera performances, with or without Thomas as conductor, and Thomas would furnish his personal orchestral library for the use of the new orchestra. With Fay and his colleagues, Thomas projected a season of at least twenty weeks with two concerts a week, to be played by an orchestra of eighty-five players. Sixty-two of these were to be members of Thomas's own orchestra, now under contract to the Association, the remaining ones to be engaged locally in Chicago, an arrangement that created some difficulty with the musicians' union. All touring was to be under the auspices of the Association, and except for the Cincinnati Festivals, for which Thomas's Chicago musicians were individually contracted by the festival management, Thomas gave up all of his private activities.

Meanwhile, on May 7, 1890, at the Church of the Ascension in Chicago, Theodore Thomas and Rose Fay were married. The music for the ceremony was an excerpt from Beethoven's Fifth Symphony played by organist Clarence Eddy. Rose Fay Thomas proved, in her own quite different way, to be as admirable a wife for Thomas as Minna had been. Utterly devoted to her husband, she played an important part in his Chicago career both because of her musical background and by virtue of her brother's role in organizing the Orchestral Association. After Thomas's death, she settled in Cambridge, Massachusetts, staunch New Englander that she always was. In Cambridge she and her sister Amy took a lively interest in musical affairs there and at the Boston Symphony. Her *Memoirs of Theodore Thomas* is a fine account of her husband's career, despite the fact that she participated only in his later years.

Thomas wound up his affairs in New York, conducting his last seasons at the Philharmonic and in Brooklyn, and taking his own orchestra for the last time to Philadelphia, Cincinnati, and Chicago; his final tours were more successful than that of 1888. He was honored in New York at a grand testimonial concert in Madison Square Garden and a gala dinner attended by a host of friends and admirers. In the fall of 1891, he took up residence in Chicago.

When Thomas founded the Chicago Symphony Orchestra in 1891, there was only one other full-time resident orchestra in this country, Major Higginson's Boston Symphony Orchestra. Though the New York Philharmonic was older, neither it nor its rival, Damrosch's New York Symphony, was a full-time operation. There had been sporadic efforts in other cities—notably St. Louis, Philadelphia, and Cincinnati—to establish permanent resident orchestras, but none had so far succeeded. The difference between the orchestras of Chicago and Boston, however, can be summarized by calling one Thomas's orchestra and the other Major Higginson's, for in Chicago the conductor was the central feature and in Boston, as we shall see, it was the sponsor. In Chicago, moreover, the Orchestral Association was created as a body structurally independent of either the conductor or the domination of any one donor: so long as a group of donors would support the orchestra, the Chicago Symphony could survive. The groundwork was thus laid for perpetuating the orchestra through a wider base of community support, wealth, and influence. It is to the credit of the organizers that their orchestra survived the death of Thomas fourteen years later, despite his being its central figure.

The corporate structure of the Orchestral Association undoubtedly owed much to the example of private business, especially as that example was being applied to such educational organizations as universities and colleges. Like the private corporation, this device made it possible for donors to support the symphony to the extent that they wished, but without unlimited liability for its debts, as was the case with Higginson in Boston. Though the conductor had full disciplinary authority over his players, their contracts were with the Association rather than with him or, as in Boston, with the sponsor. Thomas was technically an employee under contract to the Association, but he was accorded special status in policy matters. The division of responsibility between artistic direction and board financing, upon which Thomas insisted unsuccessfully in Cincinnati, was achieved in Chicago because the board had complete faith in its beloved and renowned conductor and because Thomas became deeply concerned over the board's financial problems. Certainly his family connection with Fay provided an avenue of understanding and cooperation, and Thomas had already learned bitter practical lessons, but he generally got the support in Chicago that he wanted for his artistic policies.

Though no analysis of the repertory of Theodore Thomas's own orchestra has been made, the Mueller studies * of American symphonic repertory include data on the New York Philharmonic and Chicago Symphony Orchestra at the times Thomas directed them. The percentage averages by composer nationality for the relevant periods show some interesting differences between Thomas's activities in New York and Chicago, as well as with the national averages for the period from 1890 to 1905 and for the most recent one covered. It must be noted, however, that the New York Philharmonic represented only half of his activity in that city, and the repertory of his own orchestra may have been markedly different.

TABLE 2-A

THEODORE THOMAS REPERTORY New York Philharmonic, 1880–90, Chicago Symphony, 1890–1905, Compared with National Averages, 1890–1905 and 1965–70; as percentage of total repertory by composer-nationality.

	New York 1880–90	Chicago 1890–1905	National 1890–1905	National 1965–70
Austro-German	81.65	64.13	63.40	51.65
Russian	8.62	11.89	12.32	14.80
French	4.55	10.87	11.53	10.09
American	——	2.91	3.73	6.66
British	0.64	2.01	1.41	3.97
Czech	4.04	3.66	4.21	3.12
Italian	——	0.34	0.74	2.89
Scandinavian	0.22	2.22	1.82	2.76
Hungarian	——	0.17	0.31	1.57
Spanish ⎱ Latin-American ⎰	——	0.02	0.01	1.47

(Percentages in repertory tables do not always add up to 100% because miscellaneous nationalities are not recorded here.)

* See Chapter XVII for a full discussion of this research.

Though Thomas may have hoped for a tranquil tenure to close his career in Chicago, he would soon encounter problems that were counterparts of those he had faced earlier. At the outset, the actual deficit of the first three years overran slightly the initial guarantee fund; to the donors this was less surprising than was their gradual realization that these losses would be inevitable in future years and were not just the result of starting a new orchestra. Under pressure to operate economically, Thomas developed a sympathetic concern for the financial sacrifices of the sponsors. To augment income it was necessary for him to tour with the orchestra, a task that he came to abhor as he grew older. In addition, the use of the orchestra for opera performances in the Auditorium, where the orchestra also gave its concerts, disrupted the discipline and schedule of the symphonic program. All concerned recognized the difficulties of financing the orchestra, and Thomas on more than one occasion informally offered to release the trustees from their commitment, but they repeatedly assured him of their faith in him and in the ultimate contribution of his orchestra. By the end of the seventh season the Association had incurred a net deficit of over $30,000 and issued a special appeal for $60,000 to defray this and to provide working funds for the future. This appeal was accompanied by an impressive list of 104 donors (including the original 49 from 1891) who had donated a total of over $255,000 in seven years; several of these donations averaged over $1,000 a year. This report also included a seven-year financial summary: [31]

Gross expenditures	$884,962.85
Gross receipts	597,258.09
Donations	255,561.79
Net deficit	32,142.97

Thomas, for his part, made a real effort to attract larger audiences: on occasion he lightened his repertory for the subscription programs, offered request programs, and generally took a deep concern with increasing attendance, though he frequently expressed his disillusionment that his decades of effort in educating the public had borne so little fruit. However, when critics complained of the heaviness of his programs, he defended his repertory by pointing to the example of the Boston Symphony: "Do you wish our programmes to be inferior in standard to those of the Boston Orchestra? . . . Well, we give every year a number of programmes without a symphony. The Boston Orchestra does not." [32] Some of the Chicago press, notably George P. Upton of the *Tribune*, strongly supported Thomas, but a considerable segment was hostile to him personally and to the orchestra in general. The trustees, however, never wavered in backing Thomas and their orchestra; they declared that it was his responsibility to give Chicago the best possible orchestra and their business to support it.

During the early years of the Chicago Symphony Orchestra, the trustees and Thomas had some difficulty in securing fully competent management: tour arrangements, box-office details, and orchestra logistics were not always as efficient as desired. In the summer of 1895, the trustees appointed Miss Anna Millar as manager; she had already shown ability in her arrangement of tours and ticket sales. She served in this post until the end of

1899, when Frederick J. Wessels was appointed business manager; he had previously been on the Association's staff. Later the following year, he appointed as his assistant Henry E. Voegeli, who became manager of the orchestra upon Wessels's death in 1926. Both Wessels and Voegeli enjoyed a close association with Thomas, and with his successor, in which the conductor played a cooperative but dominant role, sharing an office with the manager and conferring with him almost daily during the active season. Despite its difficulties, working conditions were better in Chicago than Thomas had known before, and he was able to build his orchestra in the manner of which he had long dreamed. Most of the great solo artists appeared with the Chicago Symphony Orchestra under Thomas, and he continued to introduce a great deal of music new both to Chicago and America on his tours throughout the Midwest and South every season. The lucrative touring territory in the eastern part of the nation was more or less preempted by the Boston Symphony, though Thomas made tours with great success to New York, Boston, Philadelphia, and other cities in 1896 and 1898. The orchestra was generally well received, and Thomas, of course, was welcomed as an old friend wherever he went.

Among the young concert artists Thomas introduced to this country was the Swiss pianist Rudolf Ganz, who made his American debut with the Chicago Symphony Orchestra on the recommendation of Ferruccio Busoni.* After his Chicago debut in 1903, Ganz played with other American orchestras —the New York Symphony, the Boston, and the Philadelphia—but he recalled the Chicago under Thomas as the best in the country then, comparable to the finest in Europe. Thomas was a "splendid conductor" by any standards and would today rank among the very best. To the end of his life, Ganz remembered with warm gratitude the courtesy of the old conductor to the young pianist making his American debut, and entertained the highest regard for Thomas's unquestioned musicianship and control of his superbly trained orchestra.

Nevertheless, Thomas was selective in his choice of soloists with his orchestra. In 1900, when one of the trustees suggested that he re-engage a young lady who had previously appeared with him, he wrote to Fay: [33]

> Does it occur to the average listener that expression in music comes from the soul—and in the interpretation of a masterwork the honesty of purpose is easily detected? Whether a thing is done for effect—for the market—or whether it is honest, but . . . mediocre. Can you imagine a greater torture than to stand before the public and the Orchestra for hours and endure in sincerity! The few years I have to work yet, I cannot be unmindful for appearances in art matters, and I cannot conscientiously give Miss Jackson my personal endorsement by conducting for her at a second appearance in our concerts. Even if we have not reached the highest standard, it is not worth the sacrifice and the support given to the institution if not guided and carried on honestly. I am sorry to say that the testimony of many European authorities is worthless.

* Ganz died in 1972 at the age of ninety-five. When I visited him in November 1970 to verify my recollection of his reminiscences of Thomas (which I had heard in much detail during the late 1950s), he was probably the last surviving artist of major stature who had played under Thomas's direction.

Thomas had little use for guest conductors as such: he felt that they inter-fered with the continuity of discipline and musical style of an orchestra. Therefore, for his entire tenure in Chicago no guest conductors were engaged, though toward the end of his life he turned some of his duties over to his assistant, Frederick Stock, who had joined the orchestra as violist in 1895 and who in 1899 was designated associate conductor. His duties included assisting Thomas in rehearsals, conducting some complete concerts on tour, and conducting the orchestra at subscription concerts in some concerto ac-companiments. Aside from Stock, the only other musician to conduct the orchestra at a subscription concert in Chicago was the composer Richard Strauss.

Thomas had "discovered" Strauss in Munich in 1880, had played his early Symphony in F minor even before it was heard in Europe, and had intro-duced to America many of the subsequent tone poems which had made Strauss an international celebrity. Strauss first visited this country early in 1904, appearing as guest conductor in New York, Boston, and Philadelphia, with his wife, Pauline, singing his songs with orchestra. For the Chicago programs, Strauss and Thomas chose to introduce to America the difficult score of his newly composed *Also sprach Zarathustra*, and Thomas prepared for Strauss's visit by drilling his orchestra intensively in this work. At the conclusion of his first rehearsal the usually reserved composer was over-whelmed by the proficiency of the orchestra, declaring in German: [34]

> Gentlemen, I came here in the pleasant expectation of finding a superior or-chestra, but you have far surpassed my expectations, and I can say to you that I am delighted to know an orchestra of artists in whom beauty of tone, technical perfection, and discipline are found in the highest degree. I know that this is due to your, by me, most highly revered *Meister,* Theodore Thomas, whom I have known for twenty years, and whom it gives me inexpressible pleasure to meet here again in his own workroom. Gentlemen, such a rehearsal as that which we have held this morning is no labor, but a great pleasure, and I thank you all for the hearty good-will you have shown towards me.

During his visit to Chicago, Strauss spent a morning in Thomas's study, discussing his orchestral music and going over the recently completed *Sin-fonia Domestica*. In every respect it was a gratifying experience for the old conductor.

When it was founded, the nucleus of the Chicago Symphony was Thomas's old orchestra from New York, but many members settled in Chicago, teach-ing and playing, as an integral part of the city's musical community. In his old age Thomas became more and more of a paternal autocrat, stern in dis-cipline but deeply understanding of the personalities of the men who played for him, though he could on occasion subject an errant player to the humili-ation of playing a passage by himself in rehearsal. Away from the concert platform, he occasionally joined his players in small groups for a drink or late evening snack, and he took great interest in the more formal parties for the entire orchestra. On one such occasion, when the orchestra players had planned an elaborate Christmas party with a concert and banquet, Thomas learned early in the evening of the sudden death in Florida of his son, Franz, but he forbade anyone to tell the players of this tragedy and attended the party; he could not bring himself to cast a pall over the pleasure of his men.[35]

The violinist Max Bendix served as Thomas's concertmaster, both before Chicago and for a few years there before returning to New York to teach. A few days after Thomas's death, Bendix was interviewed in New York and reminisced about Thomas's relations with his players. Among these reminiscences is the story of the conductor's wig. While in Chicago, Thomas began to grow bald at the back of his head and conceived the idea that this bald spot was aggravating his catarrh. He therefore had a wig made to cover his head, but characteristically prescribed that it had a matching bald spot. When he wore this wig for the first time to rehearsal, he gravely removed it and waved it before the assembled orchestra, saying, "Now, gentlemen, have your laugh and get it over with." [36]

An equally characteristic gesture of Thomas was his refusal in 1900 of the invitation of Édouard Colonne to conduct in Paris during the Exposition there. Invited both to conduct and to allow his name to appear on a sponsoring list of internationally distinguished musicians, Thomas declined to visit Paris as a protest against the official attitude there in the Dreyfus affair.

The orchestra quickly became an important feature of Chicago's cultural life. It joined forces with visiting opera companies, including the Metropolitan from New York, in visits to the Auditorium, and appeared with local amateur choruses, notably the Apollo Club, with which at least one trustee, Philo Otis, was closely associated. Its participation in the Columbian Exposition of 1893 was the occasion, however, for a rather extensive public attack on Thomas personally, an indication that, despite the support of his trustees, Thomas was still a controversial figure. When he arrived in Chicago, plans were already under way for a mammoth world's fair to celebrate the four-hundredth anniversary of Columbus's discovery of America, Chicago having won over New York in gaining Congressional designation as the site of this celebration. The Columbian Exposition of 1893 was a cultural landmark—architecturally and industrially—celebrating the coming of age of Chicago and of the Middle West in general. Theodore Thomas was invited by the local Chicago committee to become director of its musical activities; he accepted the post eagerly and made elaborate plans which reflected both his educational objectives and the lessons he had learned in 1876 in Philadelphia.[37] Creating a summer-long festival around his orchestra and a local chorus, he invited many of the most renowned artists and orchestras of Europe and America to participate in these musical festivities, which took place in a special building that was an integral part of the Exposition site.

Once again, alas, Thomas suffered personal humiliation. For one thing, the audiences proved as disappointing as they had been in Philadelphia in 1876, despite location of the concerts on Exposition grounds. Had they drawn a larger audience, Thomas's other difficulties might have been resolved, but the visitors to the Columbian Exposition were more interested in Cyrus McCormick's farm machinery and the gyrations of Little Egypt than in Theodore Thomas and his concerts, a further demonstration to him of the failure of his great educational mission. Thomas's conflict with the Exposition management came to a head over a strictly commercial question. The Exposition management, which was divided between a federal committee of bureaucrats and a local civic group, had stipulated that no products could be used at Exposition functions unless they were officially exhibited. The Steinway firm of New York, for reasons of its own, had declined to exhibit its pianos commercially in competition with pianos made by Midwest firms. These latter insisted that their pianos, and not those of Steinway, should be used at the Chicago Symphony concerts. Thomas agreed to use these acceptable pianos in the orchestra itself and for rehearsals, but refused to dictate that visiting soloists under contract to Steinway be required to abandon that instrument. The exhibiting piano manufacturers charged that Thomas was in the pay of Steinway and that he had intentionally engaged these artists on that basis. As the issue come to a head, the exhibitors had the full support of the national committee, while Thomas was backed by the Chicago committee who had engaged him. Matters took a comic-opera turn when Paderewski's Steinway piano was smuggled into the Exposition grounds in the middle of the night before his appearance with Thomas. The anti-Thomas press, already critical of his autocratic ways, delightedly joined the outraged federal officials in demanding Thomas's removal as musical director of the Exposition. Thomas refused to meet with, or even reply to, the federal group on the grounds that he was responsible only to the Chicago committee, which supported him fully. In the end he was forced to resign, but this episode in no way jeopardized his relations with the Orchestral Association.

Between 1900 and 1902 the trustees of the Orchestral Association held discussions with President William R. Harper of the University of Chicago concerning the possibility of joining forces in organizing a music school affiliated with the university. The principal argument in favor of such a merger was the financial stability and continuity which would accrue to the orchestra. Thomas was of two minds on this question, undoubtedly recalling his sad experience in Cincinnati, but still cherishing his larger educational objectives. He was eventually agreeable to the plan, providing that the school not offer instruction in piano and voice, since these were not part of orchestral performance and because their inclusion in the curriculum would antagonize other music schools and private instructors. This condition was not acceptable to the university. Moreover, though the trustees could see financial benefits that would relieve them of the onerous task of raising money for the orchestra, they were unwilling to sacrifice the identity of their orchestra in this arrangement; in so deciding, they reiterated their responsibility for the orchestra's financial support.[38]

During these years Thomas's health began to decline; he no longer had the tireless energy of his youth, and he came to resent bitterly the necessity of frequent touring. Some years earlier, he and his first wife had purchased a summer home at the shore in Fairhaven, Massachusetts, where he spent what little portion of the summer remained after his concert seasons. After

1891, and except for the summer of the Exposition, Thomas and his wife returned to Fairhaven for long vacations, which gave him the rest he so badly needed. However, a few years after moving to Chicago he became increasingly afflicted with chronic catarrh, which was apparently first evident when he had to rehearse his orchestra in the damp and drafty uncompleted Exposition building in 1893. Finding that the damp seaside climate at Fairhaven further aggravated his condition, he and Mrs. Thomas bought another summer home in the White Mountains of New Hampshire, named Felsengarten, where he found considerable relief.

Orchestra Hall

Despite his loyalty to Chicago and the sponsors who had finally made it possible for him to realize his ambition of a permanent orchestra—a loyalty that moved him to decline an invitation from Higginson in 1892 and one from the New York Philharmonic in 1894 [39]—Thomas was not completely happy in Chicago. For one thing, he believed that the climate there made his chronic catarrh worse. Another factor was his growing attachment for New England, undoubtedly encouraged by his wife Rose. In 1899 he actually wrote formally to the trustees asking to be relieved of his duties. Philo Otis, in reporting this letter, cites no specific occasion for it, and Mrs. Thomas in her *Memoirs* does not even mention the letter, but Otis and she agree generally that Thomas was increasingly fatigued and discouraged. Thomas met with the trustees a few weeks later and was persuaded to remain in Chicago by the strong expression of faith in him, represented by the comment of one trustee: "You are engaged to play only the great works of ancient and modern times, and nothing else. If there are deficits in giving the concerts, we will take care of them." [40] However, the trustees must have had this episode in mind when, in 1903, Thomas advised them that they must build their own hall for the orchestra or disband it. Though he had made similar proposals, less strongly advanced, as early as 1896, he now pressed the matter urgently, encouraged no doubt by the recent completion of Symphony Hall in Boston.

The great Auditorium * of Sullivan and Adler, still one of the supreme large theaters of the world, was simply not suitable for regular symphonic concerts. Though the acoustics of this hall was, and still is, of exceptional quality for opera and other spectacular productions, Thomas was never satisfied with the sound of his orchestra there, and he continually experimented with the arrangement of his players on the stage and with

---

* Designed by Louis H. Sullivan and Dankmar Adler, the Auditorium opened in 1889. It served as the home of the Chicago Symphony until 1904, as well as for a variety of visiting opera companies, political conventions, and theatrical attractions. It was for many years the home of the Chicago Civic Opera until Samuel Insull moved the company in 1929 into the new skyscraper building that he planned as a means of supporting the opera company. The Auditorium, having survived threats of destruction and use as a USO bowling alley, has recently been restored and is once again in use as a theater, thanks to the efforts of Roosevelt University, which owns the building, and a civic committee.

the placement of reflecting panels around and above the orchestra to improve its sound. Moreover, the large capacity of the Auditorium, over thirty-five hundred, seldom sold out for symphony concerts: as a result, patrons knew that they could always get tickets at the last minute and failed to purchase season subscriptions. Finally, for its rehearsals and concerts, the orchestra had to share the Auditorium with other attractions, making it impossible to hold all rehearsals in the hall in which the concerts were given. In 1903, Thomas advised the trustees: [41]

> It is useless to attempt to make an orchestra permanent without its own building. I found this to be the case in New York, and was obliged to give up my orchestra there for lack of a building. Conditions in Chicago are similar. We now have here a large and cultivated public which demands the highest forms of music, and I believe, would not be willing to give up the orchestra. But what is everybody's business is nobody's business, and the people will do nothing unless the situation is brought before them strongly. I therefore ask you to announce to the general public that, unless in the next six months a sufficient endowment can be raised to provide a suitable building in which to carry on the work of our institution, I shall resign my position and go elsewhere.

Otis does not mention this communication from Thomas, nor does he anywhere imply that the trustees were under such extreme pressure from Thomas. He reports that the trustees first considered the present location of Orchestra Hall in the summer of 1902, as an outgrowth of the final rejection of the University of Chicago proposal. He also reports that while affiliation with the university was still under consideration, there were also discussions with Northwestern University of a proposal that the orchestra occupy a new building projected on university property at Lake and Dearborn Streets. In any event, the trustees' deliberations were undoubtedly influenced by Thomas's desire for a new hall at this time and their planning proceeded in close consultation with him.[42] The trustees subscribed $100,000 to take an option on a Michigan Avenue site, secured a mortgage of $350,000 on the property, and raised another $750,000 in contributions from the public, the first such intense general fund-raising. Despite some community loyalty to the old Auditorium, and despite the revival of anti-Thomas criticism in the press, the sum was subscribed by between eight and nine thousand individual contributors, large and small, millionaire and shop clerk alike. The campaign for the construction of Orchestra Hall became the rallying point which expressed the community's recognition of the importance of its orchestra and its affection for Thomas.

Orchestra Hall was designed by Daniel H. Burnham, a distinguished architect of national renown who had created many of the buildings at the 1893 Exposition and had developed a long-range plan for Chicago's lakefront parks. As a trustee of the Orchestral Association, he was a close friend of Thomas, whom he consulted intensively; Orchestra Hall incorporates many of the ideas on the design of concert halls which Thomas had developed in his many years of touring and conducting orchestra concerts in a wide variety of halls and theaters. Thomas certainly had more experience of this sort than any other musician of his time, and he had developed detailed notions on physical arrangements and acoustics from this practical experience.* Thomas's first requirements for a concert hall were that its walls be finished in wood and that its physical shape be a continuous single space enclosing both the orchestra and the audience. He favored a high, deep gallery for the dispersal of sound, but specified that it not overlap the main floor of the auditorium. He was much concerned with the different kinds of music performance and their different requirements for resonance and clarity. In most respects his views agree with those of modern acousticians, though they were not presented in quantitative or engineering terms.

Thomas's ideal was only partially realized in Orchestra Hall for several reasons beyond his control. The most serious limiting factor was the size and shape of the building lot, which precluded the construction of a building of optimum shape: the lot is too shallow, from street to back alley, with the result that the longitudinal dimension of Orchestra Hall is extremely cramped. This is reflected not only in the inadequate depth and excessive width and height of both performing area and auditorium but also in the inconvenient location of dressing rooms and supporting facilities in the basement. The inclusion of an organ in this narrow space violated Thomas's injunction against having any openings in the walls surrounding the orchestra and audience. Nor is it possible to convert Orchestra Hall easily into use for popular concerts, as Thomas had suggested in his 1873 notes and as was provided so well at Symphony Hall in Boston. Finally, the tragic Iroquois Theater fire occurred during the planning of Orchestra Hall: it resulted in changes in city regulations limiting the use of wood in the hall and requiring inconvenient arrangements of seating, exits, and public traffic in and around the auditorium itself.

Thomas's actual experience with Orchestra Hall for rehearsal and concerts was extremely limited, for he was already mortally ill when it was completed. He expressed enthusiasm for its acoustics both in a wire to Burnham, "HALL A COMPLETE SUCCESS. QUALITY EXCEEDS EXPECTATIONS," and in his comment on the spot after his first rehearsal there: "Gentlemen, your hall is a success, a great success." But he tempered these expressions by an explicit statement to Mrs. Thomas that it would take some time to adjust the playing of the orchestra to its new home.[43] The hall, as it stands today, has undergone some changes, but it remains substantially as Burnham designed it; as such it does not rank with the greatest halls of this country—Symphony Hall in Boston, the Academy of Music in Philadelphia, or Carnegie Hall in New York—but it is still an excellent setting for orchestral concerts and even better for solo recitals.†

* In 1873, when there was a possibility that a group of New Yorkers would underwrite a Thomas orchestra, he prepared *Plans for the Construction and Uses of an Orchestral Building.* In 1897, the architectural writer Russell Sturgis asked Thomas to write an article on concert halls for a *Dictionary of Architecture.* Both dissertations, quoted extensively in Mrs. Thomas's *Memoirs of Theodore Thomas,* contain extremely sensible ideas about acoustics and theater arrangements.
† My own knowledge of Orchestra Hall predates the extensive remodeling undertaken in the 1960s, which greatly improved the accommodations in the basement, but seriously altered the acoustics of the hall itself; the orchestra players now report that they can hear one another better, but there remains some question of whether the sound heard in sections of the hall has not been adversely affected.

From its opening, however, Orchestra Hall achieved Thomas's other objectives in encouraging season subscriptions and in providing the orchestra with a home completely under its control. Thanks to its more limited capacity and to the stimulation of public interest in tthe orchestra by the campaign for construction funds, the Chicago Symphony secured a much stronger base of audience support, which it needed in the next months and years to survive the death of Thomas. At the outset, the trustees also hoped that rental of the hall itself and of office space in the building would bring in enough income to defray the deficit of the orchestra's operation; this developed only to a limited degree, though such income has always helped the orchestra's finances.

Because of the delay in the completion of Orchestra Hall, the season began in the fall of 1904 in the Auditorium, much to Thomas's disappointment. During the preceding summer, his health was breaking down rapidly. Mrs. Thomas recalled: "One ear was completely deaf and one eye was nearly blind. . . . The catarrh of the throat was so deeply seated that even the air of Felsengarten no longer gave him any relief." His return to Chicago in the fall was more deliberate than usual, as he stopped to visit in Boston and New York with friends and family. In Boston he visited Mt. Auburn Cemetery in Cambridge to select a grave site for himself and Mrs. Thomas.[44] Earlier that year, in the spring, he had received a pressing invitation from the New York Philharmonic to return as guest conductor in 1905, which he first refused and then accepted only when the Philharmonic concertmaster made a special trip to Chicago to persuade him.[45] Despite his condition he returned to Chicago to open the season in the Auditorium and to oversee the completion of Orchestra Hall. On December 6, while construction material still littered the building, Thomas held his first rehearsal there on a drafty, unheated stage. Describing conditions as "working on top of the ruins of Athens," he rehearsed the orchestra and chorus of the Apollo Club for the dedicatory concert of December 14:

WAGNER: *Hail, Bright Abode* from *Tannhäuser*
WAGNER: Overture, *Tannhäuser*
STRAUSS: *Death and Transfiguration*
BEETHOVEN: Symphony No. 5, C minor, Op. 67
HANDEL: *Hallelujah* from *Messiah*

A few days later he conducted an all-Beethoven program at a pair of subscription concerts, and on December 23 and 24 a more popular program of the lighter music for which he was so beloved. He celebrated Christmas quietly, alone with his wife, and then announced, "I am tired, so tired. I must go to bed." The following morning he rose to go to rehearsal, but turned back at the front door and returned to bed, suffering from acute influenza and possibly pneumonia. Nine days later, in the early morning of January 4, 1905, he died.[46] He was buried, as he had planned, in Mt. Auburn Cemetery in Cambridge.

The city of Chicago, the nation, and the international musical world joined in mourning his passing with lavish tribute to his talent and achievement. The trustees of the Orchestral Association moved to rename their orchestra the Theodore Thomas Orchestra. Mrs. Thomas divided Thomas's personal library between the orchestra and the Newberry Library of Chicago, the orchestra receiving the conductor's entire working library of symphonic materials with Thomas's own performance markings, which he had assembled over his long career.*

The Chicago Symphony after Thomas

Thomas's death in January, 1905, left the Orchestra Association board and the community of Chicago in something of a state of shock.[47] The trustees immediately designated Frederick Stock as acting musical director while they sought a permanent successor to Thomas. This search, involving approaches to such major German conductors as Mottl, Weingartner, and Nikisch, lasted more than a year and eventually proved fruitless. In the meantime, young Stock was demonstrating his ability to carry on the work of Thomas in a manner that vindicated the older conductor's choice of him as his assistant. As Thomas's successor, Stock carried on the German tradition of the Chicago Symphony, both in its repertory and in retaining and building its basically German personnel. Despite the pressure of his conducting duties, Stock continued to compose, and to arrange for orchestra such music as the organ works of Bach. Though his own stylistic inclination was very conservative in composition, his repertory was fully as enterprising as that of Thomas. Before World War I, he presented a great deal of the late romantic Russian music that was beginning to enjoy wide public favor at this time, offered Chicago its first hearing of the newly emerging French impressionist music, and introduced the music of Arnold Schoenberg, Scriabin, and Mahler. After the war Stock became gradually less adventurous, but he did bring to the public important new music by Hindemith, Stravinsky, and Prokofiev; the latter, whose opera *The Love for Three Oranges* was premiered in Chicago in 1921, also played the first performance of his Third Piano Concerto with the Chicago Symphony under Stock.

Though Stock never suffered the extreme persecution experienced by Muck in Boston during World War I, he was obliged in 1918 to take a leave of absence because of anti-German feeling at the time; a resident of the United States since 1895, he had neglected to complete taking out American citizenship, an omission that subjected him to serious criticism in the Chicago press. Once he had obtained his final naturalization papers in the summer of 1918, his return to his post was the occasion for a heartwarming public demonstration. This experience demonstrated to Stock, however, the precariousness of maintaining an orchestra so pre-

---

* Apparently not all of Thomas's papers were entrusted to the Newberry Library: in her *Memoirs of Theodore Thomas,* Mrs. Thomas quotes diaries and letters that were still in her possession in 1910. She may have kept other such papers, present whereabouts unknown.

dominantly German, and he prodded his board of trustees to take three important steps to correct this situation. The first of these was the institution of a regular subscription series of youth concerts, aimed at developing the new audience for symphonic music; unlike some other major conductors (Stokowski excepted) Stock conducted most of these concerts himself, thus becoming a genial father-figure to a generation of Chicagoans. He also persuaded the trustees to establish an endowed and fully funded pension program for the orchestra players; Major Higginson had set up a pension program earlier in Boston, but it was funded on a year-to-year basis from Higginson's personal resources and from pension-fund concerts played by the orchestra.

Of equal importance was the foundation, at Stock's instigation, of a training orchestra of professional quality, under the auspices of the Orchestral Association. Stock, convinced that American orchestras would have to rely upon native American players in the future, conceived the idea as a means of training young musicians both in special individual coaching and in full orchestra performance. Virtually all of the private coaching was done by members of the Chicago Symphony, and the actual conducting was done partly by Stock, but mostly by his assistants under his guidance. The Chicago Civic Orchestra, as it is known, has provided a large number of players who have either "graduated" into the symphony orchestra or have found positions throughout the nation. In the case of the Chicago Symphony, this has meant the establishment of a strong musical and technical tradition that is the basis for that orchestra's characteristic style and high quality. Though there have been periods when the Civic Orchestra suffered neglect, its function has recently been revitalized in a very significant manner.

Both the pension fund and the Civic Orchestra were financed at their outset by what were then substantial endowment funds contributed mainly by the Byron Lathrop, Albert Sprague, and Elizabeth Sprague Coolidge families. Other important Chicago families, notably the Swifts and the Carrs, established major endowment funds for the annual maintenance of the orchestra, the basic financial policy being aimed at covering the annual operating deficit by the income from these endowments and from the profits in operating Orchestra Hall, both as a concert hall and as an office building. During the depression, however, this income decreased and the orchestra suffered from severe financial limitations, which Stock in his old age was forced to endure. Stock died in 1942, after forty-seven years of service to Chicago, thirty-seven of them as conductor; this is the longest tenure so far enjoyed by a conductor of an American orchestra, though Eugene Ormandy is now well on his way toward matching this record in Philadelphia.

The period between Stock's death in 1942 and the appointment of Fritz Reiner in 1953 was one of considerable turmoil over the leadership of the orchestra. During this period the critic Claudia Cassidy, first on the *Journal of Commerce* and then on the *Chicago Tribune,* became a major force in the affairs of Chicago's performance arts in general and with the symphony in particular. Motivated by a determined and fervently felt concern for Chicago's cultural welfare, Miss Cassidy went far beyond re-

porting and criticizing individual performances into a devastating attack
upon the musical and managerial policies of the orchestra. Writing in brilliant and highly personal style, she espoused her favorites (Artur Rodzinski
in particular) with lavish eloquence and castigated her foes (Désiré Defauw, Rafael Kubelik, and the orchestra board and management) with viru-
lent animus. At least two conductors parted from the orchestra under her
criticism, and the trustees' failure to retain Artur Rodzinski brought forth her
most violent public attacks.[48] The breach was healed to a considerable
degree by the appointment of Reiner: he was favored by the trustees, and
was one of the few major conductors who enjoyed Miss Cassidy's esteem.

Reiner inherited an orchestra which had been considerably strengthened
with important personnel selections by Rodzinski, Kubelik, and Eugene
Ormandy, who served for a time as musical adviser to the Chicago Symphony. During Reiner's most active seasons as musical director, the orchestra developed into one of the supreme symphonic ensembles this country
has produced. The conductor's illness in 1960 led eventually to his retirement three years later, followed by the choice of the French conductor Jean
Martinon, who was first welcomed, and then rejected, by Miss Cassidy. As
previously, though more expeditiously, in 1969 the Chicago trustees selected
another musical director in the Germanic tradition, Georg Solti; because
of his international commitments he shared the Chicago conducting duties
with Carlo Maria Giulini, the principal guest conductor, and others.

Like other major orchestras, the Chicago Symphony experienced a general increase in its deficit, for a time checked largely by holding down the
salaries of its players. Even during the Reiner years, when audience support
and national acclaim were at their height, the trustees were regularly covering a portion of the annual deficit by invading the unrestricted portion of
the endowment capital, sometimes in amounts approaching two hundred
thousand dollars a year.[49] Reiner's retirement coincided with the impact
in Chicago of the nationwide militancy of orchestra players, who demanded
and received substantial increases in pay. These additional expenses were
not sufficiently covered by annual fund-raising efforts, and the financial
problems of the Chicago Symphony were further compounded by an ill-
advised, to say the least, decision to remodel Orchestra Hall with only the
weakest assurances of financial backing. Acting upon legally unsubstan-
tiated promises of a large bequest, the trustees undertook a thorough renovation of Orchestra Hall, borrowing from their unrestricted endowment
in anticipation of the bequest and even exceeding those prospects when
costs grew beyond the original anticipation. When it became known publicly that one condition of the bequest was that Orchestra Hall be renamed
in honor of the donor's late husband, the resulting general protest caused
the prospective donor to withdraw her promised gift, leaving the Orchestra
Association with a sorely depleted endowment.

The Chicago Symphony remains, after more than eighty years, a testimonial to Theodore Thomas's vision of the permanent American orchestra.
Though large individual benefactors have always played an important role
in building and maintaining orchestras, as they were established across the

country, the institutional stability that grew out of the original plan to base the support of the Orchestral Association on a group of wealthy sponsors became the model for others. At the time of Thomas's death, Philadelphia, St. Louis, Cincinnati, Minneapolis, and Pittsburgh had started orchestras on the Chicago model; all save Pittsburgh, which failed in 1910 and was revived only in 1937, became the kind of permanent orchestra of which Thomas had dreamed. Four years after Thomas's death, the Philharmonic Society of New York finally abandoned cooperative control by its player members and accepted the financial underwriting of a board of directors.

Of tangible monuments to Thomas's memory, Orchestra Hall remains, its façade on Michigan Avenue bearing at either side plaques on which his name is inscribed. Though the decision to rename the orchestra for Thomas was revoked in 1913, over Mrs. Thomas's public protest, the trustees softened the blow by decreeing that the orchestra was to be officially known as the "Chicago Symphony Orchestra, Founded by Theodore Thomas." * A Thomas Memorial, erected in 1924 in Grant Park, facing Orchestra Hall, was "temporarily" removed in the 1950s during construction of an underground parking facility. Located in front of the Art Institute, it showed a conductor and an orchestra in low relief. It was never restored to its location, according to good Chicago authority, because the Art Institute objected to it; from last reports, it rests in a Parks Department storage yard. In Cincinnati, where Thomas played so great a role in that city's musical life, his statue still stands in the lobby of the recently renovated Music Hall, headquarters for the Cincinnati Symphony Orchestra.

Most important of all, Thomas's greatest legacy is an intangible one. More than any other conductor of his time, and more than most since, his moral dedication to the art of symphonic music has been the model to which our orchestras, at their best, have aspired. As the first great American conductor, he established the preeminent role of the music director—the resident leader of the permanent orchestra—as a unique and integral feature of the symphony orchestra in America.

---

* Apparently the trustees feared that another orchestra would preempt the Chicago Symphony Orchestra designation; Mrs. Thomas, who had moved to Cambridge by this time, expressed her unhappiness at this change in no uncertain terms.

CHAPTER III

Henry Lee Higginson–Patron

On the night of April 27, 1914, as the Boston Symphony Orchestra assembled on the stage of Symphony Hall for the final concert of its thirty-third season, Henry Lee Higginson stepped out on the stage to deliver a brief speech. Approaching his eightieth birthday, he was very much the figure of Boston aristocracy portrayed by Sargent in his memorable portrait: dignified of bearing, his face dominated by a goatee and mustache and slightly peering eyes. He spoke not to the audience of Boston socialites and music lovers but directly to the members of the orchestra, to whom he addressed this account of his founding the orchestra and his custody of it for thirty-three seasons:

Sixty years ago I wished to be a musician, and therefore went to Vienna, where I studied two years and a half diligently, learned something of music, something about musicians, and one other thing—that I had no talent for music. I heard there and in other European cities the best orchestras, and much wished that our country should have such fine orchestras. Coming home at the end of 1860, I found our country in trouble, and presently in a great war. Naturally I took part in that war, at the end of which time I did various things, and at last came to our present office in State Street, where I was admitted as a partner.

For many years I had to work hard to earn my living and support my wife. Originally I had a very small sum of money, which had been used up while studying in Vienna and during the war. All these years I watched the musical conditions in Boston, hoping to make them better. I believed that an orchestra of excellent musicians under one head and devoted to a single purpose could produce fine results, and wished for the ability to support such an undertaking; for I saw that it would be impossible to give music at fair prices and make the Orchestra pay expenses.

After consulting with my European friends, I laid out a plan, and at the end of two very good years of business began concerts in the fall of 1881. It seemed best to undertake the matter single-handed, and beyond one fine gift from a dear friend, I have borne the costs alone. All this is a matter of record, and yet it may interest you. It seemed clear that an orchestra of fair size and under possible conditions would cost at least $20,000 a year more than the public would pay. Therefore, I expected this deficit each year, and faced contracts with seventy men and a conductor. It was a large sum of money, which depended upon my business each year and on the public. If the concert halls were filled, that would help me; if my business went well, that would help me; and the truth is, that the great public has stood by me nobly.

In my eyes the requisites about the Orchestra were these: to leave the choice and care of the musicians, the choice and care of the music, the rehearsals and direction of the Orchestra, to the conductor, giving him every power possible; to leave to an able manager the business affairs of the enterprise; and, on my own part, to pay the bills, to be satisfied with nothing short of perfection, and always to remember that we were seeking high art and not money; art came first, then the good of the public, and money must be an after consideration.

We began with Mr. Henschel as conductor, taking the musicians of the town. I told Mr. Henschel that the Orchestra should play under one leader and only one, to learn his ways and to get the proper discipline; and he agreed with me. He conducted the Orchestra with much success for three years, during which we drew men from Europe. He and the Orchestra worked hard, and gave us fair results.

Then I engaged in Vienna Mr. Gericke, who came here for five years, brought in his second year many good musicians from Europe, and really created our Orchestra. He became a great favorite with the public, which was very sorry to lose him. After Mr. Gericke came Mr. Nikisch, who did much brilliant work during four years; but, owing to a tempting offer from Europe, he left us and was succeeded by Mr. Paur, who stayed five years. He also gave us good concerts, and then Mr. Gericke came back for eight years, which many of you will remember well. He found the Orchestra in good condition, and, with his skill and admirable taste, brought it to a high pitch. Then came Dr. Muck for two years, then for five years Mr. Fiedler, to whom we also owe many beautiful concerts, and now Dr. Muck is here again.

Mr. Ellis suggested the summer concerts, in order to give more work to the members of the Orchestra; and this step met a want which was keenly felt. Mr. Gericke suggested the system of pensions, which was put in force and has given help to many past members of the Orchestra, and must be a comfort to you gentlemen of the Orchestra to-day as something to look forward to when you leave off work.

For the term of thirty-three years the total deficit is about $900,000. My friends begged me again and again to stop the concerts because the strain was too great; but the work has gone on, and the result is the beautiful Orchestra, of which we are all proud.

We had been driven out of the old Music Hall in Hamilton Place because the city planned to put a street through the hall, and I welcomed the change, as the old hall was not well-aired, and was not very safe. Friends built the present hall, which I leased for a long term of years, as we must have it free for our use at all times. The hall is not rented so much as we could wish, the costs of keeping it in order are large, and therefore the yearly deficit ranges from $13,000 to $19,000. Now what does each of us do for the Orchestra? Dr. Muck chooses the music, prepares everything for the public, conducts the rehearsals and the concerts. Each of you gentlemen does his part excellently, and each of you is as well treated as lies in my power. My part is to run the risk of each year's contracts, and to meet the deficit, which will never fall below $20,000 yearly, and is often more. At present we have luck in cities other than Boston, but it is luck on which we cannot count, for good orchestras exist everywhere, and presently we may not be needed beyond our home. In Boston I have had to take my luck, which thus far has been good; but there is always a chance, and you have only to reckon how many contracts I must sign, to see what a heavy burden would be on my shoulders if the concerts were not successful, and the audiences were small. Pray remember that I must go to my office daily, in order to earn enough money to carry on this enterprise yearly and to accumulate $1,000,000, on the interest of which the Orchestra will depend after my death. I do not wish to make too much of this point, but if our concerts were to cease, my work would cease, as my friends wish; and please bear in mind that I shall be eighty years old next autumn.

There is the story. I am content and happy to go on with my work, and fully expect to get together enough money to carry on the Orchestra long after my death, if it is wanted; but without peace we cannot have a noble orchestra, and we cannot keep our reputation without excellent work by high-grade artists and as good a conductor as exists. All these things we have now; but if we do not have a peaceful life, it will drive me out of business, and will destroy the Orchestra.

We have had to dismiss various men for good reasons, and we have replaced them by able, conscientious musicians—real artists, who play for the joy of music. Do not suppose that I am ignorant about the various members of the Orchestra. At one time I knew every man; and if that is not the case now, I know many of you, and listen carefully to the playing of this or that man; know well when Witek is doing his best, hear Ferir, hear Warnke, never miss a note of Longy or Maquarre or Grisez or Wendler or Sardony; I know very well what the trumpets are doing, and the trombones, and watch the drummer, and listen for the tuba; I watch with pleasure the double basses as they stand behind you all. We lost Schuecker last year, and have in his place an admirable artist whose skill gives us much pleasure. In short, I watch the musicians almost too much, for it often interferes with my pleasure, thinking whether they are playing their best, and listening for the various points instead of listening for the whole. Whenever I go to a concert, there is always a sense of responsibility on my mind, and there is always a great joy.

Gentlemen, to sum up: You see that I know your work, and now you know mine; I know your share, and know that you try to give us the best music in the best way; and on my part, I try to make your position as comfortable as possible. It would be a great pleasure to raise your pay to a still higher point, but I cannot. One last word. Ever since my boyhood I have longed to have a part in some work which would leave a lasting mark in this world. To-day we have a noble orchestra—the work of our hands—which gives joy and comfort to many people. Dr. Muck and I are glad to do our part, and, with your hearty cooperation, the work will last.[1]

Early Music in Boston

Henry Lee Higginson was an active participant in the Harvard–State Street, Cambridge–Beacon Street business and cultural axis that played such an important role in the efflorescence of New England in the 19th century.[2] Though its influence extended far from the banks of the Charles, its source was a relatively compact and closed society: unlike New York, whose business community was continually enlarged by immigrants from Europe and by emigrants from the West and South, Boston's mercantile and financial circle was by comparison relatively circumscribed, not only by economic status and function but by ancestry and family connection. But its leaders had been exposed in their student days at Harvard to influences strongly shaped by the German culture and philosophy of the pre-Imperial era, an influence which combined with native forces extending back to Puritan times to produce a social attitude of respect for cultural and intellectual activity and a deep-rooted sense of civic stewardship.

Until the early years of the 19th century, music in New England was centered in religious activity, but there then developed an interest in instrumental and choral music no longer concerned solely with the church. The Handel and Haydn Society regularly employed instrumental musicians —amateurs and professionals from the local theaters—for some of its performances, and by 1823 it was sufficiently ambitious to offer a commission to Beethoven, an invitation that the composer considered seriously. In 1840–41, an orchestra of the Boston Academy of Music, founded in 1833, gave a series of concerts that included the first performances in Boston of several Beethoven symphonies.

A major figure in musical developments in Boston was John Sullivan Dwight (1813–93), a Harvard graduate who began his career as a Unitarian minister, but whose intellectual interests included German poetry (which he translated for publication) and music. Giving up the ministry, he joined the Brook Farm colony in 1840 as instructor in German literature and music. He returned to Boston in 1848 and, in 1852, founded *Dwight's Journal of Music*, which was until its discontinuance in 1881 the leading musical periodical in this country and is still an indispensable source of firsthand information on American musical life for the period. Dwight's musical orientation was strictly toward the German "classics"—Bach, Haydn, Mozart, Beethoven, Schubert—and such new music as that of Schumann, Mendelssohn, Spohr, and Raff. He viewed the rise of the "Music of the Future" of Wagner and Liszt with considerable hostility, though his *Journal* was the first in this country to publish the polemical writings of Wagner. He also published correspondence from Europe by such fellow-Bostonians as Alexander Wheelock Thayer and the young Henry Lee Higginson.

Dwight dominated the Harvard Musical Association, formed in 1837 from alumni who desired to carry on their undergraduate musical activities in the Pierian Society. This Association, under Dwight's leadership, was instrumental in the construction of the Music Hall in downtown Boston, which was from its opening in 1852 the site of Boston's major concerts and opera performances; as Dwight remarked in his *Journal*, it was no longer necessary for Jenny Lind to sing in the Fitchburg Railroad Station. One of the wonders of the American musical world was the "Great Organ" of the Music Hall, installed in 1863; with it were performed not only the music of Bach but also such novelties as a fantasia duet for mouth harmonica and organ. The frequent visits of the Germania Society only whetted the Bostonian appetite for more symphonic music and the dissolution of that orchestra in 1854 was followed by several seasons of symphony concerts by a group of local musicians under the sponsorship of the Musical Fund Society and the Philharmonic Society; the latter was conducted by Carl Zerrahn, a former member of the Germania. These finally ceased under the pressure of the Civil War, at the end of which the Harvard Musical Association, again with Zerrahn conducting, presented annual series of orchestral concerts for seventeen years until the organization of the Boston Symphony Orchestra. In all this activity Dwight played an important role, both in guiding the policies of the Harvard Musical Association and in promoting the concerts in his *Journal*.

Boston was also frequently visited by touring musical groups. Virtually all of the successful opera companies based in New York considered Boston an indispensable stop on their tours, and that city heard all of the great singers—Grisi, Mario, Patti, and others—who visited this country. From his first tours, Theodore Thomas brought his orchestra to Boston frequently and for extended engagements; these visits created a symphonic audience and established musical standards that aroused considerable interest in establishing a resident orchestra there. Like Thomas, Dwight very early saw the need of a permanent resident orchestra and agitated for it in his *Journal*, using the standards set by Thomas as a goal toward which Boston should aspire for its own orchestra.

Young Higginson

Though no account remains of Higginson's exposure to music in his youth, there is ample circumstantial evidence that he was already an experienced opera- and orchestra-goer before he went to Europe in his eighteenth year.[3] Though born in New York on November 18, 1834, Higginson grew up in Boston, where he attended the Latin School with the sons of the best Boston families. Higginson's own genealogy extended back for nine generations to the Reverend Francis Higginson, who had emigrated from England to the Massachusetts Colony in 1629, and through his mother's family he was related to the Lees and Cabots. In a community where family connections played so important a role, Higginson moved securely in the very top rank, a privilege that he fully exploited but also considered a great responsibility for public service. His health in childhood was poor, and having entered Harvard College in the fall of 1851, he became so afflicted with headaches and eye trouble that he was forced to withdraw before the Christmas vacation.

A love for music must have been implanted by this time in young Higginson, for, after a recuperative holiday in Vermont, he undertook an extensive tour of Europe, ostensibly as a substitute for his formal education, but undoubtedly also motivated by a desire to hear music there. From his arrival in London in June, 1852, his letters were much concerned with opera and concerts, and, by the time he reached Germany and Vienna, music had become a major preoccupation. His family expected him to return, after a reasonable exposure to Europe, to enter business in Boston, but after a few months in an office at India Wharf the pull of music and Europe became irresistible, and he returned to Vienna, for the explicit purpose of studying music. Again he was deterred from activity for which he was certainly unfitted by natural talent: his return to piano practice too soon after being bled for an illness rendered his left arm useless for piano playing. He next turned to the study of singing and composition, but, as he told the orchestra players in 1914, he came to realize his complete lack of talent.

In these formative years in Vienna, Higginson developed the musical taste and passion for symphonic music that would eventually shape his concept of the Boston Symphony Orchestra. Wagner was only becoming a major musical force, though Higginson heard his first operas and orchestral performances of excerpts from them, and became acquainted with that composer's early writings. But the real center of Higginson's musical cosmos was Beethoven, the revolutionary and ethically progressive giant dominating the Austro-German music world. Living in Vienna only a generation after Beethoven's death, Higginson was caught up in the same almost fanatical idealization of Beethoven that also played an important role in Thomas's view of his mission. For Higginson in Vienna, as for Thomas in America, Beethoven was not only a great musician but also a unique ethical and moral force, embodying human aspiration and idealism, and making music a positive uplifting force. This concept of music, exemplified by the figure of Beethoven, had a strong appeal to the New England conscience of Higginson and Dwight. In Vienna, moreover, Higginson also made personal friendships with musicians that were to prove of great value in later years. In every respect, therefore, the young man developed a commitment to music that already involved his dream of founding a great orchestra in his home city.

The growing national crisis at home in 1860 provided the occasion for Higginson to return to Boston. His family had for some time been pressing him to forsake his music studies and resume life in Boston, and his deep Abolitionist sympathies, combined with a strong sense of patriotism, aroused in him increasing concern with developments in the United States. Immediately after the outbreak of the Civil War, he enlisted as an officer in the Second Massachusetts Regiment; though his military career was hardly distinguished, he ever after fancied being addressed as Major Higginson. He saw little action until the early summer of 1863, when he was wounded at Aldie, Virginia, in a skirmish that preceded the battle at Gettysburg, receiving a saber cut in his face and a bullet at the base of his spine. He spent the rest of the war recuperating and writing letters to public officials in favor of making "suitable" appointments of officers. During his recuperation, in the fall of 1863, he married Ida Agassiz, the daughter of the distinguished Harvard scholar Louis Agassiz.

Once the war was over, Higginson did not immediately join his father and uncle in the newly organized brokerage banking firm of Lee, Higginson, and Company, but instead embarked on two unsuccessful business ventures—an effort to operate a cotton plantation in Georgia with freed slaves, and a stint of work in the oil fields of Ohio. In 1868, however, he finally joined Lee, Higginson, and Company as a member of the firm. His own business ability was never spectacular, his major contribution being his unquestioned reputation for conscientious honesty and gentlemanly conduct. The firm, however, prospered greatly: its role in the financing of such ventures as the Calumet and Hecla mines in Minnesota and the Chicago, Burlington, and Quincy railroad played an important part in the establishment of a number of Boston fortunes, including those of the members of the firm itself. By 1881, therefore, Higginson had established sufficient financial security to contemplate the realization of his youthful dream.

The Boston Symphony Orchestra

During these years, Higginson continued to observe musical life in Boston, interesting himself in the affairs of the Harvard Musical Society, despite growing misgivings over the autocratic conservatism of John S. Dwight. He undoubtedly attended Thomas's concerts in the Music Hall frequently, and may well have made the conductor's acquaintance at this time. From his European experience, as well as from Thomas's concerts, he was painfully aware of the shortcomings of the symphonic efforts of the Harvard Musical Society and its conductor, Carl Zerrahn. He probably also had his doubts about the quality of the local Boston players, but, at the outset at least, he was prepared to see what they could do under strong leadership and adequate financing.

In 1881, therefore, Higginson was ready to start his orchestra.[4] In the young George Henschel * he thought he had found a good musical director. Henschel was then thirty-one years old; a singer and pianist of considerable ability and a composer of skill, he was still inexperienced as a conductor, though he had made a very strong impression the year before conducting the Harvard Musical Society orchestra. From the outset, Higginson was under no illusions about the cost of a good permanent orchestra: his long-range goal was the establishment of a million-dollar trust fund to cover the operating deficit of the orchestra. Until that could be set up, Higginson was ready to defray the operating loss on a year-to-year basis. It must be noted here that Higginson, though reasonably affluent in terms of annual income, did not enjoy the really great wealth of a Carnegie or a Frick: though he lived well in a Commonwealth Avenue mansion, had a summer home on

---

* George (later Sir George) Henschel (b. Breslau, 1850; d. Scotland, 1934) was already a British subject when he arrived in Boston, and, after his return to London, played a major role in the musical life of England for the next fifty years as conductor and singer. In October, 1930, he returned to Boston to repeat his inaugural program as a part of the orchestra's fiftieth anniversary season.

Lake Champlain, and enjoyed the comforts and amenities of wealth, his generosity to Harvard University and his support of the Boston Symphony by and large came out of his yearly income. Thus, as he met these annual obligations, he had little opportunity to amass the capital with which he could endow the orchestra during his lifetime; as time went on, therefore, this endowment came to be an intention for a bequest on his death.

Accordingly, in the spring of 1881, Higginson wrote and distributed in Boston, both privately and in the press, a letter, *"In re* the Boston Symphony Orchestra," in which he proposed in part: [5]

> To hire an orchestra of sixty men and a conductor, paying them all by the year, reserving the right to myself to all their time needed for rehearsals and for concerts . . . to give in Boston as many concerts of serious music as are wanted . . . to keep prices low always . . . 50 cents and 25 cents being the measure of prices. . . .

> Such was the idea, and the cost presented itself thus: Sixty men at $1500 = $90,000 + $3000 for the conductor and + $7000 for other men = $100,000. Of this sum, it seemed possible that one-half should be earned, leaving a deficit of $50,000, for which $1,000,000 is needed as principal. . . .

> The plan adopted has been to engage such good musicians as are in Boston for twenty concerts in Boston, paying them each $3.00 for every rehearsal (two private and one public rehearsal) and $6.00 for every concert.*

Higginson's Boston Symphony Orchestra gave its first concert (preceded by a public rehearsal the previous afternoon) the evening of Saturday, October 2, 1881; on that occasion Henschel offered the following program:

BEETHOVEN: Overture, *The Consecration of the House,* Opus 124
GLUCK: Air from *Orpheus and Euridice*
HAYDN: Symphony in B-flat
SCHUBERT: Ballet Music from *Rosamunde*
MAX BRUCH: Scena from *Odysseus*
WEBER: *Festival Overture*

From the beginning both Henschel and Higginson encountered problems with an orchestra personnel not accustomed to the discipline required of such a venture. Early in the season, the conductor issued a letter to every player setting forth in detail the decorum of rehearsals and the need for punctuality and close attention.[6] In February of 1882, in anticipation of a second season, Higginson aroused consternation among the players by submitting to them contracts for re-engagement that specifically obligated their presence at symphony rehearsals and stipulated that symphony work be given strict priority in their professional activities, including restrictions on their performance in other orchestras. These provisions provoked considerable publicity in Boston,[7] and very likely were the cause of an independent approach to Thomas to start another orchestra in Boston. Despite accusations that he was trying to "corner" musical activities in Boston, Higginson held his ground, thus winning the first of many battles with his players

* Despite the vagaries of Higginson's arithmetic, this projection gives a rough idea of symphony economics in the 1880s.

by taking an uncompromising stand backed up by his absolute financial control. In the files of the Boston Symphony Orchestra there is a list of the orchestra players' payroll for 1882–83, apparently in Higginson's hand, showing a minimum weekly pay of twenty-one dollars for most of the orchestra; most of the first-desk players and some important wind players are listed at thirty-five dollars, the principal cellist at fifty dollars, the principal bass at forty dollars, and the harpist at forty-five dollars. During the next two seasons, Henschel began to import a few key players from Europe to strengthen the orchestra, again arousing resentment, which was invariably quelled by Higginson's absolute authority; but the major influx of European players did not come until Gericke's regime.

However, it soon developed that Henschel was not the man to build this orchestra: despite his impressive musicianship, he simply had not the experience to weld it into the kind of orchestra Higginson wanted. In his third season, he agreed amicably to step down, and Higginson sought a more authoritative successor. In Vienna, friends urged him to attend a performance of *Aida* at the Imperial Opera, conducted by Wilhelm Gericke, a young Austrian conductor, who immediately impressed Higginson with his overall skill as a director.* In his first tenure of five years, Gericke brought to the Boston Symphony Orchestra the authority and musicianship that produced true orchestral quality, though many found Gericke's musical ideas somewhat unexciting. Much of Gericke's success derived from his engagement of a good number of European players, these "importations," as before, creating no little resentment among local musicians.[8] Also, at the suggestion of Gericke and manager Charles Ellis, Higginson began in 1885 to extend the season of employment by adding several weeks of popular concerts, which to this day, as the Boston "Pops," are an indispensable feature of the season. Gericke directed the Boston Symphony in its first appearance in New York in 1887; Higginson had long wanted to display his orchestra there, but Gericke refused to permit so important a debut until he was certain that the orchestra was ready. This established the Boston Symphony as a major event in New York ever after; under Gericke, too, the orchestra extended its tours greatly, and his successor, Nikisch, took it into the Midwest, appearing in 1893 at the Columbian Exposition in Chicago at the invitation of Theodore Thomas. But Gericke was never happy in Boston: despite Higginson's efforts to find him comfortable lodgings and to introduce him to congenial friends, he remained a homesick bachelor, who complained of the arduous strain of being a full-time musical director for a long concert season. In 1889, at the end of his five-year contract, he returned to Europe, much to Higginson's regret.

His successor provided a complete contrast: whereas Gericke had been

* Wilhelm Gericke (b. Styria, 1845; d. Vienna, 1925) was Hans Richter's assistant at the time of his engagement by Higginson and had in 1880 succeeded Brahms as conductor of the Gesellschaft concerts in Vienna. Between his two engagements in Boston, he was again a leading conductor in Vienna, but after leaving Boston in 1906, he spent most of his remaining years in retirement.

a rather colorless drillmaster, the young Arthur Nikisch * brought a dramatic flair, both in gesture and musical ideas, that Boston had not seen since the days of Jullien. Nikisch was, of course, a far greater and more honest musician, then at the outset of a brilliant international career. On Gericke's solid foundation of discipline and ensemble, he built a kind of symphonic excitement that had never been heard in this country. After four years in Boston, however, he was lured back to Europe in 1893. Higginson's first choice to succeed Nikisch was Hans Richter, with whom he actually signed a contract that proved to conflict with the conductor's other obligations. He then turned to Theodore Thomas, for the first time, but Thomas was by now fully committed to Chicago.† It is interesting to speculate what might have happened had Higginson turned to Thomas earlier, before he went to Chicago: Thomas would probably have accepted the invitation, but one wonders how long two such strong-minded men as Henry Lee Higginson and Theodore Thomas would have worked together. For despite all his protestations of leaving musical matters strictly to the conductor, Higginson certainly involved himself deeply. Nor was this limited merely to an *ad hoc* day-to-day relationship with the conductor: his contract with Nikisch sets forth in no uncertain terms the relationship between patron and music director, and the same provision was included in all of Higginson's contracts with conductors. (Nikisch's contract, incidentally, provided for a salary of eight thousand dollars for the eight-month season, during which he could undertake no other work.) These contracts, moreover, like those with each player, were between Higginson personally and the employee; there was no corporate entity or official organization running the orchestra. It was first and foremost Higginson's private venture.

> The said Arthur Nikisch hereby covenants and agrees with the said Henry L. Higginson, as follows, to wit:
> To train the orchestra so far as may in his judgement be necessary for their successful performance of their work; to give concerts in said Boston, or elsewhere in the United States, as said Henry L. Higginson may direct; to train, if necessary, and use, a chorus of voices; to select the music for the concerts and other musical performances of said orchestra; to assign the parts and places to the members of the orchestra; and in general to give his best endeavors and all needful time and labour to the furtherance of the musical work which the said Henry L. Higginson shall require from the said Boston Symphony Orchestra.
> . . . It is further agreed that the said Arthur Nikisch shall, subject only to the approval of said Higginson, have the sole artistic direction of said orchestra; that it shall accordingly be his duty, subject as aforesaid, to make the programmes, to select the soloists; and in case of vacancies among the members of said orchestra to select persons to fill the same, provided, always, that it shall rest with

---

* Arthur Nikisch (b. Szent-Miklos, Hungary, 1855; d. Leipzig, 1922) was one of the leading conductors in Leipzig, along with Anton Seidl, when Higginson brought him to Boston. After leaving there in 1893, he served for two years as director of the Royal Opera and Philharmonic concerts in Budapest, and then became conductor of the Gewandhaus concerts in Leipzig. For a more detailed account of his brilliant career, see Harold C. Schonberg, *The Great Conductors*.
† The "official" Boston accounts do not mention this invitation, but it was reported by both Philo Otis and Mrs. Thomas in their accounts of Theodore Thomas's career in Chicago.

the said Henry L. Higginson to decide whether any member or members of said orchestra shall be engaged, retained or dismissed." [9]

Higginson's recollections that began this chapter review the succession of conductors that followed Nikisch, including the successful return of Gericke for eight more years in Boston. By the end of the second decade of the orchestra's life, however, its basic pattern under Higginson's direction was well established. In his relations with the players of the orchestra, Higginson combined a paternalistic interest in their professional and personal welfare with an autocratic firmness in financial dealings and working conditions. He steadfastly refused to countenance any organization of the players, either by the union or among themselves, for joint action on their part, insisting on dealing individually with every player, each of whom signed his annual contract directly with Higginson. It was this patron's firm belief that any intermediary union or organization between him and his men would impede the full artistic development of the orchestra and undermine the conductor's authority. In this he not only reflected a conservative Republican business executive's point of view but also expressed his deeply paternalistic attitude toward the musicians. As sole financial support of the orchestra, he had the responsibility of balancing the requirements of his players against his own financial resources. Because so many of his players were brought over from Europe at his conductor's behest, they became solely dependent upon Higginson and were relatively immune from the organizing efforts of the union. At the same time, Higginson made every effort to run his orchestra in a manner that would provide a decent living for his players: not only did he maintain the only resident symphonic season in this country but he extended his players' work into late spring and early summer with "Pops" concerts and eventually established a pension system for retiring players, supported in part by special pension-fund concerts and partly from Higginson's own purse. (So far as can be determined this pension fund was administered entirely by Higginson, according to his own views of a player's needs.)

Higginson chose for his orchestra a succession of conductors trained in the Austro-German tradition of symphonic music. Nearly two-thirds of the music they offered was by composers of that same national origin, as can be seen in Table 3-A, a summary by nationality of composer of the Boston Symphony Orchestra repertory during the Higginson era; it is here compared to the overall nationwide averages for the same period and for the most recent half decade, as well as with the latest data for the Boston Symphony Orchestra itself.*

At first Higginson attended to the operating details of the orchestra himself, but shortly assigned one of his staff from the Calumet and Hecla operation at Lee, Higginson, and Company to assist him in running the orchestra's day-to-day affairs. Charles A. Ellis thus became the first full-time orchestra manager in the country, acting as Higginson's trusted deputy in

---

* These percentages are based on information assembled in the Mueller repertory survey that is discussed in detail in Chapter XVII.

TABLE 3-A

Boston Symphony Orchestra Repertory Summary 1880–1915
Composer-Nationality Percentages Compared with National Percentages,
1890–1915, 1965–70

	Boston 1880–1915	National 1890–1915	Boston 1965–70	National 1965–70
Austro-German	63.71	61.61	56.70	51.65
Russian	9.03	12.98	16.06	14.80
French	11.51	11.58	7.46	10.09
American	4.71	3.98	6.01	6.66
British	1.87	1.72	2.80	3.97
Czech	4.00	3.95	4.80	3.12
Italian	0.89	0.95	1.41	2.89
Scandinavian	2.24	2.21	3.11	2.76
Hungarian	0.13	0.31	0.26	1.57
Spanish Latin-American }	0.01	0.01	0.46	1.47

all matters. As time went on, Ellis developed his own management of concert artists, utilizing the contacts he established with soloists who appeared
with the orchestra. Arthur Judson, who knew Ellis well in his later years,
considered him to be the finest manager he had ever known.

Under Higginson, the Boston Symphony became not only Boston's
premier cultural institution but an integral part of the city's social life. Members of the orchestra, as soloists or in groups, played in Boston homes or
clubs for charity benefits, and Higginson frequently donated the services of
the full orchestra to special events at Harvard, Yale, or Princeton, and
other public celebrations. When Mrs. Jack Gardner opened her fabulous
Fenway Palace in 1903, the music for the occasion was provided by an ensemble of Boston Symphony players, and this was by no means the only
glittering social occasion that was so embellished.* The long-time (1885–
1903) concertmaster of the orchestra, Franz Kneisel, in 1886 organized a
distinguished string quartet with three of his colleagues from the orchestra
with Higginson's encouragement and with financial support from Boston
music lovers, appearing until 1917 throughout America and Europe.
Georges Longy, the French oboist of the orchestra from 1898 to 1925,
founded his own music schools in Boston and Cambridge. The Alsatian-
born violinist and violist Charles Martin Loeffler, who also played in Thomas's orchestra on tour, was a member of the Boston Symphony from 1882
until 1903, when he resigned to devote himself to a full-time career of composition; he made notable contributions to Boston musical life until his
death in 1935. Nor were Higginson's musical interests confined exclusively
to his orchestra: a pocket notebook in the symphony files contains jottings
that indicate he raised funds from other Bostonians for the support of

* Louise Hall Tharp, *Mrs. Jack,* has many interesting vignettes of Mrs. Gardner's interest in the
Boston Symphony and of her friendship with Higginson.

Thomas's American Opera Company, contributing five thousand dollars himself to that venture and serving on its board of directors.[10]

Nor was the Boston Symphony the sole recipient of Henry Lee Higginson's generosity of time and money.[11] Though he had spent only a few months as a student at Harvard College, he became a loyal alumnus. When he returned from Vienna in 1860, he brought back a number of books and scores for Harvard's music library. In 1882, though already deeply involved with his orchestra, he joined his mother-in-law, Mrs. Louis Agassiz, in establishing a "College for Collegiate Instruction of Women," which became Radcliffe College, on whose board Higginson served for many years. In the same year, Harvard recognized his efforts in founding his orchestra by awarding him an honorary M.A. degree. Despite his preoccupation with the Boston Symphony, he found time throughout the 1880s to raise money for Harvard. In 1890, he purchased and donated to the university the land across the Charles River now known as Soldier's Field, in memory of five of Higginson's youthful friends who had died in the Civil War. He had long had many close friends at Harvard, including President Eliot, Oliver Wendell Holmes, and William James (to whom he addressed letters as "My dear boy"). In 1893, he was elected as one of the seven Fellows of the Harvard Corporation, the governing board of the university; he served in that position until his death in 1919. In addition, he took an interest in other universities, notably Yale (which awarded him an honorary LL.D. degree in 1901) and Princeton. In 1901 he was invited by Andrew Carnegie to be a member of the first board of the Carnegie Institution. In politics he considered himself basically a Republican, though he voted for Cleveland against Blaine and for Wilson in 1912. His voluminous correspondence, which Bliss Perry quotes generously, was carried on with an incredible variety of public and business figures—Congressmen, cabinet members, presidents, and corporation executives. Through his banking contacts in London, he had many friends in business as well as university circles in England. He was, in every way, a complete Boston aristocrat and man of affairs nationally and internationally.

Symphony Hall

As did other touring and local music organizations, the Boston Symphony Orchestra played its concerts in the old Music Hall in downtown Boston from its first season. This vast auditorium was a notoriously drafty and uncomfortable hall, its acoustics badly flawed by the presence at the back of the stage of the famous "Great Organ." (This was eventually dismantled in 1884 because Higginson persuaded the owners of its acoustic disadvantage.) In 1892 the city officials of Boston announced a plan to open a new street that would run through the site of the Music Hall, and Higginson was naturally concerned with the fate of his orchestra should no hall be available for it. He had already been discontented with the Music Hall as a site for his concerts, especially after the construction of the Auditorium in Chicago and Carnegie Hall in New York, but he preferred to concentrate his efforts and financial resources on supporting the orchestra as a performing body. With the threat of losing the Music Hall, however, he turned to wealthy friends in Boston to provide him with a suitable hall. Though there was no formal agreement, there was a tacit understanding between Higginson and those who organized the financing of the new hall that Higginson would continue to support the Boston Symphony, both in his own lifetime and by endowing it in his will, if the others would underwrite the costs of the new auditorium; Higginson also promised to lease the new hall outright and to operate it, giving first priority to his orchestra, but renting it out to others when the orchestra did not need it. Moreover, he would have complete responsibility and authority for its design.

Higginson decided that the design of the new hall should be entrusted to the New York firm of McKim, Mead, and White, and was in touch ("Keep this secret") with Edward McKim as early as 1892.[12] Meanwhile his friends acquired the site on which Symphony Hall now stands. McKim moved slowly on the plans, for the city's project to demolish the Music Hall had become an on-again-off-again matter. During this period, McKim developed a rather unusual design in which the audience surrounded the orchestra in a manner reminiscent of the ancient Greek amphitheater. Late in 1898, Higginson expressed some strong reservations, based on conversations with several conductors, about this scheme in a letter to McKim: "While we hanker for the Greek Theater plan, we think the risk too great as regards results, so we have definitely abandoned that idea. We shall therefore return to the general plan of our Music Hall and the halls in Vienna and Leipzig, the latter being the best of all." [13] At the same time, Higginson was confiding his misgivings to his good friend President Eliot of Harvard, who then recommended that Higginson consult with a young physicist at the college, Wallace C. Sabine,* who had successfully corrected the poor acoustics at the Fogg Museum. When consulted by Higginson, Sabine strongly backed his reservations over McKim's Greek Theater, and was thereupon pressed on McKim as an acoustical consultant. Higginson also took the precaution of checking Sabine's views with an M.I.T. physicist, who reassured him on Sabine's expertise. Though other great theaters, notably Sullivan and Adler's Auditorium in Chicago, had been built with acoustic considerations in mind, Sabine was the first nonarchitectural expert engaged with broad authority as a consultant for a concert hall anywhere. He not only conferred with a number of musicians about halls in this country and Europe but also visited many of those most highly thought of by musicians. The final plan for Symphony Hall, in which Sabine had a strong hand, follows the general shape of the Leipzig Gewandhaus, with such modifications as were required by its increased capacity by more than a thousand seats.

* Wallace Clement Sabine (1868–1919) later worked on other acoustic projects and, during World War I, for the French, British, and American military on matters involving the physics of acoustics. A plaque honoring his memory and his contribution to Symphony Hall is located in its main corridor, and he was the subject of a biography by William Dana Orcutt, *Wallace Clement Sabine, a Study in Achievement.*

Many of Higginson's letters to McKim concern the effect of architectural plans on the seating capacity: Higginson had originally called for 2,200 to 2,500 seats, later strongly favoring the higher figure, and in one letter deplored the loss of 100 seats, which he said would cost him five thousand dollars a year. There was also much discussion of the statues to be placed in the niches surrounding the hall: always an important part of Sabine's acoustical scheme, their selection involved extensive consultation between Higginson, the architects, and Boston art connoisseurs.

The name to be bestowed on this building was a secret kept by Higginson almost to the day of its opening; in correspondence it was usually referred to as the New Music Hall. Symphony Hall opened to great fanfare on October 15, 1900, and everyone agreed that it was a triumph architecturally and acoustically, fully worth the $750,000 it had cost Higginson's friends. It proved then, as it has for nearly three quarters of a century since, one of the supreme concert halls of the entire world. Sabine's acoustic planning was such that the reverberation measurements, with the hall full of people, precisely matched his projections (2.31 seconds), and the distribution of sound, at a full range of sonic frequencies, was remarkably smooth and mellow. For rehearsals, however, the hall has always been too reverberant, and at these times the orchestra uses a curtain across the auditorium to reduce the echo. For the same reason, Symphony Hall has presented recording engineers with acoustic problems; for most recordings, the orchestra is seated on the floor of the auditorium itself, rather than on the stage. This floor, made of wood, can be leveled with special platforms to accommodate tables and chairs for the Boston "Pops" season.

Wartime and the Muck Affair

In the second decade of the present century, the Boston Symphony was established as the peerless orchestra of this nation achieving new wonders under Karl Muck,* who could stay there only because of special dispensation from the German Emperor allowing him leaves of absence from the Imperial Opera in Berlin. Other cities had followed Boston's example in establishing resident orchestras: Thomas had realized his dreams in Chicago, even to the extent of building his own hall; the New York Philharmonic Society was established on a firm financial basis; and new orchestras had been formed in St. Louis, Philadelphia, Cincinnati, Minneapolis, and San Francisco.

But the outbreak of the war in 1914 placed Higginson, his orchestra, and his conductor in a difficult position. Though a deep admirer of German

* Karl Muck (b. Darmstadt, 1859; d. Stuttgart, 1940) made his debut as piano soloist with the Leipzig Gewandhaus orchestra, but eventually turned to conducting in several German cities, Prague, and St. Petersburg. At the time of his engagement by Higginson, he was conductor of the Imperial Opera in Berlin and had conducted in London and Bayreuth. After his return from the United States in 1919, he resumed his German career with great success, notably at Bayreuth.

culture, especially as expressed in music, Higginson was by no means sympathetic to the German cause in the war, partly because of German atrocities in Belgium and partly because of his close associations in London banking circles. As the war progressed in Europe, Higginson saw with increasing clarity the inevitability of American participation on the Allied side, and this prospect aroused every patriotic instinct in him. He was, however, in a very difficult position with his orchestra: most of the members were of German or Austrian birth, many were not naturalized American citizens, and the conductor was an employee of the German Emperor on leave of absence, although he was technically a Swiss citizen. In Boston, as elsewhere, Higginson was widely regarded as a pro-German, because he did not speak out in favor of the Allied cause for fear of injuring the morale of his orchestra. His "work" there had become the all-engrossing concern of this octogenarian, torn, as we know from his private letters, between patriotism and concern for the symphony. He hoped that the cause of great musical art could surmount national differences and sought to preserve his orchestra on that basis. His position was further complicated by the fact that, in 1915, the firm of Lee, Higginson, and Company suffered such serious financial reverses that his partners were forced to request him to cut back on his support of the orchestra; he was able to keep it going only through the generosity of his brother Francis, who dipped into his personal savings for this purpose.

Although Higginson was deeply troubled by the impact of the war on the members of his orchestra, Karl Muck became the central problem as time went on. As early as September, 1914, after the outbreak of the war, Higginson presented the problem as he saw it to Ellis, then in London, in anticipation of Ellis's meeting shortly with Muck in Germany: [14]

> Now it is only fair that Dr. Muck shall understand the sentiment about himself: there is one feeling universally, and that is great admiration and gratitude for the beautiful concerts he has given, and which people hope he will continue to give . . . but you will also agree that the passions of men have been inflamed to a degree not seen in our lifetime. . . . Since the War began, it has seemed to me a very difficult problem for Dr. Muck to make all his men play together. I have doubted whether he would care to play at all unless he got his best men. . . . It isn't the lessened *numbers* but it is the lessened *quality* which I dread, and which may disturb Dr. Muck very much. You remember that we cannot get any outside musicians, for they are all in the Union . . . and Dr. Muck will not live with the Union, nor will I.

By 1917, however, he was less concerned with his problems with his men than he was with the conductor. Writing on March 22, 1917, to his "Dear Old Friend" President Eliot, he said: [15]

> We have come to a strange pass. Our contracts provided for war and other accidents, gave me the power to break up the work at any time if the Orchestra was injured seriously; and it was left for me to decide. We have a dozen nationalities in the Orchestra, and the men have behaved perfectly well toward each other since the war began. Dr. Muck is a hearty German, who wished to enlist and was refused for lack of strength. He behaved well, and has been cordial to

me since the war began, as before; and he has been most kindly received by
audiences here and in other cities. . . . I trust him entirely as an artist and as a
man, and he has worked as no other conductor has worked.

Query: Shall I go on with him and the Orchestra? He is the only man I know
who can conduct for us. The Orchestra is fine, and has set the pace for the
country, following out Theodore Thomas. . . . My connection with the Orchestra has shut my mouth many times, to my great regret, since August, 1914.
. . . Turn it over, and advise me.

In later correspondence with Eliot, Higginson expressed himself more
categorically about the indispensability of Muck: "I could not keep the
Orchestra going without Dr. Muck, and should not try. In the first place,
conductors who like old and new music are very rare; next, Dr. Muck
is the most industrious, painstaking and the ablest conductor we have ever
had. . . . I do not want the modern men, that is, the men who believe in
modern music only and have little respect for the old music; and that is the
tendency of the conductors." [16] (This was possibly a reference to Stokowski.) Nevertheless, Muck became the focal point of a great deal of anti-
German sentiment: such important national figures as Theodore Roosevelt
and Walter Damrosch joined the outcry against him, though they did not
lend their support to such wild rumors as were circulating to the effect that
he was operating a clandestine radio for espionage during his summer vacation at Bar Harbor. Eliot's replies to Higginson generally supported him in
his determination to keep the orchestra going and to retain Muck and the
German players until such time as their loyalty was definitively questioned.
However, though he doubted the statement that Muck was indispensable,
he reassured Higginson on the matter of his own loyalty: "Everybody
knows what your position really is in regard to national defense and the war
on Germany. They must know, for instance, how active your firm has been
in floating war loans of the Allies." [17]

When America entered the war in April, 1917, the Boston Symphony
personnel included one hundred players: fifty-one were American citizens,
some thirty-four by naturalization; twenty-two were German, of whom nine
had applied for citizenship; and there were eight Austrians, six Dutch, three
French, and two each from Italy, Great Britain, Russia, Belgium, and Bohemia.[18] Muck was a South German by birth, a fact which Higginson
stressed as distinguishing him from the Prussians; however, he was legally
of Swiss nationality and traveling on a Swiss passport, and was therefore
not liable for internment as an enemy alien.

When the season opened in the fall of 1917, there was some grumbling
over the orchestra's failure to display the American flag at its concerts, an
omission that Higginson admitted was his own oversight in the press of
starting the season. He quickly rectified this omission, but refused to sanction playing *The Star-Spangled Banner* at the beginning of each concert.
Though this was already the practice at the summer "Pops" concerts, he
felt that the anthem was musically out of place at a serious concert. "I had
considered carefully the playing of the National Anthem at our concerts,"
he later wrote. "One good friend advised me to have it played. My objection

had been that it did not belong in the programme and that nobody of value to me had asked for it." [19] Before this could become a public issue in Boston, however, it precipitated a crisis on tour at the orchestra's first concert in Providence on October 30, 1917, when Higginson and Ellis in Boston received a demand from some Providence subscribers that the national anthem be played. Without consulting Muck, Higginson deemed the request impossible to meet; for one thing, there would have been no time to rehearse the piece, although the orchestra must have been familiar with it from the "Pops" seasons. Higginson and Ellis took the next train to Providence and attended the concert, which proceeded without further incident. However, they refused to see the press after the concert and returned that night to Boston. Muck heard nothing of the matter until the following day when a hue and cry was aroused in the Providence press, blaming him for the omission of *The Star-Spangled Banner.*

When the orchestra and Muck returned from the tour a few days later, Higginson called the conductor to his office and requested him to play the national anthem at future concerts. Muck replied, "What will they say to me at home?" Higginson answered, "I do not know, but let me say this: when I am in a Catholic country and the Host is carried by, or a procession of churchmen comes along, I take off my hat in consideration— not to the Host, but respect for the customs of the nation." Muck agreed to Higginson's request, but also submitted his resignation effective upon the completion of the current season. At the next concert, Higginson announced Muck's resignation from the stage of Symphony Hall and further stated that the conductor had agreed to his request to conduct the national anthem.[20]

For the next few months the season proceeded smoothly; the orchestra and Muck were well received by sellout audiences everywhere, though public outcry against Muck forced the orchestra to curtail its scheduled touring. Yet, through all this concern over Muck, Higginson had far more pressing matters on his mind, namely his intention to turn the sponsorship of his orchestra over to a committee or board similar to those of Chicago, Philadelphia, and New York. He must have had such a prospect in mind for some time, but so far had not articulated it. However, a month after the announcement of Muck's resignation, President Eliot tactfully suggested: "I wish it [the Boston Symphony Orchestra] had a more institutional aspect. It, of course, appears now as the creation of an individual, which may cease whenever that individual dies or is disabled." [21] A few months later, on February 25, 1918, Higginson wrote to his friend Judge Frederick P. Cabot: [22]

> My present plan is to keep absolute silence until the end of the last concert, and then to state my case from the stage—*viz:* that the conductor has been so harassed that he can only go; and that I quit also. . . . We have reached a time, through circumstances, when I can drop this task without comment as to my motives, because the Orchestra and conductor have been attacked, and I also, as a man who employs Germans and, therefore, whose loyalty can be doubted. As you know, various decent people here and in other cities have joined in this attack; so the moment appears opportune. . . .

Do you suppose a committee can be found that will sign yearly contracts, or longer, say for $400,000 a year and who will hire the hall at a loss of $15,000 a year, and supply the music, and get and keep the confidence of the men, as well as find a great conductor, and take him for a period of years? The hardest of all is that they must keep their hands and tongues off the conduct of the art side, or they will make trouble.

I could not have stopped prudently at the beginning of the War, because it might have looked as if I had been badly hit by the War, and you know what a ticklish thing credit is. Now an excellent reason has arisen."

A month after Higginson wrote this letter, United States marshals arrested Dr. Muck following his final rehearsal for a performance of the Bach *St. Matthew Passion;* only the pleas of Higginson and Ellis prevented their actually arresting him on the stage during the rehearsal. No specific charges were ever lodged against him, though an official hinted darkly at information received in confidence. Muck was held for several days in jails in Boston and Cambridge and then interned at Fort Oglethorpe, Georgia. His arrest created a sensation in Boston, but he still commanded the loyalty of a number of influential friends, among them Mrs. Isabelle Stewart Gardner, who attempted to visit him in jail and left him a basket of food when she was refused permission to see him.[23] Muck remained at Fort Oglethorpe, without any charges being formally lodged against him, until his release after the conclusion of the war, when he returned to Germany. There he continued his career as a distinguished conductor of orchestra and opera, deeply embittered by his American experience.

In retrospect, Muck's treatment aroused much sympathy for him, and some blamed Higginson for placing him in an untenable situation over the failure to play *The Star-Spangled Banner* in Providence. However, culpable as Higginson may have been in that instance, he stood loyally behind Muck as long as he could. He must have known that the conductor harbored intensely anti-American feelings well before that crisis, and ignored them in the interest of maintaining his orchestra. Nothing in Higginson's papers indicates this awareness, but he can hardly have been ignorant of opinons held so strongly by a man with whom he was so closely associated. The full intensity of Muck's opinions did not come to public attention until after Higginson's death and they were revealed by the disclosure in the *Boston Post* late in 1919 that Muck had been carrying on an affair with a twenty-year-old girl in Boston's Back Bay to whom he wrote letters that were reported eventually to have reached the Attorney General's files in Washington; these letters were probably the confidential information alluded to so cryptically in public. In one of these letters, Muck wrote: "I am on my way to the concert hall to entertain the crowds of dogs and swine who think that because they pay the entrance fee they have the right to dictate to me my selections. I hate to play for this rabble. . . . [In] a very short time our gracious Kaiser will smile on my request and recall me to Berlin. . . . Our Kaiser will be prevailed upon to see the benefit to the Fatherland of my obtaining a divorce and making you my own." [24]

Higginson did not live to suffer the public indignity of such revelations about the musician he considered indispensable to his orchestra and whom

he backed so firmly, but he knew something of this affair after Muck had
left. "Major Higginson also learned, for the first time, that there was indisputable proof of Dr. Muck's base personal character. This narrative will not
touch further upon that matter," [25] wrote Perry. On May 4, 1918, Higginson carried out his intention, expressed the previous February to Judge
Cabot, to announce publicly his retirement from the orchestra, but his remarks on this occasion betrayed none of the bitterness he had expressed in
his February letter to Judge Cabot. Instead he bade farewell to the audience and to the players in eloquent, if somewhat platitudinous, terms.[26]
Higginson had but eighteen months to live after his farewell from the stage
of Symphony Hall. His health, already undermined by the exhausting experiences of the war years, declined rapidly. Except for a few ceremonial
appearances at Harvard, he devoted himself to carrying on his voluminous
personal correspondence from his home on Commonwealth Avenue. Finally, in November, 1919, he left that home under his own strength, refusing
the use of an elevator to descend from his room, for the last of several
trips to the hospital. He died on November 15, 1919, four days short of his
eighty-fifth birthday. At his funeral services members of the Boston Symphony played Handel's *Largo* and there was an honor delegation of undergraduates and alumni from Harvard. He was buried, as was Theodore
Thomas nearly fifteen years earlier, at Mt. Auburn Cemetery.

Higginson's Legacy

The trustees to whom Higginson turned over the Boston Symphony in 1918
assumed a burden of unexpected dimensions. The orchestra had lost not
only its conductor, its patron, and many of its musicians but also its long-
time manager, Charles E. Ellis, who resigned when Higginson did. Moreover, little more than a year after they took over the orchestra from Higginson, his will disclosed that contrary to general expectation, he had not
bequeathed it the million dollars he had hoped to; such were his financial
reverses late in life that he could provide only for his family and leave nothing to his orchestra or to Harvard.

The trustees' first task was the selection of a new conductor; a continuation of the German tradition was obviously out of the question in 1918, and
the choice of a Frenchman was equally in order. It fell to Henri Rabaud, a
composer of moderate distinction and limited conducting experience. Prior
commitments prevented his opening the season and he recommended that
Pierre Monteux * conduct the orchestra until he could come to Boston. Dur-

* Pierre Monteux (b. Paris, 1875; d. Hancock, Maine, 1964) had started his career as violinist
and violist, playing under Richter at Bayreuth and elsewhere. He became conductor for Diaghilev's Ballet Russe in 1911, touring this country with them in 1917. After leaving the Boston
Symphony in 1924, he pursued a brilliant international conducting career, returning to this
country as musical director of the San Francisco Symphony from 1936 to 1952. He was a frequent guest conductor with virtually every important American and European orchestra, returning frequently to Boston in his last years. He made his home at Hancock, Maine, where he
had a summer school for young conductors. Schonberg, *The Great Conductors*, deals all too
briefly with him. His widow, Doris, has written a memoir of her husband, *It's All in the Music*.

ing the rest of the season, Rabaud's shortcomings as a director and the limitations of his repertory—he presented the Franck Symphony in D minor twice for want of variation—became increasingly obvious to all concerned, and he was allowed to resign. Pierre Monteux, then forty-five years old, took over the musical direction of the orchestra. He brought to this post a wide and intensive experience as an orchestra violist and conductor of international renown, having introduced such major new scores as Stravinsky's *Petrouchka* and *The Rite of Spring* and Ravel's *Daphnis et Chloé*. Throughout his five years as director of the Boston Symphony, however, Monteux was hampered by the necessity of rebuilding the personnel of the orchestra and restoring its morale as a performing unit. Moreover, Monteux's repertory—non-German and modern—aroused considerable complaint from patrons brought up in the Higginson era.

Finally, it fell to Monteux to carry the orchestra through the turmoil of the musicians' strike of 1920. Higginson had, throughout his domination of the orchestra, staunchly and uncompromisingly resisted all efforts to organize its musicians, either through the union or through the players' own organization. A major weapon in his hands was the players' knowledge that if they were discharged by Higginson for any reason, they had no place else to play in America, since virtually all other employment opportunities were unionized; for most of them, the alternative to playing for Higginson was return to Europe. Higginson succeeded in this policy partly because he treated his players firmly and, at least by his lights, fairly: his scale of annual pay and length of season were matched by no other American orchestra of the time. Moreover, his old-fashioned paternalism and his intense personal involvement with each and every player staved off efforts that might have resulted in the players' organizing for bargaining purposes. Though Higginson in his last years no longer had that close personal association, Charles Ellis carried on as his surrogate. With Higginson gone, however, the musicians assumed a quite different relationship *vis-à-vis* the orchestra. They were no longer the personal employees of a dedicated, though opinionated, aristocratic father-figure, but became the hired employees of an impersonal organization.

By the 1919–20 season, the undercurrents of organization developed into a full-scale effort to unionize the orchestra.[27] This led not only to a confrontation with the trustees and manager but also to strained relations between Monteux and the players themselves, including the concertmaster, Frederic Fradkin. Matters reached a public impasse when Fradkin refused to obey Monteux's signal for him to rise and lead the orchestra in an acknowledgment of the audience's applause. Fradkin's public challenge to the disciplinary authority of the conductor left the trustees no choice but to discharge him forthwith, and a majority of the orchestra resigned in protest. For the remainder of the season, Monteux carried on the schedule of concerts, on one occasion with only twenty-two players on the stage, by recruiting replacements as the season progressed.

In their intransigent attitude toward unionization, the trustees carried on Higginson's own policy, which was a compound of deeply conservative anti-union bias in general and a conviction that unionization was incompatible with the artistic standards of the orchestra. During this crisis, and in fact for many years after, there were reports that Higginson's will, the terms of ownership of Symphony Hall, and other legal restrictions prevented the trustees from recognizing a union. The only basis for this impression was a clause in Higginson's bequest of the orchestra library and physical equipment wherein he stipulated that his executor could cancel this bequest, "guided by the manner in which the Symphony Orchestra shall have been and is managed" for a period of five years after Higginson's death.[28]

The trustees to whom Higginson entrusted his orchestra were originally headed by Judge Frederick Cabot, who later relinquished that post to Ernest B. Dane, under whose leadership the Boston Symphony prospered for many years. Dane was intensely dedicated to the orchestra and was for many years its principal financial supporter either through his own funds or those he raised from others. He was also intensely conservative in politics and social views —a conservatism reflected in the manner in which the orchestra conducted its affairs during the two decades following Higginson's death, and in its stubborn resistance to unionism. Throughout this period, the orchestra was run as a private matter: financial data were kept in strictest confidence, policy decisions were made by the trustees without outside consultation or justification, and the operation of the orchestra continued to be the private affair of a small group that acted on its own responsibility every bit as arbitrarily as in the days of Higginson.

Nevertheless, under this trusteeship, the Boston Symphony grew in stature to a degree that exceeded even Higginson's most ardent hopes. Monteux's position, already weakened in other respects, was made impossible by the strike of 1920. In the fall of 1923, with Monteux still under contract for another season, the trustees announced the engagement of Serge Koussevitzky * to take effect the following year. As is well known, Koussevitzky's tenure in Boston produced one of the greatest orchestras this country, or the world in general, has ever known. With the solid support of the trustees and the use of outstanding European players to rebuild the personnel of the orchestra, Koussevitzky, for all his artistic and personal idiosyncrasies, proved to be a unique conductor, notable not least for his generous sponsorship of American composers. With Stokowski in Philadelphia, Toscanini in New York, and Koussevitzky in Boston, America enjoyed a symphonic golden age of legendary proportions.

Yet, behind the glories of the Koussevitzky era, behind the greatness of the Boston Symphony to this day, and behind the very concept of the symphony orchestra in America lay the foundation established by Henry Lee

---

* Serge Koussevitzky (b. Vishny-Volotchek, Russia, 1874; d. Boston, 1951) began his career as a formidable virtuoso on the double bass. With help from a wealthy wife, he embarked on a conducting career, first with the Berlin Philharmonic in 1908, later in Russia before the Revolution. He had settled in Paris when he accepted the Boston position. His career has been fully chronicled, most notably by Arthur Lourie, *S. A. Koussevitzky and His Epoch;* Hugo Leichtentritt, *Serge Koussevitzky, the Boston Symphony, and the New American Music;* Moses Smith, *Koussevitzky;* and a chapter in Harold C. Schonberg, *The Great Conductors.* Harry Ellis Dickson, *Gentlemen, More Dolce, Please!,* offers a view of Koussevitzky from the players' perspective, including a number of characteristic anecdotes about him.

Higginson. His contribution, far more important than nearly a million dollars of his own funds, grew out of a distinctly New England sense of public service, a sense that overrode his personal limitations, his social and political conservatism, and his autocratic snobbery. His youthful frustration in planning a career in music was sublimated in a form distinctive to the business enterprise of 19th-century America, but his intense devotion to the art of music became the driving force of his sense of civic responsibility. This sense of responsibility also produced great contributions to Harvard University, his alma mater of but a few months, but his unique achievement was the creation of the Boston Symphony, the first truly permanent orchestra in America. None of his ideas was particularly original: a sense of public service arising from business enterprise motivated such diverse entrepreneurs as Carnegie and Rockefeller; the ambition for a permanent orchestra was felt as keenly by Thomas as by Higginson. But Higginson alone in his time had the vision, the social position, and the business acumen to bring all these forces together to achieve his purpose. At the end, he left his orchestra in grave difficulties—some of his own making, but mostly the consequence of forces beyond his control. He brought it to so firm a place in the life of Boston, however, that the trustees who succeeded him had a solid basis on which to build its future. Though the scope of the modern symphony is now so great that no one single individual can fully support a major orchestra, the Higginson tradition remains strong. He set an example for other philanthropists, admonishing them never to expect an orchestra to pay its own way, and created a tradition of paternalism that lingers yet among the leaders in present boards of directors and trustees, many of whom still look upon their orchestras as a private domain. But in the best of these is preserved another aspect of Higginson's heritage—his sincere dedication to music.

Among the last letters that Higginson wrote, in the months between his withdrawal from the orchestra and his death, is one to Wilhelm Gericke—the conductor, of all with whom he had worked, who was closest to Higginson as a friend and as an artist. As soon as he could write after the Armistice, Higginson sent Gericke a long letter, in which he reported the changes that had taken place in their orchestra and assured the conductor that he was still remembered fondly in Boston. He ended the letter on a personal note:

> But I often long for a concert such as you gave us—Haydn, Mozart, Beethoven and Schubert. Only a Wiener Kind can play Schubert. You, Nikisch, and Muck were great conductors, and the others were good.[29]

CHAPTER IV

Arthur Judson—Manager

Looking back on more than seventy years in music, Arthur Judson likes to assert that in some fifty-four years as manager of the Philadelphia Orchestra and the New York Philharmonic,* he never interfered in the artistic policy of these orchestras, nor does he recall any occasion when a board of directors with which he was associated did so.[1] Apart from the semantic definition of "artistic policy," this contention of Judson's is corollary to his larger view of the structure of the symphonic institution, in which the separation of authority between conductor, manager, and board of directors is as sacrosanct as the traditional separation of powers between the legislative, executive, and judiciary in our national constitutional government. As we explore the actual interrelations between the conductor, manager, and board of directors of American orchestras, however, we shall see that the lines of division there are every bit as blurred as they are in national politics, and Judson's own varied career illustrates the difficulties of making rigid distinctions of this sort. It is characteristic of Judson, immediately after making his general disclaimer on artistic policy, to launch into a colorful anecdote about his problems with Artur Rodzinski or the trouble he had in getting sufficiently varied repertory from Wilhelm Furtwängler.

Many who knew Judson during the days of his greatest power in symphony and artist management question his disavowal of involvement in artistic policy; others who knew him equally well agree that his statement is essentially correct, once one appreciates the actualities of the role of the manager. All agree that from 1915 to 1956, at least, Arthur Judson exercised a power and influence in the symphony and concert affairs of this country without equal then or at any other time. When he became manager of the Philadelphia Orchestra, there were possibly eight other fully professional orchestras in the United States; when he retired as manager of the New York Philharmonic in 1956, there were more than three times that number. During this period

* Strictly speaking, this orchestra has been known under more than one corporate title: the Philharmonic Society of New York, from 1842 to 1928, and the Philharmonic-Symphony Society of New York after 1928. Except when required by the context, I shall refer to this orchestra by its generally used term, the New York Philharmonic.

there was hardly a conductor, manager, or board leader who did not seek his advice. Most of those interested in organizing orchestras turned to him for counsel on general matters of organization and specific recommendation of managers and conductors. Outside the fully professional orchestras, many organizers of "community" orchestras looked to Judson as a source of expert guidance; despite their differences in philosophy, Helen M. Thompson still recalls with appreciation Judson's counsel in her organization and leadership of the American Symphony Orchestra League.[2]

A giant of a man physically—tall, handsome, and with an immediately commanding manner—he was also a monumental figure metaphorically. No one encountering Judson in person ever doubted the extent of his influence or his power to carry out his designs. Even today, at over ninety, there still emanates from Arthur Judson an aura of authority: he remains erect in stature, outspoken in opinion, vivid in recollection, and determined to set the record straight as regards his own career. Though he is still active in artist management, his days of great power are now a matter of history—the time when he managed two of our greatest orchestras, represented virtually all of the conductors active in this country, headed its largest concert bureau, organized one of the leading radio networks, and was valued adviser to the conductors, managers, and directors of symphony orchestras across the nation. Despite his denial of participation in artistic policy, he was a trained musician, with extensive experience in music education; unlike Charles Ellis, who moved into the management of the Boston Symphony from Henry Higginson's State Street investment office, Judson had a sound musical background. It is hard to believe that this ambitious and extremely able man, with his own experience in music, would not have artistic ideas of his own and express these ideas to his colleagues in the orchestras he managed.

In Philadelphia

As a young man I was for many years a violinist and teacher. I aspired to be a virtuoso. One day when I was professor of music at a midwestern university, I sat down and began to appraise my assets. I soon realized the truth, when I compared my talent with that of the great violinists I knew. There was no use to be pushed on by well meaning relatives and friends. I resolved to get into my present field. If I had not, I am quite sure I might still be back in my position at that university.[3]

With Arthur Judson became manager of the Philadelphia Orchestra in 1915, he had already had extensive musical and business experience. Born in Dayton, Ohio, on February 17, 1881, he studied the violin intensively, finishing his studies with Max Bendix, who had been Theodore Thomas's concert-master both in his own orchestra and in Chicago. At Denison University in Ohio, Judson developed one of the earliest independent music departments in the Midwest, acting both as administrator and as teacher; in these capacities he also conducted the student chorus and orchestra. He left Denison in 1907 to join the staff of *Musical America,** where he soon switched from writing to the business side of the magazine's operation; in both his editorial and business activities, he established his first contacts with the national concert scene and with major artists and managements.

Judson joined the Philadelphia Orchestra three years after its directors had hired the sensationally successful conductor of the Cincinnati Symphony, thirty-year-old Leopold Stokowski. Founded as a fully professional orchestra in 1900, the Philadelphia Orchestra had established itself in its community following much the same pattern as the orchestras of Boston and Chicago. Before Stokowski, its conductors had been German—Fritz Scheel from 1900 to 1907, and Karl Pohlig until Stokowski's advent in 1912.

Leopold Stokowski was born in London on April 18, 1882; at one time he tried to place his birth five years later, but both Slonimsky and Kupferberg confirm the earlier date.[4] His father, Kopernik Stokowski, was a cabinetmaker from Lublin, Poland, and the conductor himself counts among his Polish ancestors an officer in Napoleon's army. His mother, born Annie Moore, was of Irish extraction. He grew up in London, studying the violin, piano, and organ. He attended both Queens College at Oxford and the Royal College of Music in London, and later studied music in Paris and Munich. At the age of eighteen, he was appointed organist at St. James, Piccadilly, and five years later took a similar post at St. Bartholomew's in New York. He apparently began conducting in England and in Europe in 1908. Judson believes, as do others, that Cincinnati's attention was first drawn to Stokowski by the concert pianist Olga Samaroff (née Lucie Hickenlooper of San Antonio, Texas), whom Stokowski married in 1911. In any event, after one Cincinnati board member heard him conduct in Paris to confirm the good reports of his ability, he was engaged with a five-year contract in 1908 to conduct the Cincinnati Symphony. He served there for three seasons before breaking his contract to go to Philadelphia.[5]

Judson has said that Stokowski took a little German orchestra and turned it into a live tone picture. Never had this country, or any other for that matter, encountered quite the symphonic excitement that Stokowski generated. If the public and the press seemed most absorbed in Stokowski's elegant appearance and theatrical style of conducting, his purely musical ability had an immediate and lasting effect on the Philadelphia Orchestra. He brought to everything he conducted a dynamism and sense of orchestra tone color that enlivened the traditional repertory and made the new music he introduced dramatically exciting. As one of the first resident American conductors outside the German tradition, he gave unprecedented importance in his repertory to Russian and French music, to which his temperament responded sympathetically. And everything he did was presented with that perfect combination of showmanship and sense of artistic mission that even today characterizes this extraordinary conductor. From the very beginning of his career in Philadelphia, he was driven by an artistic restlessness, a continual search

---

* While at Denison, Judson wrote a book, *History of Music (An Investigation of Causes and Results)*, which was published "for the benefit of the Granville Spring Festival." During his years at *Musical America* he contributed many pedagogical articles to *Musician*.

for new sounds and new musical ideas, that made his more than two decades there an era of unique excitement and were eventually to cause his departure from that city.

With such a conductor, the Philadelphia Orchestra needed a comparable manager, whom they found in Arthur Judson. His first question upon assuming office was to ask the board for its budget. Hearing that none existed, he immediately prepared one, for, to Judson, the budget is the essential tool of orchestra management. It sets forth anticipated expenditures and income so that all concerned know the financial prospects in advance and the board can go about raising enough money to meet the projected deficit. The budget provides a constant standard against which ongoing operations can be reviewed from time to time, to make sure that all is going as expected during the progress of the season, and it also defines the structure of the responsibility of manager and conductor respectively. In Judson's ideal view, the budget tells the conductor how much he can spend on musical performances and allows him to determine artistic policy freely within the precise limits thus determined. The manager, in turn, is responsible for the business and promotional functions, again operating within the budget, and for businesslike accounting to keep the board of directors fully advised of the overall operation. It is further his responsibility to advise the board if the conductor's musical performance is running over budget and to compute the cost of the conductor's artistic proposals in concrete money terms as a guide to the board in its evaluation of artistic policy.

Through most of the Stokowski-Judson era in Philadelphia, the president of the Orchestra Association was Alexander Van Rensselaer, who had been one of the organizers of the Association in 1900 and served as its president from 1901 until his death in 1933. "Mr. Van," as he was known and is still remembered, was related by marriage to the wealthy and powerful Drexel family, and had as ready access to the social and business establishment of Philadelphia as Higginson had in Boston, though he did not have the personal fortune with which to support the orchestra alone. However, through his influence and that of other directors, the Philadelphia Orchestra was well supported and controlled by people listed in that city's prestigious Social Register.[6] Van Rensselaer's most important function, however, was as a member of the triumvirate who really ran the orchestra. He was a close and trusted friend of both Judson and Stokowski and their staunchest supporter in controlling the criticism of them that developed, especially in the late 1920s, in the board of directors itself. More than any other single person, he mediated between the enterprising conductor and the conservative board when Stokowski's costly musical projects had to be financed by the Association; Judson's function in this relationship involved keeping Van Rensselaer and the board informed of the financial consequences of Stokowski's plans and then managing affairs in a way that implemented the decisions of the board.

One of the most dramatic episodes of Stokowski's early years in Philadelphia was his presentation of the American premiere of Gustav Mahler's Eighth Symphony, called the "Symphony of a Thousand" because of the extensive orchestral, choral, and solo forces required. The presentation of this

Mahler symphony—in nine performances in Philadelphia and one in New York, at the Metropolitan Opera House, in March and April, 1916—was an event given news coverage of proportions unprecedented in the symphonic scene. The excitement generated by this production was due, of course, to Stokowski's imaginative artistic policy and presentation, but its exploitation as a major news event was masterminded by Judson.

In 1916, the Philadelphia Orchestra embarked on a major campaign to establish a substantial endowment fund, the income from which would cover annual operating deficits and relieve the Association from making annual appeals for funds. Though he remained anonymous at the beginning of this campaign, the prime mover was Edward Bok, editor and publisher in the highly successful Curtis publishing enterprises and son-in-law of their founder. Both Bok and his wife had a deep and informed interest in music, as did their son Curtis; all three were at various times members of the Association board and a portion of the family fortune was eventually set aside to endow the Curtis Institute of Music, one of this nation's great conservatories. Edward Bok had first shown an interest in the Philadelphia Orchestra early in Stokowski's tenure; he had, for instance, supported (with money and influence) the conductor's desire to hold all rehearsals of the orchestra in the Academy of Music, where the concerts were given.[7] All of the Bok family became close friends and ardent supporters of Stokowski. In 1916 the Association announced that an anonymous "friend" of the orchestra had offered to defray the annual operating deficits for five years and that during this time the Association was to raise $500,000 in endowment funds, income from which would permanently cover future annual deficits; one condition attached to this offer was that Stokowski be given a five-year contract. Eventually this campaign was extended to seven years, in the course of which nearly $800,000 was raised. Meanwhile, it was learned that the anonymous "friend" was none other than Edward Bok and that his personal contributions during this period exceeded $250,000. The endowment raised in this manner, plus future gifts and bequests, became the financial foundation on which the orchestra prospered until the depression. However, it also served as a kind of brake on artistic innovation and expansion of expenditures, as the board of directors tried to hold expenditures within such limits as could be financed by this endowment without seeking further annual funds from the community. Actually, though such information is still hard to confirm, there is every indication that during the 1920s the Association managed to accumulate a considerable surplus from operations and endowment income, which was administered with all of the conservative skill for which Philadelphia bankers are noted.*

As the Philadelphia Orchestra entered its third decade its eminence was assured: not only did it have a firm financial backing but it had in Stokowski a conductor whose rank would be challenged later in that decade only by Koussevitzky and Toscanini. It was a period of consolidation for the orchestra.

---

* Though Judson and others privy to financial matters in the Philadelphia Orchestra are reticent on this accumulated surplus, in their accounts of the "opera fiasco" of 1934–35 they state that the loss on that venture (amounting to $250,000) wiped out the Association's reserves.

Its women's committees, under the dynamic guidance since their establishment in 1904 of Miss Frances A. Wister, drew into their fold the leading
representatives of the distaff side of the Philadelphia establishment, providing the basis for the Friday afternoon audience. From fifty-two concerts in
1901–02, to eighty-five in Stokowski's first season, and to 107 in 1924–25, the
orchestra's activities had expanded greatly; in addition to the regular series
in Philadelphia, the twenty-nine-week season in 1924–25 included subscription series in New York, Washington, and Baltimore.[8] Except for occasional guest conductors, Stokowski conducted most of the programs, including
many memorable presentations of concerts for children from 1921 on.
Throughout this period, Stokowski continued to explore new ideas in repertory
and experimented with various innovations in performance, such as placing
the orchestra behind a curtain, reseating the orchestra, and abolishing the
time-honored custom of uniform bowing in the string sections.

Stokowski had taken his orchestra across the Delaware River to the Camden, New Jersey, studios of the Victor Talking Machine Company in October, 1917, and continued to record periodically during the next nine
years via the early acoustic recording process; in addition to short selections
tailored to fit one side of an old record (78 RPM), the Philadelphians made
two major albums: the Schubert *Unfinished Symphony* and Stravinsky's *Firebird Suite.* After the advent of electrical recording in 1926, however, Stokowski and the Philadelphia Orchestra became more active than any other
American group in the recording studios. The conductor's zeal for bringing
music to the masses and his insatiable curiosity about anything new involved
him deeply in a study of recording technique itself. In 1929, he led the
Philadelphia Orchestra in the first national commercially sponsored radio
broadcast on the NBC network.* He made frequent trips to the Bell Telephone laboratories in New York and experimented with the use of electronic devices in his concerts in Philadelphia. With the advent of the talking
picture, he took an interest in Hollywood, which exerted a strong attraction
on him as an opportunity for carrying forward his crusade to bring music to
the widest audience. He not only appeared in several motion pictures himself, but climaxed his Hollywood career with his collaboration in 1940 with
Walt Disney in *Fantasia,* for which he conducted the Philadelphia Orchestra
after he had relinquished its musical direction.

In his basic artistic policy, moreover, Stokowski continued his adventure-
some programming. Even after he reduced the time he devoted to the Philadelphia Orchestra in 1927, he continued to offer such major productions as
a staged performance of *The Rite of Spring* in 1930 (he had conducted the
first concert performance in this country in 1922), a staging of Berg's *Wozzeck* in 1931, and Schoenberg's *Gurrelieder* in 1932, recording the latter
from the concert performances. All three of these projects were sponsored in
part by the League of Composers and all three were taken to New York for

---

* Kupferberg (p. 74) refers to this occasion as "the first orchestra ever to make a commercially
sponsored radio broadcast"; this may have been the first national network broadcast under commercial sponsorship, but the New York Philharmonic had made local sponsored broadcasts as
early as 1922.

highly acclaimed presentations there. Following the first of these productions, Stokowski's portrait graced the cover of *Time Magazine* on April 30, 1930, the first conductor to be so honored.

In 1927, however, he started to reduce the time he devoted to the Philadelphia Orchestra; that year he conducted only half the season, sharing the podium with such distinguished guests as Fritz Reiner, Ossip Gabrilowitsch, Willem Mengelberg, Frederick Stock, Thomas Beecham, and Pierre Monteux. The practice of assigning a major part of the season to guest conductors remained in effect for the rest of Stokowski's tenure. Many Philadelphians, including a strong faction on the board of directors, resented Stokowski's absence from Philadelphia, but Judson, who was by this time managing the conductors who appeared as guests, was generally in accord with the scheme: he felt that Stokowski, with his restless ambition for new worlds to conquer, was too confined in Philadelphia, that he was exhausting his repertory, and that he was by no means artistically or temperamentally inclined to settle down into a routine sort of musical life. Nevertheless, there grew up within the board of directors a substantial anti-Stokowski faction, as well as one that was pro-Stokowski—a process of polarization that required all the skill that the aging "Mr. Van" could summon up to mediate.* Stokowski himself seldom engaged in direct confrontations with the board, preferring to have his point of view advanced by loyal friends within the group. On some occasions, he obliquely referred to policy differences in statements to the press or in little impromptu speeches to the concert audience; on many occasions, the prospect of such an "impromptu" speech from the stage of the Academy of Music was known in advance, not only to the Philadelphia press but to New York reporters as well.

As long as Alexander Van Rensselaer was at the helm of the Association, the tensions within it could be resolved. Judson himself wanted to leave the Philadelphia Orchestra as his commitments in New York increased, but he continued in his post at the behest of "Mr. Van." When the latter died in 1933, however, pressures long under his control erupted in the board. Curtis Bok succeeded Van Rensselaer as president of the Association, with the support of Stokowski and his friends on the board of directors. Early in the fall of 1934, Judson advised the directors of his desire to retire the following May. Stokowski, in the following December, shocked Philadelphia by announcing that he too was resigning; he gave as his reasons the failure of the Association to select a successor to Judson and their refusal to grant him a full year's leave of absence, rather than just the half season as in recent years.

These resignations came in the midst of one of the most ambitious, and at the same time financially disastrous, undertakings ever in Philadelphia—a full season of grand opera under the auspices of the Philadelphia Orchestra Association. The city had long enjoyed weekly visits from the Metropolitan Opera, as well as sporadic local efforts of varying quality. The

---

* Stokowski has recalled, in his interview with Kupferberg (pp. 108–09) and elsewhere, how tactfully "Mr. Van" transmitted to him the misgivings of the board concerning the programming of modern music.

best of these had the support of the Bok family and involved such distinguished musical directors as Fritz Reiner and the young Artur Rodzinski, who
had been brought to Philadelphia as Stokowski's assistant in 1926 and had
served on the Curtis Institute faculty before going to Los Angeles in 1929.
In 1934, the Metropolitan Opera announced that in view of the depressed
economy it was giving up its weekly visits to Philadelphia. Curtis Bok, by
now president of the Association, decided that the time was ripe to put the
orchestra into opera production. By this time Reiner was on the faculty of
the Curtis Institute, and he, Bok, and Judson planned what was by all
accounts one of the most notable seasons of ten operas ever given in this
country. Herbert Graf was brought over from Vienna as stage director,
Norman Bel Geddes designed several of the productions, and a considerable
investment was made in theatrical equipment.

By the end of the 1934–35 season, the Philadelphia Orchestra's venture
had run up a deficit of $250,000, completely wiping out the surplus carefully
nurtured by the Association during the 1920s. When the opera project was
first proposed, both Judson and Stokowski had been in favor of it, though
Stokowski, with increasing interests outside Philadelphia, took little part in
its planning. Judson, however, saw in the operas a way to diversify the activities of the Philadelphia Orchestra at a period when its central figure was
giving less and less time to it. Moreover, he assumed at the outset that the
repertory would concentrate on standard popular operas. In fact, the season
eventually offered a repertory of less than surefire box-office appeal—Wagner's *Tristan und Isolde* and *Die Meistersinger,* Strauss's *Der Rosenkavalier*
(with Lotte Lehmann, Elisabeth Schumann, and Emanuel List, and Reiner
conducting), a double bill of Humperdinck's *Hänsel und Gretel* and the
American premiere of Stravinsky's *Mavra,* Musorgsky's *Boris Godunov,*
Shostakovich's *Lady Macbeth of Mtzensk,* Gluck's *Iphigenia in Aulis,* Verdi's *Falstaff,* and Debussy's *Pelléas et Mélisande,* with only Bizet's *Carmen*
from the safe and sound repertory. One consequence of what came to be
known in Philadelphia as the "opera fiasco" was strong opposition within the
board of directors to Bok's leadership, since he had been the prime advocate
of the opera season. Moreover, Bok strongly backed Stokowski's effort to
get his own way—in the matter of a year's leave of absence and elsewhere.
One of the first issues was over the selection of a manager to succeed Judson:
after rejecting an effort by Bok to engage a lady who had been associated
with him in his local philanthropies, the board selected Reginald Allen. The
son of a prominent member of the women's committees, Allen had been for
several years on the board of directors, where he was on good terms with
both the pro- and anti-Stokowski factions; with previous experience in publicity and advertising for the Victor Talking Machine Company and in New
York, Allen had the requisite background, as well as social standing in
Philadelphia, to gain the support of a wide segment of the board. He served
as manager for nearly half a decade during the difficult transition which the
Philadelphia Orchestra faced in the next years, and which will be recounted in a later chapter.

Founding CBS

Meanwhile, Arthur Judson was expanding his own activities far beyond the management of the Philadelphia Orchestra, though it must be emphasized that he by no means neglected his duties there. He had from the outset a knack of organizing his activities expertly and hiring able and responsible people whom he could trust and who carried out his orders with genuine devotion and skill. Thus, as he came to spend less time personally in Philadelphia, he had there a good staff to carry on the managerial functions. From the very beginning of his term as manager of the Philadelphia Orchestra, however, he had engaged in the personal management of solo and concert artists in much the same way that Charles Ellis and Henry Voegeli did in Boston and Chicago respectively, drawing upon his contacts with orchestra soloists and with artists whom he had known as advertising manager for *Musical America* to build his "list." His firm, Concert Management Arthur Judson, first had its offices in Philadelphia, but soon moved to New York, the center of national booking of concert artists. (As we shall later note in detail, his shift to New York also involved his becoming manager of the New York Philharmonic.) Judson's growing activity as a manager of concert artists, and of conductors as well, not only expanded rapidly to the point of making him the most important manager in the country but also brought him into radio broadcasting.

Judson recalls that his first contact with radio was with a crystal receiver which his son had as a toy; even then, he now recalls, he foresaw the potential of radio as a means of disseminating music.[9] Nor was he alone in this belief: General David Sarnoff, who had played a major role in developing the pool of radio patents that laid the basis for the organization of the Radio Corporation of America, also saw the potential of linking together radio stations across the country by telephone service for the simultaneous presentation of program material in which music was to play an important part. Sarnoff may not then have realized the importance of having access to performing talent, for he was not responsive to Judson's overtures in this regard, but he may well have had plans of his own in the back of his mind when he rejected Judson's offer to supply musical talent, for a weekly fee, to the Red and Blue networks. Certainly it was not long before Sarnoff, Judson, and others in radio placed a very high importance on broadcasting as a means of spreading the cause of good music across the country, and as a source of employment and public exposure for concert artists.

For the programs produced by the Judson Radio Corporation, Judson sought the best artists he could persuade to appear, and his involvement in radio became a powerful incentive for artists to engage Judson as their manager. An early failure, however, was the violinist Fritz Kreisler, whom Judson approached through Clarence Mackay, then chairman of the New York Philharmonic and a friend of the artist: Kreisler refused an attractive fee, holding out for being paid one dollar for every listener, a completely impractical condition in those pre-Nielsen days. In addition to established concert artists, Judson discovered new ones whose first reputations were established on radio before they became major concert attractions; Nelson Eddy was one of these. The manager soon learned that solo recitals enjoyed little success on radio and that his artists had to be presented with orchestral accompaniment. To conduct these orchestras, Judson needed directors who were flexible and accommodating to the peculiar requirements of broadcasting, and he found them in such musicians as Eugene Ormandy (then conducting the pit orchestra at the Capitol Theater in New York), André Kostelanetz, Howard Barlow, Donald Voorhees, and Alfred Wallenstein.

When Sarnoff turned down Judson's first proposal to supply talent to his networks, Judson decided to organize a network to buy productions from his own Judson Radio Corporation. Between 1926 and 1928, Judson became involved in a succession of efforts to obtain financing for his struggling radio network. At first he was helped by Betty Fleischman Holmes (of the Cincinnati yeast fortune and a member of the New York Philharmonic board); then he had brief support from the Columbia Phonograph Company, which withdrew when the financial going got rough, but left its name on the venture; * and finally he found backing in Philadelphia from the Levy, Louchheim, and Paley families. In the end, of course, young William Paley, whose family had sold their cigar business for twenty-five million dollars, bought out most of the other investors, and won control of what now had become the Columbia Broadcasting System. However, Judson remained an active stockholder in CBS, retaining to this day an interest second only to Paley's.

Artist Management

Judson's part in the formation of CBS was of importance to his career, not only because it affiliated his management of artists with radio broadcasting but also because CBS eventually provided the capital for Judson's organization of a major concert-management corporation in 1930, which was to have an impact on the music business across the nation.[10] Judson had, in 1928, purchased the oldest artist-management firm in the nation—the Wolfsohn Musical Bureau, founded in 1884—thus greatly strengthening his list, as well as acquiring several excellent personnel. Concert management at this time was in a rather chaotic state of cutthroat competition. Not only were rival managers engaged in fee-cutting to obtain dates for their artists, but a few powerful local impresarios were playing one artist manager off against

* Ironically, the Columbia Phonograph Company, which continued to suffer financial reverses through the depression years, was eventually bought out by CBS in 1938 for approximately $800,000; CBS Records is now one of the world's most prosperous recording enterprises. After CBS's acquisition of Columbia Records, it succeeded in signing exclusive contracts with both the Philadelphia and New York orchestras which provided the core of an impressive repertory of symphonic music that contributed much to the success of this record company.

the other to obtain better terms.* In theory, of course, these artist managers were supposed to act as agents for their clients, but often they tended to look upon them as merchandise to be bought and sold. Moreover, Sarnoff's National Broadcasting Company, having rebuffed Judson in 1926, was now showing an interest in entering the artist-management field.

More important, however, were developments in Chicago aimed at a novel type of local concert presentation. Growing out of the old Lyceum, Chautauqua, and Redpath booking circuits for lecturers, entertainers, and occasionally concert artists, which brought these attractions into the smaller cities and towns across the country, there developed a new concept of the "organized audience." One of the banes of these booking operations, as of Theodore Thomas's touring activities, was the risk of not being paid by the local sponsor or committee. To correct this problem a Redpath executive, Dema Harshberger, took a novel plan to Samuel Insull to gain his financial support: instead of waiting for payment until the attraction arrived in a town, Miss Harshberger conceived the idea of having the local committee raise all of the money needed for a series *before* contracting for the attractions. Moreover, Miss Harshberger decided very early in her scheme to confine it to organizing concert audiences, a decision that appealed to Insull because of his interest in opera. Though Miss Harshberger's Civic Music Service was barely started before the depression hit the country and her backer, the scheme was sufficiently impressive to frighten the New York artist managers, who did not relish the idea of having to do business with a nationwide system of such potentially strong bargaining power.

Merger being the corporate fashion of the day, Judson organized a consolidation of a number of New York concert agents—the number varied from four to eight, depending on the degree to which the components themselves represented previous mergers. The main constituents of this merger were Judson and his enterprises; F. C. Coppicus and Frederick C. Schang, Jr., of the Metropolitan Musical Bureau; Hansel and Jones; and Evans and Salter. To this group, then known as Columbia Concerts Corporation, was added an "organized audience" division known as Community Concerts. The capital for this merger and for setting up of Community Concerts was supplied by CBS and Judson himself. Thus CBS, which had started out as an adjunct of concert management, returned to the field as a financial backer.

Community Concerts was an essential part of this scheme, possibly *the* essential factor. By organizing local Community committees to raise money in advance for a concert series, the booking agents minimized the risk of financial loss through nonpayment of the artist's fee. Moreover, since Community was a part of the Columbia Concerts combine, it obviously would buy its artists from the agencies in that combine. Thus, the Community representatives, who worked in the field to help local committees sell their annual memberships, were also salesmen for the Columbia Concerts agencies. With such ad-

---

* The violinist Albert Spalding once told me that a major factor in persuading independent managements to merge was the stranglehold exercised by the Los Angeles impresario L. H. Behymer over all bookings in an area covering Southern California and portions of four or five more states.

vance information of the market, these managers could plan their bookings
in a most economical way and reduce the evils of fee-cutting between managers. Actually, as the scheme developed, each local Community campaign
was based on one headliner attraction, the remainder of the offering being
determined by what the local group could afford to pay once its annual membership drive was over; no single tickets were sold, and no memberships
offered, once the annual campaign was over, so prospective concert-goers
were more or less forced to subscribe to the campaign if they wanted to hear
any concerts at all.

For the first two years, Community Concerts was headed by Sigmund
Spaeth, a popular lecturer on music, well known in his day as the "tune detec-
tive." But Spaeth was neither the business executive nor the organizer that
this project needed; too many local committees were booking him as a
lecturer instead of a concert artist. Dema Harshberger's Civic Music Service having fallen on bad times when Insull was forced to withdraw his backing,
Community succeeded in hiring her assistant, Ward French.* French proved
to be an extraordinary organizer for Community, not only in business matters
but in the almost religious zeal with which he imparted a sense of crusade to
his staff. Schang recalls how he himself once addressed a meeting of field-
workers for Community, citing "the pursuit of happiness" in the Declaration
of Independence to inspire the staff by identifying this right with the cause
of music in every hamlet and city across the nation. In the depths of the
depression, this "organized audience" movement grew and expanded at a
remarkable rate; moreover, NBC had organized its own concert-management bureau, complete with the acquisition of Civic Music Service. The two
giant bureaus engaged in outward competition, frequently aggressive but
more often controlled by gentlemen's agreements behind the scenes: Civic
and Community seldom attempted to organize one another's "towns" except
in special circumstances, and Columbia Concerts and NBC Concerts usually
succeeded in agreeing to deal only with selected local concert managers, to
the exclusion of the few artist representatives outside their fold.[11] At the
height of their power, the two "organized audience" operations claimed more
than two thousand towns in their combined rosters.

But the very size of these two booking agencies, of which Columbia was
definitely the larger and more forceful, raised misgivings among the artists
so booked and attracted the attention of the Department of Justice. Many
artists, some of whom owed their early establishment in the concert field to
the "organized audience" process, found it increasingly restrictive: generally
they had to play the same program in all Community or Civic appearances,
a program that French and his associates often dictated, chosen to appeal to
the broadest segment of the audience. The Justice Department, moreover, saw
definitely monopolistic tendencies in both agencies. At first, they called for
a divorce of these two agencies from their respective radio-network affiliations: by the time this was put in effect, in 1940, the agencies were strong

* Schang, who was then chief salesman and publicist of Columbia Concerts, in addition to being
a partner in the Metropolitan Musical Bureau, recalls how he and Coppicus encountered a
despondent French on Fifty-seventh Street in 1932 and promptly hired him for Community.

enough to survive on their own, and the only real consequence was that the networks engaged artists from their former rival agents for what was by then, in fact, an already declining presentation of concert artists on radio. Somewhat more effective was the agreement of the agencies, which had changed their names after 1940 to Columbia Artists Management, Inc., and National Concert and Artists Corporation, to a consent decree in 1952 which required each "organized audience" division to open its bookings to artists represented by all managers. The negotiation of this consent decree caused severe strains within the Columbia organization, French being thwarted by his partners in his attempt to take the entire Community operation out of Columbia. NCAC, however, encountered a series of difficulties with personnel, losing its very important function of handling bookings for the independent Hurok list and eventually its major position in the concert field. The Hurok agency, and a number of others that grew up after the loosening of ties between Columbia and Community, now share the concert-management field with the still strong Columbia Artists Management combine.

Though the "organized audience" scheme, now essentially all operated by Community, has declined appreciably to probably less than a thousand towns, it has had a lasting effect in stimulating the organization of local committees, often with former Community committee members, which have organized their own concert series and symphony orchestras.

In all of this Arthur Judson played a leading role: his was the most important list in the Columbia combination, and for many years he assumed a strong leadership in holding together the various partners in the complex despite frequently tense relations between them. To this day, he recalls with pride the financial investment he made in first organizing Community as a move toward spreading the cause of good music to thousands of cities and hamlets across the nation.

The New York Philharmonic

When Arthur Judson became manager of the New York Philharmonic in 1922, that orchestra was but one of several playing in New York.[12] Walter Damrosch's New York Symphony continued with the virtually sole backing of Henry Harkness Flagler. The City Symphony, under Dirk Foch, was enjoying a precarious existence prior to its merger with the Philharmonic in 1923, and the Philharmonic had only a year before absorbed the National Symphony. This latter was conducted by Willem Mengelberg and backed by Adolph Lewisohn, who had encountered Mengelberg through his banking connections in Amsterdam. Lewisohn had first become involved in symphonic music in 1918 at the behest of Mrs. Charles S. ("Minnie") Guggenheimer, who secured his backing for a series of outdoor concerts in Lewisohn Stadium on the campus of the City College of New York, which were a summer fixture of New York's musical life for nearly five decades. Lewisohn was also an amateur singer, and Judson recalls taking the young Fritz Reiner to

Lewisohn's home for a musical soirée; Reiner's ability to read and transpose every accompaniment set before him so impressed his host that he became an immediate favorite of Lewisohn's and a frequent conductor of the Stadium concerts.

The Philharmonic had for some years ceased to be the musicians' cooperative it had been since 1842. Until the death in 1898 of Anton Seidl, who had been elected Thomas's successor in 1891, the Society continued to prosper, but during the next decade, under such conductors as Emil Paur (1898–1902), Walter Damrosch (1902–03), and Vassily Safonov (1906–09), there was increasing pressure on the player-members of the Philharmonic to relinquish their cooperative control of the orchestra and to accept the financial support of contributors who would select a musical director. Much of this pressure came from wealthy patrons who wanted to establish in New York an orchestra as stable and distinguished as those of Boston, Philadelphia, and Chicago. Similar pressure came from many orchestra members themselves who wanted to be relieved of the uncertainty of compensation from shares of the profits and who desired the financial security enjoyed by their counterparts in other cities. Finally, in 1909, the Philharmonic players agreed to a reorganization of their orchestra, setting up a board of lay directors who would finance an orchestra on a salaried basis and engage as conductor the renowned Gustav Mahler. It was further aided in 1911 by a bequest in the will of Joseph Pulitzer endowing the Philharmonic with one million dollars on two conditions: that the testator's favorite composers—Beethoven, Wagner, and Liszt—play a prominent part in the orchestra's repertory, and that the Philharmonic Society become a legal membership corporation, with not less than a thousand dues-paying members. Mahler conducted the Philharmonic with great success for two seasons before his death in 1911, and was followed by Josef Stransky, who remained in the post until 1923.

When Judson joined the Philharmonic in 1922, its board chairman was Clarence Mackay, who had made a large fortune in investments and communications. He was a dedicated lover of music as well as a generous man. He was able to allocate to various board members the sums of money they were expected to contribute or raise and then write his own check for the remainder of the deficit. Judson recalls that at the end of each season he would give Mackay an accounting of the operations, whereupon Mackay would cover the amount that was lacking. With the 1921 absorption of the National Symphony, the Philharmonic had acquired the services of Willem Mengelberg, who could give the Philharmonic only a portion of his time since he was also committed to the Amsterdam Concertgebouw. For two seasons, Mengelberg shared conducting duties with Stransky, Henry Hadley, and Willem Van Hoogstraten; in 1924–25 Wilhelm Furtwängler made his first appearance as guest conductor, joined the next year by Arturo Toscanini. For two seasons, 1925–27, the Philharmonic enjoyed the services of Toscanini, Mengelberg, and Furtwängler, but the latter was dropped from the list in 1927, though Mengelberg continued to appear with the Philharmonic until the 1929–30 season. During this period, Toscanini rapidly established himself as the dominating conductor of the Philharmonic, both through his popularity with the critics and the public and through an increasingly close association with Mackay. The Philharmonic European tour in 1930, financed by Mackay at Toscanini's insistence, was conducted by Toscanini, except for a concert in Amsterdam which Mengelberg directed. Officially, Toscanini was listed as guest or associate conductor from 1925 to 1929, when he became musical director until 1936; he returned once as guest conductor, in 1941, as part of the Philharmonic's centennial season.

The Philharmonic was the first American orchestra to broadcast regularly. From 1922 to 1926, it presented commercially sponsored children's concerts locally over WEAF, and from 1927 to 1930 a large portion of its subscription concerts, as well as children's concerts, were broadcast locally in New York. These activities reflect Judson's growing involvement with radio at the time, as does the commencement in 1930 of the Sunday afternoon broadcasts of the Philharmonic over the national CBS network, which were to continue for nearly four decades as a major feature of this nation's musical life. The Philharmonic also began to record in 1922, playing for Victor under Mengelberg, Beecham, and Toscanini during this period; the Toscanini recordings still available offer a good example of the quality of the orchestra under his direction.

In 1928 the Philharmonic Society merged with the New York Symphony, the only remaining orchestra in New York. As noted earlier, the New York Symphony had been founded in 1878 by Leopold Damrosch, upon whose death in 1885 his son, Walter, succeeded him.[13] Under Walter Damrosch, the New York Symphony pursued a precarious existence, depending upon the conductor's ability to secure financing from various backers in the New York social circles with which he enjoyed such good relations. After an unsuccessful effort to take over the New York Philharmonic in 1902–03, Damrosch continued to lead his New York Symphony with increasing support from Henry Harkness Flagler, who by World War I was virtually that orchestra's sole sponsor. Flagler was a close friend of Damrosch, completely dedicated in his faith in the conductor's leadership. However, by the mid-1920s, the cost of supporting the New York Symphony ($100,000 a year) was becoming more than Flagler wanted to bear, especially in the face of the competition from the Philharmonic under the direction of Toscanini, Mengelberg, and Furtwängler. When Flagler approached Mackay with a proposal to merge the two orchestras, Judson had great misgivings: he saw major problems in absorbing the Symphony players into the Philharmonic, retaining Damrosch as a conductor, and in financing the enlarged operation needed to serve the Symphony's subscribers. However, Flagler and Mackay prevailed and the orchestras were merged: the personnel of the Philharmonic-Symphony was enlarged and Damrosch was included in the roster of conductors for one season before joining the staff of the National Broadcasting Company, where his great charm and the sense of artistic mission he brought to his concerts and children's programs entertained a national audience. After the merger, Mackay remained as chairman of the combined board of the New York Philharmonic-Symphony Society and Flagler served as its president until he relinquished the post to Marshall Field in 1934. As Judson anticipated, the expanded operation of the Philharmonic involved a greater deficit than the one orchestra had accumulated, but Flagler made substantial contributions to help defray it.

National Influence

Upon relinquishing the Philadelphia management in 1935, Judson was able to center all of his activities in New York. His private office, in a corner on the top floor of the Steinway Building on Fifty-seventh Street, was elegantly furnished in Early American style and contained a handsome "stand-up" antique desk rather than the conventional office type. The offices of Judson's concert management and radio programming were located a floor below in the complex occupied by his partners in Columbia Concerts; there the routine of booking and management was under the supervision of Ruth O'Neill, who had started in the Philadelphia Orchestra office in 1911. In the Philharmonic offices on the top floor, adjacent to Judson's private quarters, Bruno Zirato was in charge; he had formerly been Enrico Caruso's secretary and was engaged by Judson in large part because of his close association with Toscanini. Judson himself was never as close to Toscanini as he was to other conductors; the Maestro's major contact with the Philharmonic was either through Mackay as board chairman or with Zirato on orchestra routine. Zirato also came to handle much of the booking routine for Judson's list of conductors. However, Judson kept close supervision over the activities which he had delegated to his colleagues. In many instances, he remained rather remote from the day-to-day operations of both his concert management and Philharmonic affairs, concerning himself with larger policy issues or with important problems as they arose. Very often policies or actions set in motion by his subordinates aroused reactions from many who blamed Judson ultimately, and it is very likely that though he may not have acted directly himself, he fully approved the actions taken by his colleagues acting in his behalf.

Moreover, Judson kept in very close touch with his board leaders—Clarence Mackay until his death in 1938, and Marshall Field, Charles Triller, and David M. Keiser thereafter—as well as with key board members of the Philharmonic. Judson, alone of orchestra managers in his time, was in a position to deal on an equal plane with such business executives, for he was himself a corporate executive, not an agent of the patron, as was Ellis in Boston. In this capacity Judson exerted a subtle influence on policy, not so much by explicit advocacy at formal board meetings, but in more informal contacts behind the scenes. When he presented a detailed outline for a season, the board knew that it was based on a comprehensive knowledge of the international music scene, and few directly questioned his authority. With the New York Philharmonic, the selection of guest conductors and soloists was as important as in Philadelphia after Stokowski had reduced his work load to half a season. Moreover, the national prestige of the Philharmonic, and its weekly radio exposure over CBS after 1930, made it a sought-after showcase both for guest conductors and soloists. Since Toscanini as musical director conducted only a portion of the season, the engagement of guest conductors and soloists was important at the Philharmonic. Contrary to popular opinion at the time, Judson did not necessarily play the sole role in the selection of guests. Some were engaged at the behest of Toscanini himself. Others were heard in Europe or elsewhere in this country by board members who suggested them to Toscanini or Judson. But Judson himself took the initiative in other instances, for, as an artist manager himself, he had ample opportunity to assess the available supply here and abroad. He visited Europe regularly, where he was constantly importuned by artists and their managers seeking American engagements. Those artists in whom Judson had faith could be virtually assured of a first-rate introduction to American audiences through appearances with the Philharmonic, national exposure on the radio broadcasts, bookings in recital through Judson's management, and engagements with the other American orchestras whose conductors were under his management or whose managers were close to Judson. In retrospect, Judson likes to point out that in offering lists of possible soloists to the musical directors of orchestras with whom he worked, he never mentioned who managed them, but few conductors were so naïve as not to know which were Judson's artists. With the conductors and managers of other orchestras, Judson had no need for such restraint: his recommendation of a new European artist carried great weight, especially when he could assure that orchestra that the soloist in question would open his tour with a nationally broadcast appearance with the Philharmonic. As manager of practically all symphonic conductors working in the United States, Judson had ample opportunity to suggest soloists in an almost casual manner, and often relied upon these musicians to recommend or give an opinion on possible concert artists to be brought over from Europe.

Similarly, just as Judson was on easy personal terms with the key members of the boards of the Philadelphia Orchestra and New York Philharmonic, his advice was eagerly sought by symphony board members throughout the country. While he was manager of both New York and Philadelphia orchestras, he also served for a time as adviser to the Cincinnati Symphony, but such formal arrangements were not required for Judson to play a crucial role in the engagement of many conductors of local orchestras. Aside from his representation of those conductors who held permanent positions, he also was the source to which orchestras turned for the booking of guest conductors, many of whom were more or less candidates for permanent positions once they opened up. In such cases where an orchestra chose a conductor whom Judson had not recommended, he often became involved in the contractual arrangements for engaging him. Thus, when Cincinnati took an interest in Thor Johnson on the recommendation of Serge Koussevitzky, Judson handled the negotiations for Johnson, even though the conductor had not been under his management previously. Similarly, he played an important part, as we shall see, in Eugene Ormandy's * engagement by the Minneapolis Symphony Orchestra, and in his replacement by Dimitri Mitropoulos when Ormandy

* Ormandy to this day gratefully acknowledges his debt to Judson. "I owe overything to him," he told me recently.

went to Philadelphia; finally, when Mitropoulos became conductor of the New York Philharmonic, Judson played a part in moving Antal Dorati from Dallas to Minneapolis and sending Walter Hendl to Dallas. It was very rare that an American orchestra, during the decades of Judson's greatest influence, did not at least consult him when it sought a resident conductor, and few failed to take his advice. Likewise, many conductors interested in an American career took great pains to seek Judson's advice and help, not only because of their confidence in his advice but also because they knew that, with Judson's support, they had very practical advantages in the advancement of their careers. Most of the conductors whom Judson represented were of European origin, many of them seeking an American career as refugees from a Hitler-threatened Europe. However, as such young American conductors as Leonard Bernstein appeared on the scene, Judson took an interest in advancing their careers as well; Bernstein, as a protégé of Reiner and Koussevitzky, was a newly appointed assistant to Artur Rodzinski at the Philharmonic when he dramatically replaced the ailing Bruno Walter at a Philharmonic concert, and he was represented for many years after by Judson in his conducting career. However, Judson also had strong opinions about conductors, based both on his evaluation of their conducting ability and on his judgment of their special capability for fitting into the musical life of a specific community as permanent director. Many conductors under his management, he felt, were best suited for guest engagements, not for permanent posts; others, he felt, needed more experience before they could be placed in any position of importance. Thanks to his virtually monopolistic management of conductors and to the confidence that all concerned placed in Judson, his views on such matters were given great weight.

Judson also took an intense personal interest in the careers of young orchestra managers. Many of them started out in management on the staff of Columbia Concerts or at the Philharmonic, moving on later into posts with orchestras across the country. As in the engagement of conductors, board members sought Judson's advice in the engagement of managerial personnel, and managers looking for competent subordinates consulted Judson in the choice of their assistants, who later assumed more important positions. A great deal of this influence was difficult to define in strictly institutional terms, for so much of it rested simply on Judson's towering prestige in concert and symphonic circles between 1915 and 1960. Often Judson's influence was exercised directly, through a phone call or wire flatly recommending a conductor, soloist, or manager.* In other cases, it could be more indirect: words of praise long before an opening actually materialized or a personal phone call to an influential manager or board member on a confi-

---

* Typical of Judson's authority is a story told me years ago by Mrs. M. Donald Spencer, long-time manager of the Portland Symphony Orchestra, in Oregon. She had engaged as the orchestra's musical director Theodore Spiering, who died suddenly during the summer of 1925, just before the season was to open. In great distress she phoned Judson, explaining her plight. "I have just the man for you," he assured her. "He is one of the conductors of the New York Philharmonic." On this simple recommendation, Willem Van Hoogstraten was engaged and served that orchestra until 1937, while also acting as principal conductor of the Lewisohn Stadium concerts in the summer.

dential basis; for Judson knew, better than anyone else in his day, precisely where the power lay in virtually every orchestra across the country. On some occasions, he himself did not act directly, a recommendation coming from a close associate such as Zirato or Ruth O'Neill, but the recipient knew without being told that "A.J." was behind it. As other orchestra managers increasingly sought Judson's advice and exchanged information with him, there grew up under his leadership an informal conference of the managers of the major orchestras which met regularly once or twice a year for discussion of problems and the exchange of information on finances, union relations, and managerial activities. After meeting separately for several decades, this conference of "major" managers now is closely affiliated with the American Symphony Orchestra League.

Turmoil at the Philharmonic

Judson by no means always got his way in every instance, nor was his control as absolute as many charged at the time. But he had a remarkable facility for waiting out his opposition and, when he had to, accepting a decision with which he might not have concurred. As he recalls the immediate post-Toscanini era at the Philharmonic, he was not in complete control of the situation. The first choice of the Philharmonic board to succeed Toscanini * was another conductor of towering repute, Wilhelm Furtwängler. Judson now says that he had serious misgivings about this choice: Furtwängler's repertory was severely limited, as Judson knew from experience in dealing with him as guest conductor of the Philharmonic earlier; he was also fearful that Furtwängler's Nazi associations, real or reputed, would arouse opposition from the important Jewish community in New York. But, on instructions from the board, he proceeded with negotiations for Furtwängler's engagement. Once the announcement was made, the expected opposition erupted, not only from the Jewish community but from a number of musicians close to Toscanini. When Furtwängler withdrew his name, Judson and the board had to look elsewhere. Again, Judson recalls his misgivings over the engagement of John Barbirolli, a great favorite with several board members: in this case he felt that Barbirolli was too inexperienced at the time and too lacking in disciplinary temperament to take over the Philharmonic after Toscanini, but he went along with the board's choice. At the time, there were some who believed that Judson actually welcomed having a musical director at the Philharmonic who would be more malleable to his influence. Barbirolli's term as conductor of the Philharmonic proved to be unpopular with the pub-

* After leaving the Philharmonic in 1936, Toscanini first helped organize the Israel Philharmonic and then returned to this country in 1937, at the invitation of David Sarnoff, to lead the newly organized NBC Symphony Orchestra, for which the regular musical staff of the network was enlarged. Except for a one-year leave of absence, he conducted this orchestra until his retirement in 1954, three years before his death. Important as the NBC Symphony was in this nation's musical life, it was not the kind of community-supported orchestra with which this book is concerned.

lic, the press, and the orchestra itself; after five seasons, during which the board and Judson held out staunchly to retain him, his contract was not renewed, though he returned as guest conductor during the centennial season of 1941–42.

After an interim season of guest conductors, the board, with Judson's full approval and encouragement, engaged Artur Rodzinski as musical director in 1943.* Judson had known Rodzinski since he had come to Philadelphia in 1926 and had played an important part in his engagement by the Los Angeles Philharmonic in 1929 and by the Cleveland Orchestra in 1933. He also knew in advance that Rodzinski was a temperamental and often difficult conductor with strong religious and mystical inclinations. Moreover, during Rodzinski's term in Cleveland, Judson knew that the conductor was frequently in conflict with Carl Vosburgh, the manager there; on one occasion, he recalls, Vosburgh had phoned him in desperation, asking him to come out to Cleveland and get Rodzinski "off his back," because the conductor was trying to get him fired. But Rodzinski had guest-conducted the Philharmonic with great success and Judson felt that he was not only the best man available to bring order to a sadly undisciplined orchestra but also one who would restore the confidence of the Jewish community in the Philharmonic.

Soon after Rodzinski took over the Philharmonic he confronted Judson with a demand that some fourteen or fifteen players be discharged from the orchestra, many of them players in what was known among musicians at the time as the "Toscanini Mafia." Judson recalls trying to explain to Rodzinski that such a drastic shake-up of personnel was totally impractical, not only as a source of conflict with the union but also doing violence to the moral obligation of the Philharmonic to players who had served the orchestra long and well. After a lengthy discussion, in which Judson pleaded that such changes should be made slowly and cautiously, Rodzinski agreed to give Judson's views his careful and thoughtful consideration. But the next morning he was again in Judson's office. He had thought the matter over, as Judson had suggested, and decided to seek Divine guidance. He prayed to God, explained his side of the problem and, he assured Judson, had also presented the manager's views conscientiously, and then received this advice: "Fire the bastards."

In the end, Rodzinski prevailed in this matter, creating considerable hostility both in the union and among the players themselves. But this episode was only the first of a number of differences between Rodzinski and the manager. They came to a climax in February, 1947, during Rodzinski's fourth season, when the conductor, without previous warning, appeared before the board to demand that it choose between him and Judson: either Judson must go or Rodzinski would resign. Confronted with this ultimatum, and after an

* Serge Koussevitzky was negotiating in the spring of 1942 a contract with the New York Philharmonic calling for him to appear as guest conductor in 1942–43 and to become musical director in 1943. Though Koussevitzky did appear as guest conductor, he eventually rejected the musical-director contract offered by the Philharmonic. This episode played an important part, as will be seen in the next chapter, in the reversal of the Boston trustees' long refusal to permit the unionization of their orchestra. (See Moses Smith, *Koussevitzky*, pp. 316–23.)

attempt to mediate between the two men, the Philharmonic board discharged Rodzinski forthwith, settling the remainder of his contract and relieving him immediately of any direction of the orchestra. Rodzinski countered with a public attack on Judson and the Philharmonic, in which the manager was the target of his charges of meddling in the artistic policy of the Philharmonic, the first occasion on which Judson was subjected to such a devastating attack in the local and national press.[14] What neither Judson nor the Philharmonic board knew at the time was that when Rodzinski presented his ultimatum to the Philharmonic, he had already negotiated a contract to become musical director of the Chicago Symphony Orchestra the following fall.[15] He lasted there but one season, during which his conflict with management and the board created an equally stormy scandal. To this day, Arthur Judson recalls this episode with bitterness and regret: he still feels not only that Rodzinski's charges were unjustified but also that the conductor showed bad taste in carrying his problems with the management and the board to the public.

Though Judson emerged as victor from the Rodzinski affair, he never quite recovered his lofty position either at the Philharmonic or in the symphonic field in general. Whatever the merits in the case may have been, Rodzinski was saying, publicly and forcefully, what many others had been saying privately—that Judson was, for better or worse, the "czar" of the concert and symphonic business. For two seasons following Rodzinski's discharge, Bruno Walter acted as principal conductor and musical adviser—not full musical director—of the Philharmonic, followed by a season in which Stokowski and Dimitri Mitropoulos shared the podium; in 1950, Mitropoulos became full musical director of the Philharmonic.

This remarkable conductor had been brought to this country by Judson, making his debut in Boston in 1936, and succeeding Ormandy in Minneapolis in 1937. Mitropoulos was, in many respects, the most completely original conductor to appear in this country since Stokowski, and his performances were often extremely controversial. His tenure in New York, from 1950 to 1958, saw that orchestra produce some of its most exciting performances and some of its most questionable ones. Under the relaxed and beneficent direction of Mitropoulos, discipline in the Philharmonic, which had deteriorated since the days of Toscanini except under Rodzinski's firm hand, was further imperiled. Mitropoulos could dazzle an orchestra with his phenomenal memory for every detail of a score and charm the players with his warm and generous personality, but he was incapable of the kind of ruthless discipline that many other conductors used to maintain their authority. Moreover, Mitropoulos's advocacy of modern music—especially that of the twelve-tone school of Schoenberg and Berg,* as well as new music by younger composers—aroused opposition from the audience, the critics, and the Philharmonic board itself. Judson, despite his reputation for meddling in artistic policy, apparently exerted no effective influence to modify Mitropoulos's crusade for new music. As a result, there was a movement within the Philharmonic board to exert

---

* Mitropoulos's presentation of Berg's *Wozzeck* in concert, broadcast over the CBS network and subsequently released on records, remains one of the memorable musical experiences of our time.

stronger administrative participation in the operation of the orchestra both in business management and musical decisions.

At least until the Rodzinski affair, the board had given Judson great latitude in managing the Philharmonic. The deficits incurred were not, even by standards of that time, oppressively large, and a few board members happily defrayed them. Judson got on well with his board, according to some observers, because he got on well with its leadership and because the board as a whole followed that leadership and Judson's domination. But the public clash with Rodzinski embarrassed some members of the board, who disliked seeing the dirty linen of the Philharmonic aired in public; nor did they like the public inference that the board was not in control of the Philharmonic. Others saw the Rodzinski outburst as a confirmation of charges, in and out of the Philharmonic, of Judson's dictatorship. Finally, the loss of audience at Mitropoulos's concerts and the growing hostility of the critics had a serious effect upon the board. As a result, a way was found to ease Mitropoulos out, with two final years in which he shared the direction with Leonard Bernstein, who succeeded him in 1958.

As part of the board's more active interest, it appointed from its membership a Music Advisory Committee. This committee, which was by no means common among the largest American orchestras but whose counterpart has long existed among some smaller ones, has been headed since its inception by David M. Keiser, a New York businessman who had in his youth received a solid musical training at the Institute of Musical Art. Keiser has served as chairman of the Music Advisory Committee, as president of the Philharmonic Society, and as chairman of its board. He has not only played an active role in the musical policies of the Philharmonic but was the Society's president during the organization of Lincoln Center and the orchestra's move to the new Philharmonic Hall. His musical interests are by no means confined to the Philharmonic, with whom he played as piano soloist (with manager Carlos Moseley and conductor Bernstein in a Bach concerto) at a benefit concert: he is also a member of the Lincoln Center board and president of the board of the Juilliard School, successor to his alma mater, the Institute of Musical Art.

The Musical Advisory Committee at the Philharmonic has taken the place of the influence of Arthur Judson on the artistic direction of that orchestra. It would have been inconceivable to have such a committee with a Stokowski, a Koussevitzky, a Szell, or a Reiner, but the tradition of the Philharmonic, where Judson wielded so strong an influence, is such that it has worked smoothly. Its functions may be divided into two main areas: the choice of the musical director and the diplomatic transmission to him of the musical opinions of the board. In the former capacity it played a major part in the selection of both Leonard Bernstein in 1956 and of Pierre Boulez in 1970. Both conductors were fully informed of the committee's role in their selection and in its function *vis-à-vis* the conductor and the board. The committee itself, composed of musically sympathetic members, the manager, and the president, and led by a knowledgeable musical layman, listens to the more general comments of the board on artistic matters, and then sits down with the conductor and presents these views as diplomatically and expertly as it can. The plans, policies, and reactions of the conductor, in turn, are carried back to the full board by the committee. It is impossible, given the confidential nature of this committee, to know just how much influence it has on either the conductor or on the board in routine artistic matters. Certainly its role in advising the selection of a conductor has not only a very important immediate impact but also a latent effect of giving its activities intervening importance in the eyes of both the conductor and the board. But such a committee is the very antithesis of the manner in which Judson would run an orchestra.

Judson Retires—Almost

Meanwhile, at Columbia Artist Management, Judson's role was also challenged, especially in the almost Byzantine office politics which have come to characterize that "partnership" of managers. A year after the Rodzinski affair at the Philharmonic, Judson stepped down as head of the corporation, following a dispute with his colleagues over his attempt to set up a lecture-bureau division of the corporation. He remained at Columbia, however, as head of his own management division. Here, as at the Philharmonic, he was also advancing the careers of several young managers—some say he was grooming them as his successors—among them George Judd, Jr. and his brother William, who were sons of the manager of the Boston Symphony, and Ronald Wilford.* The latter had started his carrer as a manager independent of Columbia, but eventually joined that organization and became Judson's closest assistant in the management of the conductor list. George Judd, Jr., was on the staff of the Philharmonic, and William was in Judson's division at Columbia. However, by the mid-1950s, Judson no longer held a complete monopoly on the representation of conductors: such rival managements as the Hurok organization, National Concert and Artist Corporation, and several independent managers were building important lists of European and American conductors.

Finally, in 1956, at the age of seventy-five, Arthur Judson stepped down as manager of the New York Philharmonic, having completed thirty-four years of service. After two years in which he shared the post of co-manager with Zirato, George Judd, Jr., became manager of the Philharmonic, serving little more than two years before his untimely death in 1961. He was succeeded by Carlos Moseley, whom Judson had earlier engaged on the Philharmonic publicity staff, and who had been Judd's assistant. Moseley, like Judson, was a trained musician and has brought to his post at the Philharmonic an extraordinary degree of managerial and diplomatic skill. In 1970 he was appointed the first professional president of any American orchestra.

Now past his ninetieth birthday, Arthur Judson is still active in concert

* Schuyler G. Chapin, now acting General Manager of the Metropolitan Opera, was another protégée in Judson's management office. Wilford is now President of CAMI, and William Judd has his own independent management office.

management. Though he withdrew completely from Columbia Artists Management in 1963, when he might have looked forward to a leisurely retirement at the age of eighty-two, he organized a new independent concert bureau the following year, at first with his long-time associate Ruth O'Neill, Frederick Steinway of the piano family, and the Boston manager Harry Beall as partners, the firm being known as Judson, O'Neill, Beall, and Steinway and immediately dubbed in musical circles as J.O.B.S. Subsequently Steinway withdrew from the firm, which was renamed Arthur Judson Concert Management. When he organized his new bureau, none of the conductors or artists whom he had previously managed followed him to the new firm; though technically under contract to CAMI at the time, a few (and no conductors) have since returned to Judson once their contracts there expired. By and large, Judson's present list of artists contains many newcomers from Europe or young Americans starting their careers, except for one or two previous Judson artists such as pianist Gary Graffman. Though his associates carry the main burden of the firm's day-to-day operation, Judson takes an active interest in it, going to the office at least four days a week, sitting in on auditions of new talent, and continually conferring with his partners on details.

Still a veritable monument of a man, physically and in his past role in the musical world, Judson likes to expound his views on the symphony orchestra in America. Much of what he now believes reflects a world long since past: his repugnance of government subsidy, his strong feelings about unions and player organizations, his conviction that only those orchestras which can maintain the highest standards should be worthy of professional support. But in his clear definition of the role of management, of the importance of sound business practices, and of the budget as a central management tool, he continues to wield a great influence, less directly now than through the many managers, conductors, and board members in whom he indoctrinated his principles. Yet, for all the influence he once wielded and for all his very real recognition of the powerful role he played, he maintains the reticence of the corporate executive who shuns publicity.* He still bridles at the thought of Rodzinski's attack on him and fervently sets forth his own cause, extending this to his firm conviction that he as manager has never invaded the artistic prerogatives of the musical director. In this, as we must know from any review of his career, Judson's protestations are not entirely justified. But one must accept first his sensitivity in the Rodzinski affair and then, from his own practice, a far more flexible view of the boundary between managerial and artistic areas than appears on the surface.

On the other hand, Judson's tendency to make a rigid definition of these areas will mislead lesser managers, boards, and conductors to mistake their roles, unless they view Judson's admonitions in the light of the realities of his own phenomenal career. For Judson exercised a great power in his time, not always wisely in the opinion of some in specific instances but firmly

---

* A rare exception to Judson's avoidance of publicity occurred in 1946, when he posed for a color portrait used in the advertising campaign of Calvert Distillers as part of a series of "Men of Distinction." Yet, even here, Judson was identifying himself with the other corporate executives in the series. The fee for this advertisement was donated to charity.

and efficiently, bringing into the symphonic institution many elements of strong and sound management. If he himself insists on deprecating his role, others must see in his career a demonstration of how a skillful and dedicated manager can exert the force of his musical experience and business sagacity in the symphonic institution. Not the least of Judson's virtues is his own brand of modesty, allied albeit with the corporate executive's strong sense of privacy in the conduct of his business. But where other managers have sought publicity, often rivaling that of the artists they represent, Judson has avoided it scrupulously: it is significant to note that except for Ralph Colin's article in *Variety,* there was no publicity or public observance, by Judson's own desire, of the ninetieth birthday in 1971 of this remarkable man who played so important a role in this country's musical life at the time of its greatest growth.

CHAPTER V

James Caesar Petrillo and the Militant Musician

Early in 1962, some two hundred members of Chicago's Local 10 of the American Federation of Musicians gathered at their union headquarters for the annual membership meeting required by its bylaws. Among these musicians was a group of forty, spearheaded by players in the Chicago Symphony Orchestra but including musicians employed in broadcasting studios and by hotels. Representing the hard core of well-employed professional musicians in Chicago, they had organized a defiance of the virtually absolute domination of Local 10 by James C. Petrillo since his election as its president in 1922. Though they acted within the rules governing the local, they knew that Petrillo could and would take drastic reprisals against many of them if they failed in this challenge to his authority.[1]

Except for the fact that it did not include the formality of election of officers, the annual meeting of Local 10, like those of others in the AFM, bore general similarities to the annual meetings of business corporations in that they were largely *pro forma* occasions for the presentation of officers' annual reports and for the transaction of certain business required by the bylaws. (In most musicians' unions the annual election of officers is held separately by secret ballot.) But, again like the annual meetings of business corporations, there are occasional outbursts from dissident members and, in very rare instances, full-scale opposition to the leadership. In the case of the 1962 annual meeting of Local 10, this opposition represented long-standing grievances against Petrillo and his ruling group, but the dissidents had decided to focus their efforts on a single item: they knew in advance that the membership would be asked to approve a lifetime pension of twenty-five thousand dollars a year to Petrillo if and when he chose to retire from the local presidency.*

To prepare for this meeting some sixty musicians had held a preliminary session, to inform themselves thoroughly of union bylaws and Robert's Rules

---

* Petrillo had, as we shall see later, already stepped down from the presidency of the national American Federation of Musicians in 1958, at which time he had been voted a generous pension.

of Order. Each of the forty members attending the annual meeting was supplied with typewritten slips of paper containing possible motions or points of order to be used as occasion demanded. These musicians knew, moreover, that the real test on the pension proposal would come early in the meeting: there would be a procedural move to change the agenda and postpone the pension issue, until after lengthy reports from officers, to the end of the meeting, when many members would have left. When Petrillo, from the presiding chair, proposed this change in agenda, several members rose immediately to their feet—so many, in fact, that Petrillo could not ignore them. The one he called on, the Chicago Symphony Orchestra's second trumpet player Rudolph Nashan, was so nervous that he dropped his typewritten slip of paper, but he remembered its contents well enough to make the proper procedural motion. This motion, the real test of the issue, carried by substantial margin. When it came time to offer the proposal for Petrillo's pension, the president, knowing he would again suffer defeat, eloquently declined the pension before it could be put to a vote.

Encouraged by this victory at the annual membership meeting of Local 10, the dissident group, still spearheaded by symphony players, decided to continue their efforts to exert influence in the affairs of Local 10 by offering a full slate of twenty-two officers and executive board members at the union election the following December. From time to time, disgruntled members had individually opposed the official Petrillo slate, but never before had a full list been offered in opposition by an organized segment of the membership. Actually, this opposition group hoped only to carry a few positions, but in the resulting election twenty-one out of twenty-two positions were filled from the anti-Petrillo slate, the president himself suffering defeat. So ended the career of one of the most powerful and colorful personalities in the music profession.

For decades James Caesar Petrillo had been a national symbol of union intransigence. He had created in his Chicago local one of the most effective union organizations in the nation, often by methods reflecting the ganster-ridden atmosphere of Chicago in the 1920s. He had led the American Federation of Musicians in battles against the recording industry that won him national publicity and involved him with the very highest government levels in the Congress and administration, even to defying a personal request by President Roosevelt. He had forced the unbending trustees of the Boston Symphony to accept the unionization of their orchestra. And, in an interunion battle with other entertainment groups, he had decreed that Jascha Heifetz, Artur Rubinstein, and other great solo musical artists must join his union. In the era of the greatest growth of unionism in this nation, he joined John L. Lewis (whom he also vilified) as this country's popular symbol of the autocratic union "czar"; not for naught was his middle name invariably mentioned in the press. He was denounced in the clubrooms of business and the halls of the Congress, and worshiped by the rank and file of his own union only a little more than by union members in general. Though he ranged over an area much wider than the symphony orchestra alone, he had great impact on our orchestras and eventually suffered his final and most humiliating defeat largely at the hands of symphony players.

More important, the leadership which Petrillo represented came eventually to be rejected in essential part by the professional core of union membership throughout the nation. The tensions between full-time professionals in the union and union leadership, long latent in the very nature of a trade union of artists, erupted in the 1950s on several fronts, by no means with least virulence among the players in our symphony orchestras.

Organization of the AFM

From earliest prehistory, the performance of music has been a social activity; even the solo pianist or organist, with a vast repertory to perform on his own, feels an irresistible urge to join with other musicians, not merely to provide the accompaniment they require but also to make music with them as an equal partner. Given the economic requirements of modern urban life, it was inevitable that the organizations which musicians formed should acquire an economic as well as an artistic function. Purely musical organizations vary in size and formality from a quartet of string players to such groups as the original Philharmonic Society of New York. When the theater musicians and music teachers of New York gathered under U.C. Hill's leadership in 1842 to organize their orchestra, economic gain was hardly their motive: they wanted the artistic satisfactions of performing great symphonic music in a manner possible only with such a joint effort. The economic motive was secondary, though eventually participation in the Society's concerts came to offer substantial income. Even in the most highly paid professional orchestras of today, the performance of great symphonic music provides an artistic attraction quite independent of economic gains; many of the first-rank players of our major orchestras could earn more in commercial music, and, conversely, there are in the commercial sphere many fine musicians who are torn between the economic stability they enjoy there and the artistic rewards that a less lucrative career in the symphonic field can offer.

Nevertheless, as the music profession grew in number in this country and as financial opportunities increased, there was a steady trend toward organizing musicians into groups for economic purposes in a manner that reflected the peculiar employment structure of the profession.[2] Following abortive efforts in Chicago and Cincinnati in 1857, the first viable union of musicians emerged in New York in 1863, its example spreading rapidly to many other cities. Because so much musical employment was part-time and casual, a central hiring place was required: in the early days of musicians' unions, German saloons and social clubs often served this purpose. From the beginning, there grew up a system of hiring musicians through other players, known as contractors or leaders,* on whom an employer, not qualified to judge the

* This term, still used in union contracts, confuses British musicians, for whom the "leader" of an orchestra is what Americans term the concertmaster, the principal of the first violin section.

artistic requirements, relied to secure for him the musical group he needed. These contractors came to wield considerable influence in the profession by virtue of their power to hire and fire their colleagues. Not only did some engage in favoritism in their choice; others required a "kickback" from players for whom they obtained jobs. One of the earliest functions of unions was to regulate the activities of those members who acted as such contractors, but these same members also played an important part in the power structure of the unions through their ability to deliver the vote of members beholden to them for employment.

In retrospect we can see that the musicians' occupation fell between the strict professionalism of doctors, teachers, and lawyers and trade or factory labor, with the added complication of being primarily a part-time occupation involving a number of employers. In some of the early unions an effort was made to limit membership only to highly skilled and reasonably full-time musicians. But owing to the part-time nature of employment, it was impossible to apply rigid restrictions on membership, especially if the competition of part-time musicians with more highly skilled ones was to be brought under control. Thus, the musicians' union has always contained in its membership a broad spectrum of professional quality, ranging from those fully employed to others who may play only a handful of engagements in any year, and even to some who once performed and no longer do so, but retain their membership for social reasons or to participate in the very favorable insurance programs offered by many locals. It is difficult to estimate precisely the degree to which the membership of the union may be regarded as truly professional: data for earlier years are extremely hard to obtain, though the proportion of professionalism was undoubtedly higher in the days before radio, the "talking picture," and recording than it is now. Reliable estimates of the proportion of truly professional membership in the union indicate that it may run as low as five percent in some local unions to as high as twelve to fifteen percent in such centers of musical employment as New York, Nashville, Chicago, and Los Angeles.[3]

The issue of professionalism played a very important part in early disputes within the musicians' unions. There was, on the one hand, a faction that looked upon their activity as an artistic profession distinguished from the common labor then in the process of unionization. Others felt that the economic hazards of employment were such as to justify alliance with the broader growth of such national labor organizations as the Knights of Labor and Samuel Gompers's American Federation of Labor. The union musicians had attempted some national organization of their own, with the National Musical Association in 1871 and with a slightly more effective National League of Musicians of the United States in 1886, but both organizations suffered from restrictions imposed by their locals' jealous preservation of their own autonomy. Finally, after bitter battles within the League, the American Federation of Labor, under Gompers's leadership, organized the American Federation of Musicians in 1896, which eventually absorbed all of the local musicians' unions. Most musicians were under AFM jurisdiction by 1904, though several locals, notably the powerful Musical Mutual Protective Association of

New York, remained outside for some time longer.* Some of the effort to achieve full jurisdiction involved litigation in the courts, and eventually the AFM added to its bylaws a strict provision that any member or group resorting to the courts in union matters was subject to immediate and automatic expulsion.

Several basic issues played a major role in the growth of unionism among the musicians. One of these, undoubtedly, was the danger of a traveling company being stranded on tour without paying its musicians; the unions required employers to post bonds to protect their members from this hazard. A second problem was the performance of military bands in situations where civilian musicians felt that their employment was jeopardized. Though the AFM secured a series of agreements with military officials restricting the use of military bands, and applied local pressure on city officials to hire union bands for parades and civic functions, this issue still crops up. Of considerably greater consequence to the growth of symphony orchestras in this country was the influx of foreign musicians, not arriving voluntarily but with contractual commitments from employers here. The AFL had secured passage of a bill in the Congress generally forbidding employers to contract with alien laborers and then import them into this country, but the Attorneys General in Washington ruled repeatedly that musicians, as artists, were not covered by this law.† Henry L. Higginson was an early target of the union, not only for his importation of orchestra players from Europe but also in his engagement of such foreign conductors as Artur Nikisch; this was certainly one basis for Higginson's implacable opposition to unionization of his orchestra. As early as 1893, Walter Damrosch was himself nearly expelled from the union for importing a nonunion cellist, and in 1903 the players in the New York Symphony attempted to boycott the orchestra for importing five principal woodwind players.[5] In the latter instance, the Federation ruled that the players could join the orchestra and union as "soloists," but that Damrosch had to pay a fine of five thousand dollars for importing the aliens in the first place.

Equally important to local symphony orchestras have been local restrictions on "importing" players, already members of other locals, into a jurisdiction covering the orchestra. A national transfer rule has long been established that though one local could not prevent a member of another local from settling in another city, it could place restrictions upon this transfer that seriously limited his ability to work in the new jurisdiction, in some cases for several years. In effect, if a local orchestra association wishes to import a player from another city, it must first convince the local union that this player is indispensable and that his position cannot be filled by a local member. Once the union agrees, the player must file his transfer with the local, which he cannot join for an interval that varies from one local to another. During this period

* AFM jurisdiction in New York was not settled until after 1921, following protracted interlocal battles and litigation in the courts.[4] The AFM assigns numbers to its locals in the order in which they were chartered; this is why Local 802, the largest local in the AFM, has such a high number.

† Not until 1932 did the AFM secure legislation applying alien-labor contracts to musicians.

he can be restricted by the union from playing any work other than that of the symphony orchestra which imported him, until he becomes a full member of the local. Some exceptions are made, but only by the local, not by national regulation.

Under the leadership of Joseph N. Weber from 1900 to 1940, the AFM grew and prospered, consolidating its jurisdiction until virtually all performing musicians, and many others, were embraced in its membership. Except for the Boston Symphony, all professional symphony orchestras operated as closed shops, negotiating basic trade agreements for the employment of their players. But barely had this almost universal jurisdiction been established when the union was threatened with revolutionary developments in the entertainment industry of which it was an essential part. The impact of electronic media in entertainment—radio and later television, recording, and the "talking picture" *—drastically curtailed the demand for live music throughout the nation. At first, all that the union could do was mount publicity campaigns on behalf of live music, but it very soon found this to be a losing battle and turned to seek a share for its members in the burgeoning technological revolution. In this movement the most effective and spectacular leader was the president of Chicago's Local 10, James Petrillo.

The Rise of Petrillo

Born in Chicago in 1892, Petrillo started to play the trumpet at the age of eight. When he left the fourth grade, after *nine* years in school, he went to work selling newspapers and peanuts on street corners and railroads, running errands, and driving delivery carts. Later he ran a cigar store and a saloon. But he also played the trumpet—in the Hull House band, in the *Daily News* band, and in a dance band that he organized at the age of fourteen. For the latter he needed to join one of several unions then active in Chicago, which made an exception for his age. Very soon, however, Petrillo discovered that his talents lay less in playing the trumpet than in the rough-and-tumble field of Chicago union politics. At the age of twenty-two, he was president of the American Musicians Union, then a rival to the AFM-affiliated Local 10. After three years in this post he failed to be reelected and, in disgust, joined Local 10, where he was assigned the task of organizing the musicians playing in Chinese restaurants. Such was his success that in 1920 he became vice-president, and in 1922, aged thirty, president of Local 10.[7]

Given the facts of life in Chicago at this time, Petrillo could have arrived at this youthful eminence only by resorting to the vigorous practices of union organizing that were legendary in Chicago at the time. His battles to organize the Chicago theaters and hotels, and then to obtain good pay, involved much violence, both physical and rhetorical. Early in his career as

---

* Employment declined from over 4,000 motion-picture houses hiring musicians in the 1920s to but 458 in 1950, out of a total of 9,635.[6]

local president he persuaded most of the Chicago radio stations to employ musicians regularly, and this was the first city in the nation to have all of its major radio stations under contract with the local. So firm was this arrangement that, in 1931, when Anton J. Cermak planned to be installed as mayor with a high-school band leading the procession, Petrillo forced the substitution of a union band on the grounds that the parade was being broadcast by a radio station under contract to his union. From 1933 until 1962 no one opposed his leadership of the Chicago local.

Of all the leaders in the AFM, Petrillo became most dramatically identified with combating the growing unemployment in the music profession, which was hit simultaneously by the depression and by the impact of radio, records, and motion pictures with sound. Before the installation of electronic sound, Chicago theaters employed some 2,000 full-time musicians; by 1935 employment was down to 125.[8] Petrillo met this challenge partly by using union influence and, in some cases, union funds to establish free summer band concerts under city sponsorship. Such was his power that he forced political rallies to employ union musicians. More important, he developed the concept of "standby music," whereby musicians were employed, without necessarily being required to play, when competitive recorded music was played in jurisdictions under union control. In his public utterances, Petrillo made no secret either of his humble origins or of his determination to work for the benefit of the union and its members. His colorful rhetoric and cocky willingness to take on anyone in a fight were never more vividly illustrated than in his feud with John L. Lewis, with whom he shared in the public mind considerable opprobrium as a "labor baron." When Lewis took his United Mine Workers union out of the AFL in 1936 to organize the CIO, AFL president William Green, originally a miner, found himself without the union membership he needed to qualify for his post; Petrillo immediately made him a member of Local 10. Such was Petrillo's hatred of Lewis that in 1939 he ordered two Chicago theaters to delete all mention of Lewis from the scripts of shows appearing there. Though the theaters in question complied with Petrillo's demand, the outcry in the national press caused the restoration of Lewis's name in the scripts. Petrillo's comment was: "They said I was unconstitutional and all that stuff. I never had nothing like that on my mind. . . . I just thought I'd push Lewis around a little." [9]

Though Joseph Weber remained president of the AFM until 1940, becoming a sort of sacrosanct father-figure with its members, Petrillo gained more and more power in its councils and in representing the union in the public eye, having been elected to the AFM executive board in 1932. He thus assumed a public image as a Chicago union leader ruthlessly assaulting the public interest that obscured the basic policies which he espoused and represented. While other entertainment unions affected by the onslaught of the electronic entertainment media responded by holding down their membership to fit shrinking employment, the AFM continued to recruit new members and actually to expand its membership at a time when employment opportunities were shrinking. Between 1896 and 1928, the AFM grew from 4,000 members in 26 locals to 146,421 members in 780 locals, the high point before a decline to 101,111 members in 675 locals in 1934. After that, despite the general shrinking of musical employment, the AFM grew steadily to 300,000 members in 650 locals in 1971.[10] Petrillo led the AFM in combating "canned music" on three fronts. First, he was a leading proponent in mounting a publicity campaign in favor of live music, but the impact of this costly maneuver on actual employment was negligible. A second front was to create new employment opportunities for musicians through pressure on politically sensitive city officials to present free band concerts in the parks, often paying from the union treasury a share of the wages received by their members. Later, when Petrillo devised a royalty on recordings, motion pictures, and broadcasts, the funds thus raised were applied toward the employment of musicians for similar free public-service performances.

Petrillo succeeded Weber as president of the American Federation of Musicians in the summer of 1940, but before he could move against the electronic entertainment media he had to complete the unionization of two important segments of the profession not under his jurisdiction—instrumental solo musicians and the Boston Symphony Orchestra. Immediately upon becoming president of the AFM, he attacked these two problems.

The Boston Symphony Orchestra

By its original charter, the AFM had always claimed jurisdiction over all instrumentalists, but it had never pressed the matter with concert soloists, though some of them, including conductors, were actually members of the union. Most instrumental soloists, however, had joined the American Guild of Musical Artists, for representation in contractual negotiations with concert managements, record companies, and broadcasters; AGMA included in its roster not only these instrumentalists but also singers and dancers. In August, 1940, Petrillo issued an ultimatum that all solo instrumentalists must join the AFM by the following Labor Day, a move strongly opposed by AGMA. Petrillo stated his position in characteristic terms: "Since when is there any difference between Heifetz playing a fiddle and the fiddler in the tavern? . . . They [AGMA] went along and took the instrumentalists. They took the piano players and they took the orchestras. They stole my people and I'm going to get them back. They're musicians and they belong to me." [11]

The ensuing battle was waged both in the public press and in the New York courts; after the latter ruled that AGMA had no legal basis for resisting the AFM, Petrillo's victory was assured. By virtue of the fact that these instrumentalists relied upon solo appearances with orchestras of union players, they knew that Petrillo could seriously limit such appearances should he so desire. Similarly, his contracts with broadcasting and recording companies gave him power in those fields necessary for the survival of the solo career. By the summer of 1941, the soloists capitulated, resigning from AGMA and joining the AFM. Rachmaninoff, Kreisler, and Hofmann were granted hon-

orary membership without having to pay initiation fees, and several foreign
soloists and one child prodigy were given special permission to appear under
AFM jurisdiction, but all other solo instrumentalists had to join the musicians'
union or, in the case of foreign visitors, obtain permission to appear in union
jurisdiction in this country.

This organization of the solo instrumentalists was a necessary pre-
condition to Petrillo's plan to unionize the Boston Symphony Orchestra,
which had long been a thorn in the side of the musicians' union, an especially
irritating one to Petrillo. As noted in an earlier chapter, the Boston trustees
had not only broken the musicians' strike in 1920 but had maintained an in-
flexible stance ever since. Though the Boston players generally received
higher annual incomes than those of other comparable orchestras, they had to
work a longer season and were subject to virtually unlimited rehearsal calls.
Since as nonmembers of the union they could not find outside employment
in areas covered by union jurisdiction, their mobility to another orchestra was
severely limited. Once a player had settled himself in the Boston Symphony
he had little choice but to make it his lifetime career, though he was subject
to the whim of the conductor so far as job security was concerned. The players had made abortive attempts in 1925 and 1926 to organize a union,
largely in response to Koussevitzky's ruthless weeding out of orchestra players who did not meet his standards, but there was no really serious effort toward unionization either in the orchestra or in the Boston local until Petrillo
took the initiative, except for an AFM move in 1938 to force the unionized
radio networks to stop broadcasting the nonunion orchestra.[12]

In 1940, however, the Federation forced RCA-Victor to cease recording
the Boston Symphony, a move that hit it financially through the loss of royalties and was seen, by Koussevitzky in particular, as a threat to his and the
orchestra's prestige. In August, 1940, Petrillo told the press, "They're
through. We've taken them off the radio and off the records."[13] Next, having brought instrumental soloists and conductors under his control, Petrillo
forbade them to play or conduct with the Boston orchestra. Koussevitzky,
who had once shared the trustees' opposition to unionization, now began to
favor it: not only had he built the great orchestra he had long dreamed of,
but he was finding his own financial interest and artistic prestige undermined
by the trustees' policy. Though he had generally avoided involving himself
in the business affairs of the orchestra, he began as early as 1939 to take an
interest in the union problem. An early factor in this interest undoubtedly was
his involvement in future recording plans with Moses Smith, formerly a Boston critic and by then director of the Masterworks division of the newly
vitalized Columbia Record division of CBS. Smith wanted very much to acquire the Boston Symphony for Columbia, knew that the RCA-Victor contract was about to expire, and made tempting overtures to Koussevitzky, to
which the conductor responded with apparent interest. But Smith and Koussevitsky knew that it would be impossible to carry out any new recording contract unless the orchestra was unionized.

The main stumbling block to unionization continued to be Ernest B. Dane.
Though a part of the orchestra's deficit was met by contributions from the

Friends of the Boston Symphony Orchestra, some fifty thousand dollars a year, about half the deficit, was paid by Dane himself, the remaining trustees contributing relatively little. All or most of the trustees still opposed unionization, but Dane's implacable opposition was the major force. So strongly did Dane feel on the issue that when RCA-Victor was forced to stop recording in Boston, Dane himself volunteered to make up the loss in royalties. When Columbia Records finally submitted its proposal to the trustees in 1941— offering guarantees to both the orchestra and conductor not included in the RCA-Victor contract, but stipulating that the orchestra must join the union —the trustees, at Dane's initiative, shelved the matter "for future consideration" without discussion. Infuriated at the board's action, Koussevitzky shortly after began discussions with the New York Philharmonic and, by the end of 1942, had reached a general agreement for him to become musical director of that orchestra.

Meanwhile, Petrillo continued to apply pressure on the Boston Symphony, both in direct union action and through confidential conferences with Koussevitzky.* He requested other theatrical unions, notably the stagehands, to refuse to allow the Boston orchestra to appear in unionized halls on tour, and it was actually barred from auditoriums in Rochester (New York), Springfield, and Northampton; in the summer of 1942 Carnegie Hall was placed on the musicians' union unfair list primarily because it refused to bar the Boston Symphony.[15] In the spring of 1942, Dane died, but the remaining trustees continued to oppose the union. However, Koussevitzky's dealings with the Philharmonic placed the trustees in a real quandary. They acknowledged for the first time in October, 1942, that they were conducting negotiations with the union, implying that a major issue was the restriction on the importation of players from one local jurisdiction to another. Petrillo then secured emergency approval by some union locals to permit the unlimited importation of symphony players, and by December, 1942, the Boston Symphony agreed to unionization.† Koussevitsky's negotiations with the New York Philharmonic were broken off, the Boston Symphony resumed its broadcasts and recordings (still with RCA-Victor), and Petrillo had completed the unionization of this nation's symphony orchestras.

Having recognized the union, the Boston Symphony of course began to enter into regular relations with the local union regarding contracts and working conditions, formally identical with those of other orchestras but differing in one important respect. Prior to the recognition of the union, the players and management had developed the organization of a committee of orchestra musicians who not only consulted with management on day-to-day working relations but also negotiated the common features of the players' contracts. Because the Boston local had never concerned itself with the symphony or-

---

* Petrillo visited Koussevitzky during the summer of 1941 at his place near Tanglewood, and later announced to the press: "Look here, the Boston Symphony wants the privilege of walking around the country as a nonunion organization, whereas ninety-five percent of its members want to join. This includes Koussevitzky himself. How do I know? He told me so personally when I visited him at his home in the Berkshires last summer." [14]

† Despite Petrillo's assurances, local importation restrictions were later reinstated and are still very much in effect in most jurisdictions.

chestra, this players' committee retained its negotiating role, leaving it to the local merely to formalize the agreements reached with management by the players themselves.

Meanwhile, having completed the unionization of the important segments of the music business not previously under union control—the instrumental soloists and the Boston Symphony—Petrillo could now move against the recording industry and motion-picture studios.

The Music Performance Trust Fund

Though often obscured by his abrasive rhetoric, Petrillo's basic goal was to obtain for the musicians a share of the prosperity generated by the vastly higher economic productivity of the electronic entertainment media by instituting a system of royalty payments from the recording (including radio transcriptions) and motion-picture industries. These activities were centered largely in a few cities—New York, Chicago, Nashville, and, most important, Los Angeles. Technically, such studio work was under local jurisdiction, in that musicians had to belong to the union local and were subject to its regulations, but the basic trade agreements with the industries were negotiated by the Federation. Thus, in Los Angeles particularly, there grew up a sort of dual jurisdiction that necessitated the Federation's assigning a special representative there to handle intraunion problems. The local, in turn, placed strict limitations on the amount of outside work that a relatively few fully employed studio musicians could do in competition with the vast majority of the local's membership, and also established rigid transfer rules to prevent too great an influx of musicians from other jurisdictions.

Upon becoming president of the Federation in 1940, Petrillo moved forcefully against the recording industry, in order to gain greater economic benefits. Previous efforts had failed to apply copyright laws to restrict the use of recordings on radio, jukeboxes, and elsewhere in competition with live musicians, and the union had to give up its hope of licensing the commercial use of records that were ostensibly made for private use in the home.* Petrillo attacked the recording industry in two protracted recording bans in 1942 and 1948. Though the real objective of these refusals to permit union musicians to make recordings was to extract some sort of royalty on record sales, Petrillo loudly proclaimed at first that he intended to stop all recording forever, and on other occasions threatened to put the union itself into the recording business.[17]

The first ban in 1942 was the more protracted because, under wartime restrictions, the record companies were operating on a curtailed basis anyhow.†

---

* The licensing of records for commercial use has long been one of the stumbling blocks in any effort to devise in the Congress an overall revision of obsolete copyright laws, which never contemplated the electronic revolution in entertainment.[16]

† Part of the delay in settling this ban stemmed from the fact that two of the largest American record manufacturers at that time (RCA-Victor and Columbia) were also affiliated with radio networks (NBC and CBS), who feared that capitulation to Petrillo on recordings would lead to major concessions in their network contracts.

Despite government pressure, including an appeal by President Roosevelt himself, Petrillo defied public opinion and held out. In the end he won from the major American record companies substantial increases in pay to the musicians making records and a royalty payment, based on record sales, to a Recording and Transcription Fund, which was distributed to local unions for the presentation of free public performances by union musicians in schools, hospitals, public parks, and at civic occasions. The Taft-Hartley Law * of 1947 contained provisions specifically aimed at this type of royalty payment, and the Recording and Transcription Fund had to be abandoned. In 1948, therefore, Petrillo again suspended all recording activity by union members. This ban did not last as long as that of 1942: the competition from foreign records in a booming postwar market was too much of a threat to both the union and the record companies. Petrillo's real objective was to arrange some sort of legalization of the royalty principle in discussions between the union, industry, and the Department of Justice. Under the new formula, the Secretary of Labor appoints an independent trustee for the Music Performance Trust Funds, later expanded to include film and other electronic entertainment media, to which the record industry pays royalties ranging from 0.6% to 1.45% of the manufacturer's suggested list prices of records and tape recordings.[18] After deduction of administrative costs, ten percent of these funds are held for allocation at the trustee's discretion, the remainder being distributed on an area basis to pay for free public-service performances. The area quota for the allocation of funds is determined by the proportionate relation of local union membership to the national.

Though the Music Performance Trust Fund is administered independently of the union, the trustee relies upon locals to recommend projects for which ninety percent of the funds are allocated. Generally speaking, these area grants go primarily to employ union musicians, at local minimum scale. These musicians are paid directly by check from the New York office of the MPFT, on the basis of payrolls certified by the local unions. In many instances, the availability of this employment becomes a factor in the power structure of the union local, whose officers thus have authority to provide employment for such of their members as they see fit. Often such musicians are those otherwise unemployed who need work, but in many cities all or a portion of the players in the local symphony orchestra are engaged for special free concerts, many times in the schools, in close cooperation with both the educational authorities and the symphony associations. The ten percent of the Music Performance Trust Funds allocated by the trustee himself has been put to significant use in many cases. One of the most important single beneficiaries of these funds has been the nationwide education program of Young Audiences.† In addition, the trustee has also made allocations to a number of amateur and youth orchestras which are not necessarily under union jurisdiction. In such cases, the trustee is still required to send payment checks to

---

* Leiter, pp. 148–63, has a full account of another antiunion statute, the Lea Act of 1946, aimed basically at Petrillo and the Federation, largely as a result of Petrillo's attack on Joseph E. Maddy's National Music Camp at Interlochen, Michigan. However, the Lea Act was declared unconstitutional in the courts in the year of its passage. Anti-Petrillo sentiment in the Congress was then diverted to covering his activities in the Taft-Hartley legislation.
† The activities of this organization are described in some detail in Chapter XVIII.

each player participating in the free performance, but the members of the group usually endorse their checks over to the organization to which they belong for the benefit of its general expenses.

Between 1950, after the dissolution of the by then illegal Recording and Transcription Fund, and 1970, the combined allocations of the various funds administered by the trustees totaled $92,650,000.[19] The current rate of allocation amounts to over $7 million a year. The original trustee appointed by the Secretary of Labor, with advice from the film and recording industries, was Samuel R. Rosenbaum, a lawyer who was for many years a director of the Philadelphia Orchestra Association. He resigned in 1969 and was briefly succeeded by his assistant, Jerome H. Adler, who was shortly afterward killed in an airplane crash in the Caribbean. Kenneth E. Raine, formerly associated with the Columbia Records division of CBS, is now trustee of all of the funds except the Film Fund, of which Rosenbaum is still technically trustee since it is involved in litigation.*

The implementation of the Music Performance Trust Funds, however, created serious problems with the Los Angeles musicians who were employed by the studios paying royalties into the Fund. In the early 1950s these players became increasingly at odds with both Local 47 and the Federation over a number of issues: their overall pay and working conditions under the Federation master contract; the limitations imposed on them by Local 47; and, most important, their failure to share in the distribution of the royalty payments. The threat of these players to secede from the Federation and organize their own union of fully professional players caused the Federation great concern: had they been successful, other fully employed musicians, in symphony orchestras and elsewhere, could have joined them and thus deprived the Federation of its very professional core. For behind the discontent of these Hollywood studio players were deep grievances based on what they felt was the failure of union leadership, nationally and locally, to understand their problems and advance their special interests.

The Federation, for its part, had a deep-seated fear of "dual unionism" going back to the days when there were frequently more than one local in a city. Beyond this symbolic threat, moreover, was a realization that the loss of such a professionally important segment of its membership could wreck the union. This was a problem that could not be handled by the roughshod tactics of Petrillo. In 1957, the executive board of the Federation designated one of its members, Herman D. Kenin,† to deal with the incipient secession movement in Hollywood. Kenin was one of the most brilliant and farsighted

---

* This prevailed technically until Rosenbaum's death in November, 1972.
† Herman D. Kenin was a native of Portland, Oregon, where he pursued an early career as lawyer and professional musician. After serving for a time as regional representative for ASCAP, he became increasingly active in the affairs of Local 99 of the AFM, eventually becoming its president. In manner and approach to union affairs, he provided a sharp contrast with the flamboyant and often abrasive Petrillo: he had a keen legal mind, combined with a clear perception of aims which he pursued with great skill. He also had a broad interest in all types of music; though he had himself been a dance-band musician, he knew symphonic music well and attended concerts frequently in Portland, Los Angeles, and New York. In Portland, he played an important role in the revival of the Portland (later Oregon) Symphony Orchestra in 1947 and thereafter. He died in 1969 and was succeeded as Federation president by Hal C. Davis.

members of the executive board: he had played an important role in setting up the public-relations program that had softened the "image" of Petrillo and the union in the public mind and was well acquainted with the intricacies of the Hollywood problem. Through diplomatic bargaining, he worked out a compromise that mollified the Hollywood dissidents by arranging that in addition to a reduced royalty paid by industry to the Music Performance Trust Funds, an equal sum would be paid to another trustee; he would distribute these funds directly to the players, in recording and film, who had actually done the work. Thus, these musicians, including those in symphony orchestras making records, shared in a royalty based on the sales of records or films. This royalty, set up in various trade agreements with the recording and film industries, is administered, not by the MPFT, but by the same trustee who handles pension funds and other benefits now incorporated in these contracts.

Although the symphonic players were only peripherally involved in recordings and the Music Performance Trust Fund, the incipient Hollywood revolt against the Federation reflected, as we shall see shortly in more detail, a growing disaffection between the union and those of its members who constituted its professional core. Especially in the larger orchestras, the players ·followed the Hollywood problem closely and were basically in sympathy with the dissident faction there. Moreover, the success of the Hollywood players in their defiance of the union made a strong impression on many symphony musicians.

The Militant Musician

With major victories over the instrumental soloists, the Boston Symphony Orchestra, and the electronic entertainment industry, Petrillo would seem to have consolidated his union's position fully. Once his great battles were over, the public began to mellow toward him, thanks in large part to a very skillful publicity campaign sponsored by the Federation. For President Truman's inauguration in 1948, Petrillo was named National Music Chairman, and early in 1949 he presented the piano-playing president with a solid-gold membership card as an honorary member of the AFM for life. But there were major internal tensions undermining Petrillo's position, especially as a result of the Hollywood dispute in the 1950s. In 1958, in an emotional scene at the annual convention of the AFM, Petrillo announced his resignation as president of the Federation and designated as his successor Herman D. Kenin, who had so successfully averted disaster in Hollywood. During the next decade, Kenin was to face intransigence among others of his members, this time the symphony-orchestra players, that was in many respects reminiscent of his problems in Hollywood.

Actually, the same disenchantment with union leadership that eventually removed Petrillo from the presidency of his Local 10 in Chicago had been brewing for a decade in other large orchestras in this country—especially in Philadelphia, New York, and Cleveland—and it has been more or less prevalent, though less explosive, in many of the smaller orchestras across the nation.[20] Symphony-orchestra players have in many cities developed an attitude every bit as hostile toward their unions as they have toward the management in matters of pay and working conditions. This hostility arises from the fact that the players do not believe their unions have represented them aggressively enough or with sufficient understanding of the special circumstances of working in a symphony orchestra. And in the past decade and a half they have learned that when they represent their own interests firmly in direct negotiation with orchestra management, they usually gain much more than their union representatives did.

To a very large degree, orchestra musicians were completely excluded from the negotiation of the periodic trade agreements reached between their unions and their employers. Except for the Boston Symphony, where the players had established a bargaining structure through their own elected committee prior to joining the union in 1942, orchestra managements bargained directly with union officials. Such bargaining affected only a small part of union membership—few more than one hundred in a total roster of thousands. Moreover, symphony orchestra employment was quite different from most other jobs with which the union officials were familiar: they were accustomed to dealing with theaters, broadcasting stations, nightclubs, hotels, and dance halls operated for a profit, who could readily pass on to their customers or advertisers the added labor costs accruing from wage increases. Furthermore, a large number of union members worked for casual employers, who seldom bargained directly with the union but merely accepted a wage scale set unilaterally for various types of work. In dealing directly with symphony-orchestra managers and board members, the union officials encountered a quite different sort of employer, one who was running a nonprofit operation of frequently precarious existence. Therefore, they inclined to relax the kind of "hard-nosed" negotiating stance that they adopted as a matter of course with broadcasting corporations or nightclub owners. In fact, they often listened with considerable sympathy to the pleas of financial hardship which symphony boards and managers put forth—for they had little specific knowledge of the financial resources of such organizations—settling for modest increments in salary and small improvements in working conditions in a way that resulted in symphony players as a group falling behind other professional groups in the nation.

According to 1960 United States Census data, musicians and music teachers earned an average of $4,757 a year, as compared with a median of $6,778 for all professions or of $4,750 for all experienced male labor over fourteen years of age.[21] Among forty-nine professional groups, musicians and music teachers ranked fortieth in annual income, below professional athletes, salesmen, therapists, and funeral directors, and only slightly higher than medical and dental technicians and librarians. Moreover, in the postwar era symphony-orchestra players failed to keep up with other professions in the increase of income: between 1940 and 1960, while the consumer price index increased by 120% and earnings of production workers in manufacturing rose by 150%, the annual income of players in eleven major orchestras grew by only 80%.[22] Throughout this postwar period, the gains of such other professionals as schoolteachers, athletes, university professors, and librarians—to say nothing of lawyers and doctors—exceeded those of symphony players by at least a third and as much as double. These are discouraging data indeed for a profession that requires intensive and dedicated study from childhood, and a degree of general and specialized education equal to college, if not graduate level, to say nothing of reasonably rare native talent.

It is not surprising that, as union members working in the intensely cohesive group context of a symphony orchestra, these musicians nursed a growing accumulation of grievances against their unions as much as against their employers. Union officials seldom prepared themselves for negotiations by canvassing the players in an orderly fashion: they relied upon the personnel manager,* the rare union officer who happened to play in the orchestra, or a few cronies for information on conditions in the orchestra, many of which had no counterpart in other areas of musical employment. For their part, symphony boards and managers, among the largest orchestras particularly, did little until the late 1950s to expand their services in a way that would offer players increases in annual income to keep pace with the other professions with which musicians liked to identify themselves.

Nevertheless, orchestra players made some gains in the negotiations conducted by their unions. Rather early in this period, the number of weekly services—rehearsals or concerts—that could be required of players was strictly defined. Tour arrangements began to be codified. Of greatest importance was the gradual establishment of security from arbitrary dismissal, once a player had served a probationary period. Of major long-range significance, moreover, the local unions, often with great reluctance, permitted players to organize their own orchestra committees to deal with management on day-to-day issues peculiar to symphony employment and outside the general terms of the basic trade agreement. These committees became the focal point for subsequent efforts by the musicians to replace union representatives as bargaining agents with management.

Until the mid-1950s, with unions acting as sole bargaining agents for the players, American orchestras enjoyed relatively tranquil personnel relations: from 1922 to 1954 there was but one work stoppage (and that for one day only) among American orchestras. But musicians' militancy, long festering under the surface, erupted spectacularly in the next decade and a half: from 1954 through 1970 there were seventeen such interruptions, totaling 439 days and involving ten orchestras.[23] The Philadelphia Orchestra stoppage in 1954, for seven days, was the first of four for this orchestra alone; in 1966 the fourth of these interruptions of activity lasted fifty-eight days.† In the early stages of this conflict, tension between the union and players

---

* In symphony orchestras the personnel manager traditionally performed the functions of contractor, or leader, and was responsible to both union and management for a variety of duties.
† A complete list of these stoppages from 1922 through 1970 will be found in Appendix C. Personnel relations in the Philadelphia Orchestra will be discussed in greater detail in Chapter VII.

was at times as great an obstacle to the settlement of differences as were the difficulties of resolving issues between management and players. The example of the Boston Symphony players, who had established direct negotiations with management before joining the union in 1942, was by no means lost on musicians in other orchestras in their efforts to gain union sanction for dealing directly with their employers. At first, the unions permitted players to send "observers" to the bargaining sessions, but eventually orchestra committees more and more took command of their side of the collective-bargaining process.

Actually, the players of the Chicago Symphony were among the last to develop the militancy which swept the larger orchestras in the 1950s.[24] Under Petrillo's domination of the Chicago local, symphony players were not allowed to form any sort of orchestra committee until 1959. Petrillo and a few officers conducted negotiations, often in his New York office prior to 1958, and then advised the "boys" what they had secured for them. The organization of the first committee of Chicago Symphony players preceded only shortly a change in management of the orchestra, when the experienced George A. Kuyper left Chicago to become general manager of the Southern California Symphony Association. He was succeeded by the music editor of the *Chicago Tribune,* Seymour S. Raven, a protégé of Claudia Cassidy who, though he had musical training, was inexperienced in orchestra management. Raven assumed that because of Petrillo's opposition to the formation of a players' committee, he would be sympathetic to the manager's taking a hard line with the increasingly militant players of the Chicago Symphony. Raven's position was made further difficult by the fact that, less than a year after he became manager, musical director Fritz Reiner suffered an incapacitating stroke which seriously reduced his ability to handle personnel problems. In the spring of 1961, prior to a round of contract negotiations, Raven discharged five players and demoted one; all were regarded, by their colleagues and management alike, as leaders in the militant group. This incident climaxed a series of petty and, sometimes, comic conflicts between the manager and the players. On one occasion, when the orchestra committee brought in a lawyer to advise the total membership on matters under consideration, Raven ejected the meeting from the Orchestra Hall building on the grounds that the presence of a lawyer was forbidden at such meetings in the building. The players had long sought to locate their own bulletin board in their dressing room and requested permission from the manager to put one up at their own expense; after Raven procrastinated for some time over the location of such a board, the players finally installed one temporarily by suspending it from balloons floating in their dressing room.

The manager sadly miscalculated the Chicago union in his efforts to discipline the militant faction in the orchestra; though he was allowed to demote one player, the union having no jurisdiction over such matters, he faced adamant opposition on his discharge of five players. Petrillo, for his part, was forced to allow two "observers" from the orchestra to sit at the formal bargaining session, primarily to keep the orchestra membership advised of their progress but, as negotiations proceeded, also to inform the union representatives of the players' point of view on specific issues. Possibly most damaging to Petrillo's leadership was the degree to which these observers found both Petrillo and his colleagues from the local executive board to be abysmally uninformed even in the most rudimentary aspects of orchestra routine and operation.

Meanwhile, to prepare for these negotiations and to brief themselves generally on the situation in orchestras elsewhere, the Chicago Symphony players' committee had started correspondence with its counterparts in other orchestras, exchanging copies of general trade agreements and much information on bargaining tactics. One reason why the Chicago players had to undertake this correspondence was their inexperience in such matters and the relative isolation of Chicago from the East Coast. Especially among orchestras visiting New York on tour, such exchanges of information had long been undertaken informally by members of the Philadelphia, Cleveland, New York, and other orchestras when visiting groups were in town. Out of the Chicago inquiries there emerged a meeting of representatives of several orchestras in Chicago in the spring of 1960. A second, larger meeting was held in Cleveland in 1961. At these meetings the orchestra players founded an International Conference of Symphony and Opera Musicians, known throughout the symphonic world as ICSOM.

Meanwhile, the Chicago Symphony players, having become suddenly and increasingly involved in union affairs and having seen Petrillo in action in a most unfavorable light, took the leadership in an effort to challenge the union president at the membership meeting of 1962. There were others involved in this campaign: hotel musicians discontented with the union's failure to deal with certain competitive situations in hotel employment, and those in broadcasting studios unhappy with the union's inability to cope with declining employment in the Chicago studios and fearful of losing their jobs. But only the symphony players had the job security to protect them from Petrillo's vengeance should they lose their battle. Unlike hotel and studio musicians, who were at the mercy of contractors beholden to Petrillo, the Chicago Symphony players had real job security: certainly the management, restrained by the union from firing players, would not allow the union to dictate their discharge. Even so, many found that their colleagues in the hotels, theaters, and studios avoided associating publicly with them for fear of retaliation by the union. As reported at the beginning of this chapter, so deep was the resentment of a much larger segment of Local 10 membership against Petrillo that he and most of his associates were swept from office. Several members of the symphony orchestra on the anti-Petrillo ticket were elected to the local executive board, participating eventually in the chaotic developments in Local 10, when extreme "democracy" replaced the autocratic rule of James Petrillo. These affairs are of less concern to the symphony situation than is the future role of ICSOM, which emerged in Chicago and Cleveland during these developments.

ICSOM

At the outset, ICSOM encountered much the same opposition from the AFM as did the orchestra players' committees with local unions.[25] In both cases, the specter of "dual unionism" in diluting union authority aggravated relations between special member groups and the overall organization. Nor was hostility confined to union leadership: many militant orchestra players eagerly sought a confrontation with the union, like that of the Hollywood studio musicians, that could lead to the formation of a more selective union representing the special professional interests of such players. One issue, therefore, was the status within the Federation of ICSOM itself; Kenin and the more moderate members of his international executive board worked to include ICSOM as a special "conference" within the overall union structure, a move that was opposed by a minority of ICSOM leaders. A majority of ICSOM representatives, however, saw definite advantages in seeking a special and active role in the Federation, especially in setting up a strike benefit fund for symphony players during work stoppages; this was finally established in 1970 under joint AFM and ICSOM administration.* A further advantage for ICSOM of formal recognition within the AFM was that such status, under the bylaws of many locals, would require these locals to pay the cost of sending representatives to the annual meetings of ICSOM and to treat local orchestra committees with certain advantages in union affairs. One result of ICSOM pressure on the Federation was the designation of one of Kenin's special assistants, Ted Dreher, to supervise symphonic and operatic affairs within the Federation as part of other duties, though many in ICSOM would like to see such an official devoting all of his time to such matters.

In its annual meetings, in the circulation of its lively and informative publication *Senza Sordino,* and in the continual exchange of data between orchestra committees,† ICSOM has encouraged the development of similar demands by various player groups across the country and a strong trend toward reasonably uniform working conditions among orchestras of the same size.

One ICSOM project that has caused widespread apprehensions is a proposal to establish a "conductor evaluation" exchange of information. The original proposal, to publish such ratings in a manner similar to the summary of wages and working conditions, met with some opposition, partly from those who questioned the legality of publishing such subjective material. Conductor rating has been a matter of much discussion within ICSOM for a number of years, and it now appears that such orchestras as so desire will keep records, in

---

* This provides $50 per week in benefits for members of orchestras on strike; members of orchestras participating in the fund pay $35 a year. The fund was set up originally in 1970 by a loan of $250,000 from the Federation.
† For several years, *Senza Sordino* published a comprehensive annual summary of contract provisions from information supplied by its member orchestras. This *Wage Scales and Conditions in the Symphony Orchestra* is now published by Dreher's office in the Federation and is an important source of statistical facts about symphony orchestras in the United States and Canada.

questionnaire form, of players' ratings of conductors, making this information available to the players of other orchestras on request. There has always been a great deal of informal gossip among orchestra players about conductors— invariably a favorite topic of conversation whenever symphony musicians get together—and the present trend in ICSOM's conductor-evaluation program seems to be something of a codification of this talk. In 1971, however, two orchestras selected new musical directors, and their respective players expressed their opinions on such choices in advance of the associations' final decision. In Houston, the players evaluated eleven possible candidates for the post of musical director and advised management of the results of the rating. As the choice narrowed down to three candidates, an orchestra vote was taken with a large majority in favor of Lawrence Foster, who was also the final choice of the Houston board.[26] In Cleveland, however, where in their 1970 negotiations the players had won the agreement of the board to consult them in selecting a successor to George Szell, the outcome was not so happy. The players felt that their representative in the selection process was being ignored, and took a vote on possible choices, which placed the eventual board selection, Loren Maazel, very low on the list of preferences.[27]

From the outset, one very crucial issue—between ICSOM and the players, on the one hand, and the unions on the other—has been the question of ratification of contracts. Not too long ago, virtually every orchestra had to accept the contract approved by the union, but, under pressure from ICSOM and the players, ratification by the players themselves, or at least a majority, is now in effect in all orchestras represented in ICSOM. This was not obtained without serious battles. In the 1967 work stoppage in Cleveland, the players rejected a contract negotiated by the union, which then required a sixty-percent vote of ratification; when less than sixty percent, but more than fifty percent, of the players voted to accept the negotiated contract, the union executive board voted to reduce the ratification requirement to a majority of the players; a protracted dispute ensued, involving litigation in the courts. In many cities the union has, either explicitly or implicitly, more or less withdrawn from actual negotiations, leaving these up to the orchestra members and merely giving formal approval to an agreement reached and ratified by the players. Where the union still insists upon conducting negotiations, player representatives are included on the bargaining team, whenever the players so desire, in virtually all orchestras at this time. Another issue between ICSOM and the players and local unions has been over the employment of special legal counsel by the players in their negotiations. In many local negotiations, the players do not accept the official union lawyer and seek to employ, often over union opposition, a lawyer of their own.* In some instances, this lawyer is a local one in whom the musicians have faith, but many player committees now retain I. Philip Sipser, of New York, as their

---

* Cleveland remains one of the trouble spots in regard to union resistance to player militancy. As recently as the work stoppage there in the fall of 1970, local union president Anthony Granata refused the players' request to engage I. Philip Sipser as lawyer in the negotiations on the grounds that Sipser was an ICSOM lawyer and that ICSOM is "a dual union, if I ever saw one." [28]

legal counsel. An expert in negotiations, Sipser is also extremely knowledgeable on employee pension plans and has, in many instances, substantially improved the administration of plans already existing and assisted in setting up new ones for the players' greater benefit. Especially when a players' committee knows in advance that it faces a particularly crucial bargaining process, it is inclined to seek Sipser's aid. He is, therefore, involved each year in a substantial number of orchestra negotiations across the country. Sipser also acts as adviser to the national ICSOM organization and plays an important role at their annual meetings.

By the end of 1970, ICSOM included representatives of thirty-six symphony and opera orchestras in the United States and Canada, of which twenty-nine were in this country. Most of these were in the Major category, with annual budgets of over a million dollars; three of the twenty-eight in this category do not belong to ICSOM: the Utah Symphony Orchestra,* Leopold Stokowski's American Symphony Orchestra in New York, and the San Antonio Symphony. The latter, once represented in ICSOM, withdrew in the fall of 1970 at the conclusion of a protracted controversy between the players on one side and the union, conductor, and management on the other.† Present membership also includes several U.S. orchestras in the Metropolitan group, those with budgets under a million dollars, and there are indications that players in orchestras in this category will increasingly seek representation in ICSOM.

During its existence, ICSOM has seen a substantial improvement in pay, working conditions, and the general status of orchestra players. According to the annual ICSOM summaries, symphony players' average annual salary has increased from $4,147 to $9,893 between 1963 and 1971. When ICSOM was founded in 1960, no United States orchestra employed its players under a fifty-two-week contract; in the 1970–71 season, six orchestras had full fifty-two-week contracts and another five had a term of forty-five weeks or more; several of the latter either had contracts committing them to a full year eventually or were making substantial progress toward that goal. To a very large degree, in the larger orchestras of this nation the players had taken control of their relations with management, either by tacit agreement with their unions or with remaining rearguard opposition from them. The Federation had recognized the special status of symphony players among its membership and had, after a period of reluctant acceptance of ICSOM, fully integrated its activities into the larger union. These achievements reflect the aggressive and often abrasive tactics of a militant leadership that developed in the past decade and a half among orchestra players.

* See Chapter VIII for a discussion of the Utah players' attitude toward ICSOM. The American Symphony Orchestra disbanded at the end of the 1971–72 season.
† The dispute between a small group of militant players and the conductor, union, and management of the San Antonio Symphony from 1967 to 1970 involved players' charges that the union failed to support them and union charges of members' insubordination, which were finally taken to court despite Federation efforts to mediate the issue. Eventually the union and orchestra management won a substantial victory, and the players of the orchestra (31 in favor, 2 opposed, out of a total membership of 76) voted to withdraw from ICSOM. Various issues of *Senza Sordino* give a running account of this dispute, and the writer has seen some of the legal pleadings reviewing the facts in this case.

It must be noted, however, that the musicians' militance among symphony orchestras developed at a time when the orchestra associations received a major financial grant from the Ford Foundation,* which materially helped them to meet the rising demands of the players. There are many managers and board members who feel that the Ford Foundation grants had a damaging effect on overall symphonic economics by stimulating player militancy faster than the orchestras could afford to meet demands. Yet, from the very outset, part of the rationale of these grants was to improve the economic status of that part of the music profession employed in orchestras by encouraging with increased funds the extension of seasons and increase of annual pay received by symphony musicians. We shall see later how, under the pressure applied by the players, the Ford Foundation funds were by no means adequate to meet the full demands of the musicians, and local associations found themselves raising money not only to match the Ford grants but also to meet increased salary costs not covered by the annual sustaining grants in the overall Ford program. There is no doubt that the availability of the Ford Foundation grants, coming in 1966 when the player movement was spreading rapidly, whetted the appetite of the players for more money, but, from the musicians' point of view, only their militant tactics assured them of their share of the benefits intended by the Ford grant.

Though ICSOM and the movement it represents among symphonic musicians has more or less consolidated its position in the past few years, they still face future problems. In the field of recording, for instance, Federation policy greatly reflects the interests of the players in a few large orchestras with lucrative recording contracts, who want to keep recording rates at what many consider to be a prohibitively high level. As a conference within the Federation, ICSOM has become directly involved in the Federation negotiations of recording contracts and in discussions of prospective policy toward the future development of video cassettes for home use. Present ICSOM policy still tends to be dominated by a few big orchestras to the point where the interests of players in the smaller American orchestras have been seriously limited. As ICSOM expands its membership to these smaller orchestras, as it seems to be doing at present, its domination by the large ones, responsible for its founding and early success, may well undergo a change.

Many players active in ICSOM affairs and leaders in local orchestra groups feel that symphony associations have approached the limit of private financial resources for supporting symphonic music in this country. The AFM has long been a leading advocate of government aid to the arts, both locally and nationally, and has usually been far more aggressive in this respect than have the local unions on a city, county, and state basis. ICSOM as an organization is on record in full support of increased government aid, but it has yet to implement this policy with much effective action. As its relations with both the Federation and local unions improve, however, ICSOM has an opportunity to work through the politically powerful union movement beyond the musicians themselves to enlist support for substantial increases in government support of the arts.

* See Chapter XIV for the full details of this Ford Foundation grant.

Because it originated as an expression of pent-up musicians' militancy, the rhetoric and tactics of ICSOM have isolated it from other elements in the symphonic institution. Nor has ICSOM involved itself in some of the more important, not strictly economic, issues facing orchestras in general. One can read a large file of *Senza Sordino* and find no mention of the problems of the black musician, of the need for orchestras to diversify their services, of the inadequacies of general music education, or of the role of the professional musician in modern urban society. There are indications, however, both in the mood of *Senza Sordino* and in attitudes expressed privately by players active in ICSOM, of a somewhat more moderate mode of expression. There seems to be an inclination to take pride in the gains made in the past twelve years, and to look to constructive ways to consolidate these gains. In December, 1970, the editor of *Senza Sordino* wrote:

> Management's side of the table has already responded to the musicians' demands with some thoughtful attempts to find answers. More and more Symphony Boards are giving real authority and real support to well-trained and imaginative managers (where available) where a few short years ago they were insistent on hiring mere lackeys. . . . The role of the Union is another matter. There have been outstanding examples of local and national leadership. But on the whole the musician has simply been *allowed* to supply much of the brain power for negotiations and *allowed* to ratify his contract—with the Union then backing up that contract.

Not long ago, a symphony musician with extensive experience in his own committee and in ICSOM affairs commented that though management and players still used such words as "No!" and "Never!," they were both coming to realize that they didn't really mean to use them and that, in a framework of mutual recognition of the realities existing on both sides of the bargaining table, there were few issues that could not be resolved in joint give and take.

There are many in the symphonic world who still look with misgivings on ICSOM, and the player militancy it represents, as a threat to the artistic and management control of symphony orchestras. There is no question that many orchestra players believe that they should have a greater voice in the policy determination of the orchestras for whom they play, and there is every indication that this sentiment will grow rather than decline as it finds expression through ICSOM. Already orchestra members, who have strictly limited the authority of conductors in hiring and firing players, are seeking a voice in the hiring and firing of conductors. Symphony boards and managers generally agree upon resisting such efforts as unwarranted intrusions on their prerogatives and basic responsibility, but there are, here and there, indications that symphony musicians are participating more in overall policy authority than they have in the past, as a result in large part of the great improvements of their status in the past decade and a half. The implications of these prospects will be explored more fully later in this study.*

At this point, however, it must be clear that any view of symphonic personnel relations in the traditional black-and-white context of union versus

* See Chapter XIX.

management far from describes the situation as it exists. The players themselves have become a major element, on their own account and not through
the union structure, in the symphonic institution. Despite conciliatory efforts
by the Federation and some locals, the union itself will never again play a
major role in relations between management and musicians, and the players
themselves, and such organizations as their committees and ICSOM, will continue to be of prime importance.

CHAPTER VI

Helen M. Thompson
and the American Symphony
Orchestra League

The title long held by Arthur Judson as manager of the New York Philharmonic has, since the spring of 1970, been conferred upon Helen M. Thompson, though the executive reorganization which brought her to the Philharmonic entailed a division of the former duties of the general manager between her as manager and Carlos Moseley as president. While Mrs. Thompson is, in her way, every bit as important a figure in the development of the symphony orchestra in America as was Arthur Judson, one may reasonably predict, with all due respect for Mrs. Thompson's work as manager of the Philharmonic, that she will be remembered most for her extraordinary contribution through the American Symphony Orchestra League. In a sense, she and Judson made their impact on the symphonic world from almost diametrically opposed points of departure: Judson working at the very top level of management and policy influence through the largest and most prosperous orchestras, Mrs. Thompson by organizing the grass roots of the institution that proliferated through literally hundreds of small orchestras across the nation.

Helen Manning Thompson is one of a notable succession of energetic, dedicated, and immensely capable women * who have played a major part on the orchestral scene, but she is the only one to have made a national impact. For in most orchestras, and increasingly in the smaller cities, the role of the symphonic ladies has become a crucial one. Not only do they raise money

* Mrs. E. D. Gillespie and Miss Frances A. Wister in Philadelphia, Mrs. Lenore W. Armsby in San Francisco, Mrs. Adella P. Hughes of Cleveland, Mrs. George W. Nichols of Cincinnati, Mrs. Leiland Atherton Irish and Mrs. Norman Chandler of Los Angeles: these come readily to mind as ladies whose devotion to symphonic music has left its mark in their respective cities.

to support their orchestras; they also provide an active community base through their concern with education, promotion of ticket sales, and generation of publicity. Wherever symphony women's committees gathered, locally or nationally, Helen M. Thompson was for two decades a dominating figure, in person or by repute, and she still represents to these ladies in the symphonic heartland a figure of personal dedication and achievement in leadership. Mrs. Thompson did not, as some believe, invent the American Symphony Orchestra League, but once she became a force in its councils she *was* the League, in a very real sense, for thousands of men and women across the nation.

From childhood in her native Greenville, Illinois, Helen M. Thompson grew up in a musical atmosphere; as a student violinist she participated in a variety of community musical activities before enrolling at the University of Illinois.[1] Following her graduation, she married Dr. Carl Thompson and eventually settled in Charleston, West Virginia. Prior to this move she had been a social worker, an experience which she still recalls as most helpful in shaping the basic concepts of the community service so important in the American Symphony Orchestra League under her leadership. In Charleston she joined the local symphony orchestra as a second violinist and, soon after, as volunteer manager. Aware of the then newly organized American Symphony Orchestra League, she became active on its executive committee in 1944, two years after its founding.

Origins of the ASOL

The founder of the League, and long an honored and active figure in its councils, was Mrs. Leta G. Snow of Kalamazoo.[2] Mrs. Snow had founded the Kalamazoo Symphony in 1921, after attending a meeting of the National Federation of Music Clubs in Davenport, Iowa. There she heard a concert by the Tri-Cities (Davenport, Rock Island, and Moline) Symphony, which inspired her to organize in Kalamazoo a similar semiprofessional "civic" symphony orchestra. As manager of this, Mrs. Snow became increasingly impressed with the importance of learning from other orchestras how they handled the various problems of producing symphonic music for their communities, and approached Arthur Judson with a request that a group of managers from smaller orchestras be permitted to attend the annual meetings of the managers of the Major * ones to find out more about management. Judson, feeling that the situations of the two types of orchestra were too dissimilar, turned down Mrs. Snow's request, suggesting that she form a separate organization dealing with the special problems of the "civic" orchestras.[3] This she did by calling a meeting in Chicago on May 21, 1942, attended by

---

* Though formal designation of orchestras had not yet emerged at this time, the term Major then referred loosely to some twenty-five of the larger orchestras to distinguish them from the smaller ones of varying professionalism. Subsequent definition of this term and others will be discussed later in this chapter.

twenty-three representatives of orchestras, most of them managers but some of them conductors, orchestra players, and board members who served also as managers,* to organize an American Symphony Orchestra League.

The League followed a precarious existence, largely due to wartime conditions, for the next few years, but did manage to hold meetings at Chicago in 1944, at Cincinnati in 1946, and at Charleston in 1948. With wartime limitations on travel and on symphonic activity, the main work of the League in these years was conducted through the mails—personal correspondence between managers and the intermittent publication of an *Inter-Orchestra Bulletin.* In 1948, this was revived on a more permanent basis as the *Newsletter of the American Symphony Orchestra League,* since 1971 renamed *Symphony News.*

In 1950, the League held its conference at Wichita, Kansas, a meeting dominated by high optimism over the revival of "civic" orchestra activity in the postwar years, but with considerable gloom over its own financial condition. Supported by modest dues from member orchestras, and most significantly by the volunteer efforts of a few key leaders, the League had funds of barely over a thousand dollars a year to meet a rising demand for information and service. Following this Wichita meeting, a few League representatives were summoned by a businessman, who was an active amateur musician in a "civic" orchestra, to hear his offer of financial assistance. He would contribute two thousand dollars to the League on two conditions: that the League hire Mrs. Thompson as its executive secretary, and that his name as donor not be revealed. The League leaders accepted this gift and set·up its headquarters in the Thompson home in Charleston, West Virginia.

Under Helen M. Thompson's leadership the League during the next decade experienced an extraordinary growth both in size and in its activities. Already by 1950, the League had an important "cause" around which it could rally the support of all American orchestras—the repeal of the wartime federal tax on theater admissions or, at least, the exemption from that tax for such nonprofit activities as symphony orchestras.† As early as 1946 and 1947, the Major orchestras and the Metropolitan Opera had attempted to persuade the Congress to grant them relief from this tax; [4] despite the good offices of the influential Senator Robert Taft of Ohio, because of his family's interest in the Cincinnati Symphony, the corporate executives and orchestra managers were practically laughed out of Washington.‡ Conferences between Judson, other Major orchestra managers, and the League leadership resulted in a grass-roots campaign that eventually in 1951 obtained relief for nonprofit organizations from the tax. This success rested on the fact that Congressmen

---

* Originally Mrs. Snow had in mind merely an organization of managers, but she soon learned that conductors and board members were equally concerned with the problems her new League dealt with.

† The American Federation of Musicians also had a stake in this effort and worked together with Mrs. Thompson and the League in lobbying at the Congress.

‡ Arthur Judson recalls that when a similar tax was proposed during World War I, he and Van Rensselaer expressed their concern to Senator Penrose, Republican boss of Pennsylvania, who assured them not to worry and that he would take care of the matter; no admissions tax was levied on symphony orchestras during that war.

and Senators across the nation heard from their constituents with appeals on the tax question, a campaign organized in large part by Mrs. Thompson through the League.

Mrs. Snow's original concept of the League was that it represent only the smaller "civic" orchestras, specifically excluding the twenty-five or so Major ones. In 1950, when Arthur Judson was principal guest speaker at the League's Witchita conference, several of these larger orchestras sent representatives as observers, and the League decided to invite such orchestras to join as non-voting members. No doubt this step was taken in the immediate interest of promoting closer cooperation on the admissions-tax campaign, but all were aware of the long-range implications of closer liaison among all orchestras, regardless of size. The Boston and New York orchestras were the first to join the League in this manner, and others followed in the next few years. In 1952 the Major managers held their annual summer conference simultaneously with the League, and in 1954 these orchestras were admitted to full membership in the League. Though Mrs. Thompson herself favored closer ties to the Major group, there were some in the League who preferred to remain apart. Similar division of opinion existed among managers of the Major orchestras, but such younger managers as John S. Edwards of Baltimore and later Pittsburgh and Chicago, Ralph Black of Buffalo and Washington, Howard Harrington of Detroit, and Richard H. Wangerin of Kansas City and Louisville took an active part in the development of the League. For some years, all of the Major orchestras and most others with budgets over a hundred thousand dollars have been members of the League.

Growth of the ASOL

From 1950 on, it was impossible to distinguish between League activities and Helen M. Thompson's leadership. An executive committee, and later board of directors, was nominally responsible for the overall program of the League, but its executive secretary actually carried out day-to-day routine activities and also initiated in a most imaginative way all manner of new projects. Sometimes suggestions for such projects came from managers, conductors, or board members active in the League; sometimes they came from others in the music profession; but most often they originated with Mrs. Thompson herself. Invariably they carried the stamp of her basic determination to help local symphony orchestras render better service to their respective communities. She was willing to accept considerably less than musical perfection in performance, if that was the best that the community could afford to support, but she always placed a high priority on the close integration of a musical program in the community—its concert presentations, its educational program, and its leadership in overall cultural activities. In later years she defined her philosophy of the role of orchestras in their respective communities as calling for "the best music they can play with the resources they can command." [5] In this idea of combining community service and artistic program,

Mrs. Thompson recalls being strongly influenced by Antonio Modarelli, a young American conductor of Italian extraction. Modarelli had been assistant conductor of the Pittsburgh Symphony, leaving it in 1939, when Fritz Reiner became musical director, to lead the Wheeling, West Virginia, orchestra. Charleston "borrowed" Modarelli for its musical leadership, and Mrs. Thompson found him an extraordinarily inspiring force, not only in artistic matters but also in his conviction that an orchestra must serve its community. Although Modarelli was not officially active in the League,* he was instrumental in shaping many of Mrs. Thompson's attitudes until his death in 1954. This concept of the League as a service organization, helping local orchestras to develop both musical quality and community service, found realization in a wide variety of specific projects, some of them short-lived but many of lasting effect.

Especially in her first years of association with the ASOL, Helen M. Thompson was an ardent champion of the "civic" or "community" orchestras —groups organized both for the artistic satisfaction that they gave to their performers and for the service they could render their communities. Some of these orchestras consisted of professional musicians who, like the members of the Philharmonic Society of New York in 1842, wanted to play symphonic music together. Others were composed entirely of amateurs with similar motives. To hire a conductor, secure orchestra scores, rent concert and rehearsal facilities, and generally carry on their activities required money, often more than the players themselves could contribute in membership fees or could raise by selling tickets to their concerts. Many amateur groups found it necessary to hire a few professionals to play essential instruments not played by the regular members; their engagement added to expenses. As these costs increased, and as the ambitions of such groups expanded, they sought outside financial help from local citizens and friends who appreciated the importance of having an orchestra in their community.

Eventually such activities had to be organized more formally, with a board of directors, women's committees, manager, bookkeeper, and the other paraphernalia of a cultural organization. Many boards of such civic orchestras included, and still include, a substantial number of orchestra members on their boards, but they also sought the participation there of citizens of wealth and influence who could help defray their operating deficit. To a great extent, these community organizations copied the institutional structure of the larger professional orchestras or of such other cultural and educational enterprises as museums, community theaters, or colleges, which had similar functions and comparable financial problems. In her activities through the League, Mrs. Thompson played an important role in telling local groups how to organize these civic orchestras and one of the first League publications was her very practical "how to" booklet *The Community Orchestra,* first published serially in the *Music Journal* from 1948 to 1950 and then issued by the League in 1952. Though her statistics tended to be somewhat optimistic, Mrs. Thompson

---

* Modarelli contributed a forward to one of the earliest League publications, Mrs. Thompson's *The Community Orchestra, How to Organize and Develop It.*

reported in 1952 that of a total of 737 symphony orchestras in the nation, 395 were civic orchestras.* [6] She also estimated that there were then more than a thousand cities in the nation with a population of over ten thousand capable of supporting some kind of symphony activity.[7]

Though the civic orchestra—or, in present ASOL definition, an Urban or Community orchestra with an annual budget of under a hundred thousand dollars a year—lies outside the purview of a study devoted to the professional orchestra in this country, it has been important in the overall institution. It was, for one thing, the base on which the ASOL first built its strength, and while the emphasis of the League has in recent years shifted more toward the professional orchestra, the civic type still plays a part in its affairs. Moreover, many present professional orchestras outgrew their civic status in a gradual process of increasing the professionalism of their players and their ability to tap the financial resources of the communities which they served.

Most significant of all, there developed in these orchestras a sense of their community service and involvement that increasingly pervaded the professional groups. The civic orchestra demonstrated that a city could enjoy the pleasures of symphonic music without the patronage of a Higginson or a Flagler: by mobilizing the city's financial resources, it could find support in the relatively modest but cumulative contributions of individuals and business firms. To merit this support, these orchestras developed their own special feeling of community responsibility by participating in local educational and cultural activities.

Somewhat akin to these community orchestras are those sponsored, entirely or in part, by colleges and universities. Sometimes, especially in the case of educational institutions with well-developed music instruction, such orchestras consist entirely of university or college personnel, teachers, and students. In other cases, a college-community orchestra includes both college personnel and citizens of the area in which the college is located. Very frequently this latter type is supported by a board representing both "town and gown," but the exclusively college or university orchestra is generally financed by the institution itself, though it may charge admission to its concerts, which are often patronized by the townspeople. Some of these orchestras engage in community activities, especially concerts for young people in the schools of the area, similar to those undertaken by the independent civic orchestra.

Though the educational program of many of these institutions is directed primarily at training teachers for elementary and high schools, an increasing number of them engage in advanced training of young musicians seeking a professional career, and the experience they give these students in orchestra playing prepares many of them for future careers as symphony players. A very important relation of these college and university activities to the professional orchestras has also developed when their instructors, themselves excellent players, are able to play in these orchestras. Many a college or university enjoys the teaching services of better than average instructors if they can

---

* Later in this chapter we shall attempt to arrive at an estimate of the total "symphony population" as of 1970–71.

also work in a local orchestra. Conversely, the orchestra benefits from shar-ing the artistic services of a higher caliber of player whom it could not afford to hire on a full-time basis.

League Services

The training of conductors and managers very early became an important concern of Helen M. Thompson. Though the League never had the financial resources to undertake a large-scale program of training conductors inten-sively—a task for which conservatories and universities were better equipped —it began in 1953 to hold summer workshops for conductors, sometimes with the cooperation of such major orchestras as the Philadelphia but more often on its own, in charge of such musicians as Richard Lert, the Austrian-trained conductor of the Pasadena Symphony. At such workshops, in addi-tion to intensive practical and musical coaching in the technique of conducting, the participants receive briefing on their wider responsibilities as musical leaders in their communities. Similarly, at managers' workshops and in special training after 1952, the League has not only offered specific advice on opera-tional procedures, but impressed on managers the importance of the broadest possible community service. In the case of conductor training, the main effect has been to improve the work of conductors in their own communities; few of these musicians have moved into posts with Major orchestras. But with the managers the League training programs have indeed been of assistance in their advance to positions of increasing importance. Equally vital has been the relation between these training programs and the League's services to member orchestras seeking managers and conductors; especially among the smaller orchestras, the League has replaced Arthur Judson as the source to which local boards turn for recommendations of management personnel.

In 1953, the League organized its first workshop for music critics, in which the writers not only received much basic musical information but had a chance to exchange views with such professionals as conductors and managers. This League project eventually developed into an independent Music Critics Association.

Another League project, under Helen M. Thompson's leadership, that eventually developed an independent existence of its own is the Associated Councils of the Arts. As far back as 1951, Mrs. Thompson started the League on research into the activities of local arts councils, which were growing in number across the country, either as official government bodies or, more frequently, as voluntary groups representing a variety of arts and cultural activities. In 1957 the League acted as a midwife at the birth of the Com-munity Arts Council, Incorporated, as a result of studies undertaken by the League with the help of financial grants from the Rockefeller Foundation.* This group eventually established itself independently of the League as the

---

* In 1959, the League published a *Survey of Arts Councils,* the first major documentation of this activity; this study was an important factor in future arts-council development.

ACA, continuing to receive substantial support as a national service organization in the arts from the Rockefeller Foundation and Rockefeller Brothers Fund. Nancy Hanks, now chairman of the National Council on the Arts, was active in the formation of the ACA.

As a symphonic service organization, the American Symphony Orchestra League has undertaken extensive publications and dispersed much information for its members. *Symphony News,* formerly the *Newsletter,* contains many facts of interest to orchestras, generally oriented toward community needs. Mrs. Thompson found that this exchange of information is a two-way street among orchestras: not only do the smaller orchestras benefit from the expertise of the larger ones, but the latter often pick up helpful suggestions on fund-raising and community services from their smaller colleagues. In addition, the League distributes a great deal of mimeographed material of timely interest to various categories of orchestras; at present, managers and board presidents receive a periodic Special Data Service letter from the League informing them of current developments on the national symphonic scene. From time to time, moreover, the League has made comprehensive studies of special symphonic problems, often with financial aid from foundations or donors, or on contract from a government agency. Such publications include Howard Taubman's excellent survey of the symphony orchestras of Europe, a large-scale study of orchestra education programs for the Office of Education, an analysis of legal documents for symphony orchestras, "how-to" pamphlets on publicity and the organization of women's committees, and an early survey of arts councils that led eventually to the formation of the ACA.*

Though the League took an active part in the repeal of the theater admissions tax in 1951, subsequent tax regulations have restricted its direct advocacy of legislation without the loss of its tax-exempt status. It was, therefore, only peripherally involved in the campaign throughout the 1960s for the establishment of federal aid to the arts. Furthermore, the orchestras which make up the League membership were among the last arts groups to take a strong stand in favor of government aid.† Because of these two restrictions, Mrs. Thompson herself did not play an aggressive role in this matter, though she did supply various legislative and government authorities with factual information on the symphonic scene. More recently, with the increasing involvement of the National Endowment for the Arts, the League has become a major source of national data for the Endowment.

In fact, of all the performance arts—symphony, opera, dance, theater— factual information about symphony orchestras has been by far the most extensive available, both to government and to private sources, thanks in large part to the reporting system that the League took over from the Major orchestra managers and expanded to include all orchestras with budgets over a hundred thousand dollars. These detailed reports, however, have been gathered annually from orchestras with a clear understanding that they will be

* A list of such publications will be found in Appendix L.
† See Chapter XV for the League's 1962 survey of its members on this question and for subsequent developments among symphony orchestras as regards government aid.

made accessible only to those whom the responding orchestras deem to have sufficient reason for seeing them. However, by special arrangement with these responding orchestras, the League has on occasion extracted relevant information for various outside groups making special studies involving the symphony orchestras. Mrs. Thompson herself was a consultant to both the Rockefeller Panel and Twentieth Century Fund studies of the performance arts in the 1960s, and many of the data on symphony orchestras in these books were made available through her. Similarly, when the Ford Foundation prepared for its 1966 program of endowment and sustaining grants to some sixty American orchestras, it consulted frequently with her on a variety of matters that required her expertise.

If these League enterprises appear prodigious and multifarious, one must remember that they were not undertaken by a wealthy foundation or trade association. Operating out of a modest office, frequently a part of her home, and assisted only by a small staff, Helen M. Thompson was the driving and inventive force behind these programs. She had the imagination to see what should be done, and an extraordinary ability to get it done. Possibly her greatest asset was a knack of dealing with people in all walks of life, no matter how humble or exalted. Her grasp of the highest power structure of government and foundations was as complete as her understanding of the symphonic grass roots. Her perception of the function of women's associations and community service was a part of a larger dedication to symphonic music that drove her to carry her cause fearlessly to top leaders of business and government. Out of her central conviction of the community role of the orchestra there proliferated a veritable host of projects, all related to her central purpose, some falling by the wayside for want of money or practical impact, but many of far-reaching importance in the development of the symphony orchestra in America.

In a very real sense, therefore, Helen M. Thompson became the spokesman for the symphonic institution, not only to its constituent members but also in the councils of government, foundations, and major research in the arts. Her key position as an organizer of the ACA brought her in touch with a variety of people involved in the other performance arts and with cultural activities in general. Throughout the 1960s, during a period of growing national concern for the health of the arts, she was a major authority on the symphonic scene. This role assumed even greater importance when the League offices were moved from Charleston to the vicinity of Washington, D.C., a move that was symbolic in many respects of the increasing importance of the League and of major shifts in its emphasis.

The ASOL Today

In 1961, in its twentieth year, the League was offered a new home by Mrs. Jouett Shouse of Washington, D.C., on part of her Wolf Trap Farm estate fifteen miles across the Virginia border from the nation's capital. Funds were raised to move the League offices into a remodeled farmhouse near the recently opened Wolf Trap Performing Arts Center on land donated by Mrs. Shouse to the National Park Service. The League still hopes to build its own quarters on this site once it can be financed.

Until 1968, League presidents * had been symphony officials who served without pay as titular head of the organization, while Mrs. Thompson as executive secretary was the top paid executive. In 1968, however, the League directors decided that Mrs. Thompson's heavy work load should be shared with a full-time salaried president, with former president John S. Edwards assuming a new position as chairman of the board of directors. The board first engaged Seymour L. Rosen, then manager of the Buffalo Philharmonic, as president, but before he could serve he took a position as manager of the Pittsburgh Symphony when Edwards moved to Chicago. Richard H. Wangerin, manager of the Louisville Orchestra, was then engaged to fill this post, with Mrs. Thompson serving as executive vice-president. This organization of League leadership remained intact until Mrs. Thompson became manager of the New York Philharmonic early in 1970. Her post of executive vice-president has not been filled, and Wangerin thus remains sole top executive of the League. In the office at Symphony Hill he has a staff of seven people, including a newly appointed editor of *Symphony News* and general publications, Benjamin S. Dunham, and Mr. and Mrs. William O. Nelms, who have long served the League in important administrative posts.

Though the American Symphony Orchestra League originated as an organization of civic semiprofessional orchestras, it has gradually shifted its interest toward the concerns of the professional orchestras. The makeup of its board of directors in late 1971 reflects the growing influence of larger orchestras. Of the thirty-one board members, eighteen are either active in orchestras with budgets over a million dollars or have recently been associated with such orchestras (four managers, two conductors, twelve board members). Six (one manager, one conductor, and four board members) are from orchestras with budgets of over a hundred thousand dollars but less than a million. Two directors, both board members of their respective orchestras, are from orchestras with budgets of less than a hundred thousand dollars, and there are five League board members not directly affiliated with local orchestras. The influence of the larger orchestras is even stronger on the executive committee of the League board of thirteen, in which eight members are either affiliated, or have been associated recently, with orchestras in the million-dollar category; three others are from professional orchestras in the group of over a hundred thousand dollars, one from the smallest category, and one member not associated with any orchestra.

Just as the League itself nurtured such projects as the development of arts councils and workshops for music critics, which eventually became the independent ACA and Music Critics Association, it has also joined forces

---

* These presidents were: Mrs. Leta G. Snow (1942–46); A. H. Miller of Duluth (1946–48); Arthur Bennett Lipkin, conductor of the Birmingham Symphony (1948–51); Alan Watrous, manager of the Wichita, and later Dallas and Seattle, orchestras (1951–56); and John S. Edwards, manager of the Baltimore, Pittsburgh, and Chicago orchestras (1956–68).

with other symphonic groups and lent them its administrative aid and the benefit of its experience. As we shall note later when discussing government aid to the arts, the presidents and managers of most of the professional orchestras met in New York late in 1969 to take concerted action in seeking substantial federal funding of symphony orchestras. Mrs. Thompson took an active part in organizing this meeting prior to becoming manager of the New York Philharmonic; the League also did much of the planning and organization for it, as well as for another in Chicago two years later, where government officials met with symphony representatives for an intensive discussion of the philosophy and logistics of federal funding. These meetings are held apart from the semiannual meetings of the managers of the larger orchestras and the annual conference of the League itself.

There is another national symphonic organization, apart from the League and actually older: the Women's Association for Symphony Orchestras. Beginning in 1937, a group of representatives of a few women's committees have held biennial meetings in various cities for mutual exchange of ideas and discussion. This is a smaller organization than the League itself and, despite some talk of affiliation with the League, remains completely independent of it, though many of its leaders are active in the League as well. It includes some thirty women's committees or associations, most of them from orchestras with budgets of over a million dollars. Its membership is restricted to those women's groups who are formally invited to join, rather than automatically open to any who wish to affiliate, as in the case of the League. Delegates prepare in advance extensive activity reports and statistical data on their respective orchestras which are printed and distributed to the participants at the beginning of each meeting, providing them with a great deal of advance information on topics for discussion. These loose-leaf collections, themselves an elaborate publication, contain many interesting data about the variety and scope of such activities and are an impressive documentation of the role of women in local orchestras.[8]

How Many Orchestras?

With few exceptions, largely of a temporary nature, the membership of the American Symphony Orchestra League includes representation of all professional orchestras and a substantial proportion of semiprofessional and amateur orchestras in the United States and Canada. The frequent assertion that there are as many as 1,400 * symphony orchestras in this country cannot be substantiated, either from League sources or elsewhere. The League maintains a mailing list of its own active members, plus people or organizations who have been members in the past or who are known through other sources to have been more or less active in symphonic presentation. The orchestra

* This figure, cited by Mrs. Thompson herself, is frequently used to support evidence for a "cultural explosion" and widespread national symphonic activity, often in appeals for corporate and government aid.

portion of that list in 1971 included over 1,000 organizations in the following groupings established by the League: [9]

	ASOL Members	Nonmembers
Major Orchestras (over $1 million)	28	
Metropolitan Orchestras (over $100,000)	73	5
Urban Orchestras (over $50,000)	26	1
Community Orchestras (under $50,000)	164	337
Community-College Orchestras	25	62
College Orchestras	30	222
Youth Orchestras	5	73
Chamber Orchestras	2	22
	353	722

In view of the fact that the estimate of nonmembers is generous, undoubtedly including organizations no longer active but still accepting mail, it is unlikely that there are more than 700 orchestras of all kinds currently active.*

The two organizations collecting royalties on the performance of copyright music, the American Society of Composers, Authors, and Publishers (ASCAP), and Broadcast Music Incorporated (BMI), reported licensing between 560 and 620 orchestras in the two-year period between 1969 and 1971; since these organizations must be generally sensitive to the extent of performance by symphony orchestras of music under copyright, and no orchestras can operate without playing at least some music so covered, their figures probably reflect symphonic activity rather accurately. It should be noted, however, that ASCAP and BMI now cover amateur activities almost as thoroughly as they do professional.

Criteria of professionalism are difficult to formulate. The narrowest would be based on year-round operation and the guarantee of a minimum annual salary to the players of $10,000; under such criteria, less than a dozen orchestras in the United States would have qualified in 1970–71. At the opposite extreme, one might accept the mere payment of a concert fee to all or most players: between 100 and 120 orchestras might meet this standard, many of them offering as little as a few hundred dollars a year to players who may be students or whose main motivation is sheer love of playing in an orchestra three or four times a year. A common measure of orchestra professionalism is the total annual budget, and if this is applied with due attention to other factors it can be a helpful guideline. As we shall note later, such an or-

---

* ASOL membership also includes individuals as well as orchestras: a large proportion of some 1,300 to 1,400 individual members are probably affiliated with orchestras also maintaining League membership, but some may represent organizations not so affiliated.

chestra as that of Louisville, with a budget of under \$500,000 and minimum guaranteed annual pay to its players of slightly over \$3000 might on these criteria alone not qualify as professional; but, because of close ties with a local university and public-school system, and because of other important performing opportunities in the community, its musicians meet the standard of professionalism, both in the level of their performance and in being fully employed in musical activity of a high quality.

Another guide to this question of professionalism is the list of orchestras which received Ford Foundation grants in 1966, for that list was prepared on the basis of the most extensive and expert study of this kind ever undertaken.[10] Of 61 orchestras offered grants in 1966, two are no longer in existence and there is one, not included in the 1966 Ford program, that might have qualified when the grants were set up. Although professionalism as such was not the explicit base for these grants, the officers preparing the list considered a number of aspects—season length, pay scale, total budget, community involvement, long-range stability, and artistic quality—that are ingredients of the overall standard of professionalism.*

In a 1971 National Endowment for the Arts publication, *Economic Aspects of the Performing Arts, A Portrait in Figures,* the symphonic data were based on information, supplied through the League, from the 101 Major and Metropolitan orchestras listed in League membership. Here again, professionalism was not explicitly stated as a criterion, but by thus defining their field of symphonic interest, the National Endowment implied certain assumptions of it.

In the face of such considerations, and with the lack of precise orchestra-to-orchestra information, we can only attempt some rough estimates of the extent of professionalism, taking a variety of factors into account. One can, by taking the Ford Foundation Major list as the *minimum* parameter and the League Metropolitan list as the *maximum,* say that there are at least 60 professional orchestras in this nation and possibly 106; somewhere, among the 46 orchestras represented by the difference between maximum and minimum, one finds a vague area of the marginally professional. In the nonprofessional segment of this country's orchestra "population" there are at least 250 amateur and semiprofessional orchestras represented by League membership. Of the 722 nonmembers on the League's contact list, League president Wangerin takes the optimistic view that most are more or less active, since mail is not returned from them, and that other orchestras are actually represented in the League by individual, rather than organization, membership. A more conservative view would discount this large list of nonmembers by two-thirds, which would suggest that there may be a minimum of 600 nonprofessional orchestras (a figure comparable to the ASCAP and BMI licenses) and possibly as many as 900, if the League assumptions are correct.

---

* Another criterion, somewhat looser than these, may be found in what the major New York artist managements look upon as their market for soloists with symphony orchestras. Such mailing lists are reliably reported to run between 250 and 300, but these agencies consider as much as 60% of the list to be relatively inactive in terms of actual bookings or the prospect of making sales.[11]

Among those orchestras which meet some standard of professionalism, one cannot safely make qualitative or statistical comparisons freely, for it is hardly fair or relevant to compare the Albuquerque Symphony with the Philadelphia Orchestra. In view of this, groupings of orchestras have been established, both for statistical purposes and to determine the participation of various orchestras in conferences of managers and other officials. Among professional orchestras, the League has maintained two principal groupings—Major and Metropolitan—based on annual budget. In 1970 the budget ranges for these two groups were established as noted earlier, but these are not rigidly applied. Classification as Major or Metropolitan is determined not by the League but by the managers of orchestras currently in the groups. Early in 1972, the managers of the Major orchestras further defined that classification by requiring that orchestras maintain a $1 million budgetary minimum for two consecutive years before being so classified, and stating that they will lose that ranking if they fall below the $1 million mark for more than one year. Such Major orchestras must also employ on a weekly basis professional musicians, "whose principal employment shall be that orchestra." The Metropolitan classification is not defined so precisely: it includes all orchestras operating at a level of more than $100,000 a year which do not meet the requirements for Major eligibility.

Each of these professional groups is too large for a meaningful application of comparative averages in statistical study. The Metropolitan group should be divided into at least two categories, roughly but not invariably along the lines of the Ford Foundation grants, with the lower category including the marginally professional orchestras. Likewise, the Major classification is too broad, including orchestras with annual budgets of $5 million with those with $1 million; it should be divided into three categories, each including orchestras of comparable relevance. The financial application of these categories will be discussed later in a general consideration of symphonic economics. However, since they will be referred to in the next section, which deals with specific orchestras, a general description of each of the categories used in this book should be noted here.*

Category A includes the six largest orchestras in the United States, with annual budgets approaching or exceeding $4 million, year-round operation, and minimum annual salary to at least 100 players in excess of $13,000. In the following section, the Philadelphia Orchestra is representative of this group.

Category B includes eight orchestras that are approaching a 52-week operation or have already attained that mark. Seven of them employ at least 90 players who are guaranteed a minimum of $10,000 a year. Their annual budgets range in the vicinity of $2.5 million. The Cincinnati Symphony is in this category.

Category C covers the remaining orchestras in the League's Major grouping. Their annual budgets are about $1.2 to $1.5 million. Most employ at least 85 players for over 35 weeks a year with a minimum annual salary in

---

* See Appendix D for a complete list of categories.

excess of $6,500. The number of concerts offered ranges from 100 to 165. Both the Buffalo Philharmonic and Utah Symphony, to be studied in the next section, are in this category.

Category D includes orchestras in the upper portion of the League's Metropolitan classification, those that may be reasonably regarded as professional in quality. All but one were in the 1966 Ford Foundation project. Season length and players' contracts vary, but most orchestras pay a minimum in excess of $2,000 a year to their players. Some may give as few as 30 concerts a year, others many as 60. In the following section, the Louisville Orchestra represents this category.

Category E includes the remaining Metropolitan orchestras with budgets over $100,000. Orchestra size varies from 65 to 85, and players may receive as little as $250 for seasons varying from 9 to 40 concerts. Though several received Ford Foundation grants, these orchestras must be generally regarded as marginally professional. From this category, the Albuquerque Symphony will be studied in the following section.

Category F covers four orchestras, all in the over-$100,000 groups and all located in or near New York City. They are not the type of community-oriented and -supported groups which are the major concern of this study.

ASOL in the Changing Orchestra World

The establishment and growth of the American Symphony Orchestra League coincided with a period of explosive expansion in symphonic activity in this country. Grant and Hettinger, in their 1940 study of *America's Symphony Orchestras,* list sixteen Major orchestras with annual budgets ranging from $100,000 to $720,000; they also cite *Music Year Book* statistics for 1937 showing a total of 238 orchestras of all sizes in the United States.[12] More than a decade later John H. Mueller, in *The American Symphony Orchestra,* reported "over twenty" orchestras in the Major category, still determined by a minimum annual budget of $100,000.* He mentions several other orchestras of possibly professional caliber and cites the League's estimate of some six hundred "community" orchestras.[13] These data not only indicate the numerical growth of orchestras in the past generation but also reveal how little interest these authors took in any but the Major orchestras. Not the least contribution of the League, under Helen M. Thompson's leadership, has been the manner in which the smaller community efforts have been given recognition, a sense of identity with even the greatest orchestras of the nation. Through the League in its manifold activities, the American symphonic institution has in a sense discovered itself and has, in so doing, become a potent force. Thus, though the League took no direct official action in the 1960s to secure federal support for the arts, one may reasonably doubt if the legisla-

---

* The tenfold increase in two decades of the minimum criterion for the Major category reflects important developments in symphonic economics that will be discussed in Chapter XIII, for this represents appreciably more than merely keeping up with general inflationary trends.

tion establishing the National Council for the Arts, and securing appropriations of funds for it, could have been accomplished without the nationwide awareness of the performance arts generated so successfully in the symphonic sector by Mrs. Thompson and the League.

On the other hand, it now appears that, as the most effective national organization in the performance arts, the League itself has entered into a period of more conservative consolidation of its position. Even in the last years of Mrs. Thompson's association with the League, it was concentrating its efforts more on providing information to foundations and the government, and on assembling data reviewing symphonic activities, than on sponsoring innovative projects. It has become an establishment within the establishment that controlled the arts, a trend increasingly apparent since Mrs. Thompson's departure for the new challenges at the New York Philharmonic. More and more, those who have watched the League through its history feel that it has come to concentrate its efforts on the pressing financial problems—deficit financing, labor negotiations, and the mechanics of government support—of the professional orchestras.* Though the grass-roots atmosphere still plays an important part in the annual conferences of the League, there is now an air of tired recapitulation with such time-worn problems as the plight of the modern composer, the by now strained ingenuity of women's committees, and the techniques of promotion, fund-raising, and ticket sales. Certainly the liveliest exchange of ideas in recent years at these conferences took place in 1971 in Seattle after speeches concerned with the problem of the black musician and the black audience. Even so, this topic generated discussion more reminiscent of the broader national concern of two decades ago than of the urban realities of the 1970s.

As a service organization, the League, possibly because of lack of funds and staff, is no longer able to satisfy either the foundations or the government as a prime source of information. Part of this problem arises, as we shall note later, from the inability of the League's members themselves to agree upon the kind of uniform accounting systems that would facilitate relevant study of available data, but in this instance the League has not shown the forceful initiative it did in the case of its 1958 study of legal documents. Despite efforts in this direction, this important aspect of League service has yet to be implemented.

Nor has the League taken a really deep look into the personnel relations of American orchestras, though this is, at first glance, a topic that concerns only its professionally oriented membership. On the few occasions conferences have included general discussion of unions and musicians' relations to them, the approach has been primarily from the management side, with little recognition either of the developing independence of musicians' militancy or of the deeper problems facing the professional musician. Nor has the League con-

---

* Thus, in 1970 and 1971, the League made strong, and eventually successful, representations to the Internal Revenue Service to eliminate from its new regulations on nonprofit organizations the requirement that salaries in excess of $15,000 be reported for public inspection. Such a requirement, resulting in disclosure of conductors' and managers' salaries as well as those of key overscale players, obviously affected only a few large orchestras.[14]

cerned itself with the implications of the semiprofessional orchestra in which professional musicians receive modest pay and many amateurs are paid professional scale. In the larger context of the symphony orchestra, beyond narrowly economic issues, the orchestra musicians could make a constructive contribution to major policy direction; the present hostility pervading personnel relations in many important orchestras creates an obstacle that must be removed if the symphonic institution is to realize its full potential, and the League could be a force in bringing these elements together in a creative manner. Unfortunately, ICSOM quite frankly looks upon the League as an employers' trade association, and though there is much basis for this feeling, both organizations could benefit from a closer and more open dialogue at least at the various national meetings each holds annually.

In the field of education, also, the League tends to accept the status quo, its massive report on that subject reviewing existing activities comprehensively with little concern for basic education philosophy or wider potential. As we shall note later, the symphony orchestras in general have backed into educational activity largely for reasons that have little relation to an understanding of the creative process in art or to an application of that understanding to the educational process.

Nevertheless, the American Symphony Orchestra League, especially under Helen M. Thompson's leadership, has made a significant impact on the American symphonic scene and has created the organizational framework within which many future contributions can be made. The shortcomings noted here reflect comparable shortcomings in the institution it represents, and the development of major new directions within the League must also come from the overall institution itself.

PART TWO

Six Orchestras
in Time of Crisis

Though each of this nation's orchestras responds in its own way
to local conditions, so many of their elements are common to
others—especially within a given category—that an account of
relatively few can provide a reasonably comprehensive picture of
the symphonic scene in the United States. Each of our five categories of professional community-oriented symphony orchestras
will be represented in the following section. The Philadelphia Orchestra, from Category A, is one of a small handful of "super-
orchestras," in artistic performance and operational organization.
At the opposite extreme, in virtually every respect, is the Albuquerque Symphony Orchestra, whose recent emergence into
the marginally professional status of Category E provides insight
into how orchestras get started. From Category B, the Cincinnati
Symphony, one of the most venerable in the nation, is using its
recently expanded musical resources for new community services.
Two orchestras from Category C, the Utah Symphony and the
Buffalo Philharmonic, illustrate some of the ways in which American orchestras do and do not succeed in establishing themselves
firmly in their communities. The Louisville Orchestra, from Category D, has a history of imaginative innovation in repertory and
integration into the music profession of the city.

All of these orchestras share certain common features. Their
performing ensemble is structured to present the traditional symphonic repertory of the past two centuries, with occasional modi-

fications required by earlier music or contemporary works. No orchestra supports its activities entirely from ticket sales or income derived from services performed, and all must rely upon some combination of annually raised contributions, endowment income, and government support to defray their operating deficits. The responsibility for financing and guiding the policy of these orchestras rests ultimately with a board of directors or trustees, themselves laymen (in the sense that they are not professional musicians or administrators) who are in a position to rally the support of their respective communities for the orchestra. This board engages a manager (a function now designated by a variety of titles), who carries out the nonartistic administration of orchestral production, and a conductor or musical director, who is fundamentally responsible for the artistic functions. The interplay of power forces and policy authority within the board may vary from one orchestra to another, as do the interrelations between the board, conductor, musicians, and manager, but these forces exert themselves within the generally common institutional structure developed in the past.

In this study of six orchestras, our center of interest will vary from one to another, depending upon local developments. These six orchestras have been chosen not only as representative of our categories but also to illustrate the regional scope and local diversity of the American symphonic institution and to offer, in their aggregate, a comprehensive picture of the symphony orchestras of this nation.

Most important, we shall discover as we study them the manner in which the very real crisis in the American orchestras in recent years has affected each in its own way and how they have responded to the turbulent developments of the past decade and a half.

CHAPTER VII

Philadelphia Orchestra

To the listener who has known the Philadelphia Orchestra only from its recordings, its actual sound in the Academy of Music will produce a considerable shock at first impact. Instead of the lush and almost overpowering quantity of orchestral tone that the recording producers engrave into the grooves of a disc, he will hear a warm, translucent sound with a far more spacious ambience than he hears from his loudspeakers. The same experience, though often to a lesser degree, will be encountered in other halls visited by the Philadelphia Orchestra on its extensive tours, but the marriage of orchestra and auditorium in its home base is still the ultimate way to experience this great orchestra at its best.

That experience has been for six decades the most consistently exciting symphonic sound produced in this country. Under the leadership of Leopold Stokowski and Eugene Ormandy, the Philadelphia Orchestra has maintained a symphonic excellence unrivaled in our time. Many elements have gone into the making of the Philadelphia sound—the acoustics of the Academy of Music, the selection of superb individual virtuosos and their blending into the ensemble, and a tradition of instrumental quality fostered by a symbiotic relation between the orchestra and the Curtis Institute of Music. But most of all these elements have been shaped for sixty years by the orchestra's two great conductors, who have given it a continuity and stability enjoyed by no other. Supporting and directing these "fabulous Philadelphians" (to borrow Herbert Kupferberg's description) is an organization of Main Line aristocrats and board of trustees and women's committees and a skilled professional staff. An earlier chapter reviewed the important roles played by Leopold Stokowski, Arthur Judson, and the leaders of the Philadelphia Orchestra Association guiding it through its first days of glory. This account brought the story of the orchestra up to the point of Stokowski's announced intention to retire, Arthur Judson's departure from Philadelphia, and to the threshold of Eugene Ormandy's assumption of direction.

Ormandy Takes Over

In succeeding Leopold Stokowski, Eugene Ormandy brought a quite different musical background to his direction of the Philadelphia Orchestra. Hungarian by birth, Ormandy's musical training was based on a great tradition of
string playing plus a sense of national color and rhythm that produced, from
the same environment in which he was trained, such composers as Bartók
and Kodály. Ormandy did not start his career as a conductor, but rather as a
violinist of virtuoso quality. The circumstances of his arrival in America
diverted the career of the violin soloist into conducting, a change that certainly reflected basic proclivities in the young musician.[1] In the 1920s Ormandy
had wide conducting experience in nonsymphonic fields: in theater pits and
radio studios he developed his conducting technique every bit as thoroughly
as the young German or Italian conductor on the staff of an opera theater.
An important lesson that Ormandy learned in the Capitol Theater and on
Arthur Judson's radio programs was that of accommodation to the realities
of the situation in which he found himself. The self-discipline that this
young Hungarian exercised in adjusting himself to the musical and working
conditions of the theater and studio must have taxed him sorely. Yet he
never wavered in his drive to become a major symphonic conductor, spending his spare time studying scores and attending the rehearsals of such masters
as Toscanini. Whatever compromises of artistic integrity were forced upon
him by circumstances, Ormandy never allowed them to modify his basic ambition or deflect his pursuit of total mastery of the symphonic idiom.

If Ormandy had a preconceived notion of orchestral sound when he
took over the Philadelphia Orchestra, he certainly did not try to impose it.
In this he was completely different from Stokowski, who would never, even as
a young man, accept anything but his own conception. Instead, Ormandy took
the orchestra as he received it, without making revolutionary changes. For
many years after he came to Philadelphia, it was commonly asserted that the
continuing greatness of the orchestra under his direction was inherited from
Stokowski. That may have been true at the outset, but it can hardly have
been valid in succeeding years: * if the Philadelphia Orchestra influenced
Ormandy's sense of orchestra tone, especially in his early years there, he also
gradually shaped it very much in his own way. With his extraordinary sensitivity to timbre and ensemble blend, Ormandy has selected the players for
his orchestra with his conception of its tone constantly in mind, not just for
the principal positions but also for the most remote back stand. He has often
said, "Selecting players for the Philadelphia Orchestra is like matching
a fine string of pearls." Nowadays, when he makes one of his rare guest

* Though recordings are by no means a reliable reflection of an orchestra's sound, some notion
of the gradual transformation of the Philadelphia Orchestra from Stokowski through Ormandy's
long tenure can be gained by comparing examples from various epochs; a very few early Stokowski records and equally few from Ormandy's first years appear from time to time in various
historical recording reissues.

appearances with another orchestra, the result is an uncanny evocation of something quite like the typical Philadelphia sound—without its ultimate polish, ensemble balance, and characteristic smooth attack, but nonetheless very similar.

Ormandy brought to Philadelphia the same flexibility and ability of accommodation that he had developed in New York theaters and radio studios. Much to the delight of the board of directors and a considerable segment of the audience, his programs seemed more conservative than Stokowski's; actually Ormandy has produced a great deal of important new music, almost as much as his predecessor, but he has not made it a focal point of promotion and personal publicity. The excitement and tension generated by Stokowski became a thing of the past under Ormandy. Nevertheless, there was in this man an extraordinary driving force. Since childhood, Ormandy has suffered from a serious hip ailment that not only drained his energy but caused him continuing and increasing pain. A combination of fantastic willpower and expert medical aid kept him going for many years on a very heavy conducting schedule. In the summer of 1971, he finally had surgery on his hip to restore its function and relieve him of pain; it is typical of Ormandy that, though aged seventy-two, he returned to the podium ninety days after undergoing this operation.

Year-Round Activity

In sheer quantitative terms, the activity of the Philadelphia Orchestra has been as impressive as its artistic quality. During the traditional winter season, it has long offered subscription series in New York, Baltimore, and Washington, in addition to a full season in Philadelphia. Under Stokowski, the orchestra made its first transcontinental tour in 1936, and since 1946 Ormandy has led more such nationwide tours, as well as many regional ones in the United States and Canada. Ormandy and the orchestra traveled overseas in 1949 for the first of four European visits, to Latin America in 1966, and to Japan in 1967. Since 1936 they have played for the annual May Festival at the University of Michigan in Ann Arbor, and since 1966 have been in summer residence at the Saratoga (New York) Festival, besides the traditional season at Robin Hood Dell in Philadelphia. In a typical full year, the orchestra plays to more than 300,000 people during the regular season of a hundred concerts in the Academy of Music, another 350,000 in some hundred concerts on tour, at Robin Hood Dell, and at Saratoga.[2] Since 1960 its radio-transcription service has made stereo tape recordings of its concerts available to radio stations throughout the country,* and, under both Stokowski and Ormandy, has made more recordings than any other American orchestra. With all this activity, it may well be said that—in this country as well as abroad—it has long been the best known of all American orchestras.

* Similar services are currently offered by the orchestras of Boston, Los Angeles, and Cleveland, the fees usually going to the orchestras' pension funds.

During a typical week in the winter season, the Philadelphia Orchestra plays the same program in the Academy of Music on Monday or Thursday evening, Friday afternoon, and Saturday evening; on Tuesdays it usually repeats it on "runouts" (trips not requiring overnight stays) in New York, Baltimore, Washington, or other cities nearby. There are generally four two-and-a-half-hour rehearsals each week to prepare this repertory. In addition, when Ormandy is in Philadelphia, the orchestra is usually busy recording in the Scottish Rite ballroom not far from the Academy of Music; sometimes the schedule requires the orchestra to rehearse in this hall, but most rehearsals are held in the Academy. Once this thirty-week "winter season" is over, the orchestra makes a spring tour, invariably including the May Festival in Ann Arbor, sometimes as far as the West Coast but often confined to a smaller region. This tour is followed by six weeks at Robin Hood Dell and four weeks at Saratoga. Out of the fifty-two weeks of the year, the musicians receive seven weeks of paid vacation. Ormandy now conducts thirteen of thirty weeks in the winter season, occasionally a few concerts in Robin Hood Dell, and about half of the Saratoga season; his long-time assistant, William Smith, and guest conductors are engaged for the remainder of the concerts. At one time, Ormandy conducted over one hundred seventy concerts a year, but has reduced his work load to half that number in recent years. He has never appeared extensively as guest conductor elsewhere; he undertakes few such engagements, and then only with the most important American or European orchestras.[3]

Since its founding, the Philadelphia Orchestra has played its home concerts in the Academy of Music, a superb music theater completed in 1857 and acoustically one of the finest halls in the world. In 1950 the Orchestra Association bought a controlling interest in the corporation that owned the Academy and subsequently set up a subsidiary nonprofit corporation that gained full ownership of the hall. The purchase (partly with funds borrowed from the endowment funds of the Association) and renovation of the Academy have been financed both by contributions and by annual benefit concerts played by the orchestra. Though operated separately, its management is closely coordinated with the orchestra's requirements, which receive priority in scheduling. The Academy corporation has also purchased property to its rear on which it hopes in the near future to develop a commercial structure that will also provide additional backstage, rehearsal, and office facilities for the orchestra.[4]

The regular season of the Philadelphia Orchestra, from late September to early May, is the basis of its year-round operation. During this period, the proportion of rehearsals to concerts is much higher than it is on tour, at Robin Hood Dell, or at Saratoga, for which programs are drawn from the repertory prepared for the regular season with considerably less rehearsal. In any one season, this repertory encompasses a liberal representation of standard and unusual works, reflecting the catholic taste of the musical director, even in the guests he invites to share his podium. Under Ormandy, as under Stokowski, the orchestra plays a smaller proportion of 18th-century music than do some other American orchestras, and in the contemporary repertory Ormandy is somewhat less experimental than other conductors; *avant-garde* music is represented on his programs, but less aggressively than, let us say, on those of the New York Philharmonic under Bernstein's or Boulez's artistic direction.

The following table (7-A) summarizes by percentage of composers' nationality the Philadelphia Orchestra repertory for representative periods: 1900–10 for the pre-Stokowski era; 1915–25 for that of Stokowski's most intensive leadership; 1940–60 covering the period when Ormandy was conducting a large proportion of the programs; and the most recent half decade for which data are available, during which Ormandy has actually conducted less, though he has remained very much responsible for artistic policy.*

TABLE 7-A

PHILADELPHIA ORCHESTRA REPERTORY Composer-Nationality Percentages for Selected Periods, Compared with National Percentages (*In Italics*)

	1900–10	1915–25 Stokowski	1940–60 Ormandy	1965–70
Austro-German	66.53	56.19	50.61	50.22
	60.24	*51.35*	*50.18*	*51.65*
Russian	13.70	17.95	17.62	18.94
	13.54	*16.38*	*16.19*	*14.80*
French	11.43	12.00	10.46	10.15
	12.15	*14.55*	*11.53*	*10.09*
American	2.27	5.56	6.82	5.17
	3.48	*6.84*	*7.35*	*6.66*
British	0.98	1.45	2.98	4.39
	2.08	*2.20*	*3.34*	*3.97*
Czech	3.95	2.50	1.97	2.91
	3.71	*2.88*	*2.19*	*3.12*
Italian	0.69	1.23	2.69	1.38
	0.90	*1.98*	*3.10*	*2.89*
Scandinavian	1.96	1.85	3.89	2.52
	2.50	*2.25*	*2.59*	*2.76*
Hungarian	0.15	0.62	3.26	2.61
	0.96	*0.63*	*2.69*	*1.57*
Spanish	——	0.17	0.74	0.83
Latin-American	*0.01*	*0.20*	*1.26*	*1.47*

In the important area of Austro-German music, it is of interest to note that though Stokowski reduced its amount in the repertory appreciably, Ormandy played even less. Conversely, Stokowski's greater emphasis on Russian music was continued and intensified by Ormandy. Though many of Stokowski's most spectacular innovations offered music by such contemporary European composers as Mahler, Stravinsky, Berg, Schoenberg, and Scriabin, he devoted considerable attention to American composers, though slightly less than the national average; Ormandy, during the period of his most intense activity,

---

* This information has been extracted from the Mueller repertory studies, which are discussed in detail in Chapter XVII.

played more American music but still trailed the national average, and more recently he has played even less.

Because of its heavy schedule of regular symphonic concerts, the Philadelphia Orchestra plays fewer programs for young people and schoolchildren than do most others. Over a period of years, this orchestra has developed such a high proportion of regular public concerts for adult audiences that it now has little time in its crowded schedule for special community-service performances. This has become a matter of concern to some people connected with the orchestra who feel that it might well cut back on some of its concert schedule in favor of education programs, but few believe that Ormandy and the board would sacrifice major symphonic activity for such purposes.*

In Philadelphia, as in New York, Washington, and Baltimore, the backbone of the orchestra's audience is season subscription. In Philadelphia some eighty-two percent of capacity is sold by subscription; this means that virtually all of the best locations in the Academy of Music are taken in this manner. The management encourages subscribers unable to use their tickets to release them for resale, making a few desirable tickets for each concert available for single sale. Ticket prices range from a dollar and a half in the upper part of the Amphitheater to eight dollars for Parquet Circle boxes on Friday afternoons; no reduction is given on season tickets.† Subscription concerts are given in Philadelphia on fourteen Thursday evenings, thirty Friday afternoons, thirty Saturday evenings, and fifteen Monday evenings. Despite the heavy subscription and demand for single tickets, the Association will move slowly in any consideration of additional concerts in Philadelphia, weighing such a prospect against the income from concerts out of town before making major changes in an already tight schedule.

The Philadelphia Orchestra continues to offer the Friday afternoon concerts that began in the early days of the Philharmonic Society of New York as "open rehearsals" and have been a staple feature in the schedule of many of the older and larger orchestras. These concerts are attended almost exclusively by women, many of whom have held their subscriptions since the days of Stokowski or inherited them (sometimes even by formal bequest) from their mothers, grandmothers, or mothers-in-law. For many a Philadelphia matron, Friday is "symphony day," an occasion for lunch downtown at a nearby club, attendance at the concert, and a hurried exit to get home before the evening rush hour begins. The "Friday ladies" are a major support to the orchestra, not only in their faithful renewal of subscriptions but also in the organization of women's committees, which only subscribers are invited to join. These women's committees, the first to be organized by any orchestra, date back to 1904 and are a testament to the dedicated efforts of Miss Frances A. Wister until her death in 1956. Invitation to join these committees, which are organized by areas of the city and suburbs, is extended only to

* The most recent contract with the players permits the Association to split the orchestra into two sections for a limited number of concerts in schools; this opportunity had not been fully implemented in 1970–71.

† One large orchestra with heavy season-ticket sale has even contemplated charging a premium price for season subscriptions, but most orchestras in the nation, a few large ones excepted, offer these with as much as a 30% discount.

subscribers and is a coveted social honor. They play an important part in the arrangements for youth concerts in the Academy of Music and the schools and in fund-raising.

According to the players in the orchestra and soloists appearing with it, who detect distinct differences in the various audiences for whom they play each weekend, the Saturday evening public is extremely conservative in its response to new music and has the most enthusiasm for standard repertory and well-known soloists. The newer Thursday and Monday evening series, with a less strongly Social Register element, respond more readily to innovation and new personalities. The Friday afternoon audiences, once a stronghold of Stokowski's support—more often for his charisma than for his innovation—are by far the most conservative of all. However, they are a vital factor in the sustained success of the Philadelphia Orchestra, not only as loyal subscribers but as major contributors to the annual sustaining funds and to such important capital campaigns as the recent one to match the Ford Foundation grant.*

Like other orchestras with a high proportion of subscription sales, the Philadelphia faces the problem of developing new audiences from people who first attend concerts with the purchase of single tickets. With so few such tickets available, especially in desirable locations, and with the necessity for planning symphony attendance weeks in advance, many young couples with small children or families living in the suburbs find it difficult to attend the concerts. For the Association this is not an immediate financial problem, but many express concern that actual attendance at symphony concerts over a period of years has not kept pace with the city's increase in population.[5] Out of town, of course, the situation is quite different, though the Philadelphia Orchestra offers subscription series of its own in other cities and in some appears as a part of a series including other concerts. Year in and year out, it has been a major concert attraction, consistently the most successful American orchestra in attracting tour audiences. In part this has been due to the unvarying excellence of its performances under Ormandy, and in part to the extraordinary sales of its phonograph records; many a record collector who first became acquainted with this orchestra on records looks forward to hearing it in person, and record sales in turn have been substantially promoted by these personal appearances.

Though other American orchestras—notably the Chicago and Boston—preceded them in the early recording studios, the Philadelphia Orchestra, thanks to its propinquity to the Camden, New Jersey, headquarters of the Victor Talking Machine Company (predecessor to RCA-Victor and RCA Records), and by virtue of Stokowski's great interest in the techniques of recording, was the first to record regularly and intensively.† The Schwann catalog, which by no means includes all records made by the Philadelphia

---

* In 1970–71 the women's committees raised more than a third of the annual sustaining contributions received by the Association.

† Under Stokowski and Ormandy the Philadelphia Orchestra recorded exclusively for RCA (and its corporate predecessors) until it joined the newly revitalized Columbia Records division of CBS in 1943. In 1968 it returned to RCA.

Orchestra in the past forty-five years (many have been deleted or replaced), lists a total of 239 entries for it in its latest Artist Issue: 231 under Ormandy's direction, 7 under Stokowski, and 1 under Toscanini; [6] in addition, the same personnel has in the past recorded as the Robin Hood Dell Orchestra under other conductors. Comparable figures for the New York Philharmonic are 209 items under 8 conductors—174 of them by Bernstein—and 128 for the Boston Symphony under 7 conductors, plus 40 for the Boston Pops under Arthur Fiedler. Among European orchestras only the London Symphony, with 274 entries under 62 conductors, surpasses the recording activity of the Philadelphia Orchestra.

Though the Academy of Music provides extraordinary acoustics for concert performance, it has never been a satisfactory location for recording, despite efforts to adapt it for this purpose. The most recent of these, by RCA in its first sessions in 1968, employed electronic devices to modify the hall acoustics for recording, but the results did not meet with critical approval or buyer acceptance. Consequently, most Philadelphia Orchestra records have been made in various lodge halls, school auditoriums, churches, and ballrooms. The orchestra has actually recorded on tour, notably with the Mormon Tabernacle Choir in Salt Lake City, and even in Boston's Symphony Hall. At present, it records in the ballroom of a Scottish Rite hall not far from the Academy of Music.

To one attending a recording session there, it seems incredible that in the resonant acoustics of this cramped room any kind of orchestral sound can be produced for recording or that the conductor can achieve ensemble balance. Employing sometimes more than twenty microphones, connected into eight stereo channels, the entire technique is based on detailed coverage of every section of the orchestra, the final balance being settled by the conductor and record producer at the mixing panel. Both Ormandy and the orchestra have had such long experience at making recordings that sessions are almost routine. Generally a work is played through once or twice, with stops to correct mistakes or when the engineers fail to hear detail they want to preserve. The final product is the result of editing and mixing that owes as much to the skill of the editors as to the sound one hears in the ballroom. Union rates for symphonic recordings * are predicated on recording music previously prepared for concert performance. In fact, the prospect of recording often influences Ormandy's choice of repertory and soloists for the subscription concerts. However, some music is recorded—mostly from the lighter concert repertory that would be inappropriate for presentation in the Academy of Music—that is not from the concert programs, such as the album from the sound track of the film *Love Story*. Since recording sessions are not included in the weekly contracted services, being additional work for additional pay at Federation scale, and since all records are now made under Ormandy's direction, recording sessions must be added to an already heavy schedule when the con-

---

* Under a three-year recording-industry agreement signed in 1969, the symphonic rate for a basic three-hour session was a minimum of $95, effective October, 1970. A new contract for 1972–75, reached in the spring of 1972, substantially maintains this scale. During such a session, no more than one hour of final recording may be produced, and actual playing time cannot exceed an average of forty minutes per hour. Principal and other overscale players receive additional compensation.[7]

ductor is in town. The logistics of planning these sessions and their repertory requires much planning by the conductor, record-company executives, and the manager: frequently schedules are set as much as two years in advance, especially if soloists are to be involved. For other orchestras in Category A recording is a major activity, but it plays a greater role with the Philadelphia Orchestra than with any other, both in quantity of recording work and in royalty income.

Symphonic High Finance

The Philadelphia Orchestra Association has for some years published an annual financial report in summary form. To the 1970–71 report we have added (Table 7-B) comparable data for 1960–61, illustrating the expansion of this orchestra during the past decade.* The percentage figures in parentheses on these tables indicate proportion of total expense or income represented by certain specific items of particular interest.

TABLE 7-B

PHILADELPHIA ORCHESTRA

Financial Summaries for 1960–61 and 1970–71

EXPENDITURES

	1970–71		1960–61	
Music Production				
Musicians, conductors, soloists	$2,283,504	(61%)	$ 946,133	(61%)
Transportation, baggage	126,490		96,771	
Musicians' travel allowance	181,708		54,129	
Hall rent, stage expense	133,724 ⎱		164,341	
Advertising, ticket selling	191,781 ⎰			
Music	31,710		44,132	
	$2,948,917	(78%)	$1,305,506	(84%)
Administration and Management				
Staff, management and development	$ 158,772		$ 129,879	
Rent and office expense	70,298 ⎱			
Pensions and Social Security	259,765 ⎰		49,354	
Miscellaneous	47,240			
	$ 535,375	(14%)	$ 179,233	(12%)
Academy of Music				
Net expense	$ 261,732		$ 61,399	
TOTAL EXPENDITURES	$3,746,024	(100%)	$1,546,138	(100%)

* These data [8] are presented here with minor modifications to illustrate a ten-year trend and to facilitate comparison with other orchestras. The most important of these is the listing of Academy of Music figures for 1970–71 (where the Association lists expense and income separately) as *net* expense, as in 1960–61. For 1970–71, Academy expenses were $480,579 and income $219,247, both included in Association totals of $3,965,274 expenditures and $4,012,083 income. By deducting Academy income from expense, a *net* expense figure of $261,732 has been determined to establish comparability with earlier data.

TABLE 7-B (continued)

INCOME

	1970–71		1960–61	
Performance:				
Concerts	$2,103,258		$ 935,027	
Record royalties	577,102			
Television	2,728			
Commercial sponsor	8,000		279,755	
Interest	42,586			
Miscellaneous	12,301			
	$2,745,975	(72%)	$1,214,782	(82%)
Supplemental:				
Endowment	$ 408,571		$ 129,667	
Contributions	538,290		136,282	
Ford Foundation	100,000			
	$1,046,861	(28%)	$ 265,949	(18%)
TOTAL INCOME	$3,792,836	(100%)	$1,480,731	(100%)
Net Income (or Loss)	$ 46,812		$ (65,407)	

The 1970–71 report also includes a consolidated balance sheet, a relatively recent additon. Among total assets or liabilities of over $10.5 million are listed three endowment funds:

Restricted	$2,724,162
Unrestricted	1,702,963
Challenge Program, restricted	3,050,820
TOTAL	$7,477,945

The first of these consists of funds going back to the 1919 endowment-fund drive and including subsequent gifts and bequests restricted to the use of income only. The unrestricted funds include gifts and bequests without such restriction, plus the accumulation of operating surpluses. The restricted Challenge Program funds were raised in connection with the recent Ford Foundation grant; actually nearly $5 million had been raised by 1971, but the Association used part of these funds for the installation of air conditioning in the Academy of Music.

In the Administrative Expense category, nearly half of the cost is now represented by pensions, Social Security, and other employees' benefits. Obviously a major portion of this item arises from present or past services by musicians. Among the items of income are the recording royalties, notably high at the present time. In 1968 the Association signed with RCA a five-year contract that reportedly guaranteed minimum royalties of $400,000 a year, including an undisclosed portion for the conductor.[9] The division of these royalties (probably 10% of the manufacturer's recommended selling price) among conductor, soloist, and Association is a confidential matter, but the total figure of $577,102 includes the Association's share of these

RCA royalties as well as those from CBS Records, with whom the orchestra recorded between 1943 and 1968.* However, the long-range prospect for record royalties indicates a probable decrease of this figure after the expiration of the present RCA contract in 1973; the orchestra cannot, given present conditions in the recording industry, expect so favorable a contract after 1973.

In its annual financial report, the Association has no special listing of funds received from government agencies for services rendered. Included in performance income are two such grants: one for $100,000 from the National Endowment for the Arts designated for programs in the schools, and another $25,000 from the Pennsylvania Commission of the Arts to share the loss on youth concerts. The $100,000 from the Ford Foundation is a nonrecurring item, the last of five such annual sustaining grants in the 1966 nationwide project of assistance by the Foundation to symphony orchestras. Moreover, the endowment income of $408,571 includes income from the Association's long-standing endowment funds, from the matching funds raised under the Ford Foundation program since 1966, and from the orchestra's share of the trust established by the Foundation in 1965.†

A comparison of the 1970–71 figures with those of 1960–61 discloses the explosive growth of this orchestra in the past decade; similar growth will be seen in other orchestras. In the case of the Philadelphia Orchestra, this growth includes the establishment of a 52-week players' contract in 1963, as well as a considerable increase in weekly salary to these musicians. The remaining increases in expenditures reflect greater operating costs necessitated by year-round operation and the general inflationary trend during the past decade. In percentage terms, the growth of the Philadelphia Orchestra during this decade was:

Performance income	126%
Supplemental income	294%
TOTAL INCOME	156%
Production expense	125%
Administration expense	198%
TOTAL EXPENSE	142%

The inclusion of pensions and welfare benefits in the administrative item undoubtedly accounts for much of the large increase there; in certain respects these actually should be considered a part of music production, as they really represent "fringe benefits" in players' compensation. These overall increases during the 1960s are typical of the professional orchestras throughout the country, and the big increase in supplemental income—almost tripling in ten years—reflects the intensity of the financial crisis that has struck American orchestras. In Philadelphia, moreover, the actual requirement for annual fund-raising has grown even more, 370% when the Ford Foundation sustaining grant is included in contributions.

* In addition to AFM scale for the actual recording sessions, the musicians receive a share of the royalties on record sales, as described in Chapter V.
† See Chapter XIV for details on the provisions of the Ford Foundation symphony grants.

The annual contribution requirement to balance the budget rose by $500,-000 during this decade, and with the present stabilization of endowment income upon completion of the first phase of the Ford Foundation program, future rises in the income gap must be met through increased contributions. Furthermore, with the prospect of decreased recording royalties after 1973, the contribution requirements during the next five years will rise even more: it is now estimated that prospective annual contribution requirements will approach $1 million during the next decade.

One purpose of establishing various categories of orchestras in the previous chapter was to provide a framework for comparing a specific orchestra with the averages for orchestras in the same grouping. Lumping together various line items in these data, Table 7-C compares the Philadelphia Orchestra with the 1970–71 averages for all six orchestras in Category A: *

TABLE 7-C

PHILADELPHIA ORCHESTRA
Financial Summary, 1970–71, Compared with Category A Averages

	Philadelphia	Averages of 6 Category A Orchestras
INCOME:		
Performance:		
Concerts	$1,978,258 (52.2%)	$2,124,151 (39.5%)
Other nongovt.	642,717 (16.9%)	1,259,020 (23.3%)
Govt. for services	125,000 (3.3%)	217,391 (4.0%)
TOTAL PERFORMANCE	$2,745,975 (72.4%)	$3,600,562 (66.8%)
Supplemental:		
Contributions	$ 638,290 (16.8%)	$1,137,686 (21.1%)
Govt. grants		92,500 (1.7%)
Endowment	408,571 (10.8%)	562,324 (10.4%)
TOTAL SUPPLEMENTAL	$1,046,861 (27.6%)	$1,792,510 (33.2%)
TOTAL INCOME	$3,792,836 (100%)	$5,393,072 (100%)
EXPENDITURES:		
Artistic personnel	$2,283,504 (61.0%)	$2,533,140 (51.8%)
Concert production †	927,145 (24.7%)	1,788,905 (36.6%)
Administration	535,375 (14.3%)	568,223 (11.6%)
TOTAL EXPENDITURES	$3,746,024 (100%)	$4,890,268 (100%)

As compared with the six-orchestra average for Category A, the Philadelphia Orchestra is below the dollar figures in every item of income and expense. One reason for this more modest operation arises from the fact that some twenty percent of its annual schedule involves services contracted to the Robin Hood Dell and Saratoga. Four of the other five Category A orchestras sponsor their own off-season activities, thereby incurring considerably higher

* See Chapter XIII for a general discussion of all financial data by category and Appendix E for complete figures.
† Net expense for Academy of Music has been included here to show comparability of Philadelphia figures with others included in the averages.

production expenses; on the other hand, these same functions produce a higher performance income, since such ticket sales in the Robin Hood Dell and Saratoga operations do not figure in the Philadelphia report. In view of this, its concert income, mainly from the regular season and tours, is extremely high. Moreover, when percentages are compared, the Philadelphia operation is even more impressive: it spends a significantly higher portion of its budget for artistic services (not including pensions and players' benefits) and receives an impressively greater portion of its income from concerts. Interestingly enough, in view of its reputedly favorable recording income, its miscellaneous income falls far behind the category average. Despite recently intensified efforts to raise annual sustaining funds, its contributions remain substantially lower than average. Most impressive, however, is the seventy-two-percent share of total income represented by performance activity, probably the highest of any orchestra in the nation today. As we shall have occasion to note in our general comparison of the various categories, the six largest orchestras as a group enjoy the highest proportion of performance income, an average of sixty-seven percent, and the Philadelphia Orchestra has long been a leader in this respect. However, when we compare 1970–71 figures with those for a decade earlier, there is a drop of ten percent in this item, a cause for deep concern in Philadelphia, as well as in other orchestras experiencing a similar decline. This decline in performance income percentage, despite a dollar increase in supplemental income, lies at the root of the financial crisis caused by the widening income gap encountered by virtually all American orchestras in recent years.* This crisis has posed a major challenge to orchestra management and board leadership.

Running the Orchestra

Administering this enterprise has become a far larger task than it was in the days of Arthur Judson. Since his departure in 1935, the Philadelphia Orchestra has had seven managers, among them Reginald Allen, the composer Harl McDonald, Donald L. Engle, Roger G. Hall, and, since 1964, Boris Sokoloff. The son of the Russian-born conductor Nicolai Sokoloff, he attended the University of Virginia and did graduate work in drama at the Yale University School of Fine Arts. After employment in Community Concerts and Columbia Artists Management under Judson, he joined the staff of the New York Philharmonic in 1947. Before coming to the Philadelphia Orchestra, he was manager of the Minneapolis Symphony from 1953 to 1964. At present his assistant is Joseph H. Santarlasci, who has served the Association for more than twenty-five years. His duties include supervision of ticket sales and subscriptions, tour arrangements, and the accounting for the orchestra's pension program and credit union. They are assisted by a modest clerical, secretarial, and accounting staff in offices located in a build-

---

* The income gap and the basic economic factors that cause it will be considered in detail in Chapter XIII.

ing near the Academy of Music. Separate from this office is the fund-raising
activity, headed by John D. Healy, with responsibilities to be discussed later.

Sokoloff himself subscribes to Arthur Judson's rather limited view of the
function of an orchestra manager: though his experience and detailed knowledge of orchestra operations undoubtedly contribute significantly to the trustees' deliberations, he probably plays a comparatively less important role in
explicitly developing new policies for the Philadelphia Orchestra than do his
counterparts in other orchestras. To a large degree, this results from old traditions in Philadelphia. Ormandy's long tenure has brought him special prerogatives, among them a separate office in the Academy from which he conducts
much orchestra business directly with artists, record companies, and managements. Similarly, a few key directors, notably former board president and
present board chairman C. Wanton Balis, Jr., take active interest both in
artistic policy with Ormandy and in many phases of the operation of the
orchestra. Balis still handles many negotiations with important players who
receive more than the minimum pay established in the basic trade agreement with the union.[10] Sokoloff is by no means excluded from such matters:
both he and Ormandy confer with Balis, but he does not have the primary
responsibility or direct contact with the players. To the degree that these employees sense this divided authority, the manager enjoys significantly reduced
influence in other dealings with them, both in formal negotiations and in
routine matters.

Nevertheless, Sokoloff has important responsibilities in the personnel relations of the orchestra. In contract negotiations he works closely with the
board of directors to set basic policy, informing them of the consequences, financially and otherwise, of specific issues under consideration. In these he is
joined by selected directors and by legal counsel.

In personnel relations he works with both the orchestra committee and
the personnel manager, Mason Jones. With the increasing power of the players' committee, the responsibilities of the personnel manager have changed
considerably, and are still, in many respects, in a state of flux. Traditionally,
he was the management's agent in dealing with personnel matters, as well
as a union member with certain obligations as contractor to the union. However, as orchestra players in general, and those of Philadelphia especially,
sought to develop more direct contract with their employers, the work of the
personnel manager has often been replaced by direct consultation between
the manager and the players' committee. Nevertheless, Jones, while still
playing part-time as first horn, provides an important liaison between the orchestra, conductor, manager, and union, and is often a major channel of
information for exploring problems that arise in interpreting the union contract and guiding the conductor and manager on specific operational questions such as extra rehearsals, scheduling of trips, and allocation of playing
responsibilities. He also works with the conductor when extra players are
needed or substitutes are hired in case of illness, and in setting up auditions
to fill vacancies in the orchestra. All of this requires consummate diplomatic
skill and a lifetime of experience in orchestra routine. In what has come to

be in Philadelphia one of the most crucial areas of musicians' militancy, both Jones and Sokoloff are in daily encounter with problems and personalities requiring utmost managerial expertise.

Unlike many symphony managers, Sokoloff is not deeply involved in organizing and managing fund-raising campaigns, as we shall see later. This task is handled by a separate development office originally set up to manage the Ford Foundation matching challenge and later embracing the annual sustaining fund. However, because of his knowledge of financial requirements and of the resources which the orchestra can apply to overall promotion, Sokoloff works closely with this development office.

The Power Structure

In Philadelphia, as elsewhere, the board of directors of the Association performs two essential functions: overall policy direction and supervision, and fund-raising to defray the annually inevitable operating deficit. To achieve these ends, membership in the board is drawn almost exclusively from the social and economic leaders of the community on the theory that such people not only have access to sources of contributions but have in their own affairs demonstrated the kind of business acumen and civic responsibility qualifying them for positions of leadership and trust. As pointed out earlier, the Philadelphia Orchestra was founded and developed largely under the guidance of men and women listed in the city's Social Register. Even with changes and expansion of board membership since 1966, this is still true: established family wealth and executive positions with major mercantile and manufacturing corporations—or with legal, banking, and insurance firms serving these corporations—remain the primary criteria for service on this board.[11] Moreover, such membership is regarded as long-term: unlike symphony boards in other cities, frequent rotation is unheard of in Philadelphia.

Like many of its kind in the arts and other nonprofit activities, the board of directors of the Philadelphia Orchestra Association, though representative of the economic and social elite of the community, tends to be dominated by a few strong leaders. This is especially the case where, as in Philadelphia, there is an established tradition that the board chairman and president hold office for relatively long periods of time. In Philadelphia, the dominant figure on the board has long been C. Wanton Balis, Jr., a leading insurance executive, who has brought to his role an intense interest in music, dedication to community interests, and conservative business judgment. Nowadays Balis's main interest in the orchestra is musical, and he and Ormandy have developed a close working friendship arising from their common concern with the artistic development of the orchestra. Though he scrupulously recognizes Ormandy's authority, his views on policy generally dovetail with those of the conductor.*

---

* On one recent occasion, Ormandy commented that he had programmed a Haydn Mass—a work certainly otherwise appropriate—as he put it, "for Mr. Balis."

In the last few years, however, there has been a music committee of board members, who meet several times a year with Ormandy for an informal discussion of repertory and guest artists. Like its long-established counterpart at the New York Philharmonic, this committee provides a two-way exchange of views between the conductor and the board, although it defers completely to Ormandy's artistic direction, its advisory role being considerably less important than in some other orchestras. Of special importance, in view of Ormandy's age, are its discussions with him of the various guest conductors, for the question of the future leadership of the orchestra has become one of great, though discreet, concern.

In administration of the orchestra, Balis always kept in close touch with the manager, as did Thomas Gates and Orville H. Bullitt, who preceded him as president. In fact, these leaders carried on Alexander Van Rensselaer's tradition of intensive personal involvement in orchestra affairs, based on a solid continuity of service on the board.

Over a period of years, however, Balis and Bullitt came to personify the conservatism of the Association in two major areas: relations with the players, and the failure to bring into the Association a wider representation of community leadership and financial support. Balis and Bullitt were its top officials through the turbulent period of musicians' militance; in their strong and frequently publicized stand against concessions in negotiations, they appeared to the orchestra players, and to the community at large, to represent implacable opposition. In this they were strongly supported by the board, who shared their concern that the financial resources of the city could not meet the demands of the players. The board leadership undoubtedly recalled the 1920s, when the Association succeeded in building a surplus from operations, endowment income, and relatively modest annual contributions, and they continued three decades later to conceive their responsibility as incurring as little deficit as possible and as covering much of that with income from endowment. Having been in the enviable position of not calling upon the Philadelphia community for substantial contributions since the endowment-fund campaign after World War I, the board underestimated its potential for greater support of the orchestra. As the financial data for 1960–61 indicate the Association was required to defray a relatively modest (considering the size and wealth of the city) annual deficit of little over $200,000, and in that year failed to cover the amount by nearly one-third. This failure was undoubtedly due to the fact that by this time the board had come to represent too narrow a segment of community leadership and financial resources.

In his study of the Philadelphia Orchestra, *Bach, Beethoven, and Bureaucracy,* Edward Arian attempts to contrast the Stokowski and Ormandy eras using Max Weber's sociological concepts of the "charismatic" versus the "bureaucratic" type of institution. He describes this difference in terms implying that prior to 1936, the Philadelphia Orchestra was dominated by the innovative and dynamic Stokowski, and that with the advent of Ormandy, the board imposed its "bureaucratic" influence. Arian sees this bureaucratization of the Philadelphia Orchestra in programming for box office and recordings, exploitation of player rivalries within the orchestra, increased emphasis on touring, efforts to maximize the utilization of the working force (the orchestra musicians) for income production, and Ormandy's apparent acquiescence in what Arian feels were artistic compromises.[12] Without minimizing the differences in personality of the two conductors, it seems that Arian's analysis is excessively doctrinaire to anyone acquainted with the actual power relations in the orchestra over this long period. During the Stokowski era, the board, led by Van Rensselaer, certainly played an important role in the development of the orchestra and exercised definite restraint on the conductor. Ormandy, since being established as musical director of the orchestra, has exercised full artistic leadership. The difference between the two eras is more one of degree than of kind. Certainly Stokowski applied far greater pressure on the Association than did Ormandy, with his greater willingness for accommodation. But it is also true that in the three past decades the Philadelphia Orchestra, like others throughout the country, has expanded its activities in ways that required an intensification of purely business concerns.

In the case of this orchestra the shift in its power structure grew out of a crisis in 1934–35 that resulted from a number of events. With Van Rensselaer's death in 1933, the presidency of the Association had been assumed by Curtis Bok, who was much more inclined than his predecessor to accede to the pressure of Stokowski. The conductor, in turn, took advantage of his greater influence through Bok to demand more time away from Philadelphia than the board wanted to give; in fact, it wanted him, as musical director, to spend more time with the orchestra. Finally, the departure of Judson in 1935, Stokowski's public announcement of his intention to resign, and the catastrophic loss on the opera season threw the board into turmoil. Having failed to persuade the board to grant Stokowski's demands, Bok resigned the presidency and, together with his mother, withdrew from the board. Out of this crisis new leadership developed: Thomas Gates, president of the University of Pennsylvania, became president, Reginald Allen was engaged as Judson's successor, and efforts were made to patch up the quarrel with Stokowski. Emissaries from the board traveled to Hollywood to persuade the conductor to return, for what all knew would be but a temporary period.

Eventually a search was started to replace Stokowski with a leader more amenable to the policies and objectives of the board leadership in facing a serious financial crisis in the midst of the depression. Ormandy,* whose successful emergency guest appearance in Philadelphia in 1931 had led to his engagement by the Minneapolis Symphony, was re-engaged as a guest conductor and, for a transitional period from 1936 to 1938, designated co-conductor with Stokowski. As we have noted earlier, Ormandy was by temperament and ambition much more inclined to fit into the board's notions of a resident conductor who would create fewer tensions than it had experienced in the previous years. Moreover, in Allen and his successors in the manage-

---

* Ormandy was not, as Arian states (p. 17), "only a young conductor with a minor orchestra." When he became co-conductor in 1936, he was thirty-seven years old and had capably taken over one of the best established Midwestern orchestras.

ment of the orchestra the board had full-time administrators who were more amenable to board direction than was Judson.* Thus, in the tripartite leadership structure of the Association, both manager and conductor relinquished important power to the board and eventually to its leadership under Bullitt and Balis in the next three decades. This new power structure, under which the Philadelphia Orchestra prospered and expanded, was not challenged again until the mid-1950s. The first of these challenges, which the Association met with stubborn rearguard resistance for more than a decade, came from the orchestra players; the other came from financial pressures, which culminated in 1966 with the Ford Foundation grant.

Confrontation with the Musicians

The polarization between symphony musicians and their employers, described in an earlier chapter, was manifest more intensely and earlier in Philadelphia † than elsewhere.[13] As early as 1948 the Association, faced by what it felt was an impasse in contract negotiations, announced the cancellation of the forthcoming season because it felt that the demands of the players "would seriously impair the finances of the organization";[14] to show that it was not bluffing, the board instructed the staff to commence returning payments received from season subscribers. In 1954, in the first significant work stoppage among American orchestras in more than three decades, the season opening was delayed by seven days; in the next decade there were two more stoppages—ten days in 1959 and nineteen in 1961—and, even when contracts were settled without interruption of work, relations with the players became increasingly hostile. As players' militancy grew, the Association tended to cling as best it could to traditionally conservative approaches to bargaining. Dominated to a large degree by executives from investment, banking, and insurance, with little direct experience in their own businesses of the realities of post-depression labor relations, the board fought a stubborn rearguard battle for what it believed to be the very survival of the Philadelphia Orchestra.

The players, for their part, developed an increasingly militant stand, fostered both by the implacable views of the board and by what they felt to be

---

* For many years after the upheaval of 1934–35, the very names of Stokowski and Judson were anathema to many board members, and not until 1960 was Ormandy allowed to invite Stokowski back as guest conductor. Though he had been scheduled to celebrate the sixtieth anniversary of his debut in Philadelphia at a benefit concert in October, 1972, he cancelled that appearance upon moving his residence to London the previous summer.

† In terms of weekly pay for various years, the players received the following *minimum* weekly salary:

During 1920s	$ 60.00	(approximately $2,000 per year)
1948–49	115.00	(approximately $3,500 per year)
1956–57	147.50	(approximately $5,000 per year)
1961–62	190.00	(approximately $7,800 per year)
1965–66	200.00	(guaranteed $12,400 per year, including recording)
1970–71	280.00	(guaranteed $16,560 per year, including recording)

intolerable working conditions. Much of the success of the Philadelphia Orchestra rested upon extensive traveling away from home—short "runouts" during the season and tours of as much as six or eight weeks following it. Through these tours management achieved a maximum utilization of its personnel to produce performance income, thus holding down the operating deficit for which it had to seek annual sustaining contributions.* The players who found themselves away from home, not only daytimes for rehearsals and recordings but many evenings for concerts in Philadelphia and other cities, were convinced that they were being exploited. However, though the working schedule was an issue in the early phases of player militancy, the main thrust of this effort was directed toward a year-round contract. In 1961, the Robin Hood Dell season was incorporated into a forty-one-week overall agreement, a major step toward this goal. This same 1961 agreement, settled only after a stoppage of nineteen days, also incorporated a provision requiring ratification of contracts by a majority vote of the players, an important victory for the musicians in their challenge to union bargaining authority.

The long stoppage in 1961 had really shaken the Philadelphia community, which suddenly learned all was not well within the great orchestra that so many took for granted as a prime civic showpiece, even if they did not take an active interest in it. The public airing of the sharply polarized views of the Association and the musicians included much misinformation from both sides. The impeccable image of the Association was tarnished, even to the extent of an abortive effort to organize a citizens' committee in support of the players. For the first time, there was widespread criticism of the Association as an ingrown group of Social Registerites controlling the destiny of a major civic activity. The players, sensing this feeling, were thus encouraged in their position, and the Association did nothing, either overtly or through improved public relations, to repair the damage to its stature in the community.

In reviewing the stormy labor relations in the Philadelphia Orchestra, one cannot ignore the extraordinary feeling of solidarity which has long existed among its players.[16] They have always taken an intense collective pride in the acclaim accorded the performances at home and on tour, in the great sale of their recordings, and in every occasion on which the orchestra has been hailed by critics in uniquely laudatory terms. They enjoyed the praise heaped on the "Philadelphia sound," and bitterly resented efforts by the conductor to lay claim to an "Ormandy sound." They viewed as inconsistent with high artistic standards the pressure of management and conductor to influence repertory for recording purposes and to make records under less than optimum conditions, even though they enjoyed lucrative income from these records. Whatever differences existed among these musicians—and there have been many—they closed ranks firmly in confrontation with their em-

---

* Arian gives graphic indication of the growing importance of touring after 1935: [15]

Season	Home Concerts	Out-of-Town Concerts	Total Concerts
1934–35	83	17 (17%)	100
1939–40	72	69 (49%)	141
1966–67	121	83 (41%)	204

ployer. This cohesive *esprit de corps* has been fostered by the fact that over sixty percent of them had studied with current or past members of the orchestra, either privately or at the Curtis Institute of Music, a circumstance contributing to the orchestra's artisic quality and continuity (although also leading to a high degree of "cronyism" that has excluded some fine players, including all but one black musician,* from the orchestra's roster). Moreover, the Philadelphia Orchestra musicians were no longer alone in their overt expression of militance; their representatives played an important part in the organization of ICSOM in 1961, and were in close touch through that organization with other orchestras across the nation.

As the time approached for negotiations in 1963, the orchestra committee dropped a bombshell by announcing publicly that the musicians henceforth should have the right to fire the conductor, if at least seventy-five percent of the players so voted.† Though this announcement expressed no specific desire to remove Ormandy, it was the first time since the members of the Philharmonic Society of New York had abandoned their cooperative structure in 1909 that players in a major American orchestra had even intimated openly their desire to become involved in such a basic question of artistic policy. The announcement served to focus attention on the musicians' militance and impressed the board as a dangerous threat, to say nothing of an unwarranted public expression of hostility. Whether this influenced the board's subsequent approach to negotiations is impossible to determine, for the Association did, in fact, start its bargaining with the long-desired commitment to employ the players on a year-round contract.‡ This offer cleared the way for a settlement without work stoppage. One reason the Association could make such an offer was that it was then planning to play a summer season in 1966, in addition to Robin Hood Dell, at a projected festival in the Pocono Mountains.

One of the concessions extracted in exchange for full employment was that orchestra players be restrained from performing other orchestral work while under year-round contract. This "anti-moonlighting" provision seemed at the time to be a reasonable provision, since the Association was now offering full-time employment, but it soon became a major matter of contention. Nevertheless, the 1963 contract agreement was hailed widely as an epoch-making step toward placing American orchestras on a sound artistic and financial basis. Orchestra musicians in Philadelphia and elsewhere, moreover, were quick to note that this contract had been arrived at primarily by direct bargaining between the employer and the players themselves with virtually no union participation. In fact, union officials were surprised that the

---

* This is not unique to Philadelphia and exists in many other orchestras. The problem of the black musician will be considered in a larger context in Chapter XIX.

† This declaration was later repudiated by the rank and file of the orchestra, who gave Ormandy a standing ovation when he entered to conduct his next public concert. The orchestra also voted to discharge the lawyer reputed to have devised this demand.[17]

‡ The Philadelphia Orchestra Association was the first symphonic employer to make such a commitment, in this case to be effective in the third year of the contract, the 1965–66 season. Shortly after, however, the New York Philharmonic became the first orchestra to employ its players year-round, effective earlier than in Philadelphia.

players could accomplish so much for themselves, and readily approved the contract, as did the players by a vote of sixty-eight to thirty-three.

The board believed that granting the players their long-sought full employment had laid the foundation for improved relations with them, even if at the cost of substantially increased financial burdens. The impact of this contract can be seen by comparing the figures for 1965–66 with the year preceding this contract.[18]

	1962–63	1965–66
Salaries of musicians and stage personnel	$ 869,719	$1,397,824
Total expenditures	1,837,593	2,975,624
Contributions	178,161	237,864
Net income (or loss)	259,830	(24,120)

Nor did the board realize that year-round employment would by no means dampen players' militance or that it would, in some respects, actually aggravate it. During the life of this three-year contract, much to the surprise of the Association, the polarization between it and the players became even more extreme. To understand how this could happen at a time when the musicians had apparently gained a major objective in guaranteed annual pay, one must turn to Edward Arian's discussion of the musicians' attitudes, which are the subject of the last portion of his study *Bach, Beethoven, and Bureaucracy.*

Though Arian's definition of the bureaucratization of the Philadelphia Orchestra in the post-Stokowski period has been questioned here, the conditions he describes in formulating that concept played an important part in the development of the musicians' sense of alienation from their work. Himself a bass player in the orchestra from 1947 to 1967, Arian describes this process from the point of view of the musicians and as reflected upon in academic terms. In his account, Arian reviews all of the factors previously described as contributing to player militance, with specific reference to his own experience in the orchestra during the time in question. Moreover, for the crucial period between 1963 and 1966, he attended most meetings of the orchestra players and had access to the minutes of these and orchestra committee meetings.[19]

Less than a year after signing the 1963 contract, the orchestra members repudiated the committee which had negotiated it, replacing it with players drawn from the minority who had voted against its ratification. Against the advice of their own lawyers, the players also drastically revised the bylaws governing committee procedures in the interests of greater "democracy," sharply curtailing committee authority to act on behalf of the orchestra and specifically forbidding the committee to meet with management or with a liaison committee of board members as specified in the 1963 contract. Thus deprived of essential contact with the players, management encountered increasing difficulty in discussing important implementations and modifications of the basic agreement. A major problem arose from the abandonment of the Poconos project in favor of accepting the invitation of the Saratoga Festival in 1966; the contract of 1963 had been drawn with the Poconos in mind and required modification to meet the special conditions at Saratoga. Though this involved relatively minor changes,* management was unable even to get any firm answer from the players for a considerable period, and finally the local union stepped in to settle the matter.

Hostility was further intensified when the players discovered the full implications of the "anti-moonlighting" provision of the contract. When the orchestra's concertmaster, Anshel Brusilow, resigned to organize his own chamber orchestra, he was not allowed to engage players from the Philadelphia Orchestra. Though for many players the increased income under a fifty-two-week contract ($12,400 guaranteed minimum per year by 1965–66) more than made up for the loss of outside employment, many of the better players in the orchestra, whose services were in demand for nonsymphonic work, found themselves losing money under the new arrangement. In any event, the general feeling developed throughout the orchestra that the fifty-two-week contract had turned out to be a poor deal. Moreover, despite the improved security of a fifty-two-week contract, many players came to resent being limited professionally to the symphonic repertory in their artistic efforts.†

As direct liaison between the players and management broke down, all of these issues engendered increased hostility toward the Association, whose good faith the players came increasingly to denounce. On one occasion, when a militant candidate for the orchestra committee chairmanship was under consideration, an otherwise moderate orchestra member was heard to state, "Let's turn him loose on the Association and see what he can do." As meetings of the orchestra more and more took over the function of committee authority, attendance at these meetings declined: fewer than forty members participated in most of them, and some twenty-seven players initiated seventy-seven percent of the topics considered during a sample period studied by Arian.[21]

These players and the elected committee members were drawn from what Arian defines as the most alienated portion of orchestra membership. Most of them were players who received minimum salary, as opposed to first-desk and other artistically important overscale musicians. A very large proportion of these most alienated players were from the string sections, musicians who, unlike principal players, have no opportunity for individual expression and who feel condemned to spend their lives in professional obscurity. Though many of these players undoubtedly benefited financially from the fifty-two-week contract, they suffered most in such artistic respects. At the same time, the group pride and morale in the Philadelphia Orchestra had its counterpart in a deep sense of resentment, aimed at the Association and aggravated by intense alienation from their work. This love-hate relation-

---

* One problem here, as in other labor-management situations, is that one side may well see the merit of the other's request, but hold off granting it in order to extract a *quid pro quo* concession in other areas.

† When Arian was asked why he had left the Philadelphia Orchestra, he replied, "When I found myself playing the fourth movement of Brahms's First Symphony for the hundred-and-first time and couldn't remember playing the first movement, I knew I had had enough." [20]

ship * produced an irrational anger that erupted in the bitter work stoppage of 1966, for by the time negotiations began in the spring of that year the most militant faction of the orchestra was in full control, and few of the more moderate players dared to risk the ostracism they would provoke by expressing opposition. (Moreover, the experience of the past decade had demonstrated to even the most conservative orchestra musician that a militant stance produced far greater material gains than moderation ever had.)

Though official liaison between the musicians and the Association had broken down, the latter knew that it faced tempestuous negotiations in the spring of 1966,[22] and many directors were bewildered at what they felt was the completely unreasonable and ungrateful attitude of the players in response to the full-year contract of three years earlier. Furthermore, though the orchestra's operation in the year prior to the 1963 negotiations had shown an appreciable surplus, the cost of the fifty-two-week contract was causing a loss. The board felt that it had gone as far as it could in the 1963 contract in making major concessions, and many of its members believed that the time had come to take a strong stand and to curb the musicians. From the beginning, negotiations were conducted in an atmosphere of distrust and hostility. At the first meeting, both sides agreed not to ventilate their respective positions publicly. Unfortunately, Balis had not attended that meeting and was unaware of this agreement: upon inquiry from the press, he replied with a typically conservative statement to the effect that the Association could not afford to meet the players' demands, and the orchestra musicians immediately took this as a breach of faith at the very outset of bargaining.

Despite wide differences between the musicians' demands and management's offers in matters of pay, vacations, touring services, and fringe benefits, the major obstacle to consideration of these issues was deeply psychological. The board considered the players' insistence on reducing touring to be more than a simple matter of working conditions: in challenging a fundamental phase of the orchestra's success, it was viewed as interference in basic policy. Some board members were tempted to stand fast on such issues, even if this necessitated suspending operations for a season. The determination to break the back of players' militance on the part of some board members had its counterpart among a minority of musicians who, considering the Association incompetent to run the orchestra, would have welcomed its demise and the assumption of sponsorship of the orchestra by a new group more favorably disposed toward the players' cause. There was, in fact, a real fear in the board that an effort would be made at the annual meeting of the Association to challenge its leadership;[23] this threat did not materialize, though there were rumors that outside contributions of as much as $500,000 would back it.

Negotiations reached an impasse well before the scheduled opening of the season in September, and the Association rejected the players' offer to perform while negotiating, provided that any settlement reached would be

---

* Arian's description of alienation in this orchestra only touches the surface of a phenomenon that should be of interest to students of group psychology. Some of the broader implications of Arian's concept are discussed in more general terms in Chapter XIX.

made retroactive to the beginning of the season.* While the stoppage continued to receive increasing publicity throughout the community and became a matter of broad public concern, Leopold Stokowski led the orchestra in a special strike-fund concert on October 14 in Convention Hall for an audience of nine thousand people, commenting favorably on the acoustics achieved by the use of a special shell there and arousing considerable resentment among the Association's directors, who had long staunchly rejected suggestions that the orchestra could reach more of the populace of Philadelphia by playing regularly in Convention Hall. By early November, it was obvious that a pay package could be worked out, but that the real stumbling blocks were the matter of work load and the intense hostility of both sides. The situation was therefore ripe for responsible intervention by outside forces. Early in November, Mayor James H. J. Tate appointed a board of public accountability, first to determine the facts at issue and then to mediate on their basis. His three-man board included his own labor consultant S. Harry Galfand, F. Bruce Baldwin of Abbott Dairies, and Dr. George W. Taylor, a professor at the University of Pennsylvania who was a nationally recognized labor expert.†

After hearing both sides, the mayor's mediators formulated recommendations that shortly became the basis for agreement after a fifty-eight-day stoppage. The musicians won less than a third of their pay demands, elimination of the "moonlighting" prohibition, progressive restrictions on touring and scheduling, and substantial improvement in fringe benefits, especially in pensions.‡ Though the added cost of weekly salary to the Association was not extreme, other concessions, such as those on touring and benefits, concealed increases in cost. Though the players had gained little in limiting their work load, they laid the basis for future bargaining on this matter. However, the stoppage was very costly to the players: prior to the establishment of the fifty-two-week contract, whenever there had been a work stoppage at the beginning of the season, the Association had rescheduled lost performances later in the season; without spare time in the full-year contract, this was not possible in 1966–67, and the players lost a major portion of their income for over eight weeks.

* Orchestra associations in general have been reluctant to accept such play-and-negotiate offers from their players for fear that a strike will be called without notice; from their point of view, such arrangements are impossible to accept because of contractual commitments with conductors and soloists and obligations to subscribers. Managements point to such deferred settlements as that of the Metropolitan Opera, when postponed bargaining nearly prevented the 1966 opening of the new opera house in Lincoln Center. However, managements' fear of continued operation "under the gun" can sometimes be allayed when players accompany such play-and-negotiate offers with a promise to serve reasonable notice before calling a strike.
† Taylor was author of the New York State law covering labor relations with government employees which bears his name.
‡ The Philadelphia Orchestra had no pension plan for its players before 1943. As of the 1968–69 season, a musician retiring at 65, with at least 25 years of service, could expect approximately $4,000 a year for the rest of his life.[24] (Retirement at 65 is obligatory, a bitter requirement to many players who have seen such colleagues as flutist William Kincaid forced out of the orchestra while still in command of his instrument.) The pension income has improved slightly in recent years, and the importance of this issue in the 1972 negotiations was indicated by the players' retention of the legal services of I. Philip Sipser, who is not only a skillful negotiator but an expert in pension programs.

In its fact-finding report, the mayor's board of public accountability deplored the deterioration of personnel relations in the Philadelphia Orchestra. Among their most urgent recommendations was a liaison committee that would bring representatives of the board and players together regularly for meaningful exchange of views and information apart from the bargaining process itself. As eventually set up, this liaison committee explicitly excluded the manager, conductor, and several board members whose past participation in negotiations had aroused personal animosities with the musicians. Selected as chairman of this committee was Henry W. Sawyer III, a member of an oldtime Philadelphia law firm, but a man of liberal political opinion and keen intelligence; known in Association circles as the "board Democrat," Sawyer's activity in the Eugene McCarthy campaign in 1968 and his public opposition to the Vietnam war gained him considerable respect among the musicians. Under Sawyer's leadership, this liaison committee now meets as informally as possible, often in a private hotel dining room, for cocktails, dinner, and relaxed discussion. Though this committee may not take specific action, information exchanged at its meetings is often communicated to the orchestra players or union, on the one hand, or to the manager, conductor, or board as a whole, on the other. In some instances, minor irritations on either side are clarified and mitigated. From conversations with several orchestra members, it is evident that even now the musicians approach their participation with considerable suspicion; however, board representatives feel that they have learned a great deal about the players' point of view, although they doubt if they have made much headway in modifying it.

Though recommended in 1966, this committee was not set up early enough to have much effect on the 1969 negotiations, which were concluded with greater dispatch and less acrimony than any in the past twenty years, undoubtedly because both the Association and the players had suffered such damage in 1966.[25] A smaller negotiating group took part; union officials did not even attend the early crucial sessions in which the foundation was laid for settlement. From the beginning, both the Association and the players agreed that the new contract should establish working conditions as good as any in the country, on the assumption that the Philadelphia Orchestra, as the nation's finest, should treat its musicians accordingly. Thus the first step was to study the contracts of other orchestras—available to the players through ICSOM and to the Association through management contacts—to select from them the features that would meet these basic criteria. The contract was settled, approved by the union and Association, and ratified by the musicians in an atmosphere devoid of crisis, before the season opened.

The Philadelphia Orchestra faced its next contract negotiations in the spring and summer of 1972. From its well-established liaison with the players, the Association knew that the players would be represented by a tough-minded committee, still drawn from the alienated segment of the orchestra.[26] There were indications that work loads and pensions would again be major issues. The most outspoken members of the orchestra still expressed great hostility toward the Association, feeling that management and the board had not done enough to raise money and expand services into areas which would attract more government and foundation money. These musicians recall with deep resentment the occasion in 1965 when Roger G. Hall, then manager of the orchestra, testified at Congressional hearings in opposition to government support of the arts; as late as 1968, Bond expressed the same feeling in an interview with Arian.[27] To the players such opposition represented a dog-in-the-manger fear of sharing power and responsibility with others outside the Social Register establishment.*

Considerable personal hostility is still directed at specific individuals on the board, and there is a tendency on the part of many player spokesmen to revive old grievances long since settled.† Generally speaking, the musicians have an inflated notion of the wealth of the directors themselves and of the ease of raising money. They also overestimate the potential audience for symphonic music in Philadelphia, contending that if concerts were given in Convention Hall, the overall seasonal attendance could be more than tripled.‡

Reorganizing the Board

In 1966, the Philadelphia Orchestra Association faced another serious challenge at the very time that its labor negotiations approached a disastrous crisis. After several years of preliminary exploration, the Ford Foundation had announced, in October, 1965, a large-scale program of endowment and sustaining grants to over sixty American orchestras, totaling in excess of $80 million. The Foundation offered the Philadelphia Orchestra a $2 million participation in a trust fund and $100,000 a year for five years, on condition that it raise another $4 million for its endowment. With the conservative thinking that dominated its financial outlook, the board seriously considered turning down the Ford Foundation offer,[28] although it knew that in doing so it would not only antagonize the Philadelphia community but make its position *vis-à-vis* the players untenable. On the other hand, there is no question that the Association's acceptance of this grant sharply whetted the appetite of the players for their share of the bounty. In this quandary, the board engaged the services of the George A. Brakeley Company, a management consultant and fund-raising firm specializing in educational and other nonprofit activities, to make a comprehensive study of the Association's position.

The Brakeley staff interviewed literally scores of Philadelphians, both in and out of the Association, and had full access to its files on finances, board

---

* The long-standing reluctance of symphony boards in general to seek major government aid was dispelled only in 1969 with the organization of Partnership for the Arts; see Chapter XV.

† In the fall of 1970, for instance, one player gave an emotional account of an occasion on which the players were forced to take a cut in pay while the conductor received a raise. When asked about the specific conductor in question, the player readily identified him as Stokowski; the incident had occurred during the depression in the early 1930s.

‡ The 1972 negotiations were concluded before the season opened in September; they resulted in a substantial increase in minimum pay over the next three years (to over $20,000 a year), major modifications of the pension program, and additional changes in working conditions.

minutes, and internal documents. Its report, rendered in 1967, recommended that the Association not only accept the foundation's challenge offer but increase its capital goal to $10 million. However, in making this recommendation, the consultants presented what is reported to have been a devastating criticism of virtually every aspect of the Association's activity save the musical leadership of Ormandy. So drastic was the first draft of this report that it was seen only by a few key leaders, a modified version being prepared for the board in general. Among other recommendations, the Brakeley report called for an expansion of the board to include full representation of the social and financial resources of the community, a more community-oriented outlook and public image, and a substantial effort to improve relations with the players. Finally it recommended that the expanded campaign for capital funds, as well as for annual sutaining contributions, be conducted by professional management.

As a result of this report, the board was restructured with new membership * and change of nominal leadership. For the first time in its history, the Association brought into its fold representatives of the wealthy and influential segment of the Jewish community. Balis was elected chairman of the board, his post as president being taken by Richard C. Bond, head of the Wanamaker department store and a strong leader in civic affairs. Bond has since been active in mobilizing business and financial support for the orchestra and promoting its relations with other civic activities. His prominence in AMERIPORT (Ports of Philadelphia) played a part in that organization's sponsoring the 1970 European tour of the orchestra. Balis, for his part, freely admits his limitations as a large-scale fund-raiser, preferring to concern himself with the orchestra's artistic activities.[29]

To secure the professional management of its capital-fund campaign, the board hired John D. Healy, a vice-president of the Brakeley firm who had been in charge of its original study. With a complete knowledge of the problems faced by the Association, and with expertise in fund-raising, Healy proved to be an exceptionally able professional organizer of this development program. Once the success of the capital-fund drive was assured,† he added to the development activity a permanent annual sustaining-fund drive, utilizing the organization of volunteers involved in the capital drive.

In this respect, the role of Healy becomes very important in the affairs of the Philadelphia Orchestra. The distinct separation between orchestra management and fund-raising, between the responsibilities of Sokoloff as manager and Healy as director of development, is sharper in Philadelphia than in many other orchestras. Both functions are closely coordinated, not only at the board level but also by daily liaison between the two men on many matters of financial and promotional planning. However, Healy represents the introduction into traditional symphony administration of a new type of pro-

---

* However, the board remained primarily representative of the inner Social Register element of the community establishment. Arian, in his analysis of board membership cited earlier, presents data showing that though new blood was brought onto the board at this time, most of it was still as blue as it ever had been.

† As of late 1971, the capital drive had raised over $5 million.

fessional expertise, based less on arts administration than on general concepts of business management and development derived from the broader field of philanthropy and counseling. The Brakeley report of 1967 included some specific criticisms of administration, and Sokoloff and Healy have conferred together on implementing changes in this area. Superficially, development and orchestra operation might seem to be distinct functions, but, in the larger sense, development cannot succeed without a product to sell, without concern for artistic performance and its management; nor can these objectives be attained without the secure financial base achieved by professionally directed funding. It is interesting to note that Healy has recently been given, in addition to his development duties, important executive responsibilities in the management of the Academy of Music and in planning and financing the proposed new commercial structure on property to the rear of the Academy.

Tension in Contingencies

As it approaches its seventy-fifth anniversary, the Philadelphia Orchestra retains the aura and glamour that its conductors and board leadership have assiduously developed in the past six decades. Yet, beneath the surface, tensions are at work that may well provoke major changes in this orchestra in the not too distant future. Some individuals in authority and responsibility are quite aware of these tensions and are giving constructive thought to the contingencies they will raise. At the same time, there is apparently no long-range planning coordinating the insights of these diverse personnel, and there remain staunchly conservative forces within the Association that will resist even the contemplation of major change. To a large extent, these conservative forces are strengthened in their position by the continued tenure of Ormandy as musical director; all too often, when an innovative proposal is brought up, the answer is: "Well, we can't really get into that as long as Gene is around."

Yet pressing problems remain. The board of directors faces the prospect, in the next decade, of having to raise a million dollars a year in contributions, a task that will require a more comprehensive mobilization of community resources than has previously been attempted. The hostile polarization between the board and the musicians must be modified from both sides, to establish a dialogue reaching beyond immediate problems and opening the way for the musicians to contribute their artistic experience to constructive consideration of some of the major problems that this orchestra, like others, will face in the near future.* If the Association, for its part, guards its prerogatives conservatively and jealously, the musicians have been all too deaf to an appreciative understanding of the contemporary realities of symphonic life, pre-

---

* The possible role of the players in developing policy will be encountered in many aspects before receiving general consideration in Chapter XIX.

ferring still to think and talk in the labor-union stereotypes of the 1930s. In discussions with players, management, and board members, it was heartening to find a few expressing hope of achieving such constructive dialogue, but disappointing to find less expression of this desire among the musicians than in the board and management. The Association has taken some steps toward reducing polarization and certain members see the necessity for further advances, but, so far at least, these steps have not broken down the intense suspicion and hostility in many of the players. Moreover, it is possible that the musicians' sense of alienation can never be overcome and put to constructive artistic use without some sort of restructuring of the work load and the type of musical activity required of them. Yet, when proposals for splitting the orchestra into smaller groups for school concerts are advanced, many musicians respond that such ideas are "not worthy of the Philadelphia Orchestra."

The implementation of such proposals runs into opposition from those who cling to the present structure of the orchestra's activity. To a very large degree the orchestra remains quite apart from the larger community of the fourth-largest metropolitan urban area in the nation. Its audience, even at Robin Hood Dell, is nowhere as extensive as that of the New York Philharmonic in its concerts in the public parks. Nor has the Philadelphia Orchestra found time in a busy schedule of concerts and tours to develop in quantity or quality anything like the education program for the community's youth that an urban area of this kind deserves; its liaison with one of the more musically progressive public-education systems is minimal at best. Despite lip service to the idea of broadening its board of directors to include wider community representation, it remains basically dominated by downtown business, investment, and banking executives. Its womens' committees, for all their contribution of funds and concern for youth programs, remain a Social Register group, whose exclusivity is preserved through membership by invitation only.

Ormandy remains the symbol of the cohesive force and stability for which the Philadelphia Orchestra stands today. Despite important changes in the board and the polarization between the Association and the musicians, Ormandy's three and a half decades of direction have been a source of continuity through periods of conflict and crisis. Philadelphians look with pride on the accomplishments of their own orchestra, but they also contemplate the future with some apprehension when they observe the changes that have affected the whole concept of musical leadership in such orchestras as those of New York, Boston, Cleveland, and Chicago. Ormandy himself recognized this concern when he reviewed the qualifications to be expected of his successor:

The conductor who comes here should be an outstanding, well-rounded musician, even if he's only thirty years old. . . . He should remember that Philadelphia is a conservative city but that it likes to look forward. . . . He should be prepared to stay—I don't think the board of directors would engage a man, even today, even with the fifty-two-week season, who would want to conduct less than half the season. He should make up his mind that this is his home, this is where he belongs. He should be willing to become a leader in the community. All of that combined would make the kind of conductor who should take over the Philadelphia Orchestra.[30]

If Ormandy here seems to call for a successor cast in his own mold, he undoubtedly also reflects the hopes of the board of directors. Everyone agrees that as long as Ormandy wants to conduct, there is no question of his remaining at his post in Philadelphia; and no one who knows Ormandy expects him to retire as long as he can perform or to share artistic responsibility with another man. The transition, when it comes, will therefore be an abrupt one. But the kind of conductor that Ormandy calls for may well be a thing of the past, at least so far as our greatest orchestras are concerned. The Philadelphia Orchestra may have to accept a quite different type of leadership than it has known for six decades of glory. At the same time, the forces at work under the surface, so far held in check in part by the innate conservatism of the Association and in part by the stabilizing force of Eugene Ormandy, may well erupt during this transition and provoke another time of decision and crisis.

The Philadelphia Orchestra has confronted, often more intensely than in other orchestras, issues of great and pervasive importance throughout the American symphonic institution during the past decade and a half. If many of the problems faced in Philadelphia seem at first glance peculiar to that city alone, most differences from other orchestras will actually prove to be only of emphasis and degree. The significance of the Philadelphia Orchestra is that it has met these major problems while building and maintaining a performing ensemble of extraordinary quality. If its experience offers helpful lessons to other orchestras, these in turn may well be developing solutions from which the Philadelphia Orchestra can learn during the next decades.

CHAPTER VIII

Utah Symphony Orchestra

At their Symphony Symposium meeting in the fall of 1969, representatives of the American Federation of Musicians and the International Conference of Symphony and Opera Musicians faced an unusual and unprecedented problem.[1] On the agenda of the meeting was an appeal by the players in the Utah Symphony Orchestra from rulings by the AFM, supported by ICSOM, effectively ending an extensive program of recording that had since 1957 produced over sixty-five long-playing records and had spread the renown of the Utah Symphony on a national and international scale enjoyed by none but the very largest American orchestras. To make these recordings, the players in the orchestra had all accepted less than the national scale established by the recording industry and the Federation; after allowing this exception for many years, the Federation, in the spring of 1969, had advised the Utah Symphony players that they could no longer record at less than basic scale. The problem facing the ICSOM and AFM representatives was that the players, to present their case, had unanimously chosen as sole spokesman their musical director, Maurice Abravanel, whom many at this meeting considered to be a representative of management rather than of the players. Despite an effort to bar Abravanel, successfully opposed by AFM president Herman Kenin, the Utah conductor was finally allotted ten minutes at the very end of the agenda; he spoke for forty-five, and with such eloquence that after the meeting he received oral assurances from Kenin personally that the Utah Symphony's recording program could proceed as an exception to the established rules of the AFM.

Given the orientation of ICSOM, it is hardly surprising that they viewed as incredible the members of a major professional orchestra selecting their conductor to represent them in such a matter. But to anyone who knows the extraordinary relationship Maurice Abravanel has established with his orchestra in Salt Lake City, it seems only natural that his players wanted him as their spokesman. For Abravanel, since going to Salt Lake City in 1947, was the driving force which created one of this nation's most remarkable symphonic institutions in a city that presented both unusual challenges and a unique community setting. Essentially, the Utah Symphony today is the product of the interaction between a conductor of international stature and the center of Mormonism. Headquartered in a metropolitan area of nearly 560,000 [2] and in a state with less than twice that population, the Utah Symphony operates on a scale considerably exceeding that population base: though Salt Lake City ranks sixty-third in metropolitan population, its orchestra ranks twentieth in budget and activity.

Between the end of August, 1970, and early July, 1971, the Utah Symphony Orchestra gave 173 performances—symphony concerts, youth concerts, ballet and opera productions, and the governor's ball—not only in its home state but also in six other states, the District of Columbia, and in ten Latin-American countries.[3] The tour to South and Central America was the second international journey taken by this orchestra; both the 1971 tour and a 1966 trip to Europe were made without any assistance from the State Department funds for culural activities abroad. Moreover, though touring within the United States was in 1970–71 confined to six states close to Utah, the orchestra has, in other years, traveled more extensively, especially west of the Mississippi. These travels and the international distribution of its recordings have made it one of the best known of American orchestras.

All this was accomplished on a budget of $1.2 million in the 1970–71 season. Of this, the Utah Symphony earns from ticket sales, concert fees, educational services, and state and foundation grants for specific projects some $803,000, or about sixty-three percent of its total budget. To defray its portion of its operating deficit, the orchestra raised $196,000 in sustaining contributions, one of the lowest proportions of total budget in any Category C orchestra. To a large degree, this has been possible because the players have been willing, and even anxious, to work harder and to make immediate financial sacrifices in the interest of long-term gains; their unanimous acceptance of below-scale recording pay is only an instance of a more general attitude. That they are willing to do so must be attributed both to faith in their conductor and to the unique Mormon ethic that dominates the community in which a large proportion of the players have been brought up.

The state of Utah, of which Salt Lake City is the capital, has been described as a theocracy, and many observers have commented upon the manner in which the religious force of Mormonism pervades every activity of the area.[4] Yet this force is exercised, especially as regards the Utah Symphony, primarily in an indirect manner—through the individuals themselves rather than by the religious institutions, powerful as they are in the affairs of Utah. Except for a one-time gift to the endowment fund raised to match the Ford Foundation grant of 1966, the Mormon Church itself makes no direct financial contribution to the support of the Utah Symphony, though by making available such church facilities as the Tabernacle for concerts at no charge, it donates substantially in kind to the operation of the orchestra.

However, the Church of the Latter-Day Saints strongly contributes to the success of the Utah Symphony through a religious ethic pervading the life of all of its practicing members and influencing the outlook of nonmember Gentiles. The state of Utah was settled in 1847, under the leadership of

Brigham Young, by a group of religiously inspired men and women fervently dedicated to good works and community responsibility, who believed with equal conviction that their devotion would receive material reward in this world. The same faith that moved an early pioneer to give up a good farm near Salt Lake City, at the behest of Brigham Young, to settle in a remote part of the state and spread the Mormon gospel still activates the civic responsibility of the players in the Utah Symphony. Where six thousand young people each year leave home to serve for two years as missionaries throughout the world, the notion of giving up present comforts for community service is a basic mode of life. Since their earliest days under the inspiration of Joseph Smith, the Mormons have been devoted to education and self-improvement: Utah claims among its population the highest proportion of high-school and college graduates of any state in the Union. Once the community accepted the importance of a major symphony orchestra to their cultural well-being, it also accepted the responsibility for maintaining it, not necessarily with lavish financial contributions but with individual effort and help. Such support has grown only gradually in the past quarter of a century, inspired to a large degree by the self-sacrificing leadership of a foreign-born musician, Maurice Abravanel.

Maurice Abravanel

Maurice Abravanel was admirably equipped by training, experience, and temperament for his role in building the Utah Symphony Orchestra. Born in 1903 of a Sephardic family in Saloniki, then still under Turkish rule, Abravanel is a descendant of the great statesman Don Isaac Abravanel, who served as chancellor to the court of Ferdinand and Isabella in 15th century Spain before the expulsion of the Sephardim in 1492. While he was still a young man his family moved to Lausanne, Switzerland, where he grew up and, at his family's behest, entered the university to study medicine. But, both in the university and before, Abravanel was always attracted to music, primarily as an amateur but increasingly as a professional performer. As a young man in Lausanne, he became acquainted with the new music of Bloch, Honegger, and Stravinsky; he recalls vividly the premiere in Lausanne of the latter's *Histoire du soldat*. His formal education, however, did not include any extensive musical training; this he picked up on the side. Thus, when he decided definitely to pursue a musical career, he was not equipped with the technical background to qualify him for acceptance by a conservatory. Fortunately, a musician friend who also knew Busoni sought the latter's advice on behalf of Abravanel. Busoni recommended that the young man study privately in Berlin with one of his most talented pupils, Kurt Weill, with whom Abravanel established a close friendship and professional collaboration. Gradually Abravanel moved up the professional ladder through which young conductors gained experience in the opera houses of Germany during the 1920s, eventually arriving at the theaters of Berlin. On the way, he also began to conduct orchestral concerts; his first role as symphonic conductor was in Mecklenburg-Strelitz, when he volunteered to direct the players of the opera orchestra in a series of popular concerts after the local theater had been destroyed by fire. Leaving Germany in 1933, he conducted ballet in Paris and opera in Australia. On the recommendation of Bruno Walter and Wilhelm Furtwängler, Abravanel was engaged in 1936 by Edward Johnson, then just beginning his tenure at the Metropolitan Opera in New York. In two active seasons there, he conducted operas from the French, German, and Italian repertory, ignoring the traditional lines of specialization then prevalent in that house. Possibly because other conductors felt threatened by the ambitions of this versatile young man, Abravanel became embroiled in internal conflicts at the Metropolitan and, in 1938, was happy to accept the invitation of his old friend and teacher Kurt Weill to become musical director of the Broadway production of *Knickerbocker Holiday;* in succeeding years he served in the same capacity for several other Weill productions.

Nevertheless, Abravanel by no means relished being stuck in the Broadway pit and, under the management of Arthur Judson, sought more musically rewarding symphonic outlets for his talent; through Judson he obtained a few guest engagements with American orchestras during the war years. At one point, he refused Judson's urgent recommendation that he accept the post of music director at Radio City Music Hall, at a salary then far in excess of anything he could expect in the symphonic field. In 1947 the opening he hoped for developed in Salt Lake City, where the recommendation of Bruno Walter again played an important part in his being offered a contract.

Shortly after accepting the Utah post, he received an invitation from Houston, which he turned down, partly because Salt Lake City's location beneath the towering Wasatch Mountains reminded him of his childhood home in Switzerland; both Seattle and Vancouver, B.C., also approached him during his early years in Utah.

Arriving in Salt Lake City to open his first season in the fall of 1947, Abravanel found an orchestra and community sorely bruised by the birth pangs of the emergent orchestra. Two years earlier, the symphony board had attempted to make long-range plans to convert a relatively unstable organization growing out of a WPA-sponsored group into a permanent professional orchestra. Werner Janssen had been the previous conductor, importing from Los Angeles a substantial number of players for key positions; these importations not only created a considerable financial burden but also aroused resentment among the resident players, who were paid less than the imports. Like many others new to Utah, Abravanel expected the theocratic Mormon Church to provide appreciable financial and promotional support for the orchestra, and in his early days in Salt Lake City aroused some indignation among the Mormon community by his rather frank criticism of the failure of the church in this respect. The governing board of the orchestra at this time was essentially non-Mormon, being dominated to a large extent by Mrs. John M. Wallace, a wealthy and generous patroness of the arts in Utah, who still takes an active interest in the orchestra and in the excellent Ballet West company headed by William Christensen.

After an artistically successful first season, in which the orchestra contributed to the centennial celebration of the settlement of Utah, Abravanel faced a serious economic problem. For some time the state of Utah had, through its Institute of Fine Arts, given modest financial support to the orchestra, and early in 1949 the orchestra board sought to defray its accumulated deficit of fifty thousand dollars and its prospective loss for the following season with an appeal to the state legislature for a subsidy of a hundred thousand dollars. After considerable negotiation with the legislative leaders, both houses passed a bill appropriating a reduced one-year subsidy of forty thousand dollars, but Governor J. Bracken Lee vetoed the bill, and the legislature, under pressure from the governor, failed to pass it over his veto. In the ensuing financial crisis, the symphony board first decided to cancel the remainder of the season, but encountered Abravanel's strong contention that the orchestra had an obligation both to audience and players to complete it. To fail in that obligation, he argued, would mean the end of symphonic music in Utah for years to come. While prodding the board, he also persuaded the players to forgo their salaries if necessary to keep the orchestra going, proposed to take a cut in his own salary, and to give up even the reduced amount completely as long as the players were not paid. Finally, he negotiated an arrangement whereby the board agreed to raise an emergency fund and the players agreed to continue playing without salary until funds from this pledge and ticket revenues were sufficient to pay them whatever was possible. In both cases, Abravanel successfully appealed to the basic Mormon principle of making present sacrifices for future benefits. Once the crisis of 1949 was overcome, Abravanel worked to place the Utah Symphony on a firm foundation, if on the more limited scale suited to the restricted funds.*

In the years that followed, the orchestra gradually grew and prospered, making progress from year to year based on a sound estimate of available resources. To a very large extent Abravanel became in these years virtually sole business as well as artistic director. In anticipation of each season, he reached an agreement with the governing board on precisely how much in sustaining contributions could be expected, himself estimated ticket and other revenue, and submitted a budget accordingly. A major portion of that budget inevitably reflected musicians' salaries, and Abravanel set the scale that the orchestra could afford and the pay of each individual player. At the same time, he was deeply conscious of the importance of making his orchestra indispensable to Salt Lake City and to the state of Utah. He wisely gave up, for the time being, explicit agitation for increased state funds, and concentrated on gaining audience and communiy support for the orchestra by building it soundly as a performing organization, developing its repertory, and expanding its activity both in and out of Salt Lake City. He early developed a close working relationship with the University of Utah, both in placing key members of the orchestra on its music faculty and in developing special programs—often of contemporary or unusual repertory—for the more sophisticated university audience. Recalling local hostility to Janssen's efforts to import more

---

* His own salary was not restored to the pre-1949 level until 1952.

than twenty players in one season, he proceeded slowly in hiring outside musicians to strengthen the orchestra in key positions. He also worked with the university to establish a resident opera company, both to broaden the musical repertory for the community and to provide additional employment for the symphony players; later he played a role in the organization of Ballet West, for whose performances the symphony provided an orchestra.

Statewide, he progressively increased the touring activity of the orchestra, at first to such major centers as Ogden and Brigham Young University at Provo and then into smaller communities. Such has been the success of this touring program throughout Utah that the orchestra has actually played for an audience of over a thousand in a town with an official population of eight hundred. At first such tours were undertaken at considerable sacrifice on the part of the players, who received nothing comparable to the out-of-town fees paid players in other touring orchestras, but gradually these tours provided better income for the players. An integral part of the activity, both in Salt Lake City and in touring, has been the presentation of concerts for children in the schools. Here the orchestra benefited from the Mormon policy of building and maintaining good public-school facilities and from the pervasive concern for self-improvement. In Salt Lake City, this educational activity was coordinated with Abravanel's efforts to place orchestra players as music teachers in the schools, and he has adjusted the orchestra schedules to facilitate this outside employment, at the same time persuading the school officials to permit the orchestra-player teachers to work irregular hours.

Abravanel has worked with extraordinarily persuasive and diplomatic skill. He has become a leading citizen in Salt Lake City and the state of Utah, effectively and socially at home with its business and political leaders at every level. He has accepted such civic assignments as heading the Community Fund drive and serving at the governor's invitation as chairman of United Nations Day. To all of this he brings a selfless devotion, not only to his orchestra but also to the community in which he lives and works. In the rather insular Utahan this courtly and sophisticated foreigner arouses a sense of participating in an important cosmopolitan venture. Abravanel and his wife live in a modest frame house close to the center of Salt Lake City. In its basement the conductor has a spacious study where he works on scores, takes care of orchestra business, holds auditions and soloist rehearsals—one of the focal points of Salt Lake City's cultural life. Upstairs, Mrs. Abravanel may be found in the kitchen, preparing for a meeting of the symphony women's committee.

Maurice Abravanel has by no means confined his outlook to the horizons defined by the Great Salt Lake and the Wasatch Mountains. From time to time he has appeared as guest conductor of other orchestras, but this activity has been further limited by his duties as director of the summer music school at Santa Barbara, where he enjoys among his faculty the collaboration of such artists as Lotte Lehmann. He has been an active member of the American Symphony Orchestra League, serving for many years on its board of directors. His national stature as a major force in American symphonic music was recognized when President Nixon appointed him in October, 1970, to the National Council for the Arts; he had previously served for some years as member of an advisory panel for the National Endowment for the Arts.[5]

Operations and Finances

Though Abravanel in his early days assumed many of the duties of the management of the orchestra, he has relied more and more upon a well-organized staff of management personnel to run it. As the orchestra has prospered, and as its activities have grown both at home and on tour, it was inevitable that he should concentrate his energies increasingly on artistic matters, leaving to management the implementation of procedures and policies long established and developed under his leadership.

Herold L. Gregory has been manager or executive director of the Utah Symphony since 1957.[6] A native of Salt Lake City, he served abroad for six years as a Mormon missionary and in posts administering missionary activities in Europe. Though without formal musical training, his interest in symphonic music was stimulated by exposure to opera, symphony, and recitals during his years abroad. He came to the Utah Symphony Orchestra after a period of considerable friction between his predecessor and Abravanel over what the conductor felt to be the manager's undue limitation of artistic and promotional activities for financial reasons. From the beginning Gregory set out with characteristically quiet competence to work closely with Abravanel, not impinging upon the conductor's prerogatives but still managing the orchestra on a sound business basis. Only gradually, and with great tact and consideration for the conductor's unique status in the community, did he take over many management functions that Abravanel had previously assumed. He has built an able staff with clear definition of responsibility and delegation of authority. One of his key associates is Shirl H. Swenson, a Mormon who had spent some years as an army officer; officially designated as director of development, and more recently as manager, he not only coordinates publicity and fund-raising but also takes charge of touring and a great deal of operational detail. The management staff of the Utah Symphony numbers ten employees, who work in an office located on the ground floor of a small building in the center of the city, convenient to patrons desiring to purchase tickets or conduct symphony business. Inevitably, the store windows on the street front of the office are filled with displays of the orchestra's recordings. On special occasions, such as annual maintenance-fund drives, season-ticket campaigns, or special benefits, the full-time office staff is supplemented by volunteer workers from the women's committee.

As executive director of the orchestra, Gregory is in full charge of negotiations with the major New York managements, both for the engagement of soloists and to arrange tours by the orchestra to areas outside Utah and nearby states, which are scheduled directly by the orchestra. These more extended trips are booked through Columbia Artists Management and its "organized audience" subsidiary, Community Concerts. The established fee for such concerts is $4,500 per concert, and the orchestra pays a commission of twenty percent to CAMI. From the net receipts of such fees it must pay all traveling expenses; the salaries of the players, conductor, and soloists; music rentals and royalties; and must supply the local sponsor of the concert with adequate promotional materials. In the aggregate, direct touring costs (exclusive of players and conductor) of all its out-of-town concerts, whether booked directly or through CAMI, amounted in 1970–71 to $68,398; the net receipts from fees, after deducting commissions, in the same period were $154,097; this "profit" compares favorably with other orchestras. However, should the cost of the players and conductor be deducted from it, there would be a substantial net loss to be absorbed by the overall deficit financing of the orchestra's annual activity.

Additionally, in the summer of 1971, the Utah Symphony tour to Latin America cost $176,976 (exclusive of musicians' and conductor's compensation); this tour produced revenue of $129,029, and the loss of $47,947 was more than made up by special contributions of $86,510 * received from supporters of the orchestra in Salt Lake City and throughout the country, many of them wealthy Mormons living outside Utah. Like other orchestras, the Utah Symphony considers its touring justified on several grounds: only in this way can the orchestra keep its players employed and earning anything like a decent income from symphonic activity; and touring extends the musical services of the orchestra, justifying its existence as a cultural institution.

The total operations of the Utah Symphony Orchestra in 1970–71 cost $1,199,649, the first time that its operating budget has exceeded a million dollars. There is no prospect of any reduction in this figure and every expectation that, even without any increase in activity, annual expenses will continue to grow. Ever since the financial crises growing out of Governor Lee's veto of state support in 1949, the Utah Symphony has managed to operate without appreciable deficit, by virtue of extremely careful budgeting and control of expenses, once a budget has been settled upon. In 1970–71, there was a slight surplus of $3,576, indicative of very accurate fiscal management. Of a total income of $1,203,225, the orchestra earned $803,909 from performance— an extremely high proportion (67%) for an orchestra of any size. Of $399,-315 of contributed income, gifts from individuals and businesses were relatively modest, though less so when one takes into account the special donations to the Latin-American tour.

Individual contributions	$ 31,004
Business contributions	29,865
Contributions in kind	38,150
	$109,019
Latin-American tour contributions	86,510
	$195,529

Financial details for 1970–71 are given in Table 8-A.[7]

* This excess revenue from special contributions did not, however, fully cover the additional musicians' payroll for this Latin-American tour.

TABLE 8-A

UTAH SYMPHONY ORCHESTRA

Financial Summary, 1970–71

INCOME:

Performance:

Ticket sales	$ 143,277 (12%)
Program advertising	24,949
Tours, local and U.S.	154,096 (13%)
Latin-American tour	129,029 (11%)
Recording income	9,620
Other productions	57,608
Grants requiring services	265,422 (22%)
Miscellaneous	19,908
	$ 803,909

Supplemental:

Individual contributions	$ 31,004
Contributions in kind *	38,150
Business and industrial contributions	29,865
Ford Foundation	188,787
Salt Lake County and City	15,000
Utah Symphony Guild (Ball)	10,000
Latin-American tour contributions	86,509
	$ 399,315
TOTAL INCOME	$1,203,225

EXPENSES

Production:

Conductor, musicians, guests	$ 729.263 (60.6%)
Music expense	5,296
Concert production	50,616
Program expense	18,127
Advertising and promotion	29,180
Tour expense (local and U.S.)	68,398
Latin-American tour	176,976
Recording expense	2,720
Other productions	6,879
	$1,087,456 (90.6%)

Administrative:

Salaries	$ 69,362
Office expense	21,438
Ford matching campaign expense	8,984
Miscellaneous	12,409
	$ 112,193 (9.4%)
TOTAL EXPENSE	1,199,649 (100%)
Excess of Income over Expense	$ 3,576

* Contributions in kind include such items as free use of the Tabernacle, the donation of rehearsal facilities, and so on.

The Utah Symphony Orchestra receives a rather high proportion of its income as grants from various government bodies that require rendering special services, mostly educational concerts or innovative projects to develop new audiences or activities. These grants amount to twenty-two percent of the orchestra's total income, as compared with a combined figure of twenty-five percent for concerts in Salt Lake City and on tour in the United States. In this report the Utah Symphony makes no distinction in reporting Ford Foundation income between the final allocation of sustaining grants and interest from trust funds held by the orchestra and by the Foundation's trustee. The termination of the five-year sustaining grant from the Foundation in 1971 will require the orchestra to raise an additional hundred thousand dollars a year if supplemental income is to be maintained at the present level. This means almost doubling private and corporate contributions in the immediate future.

Table 8-B shows how the Utah Symphony compares, in major groupings of income and expense, with the average for the other orchestras in Category C.

Certainly the most extraordinary comparison here is the high percentage of performance income enjoyed by the Utah Symphony—67% against a category average of 49.5%. As we shall note later (Chapter XIII), all but the Category A averages show a generally equal (48% to 52%) distribution

TABLE 8-B

UTAH SYMPHONY ORCHESTRA

Financial Summary, 1970–71, Compared with Category C Averages

INCOME	Utah Symphony	Averages of 12 Category C Orchestras
Performance:		
Concerts and tours	$ 481,782 (40.0%)	$ 418,583 (31.7%)
Other nongovt.	56,705 (4.7%)	35,065 (2.6%)
Govt. for services	265,422 (22.1%)	198,055 (15.0%)
TOTAL PERFORMANCE	$ 803,909 (66.8%)	$ 651,703 (49.3%)
Supplemental:		
Contributions (incl. Ford Foundation grants and income)	$ 384,316 (31.9%)	$ 605,597 (43.2%)
Endowment income (as above)		
Govt. grants	15,000 (1.3%)	64,394 (7.5%)
TOTAL SUPPLEMENTAL	$ 399,316 (33.2%)	$ 669,991 (50.7%)
TOTAL INCOME	$1,203,225 (100%)	$2,321,694 (100%)
Net Income	$ 3,576	
EXPENDITURES		
Artistic personnel	$ 729,263 (60.8%)	$ 859,962 (66.2%)
Concert production	358,193 (29.9%)	264,969 (20.4%)
Administration	112,193 (9.3%)	174,012 (13.4%)
TOTAL EXPENDITURES	$1,199,649 (100%)	$1,298,943 (100%)

between performance and supplemental income, but the Utah Orchestra percentage is equal to the Category A average and only 5% below that of the Philadelphia Orchestra. Each of the three components of performance income is substantially higher than average. Conversely, supplemental income, especially contributions, accounts for a considerably lower proportion of total income. (In Table 8-B it was necessary to combine contribution and endowment income because the Ford Foundation item was not reported in these separate categories.)

One reason why the Utah Symphony enjoys such a favorable relation between performance and supplemental income is that it succeeds in holding its expenses down. A measure of efficiency of operation is the ratio of performance income to total production expense (artistic services and concert production combined): with the Utah Orchestra, performance income is 75% of total production cost, whereas the category average shows 58%. Except for the higher concert production cost (because of the extensive touring by this orchestra), administrative and artistic personnel expenses are well below average—both in dollar amounts and in percentage of total expenditures—due in large part to a substantially lower scale of pay for orchestra players and administrative staff. Minimum pay for the fully employed Utah Symphony musician is just over $7,000 a year (some with contracts calling for fewer services received around $4,700), whereas the Category C average is $8,210.

Another important difference between the Utah Symphony and the Category C average is the higher percentage of government funding: though outright grants are lower, income from services is substantially higher, contrbuting appreciably to overall performance income. Despite the defeat of deficit financing by the state in 1949, the Utah Symphony continued to receive, through the Institute of Fine Arts, modest but increasing state funds, ranging from $6,800 in 1949–50 to $30,000 in 1969–70. However, after the crisis of 1949, the orchestra and Abravanel wisely refrained from further agitation for major state aid, instead arousing grass-roots support through extensive statewide touring, in which youth concerts were an integral part of the local appearances. Eventually, virtually every state legislator was acutely aware of the orchestra's activities in his own district, and when major support for the orchestra was proposed in 1969 by Governor Calvin L. Rampton, the legislature responded enthusiastically; not a voice in either house was raised in opposition. These funds, amounting to over $128,000, are specifically earmarked for school concerts; in 1972–73 the amount will increase to $160,000, so that the orchestra will no longer have to make a charge to the schools themselves for such services. The Rocky Mountain Federation, a regional commission supported partly by state and partly by private funds, contributed $11,150 for the orchestra's interstate touring programs. As noted in the financial report, the orchestra also receives $7,500 each from Salt Lake City and Salt Lake County. In addition, the Utah Symphony received $100,000 from the National Endowment for the Arts, specifically designated for regional touring and educational activities, many beyond the boundaries of the state itself. Thus, in 1970–71, from all government sources, the Utah Symphony Orchestra received:

For services:

National Endowment for the Arts	$100,000
Rocky Mountain Federation	11,150
State of Utah	128,010
Other	26,262

Outright grants:

Salt Lake City	7,500
Salt Lake County	7,500
	$280,422

These funds, most of them designated for specific innovative activities and some (that of the National Endowment) requiring local matching, amounted to slightly over 23% of the total income of the orchestra.

When, in 1965, the Ford Foundation representatives presented their proposals to the Utah Symphony officials, including Abravanel, they originally contemplated an endowment grant of half a million dollars, to be matched by an equal sum raised locally. Largely at Abravanel's insistence, this grant and its accompanying local obligation were doubled, despite the feeling of some that this involved too great a commitment for local fund-raising. However, as in other instances, Abravanel's ambition for his orchestra proved justified, for it met the Ford Foundation commitment by the spring of 1971, raising over a million dollars. Even those who had had misgivings over the size of the 1966 commitment to the Ford Foundation now feel that the high goal set at that time for local matching has proved in the end of benefit to the orchestra. Not only did this goal force the symphony backers to extend themselves in fund-raising to a degree hitherto considered impossible, but the campaign reached a number of substantial donors previously unrepresented among symphony contributors. The leaders in this campaign were careful not to approach potential donors, with the exception of the church itself, with any indication that gifts to this challenge fund were to be considered final or one-time, and they felt that once the pledges were paid in by June, 1971, there remained good possibilities for continued long-term annual support from donors whose resistance was broken down in the Ford Foundation drive.

Should this be the case, the Utah Symphony stands a good chance of improving substantially what has been in the past a relatively small amount of contributions toward its operations. Except for such special efforts as those directed toward underwriting tours of Europe and Latin America, the Utah Symphony has not enjoyed as high a proportion of contributed funds as its overall operations and excellent community status might indicate. One reason for this is the extremely heavy demand made by the Mormon Church on its members both for contributions and for work in raising these. Tithing is one of the basic tenets of the Latter-Day Saints and church work is expected of every member; for many of them, the church comes first and other activities—including fund-raising for the orchestra—receive little attention or financial support. The church itself has not considered the Utah Symphony to be a part of its service, though it has helped indirectly in many ways. Therefore, except for a unique $100,000 gift to the Ford Foundation matching campaign, it has not given direct financial support to the orchestra.

As we have observed, the Utah Symphony's scale of operations compares very favorably to its population base; while the Philadelphia Orchestra's budget represents a per-capita cost of $0.81, the comparable cost for Salt Lake City is $2.15. In annual sustaining contributions, however, the Philadelphia Orchestra receives an average of $0.12, whereas Salt Lake City raises $0.165 per capita. In seeking major contributions, moreover, the Utah Symphony confronts the fact that there is relatively little great wealth in the state. The largest industries—mining and railroads—are national corporations with headquarters elsewhere, and, like most, give relatively little support to the cultural activities of their "provincial" outlets.* Finally, many local businesses that in other cities help orchestras—retail stores, newspapers, banks—are in Salt Lake City often owned by the Church of the Latter-Day Saints.

The Musicians

To a significant degree, the Utah Symphony has been subsidized by its players, though certainly not as much recently as in earlier years. Their annual minimum pay is lower than in other orchestras of similar budget, and the players work a longer season, and play more on tour, than do their counterparts elsewhere. Moreover, all agree that conditions in 1970–71 represent a major improvement in the past decade in their comparative status. The contribution of the musicians, both in the past and at present, is by no means ignored by either the conductor or the governing board, who give high priority to long-range improvement of orchestra pay.

The personnel of the orchestra consists primarily of local residents, plus a few key players who have been "imported" from time to time. Abravanel's efforts to improve the quality of his orchestra required him to bring in as many as eleven players in two of his first three years in Salt Lake City, but thereafter the number of out-of-town players declined to less than five. Moreover, in this process Abravanel succeeded in introducing musicians who actually settled in Salt Lake City as permanent residents: eleven players, originally imported, remain with the orchestra. One of Abravanel's proudest achievements has been the development, over a period of more than a quarter of a century, of young local musicians, trained by other players in the orchestra. Some eighty percent of the members of the orchestra are Mormons, a proportion that reflects the general population of Salt Lake City. The average age of these players is probably lower than that for the nation as a whole—about thirty years. As is the case in many smaller American orchestras, the proportion of women (thirty-two percent) is higher than encountered in the largest cities but comparable to other Category C orchestras.

* As we shall note later, in Chapter XIV, there have been, however, significant changes in corporate attitude toward the arts, which may in the future offer greater hope for orchestras in cities with branch operations of national corporations.

The players in the Utah Symphony are divided into two groups for contractual purposes: an "A" contract (304 services) calls for all performances, including opera, ballet, and youth concerts; the "B" contract (200 services) requires the musician to play only in the symphonic concerts. The distinction between these two groups is, of course, partly qualitative, but there are some "B" players who hold such contracts because outside work or family obligations prevent their playing the nonsymphonic performances. Minimum pay for the thirty-eight-week season is $7,000 for "A" players and $4,700 for "B" players; in addition, the musicians receive extra pay for touring and travel to cover the cost of meals and other expenses. First-desk and other key players, including some with long seniority, receive overscale pay, generally set by Abravanel.

Under these circumstances, many musicians must rely upon some other work to supplement their symphonic income, but the amount and scheduling of rehearsals and concerts severely limit the kind of work open to them. Since ballet and opera performances are included in the "A" contract, strictly musical performance opportunities outside the symphony are scarce; a few players can count on weekend dance or club jobs, but the major portion of them, being string players, have no chance for these. About a third of the orchestra musicians hold teaching jobs in the Salt Lake City public-school system or at the University of Utah. For the professional musician, such teaching work offers far greater artistic satisfaction than nonmusical employment.

The university, which has long included Abravanel among its faculty, benefits from the teaching services of top orchestra players of professional competence that it might not otherwise afford; it recognizes, moreover, that musicians actively engaged in performance often make better teachers than those who are not so deeply involved. The public-school system has found similar advantages in its tie with the orchestra, despite problems of scheduling. Because Abravanel finds this preferable to evening rehearsals when the players are tired, he schedules most of his rehearsals at 8:15 A.M., making it impossible for teachers to report for work until late in the morning. These early morning rehearsals create no major problems for university instructors, whose schedule can be more flexible, but there are mounting pressures on the public-school teachers. Though the school system has apparently been rather lenient in application of teachers' certification to orchestra players, there are indications that other teachers in the system look with some resentment on the special status accorded the music teachers who also play in the Utah Symphony.

Moreover, as the orchestra's season lengthens, especially with tours taking the players away from school jobs for weeks at a time, there is considerable danger that orchestra musicians may be forced out of the public-school system. This will certainly deprive the schools of teachers with special qualities and experience, and may well place the orchestra in the difficult position of making up the income lost to the musicians. Another less tangible but very important advantage of the liaison between the schools and the orchestra is the degree to which the presence of orchestra players as teachers in the schools has stimulated the interest of young people in the symphony orchestra.

Anyone attending the Tabernacle concerts will be impressed by the large number of young people in the audience; orchestra officials estimate that as much as one-third of the subscription audience is aged between eighteen and twenty-three, and many of these young people will be found backstage after the concert, meeting with players in the orchestra whom they knew as teachers in school.

By comparison with other orchestras of similar or larger size, the Utah Symphony is singularly free of militance among its personnel.[8] In part this can be attributed to the ethic of Mormonism, but major credit is due Abravanel. In the first place, Abravanel not only brings to his work a thoroughly sound musical authority and old-world courtliness but also treats his players with consideration and patience. Without relaxing the strict discipline essential to musical leadership, his manner both in rehearsal and away from the podium conveys sincere understanding and sympathy toward his players. On the podium he accepts the limitations of his musicians, knowing what can be expected of each and avoiding pressing them beyond their capabilities. As a result, he not only extracts from them their best effort but builds their affection and respect. Off the podium, he never ceases to display friendly concern for the personal welfare of each and every player. He knows intimately the personal life and problems of each player. This knowledge plays an important role in Abravanel's annual decisions concerning the variations in pay scale among the players, and few question his decisions. It is noteworthy that the Utah Symphony musicians' contract makes no specific provision for tenure or dismissal: the assumption has always been that Abravanel will be eminently fair and considerate in dismissing such players as he feels he must. The players find Abravanel singularly available and responsive to discussions of their personal and professional problems. One of the conductor's fondest boasts is: "Every player in the orchestra knows my unlisted phone number." Many other conductors like to think they are on intimate terms with their players, but very few actually enjoy this relationship to the degree that Maurice Abravanel does.

Like all other professional orchestras, the Utah Symphony is completely unionized. However, the local union itself plays a relatively limited role in the operation of the orchestra. The players themselves have an elected committee which acts as their spokesman *vis-à-vis* the union and the management. Contract negotiations are held annually, and it is said that neither the players nor the union have ever gone into them with a demand for a raise in pay; instead, such bargaining is based on what the management itself proposes as a practical basis for discussion. This does not necessarily mean that there are no issues between the musicians and management, but most of these concern the delicate adjustments of work schedules to the requirements of outside work. To a large degree, these matters are worked out in a preliminary way between the orchestra players' committee and management, which maintains close liaison with Abravanel throughout negotiations. Once an agreement is reached and formally ratified by the players and local union, it provides the framework within which Abravanel determines the designation of "A" and "B" players and those to receive overscale. To a great extent the conductor makes these arrangements directly with the personnel manager, Sheldon Hyde, rather than involving Gregory.

Under these conditions, it is not surprising that, among the Major orchestras, the players of the Utah Symphony are one of the two not represented in ICSOM.* The matter has come up frequently in the past ten years and the players have voted, almost annually, by substantial majorities not to affiliate, though there is a growing sentiment in its favor. Some players predict that the vote will go in favor of joining ICSOM in the next few years, but less out of a feeling of militance than out of a desire to be a part of an important force in the symphonic profession. Many symphony musicians in other states look upon the players in Utah as backward and naïve at best or, at worst, as "scabs." These players are critical not only of the willingness of the Utah musicians to accept the limitations of pay imposed on them by their management, and to work longer hours for less pay than in other orchestras, but also of the recording program of the Utah Symphony, in which they feel that the Utah players are competing unfairly with the larger orchestras.

Recording and Repertory

The recording program of the Utah Symphony began in 1957, when Abravanel, who had been recording abroad for Westminster Records, persuaded that company to make records with his own orchestra in Utah. Between then and 1969, the Utah Symphony and Abravanel made sixty-five long-playing records for the Westminster and Vanguard labels under a special royalty arrangement. For actual performance at recording sessions, the musicians in the orchestra have in the past received a pro-rata portion of their weekly pay; this amounted to between twenty and twenty-five dollars a recording session, at a time when the national AFM scale called for as much as ninety-five. In a sense, the players gambled on making up the difference: all royalties—ranging from ten to fifteen percent of the retail price of the record—are distributed to the players until they receive the equivalent of AFM scale; thereafter, the orchestra and musicians share equally in the royalty income. This arrangement required the unanimous consent of the musicians, given at a closed meeting by secret written ballot. Actually, very few of the orchestra's recordings have generated sufficient royalties to bring the players' total compensation up to the established national AFM scale. Although a few other American orchestras have occasionally recorded under similar arrangements,† no other has done so as extensively as the Utah Symphony, and several of the smaller orchestras which have issued commercial records, such as the Seattle Symphony, have worked under arrangements whereby a local subsidy was raised to meet the higher AFM recording scale.

* The Utah orchestra players have never belonged to ICSOM; those in San Antonio once did, but resigned in 1972 under circumstances noted in Chapter V.
† Some orchestras have devised special arrangements involving the allocation of a few contracted services to recording with additional payments to bring compensation up to AFM scale.

Nor has any of the "major" American recording companies (RCA, Columbia, Decca, Capitol, or Mercury) entered into agreements with an American orchestra similar to that between the Utah Symphony and Vanguard or Westminster: some of their officials state privately that to do so would jeopardize their relations with the large orchestras receiving full AFM scale.

Early in 1969, the recording industry and the AFM negotiated a new three-year master trade agreement covering the use of union instrumental musicians in all types of recording in the United States, of which symphonic recording is but a small part. In the 1969 recording negotiations, largely at the instigation of ICSOM, the views of symphonic players involved in recording were sought by the union representatives, but the players of the Utah Symphony were not among these. Furthermore, in the closed negotiating sessions, the question of underscale recording activity such as that of the Utah Symphony was reported to have been raised, but the final trade agreement did not specifically prohibit such local underscale arrangements—previously considered matters of local jurisdiction—so long as the players concerned gave unanimous consent by secret ballot. However, after the trade agreement had been reached by the AFM and the recording industry, .the Federation issued a ruling that effectively barred such local arrangements as that of the Utah Symphony; there is good reason to believe that though this was not incorporated formally in the agreement, it was tacitly and informally settled during the negotiations, under pressure both from the musicians and managements of the larger orchestras and from the large recording companies.

The impact of this AFM ruling upon the players of the Utah Symphony was, of course, devastating. Not only did it cut off some of their income but it deprived them and their orchestra of a promotional device that they considered important both at home and on tour. By unanimous vote they appealed to their local union to seek an exception from the AFM. Finally, Herman Kenin advised the union to suggest that the orchestra players themselves choose a delegate to appear before the ICSOM-AFM Symposium in the fall of 1969. The players then met and unanimously designated Abravanel as their representative, with consequences noted earlier. Following this meeting, Abravanel received Kenin's oral assurance that an exception to the AFM ruling would be made for the Utah Symphony only. Kenin's death a few months later created a further problem of securing a similar commitment from his successor, but, thanks to Abravanel's untiring efforts, this was obtained before the 1970–71 season opened. During that season Abravanel led his orchestra in several recording sessions, producing enough music for four LP records. Subsequently, however, the AFM again reversed its policy and ruled that the Utah Symphony could no longer record in its customary manner. Abravanel and Gregory continued to explore ways of resuming recording and both are active in general discussions by a number of orchestras, not only of current recording problems but also of long-range policy regarding recording for cable television and video cassettes.

The Utah Symphony Orchestra has recorded over one hundred compositions, released on sixty-five long-playing records; about two-thirds of these are currently available in this country and many have been released abroad on some thirty different labels. It has been estimated that over a million copies have been sold. By and large, Abravanel and the record producers have avoided adding further to the list of heavily recorded standard repertory. Records by the Utah Symphony included Handel oratorios and Mahler symphonies well in advance of the recent popularity of such music. They also reflect certain specialized interests arising from the conductor's own background —music by Bloch, Varèse, Satie, Honegger, and Milhaud, for instance. In its representation of American music the repertory inclines toward more popular compositions, such as the lighter works of Copland, Grofé, Gershwin, Gould, and Salt Lake City resident LeRoy Robertson. Among its best-selling records, however, are Tchaikovsky ballet suites, which reflect the role of the Utah Symphony as the orchestra for Ballet West productions. Though it has recorded several major choral works—the Berlioz Requiem, Handel oratorios, Milhaud *Pacem in Terris,* and Honegger *Le Roi David*—the records have been made with university choruses, not with the Mormon Tabernacle Choir. The latter has never appeared with the Utah Symphony, since both organizations prefer to maintain separate identities, and the choir has had a recording contract with Columbia.

Though impossible to document statistically, there is a strong conviction on the part of all concerned that recordings play an important part in public relations both in the orchestra's home base and in its touring program. The residents of Utah take great pride in reading the favorable reviews given the orchestra's recordings not only in the American press but by critics in Europe and South America, reviews that reflect admiration of the major cultural achievement of Utah. Similarly, these records have aroused the interest of the musical public beyond the borders of its home state and have paved the way for the orchestra's extensive tours. In many cities outside Utah, a prime factor in building the orchestra's concerts has been the use of these records by local Mormons in concert promotion. The missionary spirit, fundamental to the Mormon outlook, extends to the pride which Mormons away from home take in the visits of this orchestra. Thus, when the Utah Symphony played in the Hollywood Bowl, it was virtually filled by a crowd of fourteen thousand —not necessarily all Mormons themselves, but brought there by an aggressive ticket-selling campaign by local Mormons. The same is true when the orchestra travels overseas: for the overseas Mormon missionary the visit of the Utah Symphony is not only a great sentimental tie to his homeland but also an opportunity to direct his missionary zeal toward the concrete enterprise of bringing an audience to hear these ambassadors of Utah artistry.

Possibly more important, though less dramatic, is the intensive touring activity of the orchestra in its own state and in the areas immediately bordering Utah. In the 1970–71 season, and exclusive of the Latin-American tour, the orchestra played fifty full concerts outside Salt Lake City, more than twice the number at home; in addition, it played for Ballet West performances in Ogden and Provo. A somewhat lower proportion of its youth concerts were also given on tour.

In Salt Lake City itself the orchestra plays a full season of fourteen regular subscription programs in the Mormon Tabernacle, whose seating capacity of

over five thousand people in wooden church pews is frequently filled by subscribers and purchasers of single tickets. The largest hall regularly used by
an American orchestra, the Tabernacle is by no means an ideal setting for
symphonic concerts, having been constructed in 1863–67 entirely from wood
and stone with little use of nails. Its most prominent feature is the vast Tabernacle organ and choir ranks, before which the orchestra seems somewhat
dwarfed. The sound is extremely resonant and regular symphony-goers have
distinct preferences as to location because of the uneven acoustics of the
hall. The usual audience at a Tabernacle concert is extremely varied in age,
and, so far as dress betrays, from a wide range of economic and social status.
An extraordinarily large proportion are in their late teens and early twenties,
some of them conservatively dressed but many most informally and a few
in "hippie" style. In its ticket promotion, the Utah Symphony makes a great
effort to involve young people, both at home and by giving concerts on tour
at universities and colleges.

Though the orchestra's recording repertory seems rather off the beaten track
its concert programs are generally comparable to those of other major orchestras. There is, in the Tabernacle subscription series at least, a strong
emphasis on the established standard classics and on the appearance of the
usual variety of visiting artists in concertos and vocal repertory. Abravanel
has complete authority over both repertory and the selection of soloists, and
he engages players from the orchestra as soloists for at least one or two of
the subscription concerts each season. In repertory Abravanel reflects both his
background and his age. Though he grew up when Stravinsky, Milhaud, Bloch,
and Honegger were novelties, he still makes an effort to play music of the
younger generation, but admits to having less and less sympathy for *avant-
garde* works. In concerts at the university, the orchestra plays a larger proportion of unusual music, and in recent years Abravanel has engaged
such composer-conductors as Gunther Schuller and Lukas Foss to broaden
the orchestra's repertory beyond his own interests. With this particular artistic
policy, the orchestra, in its home base at least, offers its audience a well-
balanced repertory, somewhat more adventurous at times than its rather conservative audience welcomes, but also somewhat more conservative than some
other orchestras.

Table 8-C, based on the Mueller analysis of symphonic repertory, indicates
the various composer-nationality components in the Utah Symphony programs since 1940. Compiled for five-year periods, these indicate the percentage of repertory contributed by each nationality of composers for the
years preceding Abravanel (1940–45), a period (1945–50) covering his
arrival in 1947, and for that during which he was sole music director (1950–
70).

The most important conclusion to be drawn from these data is the great
emphasis that Abravanel has given American music, especially between 1950
and 1960; his twenty-year record is substantially better than the national
average, and in 1950–55 was actually more than double the national figure
and second only to Austro-German music. He has consistently presented
a higher proportion of American music than French, unlike the other or-

TABLE 8-C

UTAH SYMPHONY ORCHESTRA REPERTORY 1940–70
Composer-Nationality Percentages Compared with National Averages
(*In Italics*)

	Various Conductors 1940–45	MA etc. 1945–50	Abravanel			
			1950–55	1955–60	1960–65	1965–70
Austro-German	40.83	46.76	45.24	50.81	55.33	53.54
	46.41	*50.75*	*52.41*	*51.15*	*52.04*	*51.65*
Russian	23.72	21.70	13.27	13.20	15.57	13.52
	19.68	*17.00*	*14.04*	*14.06*	*14.64*	*14.08*
French	15.22	8.81	12.22	8.36	6.84	9.57
	10.39	*12.23*	*12.09*	*11.41*	*10.76*	*10.09*
American	6.78	12.42	14.56	12.72	8.00	9.82
	8.47	*7.00*	*6.79*	*7.12*	*7.32*	*6.66*
British	4.28	2.25	3.54	6.55	4.34	5.31
	3.65	*2.87*	*2.85*	*4.13*	*3.35*	*3.97*
Czech	5.44	1.17	3.10	1.66	3.51	1.45
	2.70	*2.25*	*2.49*	*2.31*	*2.97*	*3.12*
Italian	1.94	4.37	3.29	0.86	1.16	2.34
	2.31	*2.58*	*3.77*	*3.75*	*3.30*	*2.89*
Scandinavian	1.50	2.25	2.78	3.15	1.65	2.71
	3.33	*2.48*	*2.35*	*2.18*	*2.09*	*2.76*
Hungarian	—	—	0.93	1.44	3.49	0.70
	0.98	*1.22*	*1.32*	*1.87*	*2.17*	*1.57*
Spanish	⎱ —	0.32	0.85	0.81	—	0.93
Latin-American	⎰ *1.52*	*0.95*	*1.25*	*1.30*	*1.12*	*1.47*

chestras studied. Even in the last decade, when his proportion of American music declined, Abravanel's American component ranked eighth out of twenty-seven orchestras in the first five years and second in the last. Though his proportion of Austro-German music was below the national average when he first came to Utah, it now slightly exceeds the average. Consequently, it is not surprising that his offering of French and Russian music has generally been low, though that of British music has been invariably higher.

Special repertory must be prepared for youth concerts and ballet and opera productions, but the fourteen programs of the Salt Lake City subscription series provide most of the repertory for touring. Abravanel usually spends more time in rehearsal than do the orchestras of larger cities. Whereas three or four rehearsals of two and a half hours each suffice for a regular program in Philadelphia or comparable cities, the Utah Symphony generally devotes five three-hour rehearsals to the average program.

Through nearly twenty-five years of conducting his orchestra and playing an active role in civic affairs, Abravanel has achieved an extraordinary artistic identity with his orchestra and the community. The orchestra, as he has built it, is very much his own, and he has won for it and for himself a unique place in the affections of his city and state by his dedicated and uncompromising musical service. He has long viewed his role as one of building an audience, not in materialistic quantitative terms but rather as enriching the artistic experience of the citizens of Utah. He sets great store by his many years of presenting symphonic programs in schools—which he calls his "musical fifth column"—but admits that in the interests of promoting good public relations he has spread his youth concerts rather thin; the orchestra seldom visits a school more than once a year and seeks relatively minimal implementation of these youth concerts in the general curriculum. Though he once presented these concerts himself, Abravanel relies more and more on his capable assistant, Ardean Watts, to carry this increasingly heavy burden of work.

Policy Direction and the Future

The grateful response of the community and the support it has given Abravanel and his orchestra are, in the last analysis, represented through the board of directors of the Utah Symphony, in whom is vested the ultimate policy direction of the orchestra and the responsibility for its maintenance. All agree that in recent years this board has gained considerably in strength. When Abravanel came to Salt Lake City in 1947, the board was dominated by a few music lovers, among them Mrs. John M. Wallace, who gave much devotion and money during its most crucial years. However, at that time the board lacked strong representation of the most influential Mormon leadership in the community, without which it could never have succeeded. In the beginning, Abravanel, as an outsider, tended to antagonize some of the Mormon leadership, but soon saw ways of better mutual understanding that eventually brought them into the symphony orbit. The current president of the board, Wendell J. Ashton, a leading advertising executive in Salt Lake City, enjoys close connections with this group.

Legally, the orchestra is a division of the Utah State Institute of Fine Arts, which has played an important role in all of the arts in the state since its establishment in 1899; * the symphony orchestra, then under WPA sponsorship, came under the Institute in 1937. By statute, thirteen of the orchestra's directors are also members of the Institute's own board, which is appointed by the governor with legislative approval. Another twenty-four directors, appointed by the board president, have only one-half vote each; thus, in theory, the Institute board members could as a group outvote the others. Though such a contingency has never arisen, there was at least one occasion in the past when the orchestra management, confronted with problems with one of the board officers, resolved them by mustering support among the Institute board members. The thirteen directors holding dual membership in both the symphony and Institute boards sometimes find themselves caught between the requirements of the symphony and other arts institutions whom they oversee,

---

* The Institute is, therefore, the oldest state body—commission or council—devoted to the promotion and support of the arts.

and subjected to pressures from their colleagues on the symphony board to seek a greater share of state funds for the orchestra.

However, despite the role of the Institute in the symphony board, it is generally agreed that the latter operates responsibly and independently under Ashton's strong leadership.[9] With all of the heavy demand on his time in his business and in church affairs—he prefers to conduct much symphony business at breakfast meetings in the Utah Club—he is, by common agreement, the dominating figure on the board. While certainly reflecting the views of his colleagues, he provides the driving force of board leadership, working closely with Abravanel and Gregory. Ever since the crisis of 1949, the Utah Symphony board has clung tenaciously to a determination that it will never again risk bankruptcy in its operations. With Abravanel's full cooperation, each season's plans are tailored to what the board, often prodded by Abravanel, decides to be the available resources, and Ashton and the board hold Gregory to strict accountability in fiscal matters. Though Ashton realizes that community support of the orchestra may not always match its contribution to the city, and is fully aware of the sacrifices of the players and Abravanel, he also takes a realistic view of community potential for support, from his perspective in business affairs and in the church.

In taking a long-range look at the orchestra's future, Ashton and others share a deep concern for the eventual decisions that must be made concerning the orchestra's artistic direction. Everyone regards Abravanel as a unique and almost saintly figure, to whom Utah will long be in great debt, and it is no reflection on their affection and gratitude that they also frankly face the fact of his age. After twenty-five years of service in Salt Lake City, Abravanel is approaching his seventieth birthday: though he has gradually cut down on his work load, he remains the central figure in the symphonic picture. When the day comes that he can no longer fill the position, the leadership of the Utah Symphony Orchestra will face its most crucial decision in decades.

It is to their credit that they will talk realistically about this prospect, invariably with genuine appreciation of "Maurice's" contribution and with recognition that, in a very true sense, he will be irreplaceable. Yet so convinced are they of this that they run the danger of accepting as his successor so different a kind of leader that much of Abravanel's work may be undone. His own close identification with the city and state understandably inclines those facing the future toward thinking in terms of other conductors, possibly less musically authoritative than Abravanel, who would seek similar ties with the city, reflecting a willingness, if necessary, to sacrifice artistic stature for community service. The orchestra may well find to its great distress that the whole structure of symphonic conducting has changed considerably in the past two decades. For all the contribution of Abravanel as an outsider, a surprisingly diverse sentiment in Salt Lake City seems oriented toward a narrowly local Mormon leadership in the future, as if forgetting that no small part of Abravanel's success has stemmed from his broad international background.

The synergistic combination of Abravanel and Mormon Utah has produced a symphony orchestra which has achieved extraordinary identification with its community. To the degree that the Mormon environment played a part in this process, the Utah Symphony is a unique case. Though the dedicated leadership of Maurice Abravanel has its counterpart in other orchestras in this nation, all too few in the last generation can boast of the peculiarly devoted contribution that he has made to Utah. In this he ranks with such American symphonic greats as Theodore Thomas, Frederick Stock, Serge Koussevitzky, and Leopold Stokowski.

CHAPTER IX

Louisville Orchestra

Robert Whitney, who served as musical director and conductor of the Louisville Orchestra † from 1937 to 1967. recalls the not too joyous Christmas season of 1949 as the worst crisis of his thirty years of service to the orchestra.[1] Though he and Charles P. Farnsley,† the orchestra's president as well as mayor of Louisville at the time, had two years earlier taken radical steps to place the orchestra on a firmer footing, it faced such financial problems that Farnsley and his board were ready to abandon the entire project. Reduction in the size of the orchestra, establishment of united arts fund-raising for the community, and the innovation of a policy of commissioning new works for premieres in Louisville had so far failed to provide the basis for kind of support, in contributions and in audience, that the orchestra needed to survive. By December, 1949, it had accumulated a deficit which it saw no way to liquidate and which would only increase unbearably if the orchestra continued operations beyond the end of the year. Whitney was ready, after twelve years of hard work in Louisville, to admit defeat, except for the fact of having in his possession a new score that he was convinced was of extraordinary importance.

In the course of setting up their commissioning program in 1947 and 1948, Whitney and Farnsley had approached the dancer Martha Graham with a proposal that she stage a new work to a score especially composed for the reduced orchestra in Louisville. At her suggestion the score was commissioned from William Schuman; the dancer and composer settled upon the biblical story of Judith as a subject, and Schuman had, by the end of 1949, sent the

---

* Actually, the Louisville Orchestra is sponsored by the Louisville Philharmonic Society, Inc., and was for some time known as the Louisville Philharmonic Orchestra. However, in this account the orchestra will be referred to throughout by its present name, and the corporate designation will be used only in that specific sense.
† Robert Whitney and Charles P. Farnsley are two of the most delightful people I have encountered in this study. Though he now seems tired and somewhat disillusioned by the trials and disappointments of his thirty years in Louisville, Whitney still sparkles with enthusiasm when he recalls the "crazy" ideas that he and Farnsley conceived. Farnsley, now an elder statesman in Louisville, combines the garrulous charm of a southern politician with a keen intellect and deep concern for civic welfare: he can make a dissertation on the difference between southern and northern politics delightfully relevant to the problems of the Louisville Orchestra.

score to Whitney, who was so excited by it that he determined to keep his orchestra alive until he could produce it for his public in a fully staged version, with decor by Noguchi and Calder and lighting by Jean Rosenthal. Such was Whitney's faith in Schuman's choreographic poem *Judith* that he persuaded Farnsley and the Louisville board not to abandon their orchestra before carrying through this project on which so much work had been done, and for which he had such enthusiasm.

Judith was produced early in 1950 with great local success and, more important, with extraordinary national publicity. Critics from all over the country attended this premiere, writing glowing accounts of it and of Whitney's efforts to further the cause of new music in Louisville. Virgil Thomson, then critic for the *New York Herald-Tribune,* was especially lavish in his praise, using Louisville as an example in his plea to the great orchestras of the nation to do more for native composers. The success of *Judith* in Louisville was repeated later in New York in 1950, when the entire production, including Whitney and his orchestra, was given in Carnegie Hall on a program that included other New York premieres of music commissioned by the Louisville Orchestra. The national interest aroused by this work had its effect at home of stimulating an interest in the orchestra that eventually led to Farnsley's success in securing a solid foundation for his then novel idea of combined fund-raising effort for all the arts there. It also led, in 1953, to the Louisville Orchestra's receiving from the Rockefeller Foundation a grant to inaugurate a project of recording a large quantity of newly commissioned music; this was the first occasion on which a major national foundation had involved itself in any sort of a project with an American orchestra. Given this stimulus, and under the devoted leadership of Whitney and Farnsley, the Louisville Orchestra not only became an important force on the national symphonic scene but, more important, proceeded in the next two decades to develop its service to the Louisville community.

Innovation of Whitney and Farnsley

Regionally, Louisville is a border community, having known extremely divided loyalties between the North and South during the Civil War; to this day there is a distinctly southern flavor to the city. Its economy is based both on the surrounding farm country of Kentucky and southern Indiana and on large industrial installations, especially a General Electric plant which employs some fifty-seven thousand people and attracts to Louisville a substantial corps of executives who contribute significantly to the community's life.

From its beginnings Louisville received a considerable influx of German immigrants, who brought with them an interest in music manifested in what can best be described as a German bandmaster tradition. Although this tradition was largely smothered during World War I, enough remained for the community to retain some interest in serious music. The Cincinnati Symphony visited Louisville frequently during the 1920s and 1930s, and there were sporadic efforts to maintain an orchestra of local performers alone. When Robert Whitney came to Louisville in 1937, he found an orchestra of some eighty players that lacked certain key performers among the woodwinds and whose string playing left a great deal to be desired. The city enjoyed considerable strong civic leadership, notably from the Bingham family, which owned the *Louisville Courier-Journal* and eventually built a communications empire in newspapers, radio, and television.

Robert Whitney, before coming to Louisville, had been a professional pianist in Chicago, working in nightclubs and radio stations while he attempted to pursue a career in composition. In Chicago, he had been a member of the first conducting class organized by Frederick Stock and Eric DeLamarter in connection with the Chicago Civic Orchestra; Stock had played one of Whitney's compositions on a subscription program of the Chicago Symphony in 1934. When, in 1937, the Louisville Philharmonic Society was looking for a young conductor to vitalize its symphonic efforts, they selected Robert Whitney largely on the recommendation of Stock and DeLamarter. Under Whitney the orchestra pursued a rather precarious existence through the war years, but began to obtain some community support in the immediate postwar era.

One of the civic leaders attracted to the orchestra was Charles P. Farnsley, an ambitious lawyer with a great interest in the city's affairs. He was already president of the Philharmonic Society in 1949, as well as an alderman on the city council, when he was unexpectedly elected mayor upon the death of the man in office. Thus, Farnsley suddenly found himself in a position to further the interests of the orchestra. In both his political career and his activities as president of the Philharmonic Society, Farnsley was motivated by a very strong sense of civic responsibility. Farnsley makes no secret of the limitations of his knowledge of music: as a youth he had heard and enjoyed the jazz performances brought up the Ohio on the Mississippi riverboats from New Orleans. At some point, he had either heard Stravinsky's *Rite of Spring* or at least heard about the great publicity that had attended its first performances in Europe and in the United States. From his wide reading in European and American history Farnsley had encountered reports of the smaller (fifty pieces or less) court orchestras for which Mozart, Haydn, and Beethoven wrote their music. When he became president of the Philharmonic Society in 1947, he made two major proposals to change its operations. The first was to reduce the size of the orchestra from the unwieldy mixture of some eighty amateur and professional musicians to a more manageable group of fifty players; such an orchestra would not only be more practical economically but would also retain in its membership the best players in the community, thereby raising the overall quality of performance. His second proposal was even more radical: he suggested that the orchestra include on every program the first performance anywhere of a new work, each commissioned by the orchestra. Farnsley was motivated less by a commitment to contemporary music as such than by the publicity such a program would generate, giving the Louisville Orchestra a national prominence that would enhance its standing at home. Whitney, as a composer himself, was more than sympathetic to the cause of contemporary music, but he had considerable misgivings about such a large emphasis on new music. Though he feared that too much contemporary music might antagonize his audiences, Whitney was persuaded by Farnsley's eloquence; after all, he later recalled, *something* had to be done to save the orchestra. The power of Farnsley's persuasion also affected his colleagues on the Philharmonic board and the program was immediately implemented. Contacts were made in New York City and elsewhere to discover which composers should be offered commissions for premieres in Louisville, with the stipulation that the compositions be written for a fifty-piece orchestra.

The success of *Judith* and the impact of national publicity on the Louisville community did not necessarily solve the financial problems of the Louisville Orchestra. Deeply aware of the heavy burden on his board colleagues in raising funds to defray the annual deficit of the orchestra, Farnsley conceived a general fund-raising drive for the established arts in Louisville, among them the orchestra, whereby funds to support all of them could be raised in one annual campaign similar to that of united charitable fund drives. Using his considerable charm and persuasiveness and his position as mayor of Louisville, Farnsley succeeded in establishing the Louisville Fund in 1949 and in strengthening its role in the community through an aggressive symphonic program that became its major constituent.

The Recording Project

Nor were Whitney and Farnsley content to rest on the success of Schuman's *Judith* in their efforts to identify the Louisville Orchestra with the cause of new music. Not only was the policy of commissioning and performing new works at every concert continued, but Farnsley had other suggestions to exploit this feature of the orchestra. At one point he tried to persuade Whitney to put on a marathon performance in which the orchestra would play new music all day long at some central location, where the public could come in and out to hear it without charge; this particular scheme was never carried out. More realistic were the ideas Whitney and Farnsley developed to present to the Rockefeller Foundation for an extensive program of recording the new music commissioned by the Louisville Orchestra.[2] They proposed that the foundation supply funds to start a project which, it was hoped, would become self-sustaining after the first year or two. This contemplated the commissioning and recording each year of sufficient new music to fill twelve long-playing records, which would be sold by subscription only to mail-order purchasers. Farnsley and Whitney believed that this would, besides providing an intrinsic service to new music, promote the stature of the Louisville Orchestra nationally and internationally. It would also give additional employment to the players, making it possible to improve the personnel of the orchestra. On the basis of Whitney's and Farnsley's presentation, the Rockefeller Foundation made an initial grant of $400,000 in 1953 to cover the costs of setting up this recording project, including the commissioning fees, recording and performance costs, and promotional expenses; a second grant of $100,000 was made in 1955, but since then the project has indeed been self-sustaining. The first twelve records, issued on a monthly subscription basis, were produced in 1955; later the annual series was reduced to six records.

Late in 1970, the Louisville Orchestra issued the hundredth record in this First Edition series. All of the compositions were first recordings and in most cases remain the only recordings available of the music; except for a few 19th-century works recorded in the past few years, all of the compositions were newly commissioned by the Louisville Orchestra for performance in this series. Until his retirement in 1967, Robert Whitney had full responsibility for the selection of commissions, but frequently consulted with other composers, publishers, and critics familiar with the contemporary music scene in making his choices. Although the series was by no means confined to native American composers, there was a strong emphasis in this repertory on the more conservative and academic style of American composition during the 1950s and 1960s.[3] To some extent this reflected Whitney's own taste in contemporary composition and to some extent it reflected the limitations of the Louisville Orchestra and the rehearsal resources.*

After Jorge Mester succeeded Whitney as musical director of the Louisville Orchestra, he and the orchestra management decided to experiment with varying the repertory in the hope of improving the sale of subscriptions. Rather than attempting to compete with the output of major American and European orchestras on commercial labels, they sought out previously unrecorded works from the 19th century, hoping thus to capitalize on the so-called romantic revival. A few releases have been made of this repertory but have not met with great success: there have been considerable protests from subscribers who preferred to have an exclusively contemporary repertory, and minimal new subscriptions have been attracted by the change. For this reason Mester and the orchestra manager, James D. Hicks, have undertaken a thorough review of the policy of this First Edition series.

Though they are now available through a limited number of high-volume record retailers, the First Edition records were for many years available only by mail-order subscription. These subscriptions were solicited and promoted primarily by advertising in national magazines in a style similar to that of book and record club promotion. Over a period of fifteen years, the subscriber list to the First Editon series has varied between two and three thousand; a considerable proportion of the subscriptions are held abroad. Although there are a substantial number of individual subscribers, many libraries and music schools maintain annual subscriptions because the service constitutes important documentation of certain aspects of American composition during the mid-20th century. It is interesting to note, for instance, that there are more subscribers in London than in Louisville itself.

During the early days of the First Edition series, Farnsley devised a rather unconventional promotional scheme of periodically increasing the price of the record subscriptions but announcing this increase sufficiently in advance

---

* By no means was all of the new music commissioned by the Louisville Orchestra actually recorded, especially after the annual program was cut to six records.

to give buyers an opportunity to subscribe beforehand; the result of these periodic increases was that eventually the records were virtually priced out of the market, finally selling for more than ten dollars apiece, nearly twice as much as commercially released records. This policy has been abandoned and promotional efforts are now more centered on the repertory that is offered uniquely in this First Edition series. In 1969, the Louisville Orchestra received a grant from the National Endowment for the Arts to undertake an intensified promotional program for these records. This campaign, created by the J. Walter Thompson advertising agency, resulted in a considerable rise in subscription. However, there has been some indication that the new subscribers are not renewing their subscriptions in the quantity hoped for by the orchestra management.

The First Edition record series has never produced anything like the profit that Farnsley and Whitney had originally hoped for. Such profits as may accrue from year to year are often wiped out by a deficit in a following year, especially as recording and advertising costs grow. For this series, the players in the orchestra are paid the full AFM recording scale; thus the project has produced important indirect benefits to the orchestra through the improved economic situation of the players; at AFM scale prevailing in 1970–71, the orchestra musicians earned between five and six hundred dollars each from recording. Another indirect benefit to the Philharmonic Society is the national publicity obtained by the records themselves and, possibly more important, by the frequent exposure through advertising of the Louisville Orchestra in national media.

Certainly a crucial question arising from this recording project is the impact on the public at large of so intensive a concentration on new music. To those deeply concerned with the cause of contemporary music, the failure of the Louisville Orchestra's First Edition series to obtain more than a few thousand subscribers at any one time has been a great disappointment. When confronted with such discouraging data, some ardent defenders of contemporary music maintain that the entire program cannot be taken as an indication of public demand for new music because the repertory has lacked progressive appeal and the orchestra itself is not well known. Even such critics admit, however, that the First Edition series has been amply publicized.

Varied Professional Life

Thanks to Whitney's and Farnsley's innovations in the early 1950s in repertory, recording, reduction in orchestra size, and the organization of the Louisville Fund, the Louisville Orchestra for the first time achieved something like a stable operation. This stability was also a result of extraordinarily good teamwork between Whitney as musical director, Farnsley and his successors in board direction, and the skillful management of Richard H. Wangerin, who came to the Louisville Orchestra from the Kansas City Philharmonic. Wangerin was not only manager of the orchestra, in charge of its operations and recording program, but also executive director of the Louisville Fund and of the Theater Alliance. The latter had taken over the lease on the old Brown Theater, a part of a real-estate complex owned by a wealthy but eccentric gentleman. The complex also included an office building, in which the symphony had its offices, and the well-known, old-time Brown Hotel. The Brown Theater thus became something of a performance arts center, housing not only the symphony orchestra but also local opera and ballet companies and visiting theatrical and concert attractions. After the death of Mr. Brown several years ago, however, the status of the theater became a matter of litigation, which has only recently been resolved in a way that will permit a new organization to renovate and continue operating the theater as a home for various community performance activities, including the orchestra.*

During the past two decades, there has developed a well-coordinated activity around the Louisville Orchestra that not only has offered the city a diversified program of performance and education but has also substantially improved the quality of the orchestra itself. A leading factor in this certainly has been the cooperative atmosphere created by the Louisville Fund itself, as a general clearing house for the fiscal stability of all of the arts organizations. An equally vital role has been played by the University of Louisville, until two years ago an independent university but now a part of the Kentucky state-university system.

The most important effect of this cooperative effort may be seen in the unusually stable condition of the music profession in Louisville.[4] Virtually all of the fifty to sixty players under contract to the Louisville Orchestra perform a variety of musical functions in the city. Besides playing in the orchestra itself, they participate in opera and ballet performances in the Brown Theater; during the 1970–71 season there were four opera productions, each giving two performances, and two ballet productions, also giving two performances each. In addition, many orchestra musicians hold some sort of teaching position, either at the University of Louisville or in the public-school system; for this reason, all rehearsals by the Louisville Orchestra are held in the evening from seven to ten. There are several active chamber-music ensembles, including a string quartet of first-desk players from the orchestra, a woodwind quintet, and a brass ensemble, whose concert activities are centered at the University of Louisville. There is also a local Bach Society, presenting Baroque instrumental and vocal music and employing orchestra members. In addition to thirty subscription concerts, offering twelve different programs in four separate series on Friday and Saturday evenings and Sunday afternoons, the orchestra plays a number of concerts in the public schools, and ensembles from the orchestra play children's concerts at the public library. The Music Performance Trust Fund employs most of the orchestra musicians for a number of free concerts in the schools. All of these schedules are carefully coordinated so that no conflicts for players will be created.

With all of this activity, the life of the orchestra musician in Louisville is an extremely busy one, but most of the players agree that it is rewarding

---

* As of late 1972, plans were under way to raise $500,000 to remodel this facility and rename it the McCouley Theater.

both financially and artistically. Over a period of years a highly skilled personnel has been assembled, both by training musicians locally (especially at the University of Louisville) and by importing them from outside the city. Actually, from the players' financial point of view, the orchestra plays rather a minor role; the minimum income guaranteed by the orchestra is somewhat under three thousand dollars, although this is augmented by several hundred dollars in recording fees and in the case of key players by additional first-desk or senority pay. Unlike the Utah Symphony, the Louisville Orchestra contract with its musicians does not include opera and ballet performances, though the schedule of these activities is closely coordinated with the orchestra's and its players are given priority in employment; thus opera and ballet income adds substantially to the basic symphony and teaching pay. For many players the major portion of income must come from teaching activity, at the university, in the public-school system, or from private pupils. Though it is hard to gain any accurate estimate, the total income of the players probably runs in the vicinity of twelve to eighteen thousand dollars a year, an amount comparable to the guaranteed salary in many major orchestras.

To earn this, the orchestra musicians must work hard over long hours in various parts of the city. Nevertheless, some of the best players in Louisville have rejected offers from larger orchestras with longer seasons because they prefer the ambience of Louisville and the greater professional variety to the more artistically restricted life of a larger orchestra. In fact, those able to command higher fees per performance actually turn down jobs in order to have some time at home with their families and for instrumental practice.

A major factor in the quality and stability of the music profession in the city undoubtedly is the University of Louisville itself, which has always enjoyed a close relationship with the orchestra. For many years Robert Whitney was the head of its music department and its current head, Jerry W. Ball,[5] is a former first-horn player in the Louisville Orchestra who still returns when additional brass players are needed for special performances. The music department of the university is generally regarded as the best in the state and attracts Kentucky's outstanding students. Several hundred students are currently enrolled in its full-time undergraduate and graduate curricula, and many others of precollege age study on a per-lesson basis in its preparatory division. All individual instruction in orchestral instruments is given by orchestra musicians, many of whom also teach group classes. However, with the entry of the University of Louisville into the state system, pressures are mounting to apply rather rigid state regulations concerning the outside work of its teaching staff. So far, the music department has been able to adjust its teaching load to the performance requirements of its faculty, but it may not be able to do so for much longer, especially in the case of a few key teachers who may be faced with a choice between teaching and outside activity. If such a choice is forced, both the orchestra and the university can suffer. The orchestra alone cannot guarantee a sufficient income to provide an adequate living for its players and probably would lose those whom economic pressures would force into the university on a full-time basis. On the other hand, the university might very well suffer in that its faculty would become increasingly separated from actual musical performance. Certainly one of the educational benefits of the present relationship between the orchestra and educational activities in Louisville arises from the fact that the teachers of music are themselves professional musicians active in performance; many educational authorities feel that this is an extremely healthy situation and that the divorce between teaching and performance would be highly undesirable.

The rich and varied professional life of the Louisville musician, involving as it does a wide variety of artistic activity and the special challenge of playing a great deal of contemporary music, has attracted and held an unusually high quality of player. Conductors and soloists who have wide experience with other orchestras across the nation generally agree that the Louisville Orchestra produces an exceptional quality of ensemble sound and has an extraordinary ability to read unfamiliar music, thanks in large part to the long tradition of performing new scores. An orchestra which takes great pride in the total contribution of the institution to the community, it enjoys good morale and seems fairly free of the internal cliques and friction that characterize many other orchestras.[6]

The players themselves did not have an orchestra committee until 1969. Although there had been some previous talk of such an organization, it never developed, partly because there was no great internal pressure from the orchestra for it and partly because it was rather strongly but quietly opposed both by the union and by the manager at the time, Richard H. Wangerin. However, when James D. Hicks became manager in 1969, he felt that there was sufficient sentiment in the orchestra to warrant encouraging the formation of a players' committee. He also believed that such a committee could furnish management a more effective formal liaison with the orchestra personnel.* Like such committees in most American orchestras, this consists of five players elected by the full membership; unlike most other committees, two of these are elected for two-year terms each in rotation, thus giving some continuity and a stability that other orchestras do not necessarily have. The committee took part in contract negotiations with the management for the first time in 1970, with the full cooperation of local union officials. A major concern then was establishing rather firm guidelines on the scheduling of rehearsals and other orchestra activities, and requiring more advance notice on changes in schedule; virtually all of these regulations were the outgrowth of the scheduling problems the musicians had experienced in taking on professional work outside the symphony activity. The committee works closely with the manager, the personnel manager, and the union shop steward. The latter is a relatively recent development in a number of orchestras, sought elsewhere by ICSOM in an effort to clarify the role of the personnel manager. His major duties concern the interpretation of union regulations and the trade agreement in such matters as scheduling and overtime, leaving to the personnel manager more general responsibilities in the employment of extra players, preparation of payrolls, and general liaison with the conductor and manager on personnel matters.

* Only recently have the players in the Louisville Orchestra considered joining ICSOM, which has not, in fact, been deeply involved in the smaller orchestras until the last year or two.

One cannot engage in discussion with the musicians of the Louisville Orchestra without being impressed strongly by how artistically important their symphonic work is to them, despite the fact that the orchestra is not the dominant economic factor in their careers. The possibility that university regulations may force them to choose between the orchestra and the university is one they view with great apprehension, for they would be extremely reluctant to cut themselves off from the orchestra's professional satisfactions. The many players whose service extends back to the days of Whitney look back on that innovative era as a period of considerable excitement, even though it involved difficulties in learning new scores. In many cases they shared the hostility, or at best indifference, of the audience toward the new music, but were devoted personally to Whitney and gave their best in performance, if only out of a sense of professional responsibility.

Finances and the Louisville Fund

Given the strong musical direction established by Whitney, the energetic community leadership exemplified by Farnsley, and the stability possible with financing by the Louisville Fund, the orchestra has for some time enjoyed extremely able management. When Wangerin left in 1968 to become president of the American Symphony Orchestra League, the board chose as his successor James D. Hicks, who had had extensive managerial experience in Indianapolis, Detroit, and at the Meadowbrook Festival in the suburbs of Detroit.* Although Hicks could not free himself of his commitments at Meadowbrook when the Louisville position was offered to him, he covered his responsibilities in Louisville by virtually commuting for a number of months, and the orchestra suffered somewhat from having a part-time manager, especially since it was then breaking in a new conductor as well. Hicks has been in full-time charge of the Louisville Orchestra, however, since late 1969. He considers that one of his most urgent tasks is to work with the board on the solution of basic problems of contributed income raised by the relationship with the Louisville Fund. He also is deeply concerned with the First Edition recording program, for he realizes that this project is presently in a very precarious condition, especially since the "romantic revival" experiment did not succeed as hoped. He is working with Jorge Mester to devise ways of strengthening the subscriber appeal of the contemporary music recorded, and has undertaken to increase sales by offering the records on a retail basis through a few selected outlets across the country. In his special efforts to establish a close and friendly working relation with both the local musicians' union and the members of the orchestra, the part that he played in supporting the organization of the players' committee is remembered with considerable appreciation by the musicians.

* Hicks's title is executive director, in keeping with the recent trend toward designating orchestra managers by various titles; however, because of the profusion of such designations, I retain the one description that applies to all, except when another title denotes unusual responsibilities.

In 1970–71, the orchestra spent just under $380,000 and received some $20,000 less. Table 9-A summarizes the orchestra's finances and compares them to the Category D averages.[7]

TABLE 9-A

LOUISVILLE PHILHARMONIC SOCIETY, INC.
Financial Summary, 1970–71, Compared with Category D Averages

INCOME		26 Category D
Performance:	*Louisville*	*Orchestras*
Concerts	$112,384 (31.5%)	$131,995 (32.9%)
Other nongovt.	3,300 (0.9%)	19,007 (4.7%)
Govt. for services	23,000 (6.5%)	41,366 (10.3%)
TOTAL PERFORMANCE	$138,684 (38.9%)	$192,368 (48.0%)
Supplemental:		
Contributions	$194,667 (54.6%)	$151,887 (37.9%)
Govt., nonservice		19,205 (4.8%)
Endowment and interest	23,041 (6.5%)	37,281 (9.3%)
TOTAL SUPPLEMENTAL	$217,708 (61.1%)	$208,373 (52.0%)
TOTAL INCOME	$356,392 (100%)	$400,741 (100%)
EXPENDITURES		
Artistic personnel	$237,560 (62.8%)	$249,080 (63.7%)
Concert production	75,738 (20.0%)	71,926 (18.4%)
Administration	65,144 (17.2%)	69,838 (17.9%)
TOTAL EXPENDITURES	$378,442 (100%)	$390,844 (100%)

When the Louisville Orchestra's expenses are compared with the category averages, both its percentages and dollar amounts fall very close to the Category D norm. But in the all-important matter of the proportion of performance income, the orchestra shows a considerably less favorable relationship than the average for its category, 39% against 48%.* Moreover, a comparison with the category averages indicates that this difference is due, not to higher than average expenditures, but rather to disproportionately low performance income: in each of its components, the Louisville performance receipts are substantially lower than the category average. Furthermore, more than one-sixth of the Louisville concert income comes from tours outside the city: its thirty concerts in the Brown Theater produce $69,000, or an average of $2,300 each. Despite the small capacity of this auditorium, well under sixteen hundred, this seems to be a rather low return on the effort expended. On the other hand, touring generated income of $25,304, against direct expense of $12,548, which of course did not include artistic services.

Income from government for services rendered, slightly more than half the category average, was primarily from the city and public library for youth concerts by the orchestra in schools and by ensembles in the library. As noted earlier, the 1970–71 grant of $40,000 from the National Endowment for the

* Appendix E indicates how the Category D orchestras, on the average, have a lower proportion of performance income than any of the four other groups.

"Presented to Theodore Thomas by Members of his Orchestra," a previously unpublished oil portrait dating from the 1870s.

(above left) Mrs. Jeanette M. Thurber, founder of the American Opera Company and National Conservatory of Music of America; *(above right)* Walter and Leopold Damrosch; *(below)* Anton Rubinstein and Henri Wieniawski join Theodore Thomas *(upper left)* on the occasion of their tour with the Thomas Orchestra in 1873.

Henry Lee Higginson, oil portrait by John Singer Sargent.

(left) Arthur Judson, portrait by H. Lane; *(right)* Leopold Stokowski and Alexander Van Rensselaer on the occasion of the 1916 performances of the Mahler Eighth Symphony in Philadelphia and New York.

The Theodore Thomas Orchestra in Steinway Hall, New York, 1890.

Mrs. Leta Snow, Alan Watrous, and Helen M. Thompson, early stalwarts of the American Symphony Orchestra League.

Three presidents of the American Federation of Musicians: Hal C. Davis (1969–), James C. Petrillo (1940–58), and Herman D. Kenin (1958–69).

(above) Willem Mengelberg and Arturo Toscanini, Holland, 1929; *(right)* Arturo Toscanini and Fritz Reiner on vacation in Italy during the 1920s; *(below)* three conductors of the Boston Symphony Orchestra: Pierre Monteux (1919–24), Serge Koussevitsky (1924–49), and Charles Munch (1949–62).

(*above*) Leonard Bernstein and Lukas Foss; (*below left*) Maurice Abravanel with composer Ned Rorem; (*below right*) Michael Tilson Thomas.

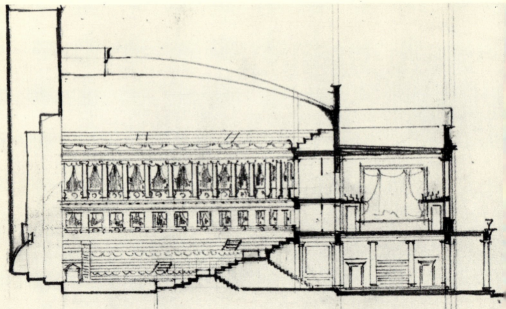

(above) Edward McKim's original proposal for the design of a "new Music Hall" in Boston; *(below)* Symphony Hall, Boston, as viewed from the stage.

(*above*) The Philadelphia Orchestra in the Academy of Music; (*below*) the Chicago Symphony Orchestra in Orchestra Hall.

(above) Kleinhans Music Hall, Buffalo, designed by Eliel and Eero Saarinen and dedicated in October 1940; (below) the Utah Symphony Orchestra in the Mormon Tabernacle, Salt Lake City.

Utah Symphony Orchestra

PAVILION MALL FORUM CENTER THEATER

Wilton Becket and Associates and The Music Center Operating Company

(top) Cross section of the Los Angeles Music Center, completed in 1967; *(above)* exterior of the Music Center; *(below)* Zubin Mehta and the Los Angeles Philharmonic in the Dorothy Chandler Pavillion at the Music Center.

Powell Symphony Hall, home of the St. Louis Symphony Orchestra, formerly the St. Louis Theater, before and after its remodeling in 1966.

Seattle Center Opera House, formerly the Seattle Civic Auditorium, before and after its remodeling in 1966.

(above left) Mrs. Fred Lazarus, longtime worker for the Cincinnati Symphony Orchestra and American Symphony Orchestra League; *(above right)* Miss Frances A. Wister, a guiding force of the Philadelphia Orchestra's Women's Committees, with Alexander Hilsberg, the orchestra's concertmaster; *(below)* Mrs. Norman Chandler, instrumental in the creation of the Music Center, with Los Angeles schoolchildren and William Severns, managing director of the Music Center Operating Company.

(above) Mr. and Mrs. W. Ralph Corbett of Cincinnati, major contributors to the musical life of their city; *(right)* Amyas Ames, president of Partnership for the Arts, receiving the ASOL's Gold Baton Award from chairman John S. Edwards in 1972; *(below)* Mayor Charles P. Farnsley and conductor Robert Whitney, with Mrs. Dann C. Byck, celebrate the Rockefeller Foundation's underwriting of the Louisville Orchestra's recording project.

Lincoln Center for the Performing Arts; photo by Kathleen Cherry

(above) Mel Marvin, Lincoln Center Resource Professional, with students in a Manhattan elementary school; *(below)* Harold Burke, a member of the Albuquerque Symphony Orchestra, with schoolchildren during an ensemble concert at Eugene Field School.

Norm Bergsma

Arts was applied toward the special promotion of the First Edition recordings, and does not appear in this financial summary, being accounted for
separately. For the 1970–71 fiscal year this showed overall expenditures of
$93,919.59, and income of $87,905.23, a net loss for the year of $6,014.36.
Both categories were higher than usual, thanks to a special promotion campaign to stimulate subscriptions. This figure does not include certain services
contributed by the J. Walter Thompson Company in this campaign. It should
also be noted that the expenditures include over $9,500 in administrative
costs, the result of an allocation of managerial and staff expenses between the
orchestra operation and the recording project.

Thus, both the orchestra operation and recording project showed a net
deficit for that year. Fortunately, unlike some other orchestras, the Louisville
Philharmonic Society did not have to borrow to meet these deficits, having
accumulated in the past modest surplus funds in both accounts. However,
neither surplus is large enough to stand repeated deficits of this sort, and
close scrutiny is being given to both the recording project and the orchestra
operation to prevent further deficits.

In its supplemental income, the Philharmonic Society faces certain problems peculiar to its dependence on the Louisville Fund. When the Fund was
established in 1949, one of Farnsley's major objectives was the financial stability of the orchestra. However, this has by no means been the primary
beneficiary of the Fund and is at the present time only one of twelve Louisville arts organizations participating in it. Some of these organizations receive
relatively nominal contributions, but several—notably the Art Center Association, the Actors Theater, the Kentucky Opera Association, the Kentucky
Dance Council, and the Bach Society—share substantially in the Fund,
which in 1970–71 totaled approximately $400,000.

One of the unique features of the Louisville Fund, it must be noted, is
that it does not publish specific suthoritative information concerning its distributions to the various beneficiaries. Each of the participating organizations
makes application for support with as much substantiating evidence as it can
provide, and is then advised how much of a stated overall goal it will receive
if that goal is reached. The Fund then conducts an annual drive throughout
the community with considerable intensity and professional skill; if it reaches
its goal, all organizations receive the amount originally allocated; if it does
not reach the goal, cuts must be made. However, no public statement is made
on the specific allocation of funds.*

Although the Louisville Fund has certainly played a very important part
in the preservation of the orchestra, it has not always been an unmixed blessing. The greatest problem arises from the fact that the Fund's overall increase
has not kept pace with the orchestra's recent explosive growth: in the past
decade orchestra expenses increased by 110%, while the Fund itself grew
only by 66%. During the latter half of this period, to be sure, the Louisville
community was being solicited for contributions to a matching fund of $500,-
000 under the Ford Foundation program for symphony orchestras. In order

---

* Because of the confidential nature of Louisville Fund allocations, the comments that follow
are based on information pieced together from off-the-record interviews.

to undertake this campaign, and assure participation in a $500,000 share of the Ford Foundation trust, the Philharmonic Society had to obtain permission from the Louisville Fund. One condition for this was that Fund contributions to the orchestra's annual requirements would be held stationary during the 1966–71 challenge campaign. Of course, the orchestra received from the Ford Foundation substantial operating grants ($200,000 in five years) to offset the normal annual increases from the Louisville Fund. However, in the absence of such increases, the orchestra has lost five years of its "base" for future annual increments. There is good reason to believe that in this process the orchestra now receives a smaller proportionate share of the total than it did a decade ago, while other arts organizations in the community have gained, in a sense at the orchestra's expense.* In the hope of rectifying this situation, the orchestra made its 1972–73 application to the National Endowment for the Arts a straightforward subsidy to carry the orchestra over a transitional period until it can improve its relative position in the Louisville Fund. The magnitude of this problem may be seen from the fact that in the 1970–71 fiscal year operating funds from the Ford Foundation (the last year in which these were available) totaled $40,000, more than 30% as much as the Fund allocation of $111,670. This is a considerable gap to close by increasing the "base" for annual increments. Another way of looking at this problem is to point out that when the $40,000 from the Ford Foundation is no longer available, its share in financing the orchestra must be filled by increases from the Louisville Fund or from government grants. This situation, plus the fact that the 1970–71 season produced a deficit of more than $20,-000, has given the leadership of the Louisville Orchestra considerable cause for concern.

Fortunately, no one in the Philharmonic Society, either in management or on the board of directors, is inclined to allow this problem to grow without control; neither further resort to dwindling reserve or a bank loan is looked upon as a possible solution. The one-time, nonmatching grant sought from the National Endowment for 1972–73 will provide only a brief respite for the orchestra, during which it can work out more favorable arrangements with the Louisville Fund and begin the long process of increasing the proportion of its performance income.

A Board Without Fund-Raising

The board of directors of the Louisville Philharmonic Society, thanks to the Louisville Fund, does not have the money-raising responsibilities of most other orchestra boards. It is a rather large group, between thirty-five and forty members; usually boards of such size are justified by the necessity of

---

* In this context, it must be noted that, generally speaking, other orchestras participating in the Ford Foundation program, in addition to receiving sustaining grants from the foundation, actually succeeded in appreciably increasing their annual contributions while raising the restricted capital funds required.

securing wide community representation for fund-raising, and there are some in the city who feel that the Philharmonic Society board actually does not have enough to do. Its recently elected president, Barry Bingham, Jr., of the *Courier-Journal* family, is quite aware of the challenge his board faces in this respect.[8] He sees as its most important function that of selecting the manager and conductor of the orchestra, but once chosen they must be given wide responsibility and full authority to proceed in their respective spheres without continual interference. This means that, short of consideration of major contracts, the board indeed should have little to do except to review the financial soundness of the operation. Bingham hopes to develop special areas of board activity to help the orchestra without meddling in management and artistic policy. Bingham would like to explore with his board and with the Louisville Fund possible areas of fund-raising that might be permitted the orchestra.* In this he enjoys a very advantageous position because he is also on the executive committee of the Fund itself.

The kind of board interference in orchestra operation which Bingham himself deplores can be illustrated by an incident that arose during the 1970–71 season, when Jorge Mester programmed an *avant-garde* contemporary work which combined orchestra performance with a prerecorded tape. The tape apparently contained what has been described as rather sensual sounds of "heavy breathing," which impressed some members of the orchestra as being in questionable taste. These misgivings reached the board, who appointed a committee to listen to the tape and decide whether or not the composition should be presented. In the end, the decision was left to Bingham and Mester, and Bingham took the position that this was, in the last analysis, an artistic choice for the conductor to make. The work was played, and in actual performance the tape itself was so submerged in the general orchestral sound that no one in the audience was aware of anything particularly offensive. In retrospect, Bingham feels that it was unfortunate that the board ever became involved in such a question and that it should never have listened to the tape; it should from the outset have taken the position he ultimately did himself, that the entire matter was up to the conductor. On the other hand, he feels that the board must at all times review the overall musical policy of the conductor, and if such a policy in the aggregate does not seem to the best interests of the orchestra and the city, the board must be prepared to make a change of musical direction. He similarly believes that it should not be the task of the board to mediate continually between the manager and the conductor when differences of opinion arise in the daily routine of running the orchestra. In general, Bingham feels such conflicts should be resolved in favor of the conductor unless they involve major financial deviations from the basically approved budget.

The imbalance of performance to supplemental income reflects a more deep-seated problem of audience support for the Louisville Orchestra. Once undoubtedly one of the most innovative orchestras in the nation and an ex-

---

* The Louisville Fund's present restrictions on independent fund-raising by the orchestra are much more stringent than exist in the comparable relationship between the Cincinnati Symphony Orchestra and that city's Institute of Fine Arts (described in Chapter XII).

citing force in community life, the orchestra seems for some time to have settled into a comfortable middle age. To the culturally oriented public of
Louisville, the opera company and especially the Actors Theater under John
Jory's imaginative leadership have captured much of the attention once
aroused by the orchestra, which is too often taken for granted. Ticket subscribers renew faithfully, but many do not actually use their tickets with reg-
ularity, and the management has had only moderate success in persuading
subscribers to turn in unused tickets for resale. At a concert in November,
1971, most of the seats in the Brown Theater were filled at the beginning of
the program, thanks to the appearance of Robert Casadesus as soloist, but
many were vacant after intermission for the first performance by this orchestra of Strauss's *Ein Heldenleben*. From all accounts this is not a new
phenomenon with the Louisville Orchestra: observers report that the middle-
age syndrome was already setting in before Whitney's retirement in 1967.
Thirty years is a long time for any conductor to retain his hold on the audience
especially when, for two-thirds of that period, he has been aggressively programming new music at every concert. In fact, the extreme emphasis on new
music may very well have contributed to the community's inclination to take
its orchestra for granted. Most observers, including Whitney himself, now
question the success of this policy, certainly in terms of building a strong audience in Louisville itself. Although it put Louisville on the national symphonic map, it apparently did not become a source of real satisfaction to the
local audience, nor did it lay the foundation for a genuine receptivity for new
music among even a small group. It has been said that most of the audience
became basically indifferent to the new music, accepting it much as one
might a dose of unpleasant medicine which had to be taken for one's own
good. Another consequence of the emphasis on this new music was that it
consumed an excessive amount of time, both in the programs themselves
and in rehearsal, not only to the neglect of considerable portions of the
standard symphonic repertory but to the virtual exclusion of much important
20th-century music. Thus, the Louisville audience had not, before 1968, encountered substantial representation of such composers as Stravinsky, Bartók, Hindemith, Prokofiev, Copland, Ives, and others who were not contacted
for commission or were at best selected only once in the twenty-year period.
The limited size of the orchestra was another factor in the neglect of much
of the standard repertory, especially the late-romantic and early-20th-century
music of such composers as Richard Strauss, Debussy, and Mahler.* The
Louisville community was continually reminded of the national prominence of
the orchestra because of its innovations and was repeatedly told how important an orchestra it was. Such admonitions implied a community responsibility to attend the concerts and support the orchestra, fostering a tendency

* Unfortunately the Louisville Orchestra's programs were not included in the Mueller studies of
symphonic repertory, so it is impossible to analyze them quantitatively and comparatively in the
national context. However, this orchestra, by including a premiere on every program, performed
a far greater proportion of contemporary music, most of it American, than any other in the
country. The degree to which this policy resulted in the omission of other 20th-century repertory has been explicitly recognized by both Whitney and Mester.

to regard it as a matter of obligation rather than of artistic pleasure and satisfaction.

In Louisville, as we shall see later in Buffalo, one is confronted in very real terms with the problem of repertory in general and with the specific challenge of presenting new music to a relatively conservative and uninformed audience. In Louisville, moreover, conditions were considerably different from those in Buffalo. The exposure of the audience to innovative programming in Buffalo lasted for little more than two seasons at the beginning of Lukas Foss's tenure as musical director, whereas in Louisville the policy of presenting new music on each program extended over two decades. Furthermore, there was a very sharp difference in the kind of music offered in the two cities: Foss was committed to a much more experimental type of *avant-garde* music than was Whitney. As one reviews the list of compositions first presented in Louisville, of which its current recording catalog is a good sampling, one is impressed with the general conservatism; among more than two hundred compositions listed, there are relatively few that can be counted as stylistically representative of strong experimentation or innovation. With rare exceptions this is music that has been played once by the Louisville Orchestra and has seldom actually entered the repertory of other symphony orchestras. There are, to be sure, a few notable exceptions, such as William Schuman's *Judith,* Elliott Carter's *Variations for Orchestra,* Peter Mennin's Fifth and Sixth Symphonies, Aaron Copland's *Orchestral Variations,* and Walter Piston's Fifth Symphony, but in its aggregate the Louisville First Edition repertory rather reminds one of catalogs of music in the 18th century, filled with composers now forgotten and only occasional mentions of such masters as Mozart and Haydn. In a general overview of musical culture, the emergence of a few major composers may require a vast mass of competent but basically uninspired creation, and the Louisville Orchestra's repertory policy and First Editions recordings certainly have served that function. But it may well be argued that such a risk is more than one orchestra of moderate size can or should undertake by itself. Certainly in terms of the Louisville audience, there is no question that the new-music emphasis during the latter two decades of Whitney's tenure as musical director failed to create any basic appetite or understanding of new music in itself.

Conductor in Orbit

In a very real sense, the selection in 1968 of Jorge Mester as Robert Whitney's successor represented a realization that basic changes in artistic policy had to be explored. Whitney had, in his long service to Louisville, become a beloved and highly respected figure in the community. He was never a showy virtuoso conductor, and his appeal rested on his obvious sincerity and dedication, and on his considerable talents as an orchestra technician and musician. When the orchestra was faced with the problem of replacing Whitney, it auditioned a number of young conductors, seeking for Louisville the excitement of youth and charisma. It found these qualities in Jorge Mester.[9]

Born of Hungarian parents in Mexico City in 1935, Mester began his musical studies with the violin, eventually coming to the attention of cellist Gregor Piatigorsky at a master class in California. In 1952 he enrolled at the Juilliard School of Music as a conducting student with Jean Morel and during the summers studied at Tanglewood, both violin and conducting with Leonard Bernstein. Following his graduation from Juilliard in 1958, he was immediately appointed to the school's conducting faculty and engaged in a wide variety of performing activities with various student orchestras and ensembles. Also on the staff of the Juilliard opera department, Mester did the preliminary preparation for the American premieres of important operas by Hindemith and Henze. When still at Juilliard he became musical director of the St. Louis Philharmonic, a post which he held while remaining on the Juilliard faculty. His professional activities expanded rapidly, including appearances as opera conductor in New York, Washington, and at the Spoleto Festival, conductor for the Paul Taylor and Harkness Foundation dance companies, and summer orchestral concerts at Philharmonic Hall in New York. In recent years he has appeared as guest conductor with the Philadelphia Orchestra, the Pittsburgh Symphony, the Cincinnati Symphony, the Indianapolis Symphony, and the New Orleans Philharmonic. Mester recently reviewed his conducting activities and discovered that he had performed in thirty-three cities on the American continent and seven cities in Europe, plus Tokyo. He has for some years been active at the Aspen Festival in Colorado and since 1969 has been designated as music director there, in charge of a considerable program of instruction and performance in conducting, orchestra, and opera. In the summer of 1971, he was invited by the Kansas City Philharmonic * to become its musical adviser in an effort to place that orchestra on a firm artistic and financial basis. His responsibilities there include conducting a few concerts and generally overseeing the musical program, selection of other guest conductors and soloists, and advising the board of directors on long-range musical policy for the revival of an orchestra which has in recent seasons experienced considerable difficulty.

From all of this activity it is obvious that Jorge Mester is a young man very much on the go in symphonic circles here and abroad, pursuing a career quite in the modern style. To his responsibilities as musical director of the Louisville Orchestra he brings the same energy and somewhat hectic atmosphere that surrounds his international career, providing a sharp contrast to the more sedate Whitney, who became and remained a resident of Louisville, with little ambition to conduct elsewhere. There is a strong feeling in that city that Mester has wider ambitions and that his service there is but a stepping-stone to more important engagements. Nevertheless, Mester has

---

* The Kansas City Philharmonic was forced to cancel the final portion of its 1970–71 season; it was one of the few orchestras that failed to raise its Ford Foundation matching fund by mid-1971. In a subsequent reorganization, its long-time conductor Hans Schwieger resigned, and Mester was invited to act as musical adviser for the 1971–73 seasons, pending choice of a full-time director.

determined to dedicate himself to the Louisville Orchestra for as long as he is associated with it. His original three-year contract, which began in 1968, was renewed for another three years at the end of his second season there.

Upon first assuming his post in Louisville, Mester set out to reduce, but by no means eliminate, the emphasis on new music, to present important 20th-century music not heard there previously, and to expand the orchestra's presentation of the traditional symphonic repertory. He was delighted to find the orchestra such an expert ensemble, both in technical quality and in ability to pick up unfamiliar music readily. For the preparation of the subscription programs Mester has four full orchestra rehearsals of two and a half hours each, plus two separate rehearsals for strings only. Of the twelve subscription programs he conducts ten, leaving the other two to visiting guest conductors. Mester also conducts about ninety percent of the high-school concerts and tour dates, although his contract requires him to conduct only fifty percent; the other children's and high-school concerts are directed by his assistant conductor, James Livingston, who is also first clarinetist of the orchestra.

In his repertory, Mester has by no means abandoned the presentation of contemporary music, although the emphasis is no longer on first performances of commissioned works; during the 1971–72 season he programmed first performances for Louisville of such important contemporary works as the Britten *Sinfonia da Requiem,* Wallingford Riegger's *Dichotomy,* and works by Kodály, and Bartók. He is also introducing a great deal more of the late-romantic and 20th-century music hitherto neglected. In presenting such works as Strauss's *Ein Heldenleben,* Debussy's *Ibéria,* and the Mahler Second Symphony, Mester is certainly stretching his limited instrumental resources; for the Strauss work he was able to engage all of the extra woodwind and brass players required by that score, but his string section was limited to a proportion determined by ten first violins. Mester justifies such risks by pointing out that the ensemble quality of the orchestra produces a reasonably good musical effect and that the Louisville audience deserves live performances of such major symphonic works, even by a reduced orchestra of quality. (The small size of the Brown Theater also makes up for the reduced orchestral volume.)

Though he maintains a home in Louisville on a year-round basis, Mester's actual time there is restricted by his outside engagements. Even when he is conducting successive subscription programs at two-week intervals, he may leave town to attend to his duties in Kansas City or to conduct at the New York City Opera. Invitations for social engagements and appointments for community functions must be arranged far in advance with Mester and adjusted to his schedule in a manner that would not be necessary were he a full-time resident of the city. However, there is no doubt that his engaging, energetic personality and the very fact that his services are in demand for important engagements outside of Louisville add to his glamour with many segments of the community. Louisville, like many other cities, must face a choice between a resident and somewhat less colorful conductor on a full-time basis, inclined to devote his life to his community, and a young, ambitious director embarked on an international career that will undoubtedly carry him beyond the city in the future. Having experienced both types of conductor, Louisville is not yet certain which it prefers.

In coming to Louisville for his first full-time post as musical director of an American orchestra, Mester was under the further disadvantage of arriving at a time of transition in management. As noted earlier, Wangerin left the orchestra in 1968, shortly after Mester arrived, and there was a considerable interval before Hicks could give his entire time to Louisville. Hicks and Mester work together smoothly, with a minimum of the differences that inevitably arise between conductor and manager in the normal course of operations. A major area of disagreement concerns Mester's desire to increase the size of the orchestra for such repertory as *Ein Heldenleben*. When he makes up his programs for a season, there apparently is no effort to review them in terms of their financial implications, a rather important matter when the basic orchestra is small. Consequently, Mester's requirements for extra personnel threaten overruns in the budget, which is Hicks's responsibility to maintain. Such problems must often be resolved by the board or board president, almost invariably in the conductor's favor, since he is the artistic director and public commitments for programs have already been made. However, repeated episodes of this sort place the manager in a difficult position: in trying to hold down personnel costs, he does not intend to interfere in artistic matters but that consequence is inevitable, and he must welcome a decision at board level on such day-to-day operating issues. In the long run, both he and Mester must seek ways of anticipating such additional personnel costs before the basic budget is approved by the board.

Curing the Middle-Age Syndrome

Mester's energy, ambition, and personal aura have yet to arouse Louisville substantially. Some say that he does not spend enough time there, others that the middle-age syndrome surrounding the orchestra cannot be broken in a short time. Despite the youthful exuberance of Mester and the keen perception of the orchestra's problems by its young board president, one cannot help but sense the contrast between the rather staid atmosphere of the Louisville Orchestra today and what must have been the excitement of the Whitney-Farnsley era two decades ago. Since the orchestra has long received its financial support through the Louisville Fund, its special needs cannot be impressed on the community in the form of fund drives. As long as other important constituents of the Fund prosper and arouse audience excitement, the problems of the orchestra will not affect the success of the Fund materially.

The youthful leadership of Bingham and Mester, working with such a highly experienced manager as Hicks, has every possibility of meeting these problems. At the moment, all three—each from his own vantage point—are aware of the relative stagnation that seems to have settled over the orchestra. Each has his own ideas about his role in vitalizing the orchestra and these ideas can be brought together in a comprehensive, long-range effort. Bingham knows clearly the role of board leadership and community representation; he knows also the need for reviewing the place of the orchestra in the Louisville Fund. Mester has a clear vision of his task in strengthening the orchestra's artistic impact on the community, arousing what has become an audience too willing to accept music in general, and new music in particular, all too complacently. Hicks, from his keen appreciation of the underlying economic problems and of the Louisville Orchestra's unique relation to the Fund, has developed concrete programs for placing the orchestra on the sounder financial base it needs to implement the objectives of the conductor and board leadership. Nevertheless, to the outside observer at least, all three seem to be thinking within the existing concept of the orchestra. There is much that it could do by way of expanding educational programs, as well as touring the smaller cities of Kentucky, Indiana, and Tennessee that are impractical for larger orchestras. Such steps will require basic changes in the nonorchestral work of the musicians, especially those teaching at the university and in the public schools, that will require substantial improvement in the share of their total needs earned from the orchestra. This, obviously, would place an even greater financial burden on the orchestra, which has still to resolve its present fiscal role in the Fund. It may well be that, in the long run, more radical changes in this relation, occasioned by substantially increased service in the area, may be easier to accomplish than some of the modest adjustments presently contemplated.

The radical and often impractical innovations of Whitney and Farnsley a generation ago, for all their unconventionality, did succeed in establishing the Louisville Orchestra on a footing that made it a significant musical force, locally and nationally, for two decades. Among the many people involved with symphony orchestras across the nation whom this writer has interviewed, Robert Whitney and Charles P. Farnsley are unique in the enthusiasm and relish with which they recall the sheer fun they had with the Louisville Orchestra in its trying times. Though they "went to hell," in a way quite different from the manner Theodore Thomas contemplated, they can also vividly summon up in recollection a sense of joy all too lacking today in Louisville and, for that matter, in much of the national symphonic scene.

CHAPTER X

Buffalo Philharmonic Orchestra

During the summer of 1969, the citizens of Buffalo, New York, were treated to an extraordinary musical demonstration. On street corners and in shopping centers; for block parties, union meetings, and club gatherings; in private homes, churches, schools, banks, and department stores—in virtually every conceivable location, there were free performances of music by groups ranging in size from soloist with accompaniment to chamber orchestras. The newspapers and other media were flooded with reports of these programs, as the city of Buffalo enjoyed a saturation musical play-in. It was a sort of Salvation Army, often in shirtsleeves: the army was the personnel of the eighty-seven-member Buffalo Philharmonic; their cause, saving their orchestra, then on the brink of disaster, from either losing its identity or being completely disbanded.[1]

The Save-the-Philharmonic campaign was the most dramatic and, for the public at large, most spectacular event in the recent crisis-ridden history of the Buffalo Philharmonic. The immediate incident that touched off this players' campaign was the announcement, in April, 1969, that the directors of the Philharmonic Society had initiated exploration with the Rochester Philharmonic of the possibility of merging the two orchestras. This announcement galvanized the Buffalo players into taking constructive steps to preserve their orchestra, steps that involved their doing the one thing they knew best —performance of music for everybody or anybody who would listen to them. Since the Philharmonic's immediate crisis was essentially financial, the players' objective was also financial. With minimal professional guidance and no experience at fund-raising, they set out to establish a $1.5 million endowment for the orchestra. From the outset, they suspected that this was an unrealistic goal: they had no idea of how much they could raise by passing the hat (actually, in most instances, an empty instrument case). Had they known that it would produce but $50,000, they might never have started this campaign to which scores of musicians contributed virtually their full time for the entire summer. But had they not undertaken this project, it is virtually certain that the Buffalo Philharmonic would not have survived, for their efforts so informed the public of Buffalo, so closely tied their cause to the community's pride, that major government sources of financial aid were forthcoming in the next two years. The players were not alone in securing these funds, but their efforts played an essential, possibly crucial, part in saving the orchestra —or, more precisely, in gaining a reprieve for the Philharmonic.

The Philharmonic's problems were far too deep-seated to admit of easy or quick solution. In turning to a possible merger with Rochester in April, 1969, its directors were responding to a financial crisis that had been accumulating for years. For a decade the orchestra had experienced a rapid increase in its budget that was far from matched by a comparable increase in income from performances. As the sustaining-fund requirements to meet this deficit grew, their ability to raise the required money annually fell far short from year to year, and the orchestra stayed in business only by borrowing from local banks; by the spring of 1969, these loans totaled nearly $300,000, and the banks were pressing the Philharmonic board to get its financial house in order. Nor was the musical program of the Philharmonic completely accepted in Buffalo: since 1963 the orchestra had enjoyed the services of the dynamic and personable American-trained conductor Lukas Foss, whose commitment to *avant-garde* music—especially in his first years as the Philharmonic's conductor and continually in his role as director of the Creative Associates in Contemporary Music at the Buffalo branch of the State University of New York—had antagonized some subscribers, alienated important contributors, and created mounting misgivings among board members. Moreover, the Philharmonic had suffered an exceptional turnover in its management: in the spring of 1969, its third manager in three years was anxious to leave his post. There has always been in Buffalo, a pervasive feeling, both in the symphonic group and in the community at large, that the city is essentially a "blue collar" town. Its metropolitan-area population of 1,350,000 [2] is basically supported by heavy industry, and its most important employers, such as steel and auto plants, though very large, are not locally owned. Ethnically, much of its population is of Polish extraction, many only a generation past actual immigration. Economically and socially, the city contains a big mass of working people, a small, old-family upper crust, and, for a city of this size, a relatively modest middle class based in professional and service vocations. Traditionally this has not provided a broad and firm base for cultural activities that call for large-scale financial support on a continuing basis.

The "Philharmonic Family"

Like other American orchestras, the roots of the Buffalo Philharmonic extend far back to the early efforts of working musicians to organize symphony concerts. In the case of Buffalo, a symphonic activity has been traced as far back as 1884, but it was not until 1932 that an effort was made to establish a permanent orchestra.[3] This led a precarious existence until 1936 when, with help from the WPA, the Philharmonic became an adequately financed body of musicians and engaged Franco Autori as its musical director. The Buffalo Philharmonic Orchestra Society was soon incorporated, and took over when WPA support was withdrawn in 1939. The completion of Kleinhans Music Hall in 1940 provided an excellent hall for its performances, rehearsals, and supporting storage and office requirements; designed by Eliel Saarinen, and owned and operated by the city of Buffalo, it is one of the finest music halls in the country. In 1945 a small group of interested people in Buffalo decided to place the Philharmonic on a more substantial basis, financially and artistically.

One of the leaders of this group was Cameron Baird, a member of a wealthy and influential family in the city, and himself a dedicated music lover.[4] Although Baird's own musical activity was largely limited to conducting an amateur chorus, his interest in music was extremely broad, encompassing not only symphonic music but also chamber music. Upon his death in 1958, he endowed the University of Buffalo with funds to perpetuate his memory with an annual Beethoven-quartet cycle, originally performed by the Budapest Quartet, but now given by the Guarneri Quartet. Although others secured financial and community support for the Philharmonic, Baird not only contributed substantial funds himself but was the musical authority of this group. He was instrumental in engaging William Steinberg as musical director of the orchestra in 1945, largely on the recommendation of Arturo Toscanini, and when Steinberg left for the Pittsburgh Symphony in 1952, Baird was prime mover in engaging Josef Krips as his successor after an interim season of guest conductors. However, early in his tenure, Krips and Baird had a serious disagreement about the role of Baird's amateur chorus in Philharmonic activities and Baird had withdrawn to a considerable degree from active influence in Philharmonic affairs before his death in 1958. Meanwhile, he had also taken a great interest in the development of the State University of New York at Buffalo, an outgrowth of the University of Buffalo, and played a major role in the long-range planning of its general scope, with special attention to the development of an important music department there. Prior to his death, Baird had conferred intensively with Dr. Allan D. Sapp, who shortly became head of the department, which he proceeded to develop aggressively, with, among other things, a great emphasis on contemporary composition and performance.* A chamber-music hall on the campus of the university was erected with funds donated by Baird and is named in his memory.

Under Steinberg and Krips, the Buffalo Philharmonic developed into a thoroughly professional orchestra, drawing some of its personnel from the locality but bringing in many players from the outside—from conservatories in Ohio, as well as from the Eastman School of Music in Rochester and Julliard in New York City. The repertory of both Steinberg and Krips, as might

---

* The development of the university in general and of its music program has been slowed appreciably in recent years due to drastic reductions in funds available from the state of New York for building construction and faculty expansion.

be expected from their respective national origins, placed considerable emphasis on such Austro-German composers as Mozart, Haydn, Beethoven, Brahms, and Bruckner. From the Mueller repertory studies it is possible to extract some general data on the Buffalo Philharmonic programming as compared with national repertory for the five-year periods when each of its three conductors since 1945 was in complete charge of musical policy. Short of a detailed composer-by-composer analysis, this can best be described in terms of the nationalities of composers represented in the repertory, in Table 10-A.

TABLE 10-A

BUFFALO PHILHARMONIC REPERTORY

Composer-Nationality Percentages Compared with National Percentages (In *Italics*)

	1945–50 Steinberg	1955–60 Krips	1965–70 Foss
Austro-German	59.70	68.59	52.29
	56.75	*51.15*	*51.65*
Russian	17.62	9.26	14.63
	17.00	*14.06*	*14.80*
French	5.87	5.73	11.14
	12.23	*11.14*	*10.09*
American	5.73	5.60	7.59
	7.00	*7.12*	*6.66*
British	2.94	2.96	1.85
	2.87	*4.13*	*3.97*
Czech	5.04	2.96	1.73
	2.25	*4.13*	*3.97*
Italian	1.32	2.02	6.50
	2.58	*3.73*	*2.89*
Scandinavian	0.83	1.18	0.61
	2.48	*2.18*	*2.76*
Hungarian	——	0.89	0.14
	1.22	*1.87*	*2.76*
Spanish ⎱ Latin-American ⎰	0.52	0.34	2.00
	0.95	*1.30*	*1.47*

More detailed attention to Foss's repertory will be deferred until discussion of that conductor's period of activity, but certain observations can be made here concerning Steinberg and Krips. The Mueller data confirm the general impression in Buffalo that these two conductors strongly oriented their repertory toward Austro-German music, Krips much more so than Steinberg. Whereas Steinberg's representation of Russian music is close to the national average, Krips's is substantially lower. Both conductors included a significantly smaller proportion of French and American music than the national average. Except for Austro-German, the only composer nationality in which Steinberg presented more than the national average was the Czech; Krips's very strong emphasis on Austro-German music was obviously at the expense of every other national grouping.

During the leadership of Steinberg and Krips, the Buffalo Philharmonic was supported by a relatively small group, some forty-five families known as the "Philharmonic Family," [5] who shared the conductors' conservative approach to programming. Both Steinberg and Krips enjoyed many close personal friendships among the "Philharmonic Family" and played a major role in the social and cultural affairs of Buffalo. With disciplinary ideals characteristic of their background, they developed the orchestra in a rather autocratic fashion both in musical direction and in selection and training of the personnel. However, when Krips left Buffalo to become conductor of the San Francisco Symphony in 1963, there was strong feeling among the leaders of the Buffalo Philharmonic that a sharp change in the orchestra's tradition was in order.

Lukas Foss

A major force in articulating these ideas was Robert I. Millonzi, an influential lawyer in Buffalo, who, like Baird, has a deep dedication to music. Millonzi comes from a family of professional and amateur musicians: his father, born and trained in Rome, played double bass in the Buffalo Philharmonic during the 1930s. Millonzi is engaged in a number of business enterprises in addition to his legal practice, and enjoys excellent connections with the city, state, and county political organizations.

With the departure of Krips, Millonzi played a dominant role in the selection of his successor. He personally visited a number of American and European orchestras to hear conductors, talking with all manner of musicians, soloists, and managers to gain a full view of possible choices to succeed Krips. Coming as he did from a musically active family, he not only had a keen critical understanding of musical performance but also spoke the language of professional musicians. Millonzi worked closely with Allan Sapp, then establishing his music department at the university, who shared Millonzi's determination to bring new vitality to the Philharmonic and envisioned a close relation between his department and the orchestra.[6] Undoubtedly impressed with the success of Leonard Bernstein with the New York Philharmonic, Millonzi very early determined to obtain the services of Bernstein's contemporary and fellow-student in classes of Fritz Reiner and Serge Koussevitzky, Lukas Foss.

Born in Germany, Foss came to this country at the age of fifteen and enrolled at the Curtis Institute of Music, where he studied piano, composition, and conducting. Like Bernstein, he was an engaging personality and a dynamic musical figure. Though his early career was not as meteoric as Bernstein's, Foss had had extensive experience under Koussevitzky in the Boston Symphony, where he served for several years as orchestra pianist and had ample opportunity to study the technique and personal magnetism of the great Russian conductor. To Millonzi and Sapp, and the others on the board who followed their advice, Foss represented the kind of American-rooted "charisma" that Buffalo needed after nearly two decades of conservative Austro-German artistic direction. Though Foss was not formally engaged by Sapp to head the university's Creative Associates program at the time he negotiated his contract with the Philharmonic, he and Sapp had already discussed the possibility of such an affiliation.[7]

When he came to Buffalo, Lukas Foss had as a composer recently undergone a radical transition, from a rather conservative style of composition to experimentation in *avant-garde* music. In many respects, the dividing line in Foss's career as a composer was his *Time Cycle,* which he completed in 1960 for soprano Adele Addison on commission from the Ford Foundation, and which received the New York Music Critics Circle award in 1961. In this work, he not only employed serial techniques for the first time in one of his major compositions, but interspersed between its sections interludes performed by an improvisation chamber ensemble, a group of four performers, including himself, which he had organized in California in 1957. This introduction of improvisatory techniques became a leading aspect of Foss's music during the next decade.

In an interview with the *New York Times* in 1969, Foss, always an extremely articulate spokesman for his ideas, reviewed this change in his compositional style and attitude toward musical performance in some detail. "The more I got interested in the new, the more concerned I became with writing something really new, really experimental. When I grew out of the new Classicism, which was my former life in composition, and when I could no longer therefore make love to the past in my compositions, I suddenly found a great hunger. My psyche demanded that I make love to the past through performing. So I found I couldn't turn back anymore. The only thing that interests me now is this process of discovery." [8]

Upon assuming direction of the Buffalo Philharmonic, Foss immediately instituted a radical change in its traditional programming. Unfortunately, the Mueller survey previously cited does not indicate the proportion of contemporary music, but much of Foss's emphasis on American music (some sixteen percent greater than the national average) reflects this, though only in part, for he played *avant-garde* music by non-American composers as well. Nor does the five-year-average method of the Mueller data fully reflect the rather intensive attention to new music in Foss's first two years, which decreased substantially thereafter. Moreover, Foss's innovative repertory was by no means confined to the *avant-garde;* he discovered to his amazement, for instance, that the Philharmonic had never presented such important twentieth-century classics as Stravinsky's *Rite of Spring* and major works by Hindemith, Bartók, and Prokofiev, long accepted in the programs of other orchestras. To the Buffalo symphony audience, accustomed to the conservative programming of Steinberg and Krips, this amounted to a radical change. The sharp reduction (from 68.59% to 52.29%) in Austro-German music and comparable increases in Russian, French, and Italian music, to say nothing of the greater emphasis on American repertory, provided a rather rude shock for conservative subscribers, many of whom responded unhappily to these changes.

Charges that Foss's repertory caused a decline in attendance, contributing to the financial woes of the Philharmonic, cannot be substantiated. Krips had, during his tenure in Buffalo, enjoyed a high of over 2,900 season-ticket subscribers, before a decline set in. The following summary shows the number of season-ticket purchasers—the best indicator of audience loyalty—for Krips's final season and the seven when Foss was musical director: [9]

1962–63	2,659 Krips	1966–67	3,008
1963–64	2,740 Foss	1967–68	2,806
1964–65	2,716 Foss	1968–69	2,556
1965–66	3,421 Foss	1969–70	2,592

The increase for Foss's first year was undoubtedly due to curiosity about the new conductor, but, despite his new repertory in his first season, subscriptions held up reasonably well. The high figure for 1965–66 resulted from a special campaign to sell season tickets to corporations for distribution to employees and customers; 160 such subscriptions were sold, indicating that after two seasons Foss's innovative programming would have maintained a substantial increase apart from the special corporation campaign. This was abandoned after one year, with promotional inconsistency characteristic of Philharmonic management. Actually, the decline in patronage set in later in Foss's tenure, reflecting factors other than repertory, for after his first two seasons Foss reduced his emphasis on new music appreciably. Though no one will claim that this change resulted from board pressure, it did take place after negotiations in 1965 for the renewal of his contract. To some extent, this change may have reflected the fact that by this time Foss was more at home in the standard symphonic repertory, which, as guest conductor, he had not previously explored.

There must, therefore, have been other causes for the decline in patronage. Some contend that the location of Kleinhans Hall at the edge of downtown Buffalo is inconvenient for suburban subscribers, who must travel congested highways and find poor parking facilities at the hall. Moreover, the concert schedule—Sunday afternoons and Tuesday evenings—may no longer be as attractive as it once was for patrons. Only recently has thought been given to changing this. Nevertheless, Foss's reputation for advocacy of new music created great concern in the "Philharmonic Family." Even if patronage did not actually decline, the unfavorable reaction of a few vocal subscribers could, in the board's mind, have an adverse reaction on conservatively inclined contributors. Thus the impact of Foss's repertory was more psychological than actual.

Foss's identification with *avant-garde* music in Buffalo was intensified by his additional position as director of the Center for the Creative and Performing Arts at the university.[10] When Allan D. Sapp became head of the music department at the State University of New York at Buffalo, one of his long-range objectives was to organize on the campus a resident performing ensemble that would devote its full time to new music. He also envisioned a close relation between the orchestra and the university, especially in employing important orchestra musicians on his faculty. Both of these objectives were much in Sapp's mind when he joined Robert I. Millonzi in searching for a new conductor for the Philharmonic in 1962. After Foss became musical director in the fall of 1963, Sapp, who had already discussed his plans with Foss informally, organized this performing ensemble with Foss and Richard Duffalo as musical directors. The Creative Associates devoted their attention to new music, much of it experimental, often with the active collaboration of the composers themselves. Founded in 1964 with a grant from the Rockefeller Foundation, this project has, since the expiration of its foundation support and the general decrease of funds available to the university, continued on a reduced basis.

Many of the concerts of the Creative Associates in Buffalo have been given at the Allbright-Knox Art Gallery, which contains one of the most distinguished collections of contemporary art in the nation, thanks in large part to the generous interest of Seymour Knox, whose father was a co-founder of the F. W. Woolworth stores and whose family has long been prominent in Buffalo. Knox, who has also been chairman of the New York State Council on the Arts, has always been less interested in music than in the visual arts, and was not a major force in Philharmonic affairs. His most important interest in music in Buffalo has been in connection with the Creative Associates' concerts in the Gallery; through these he and Foss found common interests, which were not carried over into Philharmonic affairs, except that Foss's continued identification with the experimental activities of the Creative Associates contributed to his general reputation in Buffalo for *avant-garde* advocacy. Even so, the Philharmonic did nothing to counteract this image with any sort of publicity to present the true facts of subscriber support. Nor did it even pursue consistently such subscription-promotion efforts as had shown success.

As musical director of an orchestra with a budget exceeding a million dollars before he left it, Foss shared with some of his present-day colleagues substantial shortcomings as an artistic administrator. In his case, however, this was all the more apparent because, with one exception, he did not work with a manager who could make up for his own administrative defects. During Foss's seven-year tenure there were four managers of the Society; of these only Seymour L. Rosen had the ability to act with authority and responsibility. Consequently, many of the actions for which Foss was widely criticized in Buffalo—his frequent changes of program, last-minute calls for extra rehearsal, and indiscreet remarks to the press that later had to be "clarified"—stood out in stark relief in the Philharmonic's image. These shortcomings could have been minimized by sufficiently expert management, of the kind that in other cities succeeds in protecting the conductor from his weaknesses. Another function of strong management would have been to create promotional programs in Buffalo that would have capitalized on Foss's indisputable charisma and on the international acclaim that hailed him for an innovative artistic policy which, left to their own devices, Buffaloans were allowed to resent.

In the total performance of the Philharmonic, moreover, Foss's interests focused narrowly on his own activities and on the occasional guest whom he personally selected to present music for which he shared an enthusiasm. He took little active interest in the other subscription concerts or, in many cases, in the soloists to appear on his own programs, leaving their choice to the manager or board members; apparently he felt that such questions were more in the nature of promotion or business management. Beyond the subscription concerts—the Saturday evening popular programs and the educational concerts—he was even less involved. For two years, his assistant conductor was a man engaged by Krips who had married into a prominent Buffalo family. When he chose his own assistants, Richard Duffalo and Melvin Strauss, they were well-qualified musicians whose approach to music was very much in sympathy with his own. Once he had engaged them, however, he gave them full responsibility and authority over their own activities, with virtually no overall artistic direction or guidance in policy.

If the subscribers found Foss's programming "bizarre," the members of the orchestra found him a refreshing contrast with the authoritarian atmosphere established by Steinberg and Krips.[11] Whereas his predecessors had taken virtually sole responsibility for the selection of new players, Foss readily consulted leading musicians of the orchestra to assist him in auditioning new players; under Foss's direction, the orchestra acquired a considerably more youthful personnel. Though a number of the players felt that Foss was basically an inexperienced conductor, they were captivated by his enthusiasm, charm, and obvious dedication to the task of making music. However, many —including those personally most sympathetic to his artistic aims and responsive to his personality—recognized his lack of musical authority in the standard orchestral repertory. Much of Foss's previous actual conducting experience had been in guest engagements in which he played his own music or his choice of contemporary specialties. Even when he came to rehearsal technically prepared for a work from the traditional repertory, several in the orchestra found his musical insight to be tentative or superficial. On the other hand, in the new music close to his heart Foss could arouse the players' full respect, even if they found the music difficult to master. Under these circumstances they gave the best performance they could to Foss and played with great vitality and enthusiasm.

But the personal charm that won the orchestra over to Foss was not felt nearly as fully in the community. He did not, like Steinberg and Krips before him, become an integral part of the "Philharmonic Family." Though he and his wife at first made their home in Buffalo, they soon moved away and eventually Foss's residence was actually in Toronto, whence he commuted to Buffalo and numerous guest engagements. Under these circumstances, the board, prominent contributors, and the important women's committee felt slighted. Nor did Foss make any substantial impact on the community as a cultural leader, despite his very positive assets of dedication and magnetic personality. Had he applied these assets to promote in the community his advocacy of new music, he might very well have counteracted the conservative opposition which he aroused. But for most of Buffalo he remained a visiting celebrity, who came only to conduct his concerts and attend to the business of the Creative Associates while he carried on an extensive international conducting career. To a degree this seems to have aroused considerable resentment growing out of the intense pride which the citizens of Buffalo, whether they were part of the "Philharmonic Family" or not, took in their orchestra. Buffalo, which in 1969 would show a broad and deep concern for the orchestra, felt that it deserved a full-time resident conductor.

Foss's contracts provided that either he or the Society give a full year's notice of a desire to terminate their agreement. On April 24, 1969, in accordance with this provision, it was announced that Foss had advised the board he did not wish to renew his contract when it expired a year later. Though the matter was publicized as a resignation, all concerned realized that the severance was by mutual agreement. The announcement came a few days after the Buffalo Philharmonic Society precipitated the "merger crisis" by announcing to the public and orchestra musicians that it was exploring with the Rochester Civic Music Association a merger of their two orchestras.

Merger Crisis

Though some of the financial problems of the Buffalo Philharmonic that came to a crisis in 1969 can be traced back to the early 1960s and before, their real impact was felt after 1965. To a large degree they arose from substantial increases in musicians' payroll incorporated in the three-year contract covering 1966–69, and from the failure of the Philharmonic to develop fully the utilization of additional services of the players for income to meet these increases in payroll. Moreover, during this period of expansion in expenditures, the level of contributions remained (with the exception of one year) relatively stable. To cover the deficit which resulted, the Philharmonic borrowed from local banks, at times using the restricted contributions and pledges to the Ford Foundation matching-fund campaign as collateral.[12] The following table shows these financial problems in terms of total annual expenditures, contributions received,* accumulated bank loans, and minimum weekly pay and season length in the musicians' contract.

Year	Expenditures	Contributions	Loans Outstanding	Weekly Minimum Pay	Weeks	Annual Minimum Pay
1965–66	$ 869,000	$228,000	$———	$145.00	34	$4,930
1966–67	1,031,000	230,000	25,000	157.50	34	5,305
1967–68	1,190,000	217,000	150,000	170.00	36	6,120
1968–69	1,283,000	324,000	291,000	182.50	38	6,835
1969–70	1,304,000	281,000	225,000	182.50	38	6,835
1970–71	1,334,000	298,000	270,000	225.00	36	8,100
1971–72				225.00	39	8,775
1972–73				237.50	42	9,975

* These figures were supplied by the Philharmonic management early in 1972. Especially as regards contributions, they do not coincide with information given me by other sources: in particular, Carl W. Shaver, in an interview, claimed a total of $425,000 in contributions for the fund-raising campaign his firm managed in 1967–68. The difference is probably due partly to the allocation of receipts to other fiscal years and to the fact that Philharmonic accounting reports *net* contributions after the deduction of campaign expenses: some of the income from the Shaver-managed drive in 1967–68 may have been credited to the endowment-matching drive.

Thus, in the four seasons from 1965 to 1969 expenditures increased by $414,000, while contributions advanced only $96,000; some of this difference was made up in performance and other supplementary income, but since loans did not cover all of the deficit, the operation ran more than $300,000 behind. Additional supplementary income during this period developed from growing support from the city of Buffalo and from Erie County; though the justification of such support was based on educational and community services, the Buffalo Philharmonic accountants have not computed such grants as performance income for services rendered but rather as contributions under supplementary income.[13] Though, as noted in the previous footnote, the accounting procedures of the Philharmonic are not entirely clear, the general trend of financial difficulty, especially as reflected in growing bank loans, is apparent here.

That this crisis was allowed to develop must be attributed in considerable degree to what can only be described as the defeatist psychology that grew like a cancer in the Philharmonic board. This was partially related to concern over Foss's real or imagined alienation of the audience and contributors with his programming. It is also certainly very deeply rooted in the general Buffalo blue-collar-town syndrome. Nor was this psychology confined to year-to-year operations; in 1966, the Ford Foundation's original offer to Buffalo was an endowment grant of $2 million, to be matched by a similar sum raised locally. The Buffalo Philharmonic was one of the few orchestras in the country that substantially reduced the Ford Foundation grant: it asked for only $1 million, with a commitment to raise the same amount locally. However, it should be noted that three-quarters of the Buffalo matching challenge were rather readily raised within sixteen months of concluding arrangements with the foundation. Certainly the board's reluctance to undertake too large a commitment can be justified in view of the bank loans, but this episode illustrates how accumulated deficits can become a deadweight deterring the acceptance of innovative challenges.

After an initial partial success in raising the Ford challenge funds in 1966 and 1967, the board decided to seek outside help to meet the remaining goal and engaged C. W. Shaver and Company of New York City [14] as consultants and as managers of the drive. Like the George A. Brakeley firm which worked on the Philadelphia Orchestra campaign, the Shaver organization is one of several specializing in advising educational and cultural institutions on their fund-raising problems. Before making specific recommendations and undertaking the management of the campaign, the Shaver staff came to Buffalo in the fall of 1967 to make a complete survey of the operations of the orchestra and their potential for the future. It soon became evident that the real problem facing the Buffalo Philharmonic was not in raising the remainder of the Ford Foundation challenge but actually in completing the season already under way. It not only found the Philharmonic in perilous condition, but explicitly traced it to weak management and unsound board policies. Repeatedly, the Shaver personnel experienced difficulty in getting consistently accurate and meaningful financial information from the Philharmonic management or its board, and found meetings which they attended poorly arranged and conducted, without adequate information for such directors as attended. Faced with these conditions, Shaver recommended that his firm's activities be directed first to organizing and managing a sustaining-fund campaign for the current year (1967–68) before attempting to complete the challenge drive for endowment funds. An essential part of this report recommended that management be reorganized and given clear responsibility and authority, and that the board, in addition to seeking wider representation of the community, revise its own methods of operation. The Society then engaged the Shaver firm to manage its current sustaining campaign, which raised $425,000, the largest amount ever in Buffalo for the Philharmonic in annual private contributions.

Though Shaver looked forward to continuing the management of annual maintenance and the endowment-matching drives, the Philharmonic Society board failed to conclude arrangements for this, more by postponement of the decision than by explicit severance of the relation.* A year later the Philharmonic found itself in such an impossible financial situation that it was forced to contemplate merger with the Rochester Philharmonic.

Prior to the 1966–67 season, at a time when orchestra players in general had extremely high expectations for expansion because of the recently announced Ford Foundation grants, the Buffalo Philharmonic concluded an extremely favorable contract from the point of view of the players. Such a contract could be absorbed in terms of musicians' services only by a considerable expansion of the orchestra's activities, and justified financially only by an appreciable increase in performance income. Previous contracts had called for minimum pay of $120 per week (eighty players for twenty-nine weeks) in 1962–63, rising to $145 per week (eighty-three players for thirty weeks) in 1965–66. The new contract increased the number of weeks to thirty-four, the weekly minimum ranging from $157.50 in 1966–67 to $182.50 in 1968–69.[15] Thus, in six years, the musicians' annual cost nearly doubled.

During the course of this contract it became increasingly apparent to the players that the Philharmonic was in ever more precarious financial condition.[16] Even without access to the detailed financial and operating records of the Society, the musicians recognized that overall policy direction (whether of the manager himself or of the board) was weak and unimaginative: they encountered passive audiences and felt the general air of defeat that permeated the Philharmonic. As early as October, 1968, members of the musicians' committee met informally (in the sense that they did not directly discuss negotiations) with the president of the Society, who outlined to them the bleak prospect of the Philharmonic in promotion, finances, ticket sales, programming, and community support. All agreed that the orchestra was in sick condition, and the musicians left with a feeling that they could make a real contribution by offering constructive suggestions to the board, which indicated that it would welcome such comments from the musicians outside the formal

---

* Shaver himself vividly recalls making a special trip to Buffalo in the spring of 1968 to discuss and conclude arrangements for the future. The lengthy executive-committee meeting, to which he was invited for this purpose, dragged on and ended without ever bringing up the subject for which he had traveled to Buffalo.

negotiations for the next contract. However, except for a formal negotiating meeting in January, 1969, the promised conferences never materialized, though the players continued to press for them and held a number of meetings among themselves to formulate specific proposals for informal presentation to the board. After repeated requests for such a meeting were either postponed or ignored by the board, a time was set for April 22, which the players assumed would be the occasion for airing informally their suggestions and ideas for assisting the orchestra in working out its problems. However, before the musicians could present their carefully formulated proposals, Millonzi, on behalf of the board, opened the meeting by announcing that the Philharmonic Society had already released to the press a statement that Buffalo and the Rochester Civic Music Association had begun to explore the possibilities of merging the two orchestras.*

This news fell like a bombshell on the musicians, and the meeting quickly degenerated into a rather acrimonious discussion of the pros and cons of the merger proposal. Though the players were obviously concerned about their own job security, they accepted Millonzi's assurance that no one would lose his job as a result of the merger; tentative plans contemplated that some 130 musicians from both orchestras would provide a pool for activities in both cities and that the personnel would be gradually reduced through attrition over a period of years, a realistic projection in view of the turnover in both orchestras at the time. To the players themselves, the issue of job security was considerably less pressing than their concern over the loss of the identity of the orchestra to which they were devoted. In subsequent discussions by the orchestra committee and by the orchestra as a whole, this latter concern assumed major importance.

In Rochester the response of both players and local union was immediate and categorical: the union issued a statement denouncing the merger and stating that the Rochester players would not be permitted to cooperate in it. In Buffalo, however, neither the players nor their union took such a drastic position. There were, of course, some players in the orchestra who argued for an outright denunciation of the Philharmonic board for mismanagement and incompetence, but there were others, eventually a preponderant group, who felt that the musicians should react more constructively to the merger proposal. To a degree this reflected a rather sharp division in the orchestra's composition: a minority were old-time professional musicians who had been in the orchestra for some time and were rather conservative in their musical tastes and dogmatic in union matters; but many intelligent and imaginative young musicians, some of them holding their first positions in a major American orchestra, wanted to take a more constructive approach. This latter group, especially under the leadership of first oboist Rodney Pierce and principal violist Jesse Levine, persuaded their colleagues to organize the Save-the-Philhar-

* Orchestra merger was very much in the air during 1969, despite the fact that the provisions of the Ford Foundation trust of 1966 specifically required beneficiary orchestras to maintain their independence until 1976. However, there was no mention of this in widespread public discussion of mergers in Cincinnati, Indianapolis, Rochester, or Buffalo, where other factors eventually caused the merger projects to be dropped. At the same time, two orchestras not included in the Ford Foundation program, those of Tampa and St. Petersburg, did successfully merge in 1969.[17]

monic campaign that had such an impact on Buffalo in the coming months.

While this campaign was in progress, the orchestra committee was also involved in negotiations with management for renewal of its contract for the coming season. Under the emergency conditions it was obvious that major advances in this contract could not be achieved, and eventually the players accepted a virtually status quo contract for one year, including the provision that the season could be canceled during its course after a certain date in midseason if sufficient funds for its completion were not in hand.

Meanwhile, the efforts of neither the musicians nor the board during the summer of 1969 produced from private sources sufficient funds to guarantee the success of the 1969–70 season. Moreover, the board had early announced that it would not commence the next season if it did not have sufficient funds to see it all the way through. During the course of the summer, while the musicians' Save-the-Philharmonic campaign was still in progress, it became known to both players and board members that a solution for the plight of the Philharmonic might lie in an increased subsidy by Erie County. Both the city of Buffalo and Erie County had for some time made outright grants to the Buffalo Philharmonic, thanks in large part to the political connections enjoyed by Millonzi; for 1968–69, the county had appropriated $93,000 and the city $50,000. During the summer of 1969 the Philharmonic asked the city for $250,000, but the grant was renewed at the prior level. However, it was known that Erie County had in its contingency and surplus funds more than $1 million which could be tapped for the Philharmonic. There began behind the scenes a coordinated effort on the part of both the players and the Philharmonic Society to secure county funds. A major force in this was the support of George S. Wessel, head of the Buffalo area AFL-CIO. Wessel had already manifested considerable interest in the arts, unusual in American unionism, when he had obtained for Buffalo one of five pilot projects in the arts sponsored by AFL-CIO, at the behest of several entertainment unions under Herman D. Kenin's leadership.* Wessel was also concerned with the plight of the orchestra players, since they were members of one of the unions in his overall organization. He not only mobilized aggressive union support for the Save-the-Philharmonic efforts, but worked very effectively behind the scenes with the county legislators to lay the groundwork for a major increase in the amount of money for the Philharmonic. Although the Erie County legislature enlarged its grant during the summer to $100,000, the orchestra knew that even more funds were available. As is so frequently the case with such negotiations, the county legislature was slow to consider the request, and at the end of August the Philharmonic board announced that since there were insufficient funds for the coming months, the season was canceled. Within a few days the county legislature appropriated an additional $100,000 to assure starting the season, and the board agreed to procede even if full funds were not yet in hand; they were protected in this by their agreement with the musicians that they could disband the orchestra in midseason if necessary.

In making the additional $100,000 appropriation in early September, the

---

* Despite some encouraging local success in Buffalo and other cities, this effort to involve unions in the wider scope of community performance arts lasted only two years.

county legislature indicated that it would entertain a request from the Philharmonic for even more funds, providing the board would make a suitable presentation of its needs. During the months that followed the board made two such presentations and was subjected to very close questioning by a number of legislators, both in formal session and in informal discussion. The first presentation of the board was so loosely formulated and its spokesmen so poorly informed when questioned by the county legislators that a second one was required; in the meantime, the musicians and Wessel informally presented their case to key legislators. This second, and more informative, proposal contained fourteen points: a promise to seek contributions amounting to $575,000 a year, broadening board representation of the community including representation of the county officials, better business management and public financial accounting, long-range planning, and increased community services in popular programs and education, among others. At this time there arose some misunderstanding about whether the county's previous commitments did or did not include the regular $93,000 allocation. Finally, after the Philharmonic had twice given notice of midseason suspension of activity, the Erie County legislature appropriated sufficient funds to bring its total grant for 1969–70 to $335,000.

Thus, the Buffalo Philharmonic was saved by massive funds from Erie County. Though all elements in the Philharmonic picture worked to obtain these funds, no one doubts that a major factor was the public concern for the Philharmonic aroused by the musicians' campaign. Even if the musicians fell far short of their goal, they did succeed in arousing a real concern over the preservation of the Philharmonic as Buffalo's own. In response to their campaign, virtually every political leader in the city and county stated unequivocally that the community could not afford to lose its orchestra.

Thanks to the county appropriation and to a substantial grant ($175,000) from the New York State Department of Education for concerts in upstate New York universities, the Philharmonic completed its 1969–70 season with a surplus of nearly $100,000. But it was by no means out of the woods. It was still saddled by a bank debt, had yet to complete by June 30, 1971, raising its $1 million matching requirement under the Ford Foundation program, was now without a musical director, and had been in the summer of 1969 advised by its manager of his desire to be replaced as soon as another could be engaged. Moreover, its image nationally and locally had been tarnished by the publicity arising from the merger crisis of 1969. Though it had in 1969–70 raised less than half of the private contributions it had promised the county legislature in the fall of 1969, it still hoped for continued support there and, more important, from the unprecedented "emergency" appropriation of $18 million for the arts that Governor Nelson A. Rockefeller had requested of the state legislature early in 1970.* With the passage of this by far the largest state appropriation for the arts even undertaken in this country, the Buffalo Philharmonic Society eventually received $360,000, in addition to $263,000 from the city and county, which once again assured its continued operation.

* See Chapter XV for further details on the New York State Council on the Arts.

Millonzi was active in a statewide citizens' committee backing Rockefeller's request, and his close friendship with State Senator Brydges, reputed to be the most powerful politician in the legislature, undoubtedly played a part in the success of this measure.

Faced with these prospects, the Buffalo Philharmonic board began to set its house in order. By the summer of 1971, the Society met the Ford Foundation deadline for raising its $1 million in endowment, including in the final total the $50,000 raised by the musicians in their Save-the-Philharmonic campaign two years earlier. Acting upon one of Shaver's recommendations, it reorganized the board of directors, reducing it considerably in size to between thirty and thirty-five members, with an auxiliary council of trustees containing a wide representation of the community. Despite this structural change, there has been little evidence of substansive change in basic decision-making in the Philharmonic Society; this still rests with a few directors, and neither the full board nor council of trustees has appreciable impact on policy. Though AFL-CIO president George L. Wessel had been elected to the board of directors, his contribution to its deliberations was limited when he decided that it would be improper for him to attend meetings of the board during a strike at a business managed by one of the Philharmonic Society officers.

Another of Shaver's recommendations was that the board upgrade the role of the manager to that of chief executive officer. In the summer of 1970 the board secured the services of Howard A. Bradley, a former business executive who had in his youth studied music intensively; in fact, his talent had been such that he was accepted at several conservatories, but he decided to study at a conventional university instead. Prior to joining the Buffalo Philharmonic he had been an executive in the Ford Motor Company, and more recently in a local manufacturing firm in Buffalo. Thus he combined a thorough knowledge of music, and a dedication to it, with extensive business experience. In engaging Bradley, the Buffalo Philharmonic explicitly stated that they expected him to undertake full management of the orchestra in a way that had not been the case in the past, when the board members themselves had deeply involved themselves in day-to-day managerial operation. In June, 1971, after Bradley had served for a year as general manager and executive vice-president of the Society, he was officially designated president,* as recommended earlier by Shaver.

Management and Finance, 1970–71

Bradley is the fifth manager of the Buffalo Philharmonic in the past ten years. There is no question that he is the strongest occupant of that post since the departure of Seymour Rosen in 1968 for the Pittsburgh Symphony; in fact,

* At the present time, two other orchestras have created the post of professional board president: Carlos Moseley, at the New York Philharmonic since 1970, and Donald L. Engle, at the Minnesota Orchestra since 1971, are both former orchestra managers—Moseley with the Philharmonic and Engle in Philadelphia. The implications of this change in executive leadership of symphony orchestras will be explored later in Chapter XIX.

there is some indication that Bradley will have considerably wider authority than any previous manager has enjoyed. One of the principal criticisms of the Philharmonic in the past has been the excessive turnover in management, reflecting both on its quality and on the board's unwillingness to delegate responsibility. Bradley's engagement indicates widespread concern about the management of the orchestra and a desire on the part of many board members to upgrade that position. His extensive experience in business undoubtedly inspires confidence on the part of the board, and it is very likely that many now strongly incline toward giving him the full administrative authority he should have. Moreover, his musical background as a trained performer gives him a good basis for working with the orchestra members and their musical leadership. There is, however, a very grave danger that the board, in relying so heavily on Bradley, may be seeking an easy solution for its problems; the manager, no matter what his title may be, cannot by himself solve all of the problems of the Buffalo Philharmonic. Bradley assumed his post after a thorough look at those problems: as a citizen of Buffalo, he was fully aware of the publicity the orchestra had been receiving, and as prospective manager, he was given access to complete information within the organization before he accepted the post.

During his first year, Bradley completely acquainted himself with all aspects of the Philharmonic's operations and community relations. Taking advantage of the extraordinarily diverse experience of the New York State Council on the Arts, he drew upon their staff, including consultant Bradley G. Morison,* for extensive advice and counsel in a variety of areas involving broader community service and long-range planning. Working closely with board president Leon Lowenthal, a radio and television executive, he overhauled the Philharmonic's public-relations activity and brought it completely under his staff supervision, rather than farming it out to an independent agency. Guided by his experience with corporate management, he is making progress in systematizing the accounting and business procedures.

During 1970–71 the Buffalo Philharmonic received almost as much as it spent, slightly under $1.5 million. Table 10-B gives a summary of finances for that season.†

Of $280,794 in performance income, less than half ($123,761) was from the regular subscription season of fourteen pairs of concerts, an average of $4,420 per concert. Popular concerts, youth programs, tours, and miscellaneous performance services accounted for the remainder, indicating a considerable reliance on activities other than the strictly symphonic. In supplemental income, the large ($250,000) item from the Ford Foundation included a

---

* Morison, a Minneapolis-based arts consultant, first became involved in arts audience promotion with the Guthrie Theater in 1962 and has since worked with various other performance organizations, primarily in the area of management and audience-building. He was consultant to a Carnegie Endowment study of the educational impact of performance arts organizations undertaken by Mark Schubart, to be cited in Chapter XVIII. He also has been retained by the New York State Council on the Arts to advise both the Council staff and a variety of arts organizations in that state on various aspects of arts management.

† Based on Buffalo Philharmonic Orchestra Society, Inc., annual financial report, with author's modifications to facilitate comparison with similar summaries for other orchestras in this study.

TABLE 10-B

BUFFALO PHILHARMONIC ORCHESTRA SOCIETY, INC.
Financial Summary, 1970–71

INCOME
Performance:

Subscription season	$ 123,761	
Popular concerts	68,104	
Youth concerts	27,943	
Tours	4,300	
Other	56,686	$ 280,794

Supplemental:

Contributions (Net after expenses of $41,114)	$ 257,019	
Ford Foundation	250,000	
Government grants	622,640	
Endowment	67,425	
Interest	623	$1,197,707
TOTAL INCOME		**$1,478,501**

EXPENDITURES
Concert Production:

Artistic services	$1,027,678	
Production expense	101,812	
Special concerts and tours	76,454	$1,205,994
Administration	$ 128,225	
Interest	20,474	
Pension funding for past service	125,000	$ 273,699
Excess of Expenditures over Income		$1,479,643

special one-time grant of $125,000 to assist in funding a pension program; the other half of this income was the final sustaining grant as a part of the five-year program. The endowment figure includes income from the orchestra's share in the foundation trust and from the matching funds it raised between 1966 and 1971.

Income from government sources, amounting to 42% of the total, is by far the largest received by any American orchestra. It included in 1970–71:

New York State Councils on the Arts	$360,000
County of Erie	212,640
City of Buffalo	50,000
TOTAL	$622,640

Under accounting procedures used by the Buffalo Philharmonic, all of these funds are regarded as outright grants, not received for specific services rendered, although the Society based its applications for them on youth programs, free concerts, and other community services. However, it makes no effort to record such services by cost accounting. The orchestra received no funds from the National Endowment for the Arts in 1970–71; in addition to $25,-000 prior to 1970, it received $73,850 in 1971–72.

As of June, 1970, the balance sheet of the Buffalo Philharmonic Orchestra Society showed an accumulated deficit, including the small addition for 1970–71 operations, of $474,018. This was covered in part by bank loans of $270,-000 and by a portion of deferred income for the following season.

In order to compare these data with the Category C averages, certain adjustments must be made. Fund-raising expense of $41,114 has been added to administrative expense, and actual contributions increased accordingly. The $125,000 pension funding has been eliminated from both income and expense. Table 10-C includes these changes in the comparison of Buffalo with the category averages.

TABLE 10-C

BUFFALO PHILHARMONIC ORCHESTRA SOCIETY, INC.

Financial Summary, 1970–71, Compared with Category C Averages

INCOME	Buffalo	Category C Averages
Performance:		
Concerts	$ 224,108 (16.1%)	$ 418,583 (31.7%)
Other nongovt.	56,686 (4.1%)	35,065 (2.6%)
Govt. for services		198,055 (15.0%)
TOTAL PERFORMANCE	$ 280,794 (20.2%)	$ 651,703 (49.3%)
Supplemental:		
Contributions	$ 423,133 (30.3%)	$ 505,761 (38.3%)
Govt., nonservice	622,640 (44.6%)	64,394 (4.9%)
Endowment and interest	68,048 (4.9%)	99,836 (7.5%)
TOTAL SUPPLEMENTAL	$1,113,821 (79.8%)	$ 669,991 (50.7%)
TOTAL INCOME	$1,394,615 (100%)	$1,321,694 (100%)
EXPENDITURES		
Artistic personnel	$1,027,678 (73.6%)	$ 859,962 (66.2%)
Concert production	178,266 (12.8%)	264,969 (20.4%)
Administration	169,339 (12.1%)	174,012 (13.4%)
Interest	20,474 (1.5%)	
TOTAL EXPENDITURES	$1,395,757 (100%)	$1,298,943 (100%)

In the distribution of its income, the Buffalo Philharmonic deviates from the Category C averages in two important, and by no means unrelated, respects: the large proportion of government funding and the lower share of performance income. In a sense, this orchestra compensates for its low "earned" income (40% of the category average) with the government subsidies detailed earlier. Performance income might show a substantial increase if the Society were to use different bookkeeping methods, but it is doubtful whether their application would allocate all of the government funds to performance income. The fact remains that even when for-service and nonservice government funding for the category averages are combined (20.3%), the Buffalo reliance on this support is more than twice that percentage.

The large part played by government funding in Buffalo also has a relation to the importance of private contributions. Nearly 30% of these in 1970–71 came from the final Ford Foundation expendable grant; in subsequent years, the maintenance of supplemental income will require greatly increased private contributions if the present level of income is to be continued. Actually, the contribution factor in Buffalo's supplemental income is already significantly lower than the category average, both in dollars and percentage.

One reaches the inevitable conclusion that this orchestra derives a substantially lower return from performance in proportion to total expenditures. This is also apparent by comparing the relation of performance income to combined production expense (artistic personnel plus concert production): for Category C, performance income is more than twice (58%) the percentage of production cost of that (28%) of the Buffalo orchestra. In addition to the low performance income, this imbalance is also due to the significantly higher cost of artistic personnel in Buffalo, 73.5% of expenditures versus a category average of 66.2%.

In its current efforts to bring about greater financial stability, the Buffalo management has recently concentrated on securing greater performance income from its heavy investment in orchestra personnel. The problem of contributions has by no means been forgotten, but there is a tendency to regard the large government funding as something of a supplement to private support, while improvements are sought in other areas.

The Orchestra as a Musical Resource

In the wider area of management, Bradley met his first test during the musicians' contract negotiations in the summer of 1971, when he sought major changes in the performance structure of the contract. In 1969, the musicians, knowing the precarious condition of the Philharmonic, had agreed to a one-year renewal at virtually the same conditions as the final year of the previous three-year contract. In 1970, shortly after he became manager, Bradley negotiated a contract that reduced the length of the season but solidly increased weekly pay. In both cases, the Buffalo musicians obtained conditions better than the average of nine other orchestras in the same category, as reported in *Senza Sordino* (May, 1970) and the AFM summary of wage scales for 1971.

	Season Weeks	Weekly Minimum	Annual Minimum
Buffalo 1969–70	38	$182.50	$6,935.00
Average 1969–70	36.3	181.11	6,227.22
Buffalo 1970–71	36	225.00	8,100.00
Average 1970–71	35.7	191.11	6,769.44

However, with sizable state support assured, with continuing grants from the city and county, and with new leadership in management and artistic direction, the musicians felt that they could again seek substantial economic gains. The eventual two-year contract negotiated in the summer and fall of 1971 called for 39 and 42 weeks at a minimum of $225 and $237.50, and an annual minimum of $8,775 and $9,975. Though these increases occasioned much hard bargaining, a major point of contention was Bradley's inovative proposal to incorporate into the contract provisions to vary radically the manner in which the Philharmonic could utilize the services of the players under contract.

Basically, Bradley sought to convert the Buffalo Philharmonic into a general musical resource for western New York. He contemplated that though the traditional symphonic services would still play a major role in Philharmonic activities, the orchestra would also provide a pool of musicians for a wide variety of ensemble, solo, and education activity far beyond the previous capability of splitting the orchestra into two halves for youth concerts in the schools. In discussing this concept of what he has on occasion called a Niagara Frontier Musical Resource, Bradley freely admitted that the notion was by no means original with him, acknowledging the influence on his thinking of Bradley G. Morison and Arthur Kerr of the New York State Arts Council, of Roberta G. Jachim, formerly manager of the Utica Symphony and currently director of the Flint (Michigan) Institute of Music, and of a similarly varied program initiated by the Syracuse Symphony Orchestra.

Bradley proposed that in exchange for guaranteeing the players their basic economic support, the Buffalo Philharmonic would become a central employment agency for a wide variety of professional performance in Buffalo and the surrounding area.[18] The Philharmonic would sell the services of its contracted musicians, at a price covering their pro-rata salary and possibly contributing to the overhead costs of the operation. In defraying a substantial portion of the payroll commitment by the Philharmonic—not by activities undertaken at a loss but at least on a break-even basis—Bradley sought to solve the problem, faced by many other orchestras, of generating income to offset mounting personnel costs. Moreover, to Bradley, such a musical resource would provide in a coordinated manner a regional musical service that would, in the long run, justify increased private and government support.

In presenting these proposals, both informally and in actual negotiations, Bradley encountered strong opposition from the musicians, despite their readiness, after years of crisis, to discuss this concept reasonably. For one thing, symphony musicians have traditionally counted on outside work—as soloists, in ensembles, and as teachers—as a part of their income, as employment to be taken or rejected by individual decision; the specter of the Philadelphia Orchestra musicians' battles over the exclusivity ("anti-moonlighting") clause in their 1963 contract haunted the Buffalo players, if not explicitly, at least not too far below overt articulation. For another thing, in some discussions of his ideas, Bradley aroused the players' concern for the artistic quality of the services he had in mind, especially when he mentioned such social occasions as a Bar Mitzvah as the sort of engagement the musicians might be required to perform. Bradley's mention of Bar Mitzvahs in this context was immediately seized upon as evidence that his entire project might involve employment which the players considered beneath their artistic dignity.* Such comments did not allay their doubts concerning the new manager's expertise in symphony matters, despite their appreciation of his genuine concern, which they shared, for the necessity of creating greater financial security for the Buffalo Philharmonic.

Negotiations, which delayed the beginning of the orchestra's customary preseason activity in September, 1971, eventually produced a compromise on Bradley's musical-resource proposals. During the first year of the contract, Bradley can split the orchestra into two balanced chamber orchestras for no more than forty concerts, including the previously permitted school appearances. In the second year, he may reduce ensembles to no less than twelve players for ten services each. However, it was agreed that if sufficient demand for the use of smaller groups should develop, Bradley could submit specific proposals for them to the orchestra. He feels that these provisions mark a workable step toward his musical-resource goal and that, if necessary, the musicians would agree to increase such activity once their fears had been allayed in actual practice. He believes, moreover, that the orchestra as a whole would be more receptive to these ideas than the committee and union were; during negotiations he was not permitted to meet with the full orchestra to explain his plans directly. Nevertheless, he faces a major challenge in overcoming the misgivings of the Philharmonic musicians concerning both his specific plans and the quality of board and management leadership in general.

Michael Tilson Thomas

Nor were all of the Philharmonic musicians completely convinced that the engagement, early in 1971, of Michael Tilson Thomas [19] as a musical director of the Buffalo Philharmonic would meet the challenge of overall artistic direction of the orchestra. Following his resignation in April, 1969, Lukas Foss had still one more year to serve under his contract. He was also engaged as guest conductor for a portion of the 1970–71 season, during which several of the other guests were obvious tryouts for the position of musical director. Among these was Thomas, then enjoying national publicity following his dramatic success when, like Leonard Bernstein a generation earlier, he substituted at the last minute for an ailing conductor—on this occasion for William Steinberg—halfway through a concert by the Boston Symphony Orchestra at New York's Philharmonic Hall in October, 1969. In the engagement of Thomas, Robert I.

* This reference was also given widespread currency in symphonic circles across the nation: other symphony managements have encountered citation of Bradley's Bar Mitzvah remark by their own musicians in negotiations seeking greater flexibility in trade agreements.

Millonzi again played the leading and dominant role: there is no question that Thomas was Millonzi's choice and that he persuaded the rest of the board to accept his recommendation.

Michael Tilson Thomas was born in Los Angeles in 1945, the son of Hollywood film writer, producer, and director Ted Thomas; his grandparents were Boris and Bessie Tomashefsky, long-time actors in the Yiddish Theater in New York. Growing up in a family deeply involved in the performance arts, young Thomas benefited from the high quality of music education in Los Angeles public schools. He is one of a new generation of young musicians— Marilyn Horne, Misha Dichter, Henry Lewis, Lawrence Foster, and Shirley Verrett, among others—who have emerged from a Southern California musical environment so vastly enriched during the 1930s and 1940s by an influx of topflight professional musicians attracted by the high pay and pleasant working conditions of the motion-picture, radio, and television studios. Their impact as teachers and participants in such projects as the Evenings on the Roof concerts and the Ojai Festival has borne fruit, among other ways, in the development of these young California musicians. Thomas served as accompanist for Gregor Piatigorsky's master classes at UCLA and worked with Pierre Boulez at Ojai. At Boulez's recommendation, he spent two years in Friedelind Wagner's classes at Bayreuth, where he also assisted Boulez. Later he attended the Berkshire Music School at Tanglewood, the beginning of his association with the Boston Symphony Orchestra.

Though less committed to *avant-garde* music, Michael Tilson Thomas will continue something like Lukas Foss's imaginative innovations in programming, if one is to judge from his work in Boston, where Steinberg's illness gave him frequent opportunities to conduct and to record. Thomas sees Buffalo as a challenge both in rebuilding orchestra quality and discipline and in attracting new and more youthful audiences. A major consideration in his repertory is the selection and scheduling of music in a manner that will give him and the guest conductors, with whom he consults intensively, an opportunity to develop the Philharmonic into a genuine symphonic ensemble.

Thomas has a flair for programs with unusual juxtapositions of music: he presented Haydn's *Farewell Symphony* on his opening concert as the Philharmonic's music director, and included on his first season's programs such non-symphonic composers as Perotin, Josquin, and Gabrieli. "I call these *whiplash* programs, but the aim is not to be sensational. I program according to density, scoring, tempo, brightness, the way pieces move—the concert must have an organic feeling." [20] In Boston, meanwhile, he has organized special concerts of small ensembles, in addition to continuing as associate conductor of the Boston Symphony; on these he explores music ranging from Bach cantatas and Mozart divertimentos to rock ensemble. In Buffalo, however, he is concentrating on the symphonic programs of the Philharmonic, directing his efforts toward the central function of the orchestra, and leaving to the other staff conductors the artistic responsibility for popular programs and educational services. He believes, in fact, that the symphony orchestra as such has only limited possibilities as an educational force; he would like to use it in creatively produced educational programs for television or film, but insists that these should be of such extraordinarily good quality as to require expensive budgets and the employment of production and performance personnel on a scale impossible within the present structure of a symphony season.[21]

The musicians' misgivings concerning Thomas stem from their apprehension that for him Buffalo is only a way-station in his progress to a larger orchestra. Their unhappy experience with the itinerant Foss will, they fear, be repeated all over again as Thomas flies in and out of town, sandwiching Buffalo between his engagements in Boston and guest conducting in this country and Europe. Board members and the women's committee have been assured that Buffalo will be Thomas's headquarters and that he will enter into the social life of the "Philharmonic Family," but many musicians are skeptical of the strength of his commitment to the Philharmonic.

Like other young Americans, Michael Tilson Thomas harbors basic doubts about the viability of the symphony orchestra today and about symphony conducting as a career, feelings possibly intensified by his own family background in the broader entertainment field:

> I'm impatient with the whole milieu as it is, and the fact that all this success has happened to me so young makes all the problems of our musical life all the more evident to me. If it happened later on, I'd be brainwashed just like everyone else. I'd like to change the proprietary interest that musicians and listeners have toward music—all this talk about favorite performances is bad. In symphonic music there is only the permissible mean deviation between the Toscanini version and the Furtwängler. . . . [In the theater] the important thing is not how *like* the last time this performance was, but how *different,* and in what ways. . . . I haven't always been in music. I have other areas of interest—academic areas. If I ever get pressed to the wall, I might retire from music and teach esthetics in some small liberal arts college in New Hampshire. I am interested in cinema, I've done TV things. I never want to be just a conductor, but even in terms of conducting I want to do special things, work with small ensembles, medieval music, opera. I'd hate to be tied to the old format of conducting symphony concerts.[22]

Unfortunately, in the eyes of many Philharmonic players, Thomas's desire for diverse performing activities does not include Buffalo, and the "old format of conducting symphony concerts" is just about all that he was engaged to undertake there. Even if he were to become deeply committed to Buffalo and involve himself in working creatively toward Bradley's musical-resource objectives, many musicians and others close to the orchestra doubt if the Philharmonic board, as now so conservatively oriented, would give Thomas the full support such a radical program would demand. To them the choice of Thomas as musical director has certain aspects of a panacea for the deep-seated and long-standing ills of the orchestra. The musicians happily recognize in him a young master of extraordinary genius; they respond to him as only a band of professionals can when inspired by charismatic leadership, and the performances he has directed in Buffalo in his first season have aroused excitement in his hearers that may well attract to Kleinhans Hall new and more youthful audiences. But the questions remain whether Thomas, directing a relatively small portion of the orchestra's activities, can successfully galvanize its total activity, and whether he will provide the artistic leadership to implement effectively Bradley's concept of the Philharmonic.

An Uncertain Future

For all the excitement generated by Michael Tilson Thomas on the podium, and for all the imagination embodied in Bradley's ideas, the Buffalo Philharmonic seems still to think in terms of piecemeal quick-cures. A meteoric young conductor, with charisma to spare, as musical director; a hardheaded businessman as professional president; dependence upon lavish grants of government funds for forty-two percent of operating requirements: these elements are all part of the new developments on the symphonic scene in the 1970s, but Buffalo has still to pull them together in a cohesive manner. The internationally jet-borne conductor may well be one of the realities with which the American orchestra must cope today, but there is in Buffalo no prospective substitute for the resident musical director with his hand in every aspect of the orchestra's activities. Professional management, recognized as such by placing it at the very pinnacle of board organization, may well be the only responsible way to run our symphony orchestras, but there is some evidence in Buffalo that board members still regard such authority as window dressing. Bradley's concept of the orchestra as a musical resource shares with other managers' proposals for greater flexibility a tremendous potential for artistic service, but in Buffalo, and elsewhere as we shall see, these innovations require the kind of cooperation that symphony musicians have yet to comprehend. In their single-minded drive to improve their own financial status, the players rested their hopes on massive increases in government funding and on applying pressure on the board of directors for greater effort in securing private contributions without realistically appraising the potential of either source of support or developing a sympathetic understanding of the underlying objectives of Bradley's efforts to diversify musical services. Nor did either the management or the players fully realize the risks inherent in large-scale dependence upon local government subsidy: were the annually voted grants of either the New York state legislature or Erie County to be withdrawn, the Buffalo Philharmonic would very likely collapse, or at best be plunged into a more devastating crisis than that of 1969.

There is, moreover, a pervasive impression among the musicians in the Philharmonic that future cooperation from the New York State Council on the Arts may be, to some degree, conditional upon the implementation of Bradley's musical-resource concept. Such an impression is as hard to justify from concrete evidence as it will be to dispel. Certainly Bradley has freely acknowledged that many suggestions have originated with Council personnel. Moreover, though both Buffalo and Rochester suffered cuts in their 1971–72 state grants, Rochester's cut was deeper, and the Buffalo musicians believe the distinction was based on the fact that Buffalo has been more responsive to the Council's ideas than has Rochester. In defense of the Council, it must be acknowledged that the Buffalo management and board have sought advice from its staff: it is likely that the Council has been as much impressed by Buffalo's desire for innovation in general as by its embrace of specific suggestions. But a clarification of the Council's role in this respect may be needed to relieve the fears of the musicians.

Behind all this there lurks the still unresolved possibility of merger. In 1970–71, the New York State Council on the Arts granted a total of $1,023,-500 to five upstate professional orchestras,* two of them deep in financial trouble. Though Council officials shudder at the thought that they might meddle in the policies of the organizations they support, the very fact of such massive grants to these orchestras encourages their separate existence. This is not to suggest that it should, by omission or commission, influence the merger question positively, but merely to point out that government support of such magnitude cannot help but play an important role in shaping the course of the various orchestras' basic direction. So long as there remains even a remote possibility of merger with Rochester, relations with the Buffalo Philharmonic players will be strained: the threat of merger may modify their demands, it may make them more amenable to agreement in the musical-resource idea, but it will continue to preclude the kind of open dialogue that the implementation of these ideas requires.

Little has been said here of the Rochester Philharmonic, whose fate is tied to state subsidy as strongly or as tenuously as that of the Buffalo Philharmonic. Long a distinguished orchestra, it too has suffered its own recent crises,† arising in part out of the same general problems that confront the Buffalo and other orchestras, but also stemming from special circumstances in its history and its unique relation in the past with the Eastman School of Music. Faced with challenges every bit as demanding as those Buffalo encountered, it has not responded as dramatically: it has only recently again secured the services of a full-time musical director, and has never had as generous a city and county as the Buffalo Philharmonic has. Yet its success in resolving these problems, and the manner in which it does or does not survive, may well have an important impact on Buffalo. Once the notion of merger was advanced, the fortunes of these two orchestras became entwined: their resolution still rests in the unpredictable future.

Yet, to meet these long-range challenges, the Buffalo Philharmonic still seems sorely underequipped in its central cohesive board leadership. Unless its artistic direction takes on wider responsibilities, and unless its new presi-

* Albany Symphony ($15,000), Buffalo Philharmonic ($360,000), Hudson Valley Philharmonic ($70,000), Rochester Philharmonic ($325,000), and Syracuse Symphony ($253,000).[23]
† A widely circulated report by C. W. Shaver and Company in August, 1969, painted a discouraging picture of the viability of the Rochester Philharmonic. Its projections of unsupportable financial requirements have been somewhat modified by the subsequent grants from the state arts council. As circulated in 1969, it provided a powerful argument in favor of a regional orchestra that could be attained only by merger with Buffalo.[24] More recently, in 1972, the Rochester Civic Music Association was torn with internal dissension, controversy with the local union, and attacks on its conductor that resulted in a drastic change in the power structure of the Association and the engagement of a new conductor.

dent can act with full authority in all areas of management on the one hand and make progress in implementing the musical-resource concept on the other, the choices of these leaders can never amount to more than wall-papering over the cracks in the symphonic structure in Buffalo. The future there is both ominous and promising, and no one can at present tell which way it will develop.

CHAPTER XI

Albuquerque Symphony Orchestra

At seven in the evening, some eighty musicians of the Albuquerque Symphony Orchestra have gathered in the basement band room of the Fine Arts Building on the campus of the University of New Mexico for a rehearsal under the direction of Yoshimi Takeda, their conductor and musical director since the fall of 1970. Though there are a few older faces among the group, youth predominates to such an extent that in many respects this might well be a rehearsal of the university orchestra itself. For many of the players, the past two seasons have been their first intensive exposure to the rigors of full-scale symphonic repertory. Few of them, even those long associated with the orchestra, would consider themselves professional symphonic musicians, economically or artistically.

From the podium, conductor Takeda begins work on the Schumann Fourth Symphony, music which he knows in detail from his two-year apprenticeship with George Szell at the Cleveland Orchestra. The players here had first rehearsed the symphony a few days earlier, most of them then encountering its special difficulties for the first time, and Takeda starts this rehearsal with certain passages, notably those involving transitions of tempo, before proceeding with a full run-through. With this orchestra, he cannot take for granted even the most elementary skills of orchestra ensemble, and few corrections or instructions are grasped the first time. Takeda must proceed slowly, with great patience and the simplest explanations, as each difficulty is encountered and corrected. Intonation is a problem, especially among the strings, and the orchestra uses an electronic "A" generator, of technical accuracy but excruciatingly ugly and penetrating quality, for frequent retuning of the instruments. Time and again, Takeda must stop to call for rhythmic accuracy and attention to the beat. As he literally plows through Schumann's instrumental difficulties, which he has revised in accordance with Szell's alterations, it seems as if Takeda must tell the players how to play every passage and cannot count on their applying his instructions in one place to a comparable one later. Yet, with all this necessity to develop these most rudimentary elements of orchestra playing, Takeda succeeds remarkably in producing a real musical effect: by the time he has finished working over a movement with his players, his technical instruction has produced a genuine approach to the style and musical expression of Schumann.

Such a comparatively subtle score is actually much harder for this orchestra to prepare than flamboyant contemporary music like Ginastera's suite from *Estancia,* with its colorful instrumental effect and more obvious rhythmic verve. In concert a few days later, the Ginastera work will evoke greater enthusiasm from the audience, but most of the players will come away from the performance with a deeper satisfaction from having really learned the Schumann. For Takeda has displayed, in his two seasons with the Albuquerque Symphony, an extraordinary ability to teach his players the rudiments of symphonic music and to inspire in them a devotion to their efforts that produces genuine artistic gratification. The fruits of this conductor's work are evident from the fact that in Takeda's second season with the orchestra the entire capacity of the University of New Mexico's Popejoy Hall (2,001 seats) has been sold out on season subscription for eight concerts; in 1972–73 the subscription season will be lengthened by fifty percent, repeating half of the programs for a second series.

Takeda came to Albuquerque in the fall of 1970 at a time when the orchestra there was ready for him: a vitalized board of directors and a community eager for symphonic music awaited the kind of catalytic leadership he provided. Economically and artistically, the Albuquerque Symphony ranks at the very extreme from the Philadelphia Orchestra: its annual budget is but one-thirtieth of the Philadelphia and its musical resources are far removed. But this orchestra represents the emergence of symphonic music—even at its marginally professional level—in an American community. Though Albuquerque has had symphonic music, sometimes under capable leadership, for four decades, only recently have the various factors that might make for stability and growth come together in that community, and some understanding of the city and state and of their financial, education, and cultural resources is essential for any assessment of the present status of the orchestra and its future prospects.

Changing Environment

With an official population of 244,000 in the 1970 U.S. Census,[1] plus another 70,000 in the surrounding metropolitan area, Albuquerque has, in the past generation, grown extraordinarily: between 1950 and 1960, its population more than doubled, and the subsequent decade saw a growth of ten percent. About a third of New Mexico's population of just over a million lives in the Albuquerque metropolitan area, over half within a hundred miles: the next-largest city in New Mexico is the state capital, Santa Fe (41,000 population), sixty-five miles to the north. Very much a "new" community,

Albuquerque sprawls on both sides of the Rio Grande across the plateau to the west and toward the towering Sandia Mountains to the east, its urban expansion laced with gaudy neon "strips" and intersected by new freeways. A few tall buildings (twelve stories are a skyscraper in Albuquerque) punctuate the generally horizontal aspect of the city, which looks much like many other new cities of the American West. Though it traces its history back to a Spanish settlement of the area in the early 18th century, the city as a whole retains little of the kind of colonial Spanish flavor that one finds in Santa Fe.

As the largest city in the state, Albuquerque is also its major economic center. The Rio Grande, bisecting the state from Colorado to the north to Texas and Mexico to the south, has long been a natural trade course; the east-west routes of the Santa Fe Railroad and interstate highways cross the Rio Grande at Albuquerque. Its business activity reflects that of the state, primarily based on the natural resources of the region—mining and ranching. The wartime establishment of the major nuclear development and research laboratory at Los Alamos, ninety miles to the north, brought a considerable air-force installation to Albuquerque and after the war attracted a number of light electronic industries to the area. Because of its transportation facilities, it is a center of distribution for consumer goods throughout the area. But little of this economic activity is of the sort that has produced great wealth. The mining of copper, uranium, oil, and natural gas in the state is controlled by large national corporations; much of the natural resources of the state—natural gas from the Permian Basin and electric power generated from soft coal in northwestern New Mexico—is carried to population centers elsewhere. Ranching, once a major activity, is on the decline, and vast "spreads" are eagerly sought by developers for speculative land subdivision. Therefore, one finds little of the "old wealth" in Albuquerque that is a basic necessity for the development of the nonprofit art and cultural activity in a community. Except for a few old families who derived their wealth from several generations in cattle-raising or land development, much of Albuquerque's most important financial resources are owned and controlled by nonresidents. Reputedly the wealthiest man in the state, Robert O. Anderson of the Atlantic-Richfield international oil company, resides at Roswell in southeastern New Mexico, but his business interests are economically oriented toward Texas; though Anderson is a member of the national Business Committee for the Arts, neither ARCO nor the Anderson Foundation contributes to the state's only professional orchestra.

Nor is Albuquerque free of the social problems one usually associates with larger metropolitan centers. Its crime rate in 1971 was the highest in the nation. In motor-vehicle deaths, Albuquerque shares a New Mexico statistic of 7.6 deaths per 100,000 vehicle miles; in this it is exceeded only by Alaska, Mississippi, and Puerto Rico.* To a degree such phenomena are carried over from the violent ways of the Old West, but they have more recently become symptoms of the social tensions that have long existed in New Mexico and have now begun to surface. Socially, Albuquerque represents a cross

---

* The comparable rate for New York is 4.5, and for California or Illinois, 4.2.[2]

section of a uniquely southwestern ethnic mix that finds its most characteristic pattern in the Rio Grande valley to the north of the city. Here one finds living together, but scarcely mixing socially, three distinct cultural and ethnic groups: the various Indian tribes indigenous to the area before the coming of the white man; the descendants of early Spanish and Mexican landowners and colonial officials who settled this area as the northernmost extension of a great Latin-American empire from the 16th through 18th centuries; and the more recently arrived but socially and economically dominant *Anglos,* who came to New Mexico after its acquisition by the United States in 1848. To these often conflicting groups, Albuquerque has added a small black population and an appreciable number of more recently arrived Mexicans, who occupy a somewhat ambivalent relation *vis-à-vis* the descendants of earlier Mexican and Spanish settlers in the region. In the state as a whole, Spanish-speaking people account for forty percent of the population, and the proportion in Albuquerque is higher. Considerable unrest has developed among these people, some of it reaching overt violence, based on their depressed economic and social status; some of them feel that historically the Anglos cheated their ancestors out of their land, property, and position. In many respects, these attitudes bear alarming similarities to the problems of the black people elsewhere in this nation.

In a very real sense, therefore, such cultural activities as the Albuquerque Symphony rest on a relatively narrow social base of the Anglo population, despite some effort by the orchestra to involve the Spanish-Mexcian population, especially through children's programs. The symphony, with a basically Anglo * artistic content, differs from such other cultural activities as art museums, for instance, which draw upon indigenous Indian and Spanish cultures for a considerable portion of their collections and materials. The orchestra is by far the most thoroughly Anglo-oriented of the various developing cultural activities of Albuquerque; on a statewide basis the Santa Fe Opera is the only other professional performance arts activity so deeply rooted in Anglo culture.

Aside from the symphony orchestra, three groups are responsible for most of the professional concert music offered in Albuquerque, where several semi-professional theater groups also flourish. For many years, a Community Concerts Association has offered a subscription-only series, usually of five concerts, often including such visiting symphony orchestras as the San Antonio Symphony; many important solo artists have also appeared on this series. The June Festival Association, which enjoys a modest endowment from a sponsor interested in chamber music, has for three decades presented a series of four or five concerts featuring a nationally known string quartet (most recently the Fine Arts Quartet) and such collaborating artists as violinist Josef Gingold and pianist Ralph Berkowitz; the latter, formerly accompanist with cellist Gregor Piatigorsky and an early administrator at the Berkshire Music School, also served as executive director of the June Music Festival and was for many years business manager of the Albuquerque Symphony. Finally, the

* One must accustom oneself to hearing the music of Beethoven, Tchaikovsky, and Debussy referred to as part of the Anglo culture in New Mexico.

University of New Mexico offers a variety of concerts in two auditoriums in its Fine Arts building at its main campus in Albuquerque. The management of Popejoy Hall presents an assortment of touring companies, including theatrical shows, popular attractions, ballets, and occasionally such major orchestras as the Los Angeles Philharmonic, the Royal Philharmonic, and the Chicago Symphony. The music department of the university offers faculty and student concerts—solo recitals, chamber music, and the university orchestra—both in the larger Popejoy Hall and in a smaller recital hall; faculty musicians also appear on weekly television concerts on the educational television station operated jointly by the university and the Albuquerque public-school system.

Popejoy Hall, a part of a Fine Arts building that includes a smaller recital hall, an art museum, library, and excellent instructional facilities in music and the other arts, is a good auditorium. Completed in 1968, it has reasonably good acoustics, of the rather brittle ambience favored by Bolt, Beranek, and Newman of Cambridge, Massachusetts, and a good stage with modern production facilities, adequate for musical and dramatic presentations. As a university facility, it must give priority in its scheduling to school activities—the requirements of its performance arts instruction and the booking of university-sponsored events. Both Community Concerts and the Albuquerque Symphony must adjust their schedules to the availability of the hall under these restrictions. Another performance facility, a small theater flexibly designed for drama, will open shortly and possibly relieve some of the pressure on the Popejoy Hall schedule. Thus, the 1971–72 symphony season of eight concerts was scheduled on three Wednesdays, one Thursday, one Friday, and three Saturdays. The hall is available generally for only one rehearsal before each concert, and the orchestra holds its evening rehearsals in a band and orchestra studio in the same Fine Arts building.

In its public-school music program, Albuquerque possesses a musical resource of considerable potential. Headed by a professional cellist, Dale Kempter, this program brings a rather rudimentary curriculum of music into all of the elementary classrooms in the city, primarily through programmed instruction via television. The effectiveness of such a technique depends very much on the ability of the classroom teacher to implement the materials presented on the screen, and Kempter's staff includes a few music specialists who move from school to school to assist these teachers. Kempter realizes that this system falls far short of optimum musical instruction, but must accept it as the best possible given the budget available. Possibly the greatest merit of this method of instruction is that it stimulates sufficient interest in some children to motivate them to study instrumental music privately, in hope of gaining admission to one of the junior- or senior-high-school orchestras which are Kempter's most effective efforts in music education in Albuquerque.

There are at present three such orchestras—two composed of junior-high-school students and one of seniors. Kempter himself directs the Youth Symphony Orchestra, the senior ensemble, and supervises assistants who lead the two junior groups, with whom he also works. Each orchestra prepares several concerts a year in programs that reflect the musical competence of the students. The senior orchestra, prior to playing its public concerts, travels to various high schools to give portions of the program at assemblies. Kempter believes that such programs are well received by high-school students because they enjoy seeing and hearing their own contemporaries play music. He is also concerned with stimulating interest in music among the large number of Spanish-speaking children in Albuquerque, and one of the junior orchestras is centered in the area where this population is most heavily concentrated. Though he finds these children less motivated by their home environment to study and practice music themselves, he has discovered that, given encouragement and direction, they will respond in performance and in listening to the essentially Anglo musical materials given them: in all groups, he uses a few arrangements of Spanish materials, but the majority of the graded repertory must inevitably be of Anglo derivation.

This intensive instrumental program involves close cooperation with the music department of the University of New Mexico, which shares its cost with the Albuquerque public-school system. Kempter also employs a number of university music students as coaches and private instructors for the young orchestra players. Since this program has been established, Albuquerque has supplied a good proportion of music students entering the university, and some young musicians have pursued their musical studies in other colleges, conservatories, and universities.

Elsewhere in New Mexico, the quality of musical education in the public schools seldom matches that of Albuquerque—Los Alamos, with its population centered on the Atomic Energy Commission research laboratories, being a notable exception. The same is true of performance facilities in New Mexico communities where the Albuquerque Symphony might play concerts. With the exception of a good auditorium in the Los Alamos high school, there are few suitable halls or stages for orchestra concerts, unlike the smaller towns of Utah. In Santa Fe, for instance, the Albuquerque Symphony must play in a small five-hundred-seat theater on the campus of the College of Santa Fe at admission charges that would be prohibitive if not for the fact that such concerts are organized as benefits for the Santa Fe Opera.

Though the potential for financial support of nonprofit music is limited in Albuquerque, this is not necessarily the case as regards the Rio Grande valley area to the north—in Santa Fe, Los Alamos, and Taos, all within a distance of a hundred and twenty miles.* Santa Fe and Taos have long attracted as full- or part-time residents an Anglo population of cultivation and, in some cases, considerable personal wealth. As a center of major scientific research, Los Alamos includes in its population an appreciable number of people interested in cultural activities. In Santa Fe, John Crosby in 1954 established a summer outdoor opera company that has won international renown as one of the most enterprising and imaginative musical ventures in this country. The Santa Fe Opera now offers a season of seven weeks, during which twenty-five performances of six different operas are presented in a handsome and

---

* In a survey of statewide cultural resources made in 1966 by the newly organized Arts Commission, there is a map showing a rather dense concentration of a variety of arts activities in the upper Rio Grande valley.

superbly equipped outdoor opera theater, with casts of young American and European singers whose talents are welded into ensemble performances of standard and modern repertory of considerable distinction. The chorus for this company is made up of young "apprentice" singers who come to Santa Fe for intensive instruction in opera, and the orchestra is drawn from various major professional symphony orchestras throughout the country; no regular players in this orchestra come from Albuquerque, a circumstance to be discussed later here.

Such a venture requires considerably more support than one might expect to find in a city of only forty-one thousand. The opera audience, which totals over forty thousand in a season, is drawn partly from the mid–Rio Grande valley, stretching from Albuquerque to Taos; many of these are year-round residents, but some are summer people who vacation in the Sangre de Cristo Mountains for relief from the heat of Texas and other areas. These audiences also include an appreciable number of tourists passing through, many of whom plan their summer vacations to take in performances at the Santa Fe Opera; the New Mexico tourist office often refers to the opera company as the state's greatest tourist attraction. For a season costing some three-quarters of a million dollars, about a third of the expense is covered by admission income, the remainder being raised in a variety of contributions from individuals, corporations, foundations, and government grants. A major source of this supplemental income is from the wealthy residents of the area, either year-round or summertime, whose personal fortunes are based in Texas, California, or elsewhere.

However, the Albuquerque Symphony has not been able to share in this support. In fact, when the orchestra appeared in 1970 and 1971 in Santa Fe, it was as a benefit for the Santa Fe Opera Guild, though the trips were partly financed by grants from the New Mexico State Arts Commission and the National Endowment for the Arts.

There is no other professional musical activity in New Mexico. The Roswell Symphony, an amateur group in the southeast of the state, is the only other orchestra. Though Roswell is located in one of the more prosperous sections of the state, close to the Permian Basin, one of the largest sources of natural gas in the United States, the extraction of natural gas is not an industry employing workers on anything like the scale of manufacturing industry of comparable economic size, and the ownership of these facilities is largely out of state. The same is true in the northwest corner of New Mexico, near Farmington: here large supplies of cheap coal available for strip-mining have attracted the establishment of plants generating electric power, primarily for the population centers of Arizona and California; though a portion of this power is used in New Mexico, the utility companies manufacturing and distributing all of it are owned outside the state, as is the case with the copper, potash, and uranium mines elsewhere in New Mexico.

Thus, though the area possesses considerable natural material resources, the wealth they produce has not been of the sort that generates financial support for cultural activities. Essentially, therefore, the Albuquerque Symphony must turn to its own community for the development of such supplementary support as it can develop. In recent years, the transformation of this forty-year-old orchestra into marginally professional quality has generated financial problems which require the fullest exploitation of this limited economic base of support.

Toward a Professional Orchestra

The Albuquerque Civic Symphony, forerunner of the present Albuquerque Symphony Orchestra,[3] gave its first concert on November 30, 1932, under the leadership of Grace Thompson Edminster, a graduate of the American Conservatory and Juilliard, who had been head of the music department at the University of New Mexico since 1925. She had previously organized a student orchestra at the university, and student players and local amateur musicians made up the personnel of the Civic Symphony. A lady of great energy and enterprise, one of her early concerts was given in the depths of a New Mexico mine. She left Albuquerque in 1942,* having a year earlier turned her orchestra over to William Kunkel.

In 1945, the orchestra came under the leadership of Kurt Frederick, certainly one of the most remarkable musicians in the city's musical history.[4] Born in Austria, Frederick studied the violin and viola in Vienna during the late 1920s, when that city was the scene of intensive activity centered around the music of Arnold Schoenberg and his followers. As a conservatory student, Frederick played in early performances of the music of Berg and Webern, attended by the composers, and also in orchestras under the direction of Webern. Coming to the United States in 1938, he joined the Kolisch String Quartet as violist; Kolisch was the brother-in-law of Schoenberg and his quartet was then the leading exponent of twelve-tone music in this country. In 1944, Frederick became disillusioned with the professional music life of New York and moved to Albuquerque, where he at first studied chemistry with the thought of leaving music altogether. There he became involved with the Albuquerque Civic Orchestra as violist and conductor. Frederick fearlessly programmed a great deal of modern music by Hindemith, Stravinsky, Milhaud, and the Schoenberg group. In 1948, he conducted his orchestra and local chorus in the world premiere of Schoenberg's newly composed *A Survivor from Warsaw,* Opus 46.

Looking back on his five years with the Albuquerque Civic Orchestra, Frederick recalls how difficult it was to arouse the interest of the community in music in general. His efforts to advance the cause of modern music encountered no greater obstacles than did any of the symphonic music he played: all of it—whether by Beethoven or by Schoenberg—was so unfamiliar to both his players and his audience that contemporary music as such was no special problem: everything he played was new music. At this time, the orchestra en-

---

* Subsequently returning to live in Albuquerque, Mrs. Edminster, now in her eighties, participated in a gala fortieth-anniversary concert of the Albuquerque Symphony Orchestra in January, 1972, by conducting Schubert's *Rosamunde Overture,* with which she had opened her first concert.

joyed a close, if unofficial, affiliation with the public-school system, primarily through the considerable number of high-school students and the few teachers who played in it. Frederick parted in 1950 from the Albuquerque Civic Orchestra over the use of so many students, which he felt placed an insuperable barrier in the way of building a better ensemble. Supporters of the orchestra in the community and in the public-school system opposed him on this issue and he retired as conductor.

Meanwhile, Kurt Frederick had joined the faculty of the University of New Mexico as violist and conductor, where he became deeply involved in the statewide development of music education. In the high schools of New Mexico, he found that in instrumental music virtually all attention was devoted to the bands. As an adjunct to the sports program, with colorful uniforms and trips to other cities, the bands offered a glamorous attraction to the average high-school student with which a more serious instrumental music program had difficulty in competing. As a string player himself, Frederick was long concerned with the development of instruction in these instruments, in which public-school ensemble and orchestra programs should play an essential part. He found massive indifference among school administrators to the inclusion of instrumental, as opposed to band, music in the curriculum and to the hiring of qualified music teachers. Frederick's missionary activities with local school officials and his contribution to the training of school music teachers at the university were a major force in developing such effective programs as have grown up in New Mexico, but Frederick still feels that, with such isolated exceptions as Albuquerque and Los Alamos, the quality of music instruction in public schools in New Mexico leaves much to be desired. In addition to teaching viola at the university, Frederick has conducted the student orchestra there, from which many players have gone into the Albuquerque Symphony. After nearly thirty years of pioneering and often frustrating contribution to music in Albuquerque and the University of New Mexico, Kurt Frederick retired in the spring of 1972, an occasion marked with special tributes from both the symphony orchestra and the university.

After Frederick's resignation from the Albuquerque Civic Symphony in 1950, his place was taken by Hans Lange, who had been associate conductor of the New York Philharmonic (1923–36) and of the Chicago Symphony (1936–46) before retiring to live in Albuquerque. Under Lange, the orchestra progressed considerably, gradually diminishing its reliance on high-school students. Upon his retirement in 1958, at the age of seventy-four,* he was succeeded by the American conductor Maurice Bonney, who remained in Albuquerque until 1969. Under Lange, the orchestra had been "professionalized" in the sense that every player, of whatever competence, received some pay for his work. During Bonney's tenure, the orchestra continued to improve both in performance and in broader community support. In this period Ralph Berkowitz was manager; his broad international background and close contacts with important celebrities in the music world greatly impressed the symphony board, who gave him a reasonably free hand in his work. With the opening of Popejoy Hall in 1968, the orchestra could abandon

* He died in Albuquerque in 1960.

performing in an oversize and acoustically uncongenial convention hall, and it took on more vitality in its new setting at the university.

During Bonney's final year in Albuquerque (1968–69), he shared the conducting duties with José Iturbi, who had been engaged, hopefully as permanent conductor, in the expectation that his international celebrity as concert pianist and Hollywood personality would vitalize the Albuquerque Symphony Orchestra * in some miraculous manner. This proved to be a vain hope; in fact, Iturbi's service as conductor was little short of disastrous, as he flew in and out of the city to rehearse (or left some rehearsals to others) and conduct concerts. Moreover, the players and community soon learned that Iturbi, for all his fame as a pianist, was totally unequipped to direct this kind of orchestra. During its 1969–70 season the Albuquerque Symphony presented six guest conductors, one of whom it intended to engage as permenent director.

From the orchestra's early days as an amateur community organization, the musicians of the Albuquerque Symphony played an important role on its board of directors.[5] They had been consulted by the board in the engagement of Lange and Bonney as conductors, but were not in the case of Iturbi, an omission which they resented considerably, all the more so when that conductor failed them so badly. Faced with the designation of another musical director, the musicians met with the symphony board and insisted that they participate in his choice, basing their decision upon actually working under the various candidates in rehearsal and concert. This was the rationale of the six-conductor season of 1969–70. Though it is reported that one of the six candidates met with wholehearted support from the musicians, actually none was engaged, and the orchestra was confronted, in the summer of 1970, with the fact that it had no conductor for the coming season. Meanwhile, Berkowitz had retired as manager, to be succeeded by Mrs. Raymond H. Dietrich. Two additional conductors were then heard, during that summer, in reading rehearsals with the orchestra. One of these, Yoshimi Takeda, immediately impressed the players and those board members who heard and met him as by far the best qualified for the post, and he was contracted for the following season.

Impact of a Conductor

Yoshimi Takeda was born in 1933 at Yokohama and graduated from the Tokyo University of Fine Arts.[6] While on the faculty of the Ueno Gaken College, he made his professional conducting debut with the Tokyo Symphony Orchestra in 1954. In 1962 he came to the United States to spend two years as apprentice to George Szell at the Cleveland Orchestra,† and then

---

* The official name of the orchestra had been changed during Bonney's tenure, in recognition of the "professionalization" of the orchestra.

† In addition to his regular staff of assistants, George Szell for many years offered two or more apprenticeships in Cleveland to young conductors, who performed certain musical duties, were given some chance to conduct the orchestra, and received much instruction from Szell. A number of important American conductors, active here and abroad, served as apprentices under Szell in this rather unique project.

became associate conductor of the Honolulu Symphony, where his duties included directing a considerable portion of the orchestra's extensive educational program in Honolulu and vicinity. He has also appeared as guest conductor of several orchestras in Japan and with the Syracuse, New York, orchestra.

Although a full analysis of the Albuquerque Symphony programs, similar to the Mueller study for major orchestras, has not been made, the following summary covers Takeda's first two seasons there. Since national percentages for these years are not available, the data for the previous five-year period are included for comparison.

TABLE 11-A

ALBUQUERQUE SYMPHONY ORCHESTRA REPERTORY

Yoshimi Takeda, 1970–72, Compared with National Percentages, 1965–70

	Takeda 1970–72	National 1965–70
Austro-German	36.5	51.65
Russian	12.8	14.80
French	12.7	10.09
American	7.0	6.66
British	6.2	3.97
Czech	4.0	3.12
Scandinavian	4.2	2.76
Italian	6.9	2.89
Hungarian	2.4	1.57
Spanish, Latin-American	3.9	1.47
Japanese	3.4	n/a

Though sixteen programs in two seasons—totaling a little less than a thousand minutes of playing time—may not necessarily be a representative profile of a conductor's repertory, they can be taken as some indication of his approach to programming and of the music heard by Albuquerque audiences in a two-year period. The low percentage of Austro-German music, as compared to recent national averages, is particularly worthy of note. Furthermore, a detailed study of Takeda's programs shows that Beethoven is represented only by an overture, Schubert, Brahms, and Schumann by one symphony each, Mozart by a symphony and a divertimento, and Haydn by a symphony and a sinfonia concertante featuring four soloists from the orchestra.

A review of Takeda's sixteen programs shows further that they included only eight symphonies from the standard repertory, whereas most other orchestras average close to one full symphony per program. Moreover, there is a heavy representation of such orchestrally colorful works as Holst's *The Planets;* Debussy's *La Mer;* the suite from *Hary Janos* by Kodály; Ravel's *Rhapsodie Espagnole,* second suite from *Daphnis et Chloé,* and his orchestration of Musorgsky's *Pictures at an Exhibition* (included in these percentages as Russian music); Respighi's *Pines of Rome;* and Richard Strauss's *Don Juan* and excerpts from *Also sprach Zarathustra* (programmed as *Space Odyssey No. 3*). Tchaikovsky is represented by two concertos but no symphony. The overall impression of these programs, both on paper and in performance, is one of emphasis on orchestral excitement and display, at the expense of the presentation of more serious musical fare. A considerable measure of Takeda's success with the Albuquerque audience, as reflected in a 1971–72 season sold out by subscription, may lie in his combining in these sixteen programs elements of both the standard symphony repertory and a lighter, popular one. On the other hand, with such music as that of Strauss, Ravel, Debussy, Respighi, and Holst, Takeda has certainly strained the orchestral capabilities of his players. Though performances of such exacting compositions have proceeded without the catastrophes that often attend the playing by orchestras of marginally professional quality, thanks to Takeda's firm control of the players, many can with greatest charity be described as only approximate. However, they are presented with such verve and dynamic impact that they arouse great enthusiasm from the audience. Takeda seems to have discovered that it is far easier to make a great impression with such extroverted music than with performances of Beethoven, Schumann, or Mozart, which require a higher degree of orchestral precision and musicianship to reach the audience effectively.

From his Honolulu experience, where in each of six seasons he conducted as many as seventy children's programs and supervised the activities of ensembles in more than eight hundred concerts in the schools, Takeda has brought with him to Albuquerque a strong interest in developing a comparable educational program. Before he came, the Albuquerque Symphony Women's Association had had as one of its major projects the presentation of three or more youth programs on Saturday afternoons in Popejoy Hall. The audience at these concerts, for which a modest admission was charged, included a good number of parents who brought their children to the programs. However, Takeda believed that these programs lacked an educationally relevant approach, and found that the diversity of ages and the presence of so many parents impeded communication with the children.

He feels, moreover, that music performance should also be brought to the schools themselves, with small ensembles of professional musicians who can make a direct contact with the youngsters. In his second season, with financing from the New Mexico Arts Commission and National Endowment for the Arts, such a program was established on a modest scale. One of four ensembles—two string quartets, a woodwind quintet, and a brass quartet from the orchestra—visited twenty-eight elementary schools for three short programs each. Takeda himself worked out the repertory and presentation with each group, drawing on his Honolulu experience for guidance. These appearances are neither simple concerts nor lecture-demonstrations, but a combination of both, aimed at bringing serious music with some personal impact to the children. Kempter's office in the public schools has given enthusiastic support to this new project and handles the bookings and scheduling. Members of the women's association have played an important role in setting these programs up and in visiting the schools where concerts are played to monitor them. Unfortunately, only twenty-eight out of a total of seventy-eight elementary schools in the Albuquerque system can be reached with funds available, nor can more than one visit be made to any school. One of Takeda's long-range hopes is to expand these ensemble programs to more schools, to give them several times a year at each school, and to coordinate them with an expanded series of orchestra concerts at Popejoy Hall. For these, he hopes, the admission charge can be eliminated, so that all children of a given age group can be brought during school hours by buses.

Educational programs are but one of several proposals made by Takeda during his second season—and given considerable publicity—to improve and vitalize the Albuquerque Symphony. With all of the seats in Popejoy Hall sold out on season subscriptions, Takeda would like to expand the regular concert activity either by adding more programs or by repeating some of them back to back. Knowing the financial costs involved, he has been inclined to advocate double concerts only when the repertory or guest soloist justifies the risk. He would also like to arrange to repeat some of the Albuquerque programs in other cities where "runouts" not requiring overnight stays are possible. A few of these have been undertaken in Takeda's first two seasons, and this is the type of project for which state and national funds can be sought.

Such expansion of activity—more concerts, increased orchestra and ensemble educational activity—would, Takeda feels, provide additional income for some players, especially for key players in school ensembles, that would make possible the importation of musicians to raise the quality of the orchestra. Such a core of better players, built up gradually through increased activity and income, would also be of such quality as to secure work during the summer at the Santa Fe Opera. This would involve genuine cooperation between the symphony and opera managements and, in view of the many evenings on which rehearsals and performances are given by the opera, some players would find difficulty in commuting the sixty-five miles. Moreover, he wants very much to break down the reluctance that is keeping faculty members at the university out of the Albuquerque Symphony, a condition that will be discussed shortly in more detail.

Despite newspaper reports that sometimes portray Takeda as being impatient with conditions in Albuquerque, he seems deeply concerned with the long-range development of that community's musical life, quite aware of the financial limitations under which the orchestra must live, and realistic in his appraisal of the potential of his orchestra.

Musicians at Work

In his first two seasons, Takeda reduced the actual number of regular players in the Albuquerque Symphony from about eighty-five to slightly under eighty members, seeking an artistically viable balance between quantity and quality: at a certain point, the marginal player detracts more from performance than he contributes to the overall sound. In his efforts to improve the quality of players, he has also engaged more university music students than had previously been in the orchestra. For each subscription-concert program, there are at least five three-hour rehearsals; youth-concert programs require an average of four and a half hours of preparation. In 1970–71, the minimum pay per concert was $62, raised to $65 in 1971–72; principal players received $10 more per concert, and a few are paid higher by negotiation. In 1970–71, the minimum season pay was somewhat under $650, and for principals just under $800. In 1971–72, with increased pay and more concerts, the annual minimum increased to between $750 and $800; those minimum players involved in ensemble concerts in the schools received between $900 and $1,000 for the season, and principal players, if they were in school ensembles, received between $1,150 and $1,200.[7]

Since earlier days the orchestra members have had their own organization of nine elected officers. Four of these are also members of the board of directors of the Albuquerque Symphony Orchestra, Inc. Though all are members of the local musicians' union, the committee itself plays the major role in negotiations with the orchestra management. To a large extent, musicians' pay has been set at what the board could afford, frequently with minimal consultation with the players; early in 1972, however, the musicians formally requested that they be consulted before the 1972–73 budget, including the allocation for payroll, was prepared.[8] For many years there was no formal contract, an oral agreement being reached by the manager, board, and orchestra committee about pay scale, which was more or less automatically ratified by the union as long as it did not violate union rules. More recently a formal contract has been negotiated, but bargaining is on a reasonably amicable basis as long as the players feel that they are being fairly treated within the resources available to the orchestra. The committee also concerns itself with details of adjusting working schedules to the requirements of outside work, liaison with conductor and manager on matters of musicians' welfare, and the logistics of maintaining an irregular schedule of rehearsals and concerts: orchestra operations here can be extremely informal, and various players pitch in to help with setting up chairs for rehearsal, distributing music, or moving heavy instruments to their proper position. Several years ago, the committee was very concerned about the role of the musicians in advising the board on musical policy, especially the choice of conductor; the success of their participation in the choice of Takeda has certainly strengthened mutual confidence between board and players.

The personnel of the Albuquerque Symphony may be divided into three general groups. About twenty-five percent are musicians by vocation: a very few earn a living playing dance jobs or in restaurants and clubs; all teach music, either privately or in the schools. A second group consists of amateurs —businessmen or housewives, and in some cases married couples—for whom playing in the orchestra provides artistic recreation; they make up approximately forty-five percent of the personnel. About thirty percent of the players are music students from the university, many of whom have had some experience in Kempter's youth orchestras in Albuquerque and in Frederick's orchestra at the university. For these university students, it is difficult to play in both the Albuquerque Symphony and the university symphony orchestra, so there is relatively little overlap in their personnel; the load of symphony work is too great to allow for much other activity in addition to regular schoolwork. Though these players have been in an orchestra in the past, many of them find Takeda considerably more demanding technically and musically than their previous experience, but they seem to relish the professional demands made on them.

The faculty of the music department at the University of New Mexico includes several good professional instrumentalists, but none of them plays in the symphony orchestra: a few graduate assistants on the staff, who had been in the orchestra as undergraduates, remain with the orchestra, however. The reasons for the absence of the faculty members are obscure and largely traditional, for the orchestra would welcome them warmly and has invited specific musicians to join on a number of occasions. Takeda continues personal efforts to gain their participation. There seems to be no basic university policy that limits their outside activity. Though it is hard to get explicit reasons from faculty musicians, there may be a reluctance to join an orchestra in which their own students are playing. For another thing the faculty is comparatively well paid and may feel that the few hundred dollars of orchestra pay does not provide sufficient economic incentive, especially when they carry a heavy workload at the university. Artistically, these musicians have considerable performance opportunity in solo and ensemble concerts at the university and on the local educational television station. At least until Takeda arrived on the scene, the faculty musicians did not view the Albuquerque Symphony seriously enough to want to join it. The improvement of the orchestra under Takeda's direction may tempt faculty musicians to review their present reluctance, especially as Takeda himself personally presses on them his invitation to join the orchestra. Certainly the experience of such orchestras as Louisville and Utah indicates the mutual benefits that can accrue from a close relation between an orchestra and the faculty of a local university.

During the 1970–71 season, the Albuquerque Symphony played a total of fourteen concerts, all conducted by Takeda, in the following categories; activity for 1971–72 is shown in a second column:

	1970–71	1971–72
Concert series	8	8
Youth series	3	3
Out of town	1	2
Youth specials	1	2
Special zoo concert	1	1
Ensembles in schools	—	84
	14	100 (16 & 84)

Following the regular concert season in 1970–71, the orchestra gave a free performance at the Albuquerque Zoo that attracted an audience numbering six thousand. Total attendance for the season, including the estimated audience at this free concert, amounted to twenty-six thousand; when, however, allowance is made for those subscribers who may have attended as many as eight subscription concerts, one may conclude that sixteen thousand individuals heard the orchestra at least once during the season,* slightly over five percent of the total metropolitan-area population of Albuquerque.

The youth concerts are presented on Saturday afternoons in Popejoy Hall by the full orchestra under Takeda's direction. He builds these programs around some central idea that will relate to the children's own experience —music that illustrates concrete things or happenings, music for the theater, symphonic musical forms. The women's association prepares an elaborate printed program, containing illustrations drawn by children, quotations from them about what they hear in music, photos of the conductor, and a seating plan of the orchestra. It also offers brief program notes on the music, greetings from the conductor, and other material of interest to the young audience. This rather extensive booklet—covering all the programs in one issue and paid for by a local bank—is the only educational material supplied the children by way of preparation for the concert; except in rare cases, there is none in schooltime. Admission to the concerts is by season tickets (three dollars for three concerts) sold by the members of the women's association. In addition, the women's association includes in its youth series at least one staged program; formerly this involved the engagement of a regional ballet or musical-comedy company, but in 1971–72 two local productions, one of Humperdinck's *Hänsel und Gretel* prepared by young Albuquerque singers under the association's direction and another by a local theatrical group, were offered. As noted earlier, Takeda wants to restructure the entire educational program and has been conferring with the boards of both the orchestra and women's association on future plans. The new series of ensemble concerts in the elementary schools, which accounts for eighty-four programs in 1971–72, has been described already.

At present, the entire educational program of the orchestra is undergoing transition, in accordance with Takeda's own concept of the importance of such activity. In discussions of his plans in this area, he seems to have some rather comprehensive notions of exposing youngsters to serious music in performance, but neither he nor Kempter has yet developed a basic educational philosophy underlying the possible contribution of the Albuquerque Symphony Orchestra to a coordinated program of music education.

The Cost of an Emerging Orchestra

For the administration of these orchestra activities, the Albuquerque Symphony has a staff of two full-time employees, a business manager and a secretary-bookkeeper who work in a modest office not far from Popejoy Hall.

* The existence of substantial season-ticket holding in the total attendance figures of any orchestra makes the traditional attendance figures publicized by orchestras highly suspect. See further comment on this matter in Chapter XVI.

Mrs. Raymond H. (Marion) Dietrich has been manager of the orchestra since November, 1969. She had recently moved with her husband from Kalamazoo, Michigan, where she had been on the publicity and management staff of the local museum and also knew Mrs. Leta Snow, the founder of the American Symphony Orchestra League. Her duties encompass virtually every phase of orchestra management, including actual writing and placement of publicity, arrangement of schedules, engagement of soloists in conference with the conductor, tour plans, preparation of applications for government grants, general responsibility for the operation of the orchestra, and accounting of its finances and affairs to the board. As a professional with experience in arts management, she advises the board in many details of policy determination.

In 1970–71 the Albuquerque Symphony spent $122,368 and received income of $109,181, with an operating deficit of $13,187. This was the first year in which this orchestra had expenditures exceeding $100,000; in 1969–70, when it gave six concerts, its annual expenditures were approximately $80,000. In 1971–72 it budgeted operations on a scale of $140,000. Table 11-B shows the financial summary for 1970–71.

TABLE 11-B

ALBUQUERQUE SYMPHONY ORCHESTRA

Financial Summary, 1970–71, Compared with Category E Averages

INCOME	Albuquerque	Category E Averages
Performance:		
Concerts	$ 54,526 (49.9%)	$ 57,340 (33.5%)
Other nongovt.	4,734 (4.3%)	11,225 (6.5%)
Govt. for services	11,318 (10.4%)	21,342 (12.5%)
TOTAL PERFORMANCE	$ 70,578 (64.6%)	$ 89,907 (52.4%)
Supplemental:		
Contributions	$ 38,188 (35.0%)	$ 60,440 (35.3%)
Govt., nonservice		15,121 (8.8%)
Endowment and interest		5,903 (3.4%)
Other	415 (0.4%)	
TOTAL SUPPLEMENTAL	$ 38,603 (35.4%)	$ 81,464 (47.5%)
TOTAL INCOME	$109,181 (100%)	$171,371 (100%)
EXPENDITURES		
Artistic personnel	$ 62,203 (50.8%)	$ 93,786 (61.8%)
Concert production *	42,452 (34.7%)	28,364 (18.7%)
Administration	17,282 (14.1%)	29,573 (19.5%)
Other	431 (0.4%)	
TOTAL EXPENDITURES	$122,368 (100%)	$151,723 (100%)

When the data for the Albuquerque Symphony Orchestra are compared with the category averages (also shown in Table 11-B), its proportion of performance income is exceptionally favorable, more than 12% higher; this

* Including $23,327 for youth concerts and tour expenses, a large but undetermined portion of which is for artistic personnel.

is due primarily to direct concert income, since both miscellaneous receipts and government funding for services rendered are substantially lower than average. Nor does this reflect higher production costs (artistic personnel plus concert production): the Albuquerque ratio of concert income to these is 51.8% compared with a category average of 46.8%. Since the Albuquerque figures for concert production include substantial artistic services, direct performance costs can be compared only in terms of total production: for Albuquerque these amount to 85.8% of expenditures, against a category average of 80.5%; Albuquerque's administrative disbursements are, therefore, comparatively low. (In Chapter XIII, we shall have occasion to note how the proportion of administrative expenses rises as orchestras grow smaller.)

Given these favorable indicators in production costs and relation of performance to total income, the rather sizable deficit of over $13,000 (10.7% of total expenditures) can largely be attributed to the relatively low share of supplemental income. Since the category averages indicate an extremely big difference between the totals for expenditures and income, the fact that Albuquerque's contributions show the same percentage as the category average can be rather deceptive: in both cases, we must conclude that the existence of the deficit reflects substantially lower government funding, which contributes 10.3% of total income compared to a combined category average of 21.3% for all public funds. The Albuquerque orchestra's receipts in 1970–71 from government sources came entirely from the New Mexico Arts Commission as matching grants for youth concerts and touring; in 1971–72, the orchestra received substantially more from government—$10,000 from the state commission as previously, and $20,000 for its ensemble programs in the schools from the National Endowment for the Arts. However, in the later years, the overall budget also increased so that total government funding in 1971–72 increased to about 20%, somewhat more in line with the Category E average in 1971–72. (Category information for that season will not be available until early 1973.)

Virtually all supplementary income was from contributions, either directly or through the women's association; miscellaneous income came from the sale of musical instruments owned by the orchestra and no longer needed. The amount of the deficit, in a season during which the new conductor so vitalized the orchestra that the next season was sold out on subscription, seems to indicate a failure of the board to capitalize on the success of the orchestra in fundraising. As it entered the 1970–71 season, the Albuquerque Symphony had a previously accumulated deficit of $6,042, covered partly by bank loans, which by June 30, 1971, had grown to $17,000, as a result of the 1970–71 deficit. During the following season, the board had the task not only of raising $50,000 in supplemental income in a proposed budget of $140,000 but also of securing sufficient additional funds to pay off the loans; even with the most careful control of expenditures, the board in 1971–72 faced the necessity of raising at least $65,000 to end that season without indebtedness. Actually, in the fall of 1971, the bank loans were retired from funds collected from early contributions and season-ticket income, and the women's association had sufficient funds already in hand or in immediate prospect to meet at least $15,000 of the supplementary income requirement. By midseason, however, the board had only half of the $50,000 it needed for the current season and had made no progress in actually retiring its accumulated deficit from previous years. Unless it could make spectacular progress by mid-1972, it faced having again to borrow from the banks to complete the season.*

A Board in the Glare of Publicity

The board of directors of the Albuquerque Symphony includes a representation of those to whom its existence is a vital matter, but it lacks a comparable representation of the business community as a whole, largely because the latter has yet to be convinced that the orchestra is important as a civic activity. This deficiency, however, is gradually being corrected, particularly as the orchestra draws bigger and more loyal—in terms of season subscribers—audiences. It is difficult for local businessmen to ignore the stature of an organization which sells out its two-thousand-seat auditorium with season-ticket sales, and which has come to be regarded as artistically impressive. In recent years, the board has attempted to add to its membership influential businessmen of Spanish extraction, upon whom many Anglos have previously looked down; the emergence in recent years of this ethnic group as a strong commercial and political force in the community will inevitably entail more and more involvement in the affairs of the orchestra. The slowness of the symphony board to recognize this group has been the occasion for considerable fault-finding in Albuquerque; some critics maintain that the board leadership is still too restrictive in this.

With a membership of between thirty-five and forty citizens, the symphony board lacks strong and continuing leadership. Meeting regularly once a month during the symphony season, it tends as a deliberative body to degenerate into aimless discussion of fund-raising and operational questions that would be better left to strong board leaders and the manager. Recognizing this, the board president in 1971–72, Gordon W. Paul, instituted the designation of a president-elect at least a year in advance in the hope of thereby indoctrinating successive leaders in the problems of symphony direction. However, such a system will not significantly limit the turnover in leadership this board has known in the past unless the designated officers have extensive experience in board functions. Paul, as a long-time executive of the Albuquerque office of the accounting firm of Peat, Marwick, and Mitchell, brought to his leadership of the board a broad knowledge of the financial resources of the community—who had money, who was in a position to support the orchestra financially, and the best manner of approach. Moreover, as treasurer of the board before becoming its president, he was fully acquainted with the orchestra's operations as reflected in its finances.[10]

As board president, Paul had keen insight into the community role of the symphony orchestra, and he was acutely aware, in Takeda's second year as director, that the orchestra was at a crucial crossroads in its history. Takeda's

---

* By the middle of the 1972–73 season, however, there were indications that current operations would be fully covered and the accumulated deficit markedly reduced.

desire for expanded activity and artistic improvement certainly pointed in one direction that the orchestra could take. On the other hand, in the typical irony of American symphony orchestras in general, the Albuquerque Symphony had accumulated its worst deficit during its greatest success. Paul knew that the kind of orchestra Takeda advocated could cost, in both total budget and requirement for supplementary income, from four to five times as much as operations in 1971–72. Though such an orchestra could provide a community musical service undreamed of under present conditions, Paul questioned whether the Albuquerque or New Mexico communities could or would support it. Sharing Takeda's realization that such objectives could be attained only gradually, he persuaded the board to appoint a planning committee to explore just how the orchestra should move in the coming years. Unfortunately, that committee had to pursue its deliberations under the cloud of an accumulated deficit, which had to be liquidated before any real progress could be made. Though there is every likelihood that Paul will continue to take a deep interest in the orchestra, his own personal long-range plans did not include further service as board president; this is regrettable because he represents the kind of civic leadership which could greatly benefit the symphony with increased experience and authority.

One of the problems peculiar to this board arises from the fact that it must conduct its business under glaring public scrutiny; its monthly meetings are open to the press and are reported extensively and frankly. This seems to be a tradition of some standing in Albuquerque, reportedly originating at a time when the board felt that it could secure better public understanding of its problems through wider publicity. Since then the policy has also become identified with a state law that requires all "public" bodies to hold meetings open to the press; the symphony board has come to be regarded in this category because it receives some state funds and seeks contributions from the community. Unfortunately, this open-meeting policy has created considerable problems for the board. On some occasions, journalists attending board meetings have reported deliberations and actions by the directors in a manner that has caused acute embarrassment, in a manner experienced by no other orchestra: possibly most aggravating in this respect has been the publication of names of potential contributors before they were actually approached. The press has similarly had access to working financial data that would ordinarily be considered internally confidential. The prospect that board discussions may find their way into public print has, in frequent instances, hampered constructive exchange of opinions by the directors and created the danger that matters of major importance would be settled informally, outside regular meetings on an ad hoc basis rather than through frank deliberation by the entire board. Moreover, the Albuquerque Symphony has been subjected in the press and in "editorial" comment on local television to occasionally reckless criticism.* No one questions the right and

* One television commentator, not among the reporters attending board meetings, delivered an irresponsible denunciation of both the Albuquerque Symphony and the Santa Fe Opera in what can be described as only the crudest terms, as organizations of interest only to wealthy people in fancy clothes.

obligation of the media to report factually on matters of public interest and to criticise artistic and community policy on an informed basis, but many in Albuquerque fear that some of the more extreme criticisms have been both uninformed and motivated by personal prejudice. However, the presence of reporters at board meetings and their disinclination to treat certain information as "off the record" has frequently placed the directors of the orchestra in an embarrassing position, from which they feel they cannot now extricate themselves gracefully.

The important contribution of women's association [11] to the supplementary income—over one-fourth in 1970–71—gives evidence of the significant role it plays elsewhere in symphony affairs. The association has five hundred members, divided into two categories: active members who pay dues of five dollars a year and are expected to work on committees, and associates who pay ten dollars but do not give time to association projects. The Young People's Series is a major continuing activity of the association: much of the organization of these concerts, including the special staged productions and all ticket sales, is handled by its committees. In addition, the women organize large-scale benefits in support of the orchestra: a biennial auction of donated merchandise that most recently netted twenty-five thousand dollars, raffles, and social occasions. Because its main fund-raising event takes place only every other year, it holds its funds from year to year, making specific lump-sum allocations to the orchestra: in 1970–71 it contributed ten thousand dollars to supplementary income and in 1971–72 was committed to at least fifteen thousand dollars. Beyond its specific financial help and its organization of the Young People's Series, the women's association carries the message of the orchestra through many segments of the community.

At the Crossroads

As Gordon W. Paul has stated,[12] the Albuquerque Symphony is at a definite crossroads, and under his leadership it was very aware of the fact. By the time these words appear in print, a great deal may have happened, either to implement the orchestra's positive potential or to undermine its recent achievements. Nevertheless, a few comments about this orchestra are in order here.

No one can look closely into the Albuquerque Symphony and its local and statewide environment without detecting the high degree of parochial fragmentation surrounding the orchestra and, to some degree, existing within the organization itself. The aggressive attitude of the media is a symptom of tensions, both within the orchestra organization itself and in the community's image of the orchestra: their ability to intimidate the board, to secure dissenting opinions from board members, reflects the orchestra's lack of stature in the community and of anything approaching widespread civic support. Some of the elements of this dissension have already been noted. The failure of the orchestra to win such respect from the professional musicians on the university faculty as to attract them into it reflects both implicit misgivings about its future artistic development and a parochial attitude toward a possible conflict between the university and the orchestra for primacy in Albuquerque's musical life. With Frederick's retirement and replacement by an as yet unannounced conductor, some local musicians expect a more assertive attitude on the part of the university in Albuquerque music. Early in his career in Albuquerque, Frederick had his fill of the orchestra and harbored no ambition either to dominate it or to compete with it. No one knows how his successor at the university will act in this respect.

Takeda's own position, despite his remarkable achievement in galvanizing the Albuquerque Symphony, is much in question, if only because he has been so successful. It is no secret in the city that in his first two years he has been considered for other positions; the board, the musicians, and the press know this. Takeda has rather ambitious hopes for the Albuquerque orchestra—more ambitious perhaps than the community can support—and if frustrated in these he may naturally look elsewhere. Many people feel that the conductor may be overqualified for Albuquerque, that he deserves a better orchestra, and that his musical and technical standards will come increasingly in conflict with the capabilities of the present musicians. Even if the board were to consider placing substantially greater resources at his disposal, the musicians themselves, with strong representation on the board, might oppose these for fear that Takeda's first step would be to bring in outsiders to displace present players who have long dedicated themselves to the orchestra.

Takeda's suggestion that the Albuquerque Symphony provide the orchestra for the Santa Fe Opera strikes as visionary anyone who knows the realities of the musical scene in New Mexico. Not only are there logistic problems already mentioned, but such a proposal would encounter another type of parochial resistance from the opera company, which seeks intensively to preserve its own identity as the pre-eminent and unique musical organization of the area. Assuming that the logistic problems could be overcome, any involvement of Albuquerque Symphony players in the Santa Fe Opera will probably be a slow process arising out of a gradual improvement of symphony personnel. For 1972–73 the orchestra board will undertake an increase in the number of subscription concerts in Popejoy Hall by repeating some programs: certainly the popularity of the orchestra justifies such expansion. Moreover, there are very real possibilities for repeating some of these programs on runouts to Santa Fe, Portales, and Los Alamos; the first two cities have been visited in the past two years and the third has a good auditorium, in many respects the second best after Popejoy in the runout area available to the orchestra. The orchestra management is pursuing these possibilities, but so far has encountered the parochial syndrome of other communities looking down on the musical life of Albuquerque. The local concert committees in these towns contain powerful elements that prefer visiting concert attractions, booked nationally, to a regional orchestra from a city that has still to establish cultural standing in their eyes.

In such developments, the state Arts Commission has already given some help and can give more in the future. But its own problems in establishing itself in the political structure of the state reflect a general attitude toward the arts that can only be described as backward in the national perspective.[13] When the National Endowment for the Arts was originally established by the Congress in 1965, an essential feature was granting funds to such state arts councils as were then organized. The availability of such funds resulted in their organization by all other states not already having arts councils, if only to get the federal funds. This certainly was the argument put forth in the New Mexico legislature in 1965 to authorize such a state arts commission: the legislators were asked to provide only the minimal funds necessary to qualify the state for a federal grant. With the Commission in existence for six years, the legislature has still shown reluctance to appropriate even modest administrative funds, nor will it authorize the appointment of a professional executive director of a commission that will probably, in fiscal year 1973, disburse over $125,000 of National Endowment funds. Present procedures for making grants, though motivated with the best intentions by conscientious and devoted commission members and advisers, can only be described as haphazard and an invitation to inflated requests.

Two state arts surveys were made in New Mexico in 1966: one by the State Planning Office, another by the newly organized State Arts Commission;[14] for the latter the Commission received a special grant of $17,840 from the National Endowment for the Arts. Both surveys outlined the resources and needs of all the arts in New Mexico. Since its establishment in 1965, the Arts Commission has received modest state appropriations for administration expenses and has shared in the statutory distribution of funds to state councils from the National Endowment for the Arts which are primarily intended as program funding to be distributed to such projects as the State Commission deems worthy. Funds available to the New Mexico Arts Commission, from state, federal, and private sources, are shown in Table 11-C,[15] together with the amount granted by the Commission to the two instate symphony orchestras—the Albuquerque Symphony and the amateur group in Roswell.*

From this chart it can be seen that state appropriations have not kept pace with federal allocations. Though total federal appropriations for the arts are increasing by as much as thirty percent a year and many other states are funding their arts councils at an even higher rate, New Mexico has remained static during the period of greatest expansion in government support for the arts.† Moreover, there is considerable thought in the National Endowment of turning over to state councils in general some of the funds it now uses to make grants to the smaller orchestras. Should such an eventuality develop,

* Differences in scheduling of grants and the inclusion of some receipts in other categories (notably the Young People's Series and women's association allocations) account for the discrepancies between these data and the figures reported in the orchestra's financial summary previously cited.
† See Chapter XVIII for a summary of the growth of state arts council funding throughout the U.S.; these data, not including the extraordinary funding in New York state, show an increase from $1,468,000 in 1966 to $6,628,000 in 1972, or over 280%, during a period when the New Mexico funding actually decreased.

TABLE 11-C

New Mexico Arts Commission

State, Federal, and Private Funding, Together with Grants to Symphony Orchestras

FY Ending	State Funds	Federal Funds	Private Funds	Total Funds	Symphony Grants	
1966	$25,000	$34,983	$11,053	$70,946	$ 2,000	Albuquerque
1967	15,000	74,276		89,726	2,000	Albuquerque
					2,000	Roswell
1968	15,000	39,383		54,383	2,000	Albuquerque
					2,000	Roswell
1969	20,000	30,909		50,909	1,000	Albuquerque
					1,212	Roswell
1970	20,000	36,363		56,363	2,366	Albuquerque
					1,183	Roswell
1971	23,000	75,377		98,377	13,438	Albuquerque
					3,539	Roswell

it is hard to see how states like New Mexico, without professional direction of their arts councils, can fairly and competently discharge the increased obligations.

The failure of the New Mexico legislature to support the Arts Commission with little more than the minimum necessary to qualify for federal funding is but another example of the parochial syndrome which confronts the Albuquerque Symphony in its immediate future. It is part of a larger pattern of businessmen's indifference to the arts, of hard-nosed journalism, and local parochialism which is a symptom of a relatively new frontier society. Even the proponents of supporting the Arts Commission could muster no stronger argument than to reiterate that the Santa Fe Opera, which receives the largest single Commission grant, is the "No. 1 Tourist Attraction" in New Mexico, as if the contribution of the opera company and other arts groups to the quality of life in New Mexico were beneath concern. The annual reports of the Arts Commission itself go to great, and sometimes ludicrously labored, pains to demonstrate how a modest state appropriation of twenty thousand dollars generates several millions of dollars in the New Mexico economy; one such presentation takes credit for attracting 95,930 out-of-state tourists spending an average of thirty-two dollars a day in New Mexico.[16]

At present writing, therefore, the Albuquerque Symphony, in attempting to emerge as a viable professional musical organization, faces formidable problems that go beyond immediate financial support to involve major community attitudes. Many other orchestras—most of them, in fact—encountered similar obstacles in their infancy and some are still so bedeviled. But the fact that other orchestras have succeeded, that the Santa Fe Opera in the same area has surmounted many of the same barriers that face the Albuquerque Symphony, should provide some encouragement to the supporters of the orchestra. Most of all, Albuquerque wants an orchestra, as its response in two years of Takeda's leadership has demonstrated. But sold-out houses alone do not assure an orchestra's success; they help, and they justify a community's support—a support that has yet to be mobilized in Albuquerque.

CHAPTER XII

Cincinnati Symphony Orchestra

Located in southwestern Ohio some seventy miles northeast of Cincinnati, with a population of ten thousand, the town of Wilmington is a small agricultural center containing a denominational college that boasts a modest music department, an auditorium seating about nine hundred people, and a sizable gymnasium.[1] Wilmington is one of thirteen cities and towns in Kentucky, Indiana, and southwestern Ohio which are currently served by the Cincinnati Symphony Orchestra in a unique regional concert program. Beginning in the fall of 1969, a local committee of townspeople has presented a comprehensive program of music in cooperation with the Cincinnati Symphony; this includes not only three evening concerts but also an extensive series of musical programs in the public schools. Each series of three evening concerts includes one appearance by the Cincinnati Symphony, under the direction of its resident conductor Erich Kunzel; a program of chamber music, usually by members of the orchestra; and a solo recital by an artist from the Cincinnati College–Conservatory of Music. On each of the three visits, the artists arrive in Wilmington in the early afternoon and give at least two and sometimes as many as four programs for the schoolchildren of the community, depending on the number of artists; when a chamber group or an orchestral ensemble visits a town, it often splits up into smaller groups, sometimes individuals, who visit classrooms in addition to performing in the school auditorium. The same artists stay over for the evening concerts for a subscription audience in the college auditorium or, in the case of the full orchestra, in the gymnasium. The Cincinnati Symphony staff handles virtually all arrangements for these concerts—transportation, meals, and motel rooms, as well as printing of tickets and programs. A local committee, organized and assisted by the orchestra staff, schedules the concerts, provides a piano when needed, and sells series subscriptions to the townspeople. Though it charges no fixed fee for this series, the orchestra hopes to receive at least nine thousand dollars from each community for what amounts to as many as ten to twelve performances during a season. In order to simplify organization and facilitate the selling of tickets, the orchestra has adopted the Community Concerts idea of selling only season subscriptions to the patrons of the evening concerts. In addition to these ticket sales, the local committee may raise money in any manner it chooses, sometimes obtaining special grants from the state arts councils of Ohio, Indiana, and Kentucky to assist in subsidizing the educational aspect of the series.

These Area Artist Series concerts are one of this orchestra's efforts to increase and diversify its activities in response to the particular challenges and opportunities confronting many American symphony orchestras in the past decade, especially among those Category B orchestras which have recently expanded their operations with full-year musicians' contracts. Whereas the larger Category A orchestras faced with the problem of giving their musicians year-round employment have generally been able to do so by using the full orchestra in summer programs and added touring, many Category B orchestras have done it primarily by adding diversity in their musical services. In so doing, they have not only had to call upon their ingenuity but have also encountered serious problems of logistics and in relations with their orchestra musicians. Though virtually all of the orchestras in Category B confront this challenge of diversification, none has worked with greater imagination than the Cincinnati Symphony, which has in recent years not only expanded its regular concert season but has reached out into a wide variety of educational projects—opera, popular concerts both indoors and out, and assorted regional musical service. In so doing, it has operated from the firm base of long-established community support in Cincinnati, and with highly dedicated and responsible leadership both on its board of trustees and in its management.

From Theodore Thomas to Max Rudolf

Cincinnati has long enjoyed a lively and solid tradition of interest in serious music—especially symphony, opera, and choral activities—undoubtedly at first stimulated by the fact that the city was a major center of the German settlement in the central Ohio valley from the 1840s on.[2] Significantly, as early as 1855 its local music profession was sufficiently strong to achieve one of the first union organizations in the nation. In the early 1850s, Cincinnati welcomed the touring Germania Musical Society and provided a local chorus for some of its concerts. Theodore Thomas had visited Cincinnati on his tours with Ole Bull and Henriette Sontag, and the city soon became a principal stop on the "Thomas highway" after he brought his own orchestra there on his first tour in the spring of 1870. During Thomas's winter tours, Cincinnati was a headquarters where the orchestra could stay for as much as two weeks, playing concerts both in the city and in surrounding areas; in some years he also brought his orchestra for an extended summer series of out-of-doors popular concerts. In 1873, Thomas was persuaded by influential backers in

Cincinnati to present the first of his May Festivals, a tradition which has continued for a century. In 1972, the May Festival combined contemporary innovation with the tradition of Thomas when its two major presentations were Leonard Bernstein's Mass—in its first performance since the premiere at the opening of the Kennedy Center in Washington—and a full-scale production of Bach's *Saint Matthew Passion*. We have already seen that despite Thomas's unhappy experience in the organization and direction of a college of music in Cincinnati,* the city retained its affection for him and supported his activities virtually to the end; during the spring before his death, he conducted the annual May Festival for the fourteenth time. One of the major tangible results of Thomas's endeavors in Cincinnati was the construction in 1884 of the Music Hall; this great auditorium, on a traditional opera-house and concert-hall plan, still seats 3,600, and is one of the largest halls regularly used by an American symphony orchestra; as we shall note later, it has recently been modernized to make it also one of the finest in the country.

Given these circumstances, it is not surprising that, in 1895, the musical leaders of Cincinnati organized a local symphony orchestra on the model of Thomas's in Chicago; it was thus the fifth city to organize and support its own symphony orchestra, being preceded by New York, Boston, Chicago, and St. Louis. The first conductor of this orchestra was Frank A. Van der Stucken,† who directed it until 1907, when its operations were suspended for two years because of serious conflict with the musicians' union. During the next two years, an exhaustive search was made to find a conductor who could reorganize the orchestra. According to one account, Hermann Thumann, a local music critic, knew of Leopold Stokowski's work as organist and choral director at St. Bartholomew's in New York. Stokowski was brought to Cincinnati for interviews and subsequently arranged to conduct a concert in Paris with the Colonne Orchestra which was attended by Lucien Wulsin, founder of the Baldwin Piano Company of Cincinnati. Wulsin was so impressed by Stokowski's mastery of the orchestra that any lingering doubts about engaging so young a conductor were dispelled. In his three seasons in Cincinnati, from 1909 to 1912, Stokowski not only justified Wulsin's confidence but established such a reputation that in 1912 he broke his Cincinnati contract to become conductor of the Philadelphia Orchestra.[4]

Stokowski was succeeded by Ernst Kunwald (1912–17) and the violin virtuoso Eugène Ysaye (1918–22). Ysaye, though a great violinist, was not cut out to be resident conductor of an American orchestra. When he retired, the Cincinnati Symphony engaged a virtually unknown Hungarian musician, Fritz Reiner, then first conductor of the Dresden Opera, where he had won

* The Cincinnati College–Conservatory of Music, now affiliated with the University of Cincinnati, continues an unbroken tradition of higher music education begun with Thomas's early efforts.
† A native of Texas (1858), Van der Stucken studied music in Antwerp, Leipzig, and with Liszt at Weimar. In the symphony programs which he conducted in Europe, he introduced music by such Americans as MacDowell, Foote, and Chadwick, most notably at the Paris Exposition in 1889 and with German orchestras. In Cincinnati he was also director of the College of Music. After leaving that city in 1907, he spent most of his life in Germany, and died at Hamburg in 1929. A bronze statue of Van der Stucken stands beside that of Thomas in the lobby of the Music Hall.[3]

high praise from Richard Strauss for his work in preparing important productions of Strauss's operas. Reiner was unhappy in postwar Germany and was flattered to be invited to succeed Ysaye by an American orchestra to whom the composer had warmly recommended him.[5]

Reiner served the Cincinnati Symphony from 1922 to 1931, a period during which he built it into one of the best performing ensembles in this country. Though his programs were based on a comprehensive representation of the standard repertory, he also introduced to Cincinnati a great deal of the new music by such composers as Stravinsky, Hindemith, Prokefiev, Milhaud, and Bartók. An indication of Reiner's enterprise and the orchestra's quality at the time was his presentation of Bartók's First Piano Concerto, with the composer as piano soloist. The year was 1928, when Bartók made his first visit to the United States expecting to present this concerto with the New York Philharmonic under Willem Mengelberg. Upon reaching New York, he was advised by Mengelberg that it was impossible for the orchestra to perform the concerto, and was forced to accept the substitution of his early Rhapsody for piano and orchestra as the vehicle for his American debut. Journeying shortly afterward to Cincinnati, where he was to appear with his old friend and pupil Reiner, he did perform his piano concerto, and the performance was taken by the Cincinnati Symphony on tour to New York, where Reiner and Bartók demonstrated to the New York audience that the work was, after all, playable. When Eugene Goossens succeeded Reiner as conductor of the Cincinnati Symphony in 1931, he reviewed the repertory of his predecessor and expressed amazement that virtually every significant work of the 20th century up to that time had been presented by Reiner in Cincinnati.

Goossens remained as conductor of the Cincinnati Symphony until 1947, serving the orchestra and the community with great musical distinction; during this period the orchestra continued to be one of the more important outside of the very largest eastern cities.

When Goossens left Cincinnati, the board of trustees of the orchestra was rather dominated by the son of the man who had discovered and brought Stokowski to Cincinnati in 1909. Recalling the success of his father's choice of a completely unknown conductor, and wanting to engage a young American rather than a European, Wulsin suggested one with whose work he was very impressed: Thor Johnson, then conductor at the Juilliard School, who had filled in for Goossens in an emergency on tour with the Cincinnati Symphony. Johnson was also highly recommended by Serge Koussevitzky, whose urgent sponsorship of Johnson overcame the misgivings that the board might have had in passing over several important European conductors in favor of the young American.[6] Although he won many loyal friends in the symphonic community of Cincinnati, Johnson's musical direction of the orchestra did not carry on the distinguished tradition of Reiner and Goossens. In 1958, therefore, he left Cincinnati for a post with Northwestern University and later became a conductor of the Nashville Symphony Orchestra. Johnson was succeeded by Max Rudolf, who had enjoyed a distinguished career as conductor and principal musical administrator at the Metropolitan Opera Company in New York. Rudolf settled in Cincinnati as a resident of that city and restored the discipline and quality of the orchestra during his eleven years as musical director. Although his German background fitted in well with the traditions of Cincinnati, he remained aloof from intensive social activities and declined to be put on show by the trustees and women's committee as a part of symphony promotion; in musical affairs however, he was actively involved in every phase of the orchestra's development and operation. Poor health made it necessary for Rudolf to submit his resignation in 1968, to be effective in mid-1969; upon his retirement from Cincinnati he joined Rudolf Serkin at the Curtis Institute of Music in Philadelphia as conductor and director of a new opera department there.

The repertory of Reiner, Goossens, Johnson, and Rudolf as conductors of the Cincinnati Symphony has been included in the Mueller survey; Table 12-A covers periods typical of their programming, showing the relative proportion, in percentages, of the nationalities of composers represented in the orchestra's subscription concerts.

TABLE 12-A

Cincinnati Symphony Orchestra Repertory

For Selected Periods, According to Conductor and Compared with National Percentages (In *Italics*)

	Reiner 1920–30	Goossens 1930–45	Johnson 1945–55	Rudolf 1960–70
Austro-German	56.59	45.10	46.96	50.46
	50.89	*47.68*	*51.58*	*51.89*
Russian	11.95	16.05	14.24	14.88
	17.04	*17.56*	*15.52*	*14.72*
French	11.75	11.92	10.98	9.17
	12.38	*11.56*	*12.16*	*10.44*
American	5.25	9.09	9.22	9.81
	6.48	*7.12*	*6.89*	*6.66*
British	1.91	6.11	4.62	2.70
	2.80	*3.52*	*2.86*	*3.66*
Czech	2.17	2.56	2.10	3.33
	1.91	*2.33*	*2.37*	*3.05*
Italian	5.43	3.02	4.39	3.52
	3.88	*2.95*	*3.18*	*3.09*
Scandinavian	0.30	2.53	2.92	2.86
	1.92	*3.41*	*2.42*	*2.43*
Hungarian	2.37	0.61	1.33	1.68
	0.89	*0.65*	*1.27*	*1.87*
Spanish ⎫	0.34	2.41	0.88	0.60
Latin-American ⎭	*0.74*	*1.10*	*1.10*	*1.29*

The most notable features of Reiner's repertory profile are an emphasis on Austro-German music, almost precisely matched by a comparable reduction of Russian, and substantially higher proportions of Italian and Hungarian music. The two latter nationalities reflect Reiner's interest in the contemporary repertory of the 1920s—the Italians Respighi, Casella, Malipiero, and Pizetti, and the Hungarians Bartók, Kodály, Dohnanyi, and Weiner. Goossens' repertory, while generally in line with the national averages in most categories, shows an understandable emphasis on British music and a rather notable interest in American. Johnson continued to present more American music than the national average and a substantially lower proportion of Austro-German music, but his repertory generally follows the national average. With Rudolf, Austro-German music returns to something like the national share, and except for a continuing emphasis on American music, his repertory shows no major deviation from the national profile. Altogether, the repertory of Goossens, Johnson, and Rudolf marked a rather sharp break from the Central European orientation of Reiner and established for four decades a consistently stronger representation of American music than prevailed nationally.

Thomas Schippers

In their search for a successor to Max Rudolf, the Cincinnati Symphony trustees realized that it might be impossible to replace him with a full-time resident conductor of national stature. They had seen profound changes in the conducting profession; the best conductors pursued international careers, guest-conducting in many cities and in some cases accepting more than one post involving major responsibilities in artistic direction. In a sense, these trustees faced a choice between a full-time resident conductor of lesser reputation and a musician of high caliber whom Cincinnati would have to share with other commitments. They decided to weigh their compromise on the side of musical quality, and, after considerable deliberation and exploration, settled upon the young American Thomas Schippers as their choice, though they were by no means certain that his services would be available. Schippers was at that time conducting opera performances at La Scala in Milan, and a delegation from Cincinnati—including manager Lloyd Haldeman and two trustees, Lucien Wulsin, Jr., and Edward J. Mack, Jr.—together with Schippers's manager, Ronald L. Wilford, went to Milan to present their invitation. They obtained his agreement to accept the musical direction of the Cincinnati Symphony for three years, with a commitment to spend at least sixteen weeks a season there. Upon the conclusion of the oral agreement, the visitors retired to an office in the hotel, where they typed out a contract on an ancient and somewhat recalcitrant Italian typewriter.[7]

Though Thomas Schippers was but forty years old when he came to Cincinnati in 1970, he had already had extensive experience in conducting opera and symphony here and abroad.[8] Born in Kalamazoo, Michigan, he enrolled at the age of fifteen in the Curtis Institute of Music to study piano, but on an impulse entered a young conductors' competition held by the Philadelphia Orchestra. He won second place in that contest, an experience that changed the course of his career. By 1950, he was working as an accompanist and coach to singers in New York and came to the attention of Gian-Carlo Menotti, who was then producing his opera *The Consul;* when the regular conductor dropped out of the production shortly after its premiere, Schippers replaced him with great success. After service with the army in Germany, Schippers returned to join the staff of the New York City Opera Company, and in 1955 was engaged by the Metropolitan Opera. Under Arthur Judson's management he secured guest engagements with symphony orchestras in this country and abroad. His operatic activity has taken him to London, Milan, Venice, Rome, and Bayreuth; he was one of the conductors with the Bayreuth company when it made its first appearances away from home, in Japan in 1967. He has appeared frequently with American orchestras, including the New York Philharmonic, which he joined for its 1959 tour of Europe and Russia. He currently divides his time between Cincinnati and Italy, where he is director of special projects for RAI and conducts opera in Milan and Venice. He was for thirteen years artistic director of the Spoleto Festival of Two Worlds, organized by Menotti.

Schippers had never conducted the Cincinnati Symphony before becoming its musical director, but from his association with Max Rudolf at the Metropolitan Opera he knew the quality of orchestra he could expect. Despite his far-flung activities, Schippers avows complete dedication to his orchestra, has purchased and remodeled a large home in Cincinnati,[9] and feels that one of his biggest problems is to convince the community that he is really devoted to Cincinnati and intends to stay there.* He does not feel that his jet-borne career will in any way diminish his contribution to Cincinnati: his youthful energy and the resources of telephone and air travel will, he feels, give him close contact with his responsibilities there. He has complete confidence in both the board of trustees and the new manager, Albert K. Webster, with all of whom he has established well-coordinated and frank working relations.

For the present, at least, Schippers concerns himself primarily with the subscription season of the Cincinnati Symphony, avoiding such related activities as the May Festival and Summer Opera. Since opera has always been an essential part of his career, Schippers by no means rejects the possibility of future involvement in opera in Cincinnati, but only on such terms as can preserve the standards which he has established elsewhere. In his international operatic work, Schippers has concentrated increasingly on a limited number of productions, working together with the producer toward an integrated conception in which all elements—singing, scenery, costumes, and staging—are coordinated on a high level of quality. Several years ago, he presented to the National Endowment for the Arts a proposal to bring to the United States a series of European productions of this sort for presentation by various regional opera companies here. Though the Endowment did not accept this scheme, partly because it involved large expenditures over a period of years, Schippers still feels that the sharing of expertly prepared opera productions by a number of American companies can result in improved artistic standards and appreciably lower costs. This seems to be the kind of operatic ac-

---

* In the spring of 1972, he further strengthened his commitment to Cincinnati by accepting a post on the faculty of the College–Conservatory.

tivity that could bring Schippers into the Cincinnati Summer Opera. Recently the opera has been preoccupied with its move into the Music Hall, and has developed a close though informal relation with the New York City Opera.* At the moment, therefore, it would seem that the Summer Opera is taking directions into which Schippers's larger plans might not easily fit.

As regards the orchestra itself, Schippers has ambitious plans for increasing its concert activity and improving its personnel. An extended European tour may have been arranged by the time this account appears in print. He hopes, as do all conductors, to make such gradual changes in the personnel as will better fit his notions of orchestral quality, though he feels that the orchestra is basically a good one. His duties as musical director of the Cincinnati Symphony have been described as coming down basically to two major responsibilities—conducting sixteen of the twenty-four subscription weeks of the winter season and overseeing the repertory and the personnel for the remaining concerts—and he is constantly in touch about them with Webster and key trustees either in person or by telephone.

In 1965, Rudolf engaged as his assistant Erich Kunzel,[10] a pupil of Pierre Monteux, who had considerable orchestral experience, especially in conducting popular concerts. During Rudolf's illness, Kunzel assumed increasing responsibilities, and was designated resident conductor in 1969, a title he still holds. As resident conductor, Kunzel is in a position to keep Schippers informed on all phases of artistic and orchestral operations. He works closely with him in auditions and in reviewing personnel and discipline. In addition, Kunzel conducts five of the twenty-four subscription programs, seven of eight popular concerts in the Saturday evening "Eight O'Clock" Series (Schippers conducted one of these in 1971–72), virtually all Young People's and Junior High Concerts, all the full-orchestra programs in the Area Artist Series and half of the chamber-orchestra concerts, and a large portion of the various summer activities of the Cincinnati Symphony—more than seventy performances a year. Within this busy schedule Kunzel finds time to accept a few guest engagements, notably with the Boston "Pops" Orchestra and Boston Symphony.

A third member of the conducting staff since 1968, Carmon DeLeone, is assigned one of the subscription programs, many of the Area Artist Series chamber-orchestra concerts, the Cincinnati in-school program, and some of the off-season concerts. A native of Ohio, DeLeone graduated from the Cincinnati College–Conservatory and is also a French-horn player and percussionist. He has his own jazz ensemble, with which he has toured Europe. Both he and Kunzel are on the faculty of the Cincinnati College–Conservatory of Music.

---

* One important link between the New York City Opera and the Cincinnati Summer Opera is W. Ralph Corbett, an extraordinary musical philanthropist, who has made major contributions both to the New York company and to a variety of Cincinnati activities, including the orchestra; more will be said of him later in this chapter.

Divers Activities

In 1970–71, the Cincinnati Symphony, either as full orchestra or split into two or three groups, played a total of 292 performances for an estimated audience of 750,000: [11]

No.	Type of Performance	Attendance
48	Subscription Series (24 pairs)	143,764
8	Popular Series	29,443
4	Open Door Concerts	9,768
4	Special Concerts	12,199
18	Young People's and Junior High	59,700
63	Cincinnati In-School (⅓ orch.)	63,000 est.
11	Area Artist Series, adult	21,125
62	Area Artist Series, student	97,678 est.
8	Runouts	24,000
5	May Festivals	15,500
17	Summer Opera (Part orchestra)	36,036
14	Summer Regional Mini-Festival (Part orchestra)	16,000
1	Stadium Concert	16,102
4	Park Concerts	55,000 est.
4	Shopping Center Concerts	18,000 est.
8	Coney Island Pops	18,000 est.
2	State Fair Concerts	15,000 est.
5	Fountain Square, CSO Week	24,685 est.
6	Television, local	75,000 est.
292		750,000 est.

Like all orchestra attendance figures, these must be regarded as approximate. Not only are certain free concerts—such as in-school programs, stadium, park, shopping center, and television—subject to extremely casual guesswork, but such paid admissions as those for subscription and popular concerts must take into account that the same ticket holder attends a considerable number of concerts. Therefore, the figure of 750,000 for the 1970–71 season is not only approximate but includes many repeaters.

The twenty-four pairs of subscription concerts, still the musical heart of the operation, include twenty-four Saturday evenings, twelve Friday evenings, six Friday mornings, and six Sunday afternoons, sold in six subscription series with savings of up to forty-five percent of combined single-ticket (four to seven dollars) cost. Schippers conducts fourteen of these programs, Kunzel five, DeLeone one, and visiting guest conductors the remaining four.[12]

An important experiment, carried on for two seasons but dropped after 1971, was the Open Door Series. Twenty-five percent of Cincinnati's population is black, much of it living in the downtown area surrounding the Music Hall itself. This building, as originally designed, not only contained a large auditorium but an adjoining ballroom and a smaller meeting hall; the latter, known as North Hall, had in recent years been used for boxing and wrestling matches and other athletic events heavily attended by the black community. When the Music Hall renovation was begun in 1968, the requirements for backstage expansion and modernization called for closing North Hall, arousing some resentment in the neighborhood. Several trustees of the orchestra contacted leaders in the black community for discussions of better involving them in the orchestra. With the help of the Corbett Foundation, a series of special concerts was given for two seasons in the Music Hall on Sunday evenings for the black community. A black publicist was engaged to promote these concerts, tickets were sold in drugstores and by residents of the community, and programs were devised to interest this special group through repertory and choice of soloists. On one occasion, a black member of the city council participated in a performance of Aaron Copland's *A Lincoln Portrait*. The concerts met with varying success in the box office, but served significantly to establish liaison between the orchestra and the black community. Though they were discontinued after two seasons, this liaison goes on. During the 1971–72 season, the appearance of Henry Lewis on the regular subscription series provided an occasion for the involvement of black patrons, and the orchestra board hopes to include blacks among its trustees once such participation can be meaningful and not mere tokenism.

Though the Cincinnati Symphony is organizationally distinct from the May Festival and the Summer Opera, it enjoys close relations with both. The May Festival was for many years a biennial event, but is now given every year; since the death of Thomas in 1905, it has employed the members of the Cincinnati Symphony as well as large numbers of local singers for its choruses. At first the Festival engaged members of the Cincinnati Symphony directly, but since the orchestra attained its year-round contract, it now plays for the May Festival as a part of this. Thanks to the tradition of the May Festival, Cincinnati has long had a number of excellent amateur and professional choruses. The programs of the May Festival rely heavily on these choruses, but also carry on Thomas's tradition of presenting major symphonic works. Julius Rudel has been artistic director of the May Festival since 1971, and the managerial responsibilities for this five-performance presentation are now handled by the Cincinnati Symphony Orchestra.

The Summer Opera, however, is a completely separate organization with its own administrative staff. For its seventeen performances at the Cincinnati Zoo (in 1972, thirteen were given in the Music Hall) it has purchased the services of a portion of the necessary musicians from the Cincinnati Symphony, since the establishment of the year-round contract; prior to this it had engaged the players directly. Although the May Festival and Summer Opera function independently, there is considerable overlap in the membership of their respective boards. The Summer Opera is also supported by the Institute of Fine Arts, as is the symphony orchestra, but the May Festival is not; we shall have more to say about the institute later.

Since the establishment of the fifty-two-week contract with the musicians, the Cincinnati Symphony has had to develop performance activity for those players not needed during the five-week opera season and for a number of additional weeks when the full orchestra is under contract for the summer. Some of these weeks are taken as vacation, four weeks in 1972. For its re-cording * and television activities, the orchestra has an arrangement with the local union whereby a certain number of services that would otherwise be available in the summer are allocated to recording on the basis of a pro-rata computation equaling Federation scale. Moreover, the musicians' contract permits the management to add to the vacation certain services arising from concerts out of town which are computed as double services in the annual total but not in those permitted weekly. However, there remains a consider-able number of musicians' services under contract that the orchestra must utilize in a variety of ways during the off-season. The concerts in the parks, shopping centers, amusement park, and state fair fall in this category. The regional Mini-Festivals during the summer represent an effort, similar to the wintertime Area Artist Series, to bring the orchestra to communities near Cincinnati in Indiana, Kentucky, and southwestern Ohio; many of these concerts are played by a smaller orchestra, either in concert or with a local ballet company, made up of musicians not playing for the Summer Opera.

Whenever possible, the orchestra attempts to secure special financial spon-sorship for the free concerts it offers. As we shall see later in connection with the Institute of Fine Arts, such solicitation of special support is permissible in Cincinnati and has become one of the major areas of board activity. Early in September, 1971, the mayor proclaimed Symphony Week in Cincinnati, during which the orchestra played five free concerts at Fountain Square in the heart of the city during the lunch hour; a total of nearly twenty-five thousand people attended. The cost of these concerts was defrayed by downtown mer-chants, newspapers, banks, public utilities, and radio and television stations. The Cincinnati Bell Telephone Company underwrote the cost of four free park concerts during the summer of 1971. On Labor Day, 1970, over sixteen thousand people attended a free concert, sponsored by the Shillito depart-ment store, in the city's new sports stadium on the bank of the Ohio River; Van Cliburn was soloist on that occasion, as he was again at a similar concert of the Fourth of July, 1971. On another occasion, the orchestra played a concert for the employees and customers of a local business firm which not only underwrote the cost of the concert but presented members of the or-chestra and staff with shares of stock in the corporation. In such projects of mutual benefit, the Cincinnati Symphony has discovered ways of identifying itself with the business community in well-publicized activities.

The educational activities of the Cincinnati Symphony are extremely varied, as one can recognize from the preceding summary of concert activity. The eighteen Young People's and Junior High Concerts in the Music Hall continue a long tradition of bringing schoolchildren to these concerts by bus.[13] There is a modest charge for series admission, and efforts are made to encourage at-tendance by each child in successive years so that all will hear a planned

---

* The Cincinnati Symphony made a number of recordings for the American Decca Company under Max Rudolf, but has no contract to record with Schippers; however, in 1971, Kunzel recorded a work by Dave Brubeck with the orchestra for Decca.

series of graded performances from grades four to six in the Young People's Series and grades seven through nine at the Junior High Concerts. Kunzel plans his materials accordingly: in any three-year period different materials will be presented each year, but each three-year period will become an integrated whole. When he first came to Cincinnati, Kunzel discussed his programming a great deal with various music educators in the schools, but as he gained in experience he has relied more on his own ideas—many of them coming from the children's reaction—to formulate his approach. The programs, which last one hour, are based on central musical concepts readily intelligible to the young audience; these may be the instrumental composition of the orchestra or an introduction to such musical elements as melody, rhythm, and harmony. In many cases, Kunzel not only selects individual movements from larger works but also presents them with considerable cuts in deference to the limited attention span of such audiences. An integral part of these programs is at least one or two numbers in which the children themselves sing with the orchestra. In many cases, Kunzel attempts to involve the children in a very direct manner; at one concert, for instance, the concept of rhythm was illustrated by having the children themselves beat various rhythms in time with the illustrative selections offered.[14]

A more recent educational innovation carries the designation of "in-school" concerts. Twenty-one schools in the city and suburbs, selected for the quality of their music instruction, receive three visits each from thirty symphony musicians. The first two consist of coaching and rehearsal sessions, in which the student players themselves rehearse alongside the symphony musicians. At the third visit, the entire student body of the school (or as many as the school auditorium will accommodate) is assembled for a concert by an orchestra consisting of symphony musicians and students together. The instrumentalists from the schools need not necessarily play the same instruments that the orchestra musicians do; it is not unusual to find a recorder or clarinet player performing beside a violinist or cellist. This project has been judged to be extraordinarily successful in stimulating the interest of musically talented children in the further pursuit of musical careers.

In the Area Artist Series previously described, an important element is the school concerts offered by the performers. These performances are usually of the more conventional type found in the Young Audiences program. The quality of these programs depends a great deal on the interest and involvement of the symphony players themselves; in a few instances, players from outside the symphony are used, especially when they appear in solo performance on the evening series. When the full orchestra or half of it is to appear at the evening concert, a number of musicians visit the schools during the afternoon, sometimes playing an assembly program, at others going into classrooms singly or in small groups to explain and play music for the children.

Such a variety and quantity of musical activity calls for a considerable commitment of staff and management: frequently they require more, in terms of audience numbers and revenue produced, than traditional symphonic work. Many of these new projects were first devised by former manager

Table 12 B

Cincinnati Symphony Orchestra
Annual Expenditures and Performance Income 1919–70

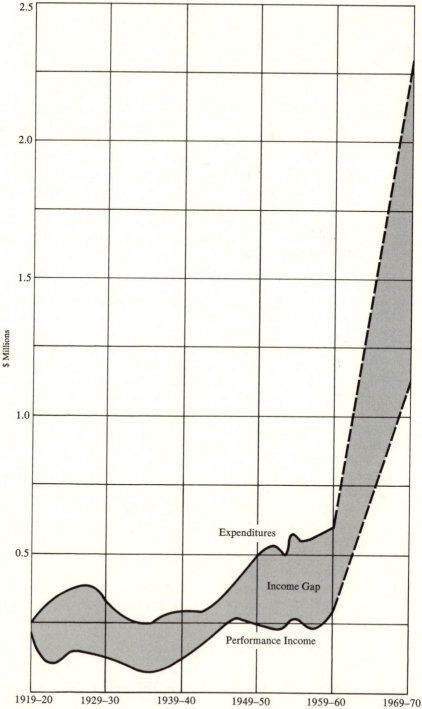

Sources: Graph to 1963 from Baumol and Bowen, *Performance Arts, The Economic Dilemma*, page 294; subsequent data from Cincinnati Symphony Orchestra indicated by broken line.

Lloyd Haldeman and have been carried on by his successor since early 1971, Albert K. Webster, who also started such new programs as the Mini-Festivals in his first summer in Cincinnati. The orchestra has been fortunate in having the services of an extremely energetic and imaginative young woman, Mrs. Judith Arron,[15] as director of regional and educational programs since her arrival in Cincinnati in 1970. A native of Seattle, where she was first introduced to symphonic music in the children's concerts presented by Milton Katims, she studied cello and was later on the staff of the American Symphony Orchestra League for four years. During her association with the League, she did fieldwork in its study of orchestra youth-concert activities in some twenty American cities. When her husband was engaged as violist by the Cincinnati Symphony, she applied for a position with Haldeman, who immediately recognized her experience and abilities and set her to work on the innovative programs that he had been developing. In this work, Mrs. Arron has also contributed a great deal of expertise to the policy direction of these programs. Her primary responsibilities are the Area Artist Series, the Mini-Festivals, and the in-school concerts in Cincinnati. With the assistance of a secretary in the symphony office, she is in charge of the coordination, planing, and logistics for nearly a hundred and fifty concerts for adults and children in Cincinnati and vicinity. In the execution of this work, she often travels as much as a thousand miles a week by auto, making personal visits to the various schools and local committees with whom she is working.

Consequences of the Income Gap

Though the Cincinnati Symphony does not publish annual financial statements, it has on occasion made data available for special studies, among these a graph published in *Performing Arts—The Economic Dilemma,* by William J. Baumol and William G. Bowen. This shows expenditures and performance income for the orchestra from 1919 to 1964 and is one of the few long-range presentations of such data ever made. Table 12-B is based on it and brought up to 1970 from information supplied by Paul Elbert,[16] the orchestra's controller.*

Although the gradual growth of this orchestra from 1920 to 1960, with a pronounced dip during the depression of the 1930s, is certainly of interest here, the most startling portion of this graph is that covering the final decade, which shows a growth that can only be described as explosive. In each instance, the Cincinnati Symphony shows a much greater expansion in the 1960–70 decade than it did for all forty years earlier:

	1920–60	*1960–70*
Expenditures	140%	233%
Performance income	100%	190%
Income gap	200%	310%

* Baumol and Bowen's original graph was in a condensed format; mine is designed to show the trends more vividly.

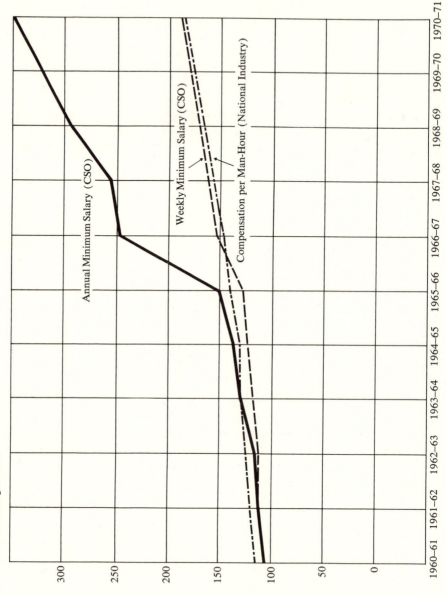

Table 12 C

Cincinnati Symphony Orchestra
Musicians' Minimum Salaries 1960-70
1957-59 Averages= 100

Though the Cincinnati orchestra is one of the few for which data over so long a period have been assembled, the 1960–70 explosion may be regarded as typical of American orchestras in general: the degree may be greater in such Category B orchestras as Cincinnati, Pittsburgh, Detroit, Minneapolis, St. Louis, and San Francisco, but these data for Cincinnati pinpoint the pervading financial crisis which American orchestras experienced during this decade, a subject which will be discussed in greater detail in the next chapter.

A major factor in this increase, over and above national inflationary trends, undoubtedly has been the rise in annual pay to musicians. During this decade the Cincinnati Symphony reached contracts with its players that not only increased weekly pay but substantially expanded the length of the contract, to the point that by 1970–71 musicians were engaged for fifty-two weeks a year; the minimum terms of the Cincinnati musicians' contract during recent years were:

	Minimum Weekly Pay	Number of Weeks	Annual Minimum
1966–67	$170.	45	$ 7,650.
1967–68	180.	45	8,100.
1968–69	190.	48	9,120.
1969–70	200.	50	10,000.
1970–71	210.	52	10,920.
1971–72	220.	52	11,440.

As the graph in Table 12-C, prepared by the controller of the orchestra, shows, weekly minimum pay just about kept pace with compensation per man-hour in industry nationally from 1960 to 1970, and minimum annual pay for Cincinnati Symphony musicians also followed this trend until 1967. However, once the extension of the number of weeks covered by the contract set in, the *annual* minimum income of these players grew much faster. From an index (based on 1957–59) of 150 in 1965–66, musicians' annual minimum wage had increased 233% by 1970–71 at the same time that industrial compensation grew by 28%. As noted earlier, there is ample evidence that in the first postwar years compensation for symphony players generally had by no means kept pace with that of other professions, and the recent rapid increases may be considered in some measure as a postponed rectification of this imbalance. In this the Cincinnati Symphony shares in all the factors producing the general "income gap" crisis during recent years in other American orchestras: increased musicians' militance, the impact of the Ford Foundation grants in 1966, and the discovery by symphony boards of previously untapped financial resources and the need to expand community services to justify their support.

In Cincinnati, the scope of this crisis can be documented by the comparative summaries in Table 12-D of its expenditures and income in 1959–60 and 1969–70.

In expenditures the expansion was relatively uniform in all categories. Income from performance was also reasonably stable, rising slightly over the

TABLE 12-D

CINCINNATI SYMPHONY ORCHESTRA

Financial Summaries for 1959–60 and 1969–70

INCOME	1959–60	1969–70
Performance	$299,000 (48%)	$ 875,000 (51%)
Supplemental:		
United Fine Arts Fund	148,000 (24%)	203,000 (12%)
Institute of Fine Arts	127,000 (21%)	75,000 (4%)
Endowments	19,000 (3%)	279,000 (16%)
Ford Foundation	——	195,000 (11%)
City	19,000 (3%)	19,000 (1%)
Other	6,000 (1%)	90,000 (5%)
Total Supplemental	320,000 (52%)	861,000 (49%)
TOTAL INCOME	$619,000 (100%)	$1,736,000 (100%)

EXPENDITURES	1959–60	1969–70
Artistic personnel	$402,000 (65%)	$1,289,000 (63%)
Concert production	163,000 (26%)	472,000 (23%)
Administration	48,000 (8%)	193,000 (9%)
European-tour deficit	——	45,000 (2%)
Other	6,000 (1%)	60,000 (3%)
TOTAL EXPENDITURES	$619,000 (100%)	$2,059,000 (100%)

halfway mark by 1969–70. But in aggregate supplementary income (49%), the components changed considerably. A new element in 1969–70 was income from the Ford Foundation, a portion of a $500,000 five-year sustaining grant, income from endowment funds raised in the matching-fund drive, and proceeds from the ten-year trust established by the foundation in 1966. The income from the Institute of Fine Arts, from the United Fine Arts Fund, and from endowments all originated through the Institute of Fine Arts: the increase from the United Fine Arts Fund reflects a general growth of annual contributions to the arts in Cincinnati, but the shift from institute income to endowment income has deeper implications. For an understanding of this, one must examine more closely the workings of the Cincinnati Institute of Fine Arts.

Like the Louisville Orchestra, the Cincinnati Symphony does not itself conduct annual fund-raising drives, but receives sustaining and endowment income from a combined arts fund.[17] During the 1920s, Mr. and Mrs. Charles P. Taft had assumed the major share of underwriting the orchestra. In 1927, they started an endowment fund for the arts in Cincinnati by offering $1 million if other donors would contribute $2.5 million. The matching fund was raised and the money was placed in a trust administered by the Cincinnati Institute of Fine Arts. At the present time, four organizations are beneficiaries of the institute's trusts: the Cincinnati Symphony Orchestra, the Taft Museum, the Cincinnati Art Museum, and the Cincinnati Summer Opera.

Since the trust was originally established, it has grown, by capital appreciation and subsequent gifts, to about $17 million, the income of which is distributed annually to the four beneficiaries. The investment policy of the institute calls for a judicious balance between capital growth and income production; the latter currently varies between 3% and 3.2%.[18] In addition, the institute administers other endowment funds, entrusted to it by the beneficiaries from contributions received by them. Finally, since 1949, the institute has conducted annual campaigns known as the United Fine Arts Fund to raise money for all four beneficiaries. Thus, the Cincinnati Symphony receives funds from the Institute of Fine Arts in three categories: its share of income from the institute's overall endowment; income from orchestra endowments which the institute administers; and its share of the annual United Fine Arts Fund drive. In recent years, however, its supplementary income requirements have exceeded these three sources, and the institute has found it necessary to invade the capital of those unrestricted endowment funds which the orchestra had entrusted to the institute for management.

In the preceding financial summary of income, that from the Institute of Fine Arts represents its share of the institute's income from its trust; that from the United Fine Arts Fund comes from the annual drive; and endowment income includes both the interest on its own endowment funds, administered by the institute, and the invasion of this capital to the extent that it is unrestricted. This diminution of its own capital resources by the Cincinnati Symphony obviously cannot continue indefinitely,* and both the institute and the symphony trustees realize that the only possible way of achieving liquidity in the orchestra's finances is to increase substantially the annual receipts from the United Fine Arts Fund Drive, which has recently brought in about $0.5 million and for which an immediate goal of double that amount has been set for the next few years. Since the orchestra now receives approximately 40% of this annual fund, it is hoped that an increase of $200,000 will reduce the reliance on unrestricted endowment funds. Officers of both the institute and the orchestra feel that such an increase is not unreasonable since the conclusion of the Ford Foundation challenge drive in the summer of 1971.

When the Ford Foundation symphony program was set up in 1965, the Cincinnati Symphony was offered an endowment grant of $2 million coupled with a five-year sustaining grant of $100,000 per year, for which the orchestra was required to raise $3 million for its own endowment fund. After securing permission from the Institute of Fine Arts to undertake this large drive, the orchestra succeeded in raising its goal without major difficulty. Before conducting this drive, it called in the services of Carl W. Shaver from New York, who was consultant to several other orchestras at this time, and received from Shaver a general management and operational evaluation; the Shaver organization also set up the drive for the $3 million campaign. Later this goal was increased substantially in order that the funds could be raised for the renova-

* Such invasion of unrestricted endowment is by no means unusual in those few orchestras which have in the past enjoyed substantial endowments: though it has occurred in other orchestras without being publicized, the financial reports of the Chicago Symphony, published annually, reveal such invasion of capital funds as far back as the late 1950s.

tion of the Music Hall, with total goal close to $7 million. Many of the contributions received in this campaign were in the form of pledges for future contributions up to the middle of 1971, so that the actual resources for music performance support in Cincinnati were rather heavily committed until then. Now that these resources are no longer under pressure from this effort, the institute sees a good possibility of making substantial increases in its annual United Fine Arts Fund.

Table 12-E presents comparative data for the Cincinnati Symphony Orchestra and the averages for all eight Category B orchestras.

TABLE 12-E

CINCINNATI SYMPHONY ORCHESTRA

Financial Summary, 1970–71, Compared with Category B Averages

INCOME	Cincinnati	Category B Averages
Performance:		
Concerts	$ 955,128 (42.7%)	$ 924,301 (38.7%)
Other nongovt.	81,968 (5.0%)	118,516 (5.0%)
Govt. for services	70,390 (5.9%)	140,254 (5.9%)
TOTAL PERFORMANCE	$1,107,486 (49.6%)	$1,183,071 (49.6%)
Supplemental:		
Contributions	$ 696,591 (31.2%)	$ 735,491 (30.8%)
Govt., nonservice	25,000 (1.1%)	144,856 (6.1%)
Endowment and interest	404,968 (18.1%)	321,880 (13.5%)
TOTAL SUPPLEMENTAL	$1,126,559 (50.4%)	$1,202,227 (50.4%)
TOTAL INCOME	$2,234,045 (100%)	$2,385,298 (100%)
EXPENDITURES		
Artistic personnel	$1,576,215 (69.3%)	$1,620,684 (69.9%)
Concert production	425,176 (18.7%)	562,942 (22.5%)
Administration	272,563 (12.0%)	314,691 (12.6%)
TOTAL EXPENDITURES	$2,273,954 (100%)	$2,498,317 (100%)
DEFICIT	$ 39,909	

In general, the Cincinnati data follow the category averages rather closely, this orchestra showing overall totals about 10% under average for the eight orchestras. Thanks to the long-established Institute of Fine Arts, its endowment income is 25% above the category average, and its larger concert income can be attributed to its management's aggressive development of diversified activities. It ranks somewhat lower in public funding, deriving most ($72,-250) of this in 1970–71 from the National Endowment for the Arts for its Area Artist and in-school programs; this rose to a net of $100,000 in 1971–72. It was one of seven Category B orchestras showing a net deficit in 1970–71, but can take some satisfaction from the fact that this was substantially lower than the category average of $179,229. Its artistic-personnel cost represents a higher percentage of expenditures, reflecting a slightly higher scale of pay for its players.

Community Support

Strictly speaking, the Cincinnati Symphony Orchestra is a subsidiary of the Institute of Fine Arts: the institute owns all of the orchestra's assets and appoints its board of trustees. In actuality, thanks in part to the considerable overlap in the two boards, the orchestra trustees have considerable independence in running the symphony, though they are fiscally accountable to the institute. The orchestra is not permitted to solicit contributions directly, though it has great latitude in seeking support for activities that can be considered as services rendered to the donor. This latitude has been essential to the success of the orchestra in developing the variety of community services outlined earlier.

The Cincinnati Symphony has long enjoyed the generosity of a number of Cincinnatians, and during the past decade it has received sizable contributions from Mr. and Mrs. W. Ralph Corbett, two incredibly generous donors to musical causes. Trained as a lawyer, Corbett first achieved success as a producer of packaged radio programs, in the course of which he found himself the owner of a small company making doorbell chimes. He built this company into a highly successful manufacturer of household appliances. Upon selling his business, Corbett engaged in an extensive program of musical philanthropy. He and his wife have an intense interest in music; they and the foundation they established have made major donations to the New York City Opera and have established fellowships to assist young musicians, especially opera singers. But the principal area of their philanthropy has been in Cincinnati itself, where they gave large support to the Cincinnati Symphony's European tour in 1969, have long been important donors to the Summer Opera, contributed substantially to the Ford Foundation matching fund, have given generously to the Cincinnati College–Conservatory of Music, and were prime movers in the recent renovation of the Music Hall. This last undertaking not only has made the Music Hall a more pleasant setting for orchestra concerts but will enable the Summer Opera to abandon its long-time outdoor setting at the zoo for a new and beautifully equipped stage in an air-conditioned building. One authoritative source estimates that in the past decade the Corbetts have contributed over fifteen million dollars to music in Cincinnati alone; others suggest a total of eight to ten million. The size and extent of the Corbetts' generosity may be compared to that of Henry L. Higginson who, in the course of over forty years of sponsorship of the Boston Symphony, is estimated to have spent approximately a million dollars of his own funds. Even when inflationary trends since the time of Higginson are taken into account, it may well be that the Corbetts are the most generous musical philanthropists this country has ever known. Like Higginson, the Corbetts base their philanthropic decisions on their own musical interests and specific artistic likes and dislikes. Though much of this philanthropy is channeled through the Corbett Foundation, this is not a professionally managed organization such as the Rockefeller or Ford Foundation; its artistic decisions are made by Mr. and Mrs. Corbett.

It is generally agreed that the board of trustees of the Cincinnati Symphony is broadly representative of the business and civic leadership of the community. Although fund-raising is not the all-important responsibility of the symphony board that it may be in other cities, access to financial support is a major consideration in determining membership among these trustees, many of whom are active in the Institute of Fine Arts and on the boards of other music organizations. However, some trustees [19] express concern that their membership does not represent certain segments of the community which ordinarily are not found on symphony boards, especially in the large and growing urban black population. We have already noted how concern for problems arising from the location of the Music Hall in the black residential area prompted efforts to bring this population into special concerts. These Open Door Concerts were underwitten in large part by the Corbetts, both out of concern for their larger urban impact and as an outgrowth of their interest in remodeling the Music Hall. It should be noted, incidentally, that these urban problems are by no means as pressing as those of the Cleveland Orchestra, where the location of Severance Hall in a similar black residential area has actually made attendance at the concerts hazardous and unpleasant for some symphony patrons.

A very important contribution to the success of the Cincinnati Symphony is its women's committee, one of the oldest in this country.[20] Though officially founded in 1924, it was preceded by various women's organizations before 1900. While this committee engages in general promotion for the orchestra, one of its most important functions is a very well organized season-ticket campaign aimed both at renewals and new subscriptions. The committee also undertakes a variety of benefit programs; in some years it presents a benefit ball, and its activities range from large social functions to sweepstakes with prizes solicited from local business firms by the women's committee. In 1970–71, the women's committee's fund-raising activities contributed nearly seventy thousand dollars to the support of the orchestra. Though the committee members are not directly involved in arrangements for the Young People's and Junior High Concerts, its members usher at these concerts and assist the Music Hall staff in handling the large crowds of children. At many of the adult concerts, the women's committee itself is extremely visible in a meaningful way; prizes to be awarded in the sweepstakes are exhibited in the Music Hall lobby, and at some concerts the ladies serve coffee, cookies, and other refreshments.*

One must also credit the women's committee of this orchestra with one of the few innovations developed in this country to counteract the declining au-

---

* I was personally impressed by the visibility of this committee on a very cold Sunday afternoon, when I arrived at the Music Hall for a concert and was welcomed at the door by a committee member offering me a steaming cup of coffee to warm me before the concert. This gesture was typical of the general friendliness I encountered with everybody connected with the Cincinnati Symphony during my visit there.

dience for the Friday afternoon concerts. The audiences at these concerts, which were dwindling in Cincinnati, are notoriously passive in their response to the music and, at least in the case of Cincinnati, consisted more and more of elderly ladies who had held their subscriptions for decades. Out of discussions of this problem among the policy committee of the women's committee, there emerged a plan in 1968 to change the time of these Friday matinees to eleven o'clock in the morning; such scheduling made it possible for younger women with family responsibilities to get their children off to school, to come down to the center of the city for a morning concert, and return home before their children were out of school and before the rush hour made traffic difficult. These concerts are preceded by a coffee hour, which is heavily attended and provides the occasion for a great deal of enthusiastic mingling among the ladies. The Friday morning series of six concerts had in 1971–72 more than doubled (2700 subscriptions) the series attendance of the previous afternoon concerts, and obviously appeals to a younger group of women, many of whom have become involved in the activities of the women's committee.

No discussion of the Cincinnati Symphony would be complete without mention of Mrs. Fred Lazarus III. This dynamic and brilliant lady has been a powerful force both in the women's committee and on the orchestra board for nearly twenty years. Although she remains an important member of the women's policy committee, her activities on behalf of the symphony extend far beyond it: she conducts her own television program featuring important civic and cultural personalities, both from Cincinnati and visiting the community, and plays an important part in policy direction of the orchestra and in securing major support for it. In addition, Mrs. Lazarus has been a leading figure in the American Symphony Orchestra League since the early 1950s, when Helen Thompson was developing it as an important force in the national symphonic affairs. She has long been a member of its executive board and a strong voice in its deliberations and policy direction. It is impossible to talk with Mrs. Lazarus without being deeply impressed by her thorough grasp of the broad and detailed problems of symphony orchestras, large and small across the country, and the changing symphonic scene in the last half of the 20th century.

Management Challenges in the 1970s

With strong board leadership, carrying on a long tradition of civic responsibility for the orchestra, it is not surprising that the orchestra is well administered. Until 1970 it was managed by Lloyd Haldeman, who left his post as general manager to explore the possibilities of prerecorded programming for video cassettes and cable television, with special emphasis on developing musical and cultural programs in these promising communications media. He was succeeded by Albert K. Webster,[21] a former assistant manager of the New York Philharmonic. A graduate in physics from Harvard University, Webster during his college years sang in the glee club and became one of its student managers, serving with notable distinction in arranging its Far East tour. When Nadia Boulanger visited Harvard and conducted the glee club, she encountered Webster and invited him to study with her in France for two summers. These activities brought him to the attention of Carlos Moseley, then general manager of the New York Philharmonic, who engaged him as assistant manager in 1962, shortly after the orchestra moved to its new home at Lincoln Center. There Webster obtained extensive and intensive experience in all phases of management of a major symphony orchestra, which he brought to his new and even more responsible post in Cincinnati. Moreover, Webster, as one of the youngest managers of a major orchestra, arrived on the symphonic scene while many of the burning issues that confronted all American orchestras in the early 1960s were being resolved; he is, therefore, free of many of the lingering prejudices and older outlooks which still prevail in many quarters. He is fortunate, too, in having inherited from Haldeman an extremely well-organized orchestra administration; by delegating responsibility to an experienced staff, he can deal with many of the larger issues which this orchestra faces in the transitional period of the 1970s, as orchestras consolidate the major changes which occurred during the previous decade.

One of Webster's major responsibilities, of course, is in personnel relations and labor negotiations. Shortly after taking office, he entered a crucial period of bargaining that began in the spring of 1971 and ended only with the conclusion of a five-week strike on April 1, 1972. The musicians of the Cincinnati Symphony are represented by the oldest musicians' union in the nation, Local 1 in the AFM. From 1907 to 1909, the orchestra suspended operations, largely because it could not meet the demands of the union representing its musicians. A one-week strike in 1958 has been described as an occasion for clarifying the terms of an agreement and as a "show of muscle" by the orchestra players in the early days of organized militance. Nevertheless, there has developed in Cincinnati a frank and open three-way relationship between the orchestra management, union, and musicians. For more than fourteen years the union has been headed by Eugene Frey, a former first clarinetist in the symphony and therefore well acquainted with orchestra realities. The orchestra itself elects its five-man committee, which has established good direct working relations with the union and with management. None of the three parties to personnel relations is under any illusions as to the position of the others: dialogue has been frank, realistic, and to the point; respective positions are expounded strongly, often with militance, but with less of the hostile invective encountered in some other orchestras.

The prolonged negotiations of 1971–72 inevitably involved questions of pay, working conditions, and pensions.[22] Having achieved a fifty-two-week contract already, the players sought increased weekly pay, an effort complicated by the presidential wage-price restrictions announced in the summer of 1971. Pensions were also a major issue: in 1970–71 a player retiring at sixty-five with thirty years' service could expect only two thousand dollars a year. But work schedules were probably the main stumbling block to an agreement. Many of the diversified activities developed by Haldeman and Webster had been scheduled into the traditional twenty-four-week season (except for Christmas vacation) and the players found these an added burden to their regular work in preparing and playing the concert season in the Music Hall.

Indicative of the good relations between the union and the players was the former's agreement to employ I. Philip Sipser, the players' choice, as lawyer for the negotiations. The musicians were represented in bargaining by their five-man committee, Frey, and the union vice-president, who was also a player in the orchestra. Partly because of the uncertainties attending the application of nationwide wage controls, both parties agreed to begin the 1971–72 season on schedule and to continue bargaining during its course, assuming that any new benefits would apply retroactively. By midseason there was hope that a settlement might be reached, but in mid-February the orchestra players voted to reject a proposed agreement and called for a strike. Despite the appeal of the mayor to continue playing, the musicians suspended operations on February 26.

During the negotiations that continued during the five-week strike, certain modifications were made in the agreement first proposed. The term of the contract was extended to three years instead of two, and major modifications in working schedule were agreed upon. The final agreement called for minimum weekly salaries ranging from $220 the first year to $245 the third (compared with $210 in 1970–71), substantial increases in medical benefits and pensions (now about $4,600 plus Social Security), and important changes in working conditions. These latter involve concentrating some of the diversification activities in weeks of their own, interrupting the consecutive scheduling of Music Hall concerts rather than interspersing them. In other respects, rules affecting scheduling achieved a workable compromise between what management and the players desired.

Webster needed greater flexibility in the utilization of the musicians' services in order to carry out the expanded activities begun by Haldeman and to secure, from programs he himself planned, better services from the resources at hand. Here he encountered resistance from the musicians similar to that already detailed in the case of the Buffalo Philharmonic. In the give and take of bargaining, he undoubtedly did not obtain all he desired in the spring of 1972, but he has expressed the view that the agreement reached then provides adequately for continuing such activities and expanding them to a limited extent.

In the overall national picture, it is a rather unfortunate commentary on the symphonic institution that it has been forced into these innovative programs, many of them of important community service, less by creative planning within the organization than by the pressure of their musicians for year-round employment. The musicians, for their part, have seldom made concrete or practical suggestions for the wider use of their talents, and have, as we have already seen, often resisted the necessary arrangements for management-devised innovations in their negotiations. These problems are more acute in Category B orchestras than in either Category A or Category C. The larger orchestras have been able to absorb the year-round services of their musicians in projects—like the Philadelphia Orchestra at the Saratoga Festival or the New York Philharmonic's free park concerts—that involve the whole orchestra. The smaller orchestras have not yet found it necessary or practical to employ their musicians for a full fifty-two weeks a year, and therefore do not yet face the problem of using these services, though some may well encounter such pressure from their musicians that they will soon find themselves forced to create additional employment. But the Cincinnati Symphony, like others in its category, must offer year-round employment if it is to maintain and build its quality as an orchestra and if it is to give its musicians economically fair treatment. Thus, in Cincinnati as elsewhere, management faces important challenges, not only in developing diversified orchestral services to the community but also in selling the musicians on the importance of them.

Filling the Policy Vacuum

As these diverse activities develop, the Cincinnati Symphony faces major problems of artistic responsibility—problems by no means unique to this city and, in fact, comparable to those that other orchestras face more and more in their own contexts. These innovative programs, as they develop across the country, often fall quite outside the traditional artistic foundation of the American symphony orchestra as we have known it for the past one hundred years. Traditionally the responsibilities of the musical director of an orchestra encompass two major areas: the overall selection and discipline of the performing ensemble, and the planning, supervision, and execution of its overall performances. However, in Cincinnati, Thomas Schippers as musical director does not concern himself with the popular concerts directed by Erich Kunzel, the school concerts conducted by Kunzel and DeLeone, or with the increasingly diversified program of presentations in the schools, during the summer, and in the smaller communities outside of Cincinnati. Nor, in fact, does Kunzel concern himself with a great deal more than the actual programs for which he is responsible,[23] though his duties also include working closely with Schippers in matters of personnel and orchestra discipline; in this latter function Kunzel, as resident conductor, plays a crucial role, since Schippers only works with the orchestra for little more than a third of the year. With Schippers and Kunzel fully occupied in this manner, there is a large and growing area of activity over which there is no central artistic direction.

One might argue that Schippers should devote more of his time to Cincinnati, overseeing all of the orchestra's activities. However, in all fairness, it is today extremely unlikely that any orchestra in this country would readily find a musician of Schippers's stature who would, given the realities of the international music scene, be willing to devote his life to any one orchestra in the manner of such conductors as Stock, Koussevitzky, Stokowski, Ormandy, and Szell.* Moreover, it may well be that his talents do not necessarily cover the specialized interests and insights required for the artistic implementation of the innovative educational, community, and regional programs that the Cincinnati Symphony is continually undertaking. To a large degree, this policy vacuum is in fact filled by management, notably Webster himself as managing director, though this seems not to be a part of his explicit duties. Certainly a major responsibility placed on Webster by the trustees is the development of new projects, but the artistic content of these—within relatively broad limits of qualitative standards—appears to be no one's particular responsibility; at best this is left up to the musicians themselves or assistant conductors. Webster's duties also involve broad concern for the orchestra's community service, but the content of an educational program, for instance, is not explicitly a part of his work.

In actuality, the Cincinnati Symphony Orchestra has in Webster a young manager with substantial musical training and an intelligent understanding of the community and educational potential of this orchestra. It is inconceivable that he would act strictly within the manager-board-conductor framework so rigidly defined by Arthur Judson. For, in fact, Webster knows that the artistic content of diversified orchestra programs is inseparable from their administrative planning, execution, and promotion. As noted earlier, these innovative activities have so far been motivated more by seeking economically productive work for the musicians under contract than by a specific analysis of community needs. If the latter should ever come to predominate in such planning, Webster possesses the qualifications for grasping and implementing them. In all of this, Webster is quite free of Judson-type illusions about his role as general manager: he knows that much of what he does carries him deep into artistic areas traditionally reserved for the musical director, but he enters into them with no illusions about rigid institutional structure.

In meeting the challenge of diversifying its activities under the pressures that have developed in the past decade, the Cincinnati orchestra is still to a large degree experimenting and improvising: the final pattern of these projects has yet to develop clearly. Here it is typical of many other American orchestras in this period of great expansion. Many factors will enter into the new patterns as they emerge: the cooperation of the local music profession as represented by the orchestra musicians, the community needs and resouces as perceived by the trustees and the manager, the availability of increased financial support from private and public sources, and, let us hope, some kind of basic educational philosophy and formulation of creative initiative that will develop opportunities rather than wait for pressures to grow. To a great extent,

* Midway in the 1971–72 season, Pierre Boulez was musical director of both the New York Philharmonic and British Broadcasting Corporation; Zubin Mehta, though spending most of his time with the Los Angeles Philharmonic, was also in charge of the Israel Philharmonic; Loren Maazel had recently accepted appointment to the Cleveland Orchestra, which would share him with the opera in Berlin; Seiji Ozawa, already musical director of the San Francisco Symphony and co-director of the Berkshire Festival, had just agreed to add the Boston Symphony to his duties in 1973, succeeding William Steinberg, who had previously been in charge of both the Pittsburgh and Boston orchestras; and Georg Solti, recently retired from the Covent Garden Royal Opera in London, had assumed the musical direction of the Orchestre de Paris and the Paris Opera, while continuing in a similar post with the Chicago Symphony Orchestra.

these orchestras, Cincinnati among them, have so far responded to pressures from the musicians and from the challenge inherent in major foundation and government support; the next decade will undoubtedly see a more orderly coordination of these efforts, hopefully with a broader concern for community needs, and there is every prospect that with the quality of trustee and community guidance it enjoys and with professional implementation by a young and able general manager, this orchestra will continue to meet these challenges in a creative manner.

PART THREE

The Income Gap

"Because of the economic structure of the performing arts, these financial pressures are here to stay, and there are fundamental reasons for expecting the income gap to widen steadily with the passage of time."

BAUMOL AND BOWEN
Performing Arts—The Economic Dilemma

Having so far considered the American symphony orchestra in terms of individuals and organizations, we now look at it in a national perspective, first within the broad economic framework. This requires consideration of such statistical data as are available to describe quantitatively and comparatively the common and diverse elements that make up the symphony economy. Though we have looked at the finances of individual orchestras in the previous section, and anticipated the forthcoming material somewhat in placing them in the economic context of the category to which they belong, the following discussion will deal with our orchestras in national economic perspective. Inevitably this account of symphonic economics describes a by no means static situation, for the American orchestra institution has, in the past decade, experienced an explosive expansion that created tensions and problems of crisis proportions. The forces at work in this have been reported in some detail already, and it remains to describe them in their more general national impact.

The most important single economic fact about symphony orchestras is the income gap, a term used by Baumol and Bowen in their Twentieth Century Fund study of the economics of the performance arts. The income gap is not at all peculiar to the symphony orchestra: it is a basic fact of life in other performance arts—opera, nonprofit theater, and dance—as well as in a host of privately supported and directed cultural, welfare, and educational activities. This income gap corresponds to that portion of costs not covered by tuition in private education or the difference between the expenses of running a hospital and receipts from patients; in certain activities, such as some museums or welfare agencies, which do not charge the public for their services, it may represent the entire cost of operation. In the performance arts, where the audience is usually expected to share the cost by buying tickets or where services are sold to schools, governments, radio and television, or other purchasers, the income gap represents the difference between the total cost of operations and the proceeds from the sale of services. For symphony orchestras the income gap ranges from a third to two-thirds of total expenditures, depending on the size of the orchestra and local conditions.

These nonprofit agencies, therefore, have traditionally depended, as do the performance arts, more or less on private funding of their operating deficit—contributions from individuals and businesses who recognize a certain community value in their activities. Sometimes, especially in the welfare field, such private funding is combined in one central community fund solicitation, with the allocation of money raised determined by a central agency representing both the community and beneficiaries. Such united funds also play a more limited part in financing education and arts activities. In the private support of arts, welfare, and education, there has grown up in this country a highly specialized form of charitable funding: the foundation. Some foundations are little more than an extension of individual or corporate giving, but others, the mega-foundations, have developed their own highly professionalized routines of allocating their resources. More recently governments—local, state, and national—have become increasingly involved in support of the arts, among them symphony orchestras. Government participation in what had originally been privately supported activities began first with education, then entered the welfare field, and only recently reached the arts.

Basic to the economic organization of these activities is a corporate structure, taken over from private business. The scheme where a board of directors determines broad policies to be executed by professional management developed in for-profit business enterprise, and prevails in the nonprofit corporation, which has a distinctive legal status, enjoys exemption from taxation to a large degree, and confers comparable exemption from taxation upon contributed funds. In certain legal and regulative respects, symphony orchestras and other nonprofit corporations are considered to be foundations themselves, although, in our discussion here, the term "foundation" will apply primarily to funding agencies as distinct from operating ones. Especially in the mega-foundations, the same kind of professional management prevails, carrying out the policies of a lay board of trustees. As government funding has come to play a part in these nonprofit activities, moreover, it operates in a similar manner, with administrators implementing the policies set by the legislative and top executive functions of government.

The central concern of all nonprofit organizations with the income gap plays a crucial role in many aspects of symphony economics. It influences the choice of trustees or directors for the governing boards and dominates much of their policy deliberations. Its funding becomes the focal point of relations with private and corporate donors, foundations, and government agencies. Most important, the phenomenal growth of the symphonic income gap in the last decade has precipitated a crisis that still pervades the orchestra field today and shows every prospect of continuing.

Symphony orchestras have developed an abhorrence of the term "deficit financing" and the traditional distinction between "earned" and "unearned" income,* with the concomitant implication of unsound business management. They prefer to distinguish two kinds of income: that earned from actual performance, and that now termed "supplemental." When their financial reports show a net surplus or deficit, it generally reflects ability or failure of performance and supplemental income combined to meet actual expenditures. Moreover, many foundations and governments specify the particular services to be rendered in exchange for their support. Such grants properly appear as performance income for services rendered, but when foundation or government funds are not tied to services, they are reported as part of supplemental income, in the same general category as private or corporate gifts or income from endowment.

In its efforts to avoid a net operating deficit symphony management—the board of directors and manager—must concern itself with three economic problems. It must first operate at the lowest cost compatible with the artistic standards it aims to maintain. It must maximize performance income in order to reduce the income gap. And it must discover and exploit every possible means of closing the income gap with supplemental income from private and corporate gifts, endowment (actually a special form of private gift), foundation grants, and government funding. The first two concerns, control of expenditures and maximization of performance income, fall within general operating finances. The third, reducing the income gap, involves private philanthropy and government support. Together they constitute the overall economics of symphony operation.

* Amyas Ames, of the Partnership for the Arts (see Chapter XV), is particularly emphatic on this point: he prefers to view supplementary income as "earned" by rendering community services.

CHAPTER XIII

Symphony Economics

There is a hoary joke in symphony circles about the efficiency expert hired to make a time and motion study of an orchestra in performance, who reported with horror that many of the musicians were actually playing only part of the time and that the overall efficiency of the orchestra was barely over fifty percent. More seriously, many a board member, schooled in the traditions of sound business practice, shudders at running an operation at an inevitable loss, and he encounters others in the commercial world who want nothing to do with the institution that cannot pay its own way.* There remains a substantial segment of the community that feels the symphony orchestra should be paid for by the people who want it. To a degree, the orchestras, because they charge admission to many of their programs, are regarded as more "commercial" than art museums or schools and therefore more subject to the laws of supply and demand. More sophisticated businessmen, such as those on the Business Council for the Arts, accept the inevitability of the income gap but still admonish orchestras and other arts groups to improve the quality of their management and accountability to convince the skeptical that orchestras are run in a businesslike fashion. The business community and public at large have been slow to understand the basic economics of the performance arts, and many still hanker for some way to put them on a break-even basis.

Yet orchestras today face the same problem encountered a century ago by Theodore Thomas and Major Higginson: Thomas learned, at the expense of his health and the risk of his own resources, that even the most efficient utilization of his playing forces in touring could not provide a sound base for artistic quality, and he turned, as did Higginson, to the permanent resident orchestra, operated at a deficit, as the only viable solution consonant with the maintenance of musical standards. Ideologically, artistic considerations and an aristocratic sense of duty motivated Higginson to subsidize his orchestra, as they did the Flaglers, Mackays, Severances, Lathrops, Clarks, and Chandlers in years to come. But as the costs of orchestras rose in response to grow-

---

* In 1971 the backers of the Dallas Symphony Orchestra were attracted by the proposals of their conductor to generate major "profits" from the presentation of nonsymphonic music events to raise performance proceeds, reduce the burden on supplemental income, and thus place the orchestra on a more businesslike basis.

ing public needs and increasing concern for the players' living standards—to say nothing of general inflation—deficit financing of symphony orchestras demanded a more comprehensive economic rationale if a broader base of support, both private and government, was to be secured. This required the kind of analysis, best represented by Baumol and Bowen in *Performing Arts —The Economic Dilemma,* that explained the fundamental economics of the performance arts in general.

Economics of the Income Gap

Artistic activity has never been a producer of goods and services for sustenance. In primitive society, the arts were an essential part of ritual or of group experience, supported as part of the religious and social life of the community. In Western civilization, as the arts became increasingly specialized, the state or church maintained them as a matter of course. But in the capitalist economy of the 19th century, centered on the profitable production and distribution of goods and services, the arts became an economic anachronism especially glaring in Anglo-American business culture. However, in the American melting pot of the 19th century, the influence of Central European artistic traditions made itself felt during the latter half of the century, as we have seen in the enterprise of Thomas and Higginson, and businesmen with wealth and a sense of community responsibility took on the task of underwriting orchestras, museums, and opera companies.

The basic economic problem of the performance arts stems from the fact that they are, in the purest sense, service functions as opposed to being producers of material goods.[1] These latter require the investment of capital for assembling the machinery and labor force for production and for further research in the constant improvement of technology that would increase the productivity of the labor force. As this happened, both the investor and the worker benefited in an expanding economy. Ideally, a rise in wages was accompanied by an increase in productivity (and vice versa), facilitated by investment in new machinery that made production more efficient. Faced with demands from his workers for more pay, the entrepreneur could weigh these extra costs against the savings anticipated by greater mechanization or efficiency in distribution.

In the performance arts, technological improvement plays a neglible role. Symphony management, faced with increased labor costs, has no recourse to labor-saving machinery to increase productivity; it can only look to the limited possibilities of increasing prices to the consumer for essentially the same product, or to new ways of utilizing its work force by seeking new markets.[2] If increase in labor cost is accompanied by the availability of additional services, the latter course is imperative, but if increases are in cost per hour only, compensating actions are much more limited. Since personnel cost commands such a large proportion of symphony expenditures (fifty to seventy percent), any increase in it involves a disproportionate requirement for supplemental income to the degree that additional performance income fails to accompany rising labor expense. For an orchestra with an equal distribution of performance and supplemental income, a five-percent increase in expenditures can necessitate ten percent greater supplemental income.

In certain marginal activities, technological advances have affected the performance arts, and deserve comment here. These concern their *distribution* more than their production. The dissemination of performance through radio, television, and motion pictures provides a tangential insight into the economics of the performance arts. These media made possible a vastly wider distribution of the performers' services, requiring substantial capital investment in technological devices. From the investor's point of view these enterprises were highly profitable, and the performers themselves sought and gained a substantial share of the increased benefits that accrued from them. Petrillo's change in the 1930s, from a position of attempting to limit and compete with the electronic dissemination of music to one of seeking, through union bargaining, a larger share of its economic benefits for the performers, illustrates the purely capitalistic forces at work. The great disparity in this country between the hourly compensation that performers receive for services in the electronic media and their pay for live performance can only be understood in these terms, and it is interesting to note that in Europe, where the capitalist approach to the arts is not nearly as firmly entrenched as it is in this country, this disparity is much narrower.

Moreover, the performance arts require that a relatively high proportion of the service rendered by its labor force be expended in preparation as opposed to actual performance: three to five or more times as much time, personnel expense, and effort are required to rehearse a symphony concert as are needed to perform it. In the commercial theater on Broadway and its "road" adjunct, these preparatory labor costs, as well as investment in designing and making scenery and costumes, can be written off over the long run of a production if it meets with the approval of a sufficiently large audience. With symphony orchestras, similar benefits are possible should there be a sufficiently large audience to justify multiple performances at home or on tour. But the latter, as Thomas discovered a century ago, is not a reliable source of such marginal income, thanks to the high costs of transportation and the vagaries of local box office. For this reason the Philadelphia Orchestra, as we have seen, enjoys a higher proportion of performance income than do most orchestras, because it has long since developed such extensive utilization of repertory once this has been prepared; the same is true of the Boston Symphony and a few others.

In eight seasons between 1963 and 1971 for which relevant data are available, average musicians' payroll increased as follows for Major orchestras: [3]

Weeks in contract:
1963–64	28	(100%)
1970–71	43.12	(154%)

Weekly minimum salary:
1963–64	$ 135.00	(100%)
1970–71	224.84	(167%)

Annual minimum salary:
1963–64	$4,365.60 (100%)
1970–71	9,958.80 (228%)

As will be noted later in this chapter, between 1961 and 1971 total artist salaries and benefits (including soloists' fees as well as conductors' and orchestra players' salaries) for twenty-eight Major orchestras rose by 173%, while the number of concerts played increased 62% and attendance by 77%.[4] Nor were artistic services the sole factor in this process: during the same period administrative expenses, in which personnel costs also play a major role, increased by 183%. Obviously, such increased artistic services as may have resulted from higher payrolls required comparable overhead in operation.

To the degree that orchestra management could utilize additional services made available under longer seasons, some of this greater labor expense could be absorbed by increased productivity, but rising costs per week could not. Moreover, since orchestras recapture only a portion of their expenditures in performance income, additional activity by no means compensated for the greater costs of extended seasons. Thus, for twenty-eight Major orchestras, the economic trends for the 1960s were: [5]

	1961–62	1970–71
Expenditures	$22,176,521	$65,764,698 (+197%)
Performance income	12,925,379	30,627,723 (+137%)
Income gap	9,242,142	35,136,975 (+280%)
Artistic personnel	14,317,100	39,060,878 (+173%)
Number of concerts	2,786	4,501 (+ 62%)

Faced with such large increases in costs, orchestra managements have three possible solutions: (1) an increase in ticket prices; (2) additional activity; (3) greater reliance on supplemental income. Generally speaking, symphony orchestras raise their ticket prices only with great reluctance, for fear of losing an already tenuous hold on the public; though price advances in the past decade have generally kept pace with the inflationary national economy, this has not been a major source of relief. Baumol and Bowen cite three basic influences that restrict increases in ticket prices beyond the normal rate of inflation: "(1) the disinclination of individual arts organizations to raise their prices, on moral grounds; (2) the place of the arts in the purchaser's hierarchy of necessities; and (3) the forces of competition." [6] To the extent that higher labor costs have been accompanied by additional services, usually in the form of longer seasons, orchestras have had to develop new areas of activity; however, as noted in the discussion of the Cincinnati and Buffalo orchestras, this requires considerable innovation and often encounters strong opposition from the players themselves. Moreover, the fact that total expenditures rose more than artistic personnel in the previous comparison indicates that such expansion of services seems to involve disproportionately higher costs of production and administration. In fact, it appears that some orchestras have been inclined to relax their requests for allowing greater diversification in exchange for players' concessions on weekly salary in negotiations.

Another method of increasing performance income is to develop special public services for which government funding can be obtained. These include school concerts, free performances in parks, and other artistic services. (As we have seen in Cincinnati, some private support for such services can also be developed.) When we trace in Chapter XV the development of government subsidy of the arts in general and orchestras in particular, we shall see how this aid was originally justified by such for-service funding, which still plays an important part in this phase of symphony finance; the recent entry of the federal government into symphony subsidy is still based on this principle. To the degree that the administrative load of such services for government is shared by public agencies, this can be a very favorable way of securing additional performance income when increased musicians' services become available from greater personnel costs.

Obviously the last solution to the problem of the widening income gap is greater reliance on supplemental income—more effort in soliciting contributions and the development of new sources of private and government support. To the degree that increased public support is tied to special projects and services, such funding appears as performance income, thereby relieving pressure on supplemental needs, but some public support comes in the form of outright grants credited to supplemental income. Before looking at the problem of the income gap in greater detail and projecting its potential impact into the future, we must place the symphony orchestras in the general context of the performance arts and examine the various components of their economics.

Symphony in the Performance Arts

In 1971, the National Endowment for the Arts prepared a financial summary of all performance arts,[7] with data both for actual operations in 1969–70 and for estimated activity in 1970–71.* These show that the hundred and one orchestras covered (twenty-eight Major and seventy-three Metropolitan) had estimated expenditures in 1970–71 of $83 million. When community, urban, youth, and college orchestras are added to this figure, it is doubtful whether the total "symphonic national product" would exceed $90 million. Compared to a gross national product of over $1 trillion, this is a relatively miniscule portion of the nation's economy. Some six hundred corporations, as

---

* The following comments are based on my version of the 1970–71 estimates, to be found in Appendix F. The symphony data used in the NEA summary were extracted from the files of the ASOL. These NEA estimates, when compared with the actual symphony figures for 1970–71, were reasonably accurate: for the Major orchestras only, they were $1 million low for expenditures, $3.7 high for performance income, and $4.6 low for gross deficit. However, since actual data on the other performance arts are not available, the NEA *estimates* for 1970–71 will be retained in this discussion of the orchestras' place in the total performance arts.[8]

reported in *Fortune Magazine,* had annual sales in excess of the *total* symphonic activity.

The relative economic importance of the nonprofit performance arts in the entertainment industry may be seen in comparing the following estimates for 1970–71: [9]

	(In millions)
Symphony, opera, theater, and dance combined performance income	$ 90.5
Symphony performance income	42.2
Estimated motion-picture grosses	250. to 350.
Broadway grosses	54.9
"Road" theatrical touring	50.1

Though symphony orchestras represent but an infinitesimal portion of the total national economy and are small by comparison with mass entertainment, they share this status with the other nonprofit performance arts, among which, however, they play a major role. Of the four principal groups surveyed —theater, dance, opera, and symphony—orchestras in 1970–71 accounted for 55% of the organizations covered, 51% of their total expenditures, 47% of performance income, and 61% of estimated attendance. Only in performance income do the orchestras fall below contributing at least half to the national performance arts total—an indication, incidentally, that symphony orchestras are serving their public at a lower cost ($3.40/person) in admission prices than the national average, and only slightly higher than the average income per person in dance. In terms of expenditures per person served, symphony orchestras ($6.60) are lower than average and higher only than dance. Their income gap ($3.20/person) and supplementary income ($2.98) are lower than average and higher only than theater. Their net deficit per person ($.22) is the lowest of the performance arts.

We shall have occasion later to discuss the reservations with which any attendance figures must be evaluated: those reported by the NEA are obviously based on estimates of varying reliability. As long as they are used only to compute costs or income per person served, they have some limited relevance, but one must not assume, from these data, that 20.5 million different individuals attended one or more arts performances in 1970–71; duplication between the arts and frequency of attendance, especially on season subscription, would reduce that figure considerably.*

Within these considerations, however, these data show that orchestras play a very important part in the nonprofit sector of the performance arts. Until such newly organized resources as the Ford Foundation data bank are in operation, it will be impossible to delineate this status more precisely, or to

---

* Baumol and Bowen [10] discuss attendance figures for 1963–64 and reach the conclusion that total attendance for comparable activity then was in the vicinity of 19 million, but did not include Metropolitan orchestras, which might increase this figure by 2-3 million. But their attendance estimate of 19 million involves, by their calculation, less than 5 million different individuals, without taking into account duplications between the arts. This entire matter will be discussed in greater detail in Chapter XVI.

place it in the overall context of all arts activity, including museums among others.

The same NEA survey gives further information about symphony orchestras, dividing them according to the ASOL classification into twenty-eighty Major (over $700,000 budget) and seventy-three Metropolitan ($100,000 to $700,000 approximately). In the various fiscal categories reported—expenditures, income, and deficit—the Major orchestras accounted for 75% to 88% of the overall totals and for 70% of estimated attendance. The Majors earned a higher portion (53%) of income from performance than did the Metropolitans (45%); they also showed a higher net deficit (4%) than did the Metropolitans (2%). Metropolitan orchestras enjoyed a portion of total attendance (30%) considerably higher than their share of expenditures (21%) or performance income (18%), reflecting their lower expenditures and income per persons.

The more conservative operation of Metropolitan orchestras may account for their lower percentage of net deficit. The estimated 4% for 1970–71 is higher than actual figures (2.2%) for fifty-eight of seventy-two Metropolitan orchestras shown elsewhere.[11] The same source reports that in 1970–71 thirty-one orchestras (nine Major and twenty-two Metropolitan) showed a surplus and the remainder (nineteen Major and thirty Metropolitan) a net loss. Over the long run, some orchestras have alternating gains or losses in a manner that generally cancels out over a period of years. Many, however, accumulate considerable deficits, some a serious problem; only a few have ever succeeded in building surpluses, probably none in recent years. However, the fact that over 61% of the orchestras reported net deficits indicates that an appreciable number may now be accumulating long-term deficits.

New Categories

The NEA figures do not break down the hundred and one orchestras surveyed into categories other than Major and Metropolitan. For this we must turn to data prepared especially for this study by the American Symphony Orchestra League. These differ somewhat from those reported in the 1971 NEA survey, in large part because the latter made projections based on a season then in progress and, in the case of the Metropolitan orchestras, estimates on the basis of fifty-two out of seventy-three orchestras. The League information here is based on the actual figures reported early in 1972 for the actual operations of the previous season; they include all of twenty-six Major orchestras * and fifty-eight of seventy-two in the Metropolitan category.[12] Insofar as these data reflect financial information, they may be considered highly reliable, being based, in virtually all cases, on the audited financial records of the orchestras.

Though the League has for some time considered changing its classification

* My three categories covered by the Major classification include only twenty-six orchestras, two less than the official League ranking, for reasons stated earlier and in Appendix D.

of orchestras, it has decided only recently to take this step retaining the Major and Metropolitan classifications,* which for purposes here do not give relevant information; we have outlined the reasons at the end of Chapter VI, where we suggested the division of the Major orchestras into three categories (A, B, and C) and the Metropolitan into two (D and E).

For each of our five categories, we have data for average expenditures, income, and general operations, combining a number of "line items" in a few summary groupings. Expenditures include cost of artistic personnel, concert production, and administration. Performance and supplementary income are subdivided to show principal sources. The operations data cover major activities of general interest. These category-average data are presented in the tables in Appendix E, on which the following comments are based.

Performance and Supplemental Income

Orchestra income includes two major items, each subdivided: concert proceeds, miscellaneous receipts (but not including government grants), and government funding for services rendered make up performance income; contributions, government subsidy not requiring specific services, and endowment comprise supplemental income.

Traditionally the series subscription is the backbone of concert income: a concrete expression of continuing patron loyalty, it is an orchestra's best insurance against the vagaries of weather, uncertain "draw" of soloists, and the impact of competition. Though attacks have been made on the subscription system,† it remains the cornerstone of an orchestra's security. The proportion of subscription income varies greatly from orchestra to orchestra, depending on many factors, among them the size of the hall: we have already noted that the Albuquerque Symphony was, in 1971–72, virtually sold out on subscription; other orchestras may enjoy a season sale of only half the capacity of their auditoriums. Some orchestras, as in Cincinnati, also sell their popular concerts on subscription, but many offer these on a nonsubscription basis. Several occasionally present nonsubscription concerts for special events, the engagement of a popular soloist, or a benefit.

Also included in concert income here are such nonsymphonic presentations as ballet and opera, when those productions are directly sponsored by the symphony association; not included are the proceeds of separate ballet or opera organizations that engage symphony musicians directly. Some Major orchestras have for years played many concerts away from home; a few even have long-established subscription series in other cities. Though touring seldom covers the expense involved, and never when players' salaries and overhead are included in cost accounting, many orchestras look to touring for

---

* The new League division between Major and Metropolitan orchestras is now determined by a $1 million annual budget; the League has also established more stringent requirements for maintaining this level of operation.[13] See Appendix D for full list of orchestras by category.
† These will be discussed in greater detail in Chapter XVI.

marginal income; gross fees from touring are considered concert income and the costs will be considered shortly in discussion of expenditures.

Some orchestras engage in occasional nonsymphonic presentations—recitals, concerts by visiting orchestras, and other ventures on which they hope both to expand their musical service and make some profit. The proceeds of such activities are listed under other (nongovernment) income. Also included in this are the net royalties received by those orchestras that make commercial recordings, fees from radio and television broadcasts, and other miscellaneous activities. This miscellaneous income can also include profit from hall rental (if the orchestra owns its hall), and special contributions from businesses and foundations to underwrite such activities as free park concerts or education programs.

As we shall have occasion to discuss in some detail in a later chapter, symphony orchestras often base their appeal for government funding on their education and community services—free programs for schoolchildren or summer concerts in the parks, for instance. Many cities, counties, states, and especially the National Endowment for the Arts, make grants to symphony orchestras on the basis of applications that specify the services to be rendered in exchange for such support. (Matching funds required for government grants, however, are included in contributions under supplemental income.) This is regarded as performance income, but when no service is specified in this manner, government funding falls into the supplemental category.

The ratio of performance to total income is a prime indicator of an orchestra's overall efficiency of operation. The average percentage of performance to total income ranges from 67% for Category A to 48% for Category D; the remaining averages cluster around 50%. In the operations of the Philadelphia Orchestra, itself enjoying 72% in this respect, we have already indicated some of the factors which contribute to the more advantageous situation of Category A orchestras in general: a greater opportunity because of greater population to repeat programs once they are prepared, and a substantially higher proportion of income from such other (nongovernment) sources as recording, more than four times that of the other categories. In the increasingly important item of government funding for special services rendered, the Category C orchestras appear to enjoy the most favorable percentage. In 1970–71 this was partly due to the fact that the National Endowment for the Arts more or less placed a ceiling of $100,000 on grants to Major orchestras, and made smaller allocations to the Metropolitans; thus, in relation to the larger orchestras, this funding in Category C became a larger proportion of their smaller budgets. All orchestras in the Major categories received government funds for services, but only twenty (of twenty-six) in Category D and twenty (of thirty-two) in Category E did.

Traditionally in the American orchestra, supplemental income has been contributed by private individuals sufficiently interested in the arts to pay an orchestra more than the admission price or convinced enough of the importance of an orchestra to the community to support it. The extreme example of such patronage, of course, was Major Higginson, who single-handed supplied the supplemental income of the Boston Symphony for nearly four decades; there have been other such lavish patrons, but the impact of income taxes on private wealth and the expansion of operations have made orchestras increasingly reliant on a wider base of support. In recent years, moreover, business corporations have been persuaded that support of the arts is as important a part of their charitable programs as are education and private welfare agencies. A special form of private or corporate charity, the foundation, has begun to play a major role in supplying supplemental income.

One type of philanthopic contribution to supplemental income is the endowment, a trust administered by the orchestra itself (or by a legal entity set up by it or by the donors) providing capital from which the orchestra enjoys the annual income. Such trusts may be restricted by their donors to specific purposes or to the use of income only; others may permit the invasion of capital. Some orchestras, which had in the past been able to accumulate unrestricted endowment through gifts or from operating surpluses, have in recent years found it necessary to withdraw substantial funds from these unrestricted endowments to meet annual deficits or to undertake major capital programs. The Cleveland and Chicago orchestras in the 1960s reduced their once formidable endowments for both of these purposes, and we have already noted how Cincinnati Institute of Fine Arts capital funds designated for the orchestra have likewise suffered similar depletion. Until 1966, endowments played a relatively minor part in symphony finances, except for the few orchestras that had accumulated large trusts, but the Ford Foundation symphony program established a trust fund for some sixty orchestras of $58 million and required them to raise even more for their own endowments; income from both sources has now become a significant factor in symphony finance. Including these still restricted (until 1976) trusts, total symphony endowment probably now totals between $350 and $400 million. All of the Category A, B, and C orchestras in this survey had endowment funds in 1970–71; twenty five (of twenty-six) in Category D and twenty-two (of thirty-two) in Category E also had endowments. Of seventy-three endowed orchestras, sixty were included in the Ford Foundation program.

As may be expected from their long-time establishment in the large centers of great wealth, the Category A and B orchestras show a substantially higher percentage (10.2% and 13.5% respectively) of endowment income. The lowest percentage (3.5%) is encountered in Category E, where few of the orchestras were included in the Ford Foundation program. Because of their higher performance and endowment income, the orchestras in the two larger categories must raise a lower portion of their income from contributions, but in dollar amounts their requirements are very high. The degree to which those in Category A rely on large donors can be seen by comparing the average size of contribution in each category: [14]

A—$244
B— 125
C— 136
D— 122
E— 112

To the extent that government grants are not designated for services, income from them is also included in the supplementary category. This can be rather substantial, as we noted in the case of the Buffalo Philharmonic, where Erie County and city funding was not specifically contracted on a service basis, even though the orchestra's plea for it was based on community services. However, this type of government funding is still relatively rare: of eighty-four orchestras only thirty-four received outright grants for which no specific services were required.

Where the Money Goes

The budget item "artistic personnel" includes the salaries of conductors, musicians' payroll, and the fees of guest artists. The most closely guarded secrets in the symphony world concern the salaries paid conductors and certain key orchestra personnel such as concertmasters and important principal players.[15] Some conductors in Category A orchestras may receive as much as a hundred thousand dollars a year, plus a share of recording royalties; at the other end of the scale, in the smaller category E orchestras, the conductor's salary may be as low as ten to fifteen thousand dollars a year. A conductor's salary in a smaller Category E orchestra can amount to as much as ten percent of the total budget, but in the larger orchestras it will be no more than two to three percent. Fees of nationally booked soloists or guest conductors generally follow the laws of supply and demand: the more popular artists, who draw larger audiences, can command higher fees; a few notable celebrities receive seven to ten thousand dollars for a symphony engagement, with others ranging from two to five thousand. A local soloist or a nationally booked artist just starting his career may accept as little as a thousand dollars, or even less, if he feels that an orchestra appearance will advance his career. Orchestra members appear as soloists for relatively modest fees, sometimes as a part of their negotiated overscale. In earlier years, it was customary for visiting soloists to play a pair of symphony concerts for their regular recital fee, but this is no longer always the case; however, additional appearances at subscription concerts or on tour are usually priced lower. Internationally celebrated guest conductors, who are in great demand, can command fees comparable to their soloist counterparts, but when an orchestra is known to be "shopping" for a musical director, candidates for the position will sometimes appear for little more than their expenses.

The largest single item in the artistic personnel budget is, of course, the orchestra payroll. This depends upon the minimum terms arrived at in negotiations between the management, the union, and the players. In all of the Major orchestras in Categories A, B, and C, these set forth the number of weeks of employment, the minimum weekly pay, and an increasing variety of fringe benefits. Though some Metropolitan orchestras have such contracts, most are drawn in terms of a minimum price per service (rehearsal or concert) or per rehearsal and per concert (at different pay), often stipulating the maximum number of services that can be called in any week and the minimum guaranteed for the season. Some orchestras have two contracts, one guaranteeing some players more work than others. Though contracts may stipulate certain minimum overscale for key players, in most orchestras these players negotiate individually for this.

Key players in a Category A orchestra—the concertmaster and the principal first-chair players—may receive as much as forty to fifty thousand dollars a year, three times the minimum scale; other first-chair musicians and those with special responsibilities or seniority also receive overscale ranging from nominal amounts to double the minimum. In some of these orchestras as many as half of the players—virtually all winds and some strings—receive overscale. An increasing number of union contracts call for "minimum overscale" on the basis of seniority or position in the orchestra. In the smaller orchestras overscale itself is paid according to a formula, sometimes fifty percent over minimum for principals, with the concertmaster's pay subject to negotiation. Though precise information on overscale is difficult to obtain, being based on private negotiations, overscale can amount to fifteen to twenty percent of the total payroll. The expenditures listed here for artistic personnel also include Social Security taxes, medical insurance, and pension contributions; these "fringe benefits," however, are found only in the larger orchestras, though they are spreading to the smaller ones.

Having already noted the manner in which rapidly rising personnel costs in the 1960s contributed to even faster widening of the income gap, we can further elaborate our data on average musicians' pay for the orchestras in Categories A, B, and C with breakdowns of the ICSOM-AFM data.[16] Though this information is not always complete, it is sufficient to show, for each of these three categories, trends in weekly minimum salary for eight years, 1963–1971.

During these eight years, the increase in length of season was greater for Category B orchestras (94%) than it was for Category A (48%) or C (78%). Weekly pay rose more in Category C (75%) than it did in B (54%) and A (56%). Because of the more rapid increase in length of season, annual pay grew more in Category B orchestras (168%) than in A (120%) or C (144%). The following graphs (Tables 13-A, 13-B, 13-C) reveal these trends in each category.

In Category A, weekly salary was rather stable at the beginning of the 1960s, the increase in annual income arising from longer seasons, but once the orchestras approached full-year operation, weekly salary rose steeply. In Category B, with shorter seasons in the early 1960s, there was a rather steady rise in all three factors: length of season, weekly pay, and annual income. In Category C, however, there was less overall lengthening of the season, and greater annual income, especially in the final four years, came almost entirely from substantial weekly increments; apparently those orchestras preferred higher weekly pay to a commitment for longer seasons as a way of meeting their players' demands for better annual income. For these latter orchestras,

Table 13 A

Trends in Musicians' Pay 1963–71

Averages for Category A Orchestras

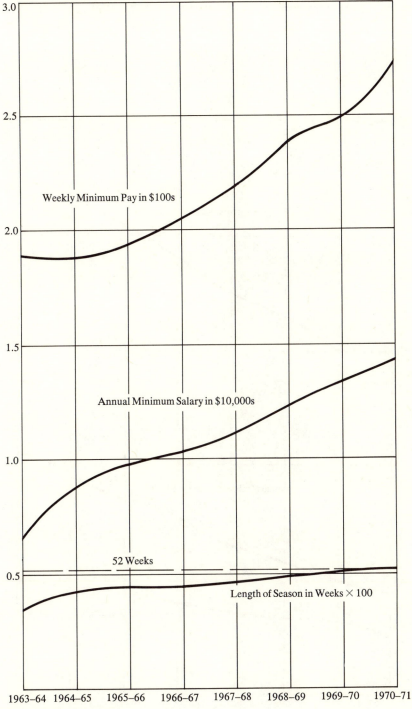

Weekly Minimum Pay in $100s

Annual Minimum Salary in $10,000s

52 Weeks

Length of Season in Weeks × 100

1963–64   1964–65   1965–66   1966–67   1967–68   1968–69   1969–70   1970–71

Source: ICSOM-AFM surveys.

Table 13 B

Trends in Musicians' Pay 1963–71
Averages for Category B Orchestras

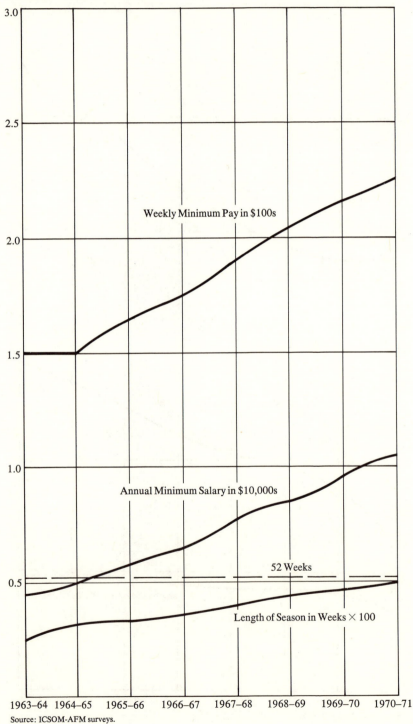

Source: ICSOM-AFM surveys.

Table 13 C

Trends in Musicians' Pay 1963–71
Averages for Category C Orchestras

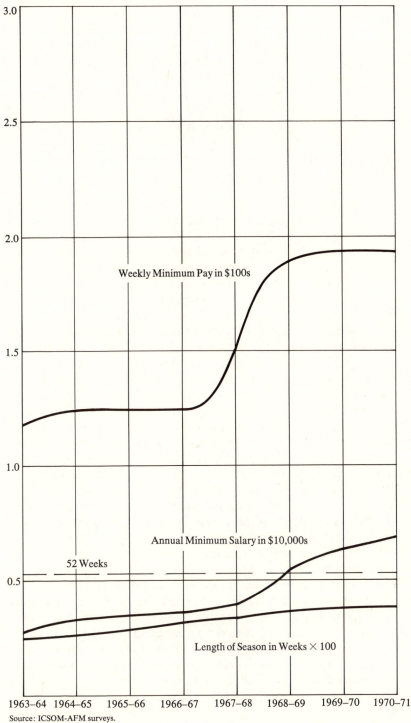

Source: ICSOM-AFM surveys.

the future may still bring longer seasons. But Categories A and B, now close to year-round operation, can only offer higher weekly pay (and various fringe benefits) to meet musicians' continuing demands and will be more limited in improving productivity, whereas those in Category C still have an opportunity to absorb advances in annual payroll with expanding services.

Concert production expense covers the whole variety of costs related to presenting concerts at home and on tour, and varies according to local conditions or traditions. These include hall rental, stagehands, ushers, ticket sellers, program and ticket printing, advertising and promotion, and the cost of touring.

A few of the orchestras in Categories A, B, and C own their own halls; others have arrangements with cities or universities giving them priority in the use of a hall or arts center for concerts and rehearsals. But most orchestras must rent facilities for concerts and often hold their rehearsals elsewhere. When orchestras own their halls, their accountants allocate a share of the cost of running the hall to the orchestra operation; in some cases, the hall itself shows a profit, which is either retained in a special fund for emergency, depreciation, or renovation, or returned to the orchestra's general fund as performance income; such cases are increasingly rare in these days of rising maintenance and material costs. Some orchestras enjoy the use of municipal or university auditoriums for their concerts and rehearsals at costs much lower than commercial rentals; others must rent local theaters at the regular rate. Virtually all halls in which orchestras play are unionized: three to six stagehands often receive more than the orchestra players, and some halls are also required to engage union ushers and box-office personnel.

Many orchestras own substantial libraries of orchestra material for the standard repertory, though considerable expense is involved in maintaining (in labor and purchase of materials), augmenting, and replacing it. Others must rent much of the performance material even for the standard repertory from music rental agencies. Some music under copyright is available for purchase by orchestras, but most contemporary music must be rented from its publishers. In either case, the orchestra must pay a royalty fee for its performance, either by the piece or, more frequently, by contracting with such publishers' representatives as the American Society of Composers, Authors, and Publishers (ASCAP) or Broadcast Music Incorporated (BMI) for an annual license based on a percentage (0.1% to 0.25%) of performance income. BMI and ASCAP, in turn, pass on these royalties to the composers and their publishers in their own manner.

Most orchestras supply their patrons with a printed program that not only lists the music to be played but also includes extensive explanatory program notes and promotional material for the orchestra. Sometimes local musicians, critics, or scholars write these program notes, but some orchestras subscribe to a national program service for them. Generally program books carry extensive advertising in an effort to defray the printing expense. A few orchestras contract with printers or publishers for securing this advertising in such a way that at least involves no net expense to the orchestra and may even return it a modest revenue. Other orchestras assign the task of advertising solicitation and program publication to their women's committees, thus providing some income for the organization.

Generally speaking, no orchestras advertise in newspapers or on radio and television as lavishly as commercial entertainment enterprises do; if a major proportion of their capacity is sold on season subscription, they need only take enough space to keep the public advised on their activities. They may take large ads once or twice a year to promote season-ticket sales, but routine concert advertising is usually confined to a few inches in the newspapers or spot announcements on radio and TV. An increasing number of orchestras engage special outside promotional counsel for fund-raising and season-ticket campaigns; the extensive use of direct-mail advertising, often to demographically selected markets, has been recently undertaken by several orchestras with such counsel. For some orchestras, a local business firm will prepare and purchase large display advertisements as a form of donation. Orchestras rely a great deal on free publicity in newspapers, spot announcements, or public-service programming; for this considerable promotional effort is required, much of it by paid staff, but in some smaller orchestras by volunteers from the women's committees. Special events—nonsubscription concerts, appearances of major soloists or benefit concerts—of course receive additional effort and, frequently, increased paid use of media.

Touring an orchestra is economically marginal, especially in recent years, but such orchestras as the Philadelphia and Boston, located with heavily populated cities nearby, find out-of-town concerts financially important, if not profitable. Any orchestra that tours considers itself fortunate if its income covers the direct travel expenses without meeting a pro-rata share of the orchestra payroll; the players are under contract in any event, and any "profit" from such touring is welcome marginal income. Some orchestras, it is reported, do not even meet direct tour costs when they travel; they do so for the prestige involved and, again, because the players are already under contract and such utilization of their services incurs less loss than would other activities. The two major components of tour expense are transportation of personnel and equipment and per-diem payments to the musicians. These latter, set forth in detail in the basic union agreement, are intended to reimburse the players for meals, overnight accommodations (if not paid by the orchestra), and the incidental expenses of travel. With the decline of railroad service, most extensive orchestra travel is by chartered airplane or bus, depending on the distances involved; exceptions, of course, are the visits of the Boston and Philadelphia orchestras to New York, which are still made by rail. Large orchestras need a full-size trailer truck to carry instruments and other equipment, including the musicians' personal luggage on long tours; some orchestras that tour a great deal own or lease their own trucks.

Next to the conductor or conductors, the most highly paid individual in the symphony organization is usually the manager, whatever his title. Again we deal here with closely guarded information, but the same educated guess applied to conductors' salaries would indicate that very few managers are paid in excess of fifty thousand dollars a year, and the salary drops appreciably in the lower reaches of Category C to about twenty thousand, with substantially less for managers of Metropolitan orchestras. In fact, among the smaller orchestras, the manager may be a part-time employee receiving as little as five thousand to seventy-five hundred dollars a year.

Like other nonprofit organizations, salaries for office staff tend toward the minimum range offered in commercial employment; not only are less skilled employees used but every effort is made to sell them on the intangible pleasures of working for a good cause. Office workers in many orchestras lag behind those in private business in such fringe benefits as medical insurance and pensions; in fact, in some orchestras the musicians enjoy fringe benefits not available to the full-time office personnel. Administrative forces vary in size and diversity, from one or two employees in the smallest Category E orchestras to over forty for the largest in Category A. Obviously the smaller staffs must do a variety of work, ranging from bookkeeping, selling tickets, and arranging concerts to publicity and advertising; in some cases they may consist of a manager and secretary-bookkeeper. As orchestras grow in size, added personnel become more specialized in their work; a first step in expansion often involves using such part-time specialists as accountants and publicists or contracting with outside firms for these services. In the larger orchestras, administration becomes extremely specialized, with one or more assistant managers assigned specific areas of operation and with full-time specialists in finance and public relations.

In comparing the average expenditures for the various categories, certain significant differences are to be noted in scale of operation and in the relative proportion of types of costs. Total performance costs (artistic personnel and concert production combined) require much the same portion of expenditures (approximately 88%) for all three categories of Major orchestras, but administrative expense is comparatively higher in the Metropolitan categories. There appears to be an almost irreducible minimum for the management of a professional orchestra, and as orchestras grow larger administrative costs do not rise in proportion. Largely due to the cost of touring and of repeated programs, the Category A orchestras spend a greater portion on concert production, and correspondingly less on artistic personnel in percentage terms. Except for the very largest orchestras, artistic personnel receive 61–65% of total expenditures.

Thirty-seven of the eighty-six orchestras covered by these data showed net surpluses from their operations in 1970–71; twenty-nine of these were in the Metropolitan categories. Half of the Metropolitan orchestras, and eighteen of twenty-six Major, showed net deficits, averaging as high as nearly $250,000 in Category A. The total net deficit for twenty-eight Major orchestras in 1970–71 amounted to $2.4 million.[17] Some orchestras must cover these deficits by borrowing from banks, which usually require individual board members to guarantee the notes personally, except in those rare instances in which an orchestra has acceptable collateral. A few orchestras with accumulated unrestricted endowment invade it to cover operating deficits. In most cases, where the deficit is not too large, the orchestra covers expenses between seasons by using prepaid subscription receipts to carry it over until, hopefully, a special fund-raising effort can be organized to restore fiscal stability. How-ever, the year-to-year financial reports of the Major orchestras show annual accumulated deficits totaling $17.3 million between 1961 and 1971.*

Operations Summarized

Before considering in more detail the implications of this large deficit and the income gap, we must comment briefly on other data presented in Appendix E, covering various operational information from these same categories in average form.

Though the Major orchestras gave an average of between 153 and 189 full orchestra concerts in 1970–71, there is a sharp drop in this number in the Metropolitan categories. The importance of diversified activities in Category B is reflected in the large number of ensemble concerts offered by three or-chestras; the even higher figure for Category D, however, includes the activi-ties of but one orchestra, that of Honolulu, which has developed such an extensive program that it distorts the average given. However, only nine of twenty-six Major orchestras, and thirty-eight of fifty-eight Metropolitans, of-fer ensemble concerts at all.

Because of different methods of contracting players, it is impossible to show data for all five categories for weekly pay, but the comparison of annual in-come for musicians shows a sharp difference between the Major and Metro-politan orchestras, and within the Major categories a range of over two to one between A and C. These data also indicate that only Categories A and B offer annual income approaching full-time subsistence and Category C may be re-garded as providing a principal source of income; few Metropolitan orches-tras play a major role in the sustenance of their players.

In accordance with previously noted reservations concerning attendance figures, those given here are useful primarily to compare categories or as a basis of computing expenditures and performance income per person; both show a progressive decline from the larger to smaller orchestras.

The use of radio or television by these orchestras is confined almost exclus-ively to the two larger categories. Actually, more orchestras made recordings in 1970–71 than appeared on the mass electronic media.

All of the Major orchestras received government funding for services ren-dered, since all but one were included in the grants of the National Endow-ment for the Arts. As noted earlier, these grants reached fewer of the smaller orchestras, an appreciable number of which, however, received local govern-ment aid, much of it as outright grants averaging from fifteen to twenty thousand dollars.

The third section of Appendix E shows the average metropolitan-area population for the cities supporting the orchestras in each category, together with certain data from the first three sections computed in ratio to the popula-tion. The largest and smallest cities in each category are:

* See "Net Deficit" in Appendix G for year-to-year figures.

Average	Largest	Smallest
Category A	New York	Cleveland
5,862,580	11,528,649	2,064,194
Category B	Detroit	Cincinnati
2,514,803	4,199,931	1,384,911
Category C	Baltimore	Utah
1,034,266	2,070,670	557,635
Category D	San Diego	New Haven
764,701	1,357,854	355,538
Category E	San Jose	Portland, Me.
438,433	1,064,714	141,625

In proportion to the total population the orchestras in Category C show considerably higher figures for expenditures and contributions per person. They also show the highest performance income per person, but only slightly higher than Category A. In estimated average attendance per person Category C significantly leads the others.

Impact of the Income Gap

Having covered in some detail the components which describe the operations of symphony orchestras of various sizes in 1970–71, we must turn again to the essential problem of their economics: the income gap, a topic given comprehensive treatment by Baumol and Bowen.[18] From their account of its importance for the performance arts in general, we can extract some significant data pertaining to symphony orchestras and, with further information from the ASOL and individual orchestras, bring their account of trends in the income gap up to date.

From a graph (Table 13-D) showing trends from 1947 to 1964 in the size of the income gap for the Metropolitan Opera, Covent Garden opera, and eleven "basic" symphony orchestras,* we have omitted Covent Garden and added 1969–71 figures obtained from the Metropolitan Opera annual reports and ASOL data, without attempting to chart the precise course of these trends from 1964 to 1971.[20]

Though the growth of the income gap in the orchestras covered is by no means as spectacular in dollars as in the case of the Metropolitan Opera,† it nearly tripled in a steady increase between 1947 and 1964, and then accelerated until 1971 to a figure more than eight times as large as in 1947 and nearly

---

* The eleven basic orchestras used extensively by Baumol and Bowen were chosen because comparable and relevant data were available for the periods studied. All were in the Major group: Chicago, Cincinnati, Cleveland, Indianapolis, Kansas City, Minnesota (formerly Minneapolis), National (Washington, D.C.), Philadelphia, Pittsburgh, St. Louis, and San Francisco.[19]

† It should be noted that during this period the Metropolitan Opera experienced the same effects of player militance that symphonies did, while its numerous other workers were making similar demands; in addition, its income-gap problems were undoubtedly aggravated by the costly move to a new opera house in Lincoln Center in 1968.

Table 13 D

Income Gap 1947–71
Eleven "Basic" Orchestras and Metropolitan Opera

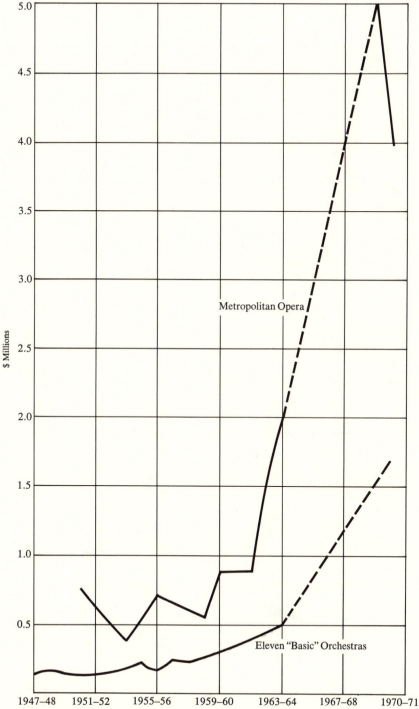

Sources: Graph to 1963 from Baumol and Bowen, *Performing Arts, The Economic Dilemma*, page 299; subsequent data from ASOL and Metropolitan Opera Association reports. Broken lines reflect estimates.

Table 13 E

Trends in Symphony Expenditures and Performance Income;
Wholesale Price Index 1937–71
Index 100=1937

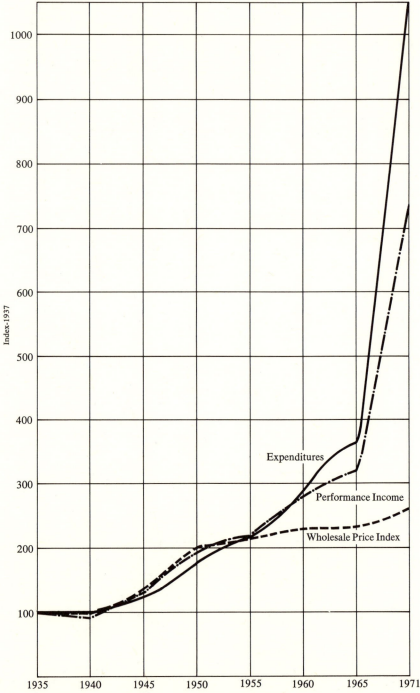

Sources: Symphony graphs to 1963 from Baumol and Bowen, *Performing Arts, The Economic Dilemma*, page 295
adapted by author; Wholesale Price Index from U.S. Bureau of Census reports.

Table 13 F

Trends in Income Gap 1937–71
Eleven "Basic" Orchestras

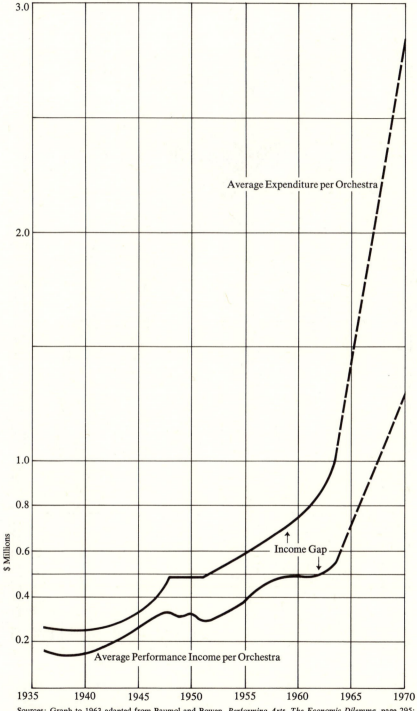

Sources: Graph to 1963 adapted from Baumol and Bowen, *Performing Arts, The Economic Dilemma*, page 295; subsequent data from ASOL.

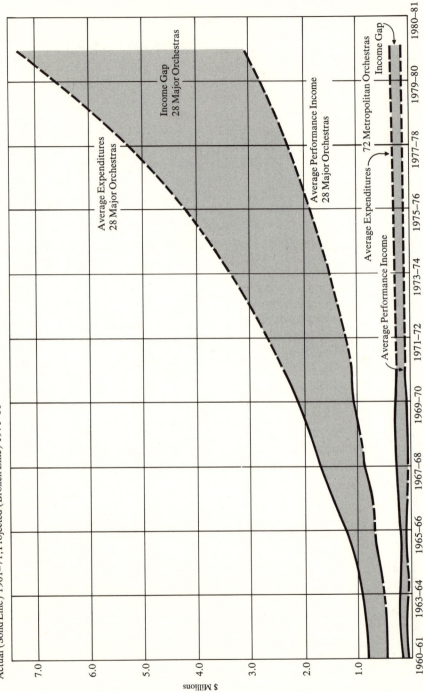

Table 13 G

Trends in Expenditure and Performance Income 1961–81
28 Major Orchestras; 72 Metropolitan Orchestras
Actual (Solid Line) 1961–71; Projected (Broken Line) 1971–81

$ Millions

7.0

6.0

5.0

4.0

3.0

2.0

1.0

1960–61   1963–64   1965–66   1967–68   1969–70   1971–72   1973–74   1975–76   1977–78   1979–80   1980–81

Average Expenditures
28 Major Orchestras

Income Gap
28 Major Orchestras

Average Performance Income
28 Major Orchestras

72 Metropolitan Orchestras

Income Gap

Average Expenditures

Average Performance Income

Sources: Macomber and Wooster for major orchestras to 1971; ASOL for metropolitan orchestras to 1971. See Appendix G
for author's projections to 1981.

three times larger than in 1963–64. In Table 13-E on page 316 trends in symphony expenditures and performance income (still the eleven "basic" orchestras) are plotted against the wholesale price index from 1937 to 1971; the former year is taken as a base index of 100 for all three items.[21] Until the mid-1950s, the symphony indicators increased in a manner generally paralleling the price index. For the next decade they rose much more sharply, but after 1965 rose at what can be described only as an explosive rate. From this graph it can be seen that the recent economic crisis of the symphony orchestras has two phases: the 1955–65 period and the even sharper crisis since then. As we shall see later, the latter phase may still be running its course.*

The total impact of these long-range trends back to 1937 is shown in the graph (Table 13-F, page 317) tracing the average expenditures and performance income per orchestra for the "basic" group.[22] Here the difference between these two items is shown as the income gap.

The preceding data from Baumol and Bowen have significance primarily in showing long-range trends, for which they are the only source of information. However, even from these it is apparent that a drastic change in symphony economics developed during the 1960s—a sudden increase in the income gap that far exceeded the normal growth to be expected in accordance with general economic rationale. For this decade there are more comprehensive data covering twenty-eight Major and seventy-two Metropolitan orchestras.† The graph on (Table 13-G, page 318) shows 1961–71 trends in expenditures and performance income for Major and Metropolitan orchestras, as well as a projection of these (on bases to be discussed shortly) to 1981.

The most obvious fact revealed by these graphs is the radically different behavior of finances in the Major and Metropolitan groups. In the former, both expenditures and performance income rose sharply, with a significant expansion of the income gap. On the other hand, the Metropolitan orchestras showed comparative stability in all three elements. Actually, were comprehensive data available in our previously defined five categories, a less extreme difference from one to another would probably be revealed: there are indications, for instance, that the trends for Category C orchestras, the smallest of the Majors, are more like those for the larger Metropolitans (Category D), and that the more extreme patterns for the Major orchestras are shaped largely by the Category A and B orchestras. However, there are equally persuasive reasons for believing that the forces at work here in Categories A and

---

* Since detailed data for the eleven "basic" orchestras are not available in a form comparable to the Baumol and Bowen graph for each year between 1964 and 1971, Table 13-E shows a straight line between these dates; the price index, however, is plotted more precisely.

† These data appear in Appendix G. Those for the Major orchestras are based on a tabulation in *How to Resolve the Growing Financial Crisis of Our Symphony Orchestras*, by John Macomber and John T. Wooster, in the June, 1972, issue of *Symphony News*. Similar statistics for the Metropolitan orchestras in Appendix G are based on information supplied me by the American Symphony Orchestra League. This Major orchestra group includes two—the Kansas City Philharmonic and the American Symphony Orchestra—not covered by my Categories A, B, and C. Since these data were originally prepared in an effort to substantiate the plea for government support, the information on this is listed separately in Appendix G; therefore neither performance income nor contributions include income from tax-supported sources.

B are likely to have future impact on Category C and, to a lesser extent, Category D.

These trends in the 1960s for the Major orchestras illustrate dramatically the extent of the financial crisis that has engulfed our larger professional orchestras and which shows many signs of continuing and spreading. Though this financial crisis struck these orchestras at various times during the decade, its impact can be pinpointed at the 1966–67 period, when in the overall total the income gap exceeded performance income. Numerically these trends can be summarized as follows: *

	1961–62	*1966–67*	*1970–71*
Expenditures	$22.2 (100%) index 100	$41.8 (100%) index 188	$65.7 (100%) index 297
Performance Income	$12.9 (58%) index 100	$20.4 (50%) index 158	$30.6 (47%) index 237
Income Gap	$9.3 (42%) index 100	$21.4 (50%) index 232	$35.1 (47%) index 380
($ in millions)			

The "index" entries show the relationship of the midpoint and final figures to those for the beginning of the decade and indicate their relative growth.

The severity of these financial pressures in the 1960s can be seen even more vividly when one computes the year-to-year percentage of growth in the income gap, alongside that of the wholesale price index.[23]

	Increase in symphony income gap	*Increase or decrease in wholesale price index*
1962–3	(−1%)	−0.53%
1963–4	13.1%	+0.21%
1964–5	18.0%	+0.95%
1965–6	18.3%	+0.21%
1966–7	48.3%	+0.20%
1967–8	6.0%	+2.50%
1968–9	21.3%	+3.90%
1969–70	10.0%	+3.66%
1970–1	16.0%	+2.30% (est)
Average	16.7%	+1.49%

Impressive as these figures are in defining the extent of the income-gap crisis in the Major orchestras in the 1960s, and especially in the last half of that decade, its full impact can only be grasped when total dollar figures are also considered. During this decade, these twenty-eight Major orchestras raised nearly $154 million in contributions; the Metropolitan orchestras received in the vicinity of $40 million during the same period. Moreover, dur-

* See Appendix G for complete figures.

ing its latter half, sixty Major and Metropolitan orchestras in the Ford Foundation symphony program raised over $84.4 million for capital funds not included in the contributions they received for annual maintenance. Thus, during this decade of crisis, the professional symphony orchestras of this nation raised over $280 million from private philanthropy.

A major factor in the increase in expenditures was, of course, the substantial rise in musicians' payroll, under the pressure of forces already discussed in Chapter V and elsewhere. The following graph (Table 13-H) plots the course of the cost of artistic services (of which musicians are a major component), together with total expenditures and the number of concerts given.

Though the increases in expenditures and artistic-personnel costs diverged slightly before 1966, the rate of that divergence increased appreciably thereafter. To a considerable degree this reflects the higher costs of administering the diversification of activities occasioned by the utilization of additional personnel available under extended contracts. From a purely economic view, these may be regarded as marginal operations. This observation is substantiated by the considerably lower rate of increase in the number of concerts actually given. The relationship between the number of concerts and expenditures is a matter of some importance, as can be seen in the next graph (Table 13-J) showing trends in *per-concert* expenditures and income, together with the total number of concerts.

Again, we note that it was in 1966–67 that important economic changes took place: in this case per-concert costs and income, after running a generally parallel course, diverged sharply. This increase in income gap per concert was further aggravated by the fact that it occurred at a time when the number of concerts increased. From these data, therefore, it is impossible to conclude that any greater economic efficiency has developed from the increase in number of concerts. If this seems to contradict the experience of the Philadelphia Orchestra, it must be pointed out that most of the new activities developed in the late 1960s were considerably more marginal financially than repetitions of full programs in heavily populated cities. Final judgment on this would require more statistical data than available here. In any event, these data should conclusively substantiate the basic economic rationale of the income gap with which this chapter opened.

Continuing Crisis

These developments produced a serious financial crisis among the American orchestras, more pressing in the larger ones but progressively affecting others in the Major categories and many in the Metropolitan. The need for increased supplemental funds to meet the income gap required an unprecedented effort to raise contributions and, as we shall see in a later chapter, finally broke down the long-standing opposition of symphony leadership to government funding. Under these pressures, this crisis coincided with the implementation

Table 13 H

Total and Artistic Expenditures 1961–71
28 Major Orchestras

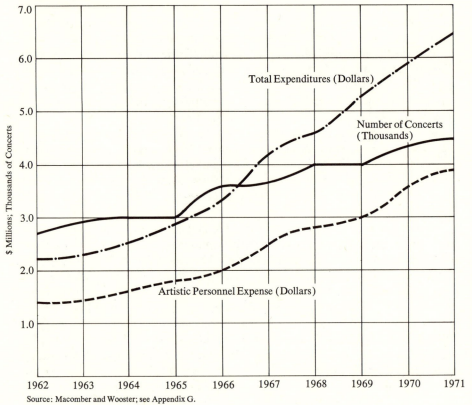

Source: Macomber and Wooster; see Appendix G.

Table 13 J

Cost and Income per Concert 1961–71
28 Major Orchestras

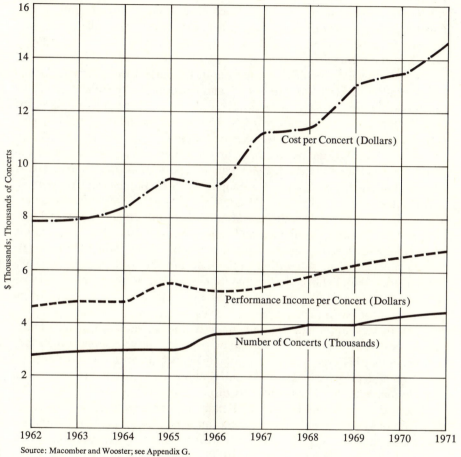

Source: Macomber and Wooster; see Appendix G.

in 1966 of the Ford Foundation symphony program, which itself contributed $24 million of the total $154 million of private philanthropy during the decade. However, the foundation program not only placed an added burden on symphony fund-raising for its endowment phase but also undoubtedly stimulated and encouraged the demands of the musicians. Even if the increases in musicians' pay had been held to a level approximating the overall inflationary trend of the national economy in the 1960s, the orchestras' income gap would still have widened in accordance with basic economic forces. But musicians' pay, in actually growing much faster than "normal" for reasons already described, contributed directly and indirectly to the extraordinary growth of the income gap.

Despite the widely publicized euphoria in the early 1960s that proclaimed the advent of a "cultural explosion" and encouraged the construction of several lavish arts centers, those closest to the performance arts detected the early symptoms of this economic crisis. The Ford Foundation symphony program itself resulted from intensive research in the field. Two other foundations undertook studies of the performance arts in general in which orchestra data figured significantly: the Rockefeller Panel Report—*The Performing Arts*—and the Twentieth Century Fund economic study by Baumol and Bowen.

Though the Rockefeller Panel Report drew together diverse information about the performance arts, their needs, and their importance to national welfare, the hardheaded economics and comprehensive statistical presentation of Baumol and Bowen proved even more effective in providing the rationale for major changes in supporting orchestras and the arts in general. To a large degree, the plight of the symphony orchestras, being more extreme on a national scale than the other arts, was the focus of concern. The cogent presentation of performance arts economics, represented and further stimulated by these studies, had three major results in the late 1960s. Individuals and corporations began to give substantially greater private support than they had previously believed necessary or possible; such organizations as the Business Committee for the Arts are manifestations of such concern. The Ford Foundation, with vast resources at its disposal, chose the symphonic field for its largest single program in the arts. Finally, conservative business executives who had long resisted major government funding of the arts not only withdrew their opposition but aggressively worked for such aid. The expansion of private philanthropy, the impact of the Ford Foundation grants, and the beginning of government funding will be considered in the two following chapters, but the forces at work during the 1960s have by no means lost their power and will continue to affect the future course of symphony economics in a drastic manner.

The trends in symphony economics during the crucial decade of the 1960s give some clues to possible future developments; * the graph in Table 13-G

---

* Writing in 1965, Baumol and Bowen computed an annual income-gap growth rate for their eleven basic orchestras of 6.9%, with lower figures for the New York Philharmonic (5.2%) and the Cincinnati Symphony (4.7%).[24] Obviously these no longer apply since the impact of the Ford Foundation grants and of musician's militance.

(page 318) projects (dotted lines) the potential scope of the continuation and expansion of the crisis of the 1960s through the following decade on the assumption that the major components of symphony finance will continue to increase at rates comparable to those of the last ten years. For these, the average annual increases were:[25]

	28 Majors 1961–71	28 Majors 1967–71	Metropolitans 1961–71
Expenditures	13%	12%	4.2%
Performance Income	10.0%	10.8%	3.2%
Income Gap	16.7%	13.3%	7.6%
Contributions	14.9%	12.3%	5.6%

The growth rates for Major orchestras have been subdivided to show more recent trends because of the previously noted changes around 1966–67; there are indications, since that watershed, of some stabilization of economic trends. For this reason the 1971–81 projections for Major orchestras are based on the 1967–71 average rate of growth, rather than the somewhat less favorable ten-year average of annual increments; the Metropolitan orchestra trends, however, are projected at the ten-year average rate.*

Obviously the projected growth is far more explosive in the Major orchestra group than in the Metropolitan. For the larger orchestras the increase in the major elements of their finances by 1981 will be:

	1970–71	Doubles by	1980–81
Expenditures	$65.8	1977	$204.3 (+210%)
Performance Income	30.6	1978	85.4 (+179%)
Income Gap	35.1	1977	118.8 (+238%)
Contributions	26.7	1978	85.3 (+219%)

($ in millions)

The increases for Metropolitan orchestras would be more modest:

	1970–71	1980–81
Expenditures	$18.3	$26.5 (+44.8%)
Performance Income	7.7	10.3 (+32.8%)
Income Gap	10.6	16.3 (+53.6%)
Contributions	8.3	13.6 (+63.3%)

($ in millions)

The crucial figures here are the differences between income gap and contributions, reflecting the ability of the private sector to continue to provide supplementary income in the traditional manner: † for Major and Metropolitan orchestras these figures for this *net financial gap* are:

* Computations of these 1971–81 projections are given in Appendix G-2.
† As noted earlier, these figures do not include income from tax-supported sources.

	1970–71	1980–81
Income Gap		
28 Major orchestras	$35.1	$118.8
72 Metropolitans	10.1	16.3
100 orchestras	$45.2	$135.1
Contributions		
28 Major orchestras	$26.7	$ 85.3
72 Metropolitans	7.9	13.6
100 orchestras	$34.6	$ 98.9
Net Financial Gap		
28 Major orchestras	$ 8.4	$ 33.6
72 Metropolitans	2.2	2.6
100 orchestras	$10.6	$ 36.2

($ in millions)

In 1970–71, a major portion of this net financial gap shown above was met by some $8 million from local, state, and national tax-supported agencies, leaving a net deficit of some $2 million to be covered by borrowing, expenditure of accumulated surplus or unrestricted endowment, or using prepaid income from the next season. But if recent trends continue, this net financial gap will grow to proportions no longer manageable by traditional devices and the present level of government support: in 1970–71, the net financial gap for all orchestras represented 12.7% of total expenditures, but it would grow, according to these projections, to nearly 16% by 1981. The problem of Major orchestras would be somewhat greater than for the overall group, with the financial gap rising from 12.8% of expenditures to 16.4%, an increase of nearly a third.

These projections, moreover, are but one scheme of computation: though others might produce a slightly lower rate of growth for the financial gap, there are real dangers that the estimates could be too low if expenditures were to grow more rapidly or if contributions or performance income should level off. A by no means improbable projection, shown as the "worst case" in Appendix G-4, would project a financial gap amounting to half of total expenditures.

These are not, it must be emphasized, predictions, but rather projections that indicate future possibilities. In assuming continuation of recent trends, they do not take into account a number of important, and at present unpredictable, variables, which cannot necessarily be analyzed here in quantitative terms. These can affect expenditures, performance income, private contributions, and government funding.

A major element in increasing expenditures has been the rapid rise in players' compensation in the past decade, especially in the larger orchestras. In those orchestras—about half of the Major group—which have in the 1960s attained something like year-round employment of their musicians, one might hope that the rate of increase in compensation might now settle down to a level approximating the overall expansion of the national economy. However, the force of musicians' militance built up in the last decade shows no signs of diminishing, with no evidence that players' demands in trade negotiations are in any way abating. Moreover, in at least some of the remaining Major orchestras, especially those in Category C offering less than forty-week seasons, players continue to press both for increased weekly salary and for more weeks of employment, the very same pressures that caused so explosive a growth of expenditures in the larger orchestras in the 1960s. The same forces may well be felt by some of the larger Metropolitan orchestras. To the degree that bargaining for longer seasons can be tied to greater flexibility of activity and to the stimulation of adequate performance income, the ultimate financial gap generated by such expansion could be held under control.

At the same time, the possibilities for greater growth of performance income must be regarded as severely limited. For reasons to be discussed in greater detail later, the potential audience for symphony orchestras is limited and significant growth in the proportion of total population that can be attracted to orchestra activities will be slow at best. Nor can substantial relief be expected from ticket-price increases that exceed the normal inflationary growth of the national economy. Moreover, there are ample indications that diversified activities by orchestras, designed to utilize the additional services of the players, are in fact more costly—in both direct expenses and administrative overhead—than the traditional subscription concert presentations.

Private contributions to symphony orchestras revealed in these summaries showed during the 1960s an average annual increase of 14.9% for Major orchestras and 5.6% for Metropolitan; the average annual increase in total national philanthropy for the same period was 7.45%.[26] Especially in the crucial group of larger orchestras, this annual increase in income from the private sector is so much greater than the national rate as to offer little hope of substantial long-range improvement in this area. The most hopeful prospect is that new sources of contributions opened up during the capital-fund drives to match the Ford Foundation challenge between 1966 and 1971 can be relied upon for continued annual contributions to supplemental income in the future. On the other hand, should government funding increase substantially in the next decade, as many anticipate, its psychological impact on private contributors is one of the most imponderable unknowns now faced by orchestras. Fears that the large grants of the Ford Foundation would depress private giving fortunately proved unfounded, but those grants were designed to encourage support from private philanthropy; this may not be the case with future government subsidy.

As will be noted in greater detail later, orchestras have turned increasingly, especially since 1969, to government funding as the ultimate solution of their financial problems. In 1970–71, the first year in which federal funding played an important role in symphony economics, total government funding was probably in the range of eight to ten percent of overall operations, falling three to five percent short of meeting the net financial gap between the income gap and contributions; to have met the full financial gap in 1970–71 total government funding, at all levels, should have been close to $11 million. By 1980–81 this requirement may at least be three times as high and possibly more, if the other elements of symphony economics behave more unfavorably than projected here. In this we are dealing with a delicate interplay of economic forces: if one or more of the components of symphony finance develops adversely in the next decade, the net financial gap can easily exceed $50 million for the professional orchestras of this nation.

If substantial increases in government funding should materialize, such an explosive growth in this financial gap is by no means unlikely unless the demands of orchestra musicians can be held under some sort of mutually agreeable control. We have already seen how the mere prospect of the Ford Foundation grants in 1966 greatly stimulated the demands of these players in their desire to assure themselves of their share of the bounty. The possibility of substantially increased government funds will have a similar effect on the militant musicians at the same time that it may depress the growth of private philanthropy to a degree not evident in the Ford Foundation grants. These are psychological forces which cannot be anticipated by quantitative projections, though the latter can provide important guidelines in estimating the consequences of specific dollar demands in player negotiations.

At present, boards, managements, and the musicians look to government support as the solution of their problems, with special concentration on the expansion of federal funding. Yet, as we shall note later in greater detail, for the federal government alone to meet the growing net financial gap of the symphony orchestras would require increasing the total 1971–72 federal arts appropriation from $30 million annually to something like $200 million a year by 1980. There are, as we shall see, prominent and influential figures in the symphony world who believe that such a goal is possible, but, given the forces outlined here, even that goal may be inadequate to meet the growing needs of orchestras unless they take unprecedented steps to hold expenditures under control and to maintain steady advances in performance income and contributions.

All of these considerations indicate that the financial crisis of the 1960s is by no means over and that considerably more attention must be given the basic underlying economic forces at work in the symphony institution than has been evident in the past. To a large degree orchestra boards and management have faced their financial problems on a year-to-year *ad hoc* basis, moving from one crisis to the next without seeking a long-range understanding of the forces at work. The kind of rudimentary analysis presented here for large groups of orchestras can be applied with far greater precision to more homogeneous groups of orchestras or to individual ones in projecting future finances and in pinpointing the critical areas of finance.

At this point it is impossible to review the rates of growth projected here without real concern for the future viability of orchestras, in some individual cases and as a group comprising the national institution. Even if one views the possible expansion of government funding as a significant force in symphony economics, there is a grave danger that it has been embraced by the orchestras as a panacea without realistically contemplating its potential. At the same time that boards, managements, and musicians look to government funding, they should also be exploring a new kind of responsible relationship among themselves—especially between the players and their employers—within a framework of sound economic projections. They must seek to replace the presently embattled and embittered adversary atmosphere with one of mutual concern for an equitable level of compensation and expansion that will maintain an orderly growth of orchestras in this nation. This goal, however, is a part of a much larger challenge that will be explored in the final chapter.

CHAPTER XIV

Private Philanthropy
and the Foundations

Reduced to its simplest denominator, securing charitable contributions requires the right person to make the right appeal to the right potential donor. He can base such an appeal on the value of the project that needs support, but more often than not his success depends on many other factors. A member of a symphony orchestra women's committee may use her social position to secure a contribution from a family desiring acceptance in an exclusive group. A man who has given to the pet charity of a friend will ask him to reciprocate by supporting his own special project. At a round-table luncheon, a number of wealthy donors will be asked to commit themselves to contributions in the presence of their fellows, each knowing that his standing in the group, and possibly his reputation for business success, will be affected by his commitment. In a variant of this technique, one large donor will offer to match, usually up to a certain limit, the contributions of all the rest. Others approached for a contribution know that the solicitor is in a position to send important business their way or to create a favorable atmosphere for securing loans from a bank or private financing. Some committee ladies are so celebrated for their persistence in seeking support for their causes that contributions are made simply to pacify them. A man of wealth may be advised by his lawyer and accountant that it is actually to his tax advantage to make a substantial donation of stock of appreciated value which the recipient organization can either hold for income or sell on the open market.

A high-level meeting of a symphony finance committee can produce the most candid and devastating evaluations imaginable of the wealth and resources of the business community, as the informed committee members review their prospect list frankly and decide how much a donor can afford and who is most likely to get the largest gift from him. The approaches are infinite in variety and intensity, the psychological ploys ingenious and sometimes ruthless, but this is how our symphony orchestras and other arts, educational, religious, and welfare activities obtain a major portion of their supplementary income. Donations may be small, coming in response to direct-mail campaigns, or they may be large, the result of a canny strategy, but each is welcome as part of the lifeblood of the symphony orchestra. In a well-organized campaign, time and personnel are carefully rationed: the most effective solicitors will be assigned to the largest potential donors and the multitude of small ones may be relegated to a direct-mail or telephone solicitation. In producing a sufficient quantity of the essential dollars the large gifts are the prime target, but sheer numbers of small donations can convince large donors of the breadth of community support and influence the size of their contributions.

Nor, in assessing the success of the American system of private philanthropy, can we disregard the impact of the Internal Revenue Service. If the graduated income tax has reduced the ability of entrepreneurs like Carnegie, Morgan, and Frick to amass great fortunes and become lavish patrons of the arts, it has also provided in the charitable deduction a major incentive for giving, whether on a modest scale or in large donations of cash or securities. Such advantages accrue both to gifts during the donor's lifetime and to bequests upon his death. The basic motives for establishing the Ford Foundation were to preserve family control of the automotive empire established by Henry Ford, avoid a monumental estate tax, and perpetuate the family tradition of concern for national and international philanthropy. In this sense, the taxpayer has long aided charitable causes indirectly, for at least a portion of the money so donated or bequeathed would otherwise have gone into state or federal coffers. But if this is a form of public subsidy, it is not accompanied by government control in deciding how these funds shall be used: the donor himself, or the foundation he sets up, retains that prerogative, selecting the recipient of his generosity, determining the amount of the gift, and often designating the purposes for which it is to be used. He may even be invited to join the recipient's governing board and thus participate in larger policy decisions.

Private Philanthropy

The individual donor remains by far the most important single source of funds in what has become a major industry in this country, that of fund-raising. It has been estimated that total philanthropy in the United States in 1970 amounted to $18.3 billion, up nearly $10 billion from 1960.[1] The 4% increase from 1969 to 1970 was the lowest in the past decade, the greatest annual increase (nearly 14%) occurring between 1965 and 1966. During this period, philanthropy has amounted to as much as 1.89% of the gross national product and has not fallen below 1.77%; even in the recession year of 1970, when many anticipated a sharp reduction in giving, the total sum grew over the previous year, amounting to 1.87% of the national product.

In 1970, 78% of all gifts to charity came from living individuals, 7.65% from bequests (a combined total of over 85% from individual sources), 9.3% from foundations, and 4.9% from corporations. Religion is by far the largest beneficiary of this philanthropy, receiving 44.8% of all giving, followed by education (16.66%), health and hospitals (16.40%), human resources (6.9%), and civic and cultural groups (5%).

The 5% of total philanthropy allocated to "civic and cultural" causes amounted in 1970 to some $900 million, of which $550 million went to the arts in general, $150 million to humanities, and $200 million to civic causes.[2] On the basis of the National Endowment for the Arts economic study for 1970–71, it would therefore appear that the performance arts as a whole probably receive about 11–12% of arts philanthropy, with symphony orchestras receiving 6–7%.[3] In the total national philanthropic picture, however, the symphony share is probably about 0.2%. Though precise figures on sources of gifts to arts organizations are difficult to obtain, individual donors contribute about the same proportion of arts philanthropy as of all giving, but bequests and corporate gifts are lower, foundation grants two to three times as high. No more detailed analysis of souces of giving to symphony orchestras is available.

It is not always easy to distinguish clearly between individual and corporate gifts. Though it makes little difference to the recipient, it may be more advantageous for a corporate executive, especially when he controls a large share of the corporation, to channel his contribution through the business he dominates rather than make the gift from his own personal funds; the impact of income taxes, personal and corporate, will often determine his decision. Nevertheless, the large corporations, with stockholders across the nation numbering in the hundreds of thousands, must be regarded by symphony orchestras as an increasingly important source of supplemental income. In many cities away from the great centers where they have their headquarters, these national corporations have factories or installations that play a large role in the local economy. Many have absorbed local businesses, the proprietors of which were formerly generous supporters of their orchestras, and the new national ownership of these businesses may not be as deeply involved in civic affairs. Traditionally, such large corporations have had to weigh requests for philanthropy against their obligation to return profits to stockholders in many other cities, who do not themselves benefit in any way from the success of an orchestra in a faraway place. At the same time, charities in the headquarters cities of great national corporations expect them to make contributions commensurate with their national wealth; corporations therefore must develop policies of allocating their philanthropy accordingly, often setting aside specific portions of their contribution appropriations for distribution by their branch operations.

However, a greater sense of corporate responsibility for the arts, orchestras included, has recently developed nationally. Directors and large stockholders, often themselves involved in the arts of their own community and therefore aware of the financial problems of all arts organizations, have assumed a broader concern for the welfare of all arts groups across the nation. Their organization of the Business Committee for the Arts works in a variety of ways to stimulate the interest of corporations in arts philanthropy and to use corporate expertise in advertising and public relations to arouse a more favorable attitude toward the arts among the general public.

Corporate philanthropy, amounting to less than 5% of the national total, has been estimated in 1959 and 1968 to have been allocated as follows: [4]

	1959	1968
Health and welfare	45%	37%
Education	39%	39%
Civic and cultural	3%	12%
Other	13%	12%

The fourfold increase in the civic and cultural share, considerably augmented in dollars by overall increases in total corporate philanthropy (from just under $500 million in 1959 to over $800 million in 1968),[5] would indicate that the arts in general received substantially greater corporation support during this period, a trend that shows every indication of continuing. Symphony orchestras are the most frequent recipients of corporation gifts.[6] Corporations prefer to give to annual sustaining campaigns for supplemental income rather than to those for capital funds, and may account for these gifts as direct business expense (32%), as company gifts (36%), or through foundations set up by the corporation (32%).[7]

Symphony Fund-Raising

The task of securing donations to any philanthropic organization is a major one in which orchestras operate under a number of serious handicaps. Unlike religion, education, or public welfare, the arts are still regarded by many as a nonessential social activity; they do not have religion's spiritual hold on large masses of people, the appeal of health and hospital services in relieving human suffering, or the prestige of education. Among the arts, moreover, symphony orchestras suffer a disadvantage, especially by comparison with museums: to the donor desiring to perpetuate his memory, the gift of a painting or sculpture has a permanence that an evanescent musical performance lacks. Furthermore, a wealthy collector may purchase art as an investment and, particularly in recent years, find that it has increased tremendously in value, making its presentation to a museum all the more welcome (and tax-deductible). There is nothing comparable to such a gift in the symphonic world.

For the symphony orchestras, the task of securing contributions is an extraordinary one. Its magnitude has already been defined in the previous chapter, but should be summarized here. In 1970–71, the Major and Metropolitan orchestras raised $35–40 million from philanthropic sources; average contributed income per orchestra ranged from $60,000 in Category E to $1.4 million in Category A, an effort involving orchestras in over a hundred cities in this nation.

To a large degree, all philanthropic activities must develop methods of fund-raising suited to their needs, the potential of their community, and the influence they wield there. In the welfare field especially, individual charities have joined together for annual united fund drives, dividing the proceeds according to the success of the campaign and their needs; the agencies receiving support from such common efforts may not engage in their own fund-raising without permission from the central group.* To a great extent, such united fund drives have been organized less from the desire of their constituents to band together than from the pressure of businesses and individuals who resent being approached for donations by several organizations. Moreover, many communities have found such combined efforts to be the most efficient utilization of the limited manpower available for solicitation. During the 1950s and 1960s and even earlier, there was a notable interest among symphony orchestras in joining in such cooperative efforts, but this trend has slowed considerably, as the symphony income gap has grown so much faster than the economy in general. Most such combined drives set their annual goal at a relatively modest increment over the previous year's actual receipts; this has, as we have seen in Louisville and Cincinnati, sometimes limited the ability of orchestras to meet their income gaps. Other orchestras and arts groups have found it preferable to confine such combined fund-raising to major corporations and businessmen, who are known to be too busy to consider each and every request they receive.

Nevertheless, the task of orchestra fund-raising boils down to the individual approach to the individual, and to a large degree this means that board members themselves must accept the responsibility for it. It also means that an important qualification for board membership is a man's or woman's ability to raise money. The organization of these efforts varies a great deal, from an informal assignment of prospects by a board chairman to year-round staffing of a separate office or engagement of outside professional management for a campaign. As orchestra operations have grown and as the pressure from the income gap has increased, orchestras have had to devote more and more attention to the organization of funding supplemental income. The day is long past when one devoted patron, such as Higginson, could defray the entire deficit, or when a Mackay could write a check to make up the difference between expenditures and such income as the Philharmonic had received from concerts and donations of others. For many years some orchestras could rely upon a relatively limited circle of board members and their friends to provide the necessary supplemental income, but this is no longer the case, as we have already seen with the Philadelphia Orchestra. Now orchestras must call upon thousands of small donors, many of them subscribers or frequent patrons at concerts, who realize that their ticket purchase may cover only half of the cost of the performances they hear, and upon wealthy individuals, not necessarily personally interested in music but convinced of the orchestra's cultural and educational importance to their community. Reaching these groups—the thousands of modest contributors and the few wealthy donors —requires a special effort and organization of that effort.

More and more, orchestras have come to realize the importance of organizing their fund drives in a systematic manner, even if this involves additional

---

* As we have seen in Cincinnati and Louisville, these restrictions can vary from city to city.

expenditure for more staff or for outside help. Sometimes a first step involves the engagement of a professional fund-raising firm, either local or national, to organize a campaign but usually only when an orchestra faces a serious financial crisis, either a crushing accumulated deficit or the prospect of extraordinary increases in the income gap. This step is taken with great reluctance: board members do not like to admit that they are unable to do the job themselves, and fear the implied criticism of their past direction and the need to reveal their fiscal secrets to outsiders. The employment of outside counsel can be a traumatic experience for a symphony board, especially when it involves, either explicitly before the campaign begins or implicitly during its progress, a searching examination by the fund-raising firm of the orchestra's total operations: many firms will not take on a campaign without first studying the organization in detail and recommending changes in operation before determining the feasibility of reaching the campaign goal.

Especially in recent years, such outside professionals have become increasingly involved in symphony orchestras: the unprecedented fund-raising challenge involved in the Ford Foundation program, requiring some sixty orchestras to raise over $76 million in endowments between 1966 and 1971, forced a number of orchestras to turn to such firms as the Carl W. Shaver Company and the George Brakeley Company for comprehensive management counseling and in direction of fund drives. At the same time, the widening of the income gap described in the previous chapter was so great and so rapid that many orchestras realized they could not deal with their financial problems without outside advice and help. These firms, with extensive experience in other fund-raising projects—education, religion, art museums, and welfare—in many cases not only effected important changes in management and board relations with their communities but convinced orchestras that they had until then failed to capture the full potential available for support. Some orchestras developed their own fund-raising staffs, under the same pressure that brought others to hire outside counsel, and many who engaged outsiders took the organization thus set up into their own staff, in some cases hiring executives from the consulting firms.

In the past, symphony boards were often reluctant to establish their own fund-raising staffs. Such staffs themselves cannot actually solicit contributions: their task is to process information concerning sources of support, confer with the solicitors as to the best approach and amount to be sought from each donor, and see to it as diplomatically as possible that the "workers" cover their prospects on schedule. Board members who hold responsible positions of prestige in their own businesses and in the community do not like to be told by employees how to conduct their solicitation, especially when they are contributing their services. Some boards believed that their manager should be responsible for the organization of fund-raising, but many soon found that friction and resentment incurred in the campaign interfered with smooth working relations between the board and manager in other aspects of orchestra affairs. On the other hand, several orchestras have elevated their professional managers to a position of president of the organization, hoping to free him from day-to-day operations for wider effectiveness in overall financial direction and fund-raising. When this requires special staffing, most orchestras now agree that it is best to give it relative independence from the manager, though as chief administrative officer he must of course be intimately involved in the major policy direction.

In recent years, with the growing importance of government and foundation funding, symphony orchestras have had to develop a special skill in formulating their requests for such support, as they have in approaching corporations for major gifts. These require more than a personal sales pitch; usually a comprehensive description of orchestra finances is necessary, as well as a detailed presentation of the specific needs for which a grant is sought. To be sure, the right word from an influential board member to a government or foundation executive can pave the way for more favorable processing of a request, but the orchestra must also present its case in terms that will appeal to the staff of the foundation or government agency. For this a certain bureaucratic expertise (in the best sense of the word) has become extremely helpful to the development personnel of symphony orchestras and will assume greater importance in years to come.

The Foundations

As the distribution of great wealth has developed over the years in this country, in response both to growing needs and to the forces impinging upon wealth through the graduated income tax, it has become increasingly hard to draw sharp distinctions in the continuum between individual charity at one extreme and highly institutionalized giving on the other. A wealthy patron of the arts today, a modern counterpart of Henry L. Higginson, may well find that major charitable giving on a personal basis is economically impossible. He may channel such charity through the corporation he controls in a manner that produces greater benefit to the recipient at less cost to him personally— the difference, let it be noted, coming from taxes not paid the government. Or he (or the corporation he controls) may set up an "independent" foundation to distribute the funds available. The choice of method will depend a great deal on the ingenuity of the donor's financial advisers in finding the applicable tax advantages.

On the other hand, the foundation may be established, originally at least, not for charitable purposes but solely in the financial interests of the donor, using the loopholes in tax regulations. The attack on foundations mounted in Congress by Representative Wright Patman was as much aimed at such devices as it was at activities by legitimate foundations in areas that aroused his opposition. Though Patman's most widely publicized condemnation was directed at a number of flagrant abuses by foundations, even the professionally directed mega-foundations have not escaped responsible criticism: though published too late for consideration here, *The Big Foundations* by Waldemar A. Nielsen (himself a former foundation executive) offers an authoritative and sometimes devastating comment on the thirty-three largest foundations whose combined assets accounted for some 44% of the total for all.

Foundations in general have become a topic of great public interest: as anyone will discover in reading the voluminous literature on them, including the reports of the Patman Committee and the Peterson Commission, or Joseph C. Goulden's popularized summary of the Patman data,[9] there are foundations and foundations. In certain technical legal respects symphony orchestras, art museums, and similar activities are themselves foundations in that they are nonprofit corporations, supported by tax-exempt contributions; however, in our discussion here, the term will be confined to those foundations that disburse their funds, either from capital or from annual income on capital, in accordance with predetermined policies and professional evaluation of causes seeking their support.

But the general term covers a multitude of sins and virtues, concerning both the intent of donors in organizing them and the manner in which they are operated. Some foundations are little more than tax-avoidance devices designed to circumvent the law and regulations of the Internal Revenue Service. Others are designed to perpetuate corporate control while reaping substantial personal benefit to the donor, sometimes in excess of that received by the supposed beneficiaries. Others may engage more or less directly in political or quasi-political action or propaganda, bordering on a violation of their tax-exempt status and arousing the ire of Congressmen. Some foundations may be established to maximize savings in taxes, stabilize year-to-year philanthropy, and establish giving on a perpetual basis extending beyond the lifetime of an individual donor or business enterprise. As we have seen in the case of such a patron of the arts as W. Ralph Corbett of Cincinnati, a foundation may be the way that an individual can best act as a modern counterpart to Major Higginson. As the Rockefellers and Andrew Carnegie discovered more than half a century ago, the professionally managed foundation not only achieves perpetuity of philanthropy but can provide such donors with institutionalized management of giving that they could not themselves achieve. The very size of such personal resources and the multiplicity of causes seeking support dictate the development of some means for evaluation of merit.

Of the three major sources of philanthropy, foundations account for 9.3% of all contributions and probably play a greater role in the arts, especially in large donations, possibly as much as one-third of the total of gifts of fifty thousand dollars or more.[8] However, because many of the biggest foundations allocate their grants on the basis of a professional evaluation of applications and because they themselves initiate special projects in the arts for local groups to implement, they wield an influence considerably greater than the share of dollars they contribute. Moreover, when foundations predicate their giving on matching by other donors, they provide an extraordinary stimulus to campaigns aimed at individuals, corporations, and other foundations.

One of the earliest of the mega-foundations, that of the Rockefeller family, arose from the twin desire of the donors to place their giving in a tax-exempt category and, in view of the unprecedentedly large sums of money involved, to institutionalize professionally the decisions on who received how much. This has been the pattern followed for more than half a century to an increasing degree by such large foundations as Ford, Mellon, Carnegie, Lilly, Mott, and Duke, among others, which interest themselves in virtually every social, religious, educational, welfare, and cultural activity imaginable. Some are directed to confine their interest to special philanthropic areas; others, though not legally bound to do so, reflect the interests of their donors or active trustees; still others attempt to divide their benefaction among a wide assortment of causes. Only recently, with the explosive increase in the cost of cultural activity, have foundations in general developed a distinct interest in the arts; the performance arts—notably symphony and opera, with their expanding income gap—have laid an increasing claim at foundation doors.

In 1970, there were an estimated 26,000 foundations in the United States, of whom 5,454 met the minimum qualifications for inclusion in the fourth edition of the *Foundation Directory*—capital assets of $500,000 and annual disbursements of $25,000.[10] In that year, these foundations held assets in excess of $25 billion and disbursed over $1.5 billion in the form of 291,000 grants. However, more than $7.6 billion out of a total of $25.2 billion in assets were held by the twelve largest foundations. The humanities field, which includes literature and the liberal arts as well as the performance arts and museums, has received seven to nine percent of foundation grants in the past ten years.[11] The proportion of grants to various fields by foundations differs somewhat from that of philanthropy in general, which is dominated by individual giving: religion receives much less from foundations, education twice as much, medicine slightly less, and welfare nearly twice as much. There are no specific data on the dollar amounts of foundation grants either to the performance arts in general or symphony orchestras specificially.

Until the Ford Foundation symphony program in 1966, foundation support of symphony orchestras was generally limited to specific and often peripheral projects, not directly aimed at reducing the income gap. To be sure, these grants underwrote worthy, sometimes indispensable programs: the Rockefeller Foundation support of the Louisville Orchestra's recording project was possibly the earliest and, before 1966, the largest single foundation effort in the symphonic field. Usually such programs as foundations did undertake were in the nature of defraying orchestras' extra costs for special programming: the Ford Foundation's commissioning of new compositions for soloist and orchestra with special funds to reimburse orchestras for the extra cost of preparing these new works, and the Rockefeller Foundation's more recent underwriting of special orchestra appearances on university campuses to perform contemporary music. These illustrate an approach in which orchestras received money for specific projects with a wider purpose of considerable significance in advancing the cause of new music, but without appreciable impact on orchestra income gap. Many local foundations have, to be sure, made substantial contributions to orchestras' supplementary income, and the Ford Foundation, in its early days when still based in Michigan, was a regular supporter of the Detroit Symphony Orchestra. However valuable as these grants were in their own special objectives and achievements, none of them faced on a national scale the central problem of the income gap in orchestra finances until the Ford Foundation undertook its massive symphony program in 1966.

Ford Foundation Symphony Program

The Ford Foundation is the largest in the country, with assets in 1970 of $2.9 billion, 11.6% of the national total; in that year it made 1,730 grants totaling $239.5 million, and spent another $34.9 million for programs. Founded in 1936 by members of the Ford family in Michigan, it concerned itself at first with such local charities as the Dearborn Museum and other projects close to the heart of the elder Henry Ford. The settlement of his estate and that of Edsel Ford placed at the disposal of the foundation unprecedentedly large assets, in the form of nonvoting common stock in the Ford Motor Company, and the foundation moved its headquarters to New York in 1951. There, under the direction of Paul G. Hoffman, its president, the Ford Foundation began a program of widespread philanthropy on an unexampled scale, which, at various times, has involved it in political controversy and subjected it to considerable criticism. These have been recounted in detail elsewhere, and we shall confine our discussion here to the foundation's symphony program instituted in 1966, which has had such an impact on orchestra development in recent years.[12]

Though this foundation had since 1951 received numerous applications for some sort of aid from symphony orchestras,* few of these received attention until the Detroit Symphony, long aided by the foundation in Michigan, asked for a major contribution in 1964 to a large-scale endowment campaign. Since previous support of this orchestra had been on a year-to-year basis as supplemental income, a donation to capital funds raised important questions of policy, which the foundation board referred to its humanities and arts staff. Eventually, the Ford Foundation contributed to the Detroit Symphony endowment campaign, but on a matching basis, and the policy deliberations leading to this decision resulted in a recommendation that the foundation explore the entire national symphonic field to determine whether it could properly and effectively support American orchestras in general.

Under the leadership of W. McNeil Lowry, and with research conducted in the field by Edward d'Arms and Sigmund Koch of the foundation staff and by special consultant George A. Kuyper (former manager of the Chicago and Los Angeles orchestras), a comprehensive symphony program was developed

---

* Between 1957 and 1970, the Ford Foundation bestowed grants, fellowships, and other awards totaling slightly in excess of $109 million in support of musical activities; these included two grants to symphony orchestras prior to 1966: the New York Philharmonic—to be matched—for costs in moving to Lincoln Center ($1.365 million), and the Detroit Symphony—also matching—for endowment ($2 million). There have been two symphony grants since 1966, to be noted later. Including the $80.2 million symphony program, symphony orchestras received 77% of the musical grants made by the foundation during this period.[13]

by mid-1965. From their discussions with symphony personnel across the nation and their evaluation of data supplied by orchestras and the ASOL, the foundation staff established three objectives for its program:

1. Improving artistic quality by making it possible for players to devote more of their time to symphony work;
2. Strengthening orchestras to enable them to increase audiences, extend their seasons, and diversify their service; and
3. Raising the income and prestige of the music profession, thus making it more attractive to talented young people.

Further, in its review of the finances of symphony orchestras, the foundation decided that its best course would be to establish and encourage the expansion of sizable endowment funds, income from which would provide an appreciable portion of supplementary income. These endowment grants were to be made conditional upon each orchestra's ability to increase its own endowment. At the same time, realizing that the task of raising endowment funds could limit their ability to maintain their annual fund-raising, the foundation provided for annual sustaining grants during the period when the orchestras were raising matching funds. Finally, they recognized that certain orchestras needed special additional financing to develop potential activities impossible with existing resources. The foundation accordingly set up a program of grants divided into two phases—endowment and expendable funds—extending over a period of ten years, from 1966 to 1976.

For the endowments, the foundation placed in trust with the Bank of New York shares of stock in the Ford Motor Company then valued at $58.75 million.[14] The trust directed the bank to hold the stock until June 30, 1976, disbursing the income to the beneficiary orchestras in accordance with a prescribed schedule set forth in the trust. Upon the termination of the trust in 1976, the bank will distribute its principal, still in the form of Ford Motor Company stock, to the beneficiaries in the same prescribed proportions.* In administering the trust, the bank must follow the direction of a Ford Foundation committee, which will advise it on such matters as the eligibility of the beneficiaries and may, if it so desires, designate substitute beneficiaries: in this, the committee will interpret the foundation's agreements with the beneficiary orchestras. In order for an orchestra to participate as a beneficiary in this trust, it must until 1976 maintain its tax-exempt status, not cease operations either by suspension or merger with another orchestra, refrain from selling or entailing its interest in the trust, raise for its own endowment a sum, set forth in the trust, by June 30, 1971, and hold it in a separate fund until 1976, using only the income from it for supplemental income. Upon the termination of the trust on June 30, 1976, each beneficiary orchestra still eligible will receive from the trustee its stipulated share of the assets in the form of Ford Motor Company stock.

At the same time that it established this trust, the Ford Foundation made

---

* These proportions are reflected in the endowment grant allocations to the various orchestras listed in Appendix H, which is a complete tabulation of endowment, expendable, and development grants, and the matching requirement for each orchestra.

expendable-fund grants to the sixty-one orchestras, payable over the first five years of the program. These were for the purpose of compensating the orchestras for any difficulty they might encounter in annual fund-raising while they were seeking the matching funds. In addition, certain orchestras received development funds for special projects the foundation deemed worthy of support. Neither of these required matching, nor were they conditional on an orchestra's meeting the endowment matching requirement. These grants totaled $21.45 million, of which $17.3 million were expendable and $4.15 million for development, to be paid over a five-year period from 1966 to 1971.

If an orchestra failed to meet the endowment matching requirement by June 30, 1971, or the other requirements set forth in the trust, it would no longer be a beneficiary receiving a share of annual income or the 1976 distribution of trust assets. To the extent that individual orchestras fail to qualify in this respect, the foundation committee can advise the trustee to pay these amounts to substitute beneficiaries or to allocate them to the remaining beneficiary orchestras in proportion to their original shares of the trust. At present writing, it appears that the trust funds set aside for orchestras losing their eligibility will be redistributed to the remaining beneficiaries in proportions set forth in the original trust.

In 1976, therefore, each orchestra that has maintained its eligibility as a beneficiary will not only have the matching endowment funds raised by 1971 and held as such until 1976 but will also receive its share in the trust distribution and will, in the meantime, have received annual income both from the trust and from its own endowment. Though the foundation has expressed the hope that orchestras will retain the trust distribution and their own matching funds as endowment, they are not required to do so as a part of their participation in this program; in effect the orchestras will, in 1976, have at their disposal upwards of $143 million for retention as endowment or for utilization as they see fit.

The scope of this Ford Foundation symphony program can be summarized by the following figures:

Endowment trust	$58,750,000
Expendable grants	17,300,000
Development grants	4,150,000
TOTAL GRANT	$80,200,000
Matching by orchestras	$85,405,000 [15]

Thus, not counting the income from the trust itself, the Ford Foundation either donated or generated over $165 million of symphony funds.

In 1966, sixty-one orchestras were included in the program, twenty-five Majors and thirty-six from the Metropolitan category. To have confined the program to the Major orchestras would have left many areas of the country, served by smaller orchestras, without this assistance. Twenty-five orchestras received funds for development in addition to sustaining grants. One orchestra, that of Puerto Rico, did not participate in the endowment trust because it is heavily subsidized by the government.

An Ingenious and Constructive Grant

The impact of these grants was profound. Most people in the orchestra world welcomed them as an epochal contribution to the stability of the American symphony orchestra, and many, possibly too optimistic, saw in them the end of decades of hard times. Some observers expressed fears that the matching provision, requiring unprecedented fund-raising efforts, would overstrain the ability of symphony boards and the potential of their respective communities; only fourteen Major orchestras had significant endowments, and they were virtually nonexistent among Metropolitans. A more serious problem was raised by the orchestra musicians, who viewed the availability of such large sums of money as an opportunity to improve their own economic position immediately. To a great extent, both the foundation and the orchestras themselves failed to impress on these players the full implication of these grants—the long-term spreading out of annual income and the Herculean task of meeting the matching challenge. It has been reported that, only after the grants were widely publicized, an official of the Ford Foundation telephoned Herman D. Kenin of the AFM to ask him to "tell the boys to go easy," an admonition that came too late and betrayed considerable naïveté concerning the then strained relations between the union and the militant symphony musicians. Especially in the early years of this program, one encountered many expressions of misgiving, sometimes explicit statements that the Ford Foundation had created more problems than it had attempted to solve.

However, to a large degree, these misgivings have proved to be unjustified. So far as the orchestra musicians were concerned, it must be noted that two of the three stated objectives of the program involved the improvement of their economic status; there can be no question that their demands outran the resources at hand, but given the degree to which they were uninformed of the full implications of the program, and given the hostility between players and management prevailing in many orchestras, this militance is understandable. More important to the long-range health of the symphonic institution was the way in which the Ford Foundation challenge stimulated the fund-raising efforts of all orchestras and, in the end, demonstrated that much community potential for their support had really not been previously tapped. We have already seen how its grant forced the Philadelphia Orchestra to revise its relations with the city: after almost rejecting the grant as involving impossible goals, that orchestra actually increased its objectives and has every prospect of reaching them by 1976. Other orchestras, such as those of Minneapolis, Cincinnati, Pittsburgh, and St. Louis, also seized upon this challenge to engage in long-needed capital-fund drives, either for additional endowment or for the acquisition of new performance facilities. It is difficult to determine just how much money, over and above the required matching, was raised in this manner, but it may run as high as twenty percent over the foundation matching.

At the same time, most of the orchestras involved learned that they could meet considerable increases in annual requirements for supplemental income while at the same time conducting their endowment campaign. This was not necessarily true of all, though: such orchestras as Utah, for instance, were able to keep their personnel costs in line. But many others found themselves meeting the demands of their players suffering appreciable increases in net deficit. A few orchestras made the mistake of approaching donors on a "one-time" basis, promising that if a contribution were made to the matching fund, no future requests would be made. Most others, however, have discovered that these new channels can be kept open for future annual sustaining contributions, and have retained the development administration, often set up by outside consultants, to carry on year-to-year efforts for supplemental income. But one of the most lasting effects of the Ford Foundation symphony program so far has been profoundly psychological: it demonstrated to symphony leadership across the nation a previously unsuspected potential for support, both in dollars and in good will, represented by a willingness to give and to work for the orchestra.

In the previous chapter, the major impact of the economic crisis was pinpointed to the 1966–68 period, precisely when the Ford Foundation grants began, leading some commentators to detect a cause-and-effect phenomenon here. Certainly this is no mere coincidence, but it is not reasonable to assume that the foundation alone triggered the crisis. In the sense that this program grew out of a recognition of the roots of orchestra financial problems, it reflected the same forces that were already coming to a head in the orchestras. To the degree that it stimulated musicians' demands and aroused general expectations, the Ford funding probably hastened and intensified the already developing process. Certainly many in the foundation and elsewhere underestimated the full extent of the income gap and its rate of increase, but one can hardly call a total outlay of $80.2 million inadequate; possibly it was all that the foundation felt that it could afford to orchestras, rather than its evaluation of their needs. Nevertheless, there is much merit in Carl W. Shaver's comment that "the Ford Foundation grants were one of the most ingenious and constructive grants in American philanthropy. They will do for the orchestras what the Rockefellers did for medical education." [16]

A few orchestras unfortunately did not meet the foundation's requirements for continued eligibility after June 30, 1971, by raising the matching funds; their failure to do so has been noted in the list of grants in Appendix H.[17] One of these, the Festival Orchestra of New York, suspended operations in 1969. Four others failed to meet the matching goal; but only one of these, the Kansas City Philharmonic, was a genuine community-oriented orchestra, typical of the American symphony institution with which we are concerned in this study.

For the beneficiary orchestras the period of greatest risk and effort ended on June 30, 1971, when they completed their matching-fund drives. The loss since then of the expendable funds from the foundation has been partly made up with the income from the endowments they raised. Since 1966 they have received their shares from the foundation trust and will continue to receive this until its principal is distributed in 1976. Their shares in that distribution will not necessarily be the actual amounts of endowment grant originally announced in July, 1966; those figures were based on the market value of Ford Motor Company stock when the trust was established, and that has increased substantially since then and may increase even more by 1976.* Moreover, since the number of beneficiary orchestras has decreased, the remaining ones will receive slightly larger distributions of the trust (as well as of income in the interim); as the trust is an irrevocable one, all of its income and capital must be distributed to orchestras by 1976.†

In its letters of agreement with the various participating symphony orchestras, the Ford Foundation stated explicitly: "This grant is made with the understanding that the Foundation has no obligation to provide other or additional support for the Orchestra," and with but two exceptions the foundation has given no further aid to symphony orchestras. The St. Paul Chamber Orchestra, not included in the 1966 grants because it was not operating then on a scale to warrant support, received in 1970 an outright sustaining grant of $96,500 but no endowment. The Symphony of the New World, a New York orchestra organized by Benjamin Steinberg to offer black musicians an opportunity to build their own orchestra, received grants in 1968 and 1970 totaling $327,252. In addition, the American Symphony Orchestra League in 1968 received $360,000 to strengthen its services to its member orchestras.[18] Otherwise, the foundation has made it clear that it will not consider symphony appeals until after 1976.

However, in 1971, it took an important step toward laying the basis for long-term examination of the needs of all performance arts in this nation. With an allocation of $618,150, it has established a computerized statistical-data bank covering two hundred professional nonprofit arts groups, extending back to 1966 and based on information supplied in a comprehensive questionnaire.[19] This resource, to be updated annually, will provide the foundation with comprehensive and (hopefully) authoritative data on which it and others can base future policies in arts support. Though it has encountered some resistance from arts organizations, including orchestras,‡ to the task of supplying this information, Ford's importance as a source of present and future financial support will obviously encourage cooperation. In its announcement the foundation pointed out that between 1957 and 1971 it had allocated nearly $238 million to individual artists and institutions. Its vice-president for the humanities and the arts, W. McNeil Lowry, defined the objective of this resource: "In a time of chronic financial difficulty for the performing arts, the new data we are collecting will give actual and potential supporters a clearer notion of how the performing arts are financed, why they cost what they do, and how these costs are met. Such information is essential for an effective

* The stock went into the trust at a market value of $50.50 per share on April 25, 1966. In early 1973, it sold for $70.
† Some of the implications of the sudden availability in 1976 of previously restricted trust funds in the amount of upwards of $160–170 million will be explored in the final chapter.
‡ The Ford Foundation data bank and its comprehensive questionnaires were a topic of considerable discussion at the ASOL conference in Seattle in June, 1971. Many managers expressed dissatisfaction with the rather modest fee offered by the foundation as compensation for the labor of answering the questionnaires.

national policy for the arts." The planning of this resource has involved such experts as William J. Baumol; Lawrence R. Kegan, formerly associated with the Committee for Economic Development; Fred S. Hoffman, formerly with the United States Bureau of the Budget; and the University of Chicago economist Albert Wohlstetter. A special audience survey, to be conducted by Eric Marder Associates, will also be undertaken. The organizations participating in this project will receive computer print-outs showing a variety of comparative data for the arts in general, for special groups of organizations, and for individual arts themselves.

To anyone acquainted with the present limited availability of reliable data on the arts, this project promises to perform an extraordinarily useful purpose. It will inform those directly involved in the arts of their own position in the total picture. The foundation itself will acquire information essential to the development of its future policies in arts support. These data will be of great significance to government agencies—the National Endowment for the Arts and state arts councils—in determining their policies, should the foundation be permitted to make them available.* In a broader context, however, the data bank implies a continuing and increasingly perceptive involvement of this mega-foundation in the arts.

Foundations under Attack

In the 1969 Congressional hearings on foundations conducted by Representative Patman, the Ford Foundation was attacked for a number of its grants, especially those in the political field such as to Robert Kennedy's associates after his death in 1968 and to groups engaged in urban, racial, and voter-registration activities. These attacks often gained more publicity than did the uncovering of more serious abuses by other foundations,[20] which resulted in the Tax Reform Act of 1969. This act called for major changes in the operations and accountability of foundations in general, the detailed provisions of which need not concern us here except as they affect symphony orchestras.

One provision of this act was to require stricter compliance with the filing of annual information returns to the Internal Revenue Service on Form 990. The original draft of this form called for listing all personnel receiving more than fifteen thousand dollars a year from all nonprofit groups—symphony orchestras as well as foundations—in an effort to expose those foundations which were paying exorbitantly high salaries to trustees or executives. For the orchestras, this would have required reporting the salaries of many managers, most conductors, and a good number of leading orchestra players, information open to public inspection at the IRS. The orchestras feared that such disclosure would create considerable difficulty with some of their employees —conductors jealous of their status, managers seeking raises in pay, or prin-

* Despite delays in computer-programming, the foundation hopes to publish summaries of certain data sometime in 1973.

cipal musicians bargaining for overscale. The ASOL argued the matter before the IRS while regulations were being formulated, pointing out that the
purpose of the law was to prevent payment of excessive salaries to trustees
who themselves set such compensation; orchestra conductors, managers, and
players have no such voice in the determination of their salaries, and board
members, who have that responsibility, serve without pay. After considerable
discussion, the orchestras won their point on this issue.[21]

An indirect consequence of the Tax Reform Act of 1969 for all beneficiaries of foundation philanthropy was its levying a tax of ten percent on all
income, the proceeds being intended to cover the cost of IRS audits of Form
990 returns. Such a tax not only reduces the funds available for allocation to
all beneficiaries but also creates a precedent of taxation of nonprofit corporations that both the federal government and states may later augment. On the
other hand, this act requires all foundations to disburse their income in accordance with their charitable purposes: since it forces them to make grants, the
entire philanthropic world, orchestras included, can benefit.

Finally, the Tax Reform Act of 1969, insofar as it applies to foundations
and nonprofit corporations, will undoubtedly encourage a greater sense of
responsibility and accountability in the orchestras and in many of the smaller
local foundations. To the degree that the act was motivated by what the Congress viewed as questionable practices, its impact on foundation policies can
only benefit such conservatively respectable beneficiaries as symphony orchestras.* The attack on the foundations, individually or collectively, in the
Patman committee hearings never questioned the propriety of such allocations
to the arts; in fact, the foundations, in defending themselves, pointed to their
support of the arts. Despite deep fears to the contrary, the mega-foundations
and the symphony orchestras emerged from the crisis with minimal damage:
the ten-percent tax on foundations certainly hurt, and the more stringent requirements for IRS accounting surely created more work for the accountants,
but no one suffered as seriously as many had feared.†

New Realism

There is no question that the Ford Foundation grants came at a crucial moment in the recent history of the American orchestra. In stimulating the players' demands, thus increasing costs faster than the new income could meet

* The reader should be reminded that here we refer only to the impact on symphony orchestras
of the Tax Reform Act of 1969 and by no means pass judgment on its entire implications for
foundations or philanthropy. For instance, its limitations on grants to individuals can have a
profoundly adverse effect on creative writers, artists, and composers. Other sections of the act,
covering the donation of property to nonprofit institutions, have even more disastrous consequences for individual creative artists.

† A *New York Times* story, *Foundations Find '69 Tax Reform Act Not as Harmful as Feared*
(May 9, 1972), stated: "But after more than two years' experience foundation leaders have
generally concluded that the law was not as damaging to their billion-dollar activities as they
had once predicted. While still discomforted by the 'rigid wording' of some provisions, they
believe the law has been enforced liberally and sensibly."

them, they undoubtedly contributed to the sharp increase in symphonic expenditures during the late 1960s, often more than their sustaining grants covered. But they also played a more subtle role in arousing concern for orchestras, a concern that in most cases resulted in a degree of private support which many had previously considered impossible. Despite hopes to the contrary—hopes not encouraged by the foundation itself, it must be emphasized—the Ford Foundation program did not solve the economic problems of our orchestras. In fact, as we have seen, the income gap widened, and the pressure for more supplemental income intensified to an unprecedented degree. To some extent these pressures were met by increased private philanthropy, and in some cases by borrowing or by invasion of unrestricted previous endowment at a time when—with the other hand, as it were—orchestras were meeting the matching challenge.

In the larger context, however, the Ford Foundation program contributed to a profound psychological change, whereby this nation became aware of the fundamental problems of the performance arts in general, but most impressively of the symphony orchestras, during a decade which began with rosy hopes generated by President Kennedy's sympathetic concern for the arts, by widespread optimism about a "cultural explosion," and by euphoric planning of elaborate arts centers. By the end of that decade, during which the militant musician had shown his power in symphony and opera, and boards of directors had faced financial problems that seemed at times insuperable, a considerably more realistic, at times pessimistic, atmosphere prevailed.

In this new atmosphere of greater realism, there emerged at the end of the decade a profound change in the attitude of the establishment, especially those directly involved on arts boards, toward government support of the arts. By the end of the 1960s, it was obvious that private resources, even the megafoundations, could not alone meet the problem of the rapidly expanding income gap in symphony economics. Reluctantly, and with surprising energy once the decision was made, the orchestras turned to government for substantial support.

CHAPTER XV

The Government

Had this discussion of government funding of symphony orchestras taken place a decade ago, a considerable portion of it would have had to be devoted to its rationale: the pros and cons of using taxpayer money to support arts activities involving only a small portion of the population and the dangers of political interference in the management of orchestras. But today government funding is an accomplished fact, by no means completely uncontroversial but nevertheless an integral and growing part of the symphonic institution. By 1969, the last hard core of opposition in the highest echelons of the symphony establishment crumbled under pressure from the widening income gap. But this sharp turnabout, leading to an aggressive campaign for more government support, was only the final step in a long process that had begun nearly four decades ago when such orchestras as the San Francisco, during the depression of the 1930s, first sought and received local government support. Since then, many smaller orchestras, a few larger ones, and the musicians' union have maintained growing pressure, locally and nationally, to achieve some measure of public funding for orchestras and for the arts in general that would augment, but not replace, the traditional pattern of private contributions to supplementary income.

In this campaign, the advocates of government funding pointed to the European system of arts support of symphony orchestras.[1] In 1970, there was not a single orchestra of importance in Europe that did not receive substantial public funds.* Some of these orchestras were independent, often musicians' cooperatives like four of the five orchestras in London, who received direct subsidy for their activities. Others were basically opera orchestras employed by states, cities, or national governments, but offering their own symphony concerts, as in such cities as Milan and Frankfort. The Vienna Philharmonic Society combined these features: a musicians' cooperative, it supplied the orchestras for the state opera theaters on a regular salary, but also played its own series of symphonic concerts. Many European symphony orchestras were

---

* Outside Europe, the same scheme may be found in Israel and, to some extent, in Latin America. Canadian orchestras, which we have regretfully omitted from this study, once showed more similarity to those of the U.S., but have recently followed the European model to a greater degree.

fully employed by state-controlled radio and television, sometimes giving public "live" concerts as well; the BBC Symphony, fully underwritten by the independent British Broadcasting System, derived its support, not directly from government funds, but from a special annual tax on radio and television receivers.

Though advocates of government subsidy in this country tended to idealize the European example, a realistic appraisal of the European symphonic scene will show that, quantitatively at least, it has by no means the scope of its American counterpart. At a time when the Boston Symphony Orchestra played more than 150 concerts a year, the Vienna Philharmonic played only 20, and the London Symphony, possibly the most active European orchestra, played 120. Moreover, the annual pay of European musicians was considerably lower than that of members of comparable orchestras in the United States; minimum salary in the London Symphony, including recording fees, was $6–7,000 a year, less than half that received by the Category A orchestras in this country. In the Vienna Philharmonic, new players on minimum scale received under $3,500 a year for opera and symphony work combined; players with considerable seniority (over ten years) received twice that much, but the maximum for a concertmaster after thirty years' service was about $20,000 a year. In these cases, we are dealing with orchestras that are on a level with the best in Category A in this country.

The European system of government subsidy for orchestras is part of an overall program of support for the arts, as a natural extension of state concern with welfare, education, and culture. To a large degree, this has grown up in the general transition from aristocratic and monarchical forms of government, under which the sovereigns and most prominent nobles maintained their own musical establishments; as popular governments took over all state functions, they assumed responsibility for the arts as a matter of course. Such a process did not occur in either the United States or England; in both of these countries the arts, especially the performance arts, continued to be supported privately. In England they long remained the province of the aristocracy and of newly wealthy businessmen, who not only received titles but also assumed some of the responsibilities of their new rank. In the United States, of course, there was no such aristocratic or monarchical tradition, but by the end of the last century the wealthy business establishment began to serve that function here, as we have already noted. Imbued with a deep suspicion of government in all its activities, and taking a certain pride in his own independence and enterprise, the American patron of the arts bitterly opposed government subsidy. The thought of seeking city or state support for his orchestra or for the construction of Symphony Hall simply never occurred to Henry Higginson or his colleagues, and this feeling persists today, even when the leaders of our orchestras find themselves forced to turn to the government.

In their long-time opposition to government funding in the arts, upholders of the status quo developed a number of arguments, which are worth reviewing briefly here in the symphonic context. In terms of conservative economic thinking, the most impressive contention was that if the arts could not pay their own way or gain the support of patrons interested in them, they did not deserve the help of the taxpayer: the fact that they operated at a loss did not necessarily qualify them for consideration. Related to this was the indisputable fact that symphony audiences were small and by no means representative of the total population,* and their activities were concentrated in a relatively few urban centers. Those concerned with raising money from private sources feared that the availability of public subsidy would encourage donors to find other recipients for their philanthropy. Others pointed out that, given the pressing economic and social problems of this nation, support of the arts had a low priority in the allocation of government funds. Finally, there was, and still is, widespread fear that government intervention in policy direction would reduce the authority and power of present boards of directors.

To each of these arguments,† rebuttals in detail have been made. To charges of small and unrepresentative audiences and deficit operations, proponents of subsidy have argued that the arts cannot be evaluated in such quantitative terms and deserve a high priority in our national culture for the experience they bring to their present audience and can bring to others who want to share it. Nor are they concerned with the possibility of government intervention in policy direction: the impact can, if desired, be controlled and in some cases can prove beneficial; there is no basis for the assumption that symphony board members are per se better qualified to pass on arts policy than informed professionals in a government bureau.‡ There are, of course, dangers that bureaucratization of government subsidy can reduce vitality and imagination in orchestra direction, but similar forces have long been at work under private control.

Though many of these questions remain to be resolved, as we shall note later, the matter of government support of the arts has now moved definitely out of the realm of argument into that of reality, less because of any one firm decision on the merits of these arguments than because the arts, especially the symphony orchestras, could not survive without this new source of funding. The about-face decision of the symphony leaders in 1969 came about, not because they accepted the logic of pro-subsidy arguments, but because financial circumstances forced them to change their minds. But this was only the final step in a process extending back for four decades, and the dramatic entry of the federal government into symphony finance in FY 1971 § should not obscure the fact that some form of government subsidy for orchestras had long been developing in this nation. By FY 1971, it was estimated that government funding—outright grants or purchase of services—by cities, counties,

---

* See the following chapter for a discussion of the size and composition of the American symphony audience.

† Baumol and Bowen also cite another by no means frivolous reason why some opposed government subsidy of the arts—the belief that poverty was good for the artist, that he performed and produced best "in the garret," and that prosperity undermined his artistic integrity.[2]

‡ In 1961 an editor of a highly respected "liberal" magazine was shocked by my suggestion, while discussing a possible article on this topic, that professional government officials might be better qualified to pass on arts policy than trustees or directors whose only claim was their ability to raise money.

§ Because most governments operate on a fiscal year (as do most orchestras) our dates here will be in that form: for instance, FY 1971 indicates the fiscal year from July 1, 1970, to June 30, 1971, unless otherwise stated.

states, and the federal government contributed approximately twelve to sixteen percent of the total income received by symphony orchestras.

"Creeping Socialism" in Symphony Orchestras

During the depression of the 1930s, governments first became involved with symphony orchestras in two quite different ways: indirect assistance to existing privately supported orchestras and sponsorship of orchestras for unemployed musicians through the Works Progress Administration Music Project.

Though a transient phenomenon on the American arts scene, the WPA Music Project is worthy of at least brief comment. To provide work for a large number of unemployed musicians, it organized many symphony orchestras of varying size which gave concerts for both free and paid admission. Some of these were in cities that already had orchestras, but elsewhere the WPA project furnished communities with their first sustained programs of symphonic activity. Drawing their personnel from unemployed, and sometimes unemployable, musicians, these orchestras varied greatly in quality, nor could they attract the services of the kind of conductor needed to build orchestral excellence; an exception, it should be noted, was Izler Solomon, now conductor of the Indianapolis Symphony, who first achieved renown for his brilliant work with the WPA orchestra in Illinois. Nevertheless, these projects laid a foundation in a number of cities—Buffalo and Salt Lake City, among others—on which permanent professional orchestras were later based. There is no doubt, moreover, that the project provided minimal but essential support without which the music profession of this nation might not have survived the double impact of electronic distribution of music and of the depression as well as it did. Whatever the merits of the later heated controversy over government activity in the arts, the WPA made an enduring contribution to the music profession and to symphonic development.

One of the first established orchestras to receive municipal subsidy was the San Francisco Symphony: in 1935, thanks to a referendum measure passed with the support of the local musicians' union, a small levy was added to the property tax to assist the orchestra, in a manner that made it possible for it to resume operations after being disbanded for one year. Administered by a local arts commission, these funds were used to purchase the services of the players for special popular-priced concerts, often under famous conductors, in a cavernous municipal auditorium. Except to the extent that these engagements covered a part of the musician's seasonal payroll, the San Francisco Symphony did not benefit directly from the tax; in later years, this city's subsidy of the arts—its museums, opera, and symphony orchestra—has increased considerably, partly with funds from a hotel tax on tourists, and the orchestra has received additional support both for general operations and for such special projects as free park concerts and youth programs.*

* The Baltimore Symphony Orchestra has also enjoyed city support, extending back prior to the depression years, but I have been unable to secure authoritative information on it.[3]

When other orchestras sought public subsidy, they followed the same pattern, selling their services for special civic purposes to a local government agency—very often the local board of education for youth concerts. Although orchestras have also received substantial direct subsidy, sixty to seventy-five percent of all government funding—federal, state, and local—is conditional in some manner upon services rendered by the orchestras. To trace in detail the precise trends and growth of local government support of orchestras * is impossible (in fact, one cannot even get completely accurate data on its present scope). Such support took varied forms, not always direct appropriation of money: a city or county would rent its auditorium to an orchestra at much less than prevailing rates, permit an orchestra the free use of high-school auditoriums or gymnasiums for rehearsal, or supply it with free office space in municipal buildings. In some cases, the orchestra benefited only indirectly from government support of music: many cities have had programs of free summer band or orchestra concerts in their parks, employing players directly, but of ultimate benefit to the local symphony orchestra in adding to the professional income of its players. The Music Performance Trust Fund, working through the local unions, often bore a share, matched from city funds, of the cost of such concerts. Later, when a symphony board would be under pressure from its musicians to lengthen the season, it would arrange to absorb such programs into its contract, with the previously allocated city money now going into the symphony funds. In many respects, government subsidy came to American symphony orchestras in a process that might well be termed "creeping socialism."

But in all probability the most frequent and direct involvement of government agencies with symphony orchestras was in the purchase of services, usually for youth concerts. For the twenty orchestras covered by the 1968 ASOL youth-concert study, twelve percent of the expense of these concerts was met from public sources. A more recent study, undertaken for Lincoln Center for the Performing Arts, reports that for all youth programs—not merely symphonic—as many as twenty-two percent of the organizations reported some kind of government funding.

Another movement affecting eventual expansion of government funding was the growth of arts councils. This term still leads to much confusion, for it covers two quite different, though occasionally overlapping, types of organizations: the "independent" or "community" council, in which a number of arts organizations band together for a consideration of common problems and pursuit of common aims; and the government or quasi-government—city, county, or state—arts councils that have in recent years engaged directly in arts funding. Though playing important and varied roles in their communities, the "independent" councils here concern us only to the extent that they have supplied leadership for the advocacy of arts subsidy, or have themselves provided the basis for the organization of the second, government, type of council. As noted earlier, the American Symphony Orchestra League played an early and important role in the national organization of these arts coun-

---

* Baumol and Bowen cite a 1958–59 Library of Congress study of municipal assistance to the arts in general and conclude that *all* local government grants to the performance arts at that time could not have exceeded $2 million nationally.[4]

cils, which eventually emerged as the Associated Councils of the Arts. The borderline between these two types is not always clear, although on a state level such councils are virtually all of the government type in order to qualify for their share of federal funds.

We have already noted how the Utah Symphony is itself a division of the Utah State Institute of Fine Arts, the oldest such state council in the nation. Minnesota established its arts council in 1902, but only four other state councils had been organized before 1960, when the New York State Council on the Arts was authorized by the legislature on the recommendation of Governor Nelson Rockefeller. By 1965, when the National Endowment for the Arts was organized, there was a total of seventeen state arts councils.* Because the legislation authorizing and funding the National Endowment of the Arts provided for the allocation of annual grants to such state arts councils, the rest of the fifty states established them by 1967.

As we shall have occasion to note shortly, these state arts councils vary considerably in effectiveness, ranging from the huge New York State Council on the Arts, whose FY 1971 appropriation was more than twice that of all other states combined, to several that do nothing more than distribute the state-federal partnership funds from the National Endowment for the Arts.

The proliferation of these activities—often more important for their involvement of people and organizations than for specific funding—gave an overall sense of direction and common concern to much of this nation's arts activity in the postwar era. It contributed to the development of such local government arts funding as was achieved and provided a foundation for major developments on the national level in the mid-1960s.

Federal Subsidy Achieved

Meanwhile, advocates of government arts subsidy continued to wage a national campaign, especially in the halls of the Congress, on behalf of their cause. During the 1950s, Representative Frank Thompson of New Jersey introduced several bills; to substantiate his legislation, he held hearings in Washington and elsewhere on the state of the arts nationally. Many data concerning the economic problems of the arts were presented by various organizations, including the American Symphony Orchestra League, and the musicians' union was also extremely active in providing witnesses, both from its membership and the music profession and from the other arts. Though the ASOL was barred by its tax-exempt status from assuming an explicit role in this campaign, as it had in repealing the admissions tax before 1951, Helen M. Thompson was active behind the scenes, and upon request furnished these Congressional committees with statistical information on the symphonic sector of the arts, information which was in most cases the most comprehensive, accurate, and impressive documentation the committee received.†

* Though these state groups are variously designated as "councils," "commissions," "institutes," and so on, we shall here refer to them by the general term "council."
† The National Council on the Arts and Government was also active in coordinating the campaign for federal funding and presented data to the Congressional hearings.

However, the League's activities in these efforts were also restricted by a sharp division within its orchestra membership on the question of government subsidy. There is no question that the smaller orchestras inclined to favor this support, that Mrs. Thompson's own personal sympathies tended in that direction, and that the larger orchestras opposed it. In 1962, with an increasingly friendly atmosphere toward government subsidy growing in Washington, the League surveyed its membership on the question.[5] An extraordinarily large proportion of the responding orchestras offered no opinion, or stated that the matter was still under consideration. The vagueness of the question, put as acceptance or rejection of the proposition that "the time had come for the federal government to show a greater concern for the development of the cultural affairs of our nation," [6] may have caused some confusion: specific spelling-out of procedures and principles of funding might have substantially reduced the proportion of those orchestras who took a middle ground or reported no decision. Table 15-A shows the results of this 1962 League survey.

TABLE 15-A

RESPONSES TO ASOL SURVEY ON FEDERAL SUPPORT OF ARTS, 1962

	19 Major Orchestras	16 Metropolitan Orchestras	200 Community Orchestras	Total Responding
Percentage of total membership responding	76%	79%	25%	235 (100%)
In favor	5%	6%	57%	116 (49%)
Opposed	21%	38%	14%	39 (16.5%)
Middle-ground position	47%	6%	3%	15 (6.9%)
No decision	26%	50%	26%	65 (27.6%)

It is obvious that the professional sector of the American orchestra was by no means ready to accept federal subsidy and that the greatest support for it came from semi- or nonprofessional groups, which, incidentally, did not receive much federal funding once it was eventually effected. Under these circumstances, the most powerful orchestras participated little in the subsequent development of federal support, though, of course, their musicians did so through the union.*

At the time the ASOL made this survey, efforts to achieve government support for the arts were on the verge of success. Presidents Truman and Eisenhower both gave lip service to the principle, but neither lent it active support. However, President Kennedy showed every sign of taking decisive, if deliberate, action on the matter, though he was fully aware of substantial opposition in the Congress. Possibly his most significant actions during his brief term of office were the appointment of August Heckscher as White House counselor on the arts and humanities and his intervention in the Metropolitan Opera labor dispute in the late summer of 1961. His designation of

---

* The resentment felt by many musicians toward their employers' opposition to federal funding certainly aggravated labor relations during this period.

Arthur J. Goldberg,* then Secretary of Labor and later a Supreme Court justice, to arbitrate the Metropolitan Opera dispute resulted eventually in Goldberg's appending to his decision a succinct, eloquent plea for government subsidy and an explicit definition of the respective roles of government, private resources, and labor in the arts.[7]

> The question before the nation, then, is how to restore the financial viability of these institutions and to promote the welfare of the artists upon whom these institutions in the final analysis do and must depend. It is, to repeat, unthinkable that they should disappear at the very moment when they have achieved an unprecedented significance to the American people as a whole. . . . The answer to this question is evident enough. We must come to accept the arts as a new community responsibility. The arts must assume their place alongside the already accepted responsibilities for health, education and welfare. Part of this new responsibility must fall to the federal government for precisely the reasons that the nation has given it a role in similar undertakings.

Goldberg elaborated this with a proposal of a six-point partnership [8] to provide "a stable, continuing basis of financial support for an artistic community that will at once be responsive to the needs and wishes of the public and at the same time to be free to pursue its own creative interests":

1. Development of a large and varied audience drawn from all segments of society;
2. Continued and substantial support by private patrons and benefactors, and the basic assumption by these enlightened patrons of responsibility for the policy of arts institutions;
3. Expansion of contributions on the part of private corporations and foundations;
4. Acceptance by the American labor movement of a responsibility for the support of arts comparable to that of American business;
5. Increase in local government support;
6. The systematic participation of the federal government in support of the arts on a national scale.

Such a partnership † would, in Goldberg's opinion, be in keeping with the pluralistic nature of American society, assure the participation of the widest base of community support, and provide the most secure protection against domination in policy making by any one force in society.

President Kennedy apparently planned to appoint, late in 1963, a special commission on the arts as part of the White House staff. After his death in November, 1963, Congressional interest in developing arts legislation grew, partly as a memorial to the slain president. By 1965, a number of proposals —ranging from the establishment of an exploratory and advisory agency with no grant funds to authorization of lavish funding of the arts—were combined

---

* An important AFL lawyer before joining the Kennedy administration, Goldberg was also personally but not officially acquainted with the problems of the Chicago Symphony musicians in the early 1960s.

† Goldberg's conception of this effort as a partnership is reflected, in part at least, by the Partnership for the Arts, an organization to be discussed shortly.

in a comprehensive measure † calling for the establishment of an independent National Council on the Arts and Humanities, with twin subsidiaries: a National Council on the Arts and a National Endowment for the Arts, matched by a similar council and endowment for the humanities.† Heading each was a chairman, with a respective advisory Council and an administrative Endowment. President Lyndon B. Johnson appointed Roger Stevens as Chairman of the National Council and Endowment for the Arts, and the Congress appropriated $2.5 million for the arts and a similar amount for the humanities in FY 1966. The original authorizing legislation was for three years, setting general levels of funding, but actual appropriations were made on a year-to-year basis; authorization was subsequently renewed for five years extending through FY 1973.

Federal Funding, 1966–71

Table 15-B shows the funding of the National Council on the Arts and National Endowments for the Arts for FY 1966 through FY 1973: [9]

TABLE 15-B

NATIONAL ENDOWMENT FOR THE ARTS

Funding FY 1966 through 1973

Year	National Grants	State-Federal Partnership	Treasury Fund	Office of Education Transfer Funds	TOTAL
FY 1966	$2.5		$0.034		$ 2.534
FY 1967	4.0	2.0	1.966		7,966
FY 1968	4.5	2.0	0.674		7.174
FY 1969	3.7	1.7	2.357	0.1	7.857
FY 1970	4.25	2.0	2.0	0.9	9.150
FY 1971	8.465	4.125	2.5		15.090
FY 1972	20.75	5.5	3.5		29.75
FY 1973	27,825	6.875	3.5		38.2
FY 1974 Requested					72.5

($ in millions)

* The devising of this structure probably owes much to Abe Fortas, Isaac Stern, Roger Stevens, and others to whom President Lyndon B. Johnson entrusted the precise drawing up of the necessary legislation.

† In the original legislation and subsequent authorizations, there is also a federal council over both the arts and humanities agencies, but it has never been actively involved in policy or operations. In effect the National Endowment for the Arts and its Council operate quite independently from their humanities counterparts. The latter, with its strong academic orientation, has concerned itself hardly at all with the arts, even in areas where the arts and humanities might overlap.

Of the categories shown here, funds for national grants were available to the NEA for allocation to such projects as deemed worthy, usually on some kind of matching basis. State-federal partnership funds were designated by the Congress for allocation, in equal amounts, to those states having active arts councils. The treasury fund was set aside to match private donations in a manner devised to encourage private contributions: for each dollar contributed privately to the treasury fund, the Endowment, by matching this gift, would grant twice as much to the beneficiary designated by the donor.

Though, as we shall have occasion to note shortly, symphony orchestras did not figure importantly in NEA funding before FY 1971, it is of some interest to report how the Endowment allocated funds (including treasury funds but excluding state-federal partnership) during its first five years:

Architecture and planning	4.8%
Dance	9.4%
Education programs	7.2%
Literature programs	6.7%
Music (including symphony)	16.2%
Public media	3.8%
Theater	22.1%
Visual arts	11.2%
Other	18.6%

Symphony orchestras received about two percent of total NEA grants during its first five years.

Until the fall of 1969, the Council and Endowment were headed by Roger L. Stevens, a highly successful New York realtor and theatrical producer. Though he developed a staff for the Endowment and sought the advice of the Council, Stevens also tended at times to back projects that especially interested him personally or were favored by individual Council members, though a major share of the Endowment grants were processed in a routine manner. Members of the National Council on the Arts and Stevens himself often exchanged ideas, both formally and informally, on initiating projects, rather than waiting for local arts organizations to file applications. Stevens was particularly successful in devising programs that would stimulate matching funds: one of the original Council members has since recalled with admiration the chairman's ability to "make one dollar do the work of four" in putting the limited resources ($2.5 to $4.25 million a year) to good use.[10] Over a third of the NEA allocations to visual arts programs in FY 1966–70 was devoted to one project, the acquisition and renovation of the abandoned Bell Telephone Laboratories building in lower Manhattan as a residence for artists;[11] the J. M. Kaplan Fund, Inc., and the FHA also shared in financing this nonprofit Westbeth corporation, to which the Endowment contributed $1 million. In another project, which failed to materialize, Stevens proposed to organize a national chamber orchestra employing first-rank musicians in an ensemble that would engage in combined concert touring and education activities, but this met with considerable opposition from symphony orchestras and music schools alike.

Among the major beneficiaries of NEA support during its first five years were the Metropolitan Opera National Company (since abandoned), Ballet Theater, Coordinating Council of Literary Magazines, National Opera Institute, Western Opera Theater in San Francisco, Young Audiences, American National Theater and Academy (nearly one-fifth of the total theater grants), Atlanta Arts Alliance, Laboratory Theater Project for Education (in cooperation with the Office of Education), and Detroit Institute of Arts.

That orchestras did not become a major factor in NEA allocations until FY 1971 should not be considered any indication of indifference on the part of the Council or Endowment or of Stevens personally: until 1969, the orchestras as a group made no concerted effort to gain government funding, though a few proposed specific projects in audience building, touring, and education. Actually, the Council, at one of its first meetings in 1965, discussed a comprehensive though modest program of funding symphony grants (some $900,000), but dropped the idea upon learning that the Ford Foundation was about to announce its $80.2 million symphony program.* However, the Council under Stevens's chairmanship continued to watch the symphony picture, and when Nancy Hanks succeeded Stevens as chairman late in 1969, she was immediately confronted with the first concerted effort by orchestras to gain substantial federal funding.

Orchestras Seek Federal Aid

When the ASOL made its 1962 survey on federal arts subsidy, only one Major and one Metropolitan orchestra expressed acceptance of that idea in principle. In many respects it was the conservative "establishment" leaders in the symphony world—managers and board members of the large orchestra —who were the last to accept this notion. In fact, many conductors, possibly because of their European background, quietly favored government support, but most refrained from being too outspoken with their views. The fact that more than half of the "community" orchestras, with budgets under $100,000 and few pretensions to professional quality, so strongly favored subsidy is a rather curious phenomenon: perhaps they saw it as the only way they could attain professional status with their limited local means; or perhaps, with a strong representation of players on their boards, they were less prone to conservative thinking.

The conservatism of the boards of larger orchestras stemmed from the political orientation of the businessmen, lawyers, and bankers who dominated these boards: not only were these men and women of wealth and influence reluctant to support any increase in government costs, and hence in taxes, as a matter of self-interest, but "in their hearts" (to paraphrase the campaign slogan of Barry Goldwater) they knew that the extension of government into any new area was wrong. Furthermore, they feared deeply—and with some justification—that public subsidy would lead inevitably to some form of gov-

---

* There have been several accounts of such an agreement between the Ford Foundation and the Endowment; mine is based on the report of a National Council member present at the meeting in question.[12]

ernment involvement in the policy-making process over which they, by virtue of their ability to raise supplementary income, had absolute control.
They knew that when they sold the services of their orchestras to the public
schools, the education bureaucracy often became involved in planning youth
concerts; they could accept this in a marginal area, but not in the central activities of the orchestra. They may not have known in detail how staunchly
Major Higginson had stood by Karl Muck against all manner of public and
political pressure in 1917–18, but they had heard of Congressmen who raised
a hue and cry over the dances of Martha Graham on her State Department
cultural tours abroad. Most of all, they looked upon their orchestras as their
own, not only to manage but also to support and to take pride in supporting.

But the yawning income gap of the late 1960s proved more than the symphonic establishment could handle on its own, either from the personal funds
of board members or the contributions they could raise in the community.
Most acutely, they felt the pressure of their musicians, a pressure to which
they reacted, rightly or wrongly, on the basis of their own ingrained hostility
to trade unionism. There were many, in this period, who talked of the demise
of the symphony, of giving it up as an impossible task, and some even lashed
out at the Ford Foundation for arousing insatiable expectations in the musicians and public alike. But in the end these leaders' commitment to the symphony orchestra prevailed and they sought to explore ways of maintaining
the institution rather than abandoning it. Many orchestras, especially in the
Major group, had called in management and fund-raising counsel to assist
them in matching the challenge of the Ford Foundation project; the most
hardheaded of these counselors not only looked at current operations but
forced symphony leaders to make future projections and, most important of
all, to decide what they wanted of their orchestras and how much they were
willing to pay for them in time, effort, and money.

The turning point came early in 1969, when the leaders of the "Big Five"
orchestras—Boston, Chicago, Cleveland, New York, and Philadelphia—
found themselves faced with mounting demands from players who were willing to strike to gain their ends and a rapid increase of income gap in their
finances. Together they commissioned a study by the Cleveland office of the
national management-counseling firm of McKinsey and Company * and
opened their files of financial records, policy deliberations, union negotiations,
and operating data to the McKinsey staff. This McKinsey report revealed an
average of sixty-four percent of 1967–68 expenditures covered by performance
income, a considerably better than average ratio; what distressed these five
orchestras was that, as late as 1963–64, this ratio had been as high as seventy-
one percent and showed signs of falling even more in 1969. Moreover, what
was a relatively low income gap in percentage of expenditure amounted for
these orchestras to over $1 million. In fact, in meeting their requirements for
supplementary income, several of these orchestras enjoyed endowment income that substantially reduced their annual need for contributions, but had

* This report, at first distributed only among the five orchestras concerned, can no longer be
regarded as a private document. It has been circulated widely, both officially and surrepti-
tiously; in at least one case, representatives of an orchestra gave copies of it to a musicians'
committee during labor negotiations. It therefore warrants specific citation here.[13]

been invading the unrestricted portion of these trusts to meet annual deficits, thus reducing their future potential as a source of income.

Completed in May, 1969, the McKinsey report informed these five orchestras that they should anticipate an increase of thirty-nine percent in their supplemental income in the next four years and that their net deficit would more than double if additional sources of supplemental income were not developed or if performance income could not be increased. Moreover, the report saw a very poor outlook for the future: concert revenue could not be expected to keep pace with rising costs, and royalties from recording, an important income item for most of the five, showed relative stability in recent years and some possibility of future decline. The report further recommended that these five orchestras work together to devise solutions to these problems, that they engage in a freer exchange of information among themselves, and that other orchestras be brought into these consultations. In view of the importance of personnel costs in the income gap, the report admonished the orchestras to improve their communications with their musicians in the hope of generating a better mutual understanding of the economic realities of symphonic affairs.

Finally, the McKinsey report advised these five orchestras, in view of the critical situation in traditional fund-raising, to formulate comprehensive plans to secure additional supplemental income from foundations and corporations and seek funding from the federal government. Though the foundation opportunity was by no means closed, the largest of the mega-foundations, the Ford Foundation with its ongoing symphony project offered no hope for immediate relief. Corporate help was explored and more aggressively pursued. And for the first time the leaders of the largest orchestras took the initiative in organizing a concerted drive for major federal funding for symphony orchestras.

In November, 1969, the presidents and managers of seventy-seven professional orchestras met as an *ad hoc* "committee of the whole" in New York at the invitation of the New York Philharmonic, with the ASOL coordinating and arranging the meeting. Nancy Hanks, then recently appointed as chairman of the National Endowment for the Arts, attended with members of her staff. Though the group made various recommendations concerning tax legislation than before the Congress and called for closer cooperation between orchestras, its most important action was to appoint Amyas Ames, then president of the New York Philharmonic, as chairman of a five-man steering committee to coordinate efforts to secure substantial funding for symphony orchestras through the National Endowment for the Arts.*

Early in 1970, a new national organization was announced: the Partnership for the Arts, headed by Ames † and embracing the whole spectrum of the arts,

---

* Shortly afterward, upon Governor Rockefeller's proposal for an $18.2 million special arts appropriation in New York for FY 1971, a similar New York State committee, the Concerned Citizens for the Arts, was organized. Ames was also active in this group.

† Amyas Ames, scion of a prominent New England family and a member of the New York brokerage firm of Kidder and Peabody, shortly afterward assumed the position of chairman of the New York Philharmonic board when Carlos Moseley replaced him as president and Helen M. Thompson became manager. Ames also succeeded John D. Rockefeller III as chairman of the board of Lincoln Center for the Performing Arts.

not just symphony orchestras, in a concerted campaign of public education to arouse support for increased government aid and to promote passage by Congress of full funding for the National Endowment for the Arts. Though the Partnership—a term reminiscent, albeit probably without intention, of Goldberg's 1961 recommendation—started out as a national organization primarily of representatives of the symphonic establishment, it sought, and still seeks, to broaden its base to include opera, theater, dance, and visual arts organizations across the country.* Since Partnership explicitly works in the political arena, it cannot offer its financial supporters the attraction of tax-exemption. As noted earlier, the ASOL may not engage in political activity without jeopardizing its tax-exempt status, though it cooperates with the Partnership.

Even before the Partnership came into existence, the *ad hoc* committee meeting of symphony orchestras and NEA staff resulted in a great expansion of grants to symphony orchestras from an average of just over $100,000 a year in FYs 1966–70 to approximately $3 million in FY 1971 alone. This provided considerable stimulus to the organization of the Partnership for the Arts in its efforts to secure full funding from the Congress.

National Endowment for the Arts
Funding of Orchestras

The economic impact of the National Endowment for the Arts on symphony orchestras since FY 1971 has been considerable, as may be seen from the following summary of direct symphony grants: *

TABLE 15-C

NATIONAL ENDOWMENT FOR THE ARTS

Funding of Symphony Orchestras, 1966–73

	Total Grants	Number of Orchestras	Percentage of Total NEA Appr.
FY 1966 to FY 1970	$ 532,200	14	2%
FY 1971	$2,975,962	67	20%
FY 1972	$4,002,256	80	14%
FY 1973	$4,088,065	97	11%

The importance of this funding can be appreciated when it is compared to the annual income from the Ford Foundation endowment trust fund, which is

---

* In November, 1972, largely because of its failure to gain financing for its own efforts, the Partnership "merged" with the Associated Councils of the Arts, where it will continue as a distinct subsidiary.

* These figures, from NEA press releases, concern only Major and Metropolitan orchestras; they do not include indirect grants through other organizations or state arts councils, and actual funding eventually may differ in minor respects from that announced in advance. They do not include private donations through the Treasury Fund.

probably producing approximately $3 million annually to be distributed among the orchestras still participating in that program. The legislation establishing these arts and humanities administrations gives them considerable latitude in organizing their procedures, the basic structure of which was established under Stevens's chairmanship, though there have been some modifications under Nancy Hanks.[14] Organizations file applications on forms provided by the Endowment, setting forth general information concerning their operations and a detailed description of the special project for which they desire federal funding; with rare exceptions, they must assure the availability of local funds to match those requested from the Endowment. The NEA staff in Washington reviews these applications and submits them to the appropriate advisory panel—in this case, one assigned to orchestra projects and consisting of professionals with experience in the field. The staff, in submitting these applications, also advises the panel concerning the merits of the projects proposed and the amount it recommends for funding in terms of overall money available; on occasion, it makes general comments about the applicants' activities. In most cases, the advisory panel approves or rejects the applications, either on staff recommendation or on its own initiative; in some cases, it refers them back to the staff for further research or clarification before making a final decision.

In strict terms, the advisory panel actually advises the chairman, who has full legal authority to act in these matters; however, in actual practice, the full National Council on the Arts receives the recommendations of the staff and advisory panel and in turn makes the final decision on grants in the form of recommendations to the chairman. However, the Council by no means automatically accepts the recommendations of the advisory group, any more than the latter follows the suggestions of the staff; at every stage, each application receives intensive scrutiny and review.*

Though not required to do so by law, the National Endowment for the Arts makes its grants for specific programs initiated by the applicant orchestras. These need not necessarily be new projects—though before FY 1971 they usually were—but the Endowment favors innovative programs or those aimed at maintaining broad community services beyond the central concert series of the orchestra. Of seventy-three projects † founded in FY 1971, thirty-one were for youth or school programs, thirty-one for expanded musical services, eight for orchestra development, and three for special professional services. In FY 1972, forty-one projects were for youth programs, thirty-four for public program expansion, eleven for professional services, four for special projects, and three for programs coordinated with other arts organizations.

It has also been possible for orchestras to obtain federal grants through the special treasury fund. In such cases, a donor contributes money to this fund, stipulating the eventual beneficiary of the grant. The NEA, after reviewing

---

* Essentially the same procedures prevail in the other arts areas covered by the NEA and in the National Endowment for the Humanities, though our description here refers primarily to the symphonic field.

† This total exceeds the 67 listed earlier because it includes several orchestras not in the Major-Metropolitan classifications and because a few orchestras' grants covered more than one type of project.

the merits of the proposal, then allocates to the orchestra twice the sum originally given by the donor. The purpose of this system was to encourage substantial private contributions by a matching incentive. In some cases, as
with the Cincinnati Symphony Orchestra, a supporting organization, not necessarily an individual contributor, can make the necessary contribution to the
treasury fund, setting this procedure in motion; in fact, that orchestra has
benefited by donations to the treasury fund from the Institute of Fine Arts as
well as from private sources. This treasury fund, one of Roger Stevens's ways
of encouraging the cooperation of private donors with the government, has
become in recent years more of a bookkeeping device.

This emphasis on funding specific projects is an administrative decision of
the NEA, established in its earliest days when money was limited. More recently, as this has increased substantially—the FY 1974 appropriations request is nearly thirty times that of FY 1966—there has been growing advocacy, in the symphonic field especially, for direct subsidy not necessarily
tied to specific projects.[15] The proponents of direct allocation of funds argue
that the present project orientation of the Endowment involves the applicant
orchestras in an excessive amount of paper work to prepare applications and of
time and planning effort to devise programs that will stand up favorably in
competition with the applications of other orchestras. Moreover, they see the
income gap as their basic economic problem and hope to establish the principle of government aid in its general solution as funding continues to increase.
One of their proposals calls for setting up automatic grants to established orchestras on some formula, such as the amount of contributions raised or total
budget, that would provide a basic NEA subsidy. Those orchestras desiring
further aid for innovative or special projects could seek it by the present application process, but each orchestra would be assured of at least a minimum
support. There is still a feeling among some orchestras that the Endowment
looks with greater favor on innovative programs, thus placing at a disadvantage those orchestras which have already developed broad programs on their
own resources; they feel that such project orientation encourages unnecessary
"make-work" projects at the expense of essential services.

The Endowment, for its part, has found itself involved in a large burden of
administrative review of applications, and the advisory panel and Council confront increasingly large stacks of applications, many of which they have some
reason to doubt their competence to evaluate conscientiously. A recent meeting of the advisory panel was forced to divide itself into two groups to cover
all of the applications on hand. Some have suggested that the NEA allocate
certain special funds, over and above the state-federal partnership, to state
arts councils for distribution to orchestras in their states, but the inadequate
staffing of many councils argues against the wisdom of so reducing the NEA's
administrative load.

In actual practice, as the Endowment has gained experience in processing
applications from orchestras, a tacit understanding seems to have developed
that orchestras of a given size and stability can count on a certain maximum
grant, providing they submit sufficient backing for an application. In FYs
1971–72, for instance, Major orchestras could expect no more than $100,000

each (an exception being made for the National Symphony in Washington, D.C.), but they could count on that amount if their projects met minimum standards and their applications were filed properly. In fact, there have been unofficial reports that a few Major orchestras, whose applications were not sufficiently documented, were advised to rectify the deficiencies with the understanding that a grant would be officially approved once they had done so.

The Endowment, moreover, has become increasingly concerned with the overall quality of some of the groups seeking its support. A large number of orchestras, to be sure, qualify for such funding on artistic grounds and in terms of their management and community service, but the Council itself has raised questions in a number of cases. Early in 1971, therefore, the Endowment attempted to evaluate music activities in a limited region, the southeastern part of the country. Here it sought to survey the major musical organizations—opera as well as symphony—in terms of their artistic quality, managerial competence, and general community standing. Teams of professional specialists visited various organizations in the area to supplement documentary information requested by the NEA for this study. This effort aroused apprehension in the orchestra world, where this evaluation was viewed as the first step toward the kind of political interference in policy direction that they had long feared as a concomitant of government aid. Despite early fears, these evaluations have proceeded smoothly and have been extended to other parts of the country, especially to specific organizations or areas where the NEA staff or advisory panels have requested more information than is given in the grant applications. As the Endowment accumulates such information for its files, its staff will be in a better position to review applications and can call on its field staff for further data.

Lingering in the background of the Endowment's procedures is a deep concern that its operations be conducted in a manner completely above criticism, especially from the Congress that authorized it, must still finance it with annual appropriations, and could at any time drastically hamper its success. Its highly organized staff of professional specialists in the arts draws upon colleges, universities, orchestras, foundations, and arts organizations for its personnel. Miss Hanks herself came to the Endowment, not as an economically and politically powerful figure in the entertainment world like Roger Stevens, but from a background in professional arts administration and philanthropy with the Associated Councils of the Arts and the Rockefeller Brothers Fund. Since its founding, the National Endowment for the Arts has therefore developed into a highly professional and thoroughly bureaucratic (not necessarily in the perjorative sense of the term) organization. Renewals of its authorization and annual appropriations have passed through the Congress with progressively less opposition, and the program in its first seven years has been remarkably free of the kind of Congressional scandalmongering that characterized the WPA arts projects in the 1930s and some of the overseas cultural programs of the State Department after the last war.

On the other hand, under Miss Hanks's chairmanship the National Endowment for the Arts has been more conservative in its approach to arts funding than under Stevens. In its major grants, it has dealt primarily with long-established organizations, honored in their respective communities and engaged in overall programs of low controversial potential: its closest approach in the orchestral field to what some Congressmen might consider politically sensitive support has been two grants of twenty-five thousand dollars each to the Symphony of the New York, a New York orchestra devoted to building the symphonic capabilities of black orchestral players. In their artistic content, of course, symphony orchestras do not present major political implications, but one may doubt, for instance, whether the NEA would allow itself to become embroiled in such controversies as that which surrounded the WPA Theater Project's efforts to produce in New York Marc Blitzstein's labor-oriented opera *The Cradle Will Rock*.* One area in which the Endowment has taken some initiative is in encouraging arts organizations to work together, often under the guidance of a state arts council, in mutually advantageous projects: working in cooperation with the Missouri State Council, the ASOL, and local "community" orchestras, the St. Louis Symphony has developed such a cooperative program with NEA funding. A review of the full listing of grants in the performance arts, though admittedly subjective, seems to indicate that offbeat ventures receive considerably smaller grants than the established orchestras, opera companies, and theaters, and even these appear to be of the sort that will arouse little criticism.† Moreover, the successive reviews of applications by staff, advisory panels, and the Council itself provide a considerable margin of protection for the Endowment from public or Congressional criticism of a specific project should controversy develop.

State and Local Arts Funding

In total public funding of symphony orchestras, however, the federal share in FY 1971 amounted to somewhat more than a third, the remainder being supplied by states, counties, boards of education, and cities, much of it developed long before the National Endowment came into existence. Unfortunately, there is no comprehensive information on past growth of these sources, or even on their present impact, of an accuracy comparable to the data on federal aid.

From its inception, legislation authorizing federal arts funding provided for state-federal partnership allocations. The availability of these funds to state councils prompted every one of the fifty states ‡ that had not done so already to authorize an arts council in order to share in the federal bounty. However,

---

* The theater is, of course, much more vulnerable to political complications. For an account of the Blitzstein opera, see John Houseman's memoirs, *Runthrough,* and Hallie Flanagan's comprehensive account of the WPA Theater Project in *Arena.*
† However, with Endowment appropriations continuing to increase at a rapid rate, both for its regular operations and in anticipation of the Bicentennial, it is possible that the NEA will support a wider variety of projects. (President Nixon's FY 1974 budget request for the arts is $72.5 million, some $34.3 over the FY 1973 appropriation.)
‡ Our data here concerns only these fifty states, although the overall NEA state-federal partnership also includes the District of Columbia, Puerto Rico, American Samoa, Guam, and the Virgin Islands.

the mere establishment of an arts council did not necessarily make it effective in the administration of state-federal funds or such appropriations as its legislature might provide. Many early councils had little more than advisory functions, and no funds with which to aid arts organizations. Beginning in FY 1967, the National Endowment for the Arts allocated an equal amount (at first slightly over $37,000) to each state arts council, which the latter in turn used for grants to arts organizations in its state. Some states either had already been making their own arts appropriations or began to do so after federal funds became available. However, as late as FY 1971, three states (Nevada, North Dakota, and Wyoming) made no state arts appropriations, and twenty-one out of fifty-three councils had fewer than three full- or part-time professional and clerical personnel on their staffs.[16] As we shall have occasion to note in greater detail, New York in that same year appropriated by far the largest amount of money for the arts, $20.3 million; next in size (after Puerto Rico with $1.7 million) was Illinois with $600,000.* The increase in total state appropriations since FY 1966 may be seen in Table 15-D, which also shows allocations of state-federal partnership funds: [17]

TABLE 15-D

STATE ARTS COUNCIL FUNDING—FYs 1966–72

(As of January 1, 1971)

Fiscal Year	Number States Funded	Amount State Funding	State- Federal Partnership	Total Funding
1966	23	$ 2,644,640		$ 2,644,640
1967	36	4,850,678	$2,000,000	6,850,678
1968	42	6,734,091	2,000,000	8,734,091
1969	44	6,847,613	1,700,000	8,547,613
1970	47	7,661,912	2,000,000	9,661,912
1971	48	26,866,942 *	4,125,000	30,991,942
1972	51	30,000,000 * est.	5,500,000	35,500,000

* Contains New York State appropriations of $20.3 million in FY 1971 and $14.4 million in FY 1972.

Included, in addition to the fifty states, are District of Columbia, Puerto Rico, Guam, American Samoa, and Virgin Islands.

The total states' appropriation for the arts was therefore about equal to the federal in FY 1966, and fell behind thereafter, except for the special New York State appropriations in FY 1971 and FY 1972. In FY 1971, total state appropriations for the arts, exclusive of the special $18.2 New York funding, were $8.2 million, as compared with a federal total of $15 million. The disparity was probably even greater in FY 1972, when federal funds rose to

* See Appendix K for a complete list of states' appropriations, shares of state-federal partnership funds, and allocations to symphony orchestras for FY 1971.

$30 million; state figures were not yet available at this writing. Of the FY 1971 total state funding, approximately $3 million went to symphony orchestras, some of them touring groups from out of state.[18] Forty-one of fifty states reported making some kind of grant to orchestras, though not all gave the amount. Total state funding therefore amounted to approximately 11% of the total, as compared with 20% in federal allocations.* (However, as federal appropriations continued to increase appreciably after FY 1971, the symphony share dropped, though the dollar amount increased; see Table 15-C.)

On the basis of special questionnaires [19] sent to all of the Major and Metropolitan orchestras, it is possible to arrive at rough estimates of city, county, and board of education funding of symphony orchestras. Of the forty-six orchestras replying, thirty-seven (80%) reported receiving some support from state or local governments, many from more than one source, and it was of interest to note the large number of smaller orchestras receiving such support; in 85% of these, grants were made for special services rendered. From these replies, it is possible to extrapolate roughly the relative roles of the various local government agencies in symphony funding:

Source	Percent Reporting Symphony Grants	Dollar Ratio to State Grants
Cities	53%	Equal
Counties	33%	Equal
Boards of education	33%	One-fourth
States	41%	Equal

Since these data indicate a considerably smaller proportion of state funding than reported elsewhere,† any attempt to draw significant conclusions from this survey must be made with caution. However, the ASOL estimates that total government funding of symphony orchestras reached $8 million. From the Missouri survey some $3 million of this came from state funds, and the National Endowment grants totaled approximately $3 million; this would indicate that city, county, and board of education grants totaled possibly $2 million.

Procedures for granting financial aid to arts organizations on state and local levels vary a great deal. In some cases, board members or managers meet more or less informally with government officials to bargain for such funding as they can obtain; in many instances, the political influence of board members plays an important part in this process. Many cities, counties, and boards of education have no overall arts budget but simply attempt to find funds somewhere for the services offered by the symphony orchestra. State councils, with a wider

* See Appendix K for a summary of state arts funding to orchestras in FY 1971.
† In view of authoritative data showing that 82% of the states made some sort of grants to symphony orchestras, we can explain this discrepancy in only two ways: (1) responses to our questionnaire may have been incorrectly stated (a by no means remote possibility); and (2) our sample, drawn from Major and Metropolitan orchestras only, did not include the smaller non-professional orchestras which received aid from their state councils, an indication that these state councils may be making grants in areas not covered by the federal program.

area to serve and enjoying specific budgets appropriated by their legislatures and augmented by the NEA state-federal partnership, must weigh the respective merits of applications from a variety of organizations; some still award grants on the basis of more or less informal pleas, but many rely increasingly on formal presentations and supporting documentation, though political pressures from influential arts board members can exert considerable influence. (It is interesting to note, incidentally, that some of those most fearful of political pressure *from* government are most adept at applying it *to* funding agencies.)

With a few notable exceptions, however, most nonfederal agencies have relatively less to disburse for the arts than does the federal government, even in proportion to population or total local budget. In the overall governmental economy it is the national sector that has the most funds at its disposal and the greatest potential for increasing them: in every aspect of their jurisdiction, states, cities, counties, and boards of education operate under increasing fiscal limitations, and the arts suffer equally with such services as education, police, and parks. There is therefore every likelihood that state appropriations will not continue to rise as fast as federal; certainly this has been the recent trend, as shown on Table 15-D, once New York is excluded from consideration. However, there are indications—in Illinois, California, and Missouri especially—of greater state interest in the arts, though so far not on the scale of New York.

New York State Arts Funding

The one state that has succeeded in securing substantial arts appropriations is New York,[20] thanks in large part to the efforts of Governor Nelson A. Rockefeller and the support of such influential citizens as Amyas Ames, Robert Millonzi, and Seymour Knox. Since its organization in 1960, the New York State Council on the Arts has enjoyed a rapid growth in the funds placed at its disposal by the legislature: [21] from an initial appropriation of $50,000 in FY 1961 these grew to $2.3 million in FY 1970 and a request for a "regular" allocation of $2.1 million for FY 1971.

Prior to FY 1971, the Council, under expert professional guidance, developed a variety of programs supporting specific arts projects—traveling art exhibitions, direct aid to artists, and assistance to touring performance groups. In the performance arts, the Council aimed its efforts less toward direct subsidy than toward encouraging local sponsors to present touring performances by underwriting the risk of loss. This involved an evaluation both of the ability of the local sponsor to handle such presentations and of the artistic quality of the performing group itself. Under the leadership first of John MacFadyen and later of John Hightower, the NYSCA developed an impressive expertise in arts support that was to prove invaluable when its program suddenly expanded in FY 1971. This included considerable experience in the evaluation of performance programs by advisory panels set up to pass on the worthiness of groups desiring state aid in their touring.

In his 1970 budget message to the legislature, Governor Rockefeller called for emergency aid to the arts in his state.[22] In citing an annual total operating deficit (in our terms, the income gap) of over $60 million for arts institutions in the state, Rockefeller reflected the same concern that impelled national symphonic leaders to seek federal aid; in fact, as a part of the national and local philanthropic establishment himself, he was acutely aware of the overall financial crisis facing all the arts. In that message he asked for a special "emergency" appropriation of $18.2 million for the arts, including $2.7 million for the sorely pressed New York Public Library.* The following year, when arts support was included in the governor's annual budget proposal as a "line item" of $14.4 million for FY 1972, the library appropriation was omitted, so that the net reduction was about $3 million for the arts. With help from the Concerned Citizens for the Arts, a statewide counterpart of the national Partnership, and with strong support from the governor himself, these appropriations received legislative approval. As noted earlier in our discussion of the Buffalo Philharmonic, the close friendship of Robert Millonzi and Senate Majority Leader Earl Brydges is reported to have been an important factor in the success of this arts legislation.

In the summer of 1970, after passage of the $20.3 million funding for FY 1971, the New York State Council on the Arts was deluged by applications for grants: 807 organizations applied, of whom 596 eventually received them. Since all of the $18.2 million "emergency" appropriation was specified for program grants only, this inundation of applications had to be processed by a staff geared to running a $2 million-a-year operation; the Council itself received some aid from the Ford Foundation to augment its professional staff. The number of applications and the scope of funding necessitated a rather significant change in the criteria previously established for funding. The Council no longer confined itself to project-oriented grants or indirect aid through subsidizing performances, but accepted applications clearly based on supplying part of the supplemental income needed by applicant arts organizations. Though its forms asked these applicants to break their general operations into component projects, showing the gross deficit for each, the central thrust of these applications was directed toward establishing their income gap as a basis for requesting state funds.

In reviewing these applications, the NYSCA employed procedures quite similar to those of the National Endowment: staff review, submission to advisory panels of outside specialists, and final approval by the Council itself. In one respect the NYSCA differs from the National Endowment: in New York the Council has the legal responsibility for final decision, whereas in the federal agency the chairman actually decides (though in practice she seldom goes against the advice of the National Council). As at the NEA, some applications were returned to the applicants or to the staff for further clarification, and in some cases the Council itself overruled the recommendations of the staff or advisory panels. In certain instances—specific organizations or types of arts activity—the Council requested that the staff, together with out-

* This was in addition to a "live item" of $2.1 million in the governor's previously submitted regular budget.

side consultants, prepare special studies, beyond the material supplied by the applicants, to guide its decisions. In the first year of its expanded funding, the New York State Council on the Arts made distributions as shown in Table 15-E.[23]

TABLE 15-E

New York State Council on the Arts

Disbursements in FY 1971

	FY 1971	
	Orgs.	Funding
Museums, galleries, historical societies	125	$ 6,548,891
Performance arts companies and studios	286	6,499,841
Performance sponsors of events	58	1,386,090
Education projects, arts centers	52	1,255,236
Film, photography, TV, audio-visual	42	1,138,804
Poetry and literature	4	206,500
Arts councils and service organizations	29	890,230
Totals	596	$17,925,592

Table 15-F lists the grants made by the NYSCA in FY 1971 and FY 1972 to Major, Metropolitan, and other symphony orchestras in the state.[24]

TABLE 15-F

New York State Council on the Arts

Grants to Symphony Orchestras, FY 1971, FY 1972

Major and Metropolitan	FY 1971	FY 1972	
Albany Symphony Orchestra	$ 15,500	$ 19,250	(126%)
American Symphony Orchestra	65,000	27,000	(41%)
Buffalo Philharmonic	360,000	306,600	(85%)
Hudson Valley Philharmonic	70,000	60,000	(86%)
New York Philharmonic	336,940	146,375	(58%)
Rochester Philharmonic	225,000	190,000	(58%)
Syrachuse Symphony Orchestra	253,000	181,000	(72%)
Others	274,560	86,100	(31%)
Total Grants	$ 1,600,000	$ 1,026,325	(64%)
	(7.9%)	(7.1%)	
Total NYSCA Appropriations	$20,287,392	$14,400,000	(69%)

In FY 1972, the orchestras as a group lost some of their share of the funding from the previous year, though some fared better than others in this respect. In both years, some orchestras also benefited from grants to local groups who in turn engaged orchestras for concert appearances. The Buffalo Philharmonic was one of the largest recipients, along with the Metropolitan Museum of Art, the Metropolitan Opera, and a statewide cultural institution covering all the arts.

Having undertaken this unprecedented funding of the arts in FY 1971, and with the promise of some degree of continuity by subsequent appropriations, the NYSCA continued to build its professional staff and services to the arts in its state. One of its most important innovations was in retaining the services of Bradley G. Morison [25] as consultant, not only to its own staff but also to arts groups throughout the state. Morison, from his headquarters in Minneapolis, had developed a special expertise in management and audience building, though he has refrained from counseling on fund-raising. The Council makes his services available to arts groups in New York State for a variety of counseling services ranging from audience promotion to assistance in filing grant applications with the NYSCA and NEA. He also advises the staff and the Council itself on general policies and on evaluating specific applications.

With what appears to be a reasonably permanent scale of operations, the NYSCA now faces considerable problems, akin to those of the NEA, in handling large volumes of paper work and formulating long-range policies in its funding. To a degree not found in the National Endowment, the NYSCA has developed certain definite ideas of what the organizations it supports should be doing. In part this results from more than a decade of working with advisory panels who had been evaluating the quality of applicants prior to FY 1971, which had brought the Council staff much closer to the activities of arts groups in the state. The regional arts-resource concept, embraced by Howard A. Bradley at the Buffalo Philharmonic, owes much to his discussions with the leadership of the NYSCA,* including Morison, and there is feeling in Buffalo, especially among the Philharmonic musicians, that the extent and size of state aid is to some degree dependent upon implementation of these ideas originating with the NYSCA.[26] This question, involving grave issues of government intervention in policy making, is obviously not one on which one can secure definite information for specific attribution, but there is no doubt that many feel, with some justification, that the NYSCA wields considerable influence. Nor is this influence necessarily resented: many arts leaders speak with admiration and gratitude of the creative force, over and above dollars and cents, exercised by the Council and its staff.

Facing the continued heavy burden of reviewing nearly a thousand applications each year, the NYSCA is reported to be considering the development of certain guidelines for funding those major organizations whose firm establishment and long continuity warrant more or less automatic inclusion in any state program of aid. Such a formula would not preclude their receiving additional funds for innovative programs of their own, nor would it prevent the NYSCA from supporting new organizations of merit. Moreover, each arts group would be as exhaustively reviewed every two or three years as it has been for each annual application. Though the NYSCA has so far proceeded with considerably

---

* The Syracuse Symphony has been especially active in developing diversified regional activities with encouragement from the Council, which in turn has regarded the orchestra as something of a proving ground in this respect.

more flexibility * in its funding than has the National Endowment, both organizations may be moving toward similar procedures from their different present position: the NEA from a strictly project-oriented framework and the New York Council from a more flexible approach to the income gap, both toward some sort of ongoing application of established guidelines with special treatment of innovative projects.

The activities of the NYSCA are by far the most extensive of any state arts council; in fact, they are comparable in scale to those of the National Endowment, exceeding the federal arts appropriation in FY 1971 for the entire nation. Funding of such proportions would not have been possible without the strong leadership of Governor Rockefeller and decisive, if sometimes reluctant, acceptance by the legislators. In its first years of massive impact, the Council was fortunate in having earlier developed an expert professional staff to assure efficient and fair allocation of the considerable funds suddenly placed at its disposal. Finally, the entire program has been supported by a statewide committee of Concerned Citizens for the Arts, a counterpart of the national Partnership for the Arts, with which it actually shares some leadership.

Partnership for the Arts

Government activity in any field with the kind of impact that the National Councils on the Arts and Humanities have developed requires widespread citizen support to assure that the Congress continues to authorize and finance it. The first and most important step in this process, of course, is the recommendation and support of the White House itself, and President Nixon has far outstripped his predecessors both in the amount of money he has recommended for appropriation and in active support of legislation to implement federal arts and humanities.† But, in any legislation affecting special interests, presidential efforts must be supplemented both by the active administrator of the program and by grass-roots advocacy across the nation.

In her first years as chairman of the National Council, Nancy Hanks proved herself an extremely able advocate both before committees and in personal contact with individual Congressmen, supplying them with the data they needed to convince themselves of the program's merit and to influence their colleagues. But she also had extensive nationwide backing through the Partnership for the Arts. In large measure, the phenomenal increases in federal funding from FY 1971 onward were the direct result of aggressive presidential recommendation, Nancy Hanks's superb Congressional liaison, and the Partnership's widespread and effective pressure.

Though originally based on the 1969 *ad hoc* committee of symphony managers and presidents, the Partnership for the Arts has gradually brought

* The reasons for its grants cited in the annual summary of the NYSCA vary a great deal from specific and limited projects to general support of an applicant's operations.
† The arts aspect has far exceeded that of the humanities in public attention, though both receive roughly equal shares.

in representatives of the other arts—theater, dance, opera, and museums.* To support its activities and the printing of large quantities of promotional material, it must rely on the nondeductible † contributions of individuals interested in its cause. As the most highly organized national group in the performance arts, the ASOL has given what help it can, under present IRS restrictions, to the Partnership.

In fact, the symphony orchestras still constitute the strongest force in the Partnership. Through the League and their large audiences and lists of contributors, they provide mailing lists and other channels for the Partnership to distribute its literature and inform the arts-oriented public of its cause and of precisely whom to write in the Congress, Moreover, of all the arts groups, the orchestras feel that they have the biggest stake in government subsidy as the most widespread performance arts activity in the nation. Though their income-gap problems may be no greater individually than in the other arts, they are in most cases more pressing and certainly more highly publicized.

The Partnership itself, in the literature it distributes publicly and which must reach at least some Congressmen, has proposed a goal of federal arts funding in the amount of $200 million, five times that proposed by President Nixon for FY 1973. There are many, both in the arts world and in the Endowment itself, who feel that this emphasis on such a high goal may alienate support by economy-minded legislators or those who are at best lukewarm to government subsidy, to say nothing of providing ammunition for those who are staunchly opposed to it. Amyas Ames, in his public statements, likes to point out that this $200 million figure represents one dollar per person in the national population, or the cost of six to eight miles of interstate freeways now under construction. In substantiating his goal, Ames estimates [27] that the national arts budget reaches an annual total of $2 billion: ‡ he suggests that federal and local governments should supply 10% each of that sum, private contributions another 30%, with the remaining 50% derived from performance income. On the basis of total expenditures by symphony orchestras in FY 1971 of $80–100 million, federal allocations to orchestras should have totaled $8–10 million § instead of the $3 million actually funded, and estimated local grants ($5 million) fell short of Ames's goal by some $3 million.

Apart from setting this $200 million goal, which many now de-emphasize in their advocacy of federal funding, the Partnership has not really attempted to define either a general allocation of government aid among the various arts of a

---

* Since the following description of the Partnership was written before its "merger" in November, 1972, with the ACA, it may not project its future activities and impact realistically in the light of its new institutional relationships.

† Several proposals have been made in the Congress to permit tax-exempt organizations to engage in political advocacy of measures under strict limitations. An early proposal, known as the Muskie-Symington bill, has since been replaced by one sponsored by Representative Al Ullman of Oregon and a large number of colleagues. Actually, arts organizations are not the only ones concerned here: such environmental groups as the Sierra Club are also anxious to have their tax-exempt status clarified in this manner.

‡ Until the Ford Foundation's new data bank or some other agency can verify such a figure, this writer can only state that it seems rather high: the NEA economic estimates in 1971 for the professional nonprofit performance arts alone run considerably under $200 million a year.

§ However, federal funding of $10 million in FY 1971 would have almost wiped out the net financial gap shown in Appendix G.

long-range projection of their overall needs. In setting these forth, it has not taken into account the likelihood that federal funding may have to assume a continually greater burden of total government aid than the local sector. Nor has it made any projections of annual increments in government funding, federal or local, that must be anticipated if it is to keep pace with the growing income gap of orchestras and the other arts. For the present, at least, the Partnership seems to confine itself to promoting the passage of annual federal appropriations for the full amount requested by the president with general advocacy of an ultimate goal of one dollar per person in the national population.

Meanwhile, there has developed in the orchestra sector itself a growing concern that it will receive its fair share of government funding, especially from the National Endowment for the Arts. To date there have been no suggestions as to what that fair share should be, but there have been considerable expressions of dismay that the FY 1972 allocations to symphony orchestras, while higher in dollar amounts, represent a cut from 20% to 14% of the total arts appropriation. The Endowment justifies this policy by pointing out that, among the arts, orchestras received massive aid in FY 1971, far beyond what would normally have resulted from the annual overall increase in funds, and that other arts must also receive similar major increases to establish a general pattern of funding: after FY 1971, for instance, the Endowment increased its allocations to museums and opera companies substantially.

At the same time, there is considerable resentment among some symphony leaders that grants to orchestras are not increasing in proportion to total funds available: by their reasoning, when total funds nearly doubled from FY 1971 to FY 1972, symphony grants should have been closer to $6 million when they were actually $4 million, and the FY 1973 symphony allocation should be closer to $8 million.* They argue, moreover, that the major effort of arousing public support for federal funding has come from symphony leadership and patrons; without the participation of symphony orchestras in the Partnership of the Arts, the annual appropriations might be far more difficult to carry through the Congress.

One manifestation of this appeared early in 1972, in a letter from Senator Charles M.C. Mathias of Maryland to the managers or presidents of all Major and Metropolitan orchestras.[28] After expressing his concern for their financial plight, Senator Mathias asked for an expression of opinion on a proposal to incorporate in the Congressional authorization for arts funding a stipulation requiring a fixed percentage of funds to be specifically allocated to symphony orchestras.

This letter raised serious questions concerning the entire process of federal funding. Should the orchestras make a concerted effort to require that a portion of funds be allocated to them in an obligatory manner, there would have been every reason to expect other arts groups to seek similarly mandated alloca-

---

* Net federal funding, including Treasury Funds but not private contributions to them, for symphony orchestras in FY 1973 was $4,088,065, or 11% of the total appropriation, as compared to 20% in FY 1971 and 14% in FY 1972.

tions, thus making the Congress an arena in which the arts would contest one another for their respective shares of support. The decision on this phase of funding would thus be removed from the professional purview of the Council and Endowment and subjected to the pressures of Congressional logrolling. The threat to the prerogatives of the Council and Endowment was obvious: in fact, one purpose of this suggestion may not have been so much the achievement of legislative determination as rather a warning to the Endowment of the consequences of their not providing better for orchestras.

Not long after this letter was circulated and widely discussed among symphony orchestras, Ames of the Partnership for the Arts explicitly disassociated himself and his organization from this effort, stating: [29]

> The Partnership is not involved in Senator Mathias's plan. We do not think it advisable for orchestras to try to solve their problems by separate legislation, but rather to work within the principles of the National Endowment and solve our problems first by getting really meaningful appropriations, and then bringing pressure to see that those appropriations are effectively distributed. I feel very strongly that the orchestras do need to receive more attention, but I believe they should work together to this end and not do it through the Congress.

Ames's statement was to be expected, coming as it did from the head of an organization concerned with representing as wide as possible a spectrum of arts activity in seeking federal arts funding, but a number of orchestra leaders also responded to Senator Mathias in similar vein, expressing their confidence in the Council and Endowment as the most capable of deciding upon such matters.

In its efforts to organize national support for government funding of the arts, the Partnership needs its own funds to carry on its campaign, and to print and distribute literally hundreds of thousands of brochures stating its case and listing key legislators to be approached. For these it must raise funds that are not tax-deductible contributions, nor may it receive support from organizations that are themselves tax-exempt. Especially when it seeks contributions from the smaller cities, it finds itself in conflict with local arts organizations, themselves already thoroughly canvassing their communities and resentful even of a few thousand dollars leaving their localities to aid a national effort. By creating a national board of directors drawn from a wide variety of cities across the nation and by selecting many of these from nonsymphonic groups, the Partnership has sought to alleviate local or parochial opposition, but it has not succeeded completely in this.[30]

Nor have the local members of the national partnership for the Arts become especially active in organizing their own efforts to gain increased aid from states, cities, counties, or boards of education. With the exception of the Concerned Citizens in New York, which directs its energies toward the state legislature, there seem to be few significant state groups modeled on the Partnership.* The primary thrust of the Partnership aims quite simply at

---

* An exception is a very recently organized group in California, again spearheaded by symphony leaders, which is reported to have had considerable impact on the state legislature there.

arousing public support for federal funding of the arts in general and at securing the passage of annual Congressional appropriations of the full amount recommended by the president.

So far, at least, there appears no sign that within its organization the Partnership concerns itself with developing any kind of a general rationale of public subsidy beyond marshaling arguments in favor of increased funding. As Ames's response to the proposal to specify fixed allocations for orchestras indicates, the Partnership remains aloof from interarts rivalries. On the other hand, it has shown no inclination to undertake a broader study of the actual needs of the arts in truly specific terms directed at the diversified requirements and services characteristic of each type of activity. As noted earlier, Ames's estimate of a total $2 billion annual arts budget may well be rather high; the Partnership should encourage efforts to ascertain and publicize more reliable data of this sort, possibly in cooperation with the Ford Foundation, the National Endowment, and such organizations as the American Symphony Orchestra League and Associated Councils for the Arts. Similarly, Ames's division of income into that from performance (50%), private contributions (30%) state (10%), and federal (10%) undoubtedly reflects his own involvement with a symphony orchestra; it may not be completely valid, especially in its distribution of the public load between local and federal sectors, and it certainly cannot be applied to art museums, for instance. Such omissions undoubtedly have occurred while the Partnership was in its formative stages, but federal funding and the Partnership itself are now established facts of life in the nation's culture: arts organizations, either on their own or through the Partnership, face an obligation to develop and refine their position on government aid as a part of their overall economic rationale.

Need for Guidelines

At a meeting late in 1971 in Chicago, many orchestra representatives pressed Nancy Hanks to abandon the Endowment's current policy of basing grants on specific projects in favor of outright subsidies. Miss Hanks, who had previously held fast to a policy-oriented approach, indicated at that meeting that she would welcome suggestions of alternative guidelines from the orchestras or from the Partnership. Though no response to this suggestion has come from the orchestras, the matter is certainly under intensive consideration. To date, however, there has not been an official exchange of views on substantive proposals between the Endowment and the orchestras. The need for the formulation of more effective guidelines for all government funding has already been implied earlier in this chapter, as well as in the discussion at the end of Chapter XIII on the potential long-range growth of the net financial gap in symphony economics. Certainly a first step would be for these to be established in the federal area: not only does the National Endowment have more funds and a wider area of activity but it can provide a model for states and local governments to follow or modify as they see best suited to their regional conditions. Moreover, with few exceptions, the Endowment has a staff of professional experts much better qualified to participate in such deliberations—a staff that, so far at least, has taken an extremely flexible approach to the diversity of the needs of the arts in general.

However, Nancy Hanks still clings rather tenaciously to some sort of project-oriented funding. Appearing before the ASOL conference at Cincinnati in June 1972, she did not repeat her previous suggestion that orchestras propose their own ideas for modification of guidelines. In fact, the central thrust of her remarks on that occasion was directed toward admonishing the orchestras that their needs had to be viewed in the context of the overall national requirements of all the arts, many of which had yet to receive support comparable to the orchestras. Moreover, from the Endowment's point of view, specific funding of projects has obvious political advantages in securing indispensable Congressional support: legislators show great interest in the specific projects funded in their districts especially when they can point to those projects with mass appeal such as youth concerts, audience-building, free services, or cooperation between diverse arts organizations.

It is obvious that a number of factors must be taken into account in formulating guidelines for government funding of orchestras, based on what is known of their requirements, operations, and diversity, and on their place in the total national arts scene. Though by no means exhaustive, the following suggestions represent an effort to define some of the problems that must be considered.

Financial needs are an obvious starting point and, as we have already seen, one for which considerable data exist in the orchestral area for the projection of future requirements, allowing especially for the unique economics of the income gap. The type of analysis reviewed at the end of Chapter XIII (and detailed in Appendix G) should be refined and expanded to provide more authoritative information about long-rang symphony economics.

Differences in orchestra size and function may require considerable flexibility in guidelines. At present, most Major orchestras could (if they completed their applications correctly) count on federal grants of $100,000 for FY 1972; for the largest this represented as little as two percent of their total budget and for others as much as ten percent.

Total expenditures have recently been suggested as a basis for government funding; Amyas Ames's rationale for annual funding of two hundred dollars is based in part on this criterion. However, as can be seen by comparing the operations of the five categories of orchestra, an across-the-board application of a fixed percentage of expenditures would not necessarily provide an equitable guideline for public support.

Musicians' income could be a major consideration if government funding accepts the responsibility for generally improving the level of professional music across the country, not as mere economic support but rather as a long-range artistic objective. In this respect, those Category C orchestras in areas that can absorb more artistic service (but cannot now afford longer players' contracts) may deserve continuing funding at levels proportionately higher than some already able to maintain year-round operation.

Level of contributions can indicate both community response to an orchestra and its ability to mobilize support. Yet there may be instances—a city with relatively little local-controlled wealth, for example, that needs a better orchestra for its artistic services than can be supported by its own private philanthropy —where such criteria cannot be rigidly applied.

Performance income, like contributions, can be another evidence of a community's response to an orchestra's services. However, low performance income alone should not necessarily deter subsidy: the quality of performing facilities, wealth of the community, and capability of an orchestra to give more concerts than it currently can afford to offer should be taken into account.

Artistic and management quality involve delicate areas of evaluation, but they must be considered in some manner, concerning both current activities and potential for improvement. Equal allocations cannot be conscientiously justified to orchestras of radically differing service and administration.

Innovative programming, both in repertory and in reaching legitimate new audiences, should be encouraged. If this suggests a return to project orientation, it must be emphasized that true innovation is the crux of the issue here. At present, many project-oriented grants are made on the basis of mere bookkeeping segregation of present activities.

Availability of public funds will obviously determine much of the substantive nature of these guidelines, as well as the actual money to be allocated. With large sums at its disposal, the Endowment could be more adventurous in encouraging innovation, for instance. Equally important, however, is the establishment of some predictable level of funding: orchestras must make commitments two and three years in advance, especially for artistic services, and must have some assurances of what they can anticipate from government.

The implementation of such guidelines, once formulated, will require special effort at the outset. Once set up, however, they can be applied on a continuing basis, with year-to-year increments to meet rising deficits and special review only of new proposals for innovation or major changes in the operations of an individual orchestra. Most important of all, any guidelines must be capable of flexible application in individual cases and of progressive change as general conditions require. However, their devising will need a better-organized process of deliberation than now prevails. At present, the initiative is in the hands of symphony leaders and, informally at least, of Endowment personnel. Symphony representation must be more explicitly formalized, possibly through the ASOL; musicians in and out of the orchestras should be involved; and Endowment officials should frankly assume a responsibility to engage in such deliberations rather than step aside and ask the orchestras to propose guidelines.

So far, moreover, we have ignored the larger issues of the relative share that orchestras should receive in total funding. On this, the Endowment and such organizations as the Associated Councils of the Arts must take an initiative not open to symphony leadership. At present, the orchestras seem best organized and most able to present financial data in support of their cause. The other arts, through their own national organizations and the ACA, must assemble comparable supporting data if an overall picture of needs is to develop. Now that the principle of extensive public subsidy of the arts has been established, the next decade should become a period of implementation and policy determination. In many respects, the symphony orchestras have gone further in this process on a nationwide institutional basis than have the other arts. In this they have already uncovered major issues that should affect government arts policy in general.

Mutual Responsibility of Government Subsidy

Though government subsidy of the arts has taken a long time to develop in this country and has grown very often in an almost haphazard manner to meet specific local problems, its greatest impact on the symphony world has been extremely recent. Only with the entry of the National Endowment for the Arts into sizable symphony grants and with the huge state appropriations in New York has large-scale funding, administered by a highly professional staff, become a major concern for symphony orchestras, in terms of the dollars involved and also in the effect of government funding on policy.

Among the feared consequences of government aid, that of reducing the private fund-raising potential of orchestras seems not to have developed. Neither the advent of federal funding nor the Ford Foundation symphony program has caused any decline in private philanthropy: in fact, this has increased, not just in spite of but possibly because of the wider community concern for the arts that these new sources of income have aroused. Nor under the strong leadership of President Nixon and Governor Rockefeller has the feared legislative opposition to appropriations developed, especially since their recommendations received grass-roots support stimulated by such groups as the Concerned Citizens and Partnership. The cause is further advanced when these programs are administered in the orderly and fair-minded fashion developed by the National Endowment for the Arts and the New York State Council on the Arts.

To those who still view the possibility of government intervention in policy direction as a grave danger, Arthur J. Goldberg offered a reasonable answer in his 1961 Metropolitan Opera arbitration statement: [31]

> Many people oppose Federal support on grounds that it will inevitably lead to political interference. This is by no means an argument to be dismissed, and the persons who make it are to be honored for their concern for the freedom of artistic expression. . . . The answer to the danger of political interference, then, is not to deny that it exists, but rather to be prepared to resist it. A vigorous, thriving artistic community, close to and supported by a large portion of the

public, need not fear attempts at interference. . . . The situation is no different from that of academic freedom in our colleges and universities: it is by defending their rights that our faculties strengthen them.

To these comments one must add that there can be different kinds of political interference. The efforts of the National Endowment for the Arts to evaluate applicants and the innovative suggestions developed by the staff of the New York State Council on the Arts are quite different from the ridicule and anger heaped on the WPA Theater Project for attempting to produce *The Cradle Will Rock* or on the State Department for sponsoring an overseas tour by Martha Graham. In the present instances, professional staffs with wide expertise in the arts seek guidance in their review of projects suggested by applicants or offer constructive suggestions to arts organizations in trouble. In both cases, these staffs attempt to place the activities of arts organizations in a broader context than their own leaders may be in a position to develop.

One must distinguish also between those instances in which the suggestions of a professionally staffed government agency challenge the authority of a governing board or management and those in which they hamper the artistic integrity of performance. There remain a number of orchestra musicians in upstate New York who oppose the NYSCA's concept of a diversified musical resource, partly as an economic threat but also because they fear that some of the work required of them will be artistically undignified. To a large degree, in the symphonic area at least, the orchestra musician has not been brought into the funding picture: conductors and board leaders are represented on the National Council, management professionals on the advisory panels, but, so far as can be determined, no orchestra musicians, whose views could be of constructive value and who could act as emissaries to their colleagues in explaining the programs proposed.

In fact, the greatest danger in the present relation between arts organizations and government funding lies, not in the present or potential intervention of these professional staffs, but rather in the degree to which existing patterns in the symphony field are, for better or worse, being preserved. There is a strong tendency to assume that simply because an organization exists and has existed for some time, it automatically qualifies for support. More than that, this emphasis on past performance—on an organization's deserving attention because, like Mt. Everest, "it is there"—makes it difficult for a new enterprise to obtain funds. More often than not, new projects require far more expensive funding to begin their programs, quite out of proportion to what long-established orchestras receive, and involve considerable risks of failure or major modification as they gain experience. The two NEA grants to the Symphony of the New World of $25,000 each, for an orchestra that sought to break new ground in training and giving dignity to the black musician, seem in this context to be modest, to say the least. To be sure, such an orchestra was a hazardous venture—in fact, at present writing it is on the verge of collapse *— but its objectives involved a potential of major significance and demanded

---

* More recently, however, it has been reorganized on what appears to be a stable basis; but such birth pangs are inevitable in this kind of innovative emergence.

greater support. Government funding cannot confine itself only to surefire successes, though these will make the task of seeking appropriations that much easier; in the arts especially, innovation carries with it great dangers of failure but also great potential for new creativity.

The implications of these concerns—the obligation and dangers of government intervention, the necessity for taking daring risks—are by no means lost on the professional arts managers involved in both sides of the process of government funding, as this important development on the symphonic scene emerges from its frail infancy. Amid the jockeying of various organizations and groups of organizations for greater favor and along with the definition of a proper advisory role of government, there must also be developed a strong sense for creative artistic direction, of service to the public and to the music profession—to composers as well as performers. This will be the ultimate justification of supporting an art that will probably always be enjoyed by relatively few, from the funds provided by the many. Even at their present level of nine to eleven percent of the national symphonic budget, public funds place our symphony orchestras under a very special obligation, and their hoped-for expansion will only increase and sharpen that responsibility.

PART FOUR

Music and Its Audience

"By 'listener,' I do not mean the person who simply hears music—
who is present when it is performed and who, in a general way,
may either like or dislike it, but who is in no sense a participant
in it. To listen implies rather real participation, a real response, a
real sharing in the work of the composer and of the performer,
and a greater or less degree of awareness of the individual and
specific sense of the music performed. For the listener, in this
sense, music is no longer an incident or an adjunct but an independent and self-sufficient medium of expression."

ROGER SESSIONS
The Musical Experience

So far this study has been concerned with the ways and means of
the symphony orchestra in the United States—the organizations
and people responsible for symphonic music, the cost of presenting it, and the sources of financing. In such a description it has
seemed at times as if the product of these efforts, the music itself,
and the audience to whom it was directed were almost incidental.
The following pages will be devoted to what certainly is the
raison d'être of the American orchestra, its repertory, its audience,
and its larger educational role. The primary function of the
symphony orchestra is to translate the composer's musical conception into sound that will communicate an artistic experience
to the listener. In institutional terms this involves both the audience and the repertory, with the orchestra acting as the bridge
between them. But this is not a passive role: artistically the or-

chestra performs a creative role of interpretation; institutionally it is motivated by a mission of enriching and expanding the musical experience of its present audience and attracting more people to it.

This effort, in its largest context, embodies in contemporary terms the lofty ideals of Theodore Thomas and Henry Lee Higginson. In what now may sound like quaintly Victorian terms, Thomas's conception of music as a morally uplifting force is but another way of stating what we today regard as the educational mission of the symphony orchestra. As a matter of fact, Thomas's formulation was far more explicit and far more encompassing than many modern statements of the role of the symphony orchestra, and the present-day failure to articulate these objectives will eventually be a major topic of our discussion here.

CHAPTER XVI

The Symphony Audience

The audience should be the most obvious point of departure for our discussion, but in the entire mass of data about the American orchestra there is less concrete information about its audience than any other aspect. We know in detail what the symphony orchestras cost, individually and collectively. We know a great deal about the music they play, as we shall see shortly. But we know appallingly little in concrete terms about the people who attend symphony concerts, and even less about those who do not attend. Even so simple a matter as precise attendance figures is hard to verify with any degree of certainty. Total symphony attendance in 1970–71, paid and free, may have reached thirteen to sixteen million, but by no means that many individuals attended one or more symphony concerts.[1]

"Counting the House"

All symphony audience data must be viewed with caution. In the first place, they are based on estimates of individual orchestras, often made from what can be best described as self-serving motives. Appeals for support of supplementary income to private and corporate donors, foundations, and governments obviously sound better the more one can point to the number of people served. Within even these limitations, one must make further distinctions. Estimates of paid attendance can be, but are not always, verified by a precise ticket count. Estimates of attendance at the growing number of free concerts for schoolchildren, in parks, in shopping centers, and for commercial sponsors are approximate at best. Sometimes such head-counts include estimates of local or national radio and television audiences. Finally, even where paid-admission attendance is based on reliable audits, the subscription series introduces an element of repeated attendance that can sharply reduce the actual number of different individuals attending an orchestra's concerts.

As a hypothetical example, let us suppose that an orchestra gives twenty subscription concerts in a hall seating 2,500 people. If it sells out all of its concerts, it reports a total attendance of 50,000. However, if it sells 2,000 of these seats on season subscription in one series, its actual season attendance, in terms of the number of individuals who attend, would be:

Season subscribers	2,000
Single tickets, 20 concerts @ 500 each	10,000
	12,000

Thus, true attendance for the season becomes only 24% of the claimed figure.* It may be argued that some of the season subscribers share their season tickets with others, but it must also be pointed out that among 10,000 single tickets sold in this example, many were purchased by nonsubscribers also attending more than one concert. Such modifications certainly are valid but we have little data describing them precisely.

We can make therefore only the most approximate estimates of the number of different individuals who attended a symphony concert at least once in 1970–71. It may be less than a quarter of the total attendance figures cited by various authorities. For 1970–71 these range from 12 million to 16 million, depending on the source of information. The National Endowment for the Arts estimated 8.75 million for the Major orchestras, 3.7 million for the Metropolitans, or a total of 12.45 million for the professional orchestras. The more recent survey of Macomber and Wooster cites actual 1970–71 attendance for twenty-eight Major orchestras of 10.6 million; extrapolating that to the Metropolitan group would give another 4.5 million and a combined total of 15.1 million. To these two groups must be added attendance for the smaller orchestras—community, university, and other amateur groups—which may add another million to these figures. All of these estimates include both paid and free attendance.

For their Twentieth Century Fund study in 1963–64, William J. Baumol and William G. Bowen attempted to estimate the total performance arts audience quantitatively and to secure some simple qualitative demographic information about it.[2] Though the quantitative data were broken down into types of performance arts—drama, dance, opera, and symphony—most of the qualitative information reported applies to the performance arts in general. In the symphonic field, Baumol and Bowen relied heavily on two main sources: the files of the American Symphony Orchestra League, and the distribution of questionnaires to the audiences at concerts of nine symphony orchestras. Table 16-A is a modification of one in which Baumol and Bowen summarized paid attendance in 1963–64 for the performance arts;[3] the items in parentheses are additions to their estimates.

The symphony orchestras accounted for 29% of the total attendance at that time and 27% of the individuals attending. However, this did not take into account those people who attend more than one type of performance art. Bowen and Baumol guessed[4] that, in 1963–64, the total number of individuals attending all of the performance arts could have not been much more than 5 million, or about 4% of the national population over the age of

---

* This phenomenon, known to all managers but seldom cited in their attendance reports, has been pointed out by such audience-development experts as Bradley G. Morison as a major factor that must be considered in any discussion of performance arts attendance data.

TABLE 16-A

ESTIMATED PAID ATTENDANCE, BY PERFORMANCE ART, 1963–64
(in millions)

	Estimated Attendance	Average Number of Times Attended in Last Year	Number of Individuals
Orchestras			
Major	6.6		
Metropolitan	2.0	4.8	1.79
Theater			
Broadway	7.0	4.5	1.56
Off-Broadway	0.9	6.5	0.14
Regional	1.5	4.5	0.33
("Road")	7.0	4.5	1.56
Opera	1.7	2.6	0.66
Dance	0.75	2.3	0.33
(Concert recitals)	2.0	4.5	0.44
TOTALS	29.45		6.81

eighteen; when the theatrical "road," recitals, and Metropolitan orchestras (omitted by Baumol and Bowen in this estimate) are added to their figure, their final projection might be increased by as much as 25% to nearly 6.3 million, or 5% of the total adult population. Allowing for a 6.5% increase in population since 1963–64, the present paid performance arts audience, in terms of individuals, may now be as much as 6.7 million.

On the other hand, by applying the 4.8 attendance factor to our earlier estimate of 13–16 million *paid and free* attendance for symphony orchestras, we arrive at a total symphony audience of 2.7–3.3 million individuals, including children, who attended symphony concerts in 1970–71, without knowing how many of these were paying patrons. This represents about 1.2–1.6% of the total population. These figures may be rather low, because the 4.8 attendance factor of Baumol and Bowen applied only to *paid* attendance, and that factor *may* be higher for free admissions; in any case, one can only conclude that the symphony audience—paid and free, children and adults— probably does not exceed 2% of the population.

Especially in recent years, free orchestra concerts—in the parks, for commercial sponsorship, and in schools—have assumed an increasing if varying importance in the overall symphony audience in certain cities. Estimates of their numbers are extremely hard to make, either in specific instances or for the nation in general. We have seen, for example, that in Cincinnati nearly half of the total attendance figure came from estimates of free-admission events; moreover, since their Young People's and Junior High Concerts, amounting to nearly 8% of the total, were, in that case, paid admission, the aggregate of all free concerts including children's, which are in many cities free, could be over 50% of the total attendance with some orchestras. However, Cincinnati probably has a higher proportion of free concerts than many other orchestras, especially in the Metropolitan groups. From a rough check of independent data [5] available at this time, it seems reasonable to estimate that free-admission attendance is 15–30% of the total reported by professional symphony orchestras.

Baumol and Bowen also traced trends in symphony orchestra paid attendance from 1937 to 1964.[6] The average annual attendance for their "basic eleven" Major orchestras shows the following major turning points:

1937	152,000	rising gradually to:
1945–46	254,000	then falling to:
1950–51	204,000	after which there is a steady rise to:
1963–64	278,000	

As Baumol and Bowen point out, the rate of increase shown here from 1947 to 1964 (about 1.1% annually) was actually less than that for the population as a whole.[7] Nor is there conclusive evidence, given comparable and controlled conditions, that the relation of growth in the paid symphony audience to that of the total population has changed in this respect. In a few instances, new areas have been served by emerging orchestras, and there has been a considerable increase in free concerts for both youth and adults. In the crucial area of paid symphony attendance during the past generation, it would appear that the so-called "cultural explosion" has been illusory so far as the orchestras are concerned.* This fact, which most symphony personnel admit only with great reluctance, is a cause for real concern, and will be discussed later in the context of symphony education responsibilities.

Symphony Demographics

For their qualitative data on the performance arts audience, Baumol and Bowen relied heavily on a questionnaire distributed to various theater, opera, dance, and symphony audiences across the country. In most cases, the distribution of these questionnaires was left up to the producer of the performance and no effort was made to control the proportion of subscribers versus single-ticket purchasers or distribution according to ticket price. A similar survey was made in London, with which the American results were compared. Though their general findings applied largely to the performance arts audience as a whole, they did comment on a number of significant differences between it and the symphony sample.[8]

In most respects the profile of the symphony audience followed that of the performance arts audience. It had a substantially higher proportion of college alumni than did the total urban poplation, reaching more than ten times as many individuals who had attended graduate school. In income distribution, the performance arts drew a smaller proportion than the national urban aver-

---

* Though this statement, admittedly based on the fragmentary evidence reviewed here, runs sharply counter to accepted symphonic gospel, it is based on the most reliable data and analysis that I have encountered in exhaustive research. Until more authoritative audience studies can be made, as I hope they will, the conclusions I have drawn seem inescapable.

age from those with incomes below $10,000, and a larger share of those with incomes above. Among those with annual incomes over $25,000 it contained over five times the proportion prevailing in the national population. The median income was nearly $13,000 in 1963–64, twice that of the national urban population. Though the data describing these audiences date back some years, there is reason to believe that, except for general inflationary trends, they still provide a fairly accurate picture.*

Although there were more men (52.8%) than women in the performance arts audience than in the national urban population (48.4%), Baumol and Bowen confirmed the general impression that the symphony orchestra attracts more women than men to its concerts.† They reported that symphony audiences contain a higher proportion of people over sixty than does the performance arts audience or the urban population in general; however, they also take note of the fact that orchestras offer more performances for children than do the other performance arts, though these are not included in their statistical study. Among the occupational groups defined in the performance arts audience, symphony patrons and concert-goers in general include a higher proportion of students, teachers, and professionals.

Occasionally, individual symphony orchestras have attempted to survey their own audiences, with varying success. Often such surveys are directed at specific local questions—parking and restaurant facilities, public transportation, performance time, type of soloists, and structure of the subscription series. One such study, which includes some demographic information as well as responses to local questions, was made by a class in marketing at the University of Washington for the Seattle Symphony.[10] It was confined, however, to mailing out questionnaires to a sample of eight hundred names (many of whom represented more than one season-ticket holder) selected at random from the subscription list for 1969–70. Of over four hundred respondents, 59% were women and the following age distribution was revealed: twenty to thirty years, 11%; thirty to forty years, 19%; forty to fifty years, 22%; fifty to sixty years, 25%; sixty to seventy years, 13%; over seventy years, 10%. These data showed considerable differences from the Baumol and Bowen 1963–64 data for the performance arts audience in general: the proportion of women is nearly 7% higher, and the over-sixty age group substantially larger. This latter figure confirms, for Seattle at least, Baumol and Bowen's general comment that the symphony audience is older than either the urban population or the performance arts audience in general.

Such data must be regarded with considerable reservations. For one thing, both surveys were directed at patrons: those actually attending performances

---

* The new Ford Foundation data bank will employ a national market-research firm to make a full quantitative and qualitative study of the arts audience in general; this should provide in the near future much more reliable information than is presently available.
† Carl W. Shaver has commented, "In a lot of families, the symphony has been like religion— it is put in the wife's name. And it is suspect to a lot of husbands, like the household checking account." [9] My own experience in record retailing and concert management left me with the admittedly subjective, but very definite, impression that record-buying decisions were made more frequently by men and concert choices by women; purchasers of records of serious music were also impressively younger than concertgoers.

in the former study, and an even more selective group of subscribers in the case of Seattle. The latter study, moreover, illustrates the difficulties of using such information in making constructive changes in policy. One would assume that the purpose of such a survey would be to improve attendance, to discover new ways of attracting more audiences. However, in directing this survey to present subscribers, who are already presumably satisfied with the orchestra's offering, the study becomes immediately biased in favor of the status quo.

Discussions of these data with orchestra managers, board members, and others acquainted with the symphony audience, often evoke the response, "So what else is new?" These people, in constant touch with their audiences, give very much the same subjective description that these rudimentary surveys have produced. It is not necessary to make a survey or distribute questionnaires to learn that blacks make up a very small portion of the symphony audience; that fact is there for anyone to see in the lobbies and auditoriums of our concert halls. Nor does an alert orchestra manager need statistics to tell him that his audience is predominantly middle-aged and affluent. Moreover, these observers recognize qualitative elements that have not been measured or described. For instance, there are, in a sense, a number of symphonic audiences —distinct components of the general audience: the ladies who almost literally inherit their subscriptions from generation to generation, the serious music students, the tired businessmen who come with their wives because they do not want the ladies driving home at night alone, the music lovers introduced to the art by recordings, the fans primarily attracted by the charisma of conductors and soloists, the socially ambitious who need to be seen at events carrying the cachet of respectability and prestige. Where an orchestra gives repetitions of the same program, such audience differences can be quite marked: they were noted earlier in the three concerts offered each week by the Philadelphia Orchestra. In other cities, all of these components gather in one audience, as in the five-thousand-seat Salt Lake City Tabernacle.

Nor do such subjective views of the audience necessarily prevail consistently from one orchestra to the next. Many in the symphony field deplore the small proportion of youth attending their concerts, but no one in the Utah Symphony audience can fail to be impressed by the large number of young people there. A new conductor may attract a younger audience, as there is some indication Michael Tilson Thomas has in Buffalo. Most observers agree, however, that the backbone of the symphony audience, the loyal and pampered season subscribers, tend to be older, more prosperous, than the population at large. They point to the increasing obstacles that modern urban living places in the way of involving the age group of twenty-five to forty-five in consistent symphony attendance: the cost and inconvenience of baby-sitters, transportation from outlying suburbs and the difficulty of finding convenient and safe parking, and the competition of other forms of live and televised entertainment. Some find that married couples who were frequent concert-goers in their youth drop out of the audience while raising their children, only to return later.

By and large, these managers and board members become extremely sensitive to the complaints and praise of their audience. Much of the decision on raising ticket prices, for instance, is made on the basis of hunches arising from such contacts—more so, actually, than on any systematic study of market elasticity. When audiences seem happy, when subscriptions hold up well, they are more likely to increase prices than when the orchestra seems in trouble. Two decades ago, most of the orchestras offered only a few subscription alternatives, generally involving a commitment to at least half the programs offered. As seasons have expanded, managements have devised a bewildering array of varied subscription formats: in Cincinnati, there are six different ways of subscribing to some or all of the twenty-four programs offered; the New York Philharmonic, with thirty weeks in its regular season, offers more than twelve subscription combinations, all devised to create attractive alternatives in terms of cost and frequency of attendance.

One of Theodore Thomas's objections to offering the new Chicago Symphony's concerts in the old Auditorium was that its large capacity did not encourage season subscriptions: patrons could select the concerts they wanted to hear and always get a good seat, leaving the orchestra at the mercy of inclement weather and the vagaries of soloist attraction. When the Chicago orchestra moved into the smaller Orchestra Hall, season subscriptions quickly created the basis for audience security. For every orchestra in this nation, the season subscription is the very foundation of its box-office support. Growing criticism, especially in New York, of the season subscription has pointed to the difficulty this scheme places in the way of building an audience from those who cannot or will not buy a series. Though some orchestras limit subscriptions and hold out a certain number of tickets for single sale, often in less desirable locations, the subscription system is, if anything, spreading to other performance arts: in New York, for instance, both the New York City Opera and the New York City Ballet have, in the past few years, intensively and successfully promoted subscription schemes, despite outcries in the press. They have no alternative if they are to secure optimum income from the box office.

Luring the Audience

Important as holding its existing audience is to the orchestra, winning the patronage of the nonaudience remains a major challenge. Actually this involves two separate problems: the determination of potentially interested individuals and groups, their possible receptivity, and their needs that the orchestra can satisfy; and then the employment of techniques to reach them and bring them into the concert hall.

In a sense, many orchestras have put the cart before the horse in devising elaborate promotional campaigns aimed at reaching beyond their present audiences without knowing precisely where to aim. The most obvious efforts to reach a broader public use the mass media of the press, radio, and television to publicize the orchestra's activities, its service to the community, and its financial needs. Such campaigns seek to create a new image of the orchestra, playing down its social exclusiveness and selling the idea that great music exists for the masses. More specific efforts to attract new audiences very frequently employ direct-mail campaigns. The mailing list of any performance arts enterprise has long been considered one of its most highly prized assets. Including not only season subscribers and contributors but also those who order single tickets by phone or mail, such lists can run into the tens of thousands for some orchestras; demographically, the occasional patron is possibly the most likely prospect for acquisition as a subscriber that orchestras currently have.

Some orchestras exchange their mailing lists with other arts groups on the principle that patrons and supporters of theater, dance, and art museums constitute a prime market of culturally inclined individuals who are a potential symphony audience. Running counter to this, however, is the zeal with which some arts groups hold their mailing lists in strictest secrecy: these are considered to be prime assets not to be shared with others.* However, such cooperation, often through "community" arts councils, is on the increase and has proved effective in many areas.

Less selective demographically are the even more extensive mailings made by some orchestras through outside promotional agencies. Danny Newman of Chicago developed such large-scale mailings first for the Lyric Opera there and later as consultant, often under Ford Foundation auspices, to a number of symphony orchestras. Newman is a firm believer in the wide distribution of dramatically designed brochures offering a variety of season-ticket subscription schemes through mailings of literally tens of thousands. Such mailings are carefully planned and directed to areas (usually selected by zip code) of known economic and social potential. Once a positive response has been received from a recipient, his name is programmed in the mailing computer as a prospect to whom future mailings will be addressed more frequently.† Many orchestras have found that such mailings, though expensive at the outset, substantially increase their patronage. These techniques have been greatly aided in recent years by computerized storage and updating of lists and actually addressing materials by electronic means.

Such campaigns are generally devoted to promoting season tickets; they may arouse the interest of some prospects in an especially attractive concert in the series, but their cost can be justified only by securing and, hopefully, holding new subscribers. Moreover, they can succeed only when an orchestra has a product to sell and when it has a reserve of reasonably good seat locations to offer. If an orchestra already enjoys a subscription for eighty percent of its capacity, it not only wastes money in trying to sell the remaining seats with an expensive campaign but also antagonizes the new patrons by being unable to assign them good seat locations. On the other hand, if an orchestra expands its subscription offering by adding a repeat performance to its series, the great increase in capacity can justify the expense and offer some assurance to the

* I recall attending meetings of the various constituents of Lincoln Center for the Performing Arts to consider proposals that all avail themselves of a central computerized mailing service. There was no question of an exchange of lists, but even when all constituents were assured that the computers could not possibly include their patrons in another's mailing, they declined to join in such a joint service.
† More than fifteen years since I last responded to one of its mailings and after four changes of address, I still receive mailings from an arts organization using Newman's services.

new patron of a reasonably good seat location. However, an orchestra that looks to such special promotion to prop up sagging patronage or overcome the unpopularity of its conductor is doomed to failure. Such campaigns work best when an orchestra offers a new series, engages a new conductor, or embarks on building a new image in the community. Sometimes a move to a new auditorium will not only stimulate public curiosity but provide the occasion for capitalizing on that by an aggressive direct-mail campaign.

The Minority Audience

Such efforts, however, concern primarily the building of new patronage within the traditional audience context, particularly the attraction of more people to the regular subscription series of the orchestra. In this, to be sure, they strengthen the financial stability of the orchestra by adding solid and reliable support to its performance income. But there are other types of audience even "newer" than this—ethnic groups in the urban centers, youth, audiences for special repertory, and those whose dispersal to the suburbs has made regular symphony attendance more difficult.

Since symphony orchestras exist in the context of the modern urban environment, they have become acutely aware of the impact of contemporary urban problems on all phases of our cultural life. Some orchestras, such as those of Cincinnati and Cleveland, find themselves actually performing their concerts in the midst of the black ghetto, into which their white affluent audiences must come to concert halls now surrounded by slums. In some instances there have been serious manifestations of interracial hostility, mostly confined to tire slashing or verbal abuse of patrons but with a potential for more serious expression. Conversely, some orchestras have attempted to bring their services to ethnic groups other than the WASP constituency to whom they have traditionally appealed. The Open Door Concerts presented by the Cincinnati orchestra have their counterpart in the Phoenix Symphony's visits to Navajo centers, where its repertory includes some music based on Indian themes.

Such efforts, commendable as they are in the context of a general recognition of the ethnic diversity of American culture, remain peripheral to the central concern of our orchestras with the musical art of Western civilization. Their future prospects will depend much on the eventual resolution of the conflicting forces in American society, challenging our traditional view of it as a melting pot, as diverse ethnic groups seek their own type of expression in their own way. In fact, some view these attempts of orchestras, like those of other arts groups, to reach hitherto neglected ethnic groups as a residue of interracial thinking of a generation ago; many, especially in the more militant segments of these groups, want nothing to do with the art of white, Anglo, or Western European culture and view its imposition on them as a form of cultural castration.

To the degree that these ethnic groups desire to become a part of the majority culture, their absorption into the symphony audience will require much more than audience promotion. If they are to feel that they are a real part of the symphony institution, they must see their "brothers" accepted in the orchestra as musicians, managers, conductors, board members, and composers. While it cannot be denied that minority-group musicians are seldom encountered in our orchestras, there is ample evidence that management and artistic direction would not only welcome such players but has been actively recruiting them. The difficulty resides in the fact that the home environment and entire social context of these groups have not been conducive to early and intensive training in instrumental music. The example of the New Orleans Philharmonic in sponsoring the training of black children in instrumental music deserves emulation by other orchestras, not so much for immediate gains as a source of talent a generation hence. Similarly, the Youth Symphony in Albuquerque can eventually introduce Spanish-speaking children to orchestral music and hopefully guide some of them to careers as musicians or future participation in the audience.*

In securing a place in the symphonic repertory for his compositions, the black or ethnic-minority composer shares with his white colleagues a more general problem to be discussed in the next chapter. Yet there has been much discussion in recent years within symphony management of the degree to which orchestras can and should modify their repertory in deference to the ethnic-minority audience. In a sense this discussion parallels the wider concern with the status of these minorities. When a music director asserts that he will be happy to program music by black composers if it is up to the standard of the rest of the repertory, he says the same thing that employers do when they express their willingness to hire blacks if they can do a job as well as their other workers. There are many who feel that orchestras should make special allowances for music by black composers, just as many in education advocate relaxing university admission standards for black high-school graduates. Others argue that music is a universal language regardless of the color of its composer's skin, but there is no doubt that, from the point of view of stimulating interest in attending symphony concerts, the inclusion of ethnically oriented repertory is a potent attraction.

In the hundred-odd Major and Metropolitan orchestras of this nation, there is now but one black musical director—Henry Lewis of the New Jersey Symphony Orchestra; there are certainly other talented and thoroughly experienced black conductors equally worthy of holding similar positions of artistic responsibility. In fact, resident conductors of Japanese origin among our orchestras outnumber native blacks. There are, to be sure, several black assistant conductors, just as there have been a few in the upper, but not top, ranks of orchestra administration. A few orchestra boards have explicitly sought black leaders for their membership. Insofar as they draw upon those minority individuals willing to be assimilated into the majority culture, the

---

* Following a legal civil-rights challenge to its hiring policies, the New York Philharmonic has recently instituted a broad program of encouraging black musicians to apply for positions in the orchestra and of actually organizing training orchestras to bring such musicians up to its performing standards.

involvement of them in artistic direction, administration, and policy making can be as essential as embracing black players and composers.

All of these efforts to secure a wider ethnic participation thrust the orchestra institution very much into the midst of contemporary urban life. Whether motivated by pressure to increase performance income, by a determination to broaden the scope of services, or by a desire to contribute through the symphony orchestra to the solution of the pressing social issues of our times, these efforts need more than patronizing good intentions, and they raise serious problems of insincerity and tokenism unless carefully conceived and implemented.

There is still another cultural minority much neglected by our symphony orchestras consisting of those, undoubtedly far fewer than the regular orchestral audience, with an interest in the wide variety of serious music for forces smaller than the full orchestra, or in the contemporary repertory, much of it composed for unusual combinations of instruments. To the degree that the symphony orchestra has become the focal point of a community's music profession, its players constitute the most obvious performing force for such programming with an appeal more limited than its central efforts. The special programs of contemporary music, often with explanation and discussion by composers, presented since 1971 by the New York Philharmonic render an important service that might well be emulated by other orchestras, a service that would be all the more valuable in other cities where such concerts are not offered by other groups as they are in New York. Quantitatively, the audiences for such efforts will be small, but the musical forces employed will also be smaller; this type of program for a different type of audience lends itself especially to those orchestras seeking diversified utilization of their players' services. For the audience, as well as for such enterprising young musicians as Michael Tilson Thomas, such programs would be a relief from the "old format" of symphony concerts.

Another specialized audience, that of young people, will be discussed in greater detail when we deal with the broader educational functions of the orchestra in a later chapter. But it, like the other "minority" audiences considered here, illustrates the profound interrelation between the audience and the music offered to it. As orchestras increasingly assume wider artistic responsibilities for community service, for their own sake or to utilize the performing staff at their disposal, the building of a far more diversified audience than traditional concert-goers becomes a major challenge to the orchestra.

The Physical Setting

Symphony orchestras have long concerned themselves with the physical facilities to which they bring their audiences for performance. On a number of occasions, Theodore Thomas expressed the opinion that part of his failure to organize a permanent orchestra in New York was due to the lack there of proper performing facilities; he played a major role in persuading Cincinnati to build its Music Hall, and both he and Higginson later recognized the importance of having specially designed halls for their respective orchestras. More recently, in the euphoric cultural explosion of the early 1960s, some performance arts organizations were tempted to succumb to the "edifice complex," but with the completion and actual use of some of these buildings, a more realistic appraisal of them set in: operating costs of modern air-conditioned buildings proved to be far greater than those of older auditoriums, and though production and audience amenities proved superior, it is no secret that some of these new halls and theaters had appreciably inferior acoustics built permanently into their steel and concrete. Some, to be sure, were vast improvements in physical environment, acoustics, and audience comfort. In some cities, universities constructed excellent new performance facilities for their own functions, but designed them also for use by local orchestras, which were thus saved the expense of constructing their own facilities. Possibly the most productive ventures worked on a more modest scale, eschewing elaborate newly constructed arts centers in favor of remodeling older existing structures: the renovation of the old civic auditoriums in Seattle and Portland, Oregon, and of the vacant but spacious motion-picture theaters in Pittsburgh and St. Louis, provided orchestras with new homes of greatly improved utility and quality without involving the organizations themselves in a crushing financial burden. Where orchestras themselves undertook the acquisition and renovation of such old structures, they combined the appeal for building funds with the drive for capital to meet the challenge of the Ford Foundation symphony program. By no means all of our professional orchestras now enjoy the use of completely adequate facilities, but a vast general improvement has been one of the more constructive aspects of symphonic developments in the past decade, and there can be no doubt that some of these new auditoriums have not only made the performance of symphonic music more agreeable for the players and conductors but have also increased audience interest.

On the other hand, some orchestras have encountered increasing problems arising from the location of their auditoriums in city centers, often in areas of urban decay. With the exodus of the affluent population into the suburbs, transportation by private automobile has created a serious impediment to frequent and regular attendance. Orchestra managements express concern, varying from serious to crucial, over the lack of convenient and safe parking facilities for their patrons. (The only major exception was Los Angeles, where the new arts center was built over a huge garage, used in the daytime for public parking and at night by those attending performances in the three theaters in the complex.) The removal of a large portion of the audience to the suburbs has also created another obstacle to regular concert attendance: the concert-goer must return from work to home in the suburbs, eat dinner, change clothes, and return to the inner city unless he or she opts for the additional expense of eating at a downtown restaurant. Some orchestras have experimented with considerable success in advancing the time of their evening concerts, and Cincinnati has moved its traditional afternoon concerts into the morning to encourage young matrons to attend more conveniently.

In some widely dispersed metropolitan areas, orchestras have met patrons' reluctance to come regularly into the urban center for concerts by taking their performances into the suburbs. This holds considerable promise for others, especially when there are adequate performance facilities in arts centers and school auditoriums in the area surrounding the core city. The New Jersey Symphony Orchestra, in fact, has shifted a major portion of its activity from the central city of Newark into the suburbs on the New Jersey shore of the Hudson. It has not, it must be noted, forgotten its role of serving the Newark community: with special programming and promotion similar to the Open Door series in Cincinnati it has sought to find an audience in the highly compacted black residential areas of the city. Though it draws some supplemental income from suburban business, it has yet to gain substantial support from those in New York City, where most of its suburban audience works.

Here we find two opposing trends: construction of more attractive facilities in the urban core and taking the orchestra out into the suburbs. With the increasing diversification of musical services by many orchestras, further dispersal and variety of activities seems likely. The more that management develops performances by ensembles and chamber orchestras, the more likely it is to find performance facilities and audiences in the area surrounding the city, thus serving those who cannot or will not come into the center for concerts. At the same time, by arousing interest in its music near the homes of its audience, it may encourage some of these patrons to make the added effort to travel into the city for concerts there.

As player contracts increasingly run for all or most of the year, managements have turned to outdoor summer concerts, held in city parks, stadiums, and other facilities where the physical setting often limits the effective presentation of serious music. Several years ago, the New York Philharmonic developed a portable shell for its park concerts that could be transported on a large trailer truck and incorporated a sophisticated audio system to amplify its sound. More recently, under a grant from the National Endowment for the Arts, the St. Louis Symphony Orchestra and the state arts council of Missouri have engaged a team of structural and acoustic engineers to develop a more elaborate "environment" for outdoor symphony concerts that holds great promise: it not only includes an imaginatively designed stage and covering for the orchestra, but also employs a highly sophisticated audio system to reinforce the "live" sound.

Electronic Media

Whatever may be one's misgivings about the relative role of "canned" versus "live" music, the importance of the electronic media cannot be ignored. An orchestra playing a concert for fewer than three thousand people in its auditorium can bring that same program to millions over the radio or television. A composition of such limited appeal as to restrict its frequent performance on the programs of any one orchestra can find a nationwide audience to justify the investment of time and money in a recording; such recordings can, in some instances, arouse a growing interest in new repertory that may eventually find a more prominent place in the concert repertory. At the same time, the electronic media have made music one of the most ubiquitous phenomena of our daily lives: in office-building elevators, from blaring transistor radios carried on the streets or on public transportation, in restaurants and places of work, and as an enhancement of the "selling" message of radio and television commercials—no one can escape hearing a constant flow of music, most of it bad and atrociously reproduced. There can be a grave danger of something like Gresham's Law in economics operating in the music experience: that bad music will drive out good. Listening to music used to be a special occasion before the advent of these various forms of Muzak: an individual chose the time and place, considered the artist and his program, and paid his admission, all of these being conscious and planned choices expressing a desire and involving his direct participation in the musical experience. To the degree that "wall-to-wall music" becomes a substitute for serious and attentive listening, it degrades the art as a valid musical experience and damages the cause of music in general and symphony orchestras in particular.

Obviously the electronic media perform a valuable service to orchestras, by no means confined to their economic benefits. Recording has produced the greatest financial return, but only in the case of the larger Category A orchestras, though many of our smaller orchestras have occasionally recorded. (Of these only the Utah Symphony and Louisville Orchestra have done it extensively.) Some orchestras broadcast on a sustaining basis all or a part of their regular concerts, often by taping performances for later broadcast to avoid competing with their concerts. So far only a very few orchestras appear regularly on television: the nationwide youth programs of the New York Philharmonic on commercial networks, the "public" television programs of the Boston Symphony, and the occasional appearance of other orchestras on their local commercial or, more frequently, "public" stations can hardly be considered extensive video exposure of symphonic music. Future developments of video cassettes for home use and of cable television are being watched by some orchestra managements, who see further potential for their orchestras in the electronic media.

Orchestras engage in broadcasting and recording for two reasons: the possibility of additional performance income and their availability as a means of disseminating their music to a wider audience. The economic benefits are limited both by the restricted audience for symphonic music, whether in actual sale of recordings or in broadcast producers' sensitivity to audience ratings, on the one hand, and by the higher musicians' pay required, on the other. In the case of the audience, of course, orchestras face the same problem here as they do in their live concert activities: it is very unlikely that the potential public for broadcasts and recordings appreciably exceeds the two percent of the population indicated in previous discussion of the symphony audience. It undoubtedly contains some music lovers who do not regularly attend concerts, but it also includes fewer of those patrons going to concerts for nonmusical reasons. Moreover, the costs of broadcasting or recording are vastly higher than they are for performance: the musicians' payroll for a typical long-playing record may run as high as $100,000, even when the music has been rehearsed for a regular concert. For this reason, American record producers and foreign companies distributing records in this country prefer to make recordings abroad, where musicians' pay for such services is less than one-third of the domestic rate.* Radio and television pay scales are comparable, though not as high in view of their evanescent nature. Given these high costs, it is obvious that commercial producers will be reluctant to risk their investment on such projects with relatively limited hope of financial return. A few of the very largest orchestras, because of their prestige or that of their conductors, have sufficient appeal to justify electronic dissemination on a profitable basis, but most other orchestras, when they succeed in making such arrangements, do so by special agreement with their players, such as was until recently in effect with the Utah Symphony. Other orchestras permit local sustaining or educational broadcasting by unanimous consent of the players, and a few tape their concerts for syndicated national distribution by allocating a considerable portion of the income to such musicians' benefits as pension funds.

From time to time, orchestra managements have sought general modification of the union scale for recording through AFM-approved schemes similar to those which some individual orchestras have negotiated locally, but they have encountered powerful resistance at the AFM both from a fear of breaking down the national scale and from the opposition of those orchestras and players who now benefit from the present scale. Symphony players' representation in the AFM negotiations with the recording and broadcasting industries has so far been limited to players from the largest orchestras working under full scale; those from the Utah Symphony or from orchestras with an interest in modifying these prohibitive scales do not participate. The ASOL has a special committee working on the problem of current scales and on the prospects for greater symphonic participation in future developments in cable TV and video cassettes. Though it has been in touch with the AFM, it apparently has not consulted ICSOM, where much of the players' power centers on such issues.

These considerations have taken on a new urgency in anticipation of the development in the near future of video cassettes and cable TV. Though the present cassette technology still remains short of full commercial application, there can be no doubt that some form will be marketed extensively in the next decade, and all of the unions concerned have already established their economic position in anticipation of these developments.† At present, there is every indication that such arrangements will follow the pattern of the current media and that costs for symphony orchestras will be comparably high. Al-

* An orchestra player in London told me that he and his colleagues considered the present American recording scale the "biggest gift" his overseas colleagues could have made; without recording activity, the London orchestras (the BBC excepted) could not survive.

† The AFM even persuaded its "brothers" in the British unions to refrain for the time being from recording material that can eventually be used in video-cassette form.

ready a number of producers have begun to tape-record program material in Europe, at lower cost, in anticipation of the development of commercial distribution of video cassettes for home use.

In cable TV there is also a great potential for symphony orchestras, less by live broadcast than for distribution through video tapes to local operators. Cable TV shares with the video cassette a great advantage for symphony orchestras: their limited appeal, which virtually excludes them from commercial broadcasting, can be compensated for by the greater diversity of choice offered by the public. With a variety of cassettes to choose from (as in disc recording) or a large number of cable-TV channels to select (a potential of nearly fifty in some systems), the possible appeal to a limited audience becomes far greater than in conventional television limited to only a few channels. However, in the case of cable TV, which requires local licensing for its distribution system, many city governments have granted franchises that do not require significant educational or cultural programming; as a consequence, all too many present cable-TV operations offer nothing more than the same programs, often syndicated reruns of old shows, that are seen on present commercial TV. In this respect, local symphony managements have a clear stake in influencing the government process whereby cable-TV franchises are granted.*

However, it is possible to overestimate the importance of these video media to the symphony orchestra. Though opera, theater, and dance can be adequately and often effectively transferred to the video tube, recitals and symphony concerts gain little in the visual medium beyond what they offer on radio or recordings; in fact, the present audio systems of television receivers, which will also be used for cassettes and cable TV, fall far short of the fidelity offered by good FM radio or recordings. Moreover, recitals and symphony concerts suffer seriously from their lack of genuine visual interest: too many producers and directors find it necessary to invent a visual interest in such productions that has nothing to do with the music.

Thus, of the various electronic media, recording for home use or radio broadcast remains the most important means by which symphonic music reaches the widest audience. In this it performs a valuable function in bringing music to an audience and in influencing its taste. Though it is impossible to know just how effective records and radio broadcasts are in building new symphony audiences, there is ample indication of its force in shaping audience preferences. In the next chapter we shall observe how the music of Mahler has in the past decade increased greatly in popularity as reflected in frequency of performance; to a large degree, the Mahler boom started with recordings of his music by such popular conductors as Leonard Bernstein. When other conductors emulated his example in their concert programming, they found a warm response from their audiences already prepared by records or broadcasts of them. The same is true of the recent surge in popularity of Baroque music and early Haydn symphonies, which first appeared on recordings and then in symphony programming, and we probably owe our acquaintance with more

---

* Though primarily concerned with the educational potential of cable TV, an "occasional paper" published by the National Education Association, *Cable TV—Protecting its Future in Education* offers general suggestions in this regard that could be of interest to orchestras.

than one or two Dvořák symphonies to recordings. A perusal of the Schwann catalog will readily demonstrate that the recorded symphonic repertory is far more extensive than that of any of our orchestras: in this respect, recordings have a continuing potential for broadening the musical experience of their listeners and thereby having an important impact on the receptivity of the symphony concert audience.

Terra Incognita

Yet, in our understanding of the symphony audience, we are faced with two very large unknowns. We know very little, as we have seen here, about the people who attend symphony concerts—regularly, as subscribers, or occasionally, as single-ticket purchasers or sharers of a season subscription. In fact, we know little about the real frequency of attendance on the part of any patrons, or of the reasons for their variation in attendance. Most important, however, for building of new audiences, we know practically nothing about those who do not attend concerts: those who attend other performance arts and those still beyond the reach of any of them.

In an activity such as the performance arts, in which 7% of the adult urban population at most can be counted as the audience for paid-admission involvement, any increase in this percentage by attracting a small portion of the rest of the population can produce rather large economic benefits to the sponsoring organization. An increase of 0.5% in the population attracted will enlarge the symphony audience by over 30%; this could produce $15 million in additional income. Yet orchestra management, for all its concern with increasing audiences, knows appallingly little about the symphonic nonaudience, what it consists of, what it wants, or how in practical terms it can be attracted. One can attend countless meetings of symphony management, at ASOL conferences or elsewhere, and hear the same tired talk of audience building—special promotions, ethnic programming, popularization of repertory, employment of Madison Avenue techniques—without hearing one comment that concerns itself either with hard facts about the nonaudience or with any understanding of the psychological process involved in artistic communication. Such failure would still be deplorable if symphony audiences were keeping pace with population growth; it becomes critical when there is good reason to believe they are not.

The symphony orchestras have been extraordinarily remiss in not placing emphasis on a systematic and statistically authoritative study of audience potential in this country. The tools for securing such data have long existed in the now highly sophisticated research facilities developed in commercial marketing techniques. Such research is expensive, requires expert programming, and is probably beyond the financial resources of any one orchestra, but, properly planned, it could be undertaken by a group. Some resources exist in this area. The ASOL has a considerable mass of information, most of it not explicitly directed toward this problem but much of it in a form that could give the programmers of such a study relevant guidance in structuring their approach. The recently organized research projects of the Ford Foundation and the National Research Center for the Arts have the facilities for undertaking this kind of study. These will need help from the orchestras themselves, both in supplying raw data and in advising on the questions most requiring answers.

To a large degree, orchestra management and boards of directors have concentrated their attention on their present audiences and on augmenting them with similarly inclined patrons. In this a major concern of managers, conductors, and boards has been to keep their present subscribers happy with the repertory offered them.

In theory, at least, artistic policy is the domain of the conductors, but there are few of them who are not sensitive, subtly and indirectly or under considerable overt pressure, to the response of the audience to their programs and performance, and fewer still whose decisions are not to some degree influenced thereby. In some orchestras, as we have seen, a music advisory committee of the board formally transmits such response. In others, the conductor, though theoretically autonomous, receives informal advice on a more or less friendly basis from the manager and trustees. In other situations, varying applause and empty seats will tell a conductor more than any music advisory committee can transmit formally.

In this there lurks a great danger that such influence on artistic policy can become regressive: the subscription audience, attracted by past performance, resists changes and threatens to depart if changes become too evident. Unless there is a good chance that defectors can be replaced by others more receptive to innovation, management would rather hold on to the subscribers it now has than risk their loss in favor of the doubtful acquisition of new ones. Nor is management alone in this: the conductor's own ego, his inner urge for success and acclaim, often prevents his taking chances with his audience. Moreover, both conductor and management are far more sensitive to a few adverse criticisms than they are to the silent acquiescence of the many. This is especially true when complaints come from trustees themselves or are expressed to trustees by major donors. Apparently this happened in Buffalo, where Lukas Foss's innovative repertory was blamed all out of proportion for the orchestra's ills at a time when objective data did not support the attack on his programming. But a stern lecture from a donor to a trustee at a country-club cocktail party, or a stream of letters to the newspapers—even if from only a score of patrons out of thousands—can carry more weight with management appraisal of artistic policy than can the passive acceptance, or even cordial welcome, of the vast majority of the audience. In symphony affairs, as elsewhere in matters involving public response, the adage of the squeaky wheel prevails. A major indicator of audience satisfaction or dissatisfaction with an orchestra's performance and programming could be the degree to which subscribers do or do not use their tickets, but it is difficult to determine the "normal" rate of such abstention, and orchestra managements that have such information are loath to share it with others.

The sensitivity of management to the audience's response to programming is by no means unjustified, however. Unless the music presented meets some need, gives some special pleasure, to the audience, an orchestra is wasting its time and the resources of community support. But an evaluation of this repertory-audience relationship requires a deeper comprehension of the content of symphony programs and of the impact of their presentation on the listener than explored so far in this study, and the conservative approach to audiences has its counterpart in the content of the programs offered by our orchestras. Neither audience nor repertory can be viewed in isolation, and no one will ever resolve the chicken-and-egg question of whether conservative audiences demand conservative programming or whether the repertory attracts its own kind of public.

CHAPTER XVII

Repertory

We often hear the repertory of the American symphony orchestra described as a musical museum, usually as a disparaging commentary on the heavy preponderance of the "Fifty Pieces" in the orchestras' programming. The repertory of our orchestras, and its consequences for their survival, has caused Oliver Daniel to complain that the "rut which programmers have gotten into is still appallingly deep," [1] and Leonard Bernstein to meditate, Hamlet-like, on the pros and cons of the "present crisis in composition and its possible consequences in the future." [2] Suspending for the moment a consideration of the merits of these criticisms, let us first attempt a description of the music played by our orchestras.

There are two major sources of information about the repertory of American symphony orchestras: a comprehensive compilation of the subscription programs of twenty-seven Major orchestras going back to 1842, complied by John H. and Kate Hevner Mueller; [3] and annual surveys of a broader sampling of programs—presented by from seventy-four to more than six hundred symphony orchestras—made by Broadcast Music, Inc., and the American Symphony Orchestra League between 1959 and 1970. [4] Though there are fundamental differences in their respective methods, these two surveys * offer an exhaustive resource for describing the repertory of our orchestras.

The first of these studies, and the most extensive in time span, was begun by John H. Mueller, a sociologist at Indiana University, author of *The American Symphony Orchestra: A Social History of Musical Taste.* Though this book contained a great deal of important general and historical information about seventeen Major orchestras, Mueller's central concern was to describe musical taste in terms of the symphonic repertory, based on a comprehensive study of the music actually played by these orchestras. He

---

* Both surveys are in danger of being abandoned. Mrs. Mueller has completed hers only through the 1969–70 season and has no intention of carrying it further. She hopes to preserve these data on computers and plans to publish a great deal of it through the Indiana University Press. In his preface to the 1969–70 BMI survey, Oliver Daniel expressed doubt about the usefulness of continuing these annual comprehensive surveys.

continued his interest in this subject after publication of his book, and since his death his elaborate system of files and charts has been continued by his wife, herself a professor of education with an interest in aesthetics. Recently, with financial help from the Rockefeller Foundation and Indiana University, and with clerical assistance from students at the university, Mrs. Mueller has brought her husband's files up to date as of the 1969–70 concert season.

In reviewing the data thus assembled by the Muellers, one must understand certain fundamental assumptions in their procedure. From the beginning of their study of the symphony repertory the Muellers realized that some type of weighting was necessary to reflect the importance of the varied compositions they dealt with: Mozart's Overture to *The Marriage of Figaro* obviously could not carry the same statistical importance as Mahler's Second Symphony. In an early publication, *Trends in Musical Taste,* published in 1941 by the Indiana University Press in its monograph series, John H. Mueller used an arbitrary weighting method, which he abandoned when he wrote his book ten years later. There he introduced into his statistical analyses a weighting in terms of performance length; one performance of the Mahler symphony (seventy-five minutes) assumes as great an importance in their summaries as do nineteen performances of the Mozart overture (four minutes). All of the data from the Mueller studies cited here are based on this accumulated total of performance times in minutes.

A second assumption embodied in these data arises from the fact that the Muellers included only the basic subscription series of some twenty-seven Major orchestras,* as classified by the American Symphony Orchestra League. They did not take into account the repetitions of the individual programs they studied; even if, in a subscription series, a program was played several times, its contents were recorded only once. Nor did they attempt to include popular or children's programs, tours, summer concerts, or any repertory played outside the basic subscription series as reflected in the published programs of the orchestras. Thus, in omitting such popular programs as the Boston "Pops" and other lighter orchestral offerings, the Muellers do limit their coverage of the total orchestral repertory.† Moreover, by confining their study to these Major orchestras, the Muellers of course tell us nothing about the repertory of some thirty-five to seventy other professional orchestras in this nation. However, outside of such rare cases as the Louisville Orchestra, anyone acquainted with the overall orchestral scene will agree that, by and large, the smaller orchestras' repertory rather closely mirrors that of the larger ones, the one possible exception being in the presentation of difficult new music.

As a first step, the Muellers recorded data from symphony programs on index file cards, each indicating the orchestra that played a given work and

* The Mueller survey includes the New York Symphony programs in its data from 1875 to 1930. Actually, only twenty-six present Major U.S. orchestras are covered. For a list see Appendix M.
† In their 1941 monograph the Muellers commented briefly on popular repertory, but their observations hardly apply to the current scene.

the season of performance. From these cards, Mrs. Mueller has prepared a five-hundred-page summary of the symphonic repertory, listed alphabetically by composer, on which is reported each performance of a work by orchestra and season. From these data, the Muellers have extracted a variety of summary analyses designed to describe the symphonic repertory from various points of view.* As we shall see, certain composers very much dominate the symphonic repertory, and the Muellers show their relative importance over a period of years both as regards the national repertory as a whole and in the repertory of specific orchestras. Similar analyses have been made in terms of the composers' nationality. Since no American composers figure in the dominant group, the Muellers made separate studies of them in tabular and graphic form. John H. Mueller's book included other special studies, such as trends in the popularity of given composers, which have been continued and elaborated by his wife.

The BMI annual surveys are based on different methods. Because all orchestras must report their programs to BMI as a part of being licensed to perform copyright music, and because the ASOL also receives concert programs from its member orchestras, a large mass of raw material was available to this joint effort, which has employed computers to record and analyze these data. From seventy-four orchestras in 1959–60, the number of orchestras covered increased by 1969–70 to six hundred and twenty. The expansion of this survey can be seen in the following summary: [5]

	1959–60	1969–70
Orchestras	74	620
Performances	4,352	26,214

("Performances" here refers to the number of times all compositions were played.)

The BMI survey differs from the Muellers' in that it studied a much larger sample of orchestras for a much shorter span of time; data were reported annually, not for the five-year periods established by the Muellers. BMI included all programs—popular, tour, children's, and so on—not just subscription, though, as we shall see later, it distinguished between types of program in its last two surveys. Moreover, the BMI statistics are in the form of number of performances of a given work, whereas the Muellers weighted these in terms of playing time; this distinction will play an important part in our efforts to correlate these two sources. Because BMI was deeply concerned with the performance of the composers of music under copyright, many of whom it represented in the collection of performance royalties, its surveys give information on the relative importance of contemporary music in the symphonic repertory not easily obtainable from the Mueller studies. However, the Muellers offer data before 1959 of major historical interest not available from BMI.

---

* I have used only a small portion of these in my more general discussion here, but the forthcoming publication of the Mueller data will include them.

Composer-Nationality Trends, 1890–1970

Compiling data from their index cards listing compositions and the orchestras playing them, the Muellers made several general analyses of repertory, based on five-year periods of activity. They charted the contribution to the repertory since 1890 * of each of more than thirty most frequently performed composers; they also made similar charts for each of some twenty-five important composers, showing their contribution to repertory of each of the orchestras studied. In their analyses of the repertory in terms of the national origin of composers, they generally assigned a composer to the country of his mature activity or to his stylistic affinity: Handel is listed as a British composer, Chopin as French, and Liszt as Austro-German, but Stravinsky is classified as Russian. These composer-nationality analyses cover the total United States symphonic repertory as well as that of individual orchestras.

The composer-nationality components of the American symphonic repertory are shown in Table 17-A, where the various percentages of nationality are indicated for each five-year interval during the eight decades studied.

This illustrates graphically the domination of the repertory by three nationalities—Austro-German, Russian, and French—followed invariably in fourth place by American music. The three leading nationalities combined contributed from 76% to 87% † of the total music played. Of the three, the Austro-German component has always been by far the largest: it has varied from a high of 65% in 1890–95 (still higher in previous years) to a low of 46% in 1940–45, the only five-year period in which this component dropped appreciably below 50%. This drop in 1940–45 undoubtedly reflects anti-German sentiment during World War II; a similar drop, from 59% in 1910–15 to 50% in 1915–20, can be traced to similar causes. However, the next four nationalities in order of importance—Russian, French, American, and British—responded in a rather different manner in the two wars:

	1910–15	1915–20	1935–40	1940–45
Russian	13.47%	15.17%	16.10%	19.68%
French	11.48%	15.99%	12.72%	10.39%
American	4.53%	7.67%	6.34%	8.37%
British	2.21%	1.55%	3.06%	3.65%

These reflect popular sympathies as regards the identity of our allies in these wars: in 1915–19, the Russians and French were favored, symphonically

* Some of the Mueller analyses go back to the founding of the Philharmonic Society of New York in 1842, but until 1890 there were only three orchestras covered: the Philharmonic, the New York Symphony, and the Boston Symphony; Thomas's orchestra was unfortunately not surveyed. Only after 1890 was there enough nationwide symphonic activity to justify national data.

† All percentages are my own computation from the Muellers' recording of performance times.

Table 17 A

Composer-Nationality Share in U.S. Symphony Repertory 1890–1970

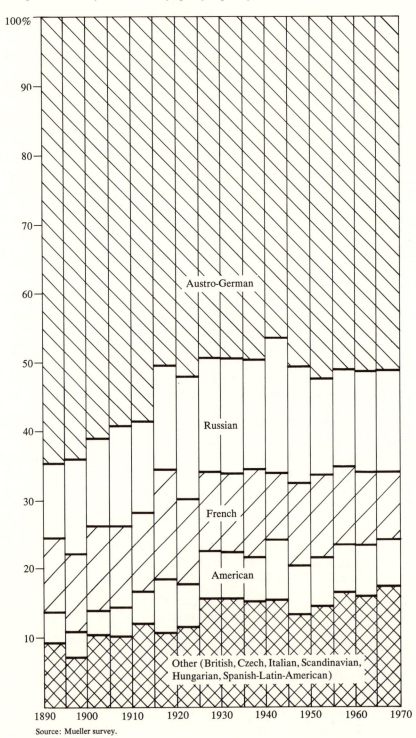

Source: Mueller survey.

at least, with the British experiencing an actual decline. However, in 1940–45, the French were not allies in the sense that the Russians and British were, and symphonic trends reflect this shift in popular sympathies. In both instances, moreover, patriotic sentiment is reflected in appreciable increases in American music.

The proportion of Russian music has increased steadily from 1890 to 1970, from 10.76% to 14.80%; in 1890–95, Russian music was slightly less favored than French, which then stood second to Austro-German, but by 1900 it had displaced French in rank. The Russian share reached two peaks: 17.58% in 1920–25 and 19.68% in 1940–45. The latter was, as noted above, undoubtedly a matter of wartime sentiment; this was the period of the premiere of Shostakovich's Seventh Symphony, and widespread performance of his and Prokofiev's large-scale works. The 1920–25 peak is more interesting, in that it coincided with general anti-Communist feeling in this country. However, an examination of the Russian repertory at that time shows emphasis on such non-Communist composers as Tchaikovsky, Scriabin, and Rimsky-Korsakov; it undoubtedly reflects, too, the preferences of Stokowski in Philadelphia, whose programming was emulated by other conductors. Since its 1940–45 peak and 17% in the following half decade, the proportion of Russian music has settled down around 14–15%.

French music, generally third in importance in the repertory, has steadily provided 10–13% of the symphonic repertory, peaking in 1920–25 at 13.11% and declining to 10.09% in 1965–70 after reaching 12.39% in 1945–50. Debussy and Ravel have shown some recent decline, while increased performances of Berlioz's large-scale works have boosted his share somewhat.

American music has consistently ranked fourth in order of importance since 1895; of the three orchestras reported before 1890, the New York Philharmonic under Thomas played virtually no American works, while Damrosch's New York Symphony and the Boston Symphony show slightly over 1% for all American music. Since 1890, however, this component has grown steadily from 4.30% in 1890–95 to wartime peaks of 7.67% in 1915–20 and 8.47 in 1940–45; between the wars its percentage hovered around 6%, and since 1945 it has averaged about 7%. The 1965–70 share of 6.66% is the lowest in the past twenty-five years.

British music, which in the Mueller survey includes Handel, has ranked fifth in importance since it displaced Czech music in the 1920–25 period. From a low of 0.87% in 1895–1900 it has increased steadily to 3.86 in 1930–35, since which time it has contributed 3–4% of the repertory, with a peak of 4.13% in 1955–60. In 1965–70 its percentage was 3.97%.

In 1890–95 music from Czechoslovakia (then a province of Austria but not included in the Muellers' Austro-German category) ranked fourth in order of importance with 5.01%. By 1925–30 it declined to 1.59%, recovered somewhat after that to 2–3%, and finally reached 3.12% in 1965–70. This last spurt was undoubtedly due to the programming of a greater variety of Dvořák symphonies; until recently that composer's repertory of nine symphonies received little attention beyond the *New World*.

Scandinavian music, which occupied 1.64% of the repertory in 1890–95 and 2.76% in 1965–70, showed a definite peak, 3.78%, in 1935–40; the increase to that date and the decline from it reflect the rise and fall in the popularity of Sibelius.

Music of Italian origin has had curious ups and downs: in 1890–95 it contributed but 0.96% of the symphonic repertory, reached a peak of 5.17% in 1925–30, dropped to 2.31% in 1940–45, rose again to 3.75% in 1955–60, and in 1965–70 had dropped again to 2.89%. The peak in the late 1920s reflects the popularity of such then contemporary composers as Respighi, Casella, Pizzetti, and Malipiero, thanks in part to the efforts of Arturo Toscanini and Fritz Reiner. Though one conductor can hardly have a strong direct effect on the national repertory, the example of such a major figure as Toscanini undoubtedly is copied by other conductors, especially when that conductor's programs are broadcast nationally. Increased interest in such Baroque composers as Vivaldi and Corelli probably accounts for the more recent increases in the Italian percentage.

Until 1945–49, Hungarian music seldom contributed 1% of the repertory, and its rise to 2.17% in 1960–65 undoubtedly came from the entrance of Bartók into the repertory.

From virtual neglect until 1925, Spanish and Latin-American music has since varied from 0.84% in 1930–35 to 1.47% in 1965–70; this includes not only such Spanish composers as De Falla, Granados, and Albéniz, but also such Latin Americans as Chavez, Ginastera, and Villa-Lobos.

Aside from these ten countries, other nations have seldom contributed as much as one percent in combination.

Changes in Repertory

One indication of the degree to which symphonic programs are static or flexible is the entry or departure of composers into and out of the repertory, the attainment of one percent of total performance time being more or less of a criterion. Since 1890, some thirty composers have, at one time or consistently, met this requirement.* Fifteen of these have been in the repertory fairly regularly for the entire period covered. Another ten entered it after 1890 and have remained there. Three, not listed in 1890–95, subsequently attained one percent and then more or less dropped out, as have two in the original list.

For the first group of fifteen composers who have figured in the repertory since 1890, we indicate (in Table 17-B) percentages and rank for the first and last half decades, their average percentage and rank for eighty years, and their high and low percentages with appropriate years.

The dominant position of Beethoven in the symphonic repertory should surprise no one familiar with programming: before 1900 he commanded

---

* The Muellers neglected to include Bartók in their analyses, and data on him have been extracted from their composer summaries by this author.

TABLE 17-B

COMPOSERS CONTINUOUSLY REPRESENTED IN SYMPHONIC
REPERTORY, 1890–1970

	1890–95 %	Average %	1965–70 %	High % & Years	Low % & Years
Bach	1.47 (13)	2.29 (10)	2.77 (6)	3.67 30–35	1.33 95–00
Beethoven	14.54 (1)	12.06 (1)	12.45 (1)	14.55 95–00	10.02 40–45
Berlioz	3.93 (7)	2.48 (8)	2.71 (8)	3.93 90–95	0.98 20–25
Brahms	6.34 (4)	8.38 (2)	7.38 (2)	10.30 45–50	5.68 05–10
Dvořák	4.60 (6)	2.45 (9)	2.54 (11)	4.61 95–00	1.32 25–30
Handel	0.70 (17)	0.72 (15)	0.87 (24)	1.87 55–60	0.20 05–10
Haydn	1.23 (14)	1.74 (14)	2.76 (7)	2.88 55–60	1.17 20–25
Liszt	2.67 (9)	1.87 (13)	0.47 (28)	3.94 00–05	0.43 55–60
Mendelssohn	2.22 (12)	1.96 (12)	1.63 (21)	3.64 95–00	1.29 25–30
Mozart	2.65 (10)	3.96 (5)	6.49 (3)	6.96 55–60	1.54 10–15
Schubert	3.13 (8)	2.18 (11)	1.79 (17)	3.52 95–00	1.79 65–70
Schumann	5.36 (5)	2.86 (7)	1.86 (14)	5.36 90–95	1.64 40–45
R. Strauss	0.75 (16)	3.18 (6)	2.56 (10)	4.39 25–30	0.75 90–95
Tchaikovsky	7.50 (3)	7.13 (3)	4.32 (5)	10.03 05–10	4.32 65–70
Wagner	10.47 (2)	5.55 (4)	1.76 (18)	10.47 90–95	1.76 65–70

one-seventh of the repertory, and except for a temporary decline during
World War II, he has retained at least a one-eighth share throughout; that
share in 1965–70 alone was more than the total of Tchaikovsky, Bach, Wagner, Debussy, and Stravinsky combined. Four composers in this group show
appreciable increases: Bach, Haydn, Mozart, and Richard Strauss. This is
to be expected from Strauss, as his works continued to enter the repertory
during this period; it is interesting to note, however, that his proportion has
declined steadily from its high of 4.39% in 1925–30. With Bach, Haydn,

and Mozart, their increase reflects a de-emphasis on the 19th-century music that has always dominated the repertory. In 1890 that music was much closer to contemporary for its time than it is today. Bach's peak in the 1930s may be due to the popularity of transcriptions of his organ music, his more recent strength to greater exploration of the Baroque repertory. Both Haydn and Mozart peaked in 1955–60, and their most recent standings—over twice those of 1890–95—are close to these high points.

Dvořák, Mendelssohn, Schubert, Schumann, Tchaikovsky, and Wagner have all declined substantially in the past eighty years. Dvořák has recovered from his low of 1.32% in 1925–30, but is still far short of his high favor in the 1890s, which was undoubtedly stimulated by his visit to this country. Schubert and Schumann have declined rather steadily over the eight decades covered; their loss, and that of Beethoven, confirms the gradual shrinkage of 19th-century music in the repertory. Greater losses were suffered by Tchaikovsky and Wagner. Tchaikovsky's high of 10.03% in 1905–10 is more than twice his low of 4.32% in 1965–70. The most spectacular change of any sort among these composers is the great decline in the importance of Wagner in the symphonic repertory: this has been steady throughout the period covered, with a sharp dip in 1915–20, but without the subsequent recovery shown by other Austro-German composers after World War I. From a rank of second in importance in the symphonic repertory in 1890–95, Wagner has fallen to eighteenth in 1965–70. One reason for the decline of Wagner in this survey is a shift away from performing extended excerpts in concert toward programming his preludes and overtures. Both Liszt and Handel have contributed a proportion to the repertory ranging more often below than above 1%; in neither case is any strong trend to be found.

The next group of composers includes ten who have entered the repertory since 1890 in the sense that they gained and retained 1% of performance time in a more or less consistent manner. Table 17-C shows the year and percentage with which they first figure in the Mueller tabulations, their high percentages and year, and their most recent ones, together with their most recent rank.

Though he barely entered the symphonic repertory as early as the 1920s, largely due to the efforts of Fritz Reiner in Cincinnati, Bartók actually did not become important until the 1940s, when he reached 0.56%; this increased to 1.01% in the 1950s and 1.70% in the 1960s. He is, therefore, the last composer to enter the repertory of American orchestras. Before him, the last was Shostakovich, who peaked during the war years of 1940–44 with 2.50%, dropped a decade later to 0.60%, and has recently regained strength. Prokofiev, the third new composer to figure significantly since 1940, entered the repertory in a minor way as early as 1915–19, showed some increases between 1925 and 1940, but exceeded 1% only after 1940, and has shown consistent strength since. The most spectacular recent gains in this group have been those of Mahler; after lingering around 1% from 1905 until 1945, he gained steadily from 1.35% in 1940–45 to 2.42% in 1960–65; in the next five years he almost doubled this to 4.57%. Bruckner has also shown recent increases, though by no means as strongly as Mahler. De-

TABLE 17-C

COMPOSERS ENTERING THE SYMPHONIC REPERTORY
SINCE 1890

	% First Years	High % & Years	1965–70 %
Bartók	0.09	1.70	1.70
	20–30	60–70	(19)
Bruckner	0.44	2.00	2.00
	95–00	65–70	(13)
Debussy	0.09	1.93	1.05
	00–05	35–40	(23)
Mahler	0.71	4.57	4.57
	05–10	65–70	(4)
Prokofiev	0.06	2.73	2.58
	15–20	60–65	(9)
Rachmaninoff	0.07	2.50	1.80
	00–05	40–45	(16)
Ravel	0.15	1.86	1.59
	05–10	45–50	(22)
Shostakovich	0.09	2.50	1.69
	25–30	40–45	(20)
Sibelius	0.57	3.63	1.84
	00–05	35–40	(15)
Stravinsky	0.02	2.43	2.43
	10–15	65–70	(12)

bussy, Ravel, Rachmaninoff, and Sibelius all reached peaks in the 1930s
and 1940s and have declined since then. Stravinsky's percentages grew
slowly to a peak of 2.22% in 1935–40 and then hovered around 1.5% until
1950–55; in the last fifteen years his percentage has shown a substantial
increase.

Three other composers entered the repertory since 1890, but no longer
enjoy more than 1% of performance time. They are shown in Table 17-D.

TABLE 17-D

COMPOSERS ENTERING AND LEAVING THE SYMPHONIC REPERTORY
SINCE 1890

	First % & Years	High % & Years	Last Years at 1%	1965–70 %
Franck	0.37	2.38	1.30	0.54
	95–00	20–25	45–50	(27)
Respighi	0.05	2.20	1.20	0.54
	15–20	25–30	30–35	(26)
Rimsky-Korsakov	1.06	2.17	1.31	0.34
	95–00	30–35	40–45	(30)

Two composers who figured with at least 1% of the repertory in 1890 have more or less dropped out since. This can be seen in Table 17-E.

TABLE 17-E

COMPOSERS LEAVING THE SYMPHONIC REPERTORY SINCE 1890

	1890–95 %	High % & Years	Last Years	1965–70 %
Saint-Saëns	2.41	2.84	1.21	0.81
	(11)	00–05	25–30	(25)
Weber	1.09	1.30	1.08	0.37
	(15)	95–00	10–15	(29)

Comparison of the Mueller data for 1960–70 with the BMI surveys for the same period casts rather interesting light on the relative importance of composers in the repertory. It is, of course, not surprising to find important discrepancies between the two surveys, given their different methods. One of the most important divergences concerns the position of Mahler, who ranked fourth (with 4.57%) after Beethoven, Brahms, and Mozart in the Mueller survey, but barely twentieth with little more than 1% in the BMI. The Muellers' time-weighting principle accounts for much of this discrepancy, but another important factor may be that Mahler's recent surge of popularity has been primarily among the Major orchestras, those better equipped technically to handle his difficult scores. To a considerable extent, the current popularity of Mahler has built up slowly from the early efforts of Bruno Walter and Dimitri Mitropoulos, and has so far centered in the Major orchestras,* though there are signs that the efforts of Bernstein, Abravanel, and, more recently, Solti in performance and recording are now beginning to stimulate interest in, and audience demand for, Mahler's music among the smaller orchestras. The same is probably true of Bruckner, who ranks considerably higher (2%) with the Muellers than he does with BMI (0.36%). Both Berlioz and Dvořák similarly show more strongly in the Mueller list, probably because much of their music in the repertory involves full symphonies of considerable length. Wagner and Ravel show greater strength in the BMI surveys, undoubtedly because their shorter works appear more frequently.

The American Share

The most extreme divergence between these two surveys concerns American music. During the 1960–70 decade, the Muellers report 7.32% and 6.66% respectively for the two five-year periods, or an average of 6.99%.

* In 1970, when the Los Angeles Philharmonic promoted a local university appearance by asking the students to vote for the composers they most wanted to hear, a full-scale campaign was mounted, dominated by heated rivalry between the backers of Beethoven and Mahler, the former winning by a very slight margin.

Table 17 F

American Music in the U.S. Symphony Repertory 1961–70

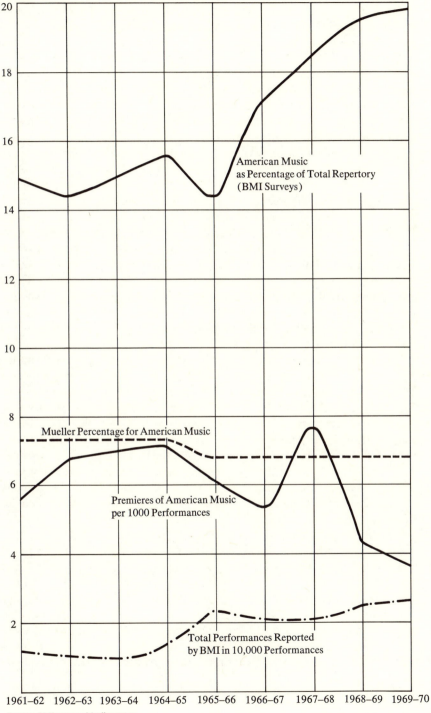

American Music
as Percentage of Total Repertory
(BMI Surveys)

Mueller Percentage for American Music

Premieres of American Music
per 1000 Performances

Total Performances Reported
by BMI in 10,000 Performances

1961–62   1962–63   1963–64   1964–65   1965–66   1966–67   1967–68   1968–69   1969–70

Sources: BMI surveys; Mueller survey.

Table 17-F shows the BMI percentage for American music (in perform-ances) in each year of that decade, indicating a share of the repertory of from 14% to nearly 20%, with a definite increase in the last half of the period, when the Muellers show a decrease. This graph also records the num-ber of premieres of American music and the total number of performances reported in the BMI surveys for this decade. It is impossible to determine whether the five-year increase in American music in the BMI survey from 1965 to 1970 is related to the fact that performances (and orchestras re-porting) more than doubled during that period. However, one can reason-ably conclude that there is no special correlation between the proportions of premieres and all American music.

Before one draws the hasty conclusion that the Major orchestras in their subscription programs (as reflected in the Mueller survey) play a smaller proportion of American music than they do on their nonsubscription con-certs or than other orchestras do in general, one must consider a number of factors. Some evidence in the BMI surveys * indicates a higher percentage of American music in the nonsubscription—popular, children's, and summer —concerts than in the subscription programs; for the one year (1968–69) in which a breakdown of data is reported, subscription and tour concerts contained 15.4% of American music, while the others had 24.2%. This can be explained by the fact that in both of the last two years reported there was a substantially higher proportion (4.82%) of popular and show music on the nonsubscription programs than on subscription and tour concerts (1.12%) between 1968 and 1970.

Two other factors, admittedly subjective impressions, must also be taken into account in any consideration of this matter. There is probably a ten-dency to program American music in shorter pieces, as compared with the popular standard symphonies and concertos. Perhaps this is "tokenism" in programming on the part of conductors, who may feel that they discharge their obligations to American music by playing short works. Moreover, de-spite the Mueller data showing a smaller American share in the subscrip-tion concerts of Major orchestras, these generally give more attention to such serious symphonic composers as Copland, Schuman, Sessions, and Ives, whose music is usually more difficult to prepare than that of Gershwin, Rodgers, and LeRoy Anderson.

Possibly the most important observation to be made about the American share of the symphonic repertory is that it is spread so widely over such a large number of composers. So far, at least, no American composer has emerged to the point where he can claim 1% of the symphonic repertory in the Mueller surveys. To be sure, achievement by any composer of that status in the repertory has become a relatively rare phenomemon since 1920: as we have already noted, only five composers—Bartók, Prokofiev, Ravel, Shostakovich, and Stravinsky—have entered the repertory and stayed there in the past half century. This extraordinary dispersal of atten-

---

* Appendix L is a summary of the BMI surveys 1961–70 from which these conclusions are drawn. It contains considerable statistical data of further interest to those who wish to pursue these matters further.

tion to American composers can be seen from Table 17-G, based on a chart prepared by Mrs. Mueller, showing the percentages of the American share enjoyed by a variety of composers in the past four decades; in it these are listed in order of importance (weighted in terms of performance time) in the repertory. (See Table 17G, pages 418-19.)

The most obvious conclusion to be drawn from this chart is that a few composers are gradually gaining a larger share of the American contribution to the repertory. Except for Gershwin in 1945–50, Barber in 1960–65 and Copland five years later were the first to claim more than 10% of the American repertory. Similarly, the fact that seven composers claimed between 5% and 10% of the American repertory in 1965–70 may indicate the emergence of a group of more frequently performed American composers to a degree not experienced in the past. Nevertheless, though Barber and Copland have begun to accumulate strong enough records to suggest that they may yet attain 1% of the overall orchestral repertory, American representation remains widely dispersed. This possibility that one or more American composers may shortly figure in the symphonic repertory with at least 1% share is further strengthened by the pronounced upward trend for all American music that can be seen from the graph in Table 17-F, where the BMI percentage for American music shows a sharp increase since 1966. Though this trend may not continue at this pace, it may serve to modify the strictures expressed by Oliver Daniel in his preface to the 1969–70 BMI survey, where he expresses such discouragement with the plight of the American composer that he announces the probable discontinuation of these surveys in the comprehensive form developed in the 1960s:

> Basically your programs seem to suffer from an overdose of ancestor worship, and about the only consolation one can take in the situation as it stands is the fact that the condition of opera is worse. The economic problems of the symphony orchestras have mounted. Performing organizations everywhere are turning to state and federal sources for funds. But none seems to recognize the fact that the American composer is also a taxpayer and, out of his earnings, is forced by way of taxation to help subsidize organizations that take little responsibility for the development of his work. No other country so ignores the creative efforts of its own citizens. And nowhere is the generation gap more noticeable. Because so little attention is given to the work of our young composers, they are turning toward smaller instrumental combinations and electronic instruments.[6]

"An Overdose of Ancestor Worship"

The problem of the American composer in the symphonic repertory is, in many respects, but a part of the larger problem of contemporary music in general. In 1905–10, when his music attained 10% of the repertory, Tchaikovsky was still very much a contemporary composer, as was Brahms when his share was approaching 7%. Certainly Daniel's comment about the generation gap is justified by trends since 1920; we have already seen ample

TABLE 17-G

AMERICAN COMPOSERS IN THE SYMPHONIC REPERTORY, 1930–70

	1930–35	1935–40	1940–45	1945–50
Over 10%				Gershwin 10%
5–10%	Bloch 6.6% Loeffler 6.4%	Bloch 7.1%	Gershwin 6.8% Copland 5%	Copland 8% Thomson 6.8% Barber 5%
Under 5%	Hanson 4% Carpenter Copland 3% Taylor Sowerby 2% Toch MacDowell 1% Piston Borowski Chadwick Gershwin Harris Barber	Loeffler 4.5% McDonald Carpenter Taylor Harris Hanson 2.5% Sowerby Barber Piston Borowski 1% Toch Chadwick Gershwin Copland	Bloch 4.5% Barber 4% Harris Carpenter McDonald 3% Creston Schuman Piston Thomson 2% Thompson Taylor Hanson Bennett 1% Foss Cowell Gould Bernstein Toch Still Diamond	Bloch 4.5% Gould 3% Piston Schuman Hanson Diamond Creston Thompson 2% Sowerby Antheil Harris Bernstein Carpenter 1% Dello Joio McDonald Foss Still Menotti

documentation of the growing emphasis of the repertory on older music. Though the Muellers have so far made no separate distinction for contemporary music, an independent analysis of their data indicates that no more than 25% of the repertory, in their terms, was composed since 1900. BMI actually shows a higher figure (43%) for all performances in 1969–70, the difference being due to factors already discussed.

A theme that runs through much criticism of the symphonic repertory is the charge—possibly Virgil Thomson invented the phrase—that our orchestras rely too much on "Fifty Pieces," which are played over and over again (to these critics at least) ad nauseam. However, in comparing successive BMI surveys, one finds considerable variations in annual lists of the fifty most frequently played compositions. In fact, comparison of BMI surveys for the beginning, middle, and end of the 1960s shows actually twenty-two

1950–55	1955–60	1960–65	1965–70
		Barber 11%	Copland 12.7%
Bloch 8%	Copland 7%	Copland 8.2%	Barber 8.7%
Copland 6.5%	Creston 6.5%		Ives 8.4%
Barber 5.5%	Barber 6%		Bloch 5.8%
Creston 5.3%			Bernstein 5.6%
Menotti 5%			Schuller 5.2%
			Schuman 5.2%
			Gershwin 5%
Gershwin 4%	Bloch 4.8%	Bloch 4.3%	Menotti 4%
Piston	Gershwin 3.5%	Schuman 3.3%	Mennin 3%
Thomson 3%	Schuman	Piston	Diamond
Dello Joio	Hanson 3%	Mennin 3%	Sessions
Hovhaness	Bernstein	Schuller	Piston
Cowell	Cowell	Bernstein	Harris
Schuman 2%	Harris	Gershwin	Foss
Still	Dello Joio 2%	Menotti 2%	Hovhaness
Hanson	Thomson	Foss	Creston 2%
Gould	Piston	Creston	Dello Joio
Foss 1%	Hovhaness 1%	Ives	Gould
Harris	Ives	Dello Joio 1%	Yardumian 1%
Lopatnikov	Sessions	Hanson	Bennett 0.5%
Krenek	Menotti	Harris	Thomson
Mennin	Foss	Sessions	Thompson
Ives	Toch	Diamond	Still
Diamond	Gould		
Bernstein			

compositions that appear every time among the fifty most frequently performed works.

BEETHOVEN Overture to *Egmont*
BEETHOVEN Symphony No. 5, C minor
BEETHOVEN Piano Concerto No. 4, G major
BRAHMS Symphony No. 4, E minor
BRAHMS Symphony No. 2, D major
BEETHOVEN Violin Concerto, D major
STRAVINSKY Suite from *The Firebird*
BEETHOVEN Symphony No. 7, A major
BRAHMS Symphony No. 1, C minor
DVOŘÁK Symphony No. 9, E minor (*New World*)
WAGNER Prelude to *Die Meistersinger*

BRAHMS *Academic Festival Overture*
FRANCK Symphony, D minor
TCHAIKOVSKY Symphony No. 4, F minor
DEBUSSY *Prelude to the Afternoon of a Faun*
WEBER Overture to *Oberon*
RAVEL Suite No. 2, from *Daphnis et Chloé*
BEETHOVEN Piano Concerto No. 3, C minor
BEETHOVEN *Leonore Overture No. 3*
SCHUBERT Symphony No. 8, B minor (*Unfinished*)
R. STRAUSS *Don Juan*
BRAHMS Violin Concerto, D major
MOZART Overture to *The Marriage of Figaro*

Beethoven is represented by six compositions, four of them symphonies or concertos; Brahms by five works, four symphonies or concertos. Austro-German compositions number sixteen out of the twenty-two, French three, and Russian two. Two of the works were composed in the twentieth century—interestingly enough, both for Diaghilev's Ballet Russe. None is by an American composer.

Though it may be impossible to pinpoint the "Fifty Pieces" precisely from these data, in terms of their consistently dominating symphony programs, lists of the top twenty composers in frequency of performance are more stable; fifteen were in this group in the BMI surveys for 1961–62, 1965–66, and 1969–70:

Beethoven	R. Strauss
Mozart	Dvořák
Brahms	Schubert
Tchaikovsky	Rossini
Wagner	Mendelssohn
Haydn	Handel
Bach	Berlioz

Moreover, by reference to Tables 17C–D showing the entrance of some thirteen composers into the repertory, it will be noted that most of them did so before 1920. This phenomenon may be summarized as follows:

Before 1920	*1920–40*	*Since 1940*
Bruckner	Ravel	Bartók
Debussy	Respighi	Prokofiev
Franck	Stravinsky	Shostakovich
Mahler		
Rachmaninoff		
Rimsky-Korsakov		
Sibelius		

This indicates a relative stability in programming since 1920, the obverse of which is a relative stagnation of the repertory during the period of the greatest expansion of the symphony orchestra in America.

These data confirm in reasonably precise terms the general impression that many observers have formed about the repertory of American symphony orchestras: domination by Austro-German composers of the past, with strong and continuing emphasis on Beethoven; a generally low proportion of contemporary music; an even lower representation of American music; the distribution of this over a large number of composers; and an increasingly static condition in the repertory. These well-known phenomena have been the source of continued criticism of our orchestras for many years, a major portion being directed at the poor treatment given contemporary and American music. In defense or explanation of the repertory of our orchestras, three principal arguments, advanced from various sources, may be cited here.

The first of these might be termed the conservative viewpoint of management—conductors, trustees, and managers. They argue that they are presenting the repertory wanted by their public and that such efforts as they make to innovate antagonize their patrons and do not draw a compensating new audience. Although some point to the experience of Lukas Foss at the Buffalo Philharmonic, we have already demonstrated that his programming did not necessarily cause a decline in subscriptions. In Louisville, even the most ardent advocates of innovative programming, including Robert Whitney himself, now believe, in retrospect, that the policy of including new music on every program did not establish an audience with either a receptivity or hunger for it. The program policy of Pierre Boulez upon assuming direction of the New York Philharmonic in 1971–72 aroused considerable hostile reaction from the subscribers, especially, it is reported, among the Friday afternoon ladies. Yet Boulez's intensive programming of Liszt, whose music is nearly a century old, and Berg, who died in 1935, scarcely qualifies as a radical departure. The issue here very probably was more a matter of lack of familiarity, and the crowding out of the programs of familiar classics, than one of a really new musical idiom. In fact, Boulez's greatest impact in innovation was his arranging programs by ensembles of Philharmonic players in smaller halls, both in Lincoln Center and in Greenwich Village, outside the regular subscription format; such ancillary programming of contemporary music may be a way for other orchestras to meet their obligations to new music by directing them to a smaller and more receptive audience. At present writing, there is no decisive evidence that the Boulez-Liszt-Berg cycle has in any major respect deterred Philharmonic attendance, despite complaints from subscribers.

A second defense of the status quo in repertory raises the question of precisely how much do these critics regard as a proper representation of new American music. BMI's own data show that over forty-two percent of the present repertory was composed in the 20th century and that American composers contribute nearly twenty percent, and one may ask the advocates of this music just how much they expect the orchestras to do. The appreciable increase in performance since 1965 may be evidence that the native composer is getting better, if belated, recognition. The problem arises partly from the fact that this nation has yet to produce a composer of commanding stature and that attention to American music is spread so widely, and thinly, over a large number of composers. A sizable proportion of performances of American music are of compositions by local musicians—residents of the community, members of nearby college faculties —who deserve attention locally. The Louisville programs included a great number of talented composers who were not nationally recognized. Perhaps our orchestras are treating native composers better by playing a large number of them rather than concentrating on a few celebrities.

One of the functions of the symphony orchestra undoubtedly is to give exposure to the music of our time, our nation, and the region in which the composer works (although not necessarily because these composers pay taxes, an infinitesimal portion of which trickles down into orchestral coffers). But a wide range of disagreement exists, and will probably continue to exist, on the precise nature and extent of this obligation. Composers and such advocates as Oliver Daniel tend to look upon this matter as the orchestras' obligation to the composer. But perhaps there is an equal obligation of the orchestra to its audience to expose it to new music, and of the composer to communicate with the audience. The partisans of new music at times incline too much to blame conductors or "elitist" trustees for placing obstacles in the way of performing new music, when some of their attention should be directed at the quality and communicability of the composers whom they support. For better or worse, the symphony orchestra is designed to reach audiences numbering in the thousands; the composers who are the objects of the "ancestor worship" which Daniel deplores wrote music that does communicate with such audiences. Nor can his implication that other countries do more for their composers be supported factually: symphony programs the world around are rather similar, and one need only point to the withdrawal of Pierre Boulez from the musical life of France as evidence of that nation's rejection of its most distinguished composer in a generation.

Finally, there is the more sophisticated argument advanced by many who are sympathetic to the cause of new music. One of these is Leonard Bernstein, who has written:

> What has happened to symphonic forms? Are symphonies a thing of the past? What will become of the symphony orchestra? Is tonality dead forever? Is the international community of composers really, deeply ready to accept that death? If so will the music loving public concur? . . .
>
> For example, are symphonies a thing of the past? No, obviously, since they are being written in substantial quantity. But Yes, equally obviously, in the sense that the classical concept of a symphony—depending as it does on the bifocal tonal axis, which itself depends on the existence of tonality—*is* a thing of the past.[7]

In broader historical perspective, the whole concept of the symphony orchestra was of Austro-German origin: nearly two hundred years ago, a handful of great composers, centered in Vienna, pulled together diverse strands of Italian, German, and French instrumental and dramatic music and created a musical idiom that flourished for more than a century, permeating symphony, chamber music, solo compositions, and even, in some cases, opera. Inspired by these Viennese masters, an increasing number of composers in other countries—France and Russia particularly—developed their own contribution to the repertory throughout the 19th century. But by the turn of the 20th century, the predominant musical style was challenged from several sources: the illustrative approach of Richard Strauss and others carrying on the ideas of Wagner and Liszt; Debussy's reaction to German classical formalism; the rhythmic and harmonic innovations of Stravinsky; and the antitonal developments of Schoenberg and his followers. Though symphonic music was by no means the only medium of this Austro-German style, that idiom dominated orchestral composition for over a century, and the orchestral institution determined by the classical symphonists remained the basis for the first breaks away from the tradition, though more recent composition may demand unprecedented modifications of the performing ensemble.

In this light, it is not surprising that the symphonic repertory continues to be dominated by the handful of composers who invented the idiom and by other composers who have worked within the tradition. Even such recent newcomers to prominence as Prokofiev, Shostakovich, and Bartók composed much essentially within these classic boundaries. Certainly, if such observers as Bernstein are correct in seeing a breakdown in the symphonic idiom, the future course of the orchestra can take only one of three paths. It may become increasingly static, as it has in recent decades, excluding from the repertory such new music as does not suit its instrumental complement. It may be open only to such composers, possibly a dying breed, who write in some contemporary version of the classical idiom. Or the symphony orchestra itself may change its composition and idiomatic responsiveness to adapt itself to new approaches to creating music.

Oliver Daniel states that young composers, shunned by the symphony orchestras, are turning to new media. Yet Gunther Schuller, a conductor who has been extraordinarily responsive to new music, reports that there are ample new scores being written by young composers for symphony orchestra.[8]

Schuller is one who contends that a major difficulty lies in the inability of many conductors—and he does not refer here to an Ormandy, a Szell, a Bernstein, or a Boulez—to evaluate new music or perform it adequately, merely from reading the score. Once they have heard a good performance of it, from commercial recordings or from concert tapes, they can judge it and perform it better.* The technical quality of many American orchestras enters into this question too: in the large mass of some six hundred orchestras covered by the BMI survey, considerably fewer than a hundred have the technical and musical competence to learn to play a difficult and un-

* Yet, at the 1971 ASOL conference in Seattle, representatives of both ASCAP and BMI, the two organizations most interested in promoting music under copyright, rejected the suggestion that their firms approach the musicians' union to seek relaxation of its ban on audition taping of first performances.[9]

familiar score. Those that do must be under the leadership of talented and dedicated conductors with the ability to teach the playing of new music, and very often such occasions succeed only at the expense of the preparation of other music on the program.

Limitations of time and money, which in a professional orchestra often come down to the same thing, are another cause of avoiding more emphasis on new music. In one of its projects, the Ford Foundation specifically allocated funds to cover the extra cost of preparing performances of the new music it commissioned for selected soloists. The Rockefeller Foundation, believing that colleges and universities would provide more receptive audiences, has underwritten preparation costs for a number of visits by orchestras to campuses to concentrate on new music. It may well be argued that were a recording project, similar to that of the Louisville Orchestra, established to involve a wider group of orchestras, its positive artistic contribution as well as its financial success might be more apparent.

Pressures on Programming

The criticisms of the symphonic repertory discussed so far are within the general framework of "serious" music in the traditional sense, and they come from what may be described as the left wing of the musical community. However, there is equally strong pressure on many orchestras, from the conservative side, to lighten programming, to include a larger measure of crowd-appealing music. Such forces, overt or implicit, seem to be reflected in the first two seasons under Takeda at the Albuquerque Symphony. To a considerable degree, they come from those who want to build larger audiences, both for the direct income they produce and as a demonstration of popular participation that can justify financial contributions from private sources and governments. In the face of the very small proportion of the total population represented in symphony audiences, such enterprises encounter considerable resistance in gaining financial support, and are tempted, within the organization, to modify artistic policy to gain wider audiences. To some degree, those orchestras upon whom the expansion of activity has been forced by musicians' demands for more employment have steadily diversified their programming into more popular areas. As far back as 1885, Major Higginson saw the Boston "Pops" as a means of simultaneously expanding his musicians' employment and his service to the community. Especially with increasing government aid, those orchestras with musicians available are expanding such activities appreciably, with popular concerts during the winter season, free concerts in parks, and such summer festivals as Ravinia, Tanglewood, Hollywood Bowl, and Saratoga.

Nonetheless, some caution must be exercised in such efforts to popularize symphony activities. In 1971–72, the Dallas Symphony, grasping at straws to survive grave internal, labor, and community problems, instituted a series of "Dallas sound" concerts, featuring popular and rock artists as special events, which by no means attracted the size of audiences required to pay the staggering fees of the guests.[10] In the 1950s, Fritz Reiner and the Chicago Symphony were persuaded by a recording company to present in concert, and to record with, a popular band in a "serious" work for jazz band and symphony orchestra; the effort to attract a new audience had little impact on symphony finances and the recording died an early death. In such instances, one can see the limits beyond which a symphony orchestra can go only with diminishing returns, artistically and financially. They also indicate that no orchestra can undertake programs of diversified and popular repertory without a solid base in traditional symphony activity.

More recently, new criticism of our orchestras has emerged as a part of the general urban upheaval of the 1950s and 1960s—the demand that orchestras become more "relevant" to contemporary life, especially in greater involvement of minority groups in the audience and direction of symphony orchestras. Though it also concerns other ethnic minorities, such as those in the Spanish-speaking Southwest, most of the discussion centers on the blacks in the large cities. Appeal to these minority audiences has already been discussed earlier, as have the dangers of tokenism in bringing their music into the repertory; the same applies to other ethnic minorities.

But a broader problem of relevance to contemporary life has been raised by such spokesmen as Elliott Carter, who has stated: "I think that unless the situation changes very drastically, not only will there be no future for new music in the symphony orchestra world, but the symphony orchestra world itself will die. . . . The old art is only interesting as it seems living to us, and it seems interesting to us because we are surrounded also with contemporary art." [11]

Reviewing these arguments should by no means minimize the problem of securing performance for our native music. Only by giving our composers adequate exposure is there any hope of advancing the historic process by which major figures may emerge and take their place in the repertory alongside Prokofiev, Shostakovich, Bartók, or Stravinsky. But entry into the repertory also involves acceptance by the symphony audience, as well as advocacy by the artistic directors. There are definite limits to general audience comprehension and enjoyment of new music. Part of the problem is sheer unfamiliarity: some New York Philharmonic subscribers objected as strongly to Liszt as to Berg, not because his idiom was offensive to their ears, but because his music was unfamiliar. At the same time, there is no denying that many of the compositional techniques of contemporary music, including American, make far greater demands on the comprehension and receptivity of the listener than does the relatively simply diatonic and tonally oriented music of Mozart, Beethoven, or Tchaikovsky.

In actuality, it is quite possible that many a symphony patron who happily accepts the music of the standard classical composers really has no deep understanding of it; that his superficial experience of it is as shallow and uncomprehending as that of the new music he does not like. Again we come to one of the unknowns of the symphony institution, the *terra incognita* of the individual's experience of creative expression. Leon Kirchner, a composer who also conducts, has spoken of the manner in which his own performance of a contemporary work illuminates his approach to a classic work:

> With this enormous investment in contemporary music, one can literally resonate the past in terms of its performance. Once one performs Webern, one can never again perform Mozart in the way that he has. And this is something which the audience picks up too.[12]

In the same statement, Kirchner points to the conflict between the past and present in composition:

> One of the most difficult things to face these days is the fact that composers for the first time have willfully separated themselves from the past. There have been composers in the past who have been great radicals but who have commanded the past before they rid themselves of it. Men like Schoenberg, or Stravinsky, or Bartók, and so many others, have literally commanded the past in the sense that they were able to manipulate these materials in their minds or on paper, in a way which was not typical of the masters of the past.

Though this conflict between the past and present is much with us on the symphonic scene, the acceptance of the radical composer who absorbs the past is as much a problem with symphonic audiences as is their receptivity to those new composers who break completely with the past. None of these problems can be solved either by conservatively holding to an increasingly static repertory, because that is what the audience wants, or by merely scolding the artistic direction of orchestras for the repertory rut they are in. In this the orchestras confront the challenge of education in the broadest sense—arousing the receptivity of the present adult audience to a broader, richer, and more intense musical experience and developing among our youth a basic understanding of the art. To the degree that there is a crisis in the symphonic repertory, the orchestras must come to grips with it through a deeper understanding of their educational function.

CHAPTER XVIII

Education and the Musical Experience

More than two thousand children filled an auditorium for a youth concert in a series long a model for other orchestras. The conductor had scheduled as his opening number the march from Prokofiev's opera *The Love for Three Oranges*, which he introduced by tossing a dozen oranges out into the audience. While order was restored in the hall, the conductor beamed from the podium as he viewed the chaos he had created by so effectively "involving" his audience in symphonic music.*

Such antics in the name of music education have had ample precedent, though by no means as irresponsible, in other orchestras, ever since they assumed the task of introducing serious music to young audiences. In Philadelphia, Leopold Stokowski enchanted youngsters at the Academy of Music by producing circus animals for a performance of Saint-Saëns' *Carnival of the Animals*, seeking a real live wolf for *Peter and the Wolf* (and settling in the end for a large dog), and arousing such expectation of the possibility of a personal appearance by Charlie Chaplin that one of the orchestra players was finally persuaded to dress up as the comedian for an appearance before the children.[1] The children's programs of few other orchestras had the benefit of Stokowski's showmanship, but many tried to devise similar stunts to arouse the interest and gain the affection of young audiences. More recently, Leonard Bernstein applied his extraordinary combination of charisma and dedication in programs, on television and in the concert hall, where he tried to convey more basic musical information to his audiences. Similar efforts by such diverse figures as Erich Kunzel in Cincinnati and Maurice Abravanel in Salt Lake City have the same aim.

Today there is hardly a professional American orchestra that does not play at least a few concerts for young people, and many have developed extensive educational programs. As the prospects for government support

* Out of consideration for all concerned in this episode, which I personally witnessed, further identification will be forgone here.

brighten, this activity will expand, since it is an obvious justification for funding by states, counties, and the National Endowment for the Arts. The format and ambience of these programs have changed considerably since the days of Stock, Damrosch, and Stokowski. In many cities, the assistant conductor is often engaged partly for his ability to conduct such concerts, and the choice usually inclines toward young Americans with an ability to communicate with the children of today, with the hope, of course, of having a director who can become a local version of Leonard Bernstein in this respect. No longer are all of the concerts given in the downtown concert hall; a growing number are taking their orchestras, often split into two or three sections, directly into the schools. The original notion of playing concerts for a select few who purchase series tickets is being either abandoned or modified by including all children, regardless of ability to pay, of a given age group. Since concerts in schools, or arrangements for children to be bussed to concert halls during school hours, require cooperation from school administrators, liaison with these officials has become a major managerial function and has, in many cases, included joint efforts to prepare the children in advance for the music they will hear.

All this has brought symphony orchestras into the education field to a degree that other independent arts activities, such as theaters and museums, have attempted only recently, and then often in emulation of the pioneering efforts of symphony orchestras. In many respects, the gradual assumption by orchestras of educational responsibilities has arisen from noneducational motives and has developed in a hasty, ill-conceived, and piecemeal manner. Though many programs were started out of sincere desire to broaden the orchestras' service to the community and instill in young people a love for music, other, less altruistic, forces were also at work. For one thing, orchestras have discovered that their programs for young people have given them a powerful selling point in their solicitation of funds from individuals and corporations, and more recently from government. The wealthy potential contributor, who himself may not like symphonic music, or the corporation reluctant to support an effort that attracts to its concerts only a small proportion of the population, is far more inclined to find justification for giving to an organization reaching thousands of local children, regardless of social status or economic advantage. Finally, as orchestras meet their musicians' demands for better overall income, they find themselves with more contracted-for services available to them than they can use in regular concert activities. To a large degree, therefore, our orchestras have drifted into these youth programs, less from a comprehensively planned program of education than out of using such projects to solve other problems. Consequently, a distressingly large portion of these efforts has been instituted without anything like a basic philosophy of objective or method. Nor has any real effort been made to establish goals for these programs and to evaluate their effectiveness. Even so elementary a factor as the success of young people's programs in building adult audiences has never been closely examined.

From Concert Hall into the School

More than other arts institutions, symphony orchestras have a long history of presenting programs for young people: possibly the earliest was the Philharmonic Society of Cincinnati, which played a special concert for children on July 4, 1858.[2] Theodore Thomas included such programs, both in actual performances and in the various schemes he proposed to civic sponsors; however, Thomas's education interests were more directed toward affiliating a professional music school with the symphony orchestra. Both the San Francisco Symphony and Detroit Symphony had already begun to present such concerts regularly when Frederick Stock began a young people's series in Chicago as a part of a wider program of music education: his own experience during World War I convinced him that his orchestra should take the initiative in introducing symphonic music to young audiences in his Children's Concerts and in training native American orchestra musicians in the Civic Orchestra; both of these projects were begun in 1919, and have continued without break ever since.

To a large degree, the success of these early concerts for children depended upon the personality of the conductor. For young Chicagoans, as for young New Yorkers at Walter Damrosch's concerts, the most lasting impression was that of the grandfather-figure recounting the stories of music as if each child were sitting on his lap before the fire. The German paterfamilias is no longer in fashion, but the role of the conductor is nonetheless important, whether it be Leonard Bernstein in New York or Milton Katims in Seattle. These concerts were given in the orchestra's regular concert hall, very often on Saturday mornings or on afternoons after school hours. A large proportion of the children were brought by their parents, who in most cases were already symphony patrons themselves. For such a selective audience, introduction to the symphony orchestra was as much a part of their indoctrination into society as Friday evening dancing school.

Gradually, however, these concerts came more and more to involve logistic, and sometimes educational, liaison with school administrators. Efforts were made to schedule concerts during school hours and to encourage group attendance under parental or teacher supervision. Before long, considerable numbers of children were released from classes and brought to the hall in school buses. In most cases, admission was charged, usually for series of several concerts to encourage more intensive exposure. The orchestra women's committees have long played an important role in relations with school officials and sometimes in handling ticket sales and concert monitoring. These programs sought to introduce children to symphonic music in something like the context in which they would later encounter it as adults. This was, for instance, a strongly stated objective of the highly organized program of young people's concerts developed in the late 1930s by Lillian Baldwin with the Cleveland Orchestra. For her, it was extremely important that the children hear music in a "normal" concert setting and that they pay at least a token admission fee.[3] Equally important were the preconcert study materials, prepared by the orchestra but distributed through the schools for teachers to use in orienting the children toward the music they were to hear. For many years the Cleveland program was a model for other orchestras, which emulated it with varying degrees of intensity and success. Such programs are still rather widespread among symphony orchestras, although they are no longer the sole channel of education efforts.

The idea of presenting orchestra concerts in the schools themselves, rather than exclusively in the concert hall, developed rather slowly, but steadily, under two major influences. One of these was the growth of the Music Performance Trust Fund after 1948, which stipulated that the musicians' services for which it paid had to be rendered without admission charge and for worthy community causes. In some cities, the schools joined the local union in presenting free concerts in the schools. For many years the Chicago union local sponsored its own series of in-school concerts with such enthusiastic cooperation from the school administration that its music supervisor issued standing orders requiring every child attending a concert to write a personal thank-you note to union president Petrillo, who of course delighted in having his picture taken for the newspapers showing him opening letters from thousands of children. But in many smaller cities, such as Louisville, school officials, the orchestra, and the union worked together to coordinate the Music Performance Trust Fund concerts into the overall symphony program.

A second factor in bringing the orchestra into the schools resulted from the development of school policies. Increasingly, educators have resisted the "elitist" implications of bussing downtown to the concert hall those children who bought tickets. They preferred to have all of the students exposed, not merely those whose parents were interested and could afford to pay for tickets. Additionally, as distances increased and traffic congestion grew, the release of children from classes for a one-hour concert downtown came to mean the loss of a full day of instruction. It made better sense to bring the orchestra out to the schools in two or three buses than to engage up to fifty to take the children in the opposite direction. Many educators believed that communication with the children was more effective in the familiar setting of the school and under strict teacher discipline. Eventually, as demand for in-school concerts grew and as more schools with limited stage facilities became involved, orchestras discovered that they could greatly increase their exposure by splitting their personnel of more than eighty players into two or three reasonably self-sufficient chamber orchestras. In many cities, the orchestra would play two forty-five- or sixty-minute youth programs in the span of two and a half hours as one "back-to-back service." Thus, a single orchestra "service" could, in theory, provide as many as six youth concerts; such arrangements vary greatly from orchestra to orchestra, depending upon the specific provisions of union agreements, and have become a major issue in labor negotiations on some occasions.

The in-school concept received a major boost from Young Audiences, Inc., a nationwide organization devoted to bringing chamber music to young people in the schools.[4] Some of its local chapters work more or less directly with symphony orchestras in engaging their players for in-school demonstration concerts. Though we will have more to say later about this important project, it must be noted here that Young Audiences pioneered in bringing music directly into the schools, in most instances before orchestras did so. Nor has the example of Young Audiences been lost on symphony managements today, when they seek employment for their musicians under contract; many have emulated the chamber-music programs of Young Audiences in their overall education programs by sending out quartets, quintets, and small ensembles in addition to orchestras, again depending on how much diversification their union contracts permit.

Rationale of Youth Programming

Today the scope of this activity is extraordinary. We have already seen how important a role in their total activity these young people's concerts, in and out of the schools, play in such orchestras as Louisville, Albuquerque, Utah, and Cincinnati. When the Office of Education commissioned the ASOL to undertake a study of youth-concert activities in the United States in 1968, it decided to concentrate on twenty cities selected for the effectiveness of their programs: of this group Cincinnati, with 114 youth concerts, had the most activity, but several small orchestras offered only two concerts; the average for all twenty was 36.35 concerts per year, which may be somewhat lower than such an average would have been two or three years later.[5]

Such an extensive education program has grown out of diverse motives, often on an improvised year-to-year development, and supported from a variety of financial sources. In a few cities, local foundations or corporations have specifically allocated funds for youth concerts; in others, municipalities, counties, or boards of education have appropriated money to help defray their costs; however, the ASOL report notes that, in the twenty cities studied, only twelve percent of the cost of youth concerts was covered by funds from government sources, seventy-five percent from the general operating expenses of the orchestras themselves, and twelve to thirteen percent from ticket sales.[6] During the 1960s, some orchestras and local boards of education took advantage of the availability of special federal education funds in the extensive programs for the disadvantaged (Title I) and for curricular innovation (Title III).* Though few orchestras took advantage of this source of support, Title I and Title III funds were put to extremely good use, as we shall see, in the Lincoln Center Student Program in New York. More recently, as the National Endowment for the Arts has substantially increased its grants to symphony orchestras, forty-two per cent of the projects funded in

---

* The impact of these education funds undoubtedly caused the sharp rise in government funding (75.6% for Major orchestras) in 1966–67 shown in Appendix G and certainly stimulated closer liaison between orchestras and public education agencies that continued after these Title I and III projects terminated.

1970–71 and fifty-five percent of money allocated were for educational purposes.[7]

This raises some basic questions of the content and objectives of the education programs of our orchestras. It is a sad commentary on these activities that there is so little evidence of fundamental educational thinking on the part of either the orchestras or the educators with whom they work. One can read literally hundreds of pages of exhaustively compiled data and descriptive commentary in the previously mentioned ASOL report * without finding any hint of a basic philosophy, either explicit or implied. There are a few truly innovative youth programs, to which we will refer later in this chapter, but to a large degree the so-called education activity of symphony orchestras has yet to come to grips with the underlying forces which they must direct to achieving the objectives rather cogently defined in the ASOL report:

1. The obligation of the orchestra to provide fine music for the youth in its community;
2. The value of developing in youth an awareness of fine music and cultural experiences;
3. The need to do all possible to develop among young people those who will become concert-goers and who will assume cultural leadership for the community in the future;
4. The need to provide children with the spiritual values inherent in listening to great music.[8]

This same study points to the difficulty in assessing the effectiveness of youth programs, either by their immediate impact on the young audience or in long-range increases in adult audiences. The most that one can obtain are personal generalizations; for instance, at one League meeting, a conductor stated that he had "indisputable evidence" that youth concerts built adult audiences, but when inquiry was pursued into the nature of this evidence, the most that could be determined was this conductor's recollection of meeting patrons in the community who told him that they had first heard him conduct when, as children, they attended his young people's concerts. No orchestra or organization has made any factual study of even this limited indicator of effectiveness of education programs.

In the light of our discussions of the symphonic repertory and the audience, the lack of evidence supporting an educational impact by the orchestras becomes a matter of deep concern. Despite years of youth programs, there is considerably more evidence that, in areas continuously served by orchestras, the symphonic audience has *not* grown in proportion to the overall population. The relative stability of the repertory during this period certainly indicates that these educational efforts have *not* opened up the receptivity of symphony audiences. Though many orchestras have developed youth programs for laudable if poorly implemented purposes, a major motive has been the utilization of excess players' services under extended contracts, and despite

* This report explicitly regrets its failure to locate any evaluation of effectiveness of the projects it studies, and implicitly avoids the larger issues of education philosophy. Within these limitations it is an extremely useful and informative study.

such notable exceptions as Milton Katims in Seattle and Maurice Abravanel in Salt Lake City, top artistic direction has often showed little interest in these developments. A few orchestras have employed educational directors, but unfortunately these are most concerned with the logistics of scheduling and liaison with the school bureaucracy. In short, these educational efforts have been undertaken with little real understanding of the basic processes whereby the music and the audience are brought together for creative communication.

Equally distressing, in this context, are the inadequacies of general education itself, both in administration and instruction. Orchestra managers, or their subordinates assigned to the youth programs, must spend an inordinate amount of time and effort, sometimes in persuading school administrators of the value of their program, and more often in the logistics of scheduling and transportation. Nor can such projects assume that their efforts will be supported educationally in the classrooms: the ASOL report comments unfavorably on the overall competence and motivation both of generalist and music-specialist teachers in the schools,[9] and we shall have occasion shortly to examine in more detail the problems encountered by the Lincoln Center Student Program in this respect. When the ASOL report cites a general belief of conductors that they can detect how well the children have been prepared for a program, and also states that a considerable number of conductors feel that preliminary instruction is useless, the only conclusion is that classroom preparation is too often inadequate.[10] Similarly, both orchestras and school officials are too inclined to plan these projects in quantitative terms, seeking the exposure of the greatest number of children, rather than directing intensive efforts to a possibly smaller number. Given the limitations of funds available to the orchestras, and the curricular pressures in the schools themselves, emphasis on numbers at the expense of intensity is the easiest choice. The school administrators thus avoid playing favorites in selecting which children should receive the programs, and the symphony orchestra can show inflated attendance figures in its efforts to gain private or public support. In a sound educational context, once-a-year exposure of a child to serious music can hardly be termed a meaningful experience; yet an amazing number of school programs are based on this scheme.

Within the orchestra community itself, little thought has been given to the fundamental psychological processes at the root of the musical experience that should shape the educational approach. A few conductors, managers, and trustees express some concern about the effectiveness of these programs, most often in terms either of the problems of holding the attention of an unruly audience or of building future audiences; occasionally this concern penetrates to questioning whether such youth programs are worth while. Nowhere in the symphonic field can one find evidence of basic educational thinking in a larger context or of efforts to evaluate and shape programs in terms of the fundamental psychological process involved. Two organizations, not directly a part of the symphony world but closely related to it, have recently sought fundamental re-examination of the very bases of their efforts. Young Audiences, after many years of presenting a rather rigidly structured type of program, has recently begun to develop completely new approaches to its programs and presentations. At the same time, Lincoln Center for the Performing Arts, which during the 1960s developed the most intensive and extensive performance arts education program in the nation, at the end of a decade of service reviewed its experience, radically and critically, in a study-report of exceptional significance not only to Lincoln Center itself but directly and by implication to the nationwide education activity of symphony orchestras.

Young Audiences, Inc.

Since its founding in 1950 in Baltimore, Young Audiences, Inc., has expanded its activities into thirty-four states, in which forty affiliated chapters presented, in 1970–71, some ten thousand performances by more than a thousand musicians, for nearly two million children, mostly in elementary schools.[11] Early in its history, it received financial support from the Edgar M. Leventritt Foundation and dynamic leadership from Mrs. Leventritt herself. Though the affiliate chapters are responsible for local fund-raising, the national organization had notable success in enlisting support from large foundations, the Music Performance Trust Fund, and in some cases government. In 1969–70, the total income of its chapters and national organization amounted to over $1.3 million, of which forty-two percent came from various local and national government sources for services rendered. Young Audiences has been a major beneficiary of the special trustee's funds of the MPTF, as well as of local allocations, to a total of nearly $232,000 in 1969–70, all of it paid directly to the union musicians employed.

From its original organization, Young Audiences worked on the principle of presenting small ensemble programs in the schools themselves, in the belief that intimate contact between a few musicians and a limited audience in familiar surroundings would provide the best possible conditions for musical communication. Some of the ensembles were touring groups, who played these programs in the schools in addition to their regular concerts. In most cases, however, local musicians were used, very often members of symphony orchestras; a few orchestra managements have worked closely with Young Audiences chapters to gain employment for their players and to coordinate schedules and school coverage, but in many cities the Young Audiences and symphony education programs are independent and sometimes competitive.

For a good number of years, the national Young Audiences leadership inclined toward prescribing a rather rigid formula of presentation: the programs combined demonstration of the instruments with explanation of the music and its performance in somewhat predetermined manner; performers were required to give the same program in each school, regardless of varying conditions or response. The national organization had a staff of music directors who supervised and often prescribed the actual presentation. More recently, however, Young Audiences, in its concern with basic problems of artistic communication and through its staff of five national and regional music directors and coordinators, has encouraged and guided the performers to seek their own mode of reaching the children with their music. Such efforts have involved encouragement of self-critical evaluations of their efforts on the part of the musicians themselves, in intensive discussions under staff leadership. In its search for new ways to bring music to children, Young Audiences has become increasingly concerned with training its performers in the special approaches needed; it has recently sought financing to implement a pilot project of intensive training and research into this problem.[12]

Like symphony orchestras, Young Audiences has not undertaken effectiveness studies; unlike symphony orchestras, it has no adult audience that can be studied to determine the long-range impact of youth programs. In this respect, its development and implementation of policies grow more directly out of a basic interest in establishing a genuine musical experience than from the other incentives found in the symphonic world. Their programs are continually subjected to review and evaluation by a young and highly motivated musical staff, which is primarily concerned not with logistics but with education performance; in this respect, it has no counterpart among symphony orchestras. As the only nationwide organization engaged in such efforts, Young Audiences presents a considerable variability in quality of performances: some reveal an informed concern for communication; others are little more than stereotyped demonstration concerts. With its nationwide staff, however, Young Audiences works diligently to locate sympathetic performers and to give them the benefit of its staff's wide experience. In its liaison with school administrations, this organization encounters a wide variety of success and problems, but again its national scope gives it considerable expertise in such matters. Its concentration of effort toward young children in the elementary schools is, as we shall have occasion to note later, undoubtedly a very sound approach. Most important, on both chapter and national levels, Young Audiences has a keen dedication to music education that is increasingly implemented with something more than mere good intentions—a growing insight into the practical realities of the musical experience of young children.*

Lincoln Center Student Program

Though it confines its operations to one area, albeit a heavily populated one, the Lincoln Center Student Program has developed an intensity and scope quite unlike any other education program in the performance arts.[13] Even in the limited district within four hundred miles of New York City, it presented in its most active year (1968–69) over fifteen percent as many performances as Young Audiences did nationally. Because Lincoln Center rep-

* Another nation-wide music organization, Affiliated Artists, Inc., is directed also at the college level, with emphasis on encouraging a close relation between artists and the community. Founded in 1966, it arranged campus and community visits of several weeks' duration by 42 artists in 1970–71. Though participating groups pay a modest fee, 84% of its annual budget of $500,000 is met by private and foundation contributions and by government grants.

resented a unique grouping of topflight constituents—the Juilliard School, the Metropolitan Opera, the New York City Ballet and Opera, the New York Philharmonic, and the Repertory Theater of Lincoln Center—it could draw upon an unrivaled pool of artistic talent and administrative leadership. As it reached the children in the schools, moreover, the Lincoln Center Student Program was also unique in offering, through one organization, a variety of different types of performance; not long after starting operations, it required each school to book at least five programs a year that would bring it performances of drama, opera, and film, as well as solo and ensemble music. Moreover, pre-existing youth programs, especially at the New York Philharmonic and Metropolitan Opera, were given financial and administrative assistance and to some extent coordinated with the overall in-school programs. Though the Lincoln Center Student Program embraced various activities for which children were brought to Lincoln Center, its most significant aspect, in this context at least, was its in-school work.

By 1968–69, its most active year, the Lincoln Center Student Program offered over 1,300 in-school performances in 329 junior and senior high schools of New York City, New York State, New Jersey, Vermont, Massachusetts, and Connecticut; in that year, an estimated 1,000,000 children attended in-school concerts, and another 35,600 attended performances at Lincoln Center. In 1970–71, however, activity decreased to 722 performances in 215 schools, attended by 637,000 children, plus another 30,000 at Lincoln Center performances.[14] To some extent, the administrative costs of this project were underwritten by special donated Lincoln Center funds allocated to education, but the major costs were borne by the schools themselves; of a total current (1971–72) cost in the vicinity of $1 million a year, approximately one-third was met by private contributions to Lincoln Center, the remainder by local school funds, state aid, and federal funding under Titles I and III of the Elementary and Secondary Education Act of 1965. One reason for the expansion of this program was that the officials at Lincoln Center very quickly established close working relations with the New York State Department of Education, one of the most progressive in this country, under the leadership of the late James H. Allen, Jr.* He and the state board of regents, with encouragement from Lincoln Center as spokesmen for its constituents, quite early determined upon the principle that education in the performance arts was an essential part of the general humanities curriculum. Moreover, again with essential assistance from Lincoln Center, the various school districts and administrations were encouraged to incorporate performance arts programs in their applications for federal funds under Titles I and III. These were "tapering" grants, in which the federal government paid all the costs for the first year, with local sources assuming an increasing share until, after three years, all funding was local. In some cases, under pressure from lack of funds, school administrations failed to continue these programs after federal financing was no longer available; this explains the decline of the program after 1969. But federal funding so effectively established the

* This extraordinary educator was later for a brief period the U.S. Commissioner of Education.

value of these programs that many schools continued, using their own resources.

While Lincoln Center administered this program, centralizing liaison with the schools in a way that five separate organizations could never have achieved individually, overall policy direction was established by an education council of representatives of all the Lincoln Center constituents. This policy council, over a period of years, became increasingly concerned with several major problems. Many of these arose in the area of educational philosophy, and the program soon uncovered basic areas of disagreement with traditional pedagogy. At the outset the Lincoln Center policy makers assumed that if first-class programs were offered to the schools, the teachers would integrate them into the curriculum. Pressure of other materials considered more important and the teachers' sheer ignorance of the performance arts made this patently impossible. Consequently, Lincoln Center itself, drawing upon talent outside the education system, devised elaborate preparatory manuals, at first for the teachers and eventually for student use.

Under the leadership of Lincoln Center, performers, performance administrators, teachers, and school officials maintained a continuing discussion on a variety of levels.* The Center itself joined the state education department in holding large-scale conferences at Lincoln Center, at which teachers, administrators, and artists discussed both the role of the performance arts in general education and the specific problems pertaining to it. In New York City itself, which involved the largest single project and presented the full variety of problems of urban education in their most intense form, there was continual dialogue between the performance administrators and the schools. Performers themselves evaluated their own efforts and the effectiveness of the schools in implementing the programs. Teachers and school administrators met frequently with the arts personnel for frank and often heated discussion.

One central question that emerged from these discussions revolved around the educational catchword "relevance." Many school personnel questioned the degree to which these arts were meaningful to children growing up in urban New York, and called upon the Center to devise programs that would relate more directly to the actual experience of these children. They reminded the Center personnel of the basic pedagogical principle of "proceeding from the known to the unknown, from the familiar to the unfamiliar." Sometimes their specific suggestions were as irrelevant as the programming they criticized, as when they suggested that piano recitals include Gershwin's *Rhapsody in Blue,* a work far more meaningful to the teachers themselves than to the students. On the other hand, some specific suggestions were incorporated in the presentations. Advantage was taken, for instance, of the relative youth of the many Juilliard performers in the program to close the generation gap very effectively: teen-age audiences were amazed and delighted to find that

---

* Lincoln Center had one advantage, not always enjoyed by local arts institutions, in having the enthusiastic support of the top officials of state and city school administrations. However, it soon discovered the *de facto* power of individual school principals, who had great latitude in following or not following the policy directives of higher officials. All arts organizations find their encounters with the school bureaucracy extremely educational in this very special sense.

their near-contemporaries could be so deeply involved in an alien culture. Dance programs, especially when presented by young students in a lively contemporary manner, were exceptionally well received. It must also be remembered that, in New York City particularly, this project was developed at precisely that moment when the entire city school system was in its greatest ethnic and administrative turmoil.

From its encounters with school principals and teachers, Lincoln Center eventually perceived the depth and breadth of the problem it faced in the integration of the performance arts into the general curriculum. In terms of audience response, such staged presentation as opera, dance, and drama usually held the attention of the audiences better than recitals or chamber music. This certainly reflects a major problem that symphony orchestras also face: how to instruct young people in the relatively abstract art of music. With a play, opera, or dance, there is a narrative content on which the teacher may base his instruction, but which most music lacks. In fact, one persistent demand of teachers in their encounters with performance representatives was for music which they could discuss in such concrete terms. This illustrates graphically the real problem of general education in the arts, for discussions of opera, drama, and dance in terms of narrative alone completely evade the issue of what makes these performances true art. The same deficiency, incidentally, pervades much teaching in the literary arts: a Shakespeare play is often discussed as a story, as psychology, as history—as everything, in fact, except what makes the play a work of art. Such instruction is like presenting Beethoven's *Eroica Symphony* as a commentary on the French Revolution or Napoleon: certainly these historical events played a part in Beethoven's conception, but a very small one as compared to his creative impulse and its realization in sound.

Educators are too inclined to look for informational content of the sort that can be easily imparted to the student and retrieved from him in response, as the criterion of effectiveness. The artistic essence of a piece of music—as of a poem, play, or opera—does not lend itself to such conventional retrieval or evaluation. A teacher may think that he has "taught" a play or an opera when the student can give evidence of having learned its story or characterization, but he has missed the whole point of it as a work of art.

In an effort to enhance creative communication to students in the New York City high schools, Lincoln Center in 1967 set up a limited experimental program that took advantage of the fact that this school system permitted professionals to assist the regular teachers in the classrooms, a scheme first devised to improve mathematics and science instruction in the 1960s. The Center enlisted the services of a small group of young professionals in the performance arts—composers, musicians, dancers, and actors, chosen both for their demonstrated ability in their own fields and for their interest and capability in the communication of their art—to undertake an intensive program of classroom instruction related to the specific performances the students would attend. These Resource Professionals, as they came to be known, worked with limited groups of not more than forty students in some twelve to fifteen high schools, a mere token sampling of the hundreds of thousands of high-school students in the city. Prior to each of five performances, they met with the students three times to discuss and explain the forthcoming performance in a freely structured manner. Sometimes a performer who was to appear later would participate in one or more of these preparatory sessions, and sometimes other artists joined the Resource Professionals in the classroom. Each planned and developed his own approach: one of them prepared for a Metropolitan Opera Studio production by guiding the students in devising an opera scenario of their own, as a basis for discussing just how and where in the narrative a specific type of music would be appropriate. Others used jazz and rock music to encourage their students to look more deeply into why certain feelings and ideas could be enhanced by musical expression. After each performance the Resource Professional returned to the classroom to review it and talk with their students about their reactions to it; on some occasions, the performers themselves took part in these review sessions, learning much about their own manner of performance.* Once a week during the school year the Resource Professionals spent a long evening together in discussion among themselves, reviewing their activities, passing on suggestions based on their own experiences, and criticizing one another's ideas.

This program, which cut across traditional methods of arts pedagogy in the freest possible manner, created extraordinary response among the students exposed to it. At the same time, the Resource Professionals themselves developed exciting new ways of looking at both their instructional work and their own creative or performing careers. Some of the most successful were young composers, able to anticipate a variety of performances without being tied to specific instruments or media. Many of these musicians, composers and performers alike, gained new insights into their own problems of artistic communication and developed a special sensitivity to audience response. Despite the limitations of scope, imposed by shortage of funds and of suitable personnel, the program demonstrated that a direct encounter between young people and professionals could implement the communication of an arts experience in ways that no traditional pedagogy could attain.† In this the Lincoln Center Student Program paralleled similar discoveries in the recent development of a more freely structured approach in Young Audiences. In fact, there was close but informal interchange of ideas

---

* Many of the performers who took part in these programs, especially the more talented Juilliard students, have gone on to important careers in the arts. Invariably they recall their participation in the Lincoln Center Student Program as an extraordinary educational experience for themselves in communicating with an audience.

† In 1970–71, the Center of Field Research and School Services at New York University undertook an evaluation of certain phases of the Lincoln Center Student Program, including schools served by the Resource Professionals. Their admittedly inconclusive findings revealed, among other things, a relatively slight impact on the children tested in terms of changes in attitudes toward the arts, as shown by controlled questionnaires. Since the study covered only one year, largely in junior and senior high schools, and since the evaluating techniques themselves were being tested, this report must be regarded as tentative, though it has been widely cited as evidence of failure in such efforts in arts education, including those of symphony orchestras which it did not study.15

between the two groups: one of the most active board members of Young Audiences, Mrs. John W. Straus, was also a member of the Lincoln Center educational policy council; and Warren H. Yost, the Young Audiences national music coordinator, was one of the original Resource Professionals in the Lincoln Center program. However, while Young Audiences directed its efforts toward the elementary schools, the Lincoln Center Student Program largely confined itself to junior- and senior-high-school students. This difference in approach has had a strong influence on the entire development of the Lincoln Center Student Program, which still faces the massive indifference to the arts that has become so strongly entrenched in teen-agers. Young Audiences, in dealing with younger children, has found a considerably more responsive audience, both nationally and in the New York area, where it overlaps the Lincoln Center Student Program geographically.

From its varied and intensive experience during the 1960s, the Lincoln Center Student Program at no point settled back into an attitude of self-satisfaction or frustration, though there was ample cause for both in various aspects of the program. With an open receptivity to new ideas and a deep desire to penetrate to fundamental principles of arts education, its leaders continually sought new solutions for problems as they arose, and re-shaped the direction of the project as their experience and "feedback" from actual performance accumulated. In 1970–71, Lincoln Center, with financing from the Carnegie Corporation, undertook a year-long study of the impact of the performance arts on young people, not only with particular emphasis on its own experience but also with reference to a number of notably successful education programs in other cities. Mark Schubart, a former journalist and Dean of the Juilliard School, who had been the Lincoln Center Vice-President for Education since 1962 and the guiding genius of its student program, took a year's leave from the Center to direct this study, which early in 1972 produced *Performing Arts Institutions and Young People —Lincoln Center's Study: "The Hunting of the Squiggle."*

This remarkable report reviews the history of the Lincoln Center Student Program in greater detail than summarized here, evaluates its effectiveness with extraordinary candor, and makes specific proposals for future innovation by Lincoln Center. Though much of it concerns a very specialized local situation and covers performance arts other than music, its general approach and many of its most important observations are applicable to the education efforts of symphony orchestras.

In Search of New Approaches

After reviewing a decade of experience with the Lincoln Center Student Program and originating a number of special research studies, this study calls for a totally new type of institution, embodying new approaches to educating young people in the performance arts. It finds that the present school curriculum and orientation and training of teachers are not conducive to the humanistic teaching of these arts. Of considerable importance to symphony orchestras, moreover, it finds that very few performance arts organizations themselves implement their responsibilities in this task. Though the study is primarily concerned with the New York area, it described certain projects across the nation that it felt represented effective activity by arts organizations. This coverage was by no means exhaustive: it mentions but one orchestral effort in arts education, that of the St. Paul Chamber Orchestra,* itself not a typical community symphony orchestra. The fact that no other orchestra within the purview of this book was deemed worthy of special comment is itself a negative comment on the symphonic scene in general.

In looking at the efforts of Lincoln Center as well as those of other groups, this study defines the scope of education in the performance arts as "the basic matter of perception and understanding of fundamental values," and goes on to say:

> For the teaching of these values can be achieved through one kind of art, or through many. Unfortunately most educational programs in the arts stress the less basic and less essential elements which are peculiar to a single artistic tradition or discipline. The *story* of the opera, the *form* of the symphony, the *history* of the ballet are stressed; the *nature* of sound, the *way* an artist works, the *function* of rhythm, the *arrangements* of movements in space are not.
>
> Consequently, it must be made clear that it is not Lincoln Center's mission to convert people to its own kind of art, or to demonstrate that one kind of art is more "cultural" than popular or folk art. It *is* the Center's mission, however, to teach values, and to demonstrate the elements found in all kinds of genuine creativity: expressivity, clarity, warmth, persuasiveness, emotional power, unity, consistency. These are qualities to be found everywhere in art and in many different kinds of artistic expression; the ability to recognize these values is the essence of aesthetic perception and should be the first goal of all education programs in the arts.[16]

Symphony orchestras, in their more limited scope, could well adapt this creed to their own efforts.

In its nationwide survey of performance arts activities, this study developed certain findings.[17] Most such activities are relatively new; less than a third were begun before 1960. A majority of them treat the students as audiences, only a few involve them as participants, and fewer still combine observation and participation. Though a small percentage of projects introduce ethnic materials or works created by young people, some 86% are based on traditional repertory: only 5% are interdisciplinary. The schools themselves initiated relatively few such projects: over 84% originated with arts organizations, nearly 80% of which financed them, fully or in part, with other fund-

---

* This orchestra, sponsored by the St. Paul Philharmonic Society and supported with considerable public and foundation funds, is a part of an arts complex that also includes drama, opera, and a museum strongly oriented toward youth. The personnel of twenty-two musicians not only gives its own public concerts but also plays an extremely diversified program of solo, ensemble, and orchestra concerts in the schools, as well as a residency program in colleges and universities. It is notable for the diversified activities in which it uses the musicians under long-term contract, and for its policy of selecting players partly in consideration of their potential for fitting into this kind of educational project.

ing coming from schools (22%), state governments (7%), federal government (8%), state arts councils (16%), and city or county governments (12%). Although they are viewed as continuing projects, little effort has been made to evaluate them; of the 21% of the programs surveyed that reported evaluation, most was in the form of reactions from students, educators, press, and project administrators. In most cases, performances do not involve top flight creative or performing artists; "the second cast is usually on hand for student performances," and only a few attempt to train the performers for the specialized approach required. Generally, performances are fixed in advance, with little or no adaptation to special circumstances to be encountered in individual schools or areas.

On the part of professional educators—teachers and administrators—the study also found very little commitment to the idea of incorporating the arts into the curriculum.[18] Many reflected a typically American ambivalence toward the arts, recognizing their importance but not considering them essential.* Some educators look upon the arts as entertainment, a passive matter of personal leisure-time pleasure, but not a vital experience. They often report that there is no room for the arts in an already crowded curriculum, especially at the high-school level, where the objective of college preparation is so important. Many educators are personally indifferent to the arts: they do not themselves attend performances regularly. Even where general humanities programs have been established in the curriculum, the performance arts are seldom included in an integrated fashion. Though the study cites a number of programs that have done this,[19] it also points out that most Title III programs in the performance arts were terminated once the federal funding stopped.

After reviewing the weaknesses of both the arts organizations (Lincoln Center included) and the school community in creating effective education programs, this study calls for a new kind of arts institution, which will bring young people into direct personal contact with the creative and performing artist at work.[20] Though the proposals for such an institution are developed in the specific context of Lincoln Center and the highly specialized and concentrated urban environment of New York, their major premises have great relevance to symphony orchestras and other arts institutions in American communities.

The first requirement laid down for such a new arts education institution is that it orient its materials and approach to young people in all their variety and diversity.

> In fact there are many who feel that the greatest single problem in American education and perhaps world education is that its size and structure prevent it from dealing with young people as people, thus assuring that almost any learning experience is likely to be wrong for a majority of the participating students. This would seem to be particularly true in matters of art and aesthetic percep-

---

* Typical of the attitude of boards of education toward the arts is the fact that during the current budgetary crises which urban education has faced, arts programs, including chorus, band, and orchestra, are among the first "frills" to be eliminated as curricula are cut back to meet the limitations of financing.

tion, areas of human experience which so personally and so individually involve cultural heritage, individual expression and response, emotions and expectations, in combination with intellectual understanding and historical perspectives.[21]

Artists themselves need to have their own creative and interpretative isolation broken down in special ways before they can successfully perform an education function; those that succeed in this often find their own artistic experience enriched in a unique manner. Similarly, educators must themselves become educated in the arts: this is less a matter of factual information than of their own personal experience, feeling the arts and learning from observation of artists working with their students. Community organizations, which use the arts as a means of involving young people in their broader religious, social, or nonschool education programs, must look upon these programs as enrichment for their own sake and not as a means of promoting their special causes. In its review of performance arts education, the Lincoln Center study found a serious shortage of available published materials and little in the media of radio, television, and recording that was useful to the basic purposes of education; the institution it has in mind would encourage more relevant developments in these areas.

Ultimately, the study points to the establishment of a Lincoln Center Project for Young People.*

> The essential fact about the Project is that it is a place of the performing arts. It is a stage for performing artists, a place where artists work at their craft and their art on the highest level of excellence. But it differs from other stages in at least two important respects: it is interdisciplinary in that it deals with drama, music, opera, dance, film, puppetry, mime, and various combinations thereof, and its efforts are directed solely to young people and those adults who have a significant role to play in the lives of the young. It is, in a sense, a school too, but it is first and foremost an arts organization with a special purpose; one in which the young are not only honored guests but active participants as well.[22]

From this summary it is obvious that the study is very much oriented toward potential developments at Lincoln Center itself, and that it pertains, as had the Center's entire student program, primarily to junior- and senior-high-school students, limiting its application to our main concern here. This emphasis on high-school students, essentially the teen-age population, has had certain important consequences in the formulation of its specific project: its proposal for a centrally located project, to which young people would come, makes much sense for teen-age youth, but it involves great logistic difficulties for younger children. One cannot help but wonder, reading these lucid and eloquent proposals, how deeply motivated these teen-agers will need to be to take advantage of the project proposed here, unless their interest in and desire for art are developed in their pre-teen years. In this respect, the study, by ignoring the earlier introduction of children to the arts, seems to cut itself off from the broader issues of arts education. Never-

* This is the "squiggle" (a small, wiggly mark or scrawl) referred to in the original title of this study; it represents the manner in which a rather amorphous original concept of this project was shaped and structured from within, through the application of observation and development of goals, rather than as an arbitrary pre-existing institution.

theless, in its radical concern for getting the facts and basing its observations on unprejudiced appraisal of the fundamental education problem, this study goes further than most in advancing constructive consideration of the problem.*

One orchestra has anticipated this proposal for a performance arts organization devoted exclusively to education. Under the dynamic leadership of Ralph and Flori Lorr, the Orchestra da Camera of Massapequa, New York, has as its sole activity the provision of orchestra and chamber music programs in the schools of suburban Long Island. Though employing no regular artistic director, the Lorrs themselves act as educators in supervising the activities of their "guest" conductors and players and in implementing close administrative and artistic liaison with the schools they serve. Though the orchestra plays exclusively for school children, it enjoys some financial support from private contributors and considerable funding from the schools themselves, the New York State Council on the Arts, and the National Endowment for the Arts. Though such an educational program could operate only in a highly populated suburban area, its promotional methods and educational philosophy deserve study by full-scale orchestras in devising their youth programs.

The Creative Experience

The arts education activities which we have so far considered all fall short of their goals to some degree, and this failure may well be the result of a lack of a comprehensive and fundamental understanding of the creative experience itself. The symphony orchestras have, to a large extent, ventured into education by the back door, as it were; audience building, surplus musicians' services, fund-raising, and a vague sense of community service have combined in various degrees to motivate their efforts. Young Audiences, after many years of a rather autocratically structured program, has recently moved toward a more flexible approach, largely because of very valuable practical experience, but with little explicit education theory. Lincoln Center, similarly, has taken a highly pragmatic approach, thanks to its extremely open-minded sensitivity, but its efforts have been directed at an age group that represents only a part of the youth population. It should be no reflection to point out that, valuable as their efforts have been, everything in their practical experience points to the need for developing a broader and more basic education philosophy, using their varied expertise and insights to implement it.

Some of the most fruitful suggestions in arts education have been advanced by Sir Herbert Read, especially in his book *Art and Society*. Though he reviews the whole span of art activity, primarily in the visual arts, from

---

* This Lincoln Center report is but the beginning of a continuing study of arts education under Mark Schubart's direction; at the June, 1972, conference of the American Symphony Orchestra League in Cincinnati, Nancy Hanks announced that the National Endowment for the Arts would in FY 1973 give financial support to its continuation and expansion.

primitive man to modern society, and has little to say specifically about the performance arts, Read's psychological approach is applicable elsewhere. After seeking a common denominator and defining specialized variants in the social context of artistic expression in all types of society, Read turns to psychoanalytic theory for a basis for his educational proposals in the arts.[23] There he finds, in the relation between the instinctual *id,* the controlling *superego,* and the conscious *ego,* a framework within which the creative process is experienced by the observer or listener. Read proposes that in artistic creation certain elements from the artist's turbulent *id* become incorporated in the finished artifact, their expression shaped by the *superego's* psychic and social forces in such a way that they arouse comparable response in the *id* of the audience. He notes that some psychoanalysts have suggested that the *id-superego-ego* relationships in the creative artist may, in some way, be different from the noncreative person, but insists that all individuals are capable of participating in this process as an audience once their own receptive *ego-superego-id* channels are opened up.*

Though Read does not do so, these hypotheses can be extended to the performance arts, in which there is an intermediate step in this creative-responding process. In his interpretation of the composer's or playwright's creation, the musician or actor develops his own *id* response to the composition or play, which he in turn fashions in his own way into the performance experienced by the audience. The functions of interpretation, of liberty or fidelity to the text, involve the interplay of psychic and social forces operating through the performer's *ego* and *superego* in varying degrees determined by his training and tradition, as well as by his own inner *id* drives.

The implications of such a theory, for arts and music education, can only be sketched here in a summary manner.[25] In his proposals for arts education, Read starts from the by no means novel premise that young children are far more responsive to the free flow of communication from *id* to *id* than older ones. He observes that in the development of the young psyche there comes a point around the tenth to twelfth years when certain psychological barriers begin to restrict the kind of communication he describes. Unless these are opened and working before that time, future development will not necessarily be impossible, but it will be difficult. In music, therefore, the experience of Young Audiences is more relevant to this observation than that of such a program as Lincoln Center's: and, where Young Audiences has moved toward a more freely structured personal involvement of children with the performances, Read's suggestions seem to be confirmed.

While it must be recognized that these observations must be tentative and superficial, certain suggestions can be made with specific reference to the education potential of symphony orchestras. In the first place, exposure to music should begin at an early age—in pre-school, if possible—and it should encompass all young children, who may be assumed at this stage to be

* The psychoanalytic approach to art and artists has been explored by a number of students—more, actually, from the point of view of individual therapy than for generalized aesthetic theorizing.[24] But even such studies, to the degree that they offer and test hypotheses of how the creative artist functions, provide data for developing education theories.

equally receptive. In this respect, the pedagogical innovations of Suzuki in Japan, Orff in Germany, and Kodály in Hungary are of special significance, for they involve the children through actual performance of music, rather than mere listening. The child who learns to produce a musical sequence of sounds on the violin under Suzuki, or with his voice under Kodály or Orff, is far more deeply involved in music than one who is listening, and the experience he gains will open his receptivity as a listener even if he never goes on to be a performer. Thus, the limited program of the New Orleans Philharmonic in sponsoring and staffing classes in the Suzuki violin method for black children will not only lay the basis for training black performers but will encourage future audiences, if it is carried on to later years. Several music schools, some of them employing orchestra players as instructors, are using the Suzuki method with considerable success in the instruction of young children. Because of their involvement in instrumental music, symphony orchestras have apparently not had any contact with the Orff or Kodály vocal approaches, but a number of private and public schools have.

Such programs should be aimed at the total group of children to bring them progressively into more and more formal contact with music. One difficulty in many cities is the shortage of professional musicians or classroom teachers capable of implementing these programs. Here the Lincoln Center study's observations on the importance of involving musicians themselves has important implications for the role of symphony orchestras in instruction. Many orchestras have long had some of their players teaching in schools, but usually as specialized instructors of a limited group of children, most often in high schools, in performance. Young Audiences, the Lincoln Center Student Program, and similar projects have shown that many professional musicians can be extremely successful in arousing young people's interest in music, once they themselves are trained in the special approach needed. In many communities, symphony personnel includes their best musicians; not all may be suited by temperament or interest to work in such programs, but many could, given proper conditions.

Such programs also need published music materials for performance, graded according to difficulty but offering substantial musical content. The scarcity of materials of authentic artistic value was the subject of a conference of music educators held at Yale University in 1964 under the auspices of the White House panel on education. Out of this conference there developed a repertory research project, financed by the United States Office of Education, in which the Juilliard School coordinated the research and study of a variety of experts in specific musical eras and styles to assemble a graded vocal and instrumental repertory for use in grades kindergarten through six. These materials, all based on authoritative musicological research or written by well-known contemporary composers, have been published as the Juilliard Repertory Project for practical use in the classroom.[26]

In addition to introducing music to the general youth population at the elementary level, such projects will soon detect those relatively few children of genuine musical talent. One of the serious problems faced by our musical profession is the lack of early detection and training of musical talent in our schools; we cannot wait until late childhood or early adulthood to start training the string players that the music profession so sorely needs today. Furthermore, to the degree that such programs penetrate into ghetto schools, black and other disadvantaged children may receive the motivation and guidance lacking in their home environment to become involved in music as a vocation. The problem of black participation in our orchestras is a complex one, but much of it cannot be solved until black children find in music a source of real satisfaction at an early age; it cannot be solved by "crash" programs of training in high school or after.*

If Read is correct in observing that children at a certain point in their growth develop a barrier to the receptivity of artistic stimulus, unless it has been developed earlier, it may well be that education programs aimed at teen-agers should not be forced on the total group, but rather should be gradually tapered off to allow those interested—those whose receptivity has been developed earlier—to receive continuing attention. These high-school students can be given academic training in the arts in which they are interested: if their instinctual experience of music has been developed earlier, they are ready now for exposure to such subjects as music history, form, and harmony. At the same time, those children with special talent will continue to receive practical performing instruction, in the course of which their talent and vocational motivation will be tested and developed. Symphony personnel can play an important role in the practical musical training of teen-age musicians, not only as instrumental instructors but also in coaching ensemble and orchestral music; the Cincinnati "in-school" project and a similar program in San Francisco, where symphony players work directly with high-school student musicians, have demonstrated how successful such instruction can be in bringing young musicians into direct contact with professionals.

At some point, those young instrumentalists of special talent should be encouraged to join youth orchestras, outside the schools themselves and run either by professional orchestras or independently. The usual orchestra programs in the schools tend to reduce the more talented children to the level of the least talented. Citywide youth orchestras offer an opportunity for a higher level of accomplishment, but they must be operated in close cooperation with school authorities if they are to avoid parochial rivalries. The structure of these can vary. Some may be undertaken on school initiative with outside cooperation, as in Albuquerque. Some may be completely independent structurally, as is the Portland, Oregon, Junior Symphony Orchestra. Others may be, as in an increasing number of cities, directly sponsored by the local symphony. On a higher level of training, designed to prepare young musicians to go directly into professional orchestras, is the Chicago Civic Orchestra, sponsored by the Orchestral Association, using players from the Chicago Symphony as private instructors and ensemble coaches, and

---

* One reason for the greater success of black singers is undoubtedly due to the fact that vocalists in general do not discover their musical aptitudes until early maturity, when they can pursue music as a vocation on their own initiative. The physical and psychic requirements for instrumental music must be met at a much earlier age.

funded through special endowments established after 1919 at the behest of Frederick Stock. Nearly a quarter of the present Chicago Symphony players received training in the Civic Orchestra, and many others trained there have gone into other orchestras. The present program of the Civic Orchestra, under the direction of Margaret Hillis, encompasses a broad presentation of theory and ensemble performance in addition to orchestral training. This area has great potential for local orchestras, who must shape such programs according to local conditions—relations with the public schools and resident conservatories, the availability of their own players as instructors, and the overall development of a total education program.

Moreover, though the musical experience of younger children will be centered in the school, teen-age youth should be encouraged to seek their musical experiences either in such special centers as suggested by the Lincoln Center report or at adult-style concerts. To some extent it may be necessary for them to attend regular adult concerts, but wherever possible, special concerts should be designed for young people at this stage. If the musical receptivity of teen-agers has been already developed, they will be able to accept considerably more substantial repertory than is now given at youth concerts. As record sales show, new trends such as increased interest in Baroque music, Mahler, or Ives have often been supported by youthful record collectors before they spread to a wider audience. Given a young audience of this sort, the whole concept of programming for teen-agers will be transformed. One of the most important features of the Lincoln Center report is its emphasis on orienting arts activity toward young people themselves, on gratifying their search for their own identity, their own "thing" in the arts.

Such an education program may have the best chance—certainly better than present programs—of producing a growing audience with artistic awareness and hunger for musical experience. Whether such an audience will respond to the present structure of the repertory is impossible to predict, but it will hear music in a quite different way and it will base its demand for music not on fashion, tradition, or the dictates of conductor, manager, or trustees but on its own musical experience. Hopefully, once a person's ears are opened to the fundamental musicality of a Beethoven or a Mozart, he will respond with equal enthusiasm to the new music of a Webern, a Carter, or a Sessions. He may also find a continuity with his own total musical experience in the most radical departures of the *avant garde*.

The Role of the Orchestra

The symphony orchestras of this nation are in a unique position to assume leadership in exploring a more relevant approach to arts education. They have been engaged in youth programs longer than other arts groups; they encompass, in most cities, the musical resources of their communities and thus have professional talent at their command; and they have established liaison with their school systems. Though the proposal of the Lincoln Center

Project for Young People is one institution's special response to the challenge presented by an intensely compacted urban area, the thrust of that study is something that all arts groups—symphony orchestras more than most—may well emulate as they review their own local challenges. However, orchestras must make every effort to involve other arts, performance and visual, in planning as integrated and interdisciplinary an approach as possible. The orchestras cannot look upon education as a narrow effort to build their own audiences or to secure favored treatment in the allocation of private and government funding. Their position of leadership should not lead to domination.

There is a crying need for arts organizations in general, again with symphony orchestras in a peculiar position of leadership, to join together on a national or regional scale to explore these questions more thoroughly. The Lincoln Center study could have been undertaken only by an organization of its eminence and wealth. Even so, its scope was necessarily limited and its conclusions confined to a special setting. No American orchestra could have made such a study, but together our orchestras might. The task of reviewing and evaluating present activities, of exploring fundamental educational psychology in the arts, and of formulating projects suitable for implementation locally calls for cooperative action on the largest scale. The ASOL study of 1968 provided much factual data, but no appraisal of effectiveness in basically creative terms, nor was it imbued with a clear sense of education philosophy, simply because this has so seldom concerned our orchestras.

Thinking through the psycho-aesthetic implications of the education function of symphony orchestras alone is a problem calling for more expertise than they now can muster from their own resources. The psychological approach suggested here is no more than that: a suggestion of the kind of thinking our orchestras must do before they can really lay claim to educational relevance. The subject cries out for more expert consideration and exploration than this book can only recommend in a very general way, and such basic thought seems more and more indicated as a primary imperative that must be met before education implementation can be even explored.

In a narrow sense, it is very much to the self-interest of orchestras to do this. If the music our orchestras play is to be carried to a greater audience, education is the most promising way. As orchestras demand an increasing share of the privately contributed dollar, they must justify this in terms of expanding service. The same is true, to an even greater degree, of the long-range hope of gaining more support from public funds: pleas for such funding can be based on general cultural welfare for only so long, before the public and its servants begin to question the overall effectiveness of symphony activities in their widest reach. Orchestras would be well advised to prepare for that day by knowing precisely what they are doing.

However, if orchestras approach the challenge of the young audience simply out of concern for their own self-preservation, just to inflate their quantitative spread, they will commit a sad disservice to the art to which they claim dedication. The most important consequence of a soundly based and creatively implemented education program will be the enrichment of the lives of the people, young and old, that it reaches. In terms of the comment by Roger Sessions quoted earlier, a true education program will transform hearers into listeners. In previous discussion of the symphony audience and repertory we have seen how difficult it is to define the motivation that brings individuals into the concert hall. Though comprehensive and precise data are lacking, we know that a considerable portion of the symphony audience enjoys only a superficial experience of the art of music. Programs of music education based on sound psycho-aesthetic principles should create for orchestras not only a larger audience but a more responsive and loyal one, in which a larger proportion of listeners will experience all music, whether by Mozart or Webern, as music and not as a superficial form of fashionable entertainment. It will be a more critical audience, not so much in rejecting that which it does not like as in demanding a deeper and broader repertory. Conductors and managements will no longer feel the deadening weight of audience resistance to new music that has increasingly stagnated the programming of symphony orchestras. Such a program will go far to give the American composer a fair chance for survival with the symphony audience, a chance based not on pleas for a hearing, not on the vagaries of conductors, managers, and trustees, but on their ability to add to the musical experience of a truly educated audience.

In one of his last essays Sir Herbert Read described how the traditional inseparability of art and society has broken down in modern industrial society.[27] He found our contemporary civilization increasingly impotent aesthetically as individual human efforts became alienated from the processes of nature, as scientific rationalism progressively stripped away the mysteries of the spirit and beauty, and as mass conformity destroyed the essentially individualistic approach to creation. To restore art to its proper and essential place in civilization is, in Sir Herbert's view, the larger role of education: man's recovery in the social context of the indispensable totality of his experience is an educational process in which art itself must play a fundamental role. Education *for* the arts thus becomes, in a larger sense, education *by* the arts.*

---

* Since these comments were written, the J.D.R. 3rd Fund has published *All the Arts for Every Child* by Stanley S. Madeja, a report on the Arts in General Education Project in the schools of University City, Missouri. Though the approach of that project to arts education differs greatly from the arts organization orientation suggested here, it uses artists of the region wherever possible and has since 1968 developed an exceptional program of great interest to other groups seeking similar involvement of children in the arts. Such efforts, made independently of arts organizations, may be an alternative to the above proposals or they may offer an opportunity for a quite different involvement of orchestras and others in broader and more intensive educational programs.

PART FIVE

Contingencies of the Future

"... *unless* ..."
Samuel R. Rosenbaum

CHAPTER XIX

Toward a
Responsible Institution

The time has come in this account of the symphony orchestra in America to forsake the editorial *we,* drop the circumlocutions of the passive voice, and abandon tentatively expressed conclusions in favor of direct statement in the first person singular. Wherever I have gone to seek information for this study, I have been impressed by the intense concern, both in and out of the symphony field itself, for the future viability of the orchestra in America. I have been asked repeatedly for my views on the current state of the orchestra and the possibilities of its survival. Often this question has been couched in such terms as, "Do you agree with Leonard Bernstein * that the symphony orchestra is dying?" or "Does the orchestra have a valid place in modern urban society?" or "How can the orchestra survive?" Naïve as these questions may sound to one who has traversed the field covered by this present study, they testify to a deep and pervasive anxiety about the orchestra in America.

The pressing financial crises in a large segment of the institution, and the degree to which awareness of them has penetrated down to orchestras by no means as deeply affected, have intensified this concern. However, this apprehension has yet to apply itself to specific problems in a wider context: all too often, the tendency is to look at the present state and future prospects of the American orchestra in a financial context, viewing such other vital issues as education, audience, community services, government funding, and artistic policy in relation to their impact on the widening income gap. Though by no means minimizing the importance of the economics of our symphony orchestras, I am convinced that the issues and challenges confronting this cultural institution require much more than a primarily financial approach. To be sure, virtually every aspect of symphonic activity has direct financial

---

* Actually, Bernstein has not explicitly proclaimed the demise of the symphony orchestra as an institution, except to question the viability of the symphonic repertory. Bernstein's views on the decline of the symphony as a form of musical expression have already been citel in Chapter XVII.

implications, and the continued viability of our orchestras rests in the last analysis on their fiscal solvency, but the degree to which economics has dominated major policy deliberations has too often obscured and distorted basic consideration of the total role of orchestras.

During the past decade and a half, American orchestras have been subjected to pressures and crises that have caused many to question fundamentally the very rationale that created them a century ago and has guided their unparalleled development since. The strongest force in this turmoil arose from the demands of the professional orchestra players for a decent income. To this extent, the major issues confronting orchestras in recent years have been economic, but these problems have also had noneconomic roots and have raised noneconomic questions: the musicians' demands for economic status involved the very survival of the music profession itself, as the Ford Foundation explicitly recognized in 1965, and utilization of the musical resources that developed from meeting these demands has presented symphonic leadership with an artistic challenge and opportunity that have not yet fully recognized or implemented.

These demands also forced the orchestras to seek a broader base of financial support, a search that inevitably aroused an unprecedented degree and breadth of public awareness of them. At the same time, they were subjected to a searching examination and sometimes devastating attack from a number of sources, some badly misinformed, some spurred by the best of motives, but many superficial and ignorant of the nature of the symphonic institution.*

Two basic attacks on the symphonic institution have been mounted on the economic front: one, largely from conservative businessmen, questions both the efficiency of management and the necessity of operating at a "deficit"; the other, arising from the left, as it were, contends that symphony orchestras and the arts in general should command a lower priority in the allocation of private and government financial resources in view of more pressing problems in modern urban society. At the same time, the symphonic institution has been attacked for its exclusivity of overall policy direction and artistic program. To both, critics have applied the term "elitism" often indiscriminately: the unquestionable degree to which our orchestras have been controlled and directed by the business and financial leadership of this nation has often been confused with the kind of music these orchestras play. It is essential, I am convinced, that we distinguish between two types of elitism in the symphonic world. The domination of our orchestras' support and control by the establishment is quite different from the qualitative element of

---

* Two such critiques have been widely publicized, despite their questionable factual basis and special pleading. A 1969 report by the Midwest Research Institute, *An Evaluation of the Performing Arts, I. The Symphony,* attempts to combine qualitative critical opinions and statistical data in a haphazard manner and uses fragmentary economic data as a basis for unjustified predictions of the demise of a number of important orchestras, which it mentions by name.[1] Janet Schlesinger's 1971 study, *Challenge to the Urban Orchestra: The Case of the Pittsburgh Symphony,* calls for a revision of the power structure of the symphony in America to make it more representative of a broader urban base; she presents her case with such obvious antiestablishment bias, factual disorganization, and naïveté of rhetoric as to vitiate the merit of her central argument.

discrimination—call it aristocracy, if you will—that is essential to any serious art.

In all of these criticisms, I find some degree of validity, as well as a considerable element of misunderstanding and misinformation. Many of these issues have already cropped up in the course of this study in a variety of contexts, and I shall here consider them in the light of what I have reported earlier. But I believe that these criticisms by no means encompass all of the issues and challenges confronting the American symphonic institution, nor do I believe that approaching them directly will necessarily produce the most revealing insight. Here again I turn to the basic institutional framework of the orchestra in this nation and offer my views in terms of the four elements that comprise it in its distinctively American form: the conductor and artistic direction, the musicians and the orchestra as a career, the audience and the creative product,* and management and policy direction. As must be obvious from my previous account of the symphony orchestra in this country—historical background, present activities and scope, basic economics, and artistic impact—many of the most pressing challenges facing our orchestras arise from the interaction of these institutional components. In my concluding remarks, I hope to define these issues in a way that will cast some light on the more general critique of the orchestra that has developed in recent years and to anticipate some of its future possibilities.

Pervading these considerations and underlying my specific judgments concerning various phases of the orchestral institution are certain basic assumptions, often implied in my account so far but now requiring explicit statement. I believe that the symphony orchestra is an essential part of American culture, as a vehicle for the preservation and presentation of a body of art every bit as important to the heritage of Western civilization as the painting of Giotto, Leonardo, and Picasso, the sculpture of Michelangelo, Rodin, and Moore, or the literature of Shakespeare, Keats, and Joyce. I believe, moreover, that the training and support of the special artistic skills of the professional musician are essential to achieving this end: to a very real degree, the symphony orchestra in America has become the primary and central force in maintaining this profession in scores of cities across the nation, without which such other performance arts as opera, dance, and theater would suffer immeasurably. However, these beliefs and my emphasis on description rather than criticism in my account so far should by no means imply that I am an uncritical apologist for the symphonic status quo: I do not believe that the institution has always operated effectively in the past, I view its present state with considerable misgivings, and I have deep concern for its future course. In this respect, my general answer to the queries pressed on me about its present and future viability can best be summarized by one word: *unless.* Here I borrow from the observations of Samuel R. Rosenbaum,† who has de-

---

* Having already presented my views on this topic in the preceding three chapters, I shall here refrain from further discussion of audience, repertory, and education.

† It has been my pleasure to encounter Colonel Rosenbaum on a number of occasions and in varying contexts during the two decades before his death in November, 1972. He served the cause of music with unique distinction as a trustee of the Philadelphia Orchestra Association

scribed the symphony orchestra as in danger of becoming a dinosaur destined for evolutionary extinction *unless* it changes its course in essential respects. Rosenbaum referred primarily to the development of broader education programs, but I believe that his qualification must be applied more generally.[2]

The Bernstein Syndrome
and Artistic Direction

The story is told [3] of the Boston lady who exclaimed ecstatically to Serge Koussevitzky after a concert, "Doctor Koussevitzky, to us you are God!" to which he replied, "I know my responsibility." * Though few other conductors have defined their role as explicitly as did this Russian autocrat, his reply reflects in colorful terms the traditional role of the conductor in the American symphony orchestra. It has long been an article of fundamental faith that only the sustained and reasonably permanent affiliation of a resident conductor can produce the high quality that our orchestras have achieved. A corollary of this assumption has been the elevation of the role of the conductor to that of a local artistic dictator, not only in his direction of the orchestra but also in his status in the community. Charismatic aura, whether of Stokowski or Koussevitzky a generation ago or of Leonard Bernstein today, is as much a necessity in Albuquerque or Salt Lake City as it is in New York or Los Angeles.

Yet profound changes have occurred in the role of the conductor in America, changes not only in his charismatic style but also in his institutional relation to the orchestra he serves. The growing number of orchestras demanding the services of internationally celebrated conductors, the increasing opportunities for them to conduct abroad, and the availability of rapid transportation by jet airplane have made possible a new kind of career that has seriously undermined the traditional concept of the resident conductor in many communities, with results that would have been unthinkable to Theodore Thomas or Henry L. Higginson. Though I described early manifestations of this phenomenon in Stokowski's conflict with the Philadelphia trustees four decades ago and in the New York Philharmonic's acceptance of part-time leadership by Toscanini, the American symphonic ideal has been typically represented by Eugene Ormandy's long-time exclusive affiliation with the Philadelphia Orchestra and by the Philharmonic's search, after Toscanini, for a succession of more or less resident conductors through the tenure of Leonard Bernstein. But Bernstein, unlike Ormandy, found after

---

and as the first trustee and architect of the Music Performance Trust Funds. In the latter, he exercised his discretion as trustee with constructive originality, often arousing the opposition of the union musicians whose labor generated the MPTF. In my meetings with him, I found him invariably acutely perceptive about the problems of the music profession and, in my discussions with him about this book, singularly sympathetic to the plight of the symphony orchestra in this country.

* Later, when a friend asked him to confirm this exchange, Koussevitzky hesitated a moment and replied, "It sounds like me."

devoting ten years to the Philharmonic that his responsibilities in New York limited the full pursuit of his artistic ambitions and capabilities, and preferred retirement from direction of the orchestra to dividing his time between it and more diversified activities, though as conductor laureate he continues to appear as a guest. In my earlier accounts of specific orchestras I have described how some must accept part-time, essentially nonresident musical direction, and how others face in the not too distant future losing the services of long-time "permanent" conductors. There and elsewhere I find every indication of a strong trend toward loosening the close bonds that have traditionally tied conductors to their orchestras in this country.

These developments reflect not only an imbalance of supply and demand on the international "conductor market" but also a very real dissatisfaction with symphony conducting as an exclusive career. To some extent this must be recognized as a consequence of the relative stagnation of the symphonic repertory. Whether or not one agrees with Bernstein [4] in asserting that the symphony, as a composition, was no longer a vital musical expression after the close of the 19th century, I doubt if conductors today await the appearance of a new symphonic work with the eagerness with which Thomas, Damrosch, and Nikisch competed for the privilege of presenting music by Wagner, Brahms, or Tchaikovsky for the first time in this country, or find an excitement comparable to Thomas's discovery of young Richard Strauss. Having already described the current state of the symphonic repertory, I can only emphasize here that the international music scene offers different artistic opportunities to those conductors who seek stimulating new musical experiences in their careers—in opera, television, recording, and with smaller ensembles.

At the same time, those conductors willing to confine themselves to symphonic music incline increasingly to restrict their repertory and to repeat their specialties more frequently in a series of guest engagements. In their times Thomas, Stokowski, and Koussevitzky—like Ormandy in ours—had their own particular favorite areas in the repertory, but they also accepted the responsibility of covering its full range. Today, the conductor can specialize, so as to assure himself the greatest personal success and run the least risk of incurring criticism because he fails to create the same excitement in the broad repertory as in his specialties. The proclivity of critics and public alike to evaluate a performance not just for its own sake but by comparison with widely distributed recordings by other conductors * becomes a serious psychological hazard: the temptation to create a performance that will withstand comparison with those of celebrated interpreters, living or dead, rather than seek one's own insight into a work, is often hard to resist.

Consequently many conductors lack enterprise in seeking new repertory, from the past or present, and tend to follow fashions established by their more glamorous colleagues. I have already described the emergence of

* Even so eminent a conductor as Fritz Reiner, when director of the Chicago Symphony Orchestra, was subjected in the press to unfavorable comparisons of his Beethoven performances with those recorded by Toscanini.

Mahler's music as an important part of the symphony repertory, thanks in large part to the performances and recordings of Bernstein. But the conductor who can establish a new trend in repertory is rare indeed, and I suggest, without any reflection on the quality of Mahler's music, that similar efforts by a conductor of Bernstein's stature on behalf of another composer or style of contemporary music might have had a similar impact.

One reason many conductors have emulated Bernstein's espousal of Mahler can be traced also to his music's suitability as a vehicle for virtuoso showmanship—not only for the orchestra itself but also, rightly or wrongly, for the conductor. Much of the frequently heard repertory from the first quarter of the present century—the tone poems of Richard Strauss, the large orchestral works of Debussy and Ravel, and the Roman suites of Respighi—fall into this category. It has often occurred to me that if a conductor were to devote the same time and effort lavished on *Also sprach Zarathustra* or *The Pines of Rome* to such orchestrally difficult works as the virtually unknown symphonies of Roger Sessions, the cause of native American music might be better served. But few conductors would regard Sessions's music as "effective" for the orchestra or easy for an audience to grasp, whereas Strauss and Respighi provide vehicles which impress the audience with their theatricality and convince it that any conductor who can evoke and control such spectacular orchestral effects is a master virtuoso.

The problem of the symphonic repertory is a complicated one, and I certainly do not suggest placing the full blame for its stagnation in the past generation on the conductor alone: symphony boards, audiences, critics, and composers themselves have been involved in that process. However, the conductor occupies the central position in programming: whatever pressures may be applied upon him, his is the final responsibility, whether he stands up for his own principles or bows to the demands of others. His own conception of how his career can be best advanced or his ideals of artistic service play a part in his decision, as do his musical ability and technical expertise. Not every conductor possesses these latter in sufficient degree to enable him to evaluate new scores (especially without the aid of records or tapes). For such conductors, as well as for some that have these qualifications, it may be easier to spend their time jetting from one engagement to another and devoting their study time to perfecting their interpretation of the surefire repertory. Nothing so satisfies the ego of some conductors as producing spectacular orchestral effects and enjoying the thunderous applause from the audience, and nothing arouses greater dismay than having these efforts received coolly.

With the possible exception of the internationally renowned tenors and sopranos of opera, the symphony conductor is the most glamorous figure today in the performance arts. Moreover, he possesses two advantages not enjoyed by even the most celebrated opera singer. In performance, he enjoys an authority unmatched by the opera star, who must—to some degree, at least—perform as a part of a team; whatever the restrictions on his power to hire and fire players, or the pressures, direct and indirect, from his employers, the symphony conductor in America comes closer than any performing artist to achieving complete control over the performance of others. Moreover, to the public outside such great centers as New York the opera star is a remote figure, known through recordings, radio broadcasts, intensive publicity, and possibly a brief visit for a concert or local opera performance, while the conductor is a deity in residence, surrounded by an aura of excitement and artistic authority (often more than his actual control over his musicians in fact justifies), and accepted uncritically by the public.

Sometimes these charismatic qualities become a conductor's main claim to his position, even in the absence of solid musical accomplishment. Though the experienced orchestra player will quickly recognize the musical and technical shortcomings of a conductor, he may well follow along, often against his better artistic judgment, under the spell of a personal force that transmits itself through the orchestra to the audience. But few conductors rely solely upon their magnetism: many—in fact, most who succeed consistently over a period of years—have the necessary artistic equipment as well.* But to a considerable degree, musicianship alone does not create a conductor of responsibility and authority: without the ego that enables one man to convince a hundred trained musicians of his and not their way of performing a piece of music, no mere musician, however well qualified, can succeed with the baton.

Until a generation ago, most of the musical directors of our orchestras were foreigners by birth and training, and their exotic remoteness added much to their charisma. But an important reason for their virtual domination of American orchestras was that they were trained at the conservatories of Europe in fundamental musicianship and received extensive conducting experience in the opera theaters there before ever daring to step onto the podium for a symphony concert. There were in Europe a host of opera houses, large and small and varying in their demands, through which a young conductor could progress before facing an orchestra of major stature or undertaking the responsibility of heading an American orchestra. Such experience involved more than music performance: life in a well-run opera theater was an excellent preparation for the logistic and practical problems a conductor confronts in the artistic direction of an orchestra here.

The native American conductor, who in the last generation has increasingly figured in the orchestral scene here, has a quite different background and training.† At best, he has received excellent general musical training in a conservatory or university music department, training as fine as can be had anywhere in the world today, but he is often thrust into major conducting responsibilities without extensive experience. Many a young music di-

---

* Pierre Monteux told me once that he had begun his musical studies on the violin, changed to viola when he learned that he was not going to be a great soloist, and then, after being stuck in the orchestra as violist, took up conducting. (Actually, Monteux was an excellent violist, playing as principal under such men as Hans Richter, from whom he learned conducting.) Finally, said Monteux, "When I can no longer conduct, I shall become a critic!"

† It is no longer true, as it was little more than a generation ago, that the native conductor is neglected by our orchestras: of twenty-six Major orchestras, half have native Americans as their musical directors. The proportion is higher in the Metropolitan group.

rector not only lacks the kind of routine that his European counterparts received as staff conductors in opera, but faces learning his repertory as he proceeds, many of his performances of even the standard repertory being his first practical encounter with the music at hand. To the task of conducting his orchestra's programs he must add administrative and public-relations duties for which his conservatory training offered no instruction whatever. If he shows exceptional talent in his youth, his services are in demand elsewhere—with other orchestras, as guest conductor of opera, or in Europe—at a time when he should be settling into the routine of directing his own orchestra. It is not surprising, therefore, that some of our most successful young American conductors are short on practical experience but long on charisma, the one element in their overall equipment that endears them most to the orchestra boards who employ them.

The very egocentricity that implements a conductor's ability to recreate music through an orchestra and makes him the leading artistic figure of a community can blind him to the wider responsibilities entailed by his position. Some times a musical director leaves to the manager or board president the choice of some guest conductors—his friends and enemies excepted—and those soloists who do not appear with him. Even when he advises the guests on their selections, it can often be in terms of avoiding conflicts with his own repertory, rather than what the guest can best contribute to the season's musical program.* Outside the central subscription season, many musical directors take little interest in their orchestras' overall artistic function in a community. Though youth programs, popular concerts, and a growing number of performances involving split orchestras or ensembles play an increasingly important role in the total activities of many orchestras, the musical director may select his associate conductors for their ability to serve his interests rather than for the larger artistic function of his orchestra. Having done so, moreover, the musical director leaves such associates on their own, except where he is himself concerned, to lead increasingly important artistic programs in which he has little or no interest. Even those who participate actively in some youth programs do so with little understanding of the special education problems that I have discussed elsewhere: they incline to accept good intentions and the widest, though shallowest, exposure of their orchestras as a substitute for the development of an education policy.

Though there are, to be sure, important exceptions to these observations, the trend seems definitely pointed toward a decreasing rather than increasing involvement of American symphonic music directors in greater diversification of their orchestras' activities. This will mean a radical departure from the American tradition of a close association between musical director and his orchestra, creating a vacuum in artistic direction. To the extent that this has already developed, the vacuum has been more or less filled by management in facing its task of finding new activities outside the traditional symphony season. Perhaps some orchestras should look for second-echelon con-

* Not infrequently, a guest conductor finds his own rehearsal schedule limited in order to give more time for the preparation of the resident director's programs.

ductors of less than overpowering charisma who can help formulate policy, as well as direct concerts, in these various new areas.

It may well be that in the long run orchestra musicians themselves will assume a more important role in policy direction. Here the European experience may provide an example: such cooperatively governed orchestras as the Vienna Philharmonic, seldom closely identified with one conductor as musical director in the American sense, have developed among their members a sense of artistic responsibility not evident in this country. Though the implications of this will be explored more fully shortly, I mention it here to point out that there are alternatives to the American tradition of building great orchestras under the autocratic control of one resident artistic director.

Nevertheless, the charismatic nature of orchestra leadership, not just in the control of the musicians in performance, will undoubtedly remain an essential feature of the symphonic institution. The style of this charisma will certainly change, as it has in the past generation from foreign and exotic glamour to the native appeal of a Bernstein. Today there is hardly an orchestra board, when faced with the task of securing a musical director, that does not hope to find, in some miraculous way, its local version of Leonard Bernstein, though his Protean gifts in conducting, composition, communication in person or on television, and his ability to bridge the gap between popular and serious music defy duplication.

Bernstein has not only become a conductor of international stature in his own right but has set the example for a new and distinctively American conception of conductor's charisma, breaking down the remoteness often inherent in the earlier foreign style of leadership, and opening up the symphonic institution to wider public interest. In emulating him, his lesser colleagues in many American orchestras have made an important impression on their communities, but they might well also heed his example—both in devoting his efforts for a decade to the orchestra to which he had committed himself, and in withdrawing from policy responsibility once the demands of his personal career led him further afield.

The Symphony Orchestra as a Career

When I was six years old I started taking violin lessons; my mother and my teacher thought I was a genius—a Mischa Elman, at least, if not another Heifetz. Sometimes I hated the violin when I was a kid, but I have to admit now that most of the time I liked it. The worst thing was not playing with the other kids when I wanted to. Every day after school I had to come home and practice before I did my homework. I never got to play ball, hang around with the other kids, or chase girls. My mother got the principal to excuse me from phys. ed. on account of hurting my hands. Anyhow, I spent most of Saturday going into town for my lesson. My father borrowed to get me my first violin, and we all saved to pay off the loan. When that was paid, he borrowed to get me a better fiddle. My teacher got me into a good music school, even before I finished high school. When I got out, he recommended me for a job with a big orchestra. Passing my audition and getting that job was the realization of my childhood ambitions and my parents' too. The kid next door played ball, hung around with the others, chased girls, and went to med school. Now he's a doctor driving a Cadillac, making fifty, sixty thousand a year, while I get a quarter of that, working sixty, seventy hours a week—playing, rehearsing, traveling away from home, and practicing—while I take orders from a sadistic egomaniac whose knowledge of music wouldn't fill my little finger nail. And when I'm sick, what do I do? I go to see my friend the doctor, sit around in his waiting room for a couple of hours; he spends three minutes with me and charges fifty bucks just to look up my ass.[5]

In this book I have indicated some of the forces at work in symphony musicians' militance: the heritage of unionism, the trauma of unemployment occasioned by the electronic entertainment media, and the growing sense of alienation from their work described by Edward Arian. The above quotation describes the degree to which their psychology is affected by a conflict between the artistic demands of their profession and the economic hardships they have suffered. An artist by talent, training, and motivation, the orchestra player is deeply concerned by his economic status, often expressing his artistic frustrations in concerted action as a trade unionist. The role that orchestra musicians play in the American symphonic institution gives them little artistic responsibility: though their training has, in most cases, included a broad musical education, and though they have been motivated since childhood by a strong commitment to music, they are, by and large, artistic eunuchs once they enter the orchestra. Their position may be summarized roughly as that of hired unionized craftsmen rather than musical artists. The long-sought full-year contracts actually aggravated rather than relaxed the psychological alienation of many players in American orchestra, intensifying their militance and evoking an equally bitter response from the managements and orchestra associations employing them. To a very large degree, musicians have for the past generation concentrated on economic issues to the virtual exclusion of their concern for the overall artistic function of the orchestras which they serve; only in such matters as the evaluation of conductors and their desire to have these opinions considered by their employers have they attempted to play a part in the musical destiny of the symphony institution.

The negative positions taken by our players, however, affect the traditional artistic policies of the orchestras: limitation of rehearsals and touring, participation in the hiring and firing of their colleagues, and assignment of orchestra seating have been among these. But the incorporation of such work rules in the trade agreements, though it has had an artistic impact, was motivated within a context of unionism as an effort to protect the players from what they saw as the arbitrary caprice of conductors and the exploitation of their services by management. Artistic considerations, certainly not those of a constructive sort, seldom entered into their demands for such protection.

More recently, moreover, this fear of exploitation has caused the players in many orchestras to resist management's constructive efforts to introduce new programs and diversify activities. As we have already seen, such management proposals themselves often arise from the necessity of a full utilization of the musicians' services made available by the extension of contracted seasons. In retrospect, the managements might have been better advised to have planned such programs on a contingent basis before meeting the demands of players for longer employment, and orchestras now facing similar demands might well make diversification of services a prior condition. To some extent, players' opposition here arises from a sincere belief that ensemble programs fall artistically outside their commitment as symphony musicians. Similarly, some opposition comes from the fear that the players will lose the outside work with which they now supplement their symphony income. Though management has failed in some instances to articulate the larger function of the orchestra as a community musical resource—in its own mind as well as in the musicians'—a major factor here is psychological: from long experience at the bargaining table, these musicians simply resist making any concessions, however constructive, as long as the proposal comes from management.

The hostile, adversary attitude of both musicians and management long pervading personnel relations still constitutes a barrier to the constructive growth of our orchestras. No responsible observer of the immediate postwar history of the orchestra in this country can ignore the degree to which orchestra players received less than they deserved for their contribution and needed for their survival: governing boards inclined too much to take their players for granted, and unions too long acquiesced in holding personnel costs down. The argument that orchestra associations paid their players as much as they could afford has been refuted by their ability to meet the vastly increased demands of the musicians, once the latter assumed the initiative in bargaining. On the other hand, the musicians, intoxicated with their success and greedy for their share of the large, though restricted, funds available in the Ford Foundation grants of 1966, often pursued economic gains and working conditions that seriously imperiled the financial stability of orchestra associations. Even when their employers submitted an accounting of their fiscal problems, orchestra musicians all too often shrugged their shoulders, saying in effect, "That is their problem, not ours." Just as the musicians retained the antagonistic attitude with which they had secured significant success on the economic front, management found it hard to forget the rancor of past negotiations. Removing this obstacle of adversary confrontation will not be an easy task, for the bitterness aroused on both sides in the past decade and a half will linger and continue to poison the future relations of musicians and management.

There are, happily, some signs of relaxation of tension on both sides. Some of the leaders of ICSOM and local orchestra committees with whom I have talked, invariably off the record, have expressed a desire to concern themselves with the larger issues of symphonic development once the fundamental economic issues are settled; it appears, in fact, that one of the remaining unresolved problems, once full-year pay has been attained, concerns the inadequacy of retirement pensions, which are still unmercifully low in all but a few orches-tras. The funding of such pensions, possibly on a national scale and either through the AFM or an independent trustee, would seem to offer a major area for immediate foundation attention.

The European experience, which I mentioned in connection with artistic direction, may provide a fruitful example to our symphony musicians, many of whom envy their colleagues' control of their orchestras, although with-out recognizing that this power involves responsibilities unknown in this country. Aside from the fact that European symphony musicians make a considerable financial sacrifice in return for their control,* these cooperative enterprises are governed by their members with considerably greater sense of artistic and financial responsibility than is evident here. Committees to whom ample authority is delegated include members who serve for long periods of time, without the turnover and turmoil so often prevailing in American players' groups.

One of the most distressing aspects of the musicians' developing mili-tancy has been the failure of orchestra players at large to accept the delega-tion of authority and responsibility to their elected committees. Not only do they limit this power by requiring constant approval by the full orchestra on relatively minor issues, but they prevent the development of a sense of responsibility by the committee through the perpetual threat of removing their members at the annual elections. Insistence on ratifying trade agree-ments has ample justification, but the authority delegated to the bargaining committee is seriously undermined when the terms reached by these representatives in arduous negotiations are summarily rejected by the play-ers. A certain amount of "democratic" turmoil is to be expected during the shift of power from the union to the musicians themselves, but the com-pletion of this transition calls for a greater recognition of responsibility by the players and their committees than prevails at present. In the crucial matter of contract ratification, my own impression is that orchestra mem-bers, by rejecting their committees' recommendation and sometimes voting to strike, have seldom won substantially more than they would have by ac-cepting the agreement, however far it may have fallen short of some de-mands in detail. From management's point of view, moreover, the fear that it may be negotiating with representatives subject to repudiation by the musicians at large creates as much difficulty in bargaining responsibly as does the committees' horror of being accused as "management stooges."

European players undertake symphonic activity because they want to and because the cooperative nature of their association gives them a direct stake in its success. If they select a musical director who may be personally ob-noxious to them, they do so because his artistic qualifications override their personal feelings. When they detect a falling-off of a colleague's perform-

---

* The average musician in the London Symphony Orchestra, the most active of these coopera-tive groups, makes less than half the annual income, for a considerably heavier working schedule, than his American colleagues earn in orchestras of comparable artistic stature; this includes income from extensive recording.[6]

ing ability, they find some way of retiring him,* despite bonds of personal friendship, in the overall interest of the orchestra. I am sure that such orchestras as the London Symphony and Vienna Philharmonic have many personal cliques and much internal dissension, but their professional attitude produces different resolution of their differences. Without suggesting that the orchestras here will adopt major features of the European tradition, I do believe that American musicians can learn much from their European counterparts in such matters as the necessity of accompanying responsibility with their newly acquired power.

On the other side, I have detected in some orchestras a genuine concern on the part of managers and board members for reducing tensions between players and their employers. In Philadelphia, one of the most aggravated situations, an effort has been made to establish communication between trustees and players through a formal liaison committee with purely informative and advisory functions; given the long history of bitterness there, this is possibly all that can be expected at present, but such a committee could hopefully develop a future climate in which constructive suggestions for the alleviation of tensions and for innovative activities could be aired from both sides. The 1971–72 trade agreement for the Seattle Symphony Orchestra [7] spells out in some detail the role of a joint player-management committee—including the conductor, manager, and board president, but with a majority of musicians—that has specific authority to modify working rules within prescribed limits in order to permit diversification of activities. The fact that this committee can be ruled by its player majority has occasioned much concern elsewhere in the conservative symphony establishment; the Seattle management, however, not only takes pride in having initiated these procedures but continues to express great satisfaction with the committee's operation in its first season. In Seattle the motive for such liaison was not so much the relief of tensions as a joint effort to seek ways of developing new services by the orchestra, which has yet to approach a year-round season. In this respect, the Seattle experience merits close watching by other Category C orchestras under pressure to expand employment. If these demands can be met with a mutual concern for diversifying artistic services without arousing the players' suspicion, such committees hold great promise for the future of the orchestra in this nation.

However, such liaison committees have a potential reaching far beyond the logistics of working conditions, into the realm of artistic policy. Within the very real limits of their place in the institutional scheme, orchestra musicians could provide a major resource of artistic expertise that is now largely neglected. They can tell the laymen on an orchestra board a great deal about the musical repertory, and about the competence of soloists and resident and guest conductors, that is otherwise unknown to management. Given an understanding of the musicians' special outlook and an awareness that

---

* The retirement problem in the cooperative orchestras in London is further aggravated by the lack of any pension programs. In other countries, where the cooperative symphony orchestra is also employed by the state opera houses or radio, however, pension provisions exist.

certain attitudes should be taken with careful qualification, orchestra players can make a very real contribution to artistic policy. Many of them are teachers themselves, with an understanding of pedagogy that could be of great value in formulating education policy for orchestras. As an important part of the community's music profession, orchestra players are sensitive to the opinions of its most culturally aware citizens, who often have no influence on a board of directors drawn from the business establishment. When orchestra associations concern themselves with "broadening their base," they should give serious thought to the ways in which the important "input" of their musicians can constructively affect overall policy. This involves some touchy and critical problems of institutional structure and of preserving clear lines of authority and responsibility, especially as regards the musical director and the formalities of union negotiations. Nevertheless, these are not insuperable problems, if the will to implement this opportunity exists on both sides. If it is possible to establish clear limits for committees concerned with logistics to prevent them from invading the prerogatives of union, management, or the conductor, it should be possible to do the same in the realm of artistic policy.

Orchestra associations and the managers who do their bidding have all too long shared with their players a narrow employer-employee approach to personnel relations, which actually involve sincerely dedicated supporters of the art on the one hand and equally serious musical artists on the other. Board members tend to lump their personnel problems in the same category as labor relations in the industrial world, bringing to the symphonic bargaining table an implacably conservative outlook derived from their private business experience, an attitude sometimes accompanied by a patronizing paternalism reminiscent of Higginson's man-to-man dealings with "his" players. To the extent that they segregate their role as symphony supporters from their business life, they expect the players to make financial sacrifices in lower pay comparable to their own contributions of money and time to the cause, forgetting that while musicians depend upon the orchestra for all or part of their living, board members do not.

Musicians, for their part, have either themselves experienced the heady success of their militance or have observed its achievements in other orchestras: its spread from one orchestra to another in the past decade and a half was due as much to proven success elsewhere as to the real needs of the players themselves. In the process, these musicians talked and thought in terms of militant unionism, using a rhetoric that inflamed their colleagues and frightened their employers. In mounting their own battle for improved working conditions they created a momentum of militance that has assumed a life of its own, even after major goals have been achieved. There is a grave danger that this militance will become an end in itself, continually seeking new issues to justify its existence. I am not suggesting that all of the musicians' economic problems have been solved, even in the largest orchestras, nor that there are not a number of orchestras which have yet to provide a decent income for their players, but rather that there are psychological forces at play here which must be understood and harnessed constructively.

In their almost exclusive preoccupation with economic problems, both sides have tended to ignore some profound psychological elements of personnel relations. Some of these aspects have their counterpart in industry, as we are beginning to learn: the deadly routine of the automated production line has its counterpart in the artistically stifling life of a majority of symphony musicians. In an orchestra there are not more than twenty players out of a hundred who have individual solo opportunities in the normal course of performance; possibly an equal number, mostly wind players, may regard themselves as individual artists in the orchestra. But the majority of players—the "side men" in the string sections, especially—find themselves condemned to artistic anonymity, not only following the musical direction of the conductor but also under the control of the principal players who lead their sections. It is hardly a surprise to learn from Edward Arian's account of the internal power structure of the musicians in the Philadelphia Orchestra that the center of frustration, of the players' sense of alienation from their work, is located in the string sections of the orchestra. I need only recall Arian's report of that paradoxical situation in Philadelphia when players' militance increased and hardened after achieving a year-round contract, which actually aggravated the psychological malaise of these players by tying them more irrevocably than ever to artistically confining work without the possibility of seeking outside musical satisfactions. The largest orchestras, especially those in Category A, which have been able to use the year-round services of their players for traditionally symphonic concerts, now find themselves faced with demands for longer vacations and for rotated weeks off during the regular season. These demands, though certainly motivated in part by the sheer momentum of militance, also reflect a desire for some relief from the routine of playing the same music in an artistically debilitating manner.

Nor are the back-desk players the only ones subject to this deprivation. I have encountered some of the best and most highly paid principal players in large orchestras who seek time off at a reduction in pay in order to engage in other types of musical activity. One such player, as he relaxed at a summer music school, remarked, "It takes at least three weeks to get that s.o.b. of a conductor off my back." Much as he enjoyed his career as a leading orchestra musician, he could not survive artistically without an opportunity for the individual expression of his talent in teaching and in playing solo and chamber-music recitals.

In my work at the Juilliard School I also encountered a considerable reluctance among talented young musicians to commit themselves to a symphonic career. On one occasion I was asked by the conductor of a Category A orchestra to recommend recent graduates for openings carrying an initial salary of upwards of fifteen thousand dollars a year, plus liberal fringe benefits. Despite a canvass of at least a score of highly qualified young people, I was unable to persuade any to apply for these positions. To be sure, many young musicians fresh out of a conservatory still harbor hopes of a solo career or at least of lucrative free-lancing in the recording and television studios of New York or Hollywood, but my inquiries also included orchestra players in smaller cities, playing shorter seasons and guaranteed pay less than a third offered by this orchestra. Several frankly stated that they were happier supplementing their modest symphony income with a varied career of teaching and free-lance work than they would be in subjecting themselves to the full-time routine of a year-round symphony contract.

There can be no doubt that, as they become almost exclusively involved in symphony performance, orchestra musicians have discovered they have attained economic security at a high artistic and psychological price. Not long ago, a team of Viennese psychologists interviewed members of the Vienna Symphony Orchestra and concluded that they worked under stress comparable to that of piloting a trans-Atlantic jet airliner or of managing an industrial complex.[8] The subjection of individual artistry to the interpretative ideas of a conductor, the absolute technical discipline, the fear of playing a wrong note, and the possible humiliation of being called harshly to task for his mistakes place a symphony musician under severe psychic strain. Over a period of years, this experience can have a devastating effect on the self-respect and emotional stability of a sensitive man or woman who started out in life, at least, to embark on a career as an artist. In my own work with orchestras I have encountered many a player who has lost his sense of artistic mission and has been reduced by long years in the orchestra to the status of able craftsmanship without a real pride in his work or genuine motivation. When I refer to the artistic aspect of symphony musicians' professionalism, I am quite aware that many players either lack it or have lost it in subservient performance in the orchestra, but I believe that the artistic impulse is very strong and that it should be cherished and encouraged as an ideal.

From this point of view, our orchestra players face a great task in recovering and maintaining their sense of identity as artists. They cannot relieve these tensions by imposing on management and the conductor more and more restrictions copied from a book of union work rules. It seems to me that they would be far better advised to work cooperatively with management on the development of diversified musical activities to their mutual advantage: the players would achieve a measure of performance variety that would be artistically satisfying, and management could develop new sources of performance income and new areas of musical service to the community. However, neither management nor musicians should fall into the trap of viewing these activities primarily as new types of employment, to the neglect of their artistic value.

The tendency, in many orchestras, to present youth programs and popular concerts with minimal rehearsal and artistic policy is deplorable. Similarly, the presentation of ensemble programs with insufficient preparation and repertory planning cannot be condoned. These ancillary activities deserve the same standards of musical quality in performance that prevail in the regular full orchestra concerts on the subscription series. Having already commented on the responsibility of artistic direction in this, I can only hope that the musicians themselves who play in ensembles will treat these with even greater personal artistic responsibility than their performance in the orchestra under a conductor. If both management and musicians approach such activities in this manner, the players will enjoy artistic satisfactions that will mitigate their sense of alienation from symphony performance and make their total involvement, including orchestra work, all the more rewarding.

The planning of programs for these diversified activities must draw upon the participants' musical experience. Ensemble performance, particularly, is a cooperative art, a blending of individual impulses into an integrated whole. Musicians should have great latitude in choosing the colleagues with whom they wish to play and in selecting the programs, for such performance is quite different from playing in an orchestra under the direction of one man. They must be encouraged to rehearse sufficiently, even if contracted services must be allocated for the purpose. Most of all, they must recognize these activities not as another way of meeting contracted obligations but as an opportunity for a wider expression of the art to which they have committed themselves.

The Ford Foundation, in announcing its symphony program in 1965, recognized the importance of providing a sound economic base for the music profession through the symphony orchestras, a responsibility which the latter have not always acknowledged explicitly. Without the economic support and artistic opportunity offered by our symphony associations, the music profession across the country would suffer irreparably. The local orchestra, in literally scores of American cities, has become the focal point of professional music. In their respective preoccupations, if not obsessions, with financial problems and union-oriented working conditions, both management and the players have lost sight of their broader obligations to the art of music and to making that art an enriching experience for the communities which they serve. The preservation and constructive development of professional music performance in this nation through the symphony orchestra demands imaginative and progressive initiative from both groups, each of which, in its own way, has tended in the past to improvise policies and strategy in response to immediate financial pressures rather than from a long-range concern for the larger functions and objectives of the symphonic institution and its role in preserving the musical heritage of our culture.

Most important of all, both management and players themselves must achieve a new respect for orchestra musicians as artists and not as hired union employees. This may involve changes in the prescribed authority of the conductor. It will certainly mean a drastic alteration of the orchestra player's own image of himself: in thinking of himself more as a respected artist, he may come to regard himself less as a union activist. Finally, though there are some indications of a change in attitude on the part of orchestra players, much of the initiative in reducing adversary hostility must come from the orchestra associations themselves: they must put aside their fear of losing control over the artistic destinies of their orchestras and implement institutional procedures and organizations that will bring the now untapped resource of their players' musical knowledge and experience into the decision-making process of their orchestras.

Professionalization of Stewardship

In the course of this account of the symphony orchestra, I have used the term "professional" rather loosely, intentionally avoiding the issues it raises when I defined my scope of interest. In its narrowest sense, professionalism implies only the payment for services rendered: if an orchestra pays all or most of its players, it meets these qualifications; and, if it is administered by a paid manager, he too becomes a professional as distinguished from a board of laymen. By now, however, it must be obvious that such a narrow definition hardly covers the manner in which I have applied the term in embracing the attitude of all concerned toward their work, beyond its limited economic reference. The musician's commitment to his art, in using it to enhance the musical experience of others, is as important as his reliance on such performance for a living. Similarly, in the overall direction of an orchestra, the professionalization of management calls for the application of special skills and experience in the context of a broad sense of responsibility that does not necessarily accompany the mere payment of a salary; in this sense, Higginson exercised a professional responsibility in his direction of the Boston Symphony Orchestra.

There are ample indications that the traditional relationship between orchestra management, in its narrowest sense, and the policy-making functions of the board of directors or trustees is undergoing a change as profound as that of artistic direction. In actual fact, the sharp division of responsibility between board and manager has never existed in the pure form prescribed by Arthur Judson. As an orchestra manager, as we have seen, he often in his own practice acted forcefully outside the narrow limits that he himself still defines, and many another has given his employers the benefit of his special expertise in different ways and with varying degrees of authority and responsibility. Nevertheless, with such rare exceptions as Judson (especially at the New York Philharmonic), managers and boards alike have looked upon the former more or less as extensions and executors of policy determined by the directors. In this, the manager's relation to the board has differed significantly from that of the musical director, for the latter has always been delegated more power in artistic matters, which boards themselves, in theory at least, have regarded as beyond their competence to exercise. By and large, orchestra administrators have not been assigned comparable authority in their areas: their boards have not expected them to assume major policy-making roles and, should they wish to introduce new programs or change the direction of orchestra activities, they must consult with the board to a degree required of few conductors when setting artistic policy.

However, as orchestras have grown in the past two decades and as their activities have proliferated beyond the traditional function of presenting a limited season of symphony concerts, many boards have been forced more and more to call upon the professional experience of their managers, to require of them a higher caliber of expertise, and to delegate to them increasing responsibility for the initiation of policy as distinct from an advisory role. This does not mean that managers have been given absolute authority, any more than boards refrain completely from concerning themselves with a conductor's musical program: conductor and manager remain responsible to their boards, both in day-to-day accountability and in the ultimate power of the board to hire and fire them. No volunteer directors or trustees, even those able to take considerable time away from their own affairs to engage in symphony board activities, can now keep up with the specialized minutiae and major challenges that confront orchestras now operating for most of the year with budgets in the millions of dollars. The manager remains the primary source of a board's knowledge about an orchestra's operations and financial health, but he increasingly assumes major responsibility for guiding its larger destinies.

This trend is reflected in the recent development of a whole new vocabulary of nomenclature: few large orchestras today designate their chief executive officer merely as manager: he now bears such titles as general manager, executive director, managing director, executive vice-president, or even president of the association. Except in the last instance, this variety of designations seems to have little substantive significance: whatever the title, it identifies his rank and importance as top professional administrator. Some orchestras have retained the position of manager, secondary to the higher executive, as an indication of division of administrative functions between those concerned primarily with operations and the larger executive responsibilities for policy and innovative development. The most advanced stage of this process places a professional executive in the association's presidency itself, a role previously reserved for a lay board member, who now becomes chairman of the board. The elevation of professional leadership to this status has long been advocated by such management consultants as Carl W. Shaver, and was first put into effect in the spring of 1970, when the New York Philharmonic elevated general manager Carlos Moseley to the presidency and engaged Helen M. Thompson as manager. The avowed purpose of such changes in New York, and subsequently in Buffalo and Minneapolis, was to give the top executive officer the authority and time to engage in a variety of development initiatives, not only in fund-raising but also in larger community relations and expansion of orchestra services, that an administrator involved in day-to-day routine could not undertake. Such status would also place the top professional executive on equal footing with the business and foundation executives, university presidents, and government officials with whom he deals in the broader phases of developing his orchestra. Professionalization of board presidency also implies the possibility of making the musical director responsible to the board via the president; this may be a gradual process accelerated by the assumption of management of considerable artistic authority in ancillary areas to be noted shortly.

These changes reflect the growing reliance of the lay directors on professional management leadership to an extent that, for my purposes here, overall management more and more embraces both the formerly narrower role of the manager and the policy-making function of the board. The importance of this change reaches far beyond mere terminology in providing a basis, previously absent in the American orchestra, for a professional approach to the challenges and problems now confronting our orchestras and imminent in their futures.

Having already discussed the challenge of developing new artistic services in other contexts, I need only repeat here that the task of planning them, of seeking the cooperation of the musicians in their implementation, and of administering them effectively falls squarely on the shoulders of management. Moreover, from my discussion of the changing role of artistic direction, it is obvious that considerable responsibility will rest there too, and not necessarily by default. Despite the rigid institutional structure set forth by Judson and his followers, many orchestra administrators have considerable musical experience and knowledge; many, like Judson himself, are well-trained musicians. Heretical as it may sound to the symphonic traditionalist, I believe that there are many managers who are better qualified to plan many phases of artistic policy, especially ancillary activities, than some conductors. Certainly the actual performance of music provides a better basis for evaluating alternative artistic options, but it need not be the only one. An orchestra manager whose musical knowledge and experience in bringing together music and an audience are embraced in a professional sense of responsibility can often develop a more objective concept of what an orchestra's overall artistic policy should be. My fear, therefore, concerns not so much the ability of such managers to formulate policies as it does the reluctance of boards and conductors to give their managers the necessary authority.

Moreover, there are major policy questions requiring greater management expertise than can be exercised by boards alone, or by the "errand-boy" type of executive so often held in contempt by musicians, conductors, and even board members. I have already cited instances where symphony leadership has faced problems only when they became crises, accepted such innovations as government funding only to prevent going bankrupt, or undertaken new programs only under the pressure of longer and more expensive commitments to their musicians; some of these were known in advance to far-sighted managers, who were, however, unable to persuade their boards to anticipate them with long-range planning. But the devastating financial crisis afflicting much of the American symphony institution is by no means over. There is, in fact, ample evidence that the orchestras will, in the next few years, confront basic economic problems every bit as serious as those they have faced in the past decade; these will require a high degree of management expertise, from both boards and professional management.

At the conclusion of my discussion of symphony economics in Chapter XIII, I presented some rather alarming projections of the widening income gap. I do not believe that this problem can be solved by increased government funding alone; the rapid rise in expenditures, of which musicians' pay is a major element, must be brought under control. This will require the new kind of cooperation between management and the players that I called for earlier in this chapter. Moreover, such control of expenditures and the establishment of a reasonable annual rate of their increase must be based on analysis of symphony economics requiring greater expertise than has to date been brought to bear on the problem.

The time has come for the economic study of our orchestras to proceed beyond a definition and projection of financial needs (important as these are) to an analysis of what the orchestras *should* do, rather than merely what they are doing. The objective should be to arrive at some reasonable and just level of operations—of rate of annual increase in expenditures— that the orchestras can live with in accordance with the prospective funding of the income gap from private philanthropy and government aid. This rate of growth undoubtedly will differ from orchestra to orchestra, depending on a number of local conditions. Some orchestras may now have achieved a level of operation that can be stabilized on the basis of a rate of growth closer to that of the economy as a whole; but their income gap will still continue to grow at a greater rate in accordance with the basic economic principles set forth at the beginning of Chapter XIII. Other orchestras may have to project a more rapid growth for a limited period until they attain a desirable scope of musical service and equitable income for their musicians; at that point, growth can recede to a more modest rate. In all cases, the orchestras must seek realistic balance between what their communities need and can support and what they can afford to pay their musicians.

In this I am not suggesting that orchestra musicians are now earning adequate compensation, but rather that future determination of compensation must balance their needs against potential financial resources more equitably than in recent years. There is no question that this balance has tipped sharply in these years from previous emphasis on the availability of support to meeting the players' requirements. What I suggest here is adjusting that balance in a manner not heretofore achieved. Orchestra boards, in particular, can no longer plead general poverty in negotiations: they and their managers must develop an economic rationale to convince the musicians that they will be treated as fairly as a sound projection of operations will permit. Establishing this confidence will not be easy, given the present adversary atmosphere, and it will require a kind of joint economic analysis never before undertaken.

Moreover, both management and musicians will be tempted to shift onto government the responsibility for meeting the growing income gap. On the basis of present distribution of funds to all the arts, federal funding would have to reach the $200 million goal set by the Partnership for the Arts well before 1981 for government funding to solve the problem of the orchestras alone. Orchestras may, of course, persuade government to increase their share of total arts appropriations, but I suspect that they will have to substantiate their case more effectively in terms of realistic economic projections and control of expenditures than they have in the past.

Nor can I ignore the possibility that the prospect of increased government funding will whet the appetites of the orchestra players and set off another round of militance comparable to that following the announcement of the Ford Foundation grants in 1965. Certainly, should such a promise (if not actuality) of public bounty appear on the symphonic horizon, these musicians, given their present power and ambitions, will not only expect their share but will also demand that managements assume the task of getting it for them from tax-supported funds. One solution to this prospective problem could be a mutual agreement between the players and management to make certain advances in pay contingent upon definite levels of possible government aid. Given the legislative and administrative uncertainties of public support, such an agreement would reduce the hazard of management's having to make long-range commitments for expenditures before knowing for sure the precise level of the income needed to meet them. Moreover, by impressing on the musicians their direct stake in government funding, managements would enlist them and their unions as more effective allies in their campaign for greater and less restricted funding. In the larger national picture, too, the musicians themselves should become more involved in the present discussions of the ways and means of increased government support of the arts; at present, at least, such questions as project-oriented grants versus direct subsidy and the anticipated requirements of orchestras are debated entirely in management and government circles. This attitude reflects a traditional management belief that such matters are not the concern of the hired help.

Aside from such practical realities, the tendency of musicians and management to look to greater government aid can become a psychological impediment to facing the real issues of the symphony crisis. Despite the uncertainties of legislative appropriations, it would seem essential that the economic analysis required include the participation of government personnel to relate expert estimates of future prospects in that area to the overall projection of operations. At the same time, government policy itself should be reviewed, both as to the philosophy of project versus sustaining grants and as to relating funding guidelines to real needs: for instance, present federal guidelines establishing the same maximum for each Major orchestra merit review to determine whether all deserve the same long-range support regardless of size or optimum rate of growth. A final danger can arise from setting a specific dollar goal for government support, without taking into account the special arithmetic of the economics of the income gap: its characteristically more rapid growth (in relation to total expenditures) must be taken into consideration in any long-range projections of annual increments in government appropriations once a "floor" has been attained.

Moreover, at the same time that the inability of contributions to meet the income gap becomes most critical, the orchestras will confront another problem with their musicians every bit as aggravating as the stimulation of the musicians' demands for their share of government funds. In mid-1976, some sixty orchestras will face important decisions arising from the completion of the Ford Foundation symphony program. At that time they will receive from the foundation's trustee substantial capital assets set aside for them, and will also have available the funds they raised as a matching requirement but were required to hold in restricted accounts until the program's termination. More than $84 million are now held by orchestras in this manner; the foundation contribution, worth $58 million in 1966, had a market value six years later of over $80 million and, assuming the continued appreciation of Ford Motor Company stock in the coming years, may provide an even greater sum completely at the disposal of orchestra boards. Having already reported the degree to which even the possibility of large but restricted capital grants to the orchestras stimulated the militancy of their musicians after its first announcement in 1965, I can only hazard a prediction of further contention once these funds, totaling well over $160 million, become available in 1976. Though precise information about how orchestra boards intend to deal with these unprecedentedly large assets has been difficult to obtain, I have been told confidentially that some orchestras, in originally setting up the trusts into which they placed their matching funds, stipulated that they should be managed as perpetually restricted endowments, with only income being available for annual operations, and that the funds distributed from the foundation trustee in 1976 are to be managed in the same manner. In some cases, a limited and temporary invasion of capital would be permitted in case of emergency.

The Ford Foundation itself has expressed concern over the management of these funds in a letter to the orchestras advising them of their continued eligibility in the summer of 1972, urging them to establish sound fiscal management of the matching funds already raised and of the further assets they would eventually receive from the trustee. Such admonition is as far as the foundation can go, in view of the fact that it specifically declined at the start to set up the entire program as a permanent restricted endowment. Nor is the foundation's concern with sound fiscal management of these endowments unwarranted: though some orchestras, especially those that have long had endowments, employ expert investment counsel in managing their portfolios, others have relied upon banker board members or, in some cases, their own managers to formulate investment policies. It should be obvious that in matters involving millions of dollars for individual orchestras, the continuous retention of outside professional investment counsel is highly desirable, as is close liaison between such counsel and management in bringing operating requirements to bear on investment policy.

However, the entire principle of restricted endowments as a basis for financing symphony orchestras has been questioned, not only by orchestra players who often urge their invasion to meet their demands but also by some economists.* The retention of large assets, returning at most a twentieth of their value in any one year, strikes some of these critics as fiscally and socially unsound: they would prefer to see such trusts invaded in an orderly

* This question has been raised in the much larger context of foundations and charitable trusts in general, especially during and after Congressional investigations of foundations leading to the Tax Reform Act of 1969. At that time, some advocated that all such foundations and trusts be required to disburse a certain proportion of their capital assets annually in addition to income.

manner over a period of years, hoping that in the future major capital drives could again be mounted to replenish the depleted funds. There are, to be sure, certain orchestra functions, notably pension programs, that depend on restricted trust management for the security of their ultimate beneficiaries and critics of limited endowment would make an exception for these.

Again we encounter what can best be described as the psychological imponderables in the delicate relations within the orchestral institution. The directors or trustees, themselves immersed in an economy of banking, law, and corporate capital, tend to regard restricted trusts as a matter of sound business practice; in fact, many look back with nostalgia to the era when such orchestras as those of Philadelphia, Cleveland, and Chicago could count on endowment as a primary source of supplemental income. The orchestra players, with little personal experience in capital investment, see such endowments as a dead and unproductive resource that could be put to better immediate use. The orchestra manager, if fully aware of the larger implications of arts management in other fields and in touch with other professionals in government, foundations, and educational institutions, can be an important source of advice, beyond mere market judgment, in the administration of such trusts.

At a time when, as I have urged elsewhere, the musicians and management should be making every effort to establish better liaison for the consideration of other broad issues, the availability of these assets in 1976 can become a bitter bone of contention, poisoning the constructive cooperation from both sides that will be needed to solve a whole range of pressing problems. Without seeming to build up an artificial straw man, I must suggest that a resolution of policy regarding these funds has implications that extend beyond the question of endowment policy: an understanding must be sought with the orchestra players to avoid rancorous dispute over these funds. Of all the problems facing orchestra leadership in its personnel relations, this one most calls for a degree of cooperation and diplomacy in personnel relations still in all too short supply.

Within the next five years, therefore, our orchestras will face large and complex questions of basic economic policy—coping with the abnormal growth of the income gap, the increasing difference between its demands and sources of private and government support, and the special problems raised by the sudden availability to sixty Major and Metropolitan orchestras of previously restricted funds. There may well be a temptation on the part of both musicians and management to use the 1976 distribution of capital assets to meet the income gap and thereby postpone the day of reckoning on control of expenditures, in the hope that government funding will meet the problem before these assets are depleted. But in view of the figures presented earlier here, even those millions will not last for long.

At the same time, with the growing importance of foundation, corporate, and government funding of the arts, the pursuit of all supplementary income must also be increasingly professionalized. Our previous projection of contributions demonstrates the magnitude of that task in the Major orchestras alone, and doubling the amount of contributions by 1977 will be difficult to achieve. The time is long since past when an orchestra with a budget in excess of $1 million could rely upon amateur fund-raising by its directors or trustees. Not only must such campaigns for individual contributions be organized and coordinated with actual operations, but in approaching corporations, foundations, and government, orchestras increasingly encounter professional staffs responsible for evaluating the merits of a fund request, whether by formal application or by personal presentation. These staffs require more factual substantiation than a mere plea of financial need and community service. In my discussion of arts philanthropy and government aid, I have already described the important new role of management in this respect and the need for its specialized competence, whether through "in house" staff or by the engagement of outside counsel and direction.

In either case, government or private philanthropy, top management within the orchestra organization must work increasingly with its professional counterparts in the funding agencies, not only to formulate and justify requests but also to exchange ideas with them. For all the long-ingrained fear of symphony boards of possible government interference in policy making, and despite the safeguards built into the developing role of public funding, orchestras must face the reality of the concern of these agencies for the substantive quality of an orchestra's overall program, both of actual musical performance and of general service to the area around it. To a considerable degree, foundation grants imply similar evaluation of the general policy and artistic performance of an orchestra, and the tendency so far of both foundations and government to designate their grants for specific projects (the Ford Foundation grants excepted) has undoubtedly had an impact on shaping policy.

Many symphonic leaders would prefer that both government and foundation funding be an unqualified contribution to supplementary income. They still entertain the delusion that they have always had full control of the destiny of their orchestras, ignoring the obvious fact that major private donors and concern for keeping contributors in general happy with the orchestra have in the past often played a part in policy decisions, affecting at times even such important matters as the choice or retention of a conductor or manager. In their apprehension of further dilution of their absolute authority and responsibility, these directors, trustees, and managers place a serious obstacle in the path of establishing realistic and constructive liaison with funding agencies essential to their continued existence.

Moreover, many foundations and government agencies have developed in their own staffs a degree of expertise not always matched by the orchestras seeking their aid. The development by the New York State Council on the Arts of counseling services has been of positive and constructive benefit to the arts organizations it serves. Whatever may be the merits of the specific substance of such advice, it can best be evaluated and implemented by an exchange of ideas between funding staff and professional management, rather than by resisting government influence as "meddling." Such cross-fertilization can be most effective when it is welcomed by a management that weighs the possibilities of application to its own situation and, in turn, contributes its ideas to the overall scene.

In some cases, suggestions by foundations and government agencies develop from their observation of especially effective programs in one locality, or in another art field; these agencies often have a broader perspective of the total arts scene than do the deliberations of symphony managers in the more restricted confines of the ASOL. The League obviously has become a unique repository for statistical data and other information about symphony orchestras and, within the limits of the confidential nature of its sources, has been most generous with its data to foundations, government agencies, and private research (the present book included). Nevertheless, by its very nature, its outlook is limited to the symphonic scene, whereas other agencies can correlate symphony data with that from other fields. Beyond these technical limitations, moreover, I detect a growing conservatism in the League's orientation, a preoccupation with the financial crisis and personnel problems as seen by the leadership of the larger orchestras. To this extent it has lost some of its former concern with the smaller orchestras, to whom Mrs. Thompson gave such a strong sense of identity in the 1950s.

There is still a strong residue of conservatism among many orchestras, which the ASOL undoubtedly reflects faithfully.* To the degree that the League acts as a channel of communication among orchestras or between orchestra leadership and private or public funding, it represents a considerably more conservative force than seems to be developing in the direct contact between some management and government agencies, though some orchestras still view public aid and the responsibilities it entails as an evil, albeit a necessary one in the face of their critical financial condition. A few still regard the Ford Foundation symphony program as a questionable blessing, though I have encountered this view less frequently since the completion of the matching-fund requirement than before. Such conservatism, by no means rare even at this late day, reflects one of the most pervading phenomena in recent symphonic history—the tendency of our orchestra leadership to undertake innovation or expansion only when forced to do so by outside pressures. I have sometimes been tempted to describe the symphonic institution as being dragged, kicking and screaming, into the last third of the 20th century. Others have criticized our orchestras for this conservatism, often more harshly than I have here, and I believe that there is considerable merit to the charges of elitism in the direction of the American orchestra— elitism in management, in repertory, in community orientation, and in general outlook. But I also believe that such blanket criticism of the orchestras as elitist requires closer examination.

* The management-oriented conservatism of the League manifested itself vividly early in 1972 when it made simultaneous presentations to federal wage-price agencies on behalf of the orchestras: one requested exemption from price control of symphony concert admission prices; the other opposed an appeal from the American Federation of Musicians to exclude symphony players' salaries from wage controls. In both cases, the government ruled for the application of nationwide controls unless an individual orchestra or local union could prove exceptional hard-ship.

In Defense of Elitism

Possibly the most pervasive criticism of the symphony orchestra in this country, the charge of elitism also has the most immediate impact on the public in general. The opening night of a symphony season all too frequently provides a spectacle of well-dressed affluence and social exclusivity that lends itself far more vividly to coverage by the media than does the artistic program of the orchestra. A large segment of the public is convinced that symphony orchestras, like opera companies, are the toy of a few rich people in evening clothes who once a week go to hear an orchestra, similarly dressed, play incomprehensible music by dead composers. As long as these affluent patrons were willing and able to support their orchestras themselves, the public concerned itself little with them, but when they could no longer meet their cost and appealed for wider private, business, and government support, many asked why they should support a plaything of the upper classes. Nor did the reluctant and piecemeal involvement of those orchestras in education and popular programming necessarily break down this resistance: it was often dismissed as public-relations strategy rather than accepted on its own merits. Finally, the insistence of governing boards on retaining control of the orchestras, and the failure to bring into their policy making representatives of the wider community or government from whom support was asked, further confirmed the change of elitism.

This almost classic criticism of the symphonic institution is warranted in many respects; there is no question that symphony boards have been dominated by the business and social elite of their respective communities. In a survey made in 1971 of Major and Metropolitan orchestras, I found the following occupational distributions * of nearly two thousand symphony board members: [9]

Industry executives	40%
Banking, finance, accounting	16%
Law	12%
Insurance	5%
Other business	12%
Education administration	6%
Musicians	2%
Government officials	3%
Other nonbusiness	4%

That some eighty-eight percent of these are drawn from the business community will surprise no one acquainted with symphony boards, but such

* My questionnaire requested that women board members without specific vocations be counted in accordance with their husbands', a request that elicited one very irate response from an orchestra manager's secretary, denouncing me for male chauvinism. My purpose, of course, was to seek some general indication of economic and social status, not to minimize the important role of women on symphony boards.

documentation emphasizes the need for further diversification. In their oversimplification of a rather complex institution, however, many critics ignore the positive virtues of the very elitism they condemn and the essential contribution that this leadership has made to the preservation and dissemination of a great art. The alternatives they offer, when they do so, seem to me impossible of achievement in a realistic context.

The suggestion that symphony boards broaden their base with a wider representation of more diversified elements of the community has great merit, and some orchestras have taken steps in that direction. However, such broadening of the base of policy making assumes that new directors or trustees can be found with a sincere commitment to symphonic music; such people are by no means lacking in our communities, but are usually found in what I can best describe as its "cultural elite"—professional and amateur musicians, artists, and avid concert-goers—whose concept of the artistic function of an orchestra may in its way be even more restrictive than that of the business establishment. Such citizens have a place in symphony deliberations, as do those other nonestablishment civic leaders who may be less personally committed to music, but as long as our orchestras rely to an appreciable extent on private contributions for supplemental income, donors and their representatives will, in the last analysis, play a dominant role on symphony boards through their control of the purse. Furthermore, as government funding assumes greater importance in symphony economics, a new type of establishment leader will play an influential role on symphony boards —the businessman or lawyer with effective political connections and power.

Nor can anyone familiar with the internal power forces within symphony boards ignore the problems created by the interplay of the personalities involved. Most board members have strong characters: in their own lives they are accustomed to wielding authority and enjoying the respect and obedience of their colleagues and subordinates. As virtually self-perpetuating groups, they draw into their circle their own friends and business associates.* Moreover, boards tend to be dominated by strong leadership, one individual or a small group willing to spend the time and energy needed, and most directors incline to go along with such leadership unless there are strongly compelling reasons for challenging it. Challenges are rare in the normal course of board activity and seldom reach public attention: boards tend to be "closed corporations" in observing the sometimes strained amenities of confidentiality and courtesy in times of dispute and have a horror of washing their dirty linen in public. Directors inclined to disagree with their leaders will often refrain from direct opposition for fear that they will have leadership imposed on them; many would rather sit out their term of office in silence and step down at an advantageous time. This reluctance to challenge leadership in the early stages of developing policy disputes often allows them to reach crisis proportions before they must be resolved with sometimes Draconic impact on the power structure of a board.

---

* Some symphony boards by legal definition designate their own membership. Those elected by membership associations, generally made up of contributors, are almost invariably chosen by nominating committees themselves appointed by boards or their officers. Only on rare occasions do associations override the wishes of boards in the selection or reelection of directors.

Moreover, individual directors can have important business relations with their colleagues which can be jeopardized by friction over symphony affairs. Only rarely do internal disputes on such nonprofit boards become public knowledge as dramatically as in the case of New York's Museum of Modern Art early in 1970, when the previously unannounced resignation of Ralph F. Colin was eventually discovered by the press. Colin, an attorney for CBS and active in the art world, had become embroiled in a dispute with his long-time friend, board chairman William Paley, over museum policy and quietly resigned from the board, but the personal animosities aroused were apparently so serious that his law firm eventually lost the broadcasting company as a client. Few directors of nonprofit boards will allow internal policy differences to go to such lengths or to reach the public ear.

A more radical alternative calls for complete government funding of supplemental income. At the present national level of symphony operation this would require annual funding of close to $50 million more than the federal government now allocates to all the arts: assuming continuation of the FY 1972 symphonic share (about fourteen percent of all National Endowment for the Arts funding), and assuming that the other arts would have comparable claims on the government, a total arts appropriation might run as high as $300 to $500 million a year. Certainly such funding would drastically alter the power structure of the American orchestra, shifting a major part of policy responsibility to government officials or government-appointed representatives, as is presently the case in such West European countries as Germany, Austria, and Italy. Such an eventuality may yet develop, but I believe that it would come only over a long period of time. Moreover, such total public funding of the orchestras would create perpetual uncertainty in immediate and long-range planning, because of reliance on annual government appropriations and the fear that such subsidy could be drastically reduced or cut off entirely.

A third, equally radical, possibility would be to turn orchestras over to the control of their players, as has been the case in a number of European centers. This scheme exists in its purest form in London, where four excellent orchestras are cooperatives governed by the musicians. However, when American orchestra players look closely at the status of their counterparts there they will discover that the latter must work harder for considerably less income, in real wages, than do their American fellows and that, under the pressure of running their own affairs, the London orchestra players have developed a tradition of responsibility, artistic and institutional, quite lacking here. Moreover, these orchestras, by their strong reliance on box-office income, generally offer more conservative programming than most of their American counterparts; much of their innovative programming has been underwritten by the British Arts Council, especially in the performance and recording of British music. These same players in London orchestras have turned more and more to government support and have even in recent years sought private contributions to secure financial stability.

Each of these alternatives to the traditional role of the governing boards of American orchestras contains elements of solid merit that warrant incorporation into the present structure. There is no question that many orchestra boards need wider community representation, not only of other business interests but also of diverse ethnic and social groups and artistic personnel. Nor is there any question that orchestra musicians and government professionals have much expertise to offer symphony boards, by direct representation, via contacts with management, or through formally established and effective advisory committees.

Nor, in considering these charges of elitism, can I ignore the extraordinary contribution that our traditional system of private support and control has made to the American symphonic institution. It has in the past century created and maintained orchestral activity without equal in quantity or quality. Particularly during the postwar generation, it has become the basic artistic and financial support of a profession threatened with extinction by radical changes in commercial entertainment. In so doing, this elitist institution has performed an artistic service that has enriched the lives of countless millions of our citizens, and it has the potential for broadening and deepening this enrichment. Since the days of Higginson's autocratic rule of the Boston Symphony there have been profound changes in broadening this leadership, but Higginson's sense of mission is still very pervasive, and much of the future destiny of the orchestra in America will depend upon the continuation and extension of that sense of responsibility.

The elitism of management in its widest context has its counterpart in the aristocracy (in the best sense of that term) of great art. Though we do not now know precisely the true potential of the audience quantitatively or qualitatively in terms of the psychology of the musical experience, there can be no doubt that, given the diversity of temperament and individuality of man in society, none of the arts or all of them together can ever be expected to have equal importance to the total population. Some, probably a considerable majority, will always prefer a game of golf, an evening of card playing, or the mass appeal of spectator sports in a stadium or on television to a visit to a museum or attendance at the theater, opera, dance, or concert. This fact of modern life must be accepted,* however reluctantly, by those deeply involved in the arts and fervently committed to them—not as a refutation of their commitment but as a definition of their role.

But these quantitative realities are only a part of the aristocratic nature of great art: the masterpieces of Beethoven, Leonardo, and Shakespeare have an artistic stature immeasurably greater than that of rock music, advertising display, or serial comedy on television. We cannot avoid distinguishing between ubiquitous illustration or entertainment and masterpieces of the rare and unique creative artist. American society, especially, has always tended to place a special value on *quantity* of appeal, in a false application of political and social egalitarianism to an essentially aristocratic activity. More recently, not only among our youth but also in much of the adult view, this egalitarian attitude has taken on a perniciously hedonistic justification for any experience that provides even the most primitive pleasures. If this were really the case, our society should legalize and encourage

---

* One often hears the American public unfavorably compared to the European as uncultured, but the audience information given in Howard Taubman's *The Symphony Orchestra Abroad* does not confirm this.

prostitution as a means of bringing intense pleasure and physical satisfaction to a large portion of the population. This is by no means a farfetched analogy: many of the proposals for popularizing art or making it more immediately satisfying to a wider audience strike me as comparable advocacy of artistic prostitution, in placing a dollar sign on what should be a private and creatively satisfying experience. For the sponsors, performers, and audience in the symphony orchestra, quality still is and must be very much the name of this game, and no one can evade it as the central issue before them.

Elitism in the symphonic world therefore has two major, and by no means unrelated, aspects: leadership by a select and dedicated group, and the inherently aristocratic nature of great art. But each aspect carries with it great responsibility. The artistocratic nature of art imposes a great responsibility on the elite leadership who have the final authority over its presentation. The sense of mission that motivated Theodore Thomas as a musician and impresario must now apply to the vastly more complicated collective leadership of the symphony orchestra a century later. The institution has reached such scope and variety that no single man can guide it as Higginson did, and even collective leadership, though often dominated by one man or a few men, has in many instances proved unequal to the challenge. This elitist leadership, recognizing the responsibilities of its mission, must more and more share its power and authority with expert professional resources inside and out of its own sphere. It can no longer direct the destiny of this complex and growing institution by the autocratic approach of a 19th-century State Street broker. In the past decade especially, the symphony orchestra has experienced a succession of crises and impact of new forces that it has yet fully to absorb. It has taken some positive steps to cope with these forces, but must take even more to survive their resolution. Whereas past response has often reacted to long-range challenges with short-term solutions to isolated problems, it seems imperative that policy must now be made in a wider context of professionalization of decision making and greater responsibility for the fundamental artistic role of the orchestra.

Theodore Thomas's eagerness to "go to hell" for a permanent orchestra must strike a responsive chord among many—orchestra musicians as well as trustees, conductors, and managers—who have survived the symphonic turmoil of recent years. They must, on many occasions, have asked themselves whether their time, effort, and money were worth the cause. If the moral uplift of Thomas and Higginson strike us today as quaintly Victorian, the same sentiment has been cast in more modern terms by Sir Herbert Read when he said, "Genius is a genetic chance and history a confused clamour, but life persists. It is a flame that rises and sinks, now flickers and now burns steadily, and the source of the oil that feeds it is invisible. But that source is always associated with the imagination, and a civilization that consistently denies or destroys the life of the imagination must inevitably sink into deeper and deeper barbarism." [10] In this "life of the imagination," so indispensable to our civilization, the symphony orchestra must play an essential role and the efforts of all of its dedicated workers find their ultimate justification.

Appendices

Appendix A

Major and Metropolitan Symphony Orchestras
in the United States, 1970–71
(Annual Budgets in excess of $100,000)

For the 89 orchestras replying to my questionnaires mailed in the latter half of 1971, all or part of the following information is given below: the name of the orchestra; its conductor(s), board president and chairman, and manager(s); summary of operating data (including government funding); previous conductors; legal name and dates of founding and incorporation; and business address. All of this information was obtained from the orchestras and was subsequently verified by them. The brief descriptions of 15 orchestras not replying is based on the roster of the American Symphony Orchestra League. I have added the population of the Standard Metropolitan Statistical Areas (according to the 1970 census) and an indication of category. Except where specifically noted, operating data is for the 1970–71 season; designation of personnel is the latest available as of spring, 1972. Though this book does not cover Canadian orchestras, those in the Major and Metropolitan groups of the ASOL are listed at the conclusion of the United States summary. Each list is in alphabetical order by city.

Akron, Ohio (679,239)
AKRON SYMPHONY ORCHESTRA. Louis Lane, conductor; John MacDonald, choral conductor; J. Ralph Gillman, president; William L. Watrous, business manager. 10 concerts, 25,000 estimated attendance; Edwin J. Thomas Performing Arts Hall, as of 1972 (3,001). 75 players under per service basis; expenditures, $132,000 ($16,000 government). Previous conductors: John F. Farinacci 1950–54; Laszlo Krausz 1954–59. Greater Akron Musical Association, founded 1949, incorporated 1953; 572 W. Market Street, Akron, Ohio 44303. (E)

Albany, New York (720,786)
ALBANY SYMPHONY ORCHESTRA. Julius Hegyi, conductor; William R. O'Bryen, president; Jack M. Firestone, manager. 101 concerts (inc. 35 ensemble, 47 Little Symphony); 80,000 estimated attendance; Palace Theater, Albany, and Troy Music Hall. 75 players; expenditures $144,000 ($7,500 government). Previous conductors: John F. Carabella 1930–37; Rudolf Thomas 1937–45; Ole Windingstad 1945–48; Edgar Curtis 1948–66. Albany Symphony Orchestra, Inc., founded 1931, incorporated 1936. Suite 26, D & H Building, Albany, New York 12207. (E)

Albuquerque, New Mexico (315,774)
ALBUQUERQUE SYMPHONY ORCHESTRA. Yoshimi Takeda, conductor; Mrs. William M. Dolde, president; Mrs. Raymond Dietrich, manager. 13 concerts, 26,000 estimated attendance; Popejoy Hall, University of New Mexico. 80 players; expenditures $123,474 ($12,378 government). Previous conductors: Grace Thompson Edminster 1932–41; William Kunkel 1941–44; Kurt Frederick 1945–50; Hans Lange 1950–58; Maurice Bonney 1958–69; Bonney and José Iturbi 1969–70; guests 1969–70. Albuquerque Symphony Orchestra, founded 1932. 122 Tulane Street, S.E. Albuquerque, New Mexico 87106. (E)

Amarillo, Texas (144,396)
THE AMARILLO SYMPHONY. Dr. Thomas Hohstadt, conductor; Mr. Travis Aaron, president; Lt. Col. James M. Alfonte, USA, Ret'd, manager. 15 concerts, 23,106 attendance; Civic Center Music Hall (2,306). Expenditures $102,000. Previous conductors: Ellis Hall, Hall Axtell, Christian Thaulow, Clyde Roller 1948–63. The Amarillo Symphony Inc.; founded 1924, incorporated 1928. Box 2552, Amarillo, Texas 78703. (E)

Atlanta, Georgia (1,390,164)
ATLANTA SYMPHONY ORCHESTRA. Robert Shaw, musical director; Michael Palmer and Donald Neuen, assistants; J. W. Kercher, president; Frank Ratka, general manager; R. W. Thompson, orchestra manager. 269 concerts; 164,675 estimated attendance; Symphony Hall (1,762). 89 players in 40-week contract; expenditures $1,600,000 ($46,000 government). Previous conductor: Henry Sopkin 1945–66. Atlanta Arts Alliance, Inc.; founded 1945; incorporated 1945. 1280 Peachtree Street, N.E., Atlanta, Georgia 30309. (C)

Austin, Texas (295,516)
AUSTIN SYMPHONY ORCHESTRA. Stuart Sankey, associate conductor; Mrs. D. J. Sibley, Jr., president; John Deford, manager. 13 concerts, 12,600 estimated attendance; Municipal Auditorium (variable: 3,000–6,060). 72–74 players; expenditures $106,000. Previous conductors:

various from 1938 to 1942; Fred Bytendorf 1942–52; Ezra Rachlin 1952–69. Austin Symphony Orchestra Society, Inc., founded 1938, incorporated 1937. 701 W. 15th, Austin, Texas 78701. (E)

Baltimore, Maryland (2,070,670)
BALTIMORE SYMPHONY ORCHESTRA. Sergiu Comissiona, music director; Stuart Knussen, general manager. 120 West Mount Royal Avenue, Baltimore, Maryland 21201. (C)

Birmingham, Albany (739,274)
BIRMINGHAM SYMPHONY. Amerigo Marino, conductor; Harold Wolfe, associate; Joseph M. Farley, president; Gordon C. Andrews, manager. 47 concerts; 102,530 estimated attendance; Municipal Auditorium (2,359). 59–66 players; expenditures $350,400. Previous conductors: Arthur B. Lipkin 1948–60, Arthur Winograd 1960–64. Birmingham Symphony Association, founded 1933, incorporated 1933. 807 City Hall, Birmingham, Alabama 35203. (D)

Boston, Massachusetts (2,753,700)
BOSTON SYMPHONY ORCHESTRA. Seiji Ozawa, music director (1973); Michael Tilson Thomas, associate conductor; Talcott M. Banks, president; Thomas D. Perry, Jr., manager. 215 concerts; Symphony Hall (2,631, winter; 2,365, Pops). 106 players; expenditures $5,000,000. Previous conductors: Georg Henschel 1881–84; Wilhelm Gericke 1884–89; Arthur Nikisch 1889–93; Emil Paur 1893–98; Wilhelm Gericke 1898–1906; Karl Muck 1906–08; Max Fiedler 1908–12; Karl Muck 1912–18; Henri Rabaud 1918–19; Pierre Monteux 1919–24; Serge Koussevitzky 1924–49; Charles Munch 1949–62; Erich Leinsdorf 1962–69; William Steinberg 1969–72. Boston Symphony Orchestra Inc., founded 1881. Symphony Hall, Boston, Massachusetts 02115. (A)
Brooklyn, New York

BROOKLYN PHILHARMONIA, INC. Lukas Foss, musical adviser and conductor; David Amram, conductor & host to youth concerts; Max L. Koeppel, president; Maurice Edwards, manager. 15 concerts, 29,221 estimated attendance; Opera House, Brooklyn Academy of Music (2,300). 60–75 players; expenditures $144,727. Previous conductor: Siegfried Landau 1955–71. Founded and incorporated 1954. 30 Lafayette Avenue, Brooklyn, New York 11217. (F)

Buffalo, New York (1,349,211)
BUFFALO PHILHARMONIC ORCHESTRA. Michael Tilson Thomas, conductor and music director: Melvin Strauss, associate conductor; John Landis, assistant conductor; Howard A. Bradley, president and general manager; Peter P. Poth, chairman of the board. 152 concerts, 325,500 estimated attendance; Kleinhans Music Hall (2,839). 87 players in 36-week contract; expenditures $1,479,643 ($557,000 government). Previous conductors: Franco Autori 1936–44; guest conductors 1944–45; William Steinberg 1945–52; guest conductors 1952–54; Josef Krips 1954–63; Lukas Foss 1963–70; guest conductors 1970–71. Buffalo Philharmonic Orchestra Society, Inc., founded 1934 and incorporated 1936. 370 Pennsylvania Street, Buffalo, New York 14201. (C)

Chapel Hill, North Carolina
NORTH CAROLINA SYMPHONY. Benjamin F. Swalin, conductor; Thomas Conlin and Alfred Haller, associate conductors; C. C. Hope, Jr., president; William H. Ruffin, chairman; L. Guilford Daugherty, manager. 169 concerts; 60–66 players; expenditures $612,468. Previous conductor: Lamar Stringfield 1932–36. Founded and incorporated 1932. P.O. Box 2508, Chapel Hill, North Carolina 27514. (D)

Charlotte, North Carolina (409,370)
CHARLOTTE SYMPHONY ORCHESTRA. Jacques Brourman, conductor; Mark R. Bernstein, president, Mrs. Marion C. Tennent, manager. 8 concerts, 14,500 estimated attendance; Owens Auditorium (2,500). 75 players; expenditures $100,304. Previous conductors: James Christian Pfohl, ten years; Henry Janiec, five years; Richard Cormier, three years. Charlotte Symphony Orchestra, Inc., founded 1932. 827 East Boulevard, Charlotte, North Carolina 28203. (E)

Chattanooga, Tennessee (304,927)
CHATTANOOGA SYMPHONY ORCHESTRA. Richard Cormier, conductor; Norman Bradley, president; Genevieve Harmon, manager. 30 concerts, 50,100 estimated attendance; Tivoli Theater (1,788). 40 contract players (40 regular extras) in 25-week contract. Previous conductors: Arthur Plettner, Joseph Hawthorne, Julius Hegyi, Charles Gabor. Chattanooga Symphony Association, Inc., founded 1932, incorporated 1945. 730 Cherry Street, Chattanooga, Tenn. 37402. (E)

Chicago, Illinois (6,978, 947)
CHICAGO SYMPHONY ORCHESTRA. Georg Solti, music director and conductor; Henry Mazer, associate conductor; Louis Sudler, president; John S. Edwards, manager. 160 concerts by full orchestra and 51 ensemble; 664,657 estimated attendance; Orchestra Hall (2,566). 108 players; expenditures $4,085,283. Previous conductors: Theodore Thomas 1891–1905, Frederick Stock 1905–1942, Désiré Defauw 1943–47, Artur Rodzinski 1947–48, Rafael Kubelik 1950–53, Fritz Reiner 1953–63, Jean Martinon 1963–68, Irwin Hoffman (acting) 1968–69. The Orchestral Association, founded and incorporated 1890. 220 South Michigan Avenue, Chicago, Illinois 60604. (A)

Cincinnati, Ohio (1,384,911)
CINCINNATI SYMPHONY ORCHESTRA. Thomas Schippers, music director; Erich Kunzel, resident conductor; Carmon DeLeone, assistant conductor; Edgar J. Mack, Jr., chairman of the board of trustees; Thomas J. Klinedinst, president; Albert K. Webster, general manager; Steven I. Monder, assistant manager. 150 full orchestra, 142 ensemble concerts, 641,213 estimated attendance; Music Hall (3,634). 92 players in 52-week contract; expenditures $2,283,097 ($25,000 government). Previous conductors: Frank A. Van der Stucken 1895–1907; Leopold Stokowski 1909–12; Ernst Kunwald 1912–17; Eugene Ysaye 1918–22; Fritz Reiner 1922–31; Eugene Goossens 1931–47; Thor Johnson 1947–58; Max Rudolf 1958–69. Cincinnati Symphony Orchestra, founded and incorporated 1894. 1313 Central Trust Tower, Cincinnati, Ohio 45202. (B)

Cleveland, Ohio (2,064,194)
THE CLEVELAND ORCHESTRA. Lorin Maazel, music director (from September, 1972); Pierre Boulez, musical adviser and principal guest conductor (to September, 1972); Louis Lane, resident conductor; Alfred M. Rankin, president; Frank E. Joseph, chairman; Michael Maxwell, general manager; Kenneth Haas, assistant manager; George P. Carmer, business manager. 182 concerts, 423,000 attendance; Severance Hall (1,980); 103 players; expenditures $4,236,000. Previous conductors: Nikolai Sokoloff 1918–33; Artur Rodzinski 1933–43; Erich Leinsdorf 1943–46; George Szell 1946–70. The Musical Arts Association, incorporated 1915. Severance Hall, 11001 Euclid Avenue, Cleveland, Ohio 44106. (A)

Columbus, Ohio (916,228)
COLUMBUS SYMPHONY ORCHESTRA. Evan Whallon, conductor; George Hardesty, associate conductor; Everett H. Krueger, president; Nat Greenberg, general manager; Glenn Norrish, assistant manager. 61 concerts, 56,400 estimated attendance, Ohio Theater (3,073). 80 players; expenditures $400,767. Previous conductors: George Hardesty, 2 years; Henry Mazer, 1 year; Claude Monteux, 2 years. Columbus Symphony Orchestra, Inc., founded 1951, incorporated 1952. 200 East Broad Street, Suite 1803, Columbus, Ohio 43215. (D)

Corpus Christi, Texas (284,832)
CORPUS CHRISTI SYMPHONY ORCHESTRA. Maurice Peress, conductor; Mrs. John Kline, manager. P.O. Box 495, Corpus Christi, Texas 78403. (E)

Dallas, Texas (1,555,950)
DALLAS SYMPHONY ORCHESTRA. Anshel Brusilow, music director and conductor; Earl Murray (1971–72) and Charles Blackman (1970–71), associate conductors; Jack L. Vandagriff, president; Kenneth R. Meine, general manager. 190 concerts; expenditures $1,375,140. Previous conductors: Hans Kreissig 1900–05; Walter Fried 1905–11 and 1918–24; Carl Venth 1911–14; Paul Van Katwijk 1925–38; Jacques Singer 1938–42; Antal Dorati 1945–49; Walter Hendl 1949–58; Paul Kletzki 1958–61; Georg Solti 1961–62; Donald Johanos 1962–70. Dallas Symphony Association, Inc., founded 1900, incorporated 1945. P.O. Box 8472, Dallas, Texas 75205. (C)

Davenport, Iowa; Rock Island, Illinois (362,638)
TRI-CITY SYMPHONY. James Dixon, conductor; Dudley Priester, president; Mrs. Richard von Maur, manager. 18 concerts; Masonic Auditorium, Davenport (2,750); Centennial Hall, Rock Island (1,750). 80 players; expenditures $120,000. Previous conductors: Charles Gigante, 11 years; Piero Bellugi, 4 years; Harry John Brown, 7 years; Oscar Anderson, 11 years. Tri-City Orchestra Association; founded 1914, incorporated 1914. P.O. Box 3865, Davenport, Iowa 52805. (E)

Dayton, Ohio (850,266)
DAYTON PHILHARMONIC ORCHESTRA. Dr. Paul Katz, conductor; Charles Harbottle, president; Mrs. Burdette Thomson, manager. 29 concerts, 70,300 estimated attendance; Memorial Hall (2,500). 80 players; expenditures $154,682 ($9,500 government). Dayton Philharmonic Orchestra Ass'n, Inc., founded 1933, incorporated 1934. Sheraton Hotel, 210 N. Main St., Dayton, Ohio 45402. (E)

Denver, Colorado (1,227,529)
DENVER SYMPHONY ORCHESTRA. Brian Priestman, music director; Allan Miller, associate conductor; Rike D. Wootten, president; David G. Kent, manager; John Gibbens, assistant manager. 148 concerts, 210,789 estimated attendance; Denver Auditorium Theatre (2,240). 85 players; expenditures $1,234,460 ($10,000 government). Denver Symphony Association, founded and incorporated 1922. 1615 California Street, Denver, Colorado 80202. (C)

Detroit, Michigan (4,199,931)
DETROIT SYMPHONY ORCHESTRA, INC. Sixten Ehrling, conductor; Pierre Hetu and Paul Freeman, associate conductors; Robert Semple, president; John Ford, chairman; Marshall Turkin, manager; Saul Bernat and Michael Smith, assistant managers. 200 concerts; expenditures $2,525,000 ($59,500 government). 101 players; expenditures $2,525,000 ($59,500 government). Detroit Symphony Orchestra, Inc., founded 1914, incorporated 1951. Ford Auditorium, Detroit, Michigan 48226. (B)

Duluth, Minnesota (265,350)
DULUTH SYMPHONY ORCHESTRA. Joseph Hawthorne, conductor; Harold Rutan, associate conductor; Dr. Dan R. Goldish, president; A. H. Miller (acting manager); 16 concerts, 14,700

estimated attendance; Municipal Auditorium (2,403). Expenditures $158,037. Previous conductors: Paul Lemay 1932–41; Tauno Hannikainen 1942–47; Joseph Wagner 1947–50; Hermann Herz 1950–66. Duluth Symphony Association, Inc., founded 1932, incorporated 1934. 401 Lonsdale Building, Duluth, Minnesota 55802. (E)

El Paso, Texas (359,292)
EL PASO SYMPHONY. William Kirschke, interim conductor; Dr. Russell L. Deter, president; Dorrance D. Roderick, chairman; Mrs. Joy Laidlaw, manager. 21 concerts, 37,200 estimated attendance; Liberty Hall (2,394). 31 contract players (30 weeks); expenditures $109,380. Previous conductors: Frederick R. Koch 1893–94, H. E. Van Surdam 1914–15, P. J. Gustat 1919–23, Anton Navratil 1924–27, Ross V. Steele 1927–29, H. Arthur Brown 1930–51, Orlando Barera 1951–71. El Paso Symphony Orchestra Association, Inc., founded 1893, incorporated 1937. Mezzanine, Hotel Paso del Norte, San Antonio at South El Paso Street, El Paso, Texas 79901. (E)

Erie, Pennsylvania (263,654)
ERIE PHILHARMONIC. John Gosling, conductor; Edward R. Bahr, associate conductor; Thomas B. Hagen, president; Douglas E. Jones, manager. 19 concerts, 22,900 estimated attendance; Memorial Auditorium (1,100). 72 players; expenditures $139,000. Previous conductors: Franz Kohler 1913–16; Henry Bethuel Vincent 1920–26; John R. Metcalf 1921–46; Fritz Mahler 1947–53; James Sample 1953–66. Erie Philharmonic, Inc., founded 1913, incorporated 1933. 720 Baldwin Building, Erie, Pennsylvania 16501. (E)

Evansville, Indiana (138,764)
EVANSVILLE PHILHARMONIC ORCHESTRA. Minas Christian, conductor; J. Michael McGregor, president; Mrs. George McCray, manager. 35 concerts; Vanderburgh Auditorium (2,001). Expenditures $130,000. Founded 1934. P.O. Box 84, Evansville, Indiana 47708. (E)

Flint, Michigan (496,658)
FLINT SYMPHONY. William C. Byrd, artistic director; Dr. Fleming A. Barbour, president; Charles B. Cumings, chairman; Roberta G. Jachim, managing director. 21 concerts, 31,000 estimated attendance; Whiting Auditorium (2,001). 75 players; expenditures $158,552. Flint Institute of Music, founded and incorporated 1965. Dort Music Center, 1025 East Kearsley, Flint, Michigan 48503. (E)

Fort Lauderdale, Florida (620,100)
FORT LAUDERDALE SYMPHONY. Dr. Emerson Buckley, conductor; A. J. W. Novak, president; Herbert W. Bromberg, manager. 87 concerts, 56,500 estimated attendance; War Memorial Auditorium (2,500). 65 players; expenditures $138,000. Fort Lauderdale Symphony Orchestra Association; 450 E. Las Olas Blvd., Fort Lauderdale, Florida 33301. (E)

Fort Wayne, Indiana (280,495)
THE FORT WAYNE PHILHARMONIC ORCHESTRA. Thomas Briccetti, conductor; Mrs. Janet Latz, president; Charles K. Winter, manager. 19 concerts, 15,466 estimated attendance; Scottish Rite Auditorium (2,197). 90 players in 31-week contract; expenditures $145,000 ($1,000 government). Previous conductors: Gaston Bailhe 1945–48; Hans Schweiger, 1945–48; Igor Buketoff 1948–66; guest conductors 1966–67; James Sample 1967–68 and 1970–71. The Fort Wayne Philharmonic Orchestra, Inc., founded 1943, incorporated 1945. 201 Jefferson Street, Fort Wayne, Indiana 46802. (E)

Fort Worth, Texas (762,086)
FORT WORTH SYMPHONY ORCHESTRA. John Giordano, music director and conductor; Robert W. Chambers, president; Mrs. Beverly H. Cardona, manager. 11 concerts, 17,469 estimated attendance; Tarrant County Convention Center Theatre (3,054). 60 players; expenditures $107,600. Previous conductors: Brooks Morris, Robert Hull 1957–63; Rudolf Kruger 1963–65; Ezra Rachlin 1965–71; Ralph Guenther 1971–72. Fort Worth Symphony Orchestra Association, Inc., founded 1929, incorporated 1957. 3505 West Lancaster, Fort Worth, Texas 76107. (E)

Fresno, California (413,053)
FRESNO PHILHARMONIC. Guy Taylor, conductor; Carlos Wilson, manager; Karney Hodge, president. 1362 North Fresno Street, Fresno, California 93703. (E)

Glendale, California (132,752)
GLENDALE SYMPHONY ORCHESTRA. Carmen Dragon, conductor; J. E. Hoeft, president; Richard F. Perry, manager. 108 concerts, 20,000 estimated attendance; Dorothy Chandler Pavilion, Los Angeles (3,204). 85 players; expenditures $145,000. Previous conductors: Amerigo Marino 1956–62. Glendale Symphony Association, founded 1923, incorporated 1956. 121 W. Lexington Dr., Glendale, California 91203. (E)

Grand Rapids, Michigan (539,225)
GRAND RAPIDS SYMPHONY ORCHESTRA. Gregory Millar, conductor; Oliver Robinson, president; Donald Cummings, manager. 13 concerts, 46,892 estimated attendance; Civic Auditorium (4,500). 85 players; expenditures $121,697. Previous conductors: Karl Wecker 1929–40; Thor Johnson 1940–42; Nicolai Malko 1942–47; Rudolph Ganz 1946–48; José Echaniz 1948–54;

Désiré Defauw 1954–57; guest conductors 1958–59; Robert Zeller 1959–64; Carl Karapetian 1964–68. Grand Rapids Symphony Society, founded and incorporated 1942. Exhibitors Building, Grand Rapids, Michigan 49502. (E)

Greensboro, North Carolina (144,076)
EASTERN MUSIC FESTIVAL. Sheldon Morgenstern, conductor; Molly Coe, executive director. 808 North Elm Street, Greensboro, North Carolina 27401. (F)

Hartford, Connecticut (663,891)
HARTFORD SYMPHONY ORCHESTRA. Arthur Winograd, conductor; Mrs. Jean S. Low, manager. 15 Lewis Street, Room 304, Hartford, Connecticut 06103. (D)

Honolulu, Hawaii (630,528)
HONOLULU SYMPHONY ORCHESTRA. Robert LaMarchina, conductor; R. Dougal Crowe, president; Richard W. Cornwell, manager. 1,140 concerts (1,009 ensemble), 230,129 estimated attendance; Honolulu International Center Concert Hall (2,100). 52–82 players; expenditures $710,000. Previous conductors: F. A. Ballaseyus 1902; W. F. Jocher 1903; Joseph Stockton 1905; various conductors 1906–14; Alf Harum 1924–25; Rex Dunn 1925–28; Arthur Brooke 1928–31; Fritz Hart 1931–49; George Barati 1950–67. Honolulu Symphony Society, founded 1900, incorporated 1922. Suite 328, Merchandise Mart Building, Honolulu, Hawaii 96813. (D)

Houston, Texas (1,985,031)
HOUSTON SYMPHONY ORCHESTRA. Lawrence Foster, music director and conductor; A. Clyde Roller, resident conductor; Charles F. Jones, president; Tom M. Johnson, general manager; Carl A. Fasshauer, assistant to general manager. 140 concerts; Jesse H. Jones Hall (3,000). 88 players in 45-week contract; expenditures $1,651,497. Previous conductors: Ernest Hoffman 1936–47; Efrem Kurtz 1948–54; Leopold Stokowski 1955–61; Sir John Barbirolli 1961–67; André Previn 1967–69; guest conductors 1969–71. Houston Symphony Society, founded 1913, incorporated 1931. Jesse H. Jones Hall for the Performing Arts, 615 Louisiana, Houston, Texas 77002. (B)

Indianapolis, Indiana (1,109,882)
INDIANAPOLIS SYMPHONY ORCHESTRA. Izler Solomon, conductor; Thomas Briccetti, associate conductor; Robert M. Seastrom, president; Hubert N. Scott, manager; Fritz Kumb, assistant manager. 120 concerts, 170,458 estimated attendance; Clowes Memorial Hall (2,176). 82 players; expenditures $1,165,000. Previous conductors: Ferdinand Schaefer 1930–37; Fabien Sevitzky 1937–55. Indiana State Symphony Society, Inc., founded 1930, incorporated 1937. P.O. Box 88351, Indianapolis, Indiana 46208. (C)

Jackson, Mississippi (258,906)
JACKSON SYMPHONY ORCHESTRA. Lewis Dalvit, conductor and musical director; James B. Campbell, president; Robert C. Bickley, manager. 42 orchestra and 125 ensemble concerts; Jackson Municipal Auditorium (2,585). 74 players; expenditures $160,000 ($49,200 government). Previous conductor: Theodore Russell for 21 years. Jackson Symphony Orchestra Association, founded 1944. P.O. Box 4584, Jackson, Mississippi 39216. (E)

Jacksonville, Florida (528,865)
JACKSONVILLE SYMPHONY ORCHESTRA. Willis Page, conductor; J. Shepard Bryan, Jr., president; Stanley D. Watson, manager, 20 concerts, 30,500 estimated attendance; Civic Auditorium (3,200). Expenditures $139,622 ($15,722 government). Jacksonville Symphony Association, Inc., founded and incorporated 1951. 221 Hemming Park Building, 46 West Duval Street, Jacksonville, Florida 32202. (E)

Kalamazoo, Michigan (201,550)
KALAMAZOO SYMPHONY ORCHESTRA. Pierre Hetu, conductor; Horace Maddux, manager. 12 concerts, 14,448 estimated attendance; Miller Auditorium (3,550). Expenditures $209,241. Previous conductors: Chester Z. Bronson 1921–24; Henry Erich 1924–26; George Buckley 1926–28; David Mattern 1928–34; Herman Felber, Jr. 1934–59; guest conductors 1959–60; Gregory Millar 1961–67; guest conductors 1967–68. Kalamazoo Symphony Society, Inc., founded 1921. 426 So. Park Street, Kalamazoo, Michigan 49007. (E)

Kansas City, Missouri (1,256, 649)
KANSAS CITY PHILHARMONIC. Jorge Mester, music adviser; Mrs. J. Clyde Nichols, president; Howard M. Jarratt, manager. 67 concerts, 98,292 estimated attendance; Music Hall (2,572). 83 players; expenditures $835,724 ($150,000 government). Previous conductor: Hans Schwieger 1948–71. Kansas City Philharmonic Association, founded 1933. 210 West 10th Street, Kansas City, Missouri 64105. (D)

Knoxville, Tennessee (400,337)
KNOXVILLE SYMPHONY ORCHESTRA. David Van Vactor, conductor; Betty Moody, office secretary. Journal Building, 618 Gay Street, Knoxville, Tennessee 37902. (E)

Los Angeles, California (7,032,075)
LOS ANGELES PHILHARMONIC ORCHESTRA. Zubin Mehta, conductor; John Connell, president; H. Russell Smith, chairman; Ernest Fleischmann, manager; Jaye Rubanoff and Robert

Mathews, assistant managers. 199 concerts, 688,725 estimated attendance; Dorothy Chandler
Pavilion (3,249). 105 players (48-week contract); expenditures $4,875,409. Previous conductors:
Artur Rodzinski 1929–33; Otto Klemperer 1933–43; Alfred Wallenstein 1943–56; Eduard Van
Beinum 1956–59; guest conductors 1959–62. Southern California Symphony-Hollywood Bowl
Association, founded and incorporated 1919. 135 North Grand, Los Angeles, California 90012.
(A)

Louisville, Kentucky (826,533)
THE LOUISVILLE ORCHESTRA. Jorge Mester, conductor; James Livingston, assistant conductor; Barry Bingham, Jr., president; James D. Hicks, executive manager; P. Thomas Fenn,
assistant manager. 78 concerts, 39,000 estimated attendance; Brown Theatre (1,453). 60 players;
expenditures $400,000 est. Previous conductor: Robert Whitney 1937–67. Louisville Philharmonic
Society, Inc., founded and incorporated 1936. 321 W. Broadway, Louisville, Kentucky 40202. (D)

Madison, Wisconsin (290,272)
MADISON SYMPHONY ORCHESTRA. Roland Johnson, conductor; Mrs. Lee A. Baron, president; Winifred Cook, manager. 20 concerts, 14,200 estimated attendance; Madison Area Technical College Auditorium (1,046). 75 players; expenditures $116,000. Previous conductors:
Sigfrid Prager 1926–48; Walter Heermann 1948–61. Madison Civic Music Association, Inc.,
founded and incorporated 1925. 211 N. Carroll St., Madison, Wisconsin 53703. (E)

Massapequa, New York
ORCHESTRA DA CAMERA. Guest conductors only, currently Herbert Grossman and Arthur
Bloom; Alfred Felberbaum, president; Ralph Lorr, manager. Long Island Auditorium. 30–45
players; expenditures $271,000. Previous conductors: Maurice Peress 1960–62; Jorge Mester
1962–64; Arthur Weisberg 1964–69; Lawrence L. Smith 1966–69; Yuri Krasnapolsky 1969–70;
Leon Hyman 1970–71. Founded and incorporated 1961. 129 East Drive N., Massapequa, New
York 11758. (E)

Memphis, Tennessee (770,120)
MEMPHIS SYMPHONY ORCHESTRA. Vincent DeFrank, conductor; Ted Cunningham, manager. 60 South Auburndale, Crosstown Station, Box 4682, Memphis, Tennessee 38104. (D)

Miami, Florida (1,267,792)
GREATER MIAMI PHILHARMONIC. Alain Lombard, conductor and music director; Richard
F. Wolfson, president; Dale Heapps, general manager. 33 concerts; Gusman Philharmonic Hall
(2,000). 75 players (27-week contract); expenditures $1,000,000. Previous conductor: Fabien
Sevitzky 1964–67. Greater Miami Philharmonic, founded and incorporated 1964. 174 East Flagler
Street, Miami, Florida 33131. (D)

Miami Beach, Florida
MIAMI BEACH SYMPHONY. Barnett Breeshin, conductor and manager; Stephen Carner,
president. 19 concerts, 58,700 estimated attendance; Miami Beach Auditorium (3,800). Expenditures $120,000 ($15,000 government). Founded 1951, incorporated 1952. 420 Lincoln Road,
Miami Beach, Florida 33139. (E)

Middlebury, Vermont
VERMONT SYMPHONY ORCHESTRA. Alan Carter, conductor; Ernest Stires, president;
Kenneth Hammer, chairman; Phyllis H. Franze, manager. 91 concerts. 72 players; expenditures
$127,000 ($5,000 government). Vermont Symphony Orchestra Association, Inc., founded 1933,
incorporated 1938. P.O. Box 548, Middlebury, Vermont 05753. (E)

Midland and Odessa, Texas (157,238)
MIDLAND-ODESSA SYMPHONY & CHORALE. Phillip Spurgeon, conductor; Jerome M.
Fullinwider, Midland co-chairman; Robert H. Latta, Odessa co-chairman; Mrs. Caroline H. Ater,
executive secretary. 14 concerts, 2 chorale; Lee High School Auditorium (1,738), Midland;
Bonham Jr. High Auditorium (1,371), Odessa. 80–85 players. Previous conductors: Dr. Lara
Hoggard 1962–67; Robert G. Mann 1967–71. Midland Symphony and Chorus Association, Inc.,
founded 1952; Odessa Symphony Association, founded 1948; Midland-Odessa Symphony and
Chorale, Inc., joined 1962. P.O. Box 6266, Air Terminal Station, Midland, Texas 79701. (E)

Milwaukee, Wisconsin (1,403,887)
MILWAUKEE SYMPHONY ORCHESTRA. Kenneth Schermerhorn, conductor; Edward
Mumm, assistant conductor; Charles A. Krause, president; Craig Hutchinson, general manager;
Richard C. Thomas, administrative director. 122 concerts, 409,155 estimated attendance; Uihlein
Hall (2,331). 86 players; expenditures $1,200,494. Previous conductors: Alfredo Antonini, 1
year; Harry John Brown, 8 years. Milwaukee Symphony Orchestra, Inc., founded and incorpo-
rated 1959. Performing Arts Center, 929 North Water Street, Milwaukee, Wisconsin 53202. (C)

Minneapolis, Minnesota (1,813,647)
MINNESOTA ORCHESTRA. Stanislaw Skrowaczewski, conductor; George Trautwein, associate
conductor; Donald L. Engle, president; Richard M. Cisek, vice-president & managing director;
David Hyslop, assistant managing director. 119 concerts, 273,164 estimated attendance; Northrop
Memorial Auditorium (4,800). 96 players; expenditures $2,500,000. Previous conductors: Emil

Oberhoffer 1903–22; guest conductors 1922–23; Henri Verbrugghen 1923–31; Eugene Ormandy 1931–36; guest conductors 1936–37; Dimitri Mitropoulos 1937–49; Antal Dorati 1949–60. Minnesota Orchestral Association, founded 1903. 807 Hennepin Ave., Minneapolis, Minnesota 55455. (B)

Nashville, Tennessee (540,982)
NASHVILLE SYMPHONY ORCHESTRA. Thor Johnson, conductor; C. B. Hunt, president; George Carpenter, manager. 45 concerts; War Memorial Auditorium (2,123). 85 players; expenditures $402,000. Previous conductors: William Strickland, Guy Taylor, Willis Page. Nashville Symphony Association, founded and incorporated 1946. 1805 West End Avenue, Nashville, Tennessee 37203. (D)

New Haven, Connecticut (355,538)
NEW HAVEN SYMPHONY ORCHESTRA. Frank Brieff, conductor; Harold Kendrick, manage. 254 College Street, New Haven, Connecticut 06510. (D)

Newark, New Jersey
NEW JERSEY SYMPHONY ORCHESTRA. Henry Lewis, conductor; Marilyn Knordle, manager, 1020 Broad Street, Newark, New Jersey 07102. (D)

New Orleans, Louisiana (1,046,470)
NEW ORLEANS PHILHARMONIC SYMPHONY ORCHESTRA. Werner Torkanowsky, conductor; Carter Nice and Robert Rohe, associate conductors; D. Blair Favrot, president; Thomas A. Greene, manager; Paul Stapel, assistant manager. 130 concerts, 240,000 estimated attendance; Municipal Auditorium (2,700). 82 players; expenditures $1,200,000 ($20,000 government). Previous conductors: Arthur Zach 1935–38; Ole Windingstad 1938–41; Massimo Freccia 1941–52; Alexander Hilsberg 1952–61. New Orleans Philharmonic Symphony Society, founded and incorporated 1935. Suite 207, 333 St. Charles Ave., New Orleans, Louisiana 70130. (C)

New York, New York (11,528,649)
AMERICAN SYMPHONY ORCHESTRA. Leopold Stokowski, music director; Cathy French, executive director. Suite 1408, 200 West 57th St., New York, New York 10019. (F). (Discontinued mid-1972.)

CLARION CONCERTS ORCHESTRA. Newell Jenkins, conductor; Thomas Newbold Morgan, president; John L. Hurley, Jr., manager; Barbara F. Austin, assistant manager. 6 concerts; Alice Tully Hall, Lincoln Center (1,096). Expenditures $130,000 (1969–70). Clarion Music Society, Inc., founded and incorporated 1957. 415 Lexington Avenue, New York, New York 10017. (F)

THE LITTLE ORCHESTRA SOCIETY. Thomas Scherman, conductor; S. Chadwick Reed, president; Herbert Barrett, manager; Thomas Matthews, associate manager. 9 concerts; Philharmonic Hall, Lincoln Center (2,836). Expenditures $150,000. The Little Orchestra Society, founded and incorporated 1947. 1860 Broadway, New York, New York 10023. (F)

NEW YORK PHILHARMONIC. Pierre Boulez, conductor; Carlos Moseley, president; Amyas Ames, chairman; Helen M. Thompson, manager; William Weissel, assistant manager. Philharmonic Hall (2,836). 106 players. Previous conductors: Ureli Corelli Hill and H. C. Timm with D. Etienne 1842–43; Theodore Eisfeld, George Loder, and others 1843–52; Theodore Eisfeld and Carl Bergmann 1852–65; Carl Bergmann 1865–76; Leopold Damrosch 1876–77; Theodore Thomas 1877–78; Adolf Neuendorf 1878–79; Theodore Thomas 1879–91; Anton Seidl 1891–98; Emil Paur 1898–1902; Walter Damrosch 1902–03; guests 1903–06; Vassily Safonoff 1906–09; Gustav Mahler 1909–11; Josef Stransky and guests 1911–21; guests 1921–27; Arturo Toscanini and Willem Mengelberg, 1927–30; Arturo Toscanini 1930–36; Sir John Barbirolli 1936–41; guests 1941–43; Artur Rodzinski 1943–47; Bruno Walter, adviser 1947–49; Leopold Stokowski and Dimitri Mitropoulos 1949–50; Dimitri Mitropoulos 1950–58; Leonard Bernstein 1958–69; George Szell, advisor 1969–70. Philharmonic-Symphony Society of New York, Inc., founded 1842, incorporated 1853. Philharmonic Hall, 65th and Broadway, New York, New York 10023. (A)

SYMPHONY OF THE NEW WORLD. Benjamin Steinberg, conductor; Benjamin Patterson, manager. 250 West 47th Street, New York, New York 10019. (F)

Norfolk, Virginia (680,600)
NORFOLK SYMPHONY ORCHESTRA. Russell Stanger, conductor; Norman C. Willcox, president; Peter W. Smith, executive director. 37 concerts, 29,448 nontour estimated attendance; Center Theatre (1,801). 80 players; expenditures $188,600 ($22,200 government). Previous conductors: Walter Edward Howe 1920–22; W. Henry Baker 1922–23; Bart Wirtz 1923–24; Arthur Fickenscher 1925; Frank L. Delpino 1925–33; Henry C. Whitehead 1934–48. Norfolk Symphony Association, founded 1920, incorporated 1949. 700 Board of Trade Building, Norfolk, Virginia 23510. (E)

Oakland, California (361,561)
OAKLAND SYMPHONY ORCHESTRA. Harold Farberman, musical director; Harry R. Lange, president; Edgar F. Kaiser, chairman; Roger R. Jones, general manager. 37 concerts, 57,650 estimated attendance; Oakland Auditorium Theater (2,002). 94 players; expenditures $529,000

($42,500 government). Previous conductors: Orly See 1933–57; Piero Bellugi 1958–59; Gerhard Samuel 1959–71. Founded 1933, incorporated 1935. 601 Latham Square Building, Oakland, California 94612. (D)

Oklahoma City, Oklahoma (640,889)
OKLAHOMA CITY SYMPHONY ORCHESTRA. Guy Fraser Harrison, conductor; Ray Luke, associate conductor; Earl Sneed, president; George K. Massad, manager; Walter W. Ashby, production manager. 154 concerts, 203,250 estimated attendance; Civic Center Music Hall (3,200). 52 players; expenditures $560,000. Previous conductors: various conductors 1938–41; Victor Allessandro 1941–51. Founded and incorporated 1938. Civic Center Music Hall, Oklahoma City, Oklahoma 73102. (D)

Omaha, Nebraska (541,453)
OMAHA SYMPHONY. Yuri Krasnapolsky, conductor; Dean R. Bartee, president; Robert P. Kelligar, manager. Omaha Civic Auditorium Music Hall (2,400). Previous conductors: Henry Cox 1921–23; Engelbert Roentgen 1924; Sandor Harmati 1925–29; Joseph Littau 1930–31; Rudolph Ganz 1936–37; Richard Duncan 1940–43 and 1947–51; Emmanual Wishnow 1952–53; Richard Duncan 1954–57; Joseph Levine 1958–69; Leo Kopp 1969–70. Founded 1921. 3929 Harney, Omaha, Nebraska 68131. (D)

Orlando, Florida (428,003)
FLORIDA SYMPHONY ORCHESTRA. Pavle Despalj, conductor; Stephen T. Dean, president; Helen E. Ryan, executive vice-president; Robert L. Landers, assistant. 73 concerts, 129,000 estimated attendance; Auditorium (2,950). 75 players; expenditures $370,203 ($20,000 government). Previous conductors: Yves Chardon, 3 years; Frank Miller, 5 years; Henry Mazer, 7 years; guest conductors, 1 year; Hermann Herz, 3 years. Florida Symphony Society, founded 1950. Suite 6A, 320 N. Magnolia Avenue, or P.O. Box 782, Orlando, Florida 32802. (D)

Pasadena, California
PASADENA SYMPHONY ORCHESTRA. Dr. Richard Lert, conductor; Mrs. Robert Buchanan, president; Mrs. Edwin A. Barnes, Jr., manager; Mrs. Martha T. Blaine, assistant manager. 15 concerts; Pasadena Civic Auditorium (2,968). Expenditures $127,000. Previous conductor: Reginald Bland 1928–36. Pasadena Symphony Association, founded 1928, incorporated 1932. 301 E. Colorado Blvd., Pasadena, California 91101. (E)

Phoenix, Arizona (968,487)
PHOENIX SYMPHONY ORCHESTRA. Eduardo Mata and Lawrence Smith, guest conductors; Lewis J. Ruskin, chairman; Kasson E. Crooker, manager. 40 concerts, 54,092 estimated attendance; Gammage Auditorium (3,019). 66 players; expenditures $466,000 ($25,000 government). Previous conductors: John Barnett 1947–49; Robert Lawrence 1949–52; Leslie Hodge 1952–59; Guy Taylor 1959–69; Phillip Spurgeon 1969–71. Phoenix Symphony Association, founded and incorporated 1947. 6328 North Seventh Street, Phoenix, Arizona 85014. (D)

Philadelphia, Pennsylvania (4,817,914)
THE PHILADELPHIA ORCHESTRA. Eugene Ormandy, conductor; William Smith, assistant conductor; Richard C. Bond, president; C. Wanton Balis, Jr., chairman; Boris Sokoloff, manager; Joseph Santarlasci, assistant manager. Academy of Music (3,000). 106 players; expenditures $3,965,271. Previous conductors: Fritz Scheel 1900–07; Karl Pohlig 1907–12; Leopold Stokowski 1912–36. Founded 1900, incorporated 1903. 230 S. 15th Street, Philadelphia, Pennsylvania 19102. (A)

Pittsburgh, Pennsylvania (2,401,245)
PITTSBURGH SYMPHONY ORCHESTRA. William Steinberg, conductor; Donald Johanos, associate conductor; John E. Ancle, president; Charles Denby, chairman; Seymour L. Rosen, manager; James L. Wright, assistant manager. 225 concerts, 500,935 estimated attendance; Heinz Hall (2,731). 104 players (48-week contract); expenditures $2,778,615. Previous conductors: Elias Breeskin 1926–30; Antonio Modarelli 1930–37; Otto Klemperer 1937–38; Fritz Reiner 1938–48; guests 1948–52. Pittsburgh Symphony Society, founded 1926, incorporated 1937. 600 Penn Avenue, Pittsburgh, Pennsylvania 15222. (B)

Portland, Maine (141,625)
PORTLAND SYMPHONY ORCHESTRA. Paul Vermel, conductor; Harold E. Woodsum, Jr., president; Russell I. Burleigh, manager. 23 orchestra and 50 ensemble concerts, 30,000 estimated attendance; City Hall Auditorium (2,340). 75 players in 36-week contract; expenditures $207,400 ($3,500 government). Previous conductors: Arthur Bennett Lipkin 1962–66; guest conductors 1966–67. Portland Symphony Orchestra Association, founded 1924, incorporated 1933. 30 Myrtle Street, Portland, Maine 04111. (E)

Portland, Oregon (1,009,129)
OREGON SYMPHONY ORCHESTRA. Jacques Singer, conductor (to June, 1972); A. Leighton Platt, president; Carl E. Simmons, assistant manager. 47 concerts, 116,832 estimated attendance; Portland Civic Auditorium (3,000). 78 players; expenditures $518,866. Previous conductors: Carl Denton 1918–25; Willem Van Hoogstraten 1925–38; Werner Janssen 1947–49; James Sample 1949–53; guest conductors 1953–55; Theodore Bloomfield 1955–59; Piero Bellugi 1959–61; guest

conductors 1961–62. Portland Symphony Society, founded 1922, incorporated 1934; reincorporated as Oregon Symphony Society, Inc. 320 S.W. Stark St., Portland, Oregon 97204. (D)

Poughkeepsie, New York
HUDSON VALLEY PHILHARMONIC. Claude Monteux, conductor; Edward Simons and Luis Garcia-Renart, associate conductors; Fred McCurdy, president; Kenneth Fricker, manager; J. Richard Webb, assistant manager. 52 concerts, 49,600 estimated attendance; Poughkeepsie High School Auditorium, Newburgh Free Academy, and Kingston Community Theatre. 80 players; expenditures $304,200. Hudson Valley Philharmonic Society, Inc., founded and incorporated 1959. Box 191, Poughkeepsie, New York 12602. (D)

Providence, Rhode Island (914,119)
RHODE ISLAND PHILHARMONIC ORCHESTRA. Frank Madeira, conductor; George Kent, assistant conductor; Martin Fischer, conductor of youth orchestra; Robert E. Grant, president; Mrs. Muriel Port Stevens, manager. 303 orchestra and ensemble concerts, 176,500 estimated attendance; Veterans Memorial Auditorium (2,199). 68 players; expenditures $263,922. Rhode Island Philharmonic Orchestra, founded and incorporated 1945. 39 The Arcade, Providence, Rhode Island 02903. (D)

Richmond, Virginia (518,319)
THE RICHMOND SYMPHONY. Jacques Houtmann, conductor; S. Douglas Fleet, president; Edmund A. Rennolds, chairman; John J. Schaeffer, manager. 155 concerts, 147,900 estimated attendance; The Mosque (3,700). Expenditures $325,000. Previous conductor: Edgar Schenkman 1957–71. Founded and incorporated 1957. 112 E. Franklin Street, Richmond, Virginia 23219. (D)

Rochester, New York (882,667)
ROCHESTER PHILHARMONIC ORCHESTRA. Samuel Jones, conductor; Mrs. Frederick J. Wilkens, president; Thomas H. Miller, chairman; Nicholas L. Jones, manager; Leland Barber, assistant manager. 109 concerts, 200,000 estimated attendance; Eastman Theatre (3,094). 53 players; expenditures $1,226,395 ($300,000 government). Previous conductors: Albert Coates 1923–25; Eugene Goossens 1924–31; José Iturbi 1936–44; Erich Leinsdorf 1947–56; Theodore Bloomfield 1959–63; Laszlo Somogyi 1964–69; guests 1969–70. Rochester Civic Music Association, Inc., founded 1922, incorporated 1930. 60 Gibbs Street, Rochester, New York 14604. (C)

Sacramento, California (800,592)
SACRAMENTO SYMPHONY ORCHESTRA. Harry Newstone, conductor; Peter F. Mancina, president; Peter P. Tencati, manager. 34 concerts, 24,441 estimated attendance; Hiram Johnson High School Auditorium (1,401). 50 players; expenditures $245,000. Previous conductors: Harry Olsen 1912–22; Franz Dicks 1923–28; Arthur Heft 1928–33; David Lincoln Burnham 1934–36; Willem Van Den Burg 1937–41; George Barr 1945–47; Fritz Berens 1948–64. Sacramento Symphony Association, founded 1912, incorporated 1948. 451 Parkfair Drive, Suite 11, Sacramento, California 95825. (D)

St. Louis, Missouri (2,367,017)
ST. LOUIS SYMPHONY ORCHESTRA. Walter Susskind, conductor; Leonard Slatkin, associate conductor; Ben H. Wells, president; Peter Pastreich, executive director; James N. Cain, manager; Peter B. Milstein, assistant manager. 167 concerts, 405,353 estimated attendance; Powell Symphony Hall (2,689). 93 players; expenditures $2,370,000. Previous conductors: Joseph Otten 1893–94; Alfred Ernst 1894–1907; Max Zach 1907–21; Rudolph Ganz 1921–27; guest conductors 1927–31; Vladimir Golschmann 1931–57; Edouard Van Remoortel 1957–61; Eleazar De Carvalho 1961–68. St. Louis Symphony Society, founded 1880, incorporated 1893. 718 North Grand Blvd., St. Louis, Missouri 63103. (B)

St. Paul, Minnesota
ST. PAUL CHAMBER ORCHESTRA. Dennis Russell Davies, music director and conductor; Louis Edouard Forner, associate conductor; Eugene M. Warlich, president; Stephen Sell, manager; John I. Jay, assistant manager. I. A. O'Shaughnessy Auditorium (1,747). 22 players. St. Paul Civic Philharmonic Society, Inc., founded 1958, incorporated 1959. Arts and Science Center, 30 E. Tenth Street, St. Paul, Minnesota 55101. (F)

St. Petersburg, Florida (1,012,594)
FLORIDA GULF COAST SYMPHONY. Irwin Hoffman, music director; Joseph Kreines, associate conductor; Fischer S. Black, chairman; Ernest Reiner, president Tampa board; Robert Ulrich, president St. Petersburgh board; Robert P. Thomson, executive director; David Ramsay, associate director. 42 concerts, 52,543 estimated attendance; Tampa, McKay Auditorium (1,763) and St. Petersburg, Bayfront Center Auditorium (2,138). 85 players; expenditures $340,000 ($10,000 government). Florida Gulf Coast Symphony, Inc., founded and incorporated 1967. P.O. Box 569, St. Petersburg, Florida 33731. (D)

Salt Lake City, Utah (557,635)
UTAH SYMPHONY. Maurice Abravanel, conductor; Ardean W. Watts, associate conductor; Wendell J. Ashton, president; Herold L. Gregory, executive director; Shirl H. Swensen, manager. Salt Lake City Tabernacle (5,000). Expenditures $1,203,225 ($280,422 government). Previous

conductors: Hans Heniot 1940–45; guest conductors 1945–46; Werner Janssen 1946–47. Founded 1940, incorporated 1966. 55 West First South, Salt Lake City, Utah 84101. (C)

San Antonio, Texas (864,014)
SAN ANTONIO SYMPHONY ORCHESTRA. Victor Alessandro, music director; Kenneth K. Caswell, manager. 600 Hemisfair Plaza Way, Suite 102, San Antonio, Texas 78205. (C)

San Diego, California (1,357,854)
SAN DIEGO SYMPHONY ORCHESTRA. Peter Eros, conductor; Robert Emile, associate conductor; L. Thomas Halverstadt, president; Philip A. Whitacre, manager; Robert Christian, assistant manager. 37 concerts, 45,117 estimated attendance; San Diego Civic Theatre (2,945). 72 players; expenditures $407,155. Previous conductors: guests 1927–40 and 1946–59; Earl Bernard Murray 1959–64; Zoltan Rozsnyai 1965–70. San Diego Symphony Orchestra Association, founded 1927, incorporated 1936. P.O. Box 3175, San Diego, California 92103. (D)

San Francisco, California (3,109,519)
SAN FRANCISCO SYMPHONY ORCHESTRA. Seiji Ozawa, conductor; Niklaus Wyss, associate conductor; Philip S. Boone, president; Joseph A. Scafidi, manager; Victor Wong and William I. Bernell, assistants. 183 concerts, 432,665 estimated attendance; War Memorial Opera House (3,252). 103 players; expenditures $2,623,597 ($190,000 government). Previous conductors: Henry Hadley 1911–15; Alfred Hertz 1915–30; Basil Cameron and Issay Dobrowen 1930–32; Issay Dobrowen 1932–34; Pierre Monteux 1934–52; guests 1952–54; Enrique Jorda 1954–63; Josef Krips 1963–70. San Francisco Symphony Association, founded and incorporated 1911. Room 107, War Memorial Veterans Building, San Francisco, California 94102. (B)

San Jose, California (1,064,714)
SAN JOSE SYMPHONY. James K. Guthrie, conductor (until June, 1972); Edward Meece, president; Don Thomson, manager; Diana Finch, assistant manager. San Jose Community Theater (2,700). San Jose Symphony Association; founded 1965. Ste. Claire Hotel, San Jose, California 95113. (E)

San Juan, Puerto Rico (455,421)
PUERTO RICO SYMPHONY ORCHESTRA. Victor Tevah, conductor; José Figueroa, associate conductor; Carlos M. Passalacqua, president; José A. Franceschini, executive director; Matías Ramos, Jr., assistant executive director. 35 concerts, 33,000 estimated attendance; Conservatory of Music of Puerto Rico (800). 62 players; expenditures $245,957. Previous conductor: José M. Castro, 7 years. Festival Casals, Inc., founded 1958. GPO Box 2350, San Juan, Puerto Rico 00936. (D)

Santa Barbara, California (264,324)
SANTA BARBARA SYMPHONY. Ronald Ondrejka, conductor; Mrs. Robert D. Cook, president; Genevieve S. Fisher, manager. 15 concerts, 17,325 estimated attendance; Granada Theatre (1,477). 70 players; expenditures $100,559. Previous conductors: Adolf Frezin, Loris Jones, Herbert Weiskopf, Ernest Gold 1953–59; Dr. Erno Daniel 1960–65; guest conductors 1966–67. Santa Barbara Symphony Association, founded 1953, incorporated 1954. Three West Carrillo, Suite 15, Santa Barbara, California 93101. (E)

Savannah, Georgia (187,767)
SAVANAH SYMPHONY ORCHESTRA. Ronald Stoffel, conductor; Alexander A. Simon, president; Dr. Peter Scardino, chairman; John Peter Chabot, manager 1971–72. 9 concerts, 10,700 estimated atendance; Savannah Municipal Auditorium (1,834). 38 players; expenditures $113,450 ($10,000 government). Previous conductor: Chauncey Kelley 1954–69. Savannah Symphony Society, Inc., founded 1954, incorporated 1955. P.O. Box 9505, Savannah, Georgia 31402. (E)

Seattle, Washington (1,421,869)
SEATTLE SYMPHONY ORCHESTRA. Milton Katims, conductor; Joseph Levine, associate conductor; Robert Denny Watt, president; Lanham Deal, manager. 159 concerts, 446,500 estimated attendance; Seattle Center Opera House (3,075). 88 players; expenditures $1,205,000. Previous conductors: Harry West 1904–05; Michael Kegrize 1907–09; Henry Hadley 1909–11; John Spargur 1911–21; Karl Krueger 1926–32; Basil Cameron 1932–38; Nikolai Sokoloff 1938–41; Sir Thomas Beecham 1941–44; Carl Bricken 1944–48; Eugene Linden 1948–50; Manuel Rosenthal 1949–52; guest conductors 1953–54. Seattle Symphony Orchestra, Inc., founded 1903, incorporated 1927. 305 Harrison Street, Seattle, Washington 98109. (C)

Shreveport, Louisiana (293,887)
SHREVEPORT SYMPHONY. John Shenant, conductor; Mrs. W. Peyton Shehee, president; Marjorie Campbell, office manager. 43 concerts, Civic Theatre (1,767). 60 players; expenditures $180,000 ($9,800 government). Founded and incorporated 1948; Symphony House, 2803 Woodlawn, Shreveport, Louisiana 71104. (E)

Spokane, Washington (287,483)
SPOKANE SYMPHONY ORCHESTRA. Donald Thulean, conductor; Scott B. Lukins, president; Maxey Adams, manager. 55 concerts, 85,000 estimated attendance; Fox Theatre (2,296). 66 players; expenditures $272,244. Previous conductor: Harold Paul Whelan 1944–62. Spokane

Symphony Society, Inc., founded 1944. 301 Great Western Building, West 905, Riverside, Spokane, Washington 99201. (D)

Springfield, Massachusetts (529,922)
SPRINGFIELD SYMPHONY ORCHESTRA. Robert Gutter, conductor; M. Mark Layne, administrative director. 49 Chestnut Street, Springfield, Massachusetts 01103. (E)

Syracuse, New York (635,946)
SYRACUSE SYMPHONY ORCHESTRA. Frederick Prausnitz, music director and conductor; Calvin Custer, associate conductor; Mrs. John R. Ralph, president; John S. Dietz, chairman; James Howland, general manager. 35 concerts; Henninger High School Auditorium (1,046). 48 players. Previous conductors: Karl Kritz 1961–69; Mihai Brediceanu 1970–71. Syracuse Symphony Orchestra, Inc., founded 1960. 113 E. Onondaga Street, Syracuse, New York 13203. (D)

Toledo, Ohio (692,571)
TOLEDO SYMPHONY ORCHESTRA. Serge Fournier, conductor; Howard S. Madigan, president; Gordon T. Coats, manager; Robert Bell, assistant manager. 233 orchestra and ensemble concerts, 77,000 estimated attendance; Masonic Auditorium (2,439). 84 players; expenditures $316,000 ($6,000 government). Previous conductors: Edgar Schenkman 1943–45; Hans Lange 1946–48; Wolfgang Stresemann 1949–54; Joseph Hawthorne 1955–63. Toledo Orchestra Association, founded and incorporated 1943. One Stranahan Square, Toledo, Ohio 43604. (D)

Tucson, Arizona (351,667)
TUSCON SYMPHONY ORCHESTRA. Gregory Millar, conductor; Norman W. Salmon, president; Douglas L. Steinriede, manager; Jimette Voorhees and Mrs. Charles Meade, assistant managers. 17 concerts, 78,101 estimated attendance; Tucson Community Center Music Hall (2,277). 45 players; expenditures $180,000. Previous conductors: Camil Van Hulse 1928–32; Joseph De Luca 1932–36; Henry Johnson 1936–37; Ivan Coleman 1937–38; William Foerster 1938–41; George Wilson 1941–46; Samuel Fain 1946–51; Stanley Schultz 1951–52; Frederic Balazs 1952–66. Tucson Symphony Society, Inc., founded 1928, incorporated 1959. 8 Paseo Redondo, Suite 10, Tucson, Arizona 85705. (E)

Tulsa, Oklahoma (475,991)
TULSA PHILHARMONIC. Skitch Henderson, conductor; Mrs. Winnifred Gillette, manager. Harwalden, 2210 South Main, Tulsa, Oklahoma 74114. (D)

Washington, D.C. (2,861,123)
NATIONAL SYMPHONY ORCHESTRA. Antal Dorati, music director; James DePriest, associate conductor; Lloyd Geisler, resident conductor; David Lloyd Kreeger, president; William L. Denton, manager; Robert J. Noerr, assistant manager; Robert Stull, operations manager. 200 concerts, Kennedy Center (2,739). 95 players; expenditures $2.7 million. Previous conductors: Hans Kindler 1931–49; Howard Mitchell 1949–70. National Symphony Orchestra Association, founded and incorporated 1931. 2480 16th Street, N.W., Washington, D.C. 20009. (B)

Wichita, Kansas (389,352)
WICHITA SYMPHONY ORCHESTRA. Francois Huybrechts, conductor and music director; Jay Decker, associate conductor; Robert G. Braden, president; Dewey Anderson, manager. 27 concerts, 43,000 estimated attendance; Century II Concert Hall (2,200). 86 players; expenditures $267,000 ($10,000 government). Previous conductors: Orien Dalley 1944–49; James Robertson 1950–70; guest conductors 1970–72. Wichita Symphony Society, Inc., founded and incorporated 1945. Suite 207, Century II Concert Hall, 225 W. Douglas, Wichita, Kansas 67202. (D)

Winston-Salem, North Carolina (603,895)
WINSTON-SALEM SYMPHONY. John Iuele, conductor; James B. L. Rush, president; Alvin R. Tyndall, manager. 15 concerts, 31,600 estimated attendance; R. J. Reynolds Auditorium (1,922). Previous conductors: Henry Sopkin and James Learch. Winston-Salem Symphony Association, Inc., founded 1947, incorporated 1950. 610 Coliseum Drive, Winston-Salem, North Carolina 27106. (E)

Youngstown, Ohio (936,003)
YOUNGSTOWN SYMPHONY ORCHESTRA. Franz Bibo, conductor; Jack W. Hynes, manager. 260 West Federal Street, Youngstown, Ohio 44503. (E)

Canadian Orchestras

Calgary, Alberta
CALGARY PHILHARMONIC. Maurice Handford, conductor; Migel Herrington, business manager. 830 Ninth Avenue, S.W. Calgary, Alberta.

Edmonton, Alberta
EDMONTON SYMPHONY ORCHESTRA. Lawrence Leonard, conductor; Jorgen R. Holgersen, general manager. 10023 103rd Street, Edmonton, Alberta.

Hamilton, Ontario
HAMILTON PHILHARMONIC. Boris Brott, conductor; Mrs. Betty Webster, executive director. P.O. Box 514, Hamilton, Ontario.

Montreal, Quebec
MONTREAL SYMPHONY ORCHESTRA. Franz-Paul Decker, music director; Denis Langelier, general manager. Place des Arts, 200 de Maisonneuve Blvd., West, Montreal 129, Quebec.

Quebec, P.Q.
L'ORCHESTRE SYMPHONIQUE DE QUEBEC. Pierre Dervaux, conductor; Francois Magnen, secretary general. 600 Grande Allee Est, Quebec, P.Q.

Toronto, Ontario
TORONTO SYMPHONY ORCHESTRA. Karel Ancerl, music director; Walter Homburger, manager. 215 Victoria Street, 5th Floor, Toronto, 2, Ontario.

Vancouver, B.C.
VANCOUVER SYMPHONY ORCHESTRA. Kazuyoshi Akiyama (1972–73), conductor; Victor White, general manager. 566 Hornby Street, Vancouver, B.C.

Victoria, B.C.
VICTORIA SYMPHONY ORCHESTRA. Laszlo Gati, conductor; T. G. McHale, general manager. 1960 Lansdowne Road, Victoria, B.C.

Winnipeg, Manitoba
WINNIPEG SYMPHONY ORCHESTRA. Leonard David Stone, general manager. 555 Main Street, Room 117, Winnipeg, Manitoba.

Appendix B

The Philharmonic Society of New York

Summary of activities from 1842 to 1890, showing conductors, number of concerts, income from ticket sales and associate memberships, and annual dividends received by each player-member.

INCOME

Yrs.	Cond.	Concerts	Total	Div.
1842–43		3	$ 1,854	$ 25
1843–44		4	2,081	32
1844–45		4	2,717	35
1845–46		5	2,671	37
1846–47		4	3,412	35
1847–48		4	1,813	26
1848–49		4	1,589	17.50
1849–50		4	2,100	32
1850–51		4	2,364	35
1851–52		4	2,618	41
1852–53	TE	4	3,032	44
1853–54	TE	4	4,425	55
1854–55		4	6,048	65
1855–56	CB	4	8,775	85
1856–57	TE	4	13,600	143
1857–58	TE	4	8,090	80
1858–59	CB	5	9,637	83
1859–60	E-B	5	10,199	80
1860–61	E-B	5	9,629	80
1861–62	E-B	5	5,253	60
1862–63	E-B	5	6,597	65
1863–64	E-B	5	11,632	100
1864–65	E-B	5	13,463	105
1865–66	CB	5	13,925	95
1866–67	CB	5	9,519	70

INCOME

Yrs.	Cond.	Concerts	Total	Div.
1867–68	CB	5	$14,061	70
1868–69	CB	6	23,635	156
1869–70	CB	6	24,302	150
1870–71	CB	7	27,057	203
1871–72	CB	6	25,610	216
1872–73	CB	6	25,035	180
1873–74	CB	6	19,022	126
1874–75	CB	6	5,760	54
1875–76	CB	6	10,039	30
1876–77	LD	6	8,291	18
1877–78	TT	6	12,499	82
1878–79	AN	6	7,157	25
1879–80	TT	6	18,735	123
1880–81	TT	6	20,749	132
1881–82	TT	6	23,465	154
1882–83	TT	6	25,003	195
1883–84	TT	6	24,279	195
1884–85	TT	6	27,191	223
1885–86	TT	6	26,241	200
1886–87	TT	6	28,443	225
1887–88	TT	6	27,693	189
1888–89	TT	6	28,247	195
1889–90	TT	6	28,246	200

NOTES: Number of concerts indicates number of programs given; gradually the final rehearsal became considered a concert, and programs were thus actually given in pairs. The dividend (Div.) is the amount received by each player-member for the entire season. Until 1852, the designation of conductor varied from concert to concert, sometimes with more than one on a program; after 1852, the conductor was elected for the full season. The initials indicate conductors as follows: TE for Theodore Eisfeld; CB for Carl Bergmann; E-B for seasons shared by Eisfeld and Bergmann; LD for Leopold Damrosch; AN for Adolf Neuendorff; and TT for Theodore Thomas. Source: Henry Edward Krehbiel, *The Philharmonic Society of New York*, p. 175.

Appendix C

Work Stoppages in Symphony Orchestras
1954–1972

Year	Orchestra	Duration (Days)
1954	Philadelphia	7
1958	Los Angeles	Less than 1 day
1959	Philadelphia	10
1961	New York	7
1961	Philadelphia	19
1963	Los Angeles	20
1963	National (Washington, D.C.)	15
1964	National	35
1966	Indianapolis	17
1966	Philadelphia	58
1966	Los Angeles	29
1967	San Francisco	49
1968	Baltimore	28
1968	Cincinnati	28
1969	National	42
1969	Rochester	42
1970	Cleveland	41
1971–2	Indianapolis	63
1971–2	Baltimore	77
1971–2	Cincinnati	35

Source: Michael H. Moskow, *Labor Relations in the Performing Arts*, p. 115, for data through 1966; more recent data from *Senza Sordino* and publications of American Symphony Orchestra League.

Appendix D

Major and Metropolitan Orchestras by Category
1972

Category A

*Boston
*Chicago
*Cleveland
*Los Angeles
*New York
*Philadelphia

Category B

*Cincinnati
*Detroit
*Houston
*Minnesota
  (Minneapolis)
*National
  (Washington, D.C.)
*Pittsburgh
*St. Louis
*San Francisco

Category C

*Atlanta
*Baltimore
*Buffalo
*Dallas
*Denver
*Indianapolis
*Milwaukee
*New Orleans
*Rochester
*San Antonio
*Seattle
*Utah
  (Salt Lake City)

Category D

*Birmingham
*Columbus
*Florida
  (Orlando)
*Florida Gulf Coast
  (St. Petersburg)
*Hartford
*Honolulu
*Hudson Valley
  (Poughkeepsie)
*Kansas City
*Louisville
 Memphis
*Miami
*Nashville
*New Haven
 New Jersey
  (Newark)
 North Carolina
  (Chapel Hill)
 Omaha
*Oregon
  (Portland)
*Oklahoma City
*Phoenix
 Puerto Rico
  (San Juan)
*Rhode Island
  (Providence)
*Richmond
*Sacramento
*St. Paul
*San Diego
 Syracuse
*Toledo
*Tulsa
*Wichita

Category E

*Akron
*Albany
*Albuquerque
*Amarillo
*Austin
*Charlotte
*Chattanooga
 Corpus Christi
*Dayton
*Duluth
 Eastern Music Festival
  (Greensboro, N.C.)
*Jacksonville
*Kalamazoo
*Knoxville
*Madison
 Miami Beach
*Midland-Odessa
*Norfolk
 Oakland
*Pasadena
*Portland, Me.
*San Jose
*Santa Barbara

*El Paso
*Erie
 Evansville
 Flint
*Fort Lauderdale
*Fort Wayne
*Fort Worth
*Fresno
*Glendale
*Grand Rapids
*Jackson

*Savannah
*Shreveport
*Spokane
*Springfield
 Tri-City
   (Davenport, Ia.)
 Tucson
*Vermont
   (Middlebury)
*Winston-Salem
*Youngstown

* Indicates orchestras included in statistical summaries by category in Appendix E.
Orchestras alphabetically listed by first name in title; where this does not indicate city, that information is given in parentheses to facilitate reference to Appendix A.

Category F

The following orchestras, listed in Appendix A and in the ASOL roster of Major and Metropolitan orchestras, are not included in the preceding five categories because they are not strictly community-supported orchestras of the type which are the primary concern of this book. All are located in or near New York City.

† American Symphony Orchestra
Clarion Music Society
The Little Orchestra Society

Symphony of the New World
Brooklyn Philharmonia
Orchestra da Camera, Massapequa

† Discontinued operations during the summer of 1972.

Appendix E (page 1)

Financial Summary, 1970–71: 82 Orchestras—Averages by Category

	CATEGORY A 6 of 6 Orchestras		CATEGORY B 8 of 8 Orchestras		CATEGORY C 12 of 12 Orchestras		CATEGORY D 26 of 32 Orchestras		CATEGORY E 32 of 40 Orchestras	
INCOME										
Performance:										
Concerts	$2,124,151	39.5%	$ 924,301	38.7%	$ 418,583	31.7%	$131,995	32.9%	$ 57,340	33.5%
Other nongovt.	1,259,020	23.3%	118,516	5.0%	35,065	2.6%	19,007	4.8%	11,225	6.5% (29)
Govt. for service	217,391	4.0%	140,254	5.9%	198,055	15.0% (11)	41,366	10.3% (20)	21,342	12.5% (20)
TOTAL PERFORMANCE	$3,600,562	66.8%	$1,183,071	49.6%	$ 651,703	49.3%	$192,368	48.0%	$ 89,907	52.5%
Supplemental:										
Contributions	$1,137,686	21.1% (3)	$ 735,491	30.8% (6)	$ 505,761	38.3% (11)	$151,887	37.9% (20)	$ 60,440	35.3% (21)
Number of contributors	(4677)		(5866)		(3718)		(1238)		(544)	
Govt. nonservice	92,500	1.7% (2)	144,856	6.1% (4)	64,394	4.9% (8)	19,205	4.8% (8)	15,121	8.8% (12)
Endowment & investment	562,324	10.4%	321,880	13.5%	99,836	7.5%	37,281	9.3% (25)	5,903	3.4% (22)
TOTAL SUPPLEMENTAL	$1,792,510	33.2%	$1,202,227	50.4%	$ 669,991	50.7%	$208,373	52.0%	$ 81,464	47.5%
TOTAL INCOME	$5,393,072	100%	$2,385,298	100%	$1,321,694	100%	$400,741	100%	$171,371	100%
EXPENDITURES										
Artistic personnel	$2,533,140	51.8%	$1,620,684	64.9%	$ 859,962	66.2%	$249,080	63.7%	$ 93,786	61.8%
Concert production	1,788,905	36.6%	562,942	22.5%	264,969	20.4%	71,926	18.4%	28,364	18.7%
Administration	568,223	11.6%	314,691	12.6%	174,012	13.4%	69,838	17.9%	29,573	19.5%
TOTAL EXPENDITURES	$4,890,268	100%	$2,498,317	100%	$1,298,943	100%	$390,844	100%	$151,723	100%
Orchestras with Surplus	$ 46,812 (1)	16.6%	$ 2,445 (1)	12.5%	$ 29,354 (6)	50.0%	$ 17,335 (13)	50.0%	$ 8,491 (16)	50.0%
Orchestras with (Deficit)	(246,909)	83.3%	(179,229)	87.5%	(37,668)	50.0%	(42,967)	50.0%	(8,455)	50.0%

SOURCE: Averages prepared according to category from 1970–71 reports from orchestras to American Symphony Orchestra League. Totals and percentages computed by author.

NOTE: Where fewer than all orchestras reporting in each category are included in average given, the number is indicated in parentheses.

Appendix E (page 2)

1970–71 Operating Data Summary—Averages of 82 Orchestras by Category

	CATEGORY A 6 of 6 Orchestras		CATEGORY B 8 of 8 Orchestras		CATEGORY C 12 of 12 Orchestras		CATEGORY D 26 of 32 Orchestras		CATEGORY E 32 of 40 Orchestras	
Number full concerts	189		178		153		45		17	
Number ensemble concerts	38	(2)	61	(3)	21	(4)	124	(19)	42	(19)
Number players	106		96		82		75		77	
Number women players	7	6.6%	16	16.6%	27	33.0%	28	37.3%	30	39.0%
Paid weeks	51+		47		36					
Minimum salary/week	$279.87		$225.81		$192.91					
Average salary/week	$329.39	118%	$260.21	115%	$228.07	118%				
Average salary/year	$18,210.		$12,230.		$8,210.		$1,600.		$710.	
Average estimated attendance	593,012		455,809		286,973		95,021		40,591	
Expenditures/person	$8.23		$5.40		$4.53		$4.11		$3.71	
Perf. inc./person	$4.98		$2.60		$2.25		$1.92		$1.98	
No. orchs. on TV or radio	4	66%	5	62%			1	4%		
No. orchs. recording	6	100%	4	50%	3	25%	1	4%	1	3%
Government funding:										
For services	6		8		12		20		12	
Nonservice	2		4		8		8		20	

SOURCE: Same as Appendix E, page 1

Appendix E (page 3)

1970–71 Finances and Operations/Metropolitan Population
82 Orchestras by Category

	CATEGORY A 6 of 6 Orchestras	CATEGORY B 8 of 8 Orchestras	CATEGORY C 12 of 12 Orchestras	CATEGORY D 26 of 32 Orchestras	CATEGORY E 32 of 40 Orchestras
Average metropolitan-area population	5,862,580	2,514,803	1,034,266	764,701	438,433
Expenditures/person	$0.83	$0.99	$1.26	$0.51	$0.35
Performance income/person	$0.61	$0.47	$0.63	$0.25	$0.21
Contributions/person	$0.19	$0.29	$0.49	$0.20	$0.14
All government/person	$0.05	$0.11	$0.25	$0.08	$0.08
Attendance % of population	10.11%	18.13%	27.75%	12.43%	9.26%
Total orchestra concerts/100,000	3.22	7.07	14.79	5.88	3.87

NOTE: Population data are based on Standard Metropolitan Statistical Areas, 1970 U.S. Census.

Appendix F

Estimates of 1970–71 Income, Expense, Attendance for Symphony, Theater, Opera, and Dance in the United States

PERFORMANCE ARTS

	Symphony	Theater	Opera	Dance	Total
No. Reporting	101	35	35	20	191
Expenditures	$82,231	$20,222	$40,648	$17,418	$160,519
Perf. Income	$42,196	$13,102	$26,587	$ 8,624	$ 90,509
Gross Deficit	$40,035	$ 7,120	$14,061	$ 8,796	$ 70,012
Suppl. Income	$37,092	$ 5,910	$12,010	$ 7,877	$ 62,889
Net Deficit	$ 2,943	$ 1,210	$ 2,051	$ 918	$ 7,122
Attendance	12,450	3,000	2,380	2,624	20,454

($ in thousands, attendance in thousands)

As Percentages of Expenditures

	Symphony	Theater	Opera	Dance	Total
Expenditures	100%	100%	100%	100%	100%
Perf. Income	51.4	65.0	65.4	49.5	56.3
Gross Deficit	48.6	35.0	34.6	50.5	43.7
Suppl. Income	45.1	29.2	29.6	45.2	39.1
Net Deficit	3.4	5.8	5.0	5.3	4.6

As Per Person Attending

	Symphony	Theater	Opera	Dance	Total
Expenditures	$6.60	$6.73	$17.10	$6.64	$7.84
Perf. Income	$3.40	$4.36	$11.20	$3.29	$4.42
Gross Deficit	$3.20	$2.37	$ 5.05	$3.35	$3.42
Suppl. Income	$2.98	$1.96	$ 4.18	$3.00	$3.07
Net Deficit	$ .22	$ .41	$ .87	$ .35	$ .35

MAJOR AND METROPOLITAN ORCHESTRAS

	Major	Metro	Total
Number reporting	28 (27.5%)	73 (72.5%)	101 (100%)
Expenditures	$64,900	$17,331	$82,231
	(78.7%)	(21.3%)	(100%)
Perf. Income	$34,397	$ 7,799	$42,196
	(81.5%)	(18.5%)	(100%)
Gross Deficit	$30,503	$ 9,532	$40,035
	(76.2%)	(23.8%)	(100%)
Suppl. Income	$27,907	$ 9,185	$37,092
	(75.2%)	(24.8%)	(100%)
Net Deficit	$ 2,596	$ 347	$ 2,943
	(88.3%)	(11.7%)	(100%)
Attendance (000s)	8,750	3,700	12,450
	(70.2%)	(29.8%)	(100%)

As Percentages of Expenditures

	Major	Metro	Total
Expenditures	100%	100%	100%
Perf. Income	53%	45%	51%
Gross Deficit	47%	55%	49%
Suppl. Inc.	43%	53%	45%
Net Deficit	4%	2%	4%

As Per Person Attending

	Major	Metro	Total
Expenditures	$7.41	$4.68	$6.60
Perf. Inc.	$3.93	$2.10	$3.40
Gross Deficit	$3.48	$2.58	$3.20
Suppl. Inc.	$3.18	$2.48	$2.98
Net Deficit	$ .30	$ .10	$ .22

SOURCE: Based on National Endowment for the Arts, *Economic Aspects of the Performing Arts, A Portrait in Figures.* My opera figures include the Metropolitan Opera, listed separately in the NEA report.

Appendix G-1

Ten-Year Trends in Symphony Finance, 1961–71 Actual

	1961–62	1962–63	1963–64	1964–65	1965–66	1966–67	1967–68	1968–69	1969–70	1970–71
MAJOR ORCHESTRAS (28)										
Total Expenditures	$22,168	$23,112	$24,820	$28,830	$33,396	$41,830	$46,306	$52,759	$58,754	$65,765
Exp./Orchestra	792	825	886	1,030	1,193	1,494	1,654	1,884	2,098	2,348
% Annual Increase		4.3%	7.4%	16.2%	15.8%	25.3%	10.7%	13.9%	11.4%	11.9%
Total Perf. Income	$12,925	$13,967	$14,474	$16,620	$18,951	$20,407	$23,591	$25,215	$28,487	$30,628
P.I/Orchestra	462	499	517	594	677	729	843	901	1,017	1,094
% P.I./Exp.	58.3%	60.4%	58.3%	57.6%	56.7%	48.8%	50.9%	47.8%	48.5%	46.6%
% Annual Increase		8.1%	3.6%	14.8%	14.0%	7.7%	15.6%	6.9%	13.0%	7.5%
Total Income Gap	$ 9,242	$ 9,145	$10,347	$12,210	$14,445	$21,423	$22,715	$27,544	$30,266	$35,137
I.G./Orchestra	330	327	370	436	516	765	811	984	1,081	1,255
% I.G./Exp.	41.7%	39.6%	41.7%	42.4%	43.3%	51.2%	49.1%	52.2%	51.5%	53.4%
% Annual Increase (decrease)		(1.1%)	13.1%	18.0%	18.3%	48.3%	6.0%	21.3%	9.9%	16.1%
Total Contributions	$ 7,910	$ 7,992	$ 8,775	$10,704	$12,048	$16,843	$17,887	$20,954	$23,883	$26,732
Cont./Orchestra	282	285	313	382	430	602	639	748	853	955
% Cont./Exp.	35.7%	35.6%	35.4%	37.1%	36.1%	40.3%	38.6%	39.7%	40.6%	40.6%
% Annual Increase		1.0%	9.8%	22.0%	12.6%	39.8%	6.2%	17.1%	14.0%	11.9%
Total Government	$ 870	$ 1,003	$ 1,068	$ 1,240	$ 1,475	$ 2,593	$ 2,618	$ 2,821	$ 3,770	$ 5,969
Govt./Orchestra	31	36	38	44	53	93	94	101	135	213
% Govt./Exp.	3.9%	4.3%	4.3%	4.3%	4.4%	6.2%	5.7%	5.3%	6.4%	9.1%
% Annual Increase		15.3%	6.5%	16.1%	18.9%	75.6%	1.0%	7.7%	33.6%	66.5%
METROPOLITAN ORCHESTRAS (72)										
Expense/Orchestra	$ 174	$ 187	$ 198	$ 181	$ 191	$ 203	$ 242	$ 263	$ 256	$ 244
% Annual Change		+7.5%	+6.1%	−8.6%	+5.4%	+6.4%	+19.1%	+8.7%	−2.7%	−4.5%
P.I./Orchestra	89	101	99	99	104	87	67	98	100	104
% P.I./Exp.	51.3%	54.1%	49.8%	54.8%	54.3%	42.8%	27.9%	37.1%	39.0%	42.6%
% Annual Change		+13.4%	−2.4%	+0.7%	+4.5%	−16.2%	−22.2%	+44.5%	+2.2%	+4.4%
I.G./Orchestra	84	86	99	82	87	116	174	165	156	140
% I.G./Exp.	48.7%	45.9%	50.2%	45.2%	45.7%	57.2%	72.1%	62.9%	61.0%	57.4%
% Annual Change		+1.4%	+16.2%	−17.7%	+6.5%	+33.2%	+50.0%	−5.2%	−5.6%	−10.2%
Contrib./Orchestra	72	70	80	74	75	94	109	112	130	110
% Contrib./Exp.	41.4%	37.3%	40.7%	40.9%	39.2%	46.3%	45.1%	42.6%	50.8%	45.0%
% Annual Change		−3.0%	+15.6%	−7.9%	+1.0%	+25.5%	+16.0%	+2.8%	+15.9%	−15.4%
Govt./Orchestra	7	7	12	10	13	20	23	21	19	25
% Govt./Exp.	4.1%	3.9%	5.8%	5.3%	6.7%	10.1%	9.7%	8.0%	7.4%	10.2%
% Annual Change		+1.8%	+59.6%	−16.0%	+32.9%	+58.9%	+14.2%	−10.1%	−10.1%	+32.5%

($ in thousands)

Appendix G-2

Ten-Year Trends in Symphony Finance, 1971–81 Estimated Projection

	1971–72	1972–73	1973–74	1974–75	1975–76	1976–77	1977–78	1978–79	1979–80	1980–81
28 Major Orchs:										
Total Exp. (12%)	$73,657	$82,496	$92,395	$103,482	$115,900	$129,808	$145,385	$162,832	$182,371	$204,256
Exp./Orch.	2,631	2,946	3,300	3,696	4,139	4,636	5,192	5,815	6,513	7,295
Total P.I. (10.8%)	33,936	37,601	41,662	46,161	51,147	56,671	62,791	69,572	77,086	85,411
P.I./Orch.	1,212	1,343	1,488	1,649	1,827	2,024	2,243	2,485	2,753	3,050
Total I.G.	39,721	44,895	50,733	57,321	64,753	73,137	82,594	93,260	105,285	118,845
I.G./Orch.	1,478	1,603	1,812	2,047	2,313	2,612	2,950	3,331	3,860	4,244
% I.G./Exp.	53.9%	54.4%	54.9%	55.4%	55.9%	56.3%	56.8%	57.3%	57.7%	58.2%
				(Approximate annual increase: 13%)						
Total Contrib. (12.3%)	30,020	33,712	37,859	42,516	47,745	53,618	60,213	67,619	75,936	85,276
Contrib./Orch.	1,072	1,204	1,352	1,518	1,705	1,915	2,150	2,415	2,712	3,046
% Contrib./Exp.	40.8%	40.9%	41.0%	41.1%	41.2%	41.3%	41.4%	41.6%	41.6%	41.7%
72 Metropolitan Orchs:										
Total Exp. (4.2%)	$18,321	$19,091	$19,893	$20,728	$21,599	$22,506	$23,451	$24,436	$25,462	$26,532
Exp./Orch.	254	265	276	288	300	313	326	339	354	368
Total P.I. (3.2%)	7,735	7,983	8,238	8,502	8,774	9,054	9,344	9,643	9,952	10,270
P.I./Orch.	107	111	114	118	122	126	130	134	138	143
Total I.G.	10,586	11,108	11,655	12,226	12,825	13,452	14,107	14,793	15,510	16,262
I.G./Orch.	147	154	162	170	178	187	196	205	215	226
% I.G./Exp.	57.8%	58.2%	58.6%	59.0%	59.4%	59.8%	60.2%	60.5%	60.9%	61.3%
				(Approximate annual increase: 4.85%)						
Total Contrib. (5.6%)	8,348	8,815	9,309	9,830	10,381	10,962	11,576	12,224	12,909	13,632
Contrib./Orch.	116	122	129	137	144	152	161	170	179	189
% Contrib./Exp.	45.6%	46.2%	46.8%	47.4%	48.1%	48.7%	49.4%	50.0%	50.7%	51.4%

($ in thousands)

Appendix G-3

Estimate of Net Financial Gap—Ten-Year Projection 1971–81 (Reasonable Basis)

	1971–72	1972–73	1973–74	1974–75	1975–76	1976–77	1977–78	1978–79	1979–80	1980–81
EXPENDITURES										
28 Major Orchs.	$73,657	$82,496	$92,395	$103,482	$115,900	$129,808	$145,385	$162,832	$183,371	$204,356
72 Metro Orchs.	18,321	19,091	19,893	20,728	21,599	22,506	23,451	24,436	25,462	26,532
100 Orchs.	91,978	101,587	112,288	124,210	137,499	152,314	168,836	187,268	207,833	230,788
PERF. INC.										
28 Major Orchs.	33,936	37,601	41,662	46,161	51,147	56,671	62,791	69,572	77,086	85,411
72 Metro Orchs.	7,735	7,983	8,238	8,502	8,774	9,054	9,344	9,643	9,952	10,270
100 Orchs.	41,671	45,584	49,900	54,663	59,921	65,725	72,135	79,215	87,038	95,681
INCOME GAP										
28 Major Orchs.	39,721	44,895	50,733	57,321	64,753	73,137	82,594	93,260	105,285	118,845
72 Metro Orchs.	10,586	11,108	11,655	12,226	12,825	13,452	14,107	14,793	15,510	16,262
100 Orchs.	50,307	56,003	62,388	69,547	77,578	86,589	96,701	108,053	120,795	135,107
CONTRIBUTIONS										
28 Major Orchs.	30,020	33,712	37,859	42,516	47,745	53,618	60,213	67,619	75,936	85,276
72 Metro Orchs.	8,348	8,815	9,309	9,830	10,381	10,962	11,576	12,224	12,909	13,632
100 Orchs.	38,368	42,527	47,168	52,346	58,126	64,580	71,789	79,843	88,845	98,908
NET FINANCIAL GAP										
28 Major Orchs.	9,701	11,183	12,874	14,805	17,008	19,519	22,381	25,641	29,349	33,569
% F.G./Exp.	13.2%	13.6%	13.9%	14.3%	14.7%	15.0%	15.4%	15.7%	16.1%	16.4%
72 Metro Orchs.	2,238	2,293	2,346	2,396	2,444	2,490	2,531	2,569	2,601	2,630
% F.G./Exp.	12.2%	12.0%	11.8%	11.6%	11.3%	11.1%	10.8%	10.5%	10.2%	9.9%
100 Total Orchs.	11,939	13,476	15,220	17,201	19,452	22,009	24,912	28,210	31,950	36,199
% F.G./Exp.	13.0%	13.3%	13.6%	13.8%	14.1%	14.4%	14.8%	15.1%	15.4%	15.7%

($ in thousands)

Appendix G-4

Estimates of Net Financial Gap—Ten-Year Projection 1971–81 (Alternative Possibilities)

	1970–71 Actual	1980–81 Table G-3	%	10-yr. Av. Median 1980–81	10-yr. %	10-yr. Av. Worst Case 1980–81	%	Worst Case 1980–81
EXPENDITURES								
28 Major Orchs.	$65,765	$204,356	13.0%	$197,558	14.8%	$259,772	15.0%	$266,019
72 Metro Orchs.	17,583	26,532	4.2%	26,515	5.2%	29,188	10.0%	45,593
100 Orchs.	83,348	230,788		224,073		288,960		311,612
PERFORMANCE INCOME								
28 Major Orchs.	30,628	85,411	10.0%	79,418	9.6%	76,570	7.0%	60,245
72 Metro Orchs.	7,495	10,270	3.2%	10,270	11.2%	21,661	7.0%	14,743
100 Orchs.	38,123	95,681		89,688		98,231		74,983
INCOME GAP								
28 Major Orchs.	35,137	118,845		118,140		183,202		205,774
72 Metro Orchs.	10,088	16,262		16,245		7,527		30,850
100 Orchs.	45,225	135,107		134,385		190,729		236,624
CONTRIBUTIONS								
28 Major Orchs.	26,732	85,276	14.9%	107,195	20.4%	171,085	10.0%	69,316
72 Metro Orchs.	7,905	13,632	5.6%	13,628	5.1%	12,995	5.0%	12,877
100 Orchs.	34,637	98,908		120,823		184,080		82,193
NET FINANCIAL GAP								
28 Major Orchs.	$ 8,405	$ 33,569		$ 10,945		$ 12,117		$136,458
% NFG/Exp.	12.8%	16.4%		5.5%		4.7%		51.3%
72 Metro Orchs.	2,183	2,630		2,617		(5,468)		17,973
% NFG/Exp.	12.4%	9.9%		9.9%		(18.7%)		39.4%
100 Orchs.	10,588	36,199		13,562		6,649		154,431
% NFG/Exp.	12.7%	15.7%		6.0%		2.3%		49.6%

($ in thousands)

Sources: For Major orchestras, John Macomber and John T. Wooster, *How to Resolve the Growing Financial Crisis of Our Symphony Orchestras,* in *Symphony News,* June, 1972. For Metropolitan orchestras, my own data from the American Symphony Orchestra League with grateful acknowledgment to William C. Nelms for his assistance.

Percentage computations are my own in all cases. For determination of percentage increments for 1971–81 see discussion in Chapter XIII under *Impact of the Income Gap.* For reasons discussed there, neither performance nor contributed income include government funding in any of these data.

Appendix H

Ford Foundation Symphony Program
Summary as of June 30, 1971
($ in Millions)

Orchestra	Endowment Trust Share	Non-Match Grant	Match Requirement	Match Achieved
American (N.Y.)	$1.0	$0.5*	$1.0	(b)
Atlanta	1.0	0.75*	1.0	$1.0
Baltimore	1.0	0.75*	1.0	1.0
Birmingham	0.6	0.2*	0.6	0.68
Boston	2.0	0.5	4.0	4.13
Brooklyn Philharmonia	0.25	0.075	0.25	0.078(b)
Buffalo Philharmonic	1.0	0.75*	1.0	1.0
Chicago	2.0	0.5	4.0	4.02
Cincinnati	2.0	0.5	3.0	3.0
Cleveland	2.0	0.5	4.0	6.5
Columbus	0.5	0.1	0.5	0.6
Dallas	2.0	0.5	2.0	2.04
Denver	1.0	0.75*	1.0	1.0
Detroit	1.0(a)	0.5	2.0	1.96
Festival (N.Y.)	0.35	0.075	0.35	(c)
Florida (Orlando)	0.5	0.1	0.5	0.52
Fort Wayne Philharmonic	0.25	0.075	0.25	0.25
Hartford	1.0	0.35*	1.0	1.0
Honolulu	0.75	0.35*	0.75	0.78
Houston	2.0	0.5	2.0	2.02
Hudson Valley Philharmonic	0.25	0.075	0.25	0.25
Indianapolis	2.0	0.5	2.0	2.35
Jacksonville	0.25	0.075	0.25	0.26
Kalamazoo	0.5	0.1	0.5	0.76
Kansas City Philharmonic	1.0	0.75*	1.0	0.13(b)
Little Orchestra (N.Y.)	0.35	0.075	0.35	0.081(b)
Los Angeles Philharmonic	2.0	0.5	4.0	4.0
Louisville	0.5	0.2*	0.5	0.56
Memphis	0.4	0.1	0.4	0.4
Milwaukee	1.0	0.25	1.0	1.24
Minnesota (Minneapolis)	2.0	0.5	4.0	7.92
Nashville	0.5	0.2*	0.5	0.51
National (Washington, D.C.)	2.0	0.5	3.0	3.11
New Haven	0.5	0.1	0.5	0.61
New Jersey	0.5	0.15*	0.5	0.52
New Orleans Philharmonic	1.0	0.75*	1.0	1.07
New York Philharmonic	1.0(a)	0.5	2.0	2.0
North Carolina	0.75	0.25	0.75	0.84
Oakland	1.0	0.35*	1.0	1.0
Oklahoma City	0.6	0.15	0.6	0.6
Omaha	0.4	0.1	0.4	0.49
Oregon (Portland)	1.0	0.25	1.0	1.07
Philadelphia	2.0	0.5	4.0	4.13
Phoenix	0.6	0.25*	0.6	0.67
Pittsburgh	2.0	0.5	3.0	3.0
Puerto Rico (San Juan)	none	0.375*	none	none
Rhode Island Philharmonic	0.35	0.15*	0.35	0.35
Richmond	0.5	0.15*	0.5	0.5

Orchestra	Endowment Trust Share	Non-Match Grant	Match Requirement	Match Achieved
Rochester Philharmonic	1.0	0.75*	1.0	1.0
Sacramento	0.5	0.2*	0.5	0.54
St. Louis	2.0	0.5	2.0	2.0
San Antonio	1.0	0.75*	1.0	1.07
San Diego	0.5	0.1	0.5	0.53
San Francisco	2.0	0.5	3.0	4.12
Seattle	1.0	0.75*	1.0	1.11
Shreveport	0.35	0.075	0.35	0.40
Syracuse	0.75	0.25	0.75	0.78
Toledo	0.5	0.15*	0.5	0.51
Tulsa	0.5	0.1	0.5	0.56
Utah	1.0	0.5*	1.0	1.05
Wichita	0.5	0.15*	0.5	0.61

a) Supplements previous Foundation grant.
b) Dropped from participation in the endowment trust fund as of 30 June 1971.
c) Discontinued operations in 1969 and dropped from participation in endowment trust fund.
* Indicates that Non-match Grant included development grant.

TOTALS: Endowment trust fund $58,750,000
          Non-match grants   21,450,000
          Matching achieved   84,405,376

(In addition, some orchestras raised more in capital funds than were reported for Ford Foundation audit between 1966 and 1971.)

NOTES:
Endowment Trust shares shown above are based on the market value of the Ford Motor Company stock placed in trust April 25, 1966. Non-match Funds include expendable and developmental grants.

Sources: Ford Foundation press release, July 6, 1966; trust agreement, April 25, 1966; special report, December 1972.

Appendix J

National Endowment for the Arts
Grants to Symphony Orchestras, 1966–72

	NEA Before FY 1970	NEA FY 1971	NEA FY 1972
Akron Symphony		$ 8,000	
Albany Symphony			$ 10,000
Albuquerque Symphony			20,000
Atlanta Symphony	$ 15,300		100,000
Baltimore Symphony		100,000	100,000
Birmingham Symphony		5,000	17,500
Boston Symphony	50,000	75,000	100,000
Brooklyn Philharmonia		15,000	
Buffalo Philharmonic	25,000		73,850
No. Carolina Symphony		25,000	20,000
Charlotte Symphony			20,000
Chattanooga Symphony			10,000
Chicago Symphony		100,000	100,000
Cincinnati Symphony	50,000	72,250	100,000
Cleveland Orchestra	32,200	25,000	100,000
Columbus Symphony		15,200	14,000
Corpus Christi Symphony			6,000
Dallas Symphony			100,000
Denver Symphony	29,500	43,510	100,000
Detroit Symphony	50,000	100,000	100,000
Duluth Symphony		10,300	
El Paso Symphony		10,000	10,000
Erie Philharmonic		8,700	15,000
Evansville Philharmonic		15,000	10,000
Fort Wayne Philharmonic			15,000
Fresno Philharmonic		17,700	24,750
Glendale Symphony			15,000
Grand Rapids Symphony			11,380
Hartford Symphony		15,000	20,000
Honolulu Symphony			84,000
Houston Symphony		50,000	50,000
Indianapolis Symphony		39,000	56,000
Jackson Symphony		30,000	35,000
Jacksonville Symphony			15,000
Kalamazoo Symphony			6,450
Kansas City Philharmonic		100,000	75,000
Knoxville Symphony		10,300	10,900
Los Angeles Philharmonic		100,000	100,000
Louisville Orchestra		20,000	16,016
Memphis Symphony		19,900	20,000
Greater Miami Philharmonic		60,900	15,000
Miami Beach Symphony		10,000	
Vermont State Symphony		10,000	15,000
Milwaukee Symphony		36,500	83,000
Orchestra da Camera			50,000
Minnesota Orchestra	27,500	106,000	112,000
Nashville Symphony		17,400	14,530
New Haven Symphony		17,800	23,500
New Orleans Philharmonic		66,000	100,000
New Jersey Symphony		72,300	82,000

	NEA Before FY 1970	NEA FY 1971	NEA FY 1972
American Symphony		$ 31,000	$ 50,000
New York Philharmonic		125,000	100,000
Symphony of New World	$ 25,000	25,000	25,000
Norfolk Symphony		16,200	12,000
Oakland Symphony			5,740
Oklahoma City Symphony		26,000	20,000
Omaha Symphony		25,000	10,675
Florida Symphony		15,000	20,000
Philadelphia Orchestra		15,500	100,000
Phoenix Symphony		25,000	13,375
Pittsburgh Symphony	50,000	100,000	100,000
Portland Symphony		12,700	20,000
Oregon Symphony		16,500	10,000
Hudson Valley Philharmonic			5,000
Rhode Island Philharmonic		35,000	25,000
Richmond Symphony		20,000	15,000
Rochestra Philharmonic		35,000	100,000
Sacramento Symphony		9,000	13,000
St. Louis Symphony	50,000	100,000	100,000
St. Paul Chamber Orchestra		25,000	25,000
Florida Gulf Coast Symphony		22,500	
Utah Symphony	15,200	100,000	100,000
San Antonio Symphony		99,500	100,000
San Diego Symphony		19,700	
San Francisco Symphony	50,000	100,000	100,000
Puerto Rico Symphony			25,000
Seattle Symphony		100,000	100,000
Shreveport Symphony		6,400	9,500
Spokane Symphony		25,000	30,000
Springfield Symphony		13,800	15,000
Syracuse Symphony		15,000	20,000
Toledo Symphony			25,000
Tucson Symphony		10,000	15,000
Tulsa Philharmonic		25,800	
National Symphony	62,500	325,000	200,000
Wichita Symphony		10,000	20,000
Youngstown Symphony		20,000	15,000
Total to Major and Metropolitan Orchestras	532,200	2,966,360	3,720,166
	(14 Orchs.)	(67 Orchs.)	(80 Orchs.)
Other Grants in the Symphonic Field	N/A	146,500	286,090

Source: Reports and press releases of National Endowment for the Arts, verified and corrected by staff.

NOTE: Detailed listing includes only direct grants to Major and Metropolitan orchestras. Final figure includes a variety of grants to orchestras not in these categories and to other organizations for cooperation programs involving orchestras or serving them. Figures are *net* government grants, exclusive of private contributions to Treasury Fund.

Appendix K

State Funding of Symphony Orchestras as Share of Total Arts Funding, FY 1971

State	State Appr.	State-Federal Funds	Total Income	Symphony Grants	Per-centage
Alabama	$ 100,000	$75,377	$ 175,377	$ 31,000	18%
Alaska	100,000	75,377	175,377	10,000	5.7%
Arizona	23,561	36,363	59,924		
Arkansas		75,377	75,377		
California	168,000	75,377	243,377	10,000	4%
Colorado	27,157	75,377	102,534	13,100	13%
Connecticut	118,702	75,377	194,079	10,000	5%
Delaware	50,000	75,377	125,377	YES	
Dist. Columbia	25,661	75,377	101,038		
Florida	83,530	75,377	158,907	83,300	52%
Georgia	88,060	75,377	163,437	15,000	9%
Hawaii	174,558	75,377	249,935		
Idaho	10,000	75,377	85,377		
Illinois	600,000	75,377	675,377	220,250	33%
Indiana	25,000	75,377	100,377	10,580	10%
Iowa	30,730	75,377	106,107	6,756	6%
Kansas	61,445	75,377	136,822	YES	
Kentucky	146,234	75,377	221,611	YES	
Louisiana	42,860	75,377	118,237	NO	
Maine	90,500	75,377	165,877	23,800	14%
Maryland	303,079	75,377	378,456	285,500	74%
Massachusetts	160,000	75,377	235,377	5,000	2%
Michigan	219,952	75,377	295,329	6,600	2%
Minnesota	115,150	75,377	190,527	24,000	13%
Mississippi	75,000	75,377	150,377		
Missouri	210,083	75,377	276,460	85,698	31%
Montana	25,000	75,377	100,377	10,600	10%
Nebraska	13,704	75,377	89,081	14,500	16%
Nevada		75,377	75,377	18,000	24%
New Hampshire	10,000	75,377	85,377	10,000	12%
New Jersey	78,776	75,377	154,153	135,624	88%
New Mexico	23,000	75,377	98,377	15,917	16%
New York	20,203,015	75,377	20,278,392	1,605,640	8%
North Carolina	120,027	75,377	195,404	12,500	6%
North Dakota		75,377	75,377	19,325	25%
Ohio	198,184	75,377	273,561	9,430	3%
Oklahoma	86,399	75,377	161,776	37,715	23%
Oregon	24,924	75,377	100,301	15,160	15%
Pennsylvania	205,000	75,377	280,377	YES	
Rhode Island	111,839	75,377	187,216	13,000	7%
South Carolina	132,917	75,377	208,294	4,980	2%
South Dakota	19,426	75,377	94,803	4,000	4%
Tennessee	72,300	75,377	147,677		
Texas	106,072	75,377	181,449	37,242	20%
Utah	83,000	75,377	158,377	29,000	18%
Vermont	34,609	75,377	109,986	32,900	33%
Virginia	140,000	75,377	215,377		
Washington	87,512	75,377	162,889	17,650	11%

State	State Appr.	State-Federal Funds	Total Income	Symphony Grants	Percentage
West Virginia	$ 159,960	$75,377	$ 235,337	$ 61,500	28%
Wisconsin		75,377	75,377	3,630	5%
Wyoming		75,377	75,377	10,500	14%
Puerto Rico	1,739,984	75,377	1,815,361		
Virgin Islands	150,000	75,377	225,377		10.3%
			$28,780,969	$2,959,397	

Average % for thirty-eight orchestras reporting symphony grants: 17.9%.

Sources: Associated Councils of the Arts Directory of State Arts Councils 1971, for state appropriations and state-federal partnership funds; Missouri Arts Council survey, August, 1971, for symphony grants by state councils or commissions; percentage computation by author.

NOTE: Some of these data do not conform to information from other sources in all details and probably are not complete; they are presented here from the above sources only in the interest of consistency. As noted in the text, completely accurate information in this area has not yet been assembled.

Appendix L
Summary of BMI Orchestral Program Surveys, 1961–70

	1961–2	1962–3	1963–4	1964–5	1965–6	1966–7	1967–8	1968–9 ALL	1968–9 S & T	1969–70 ALL	1969–70 S & T
Major Orchestras	28	28	28	28	27	28	28	27		29	
Metropolitan	22	23	22	22	43	44	46	63		63	
Urban, Community	177	173	175	195	276	350	238	327		351	
School, youth, etc.	44	37	38	39	146	135	105	165		177	
ALL ORCHESTRAS	271	262	263	284	492	557	417	582		620	
Subscription Concerts	2,103	1,961	2,155	2,324	2,950	3,233	3,064	3,338		3,554	
Tour Concerts	233	146	192	342	589	572	606	749		862	
Young People's Concerts	422	345	207	450	763	822	769	950		1,297	
Special	145	134	100	176	379	390	384	235		258	
Pops						221	213	209		196	
Summer				292	190	309	244	396		370	
Schools						137				221	
TOTAL CONCERTS	2,903	2,586	2,654	3,584	4,871	5,684	5,280	5,877		6,758	
Orchestra Works Performances	8,545	7,808	7,206		14,258	16,948	15,994	17,937	10,754	18,808	10,600
Concertos	1,875	1,749	1,709		2,905	3,860	3,223	3,991	2,940	4,119	3,023
Vocal	785	667	695		1,058	1,367	1,068	507	339	365	274
Choral	435	384	397		665	558	723	732	620	855	596
Opera Excerpts	67	51	54		124	198	337	909	645	1,245	855
Ballet Music	116	136	78		95	192	156	68	37	99	23
Show Music								518	143	662	164
Popular Music										63	4
Other		37	2			2					
TOTAL PERFORMANCES	11,823	10,832	10,141	14,609	19,375	23,126	21,501	24,662	15,478	26,214	15,539
American Composers, 20th Cent.	348	270	271	317	390	547	593	667	475	567	
Other 20th Cent. Composers	264	182	187	204	183	265	241	307	261	312	
Standard, Pre-1900 Composers	179	158	167	167	210	238	213	257	211	233	
ALL COMPOSERS	791	610	625	688	783	1,050	1,047	1,231	947	1,112	
American Works, 20th Cent.	590	479	503	961	989	1,043	1,147	1,252	845	1,150	
Other 20th-Cent. Works	397	452	490	511	537	859	773	853	697	801	
Standard, Pre-1900 Works	411	812	941	745	1,228	1,464	1,319	1,366	1,462	1,323	
ALL WORKS	1,398	1,760	1,934	2,217	2,754	3,366	3,239	3,471	2,998	3,274	
American Performances, 20th-C.	1,676	1,506	1,516	2,275	2,790	3,974	3,956	4,812	2,391	5,190	
Other 20th-Cent. Performances	2,339	2,173	1,986	3,198	3,930	5,197	4,921	5,750	3,740	6,067	
Standard, Pre-1900 Performances	7,808	6,934	6,639	9,136	12,655	13,955	12,624	14,100	9,347	14,957	
ALL PERFORMANCES	11,283	10,382	10,141	14,609	19,375	23,126	21,501	24,662	15,478	26,214	
World Premieres, American Wks.	63	71	71	104	121	123	165	108		96	
American Premieres, Other Wks.	31	19	26	32	33	55	49	55		25	
TOTAL PREMIERES	94	90	97	136	154	178	214	163		121	

Appendix M

U.S. Symphony Orchestras Included
in Mueller Repertory Survey

Atlanta Symphony Orchestra (1945)
Baltimore Symphony Orchestra (1935)
Boston Symphony Orchestra (1880)
Buffalo Philharmonic Orchestra (1940)
Chicago Symphony Orchestra (1890)
Cincinnati Symphony Orchestra (1895)
Cleveland Orchestra (1915)
Dallas Symphony Orchestra (1925)
Denver Symphony Orchestra (1945)
Detroit Symphony Orchestra (1915)
Houston Symphony Orchestra (1915)
Indianapolis Symphony Orchestra (1930)
Kansas City Philharmonic (1930)
Los Angeles Philharmonic (1915)
Milwaukee Symphony Orchestra (1960)
Minnesota (formerly Minneapolis) Orchestra (1920)
New Orleans Philharmonic Orchestra (1945)
New York Philharmonic Orchestra (1840)
New York Symphony Orchestra (1877–1927)
Philadelphia Orchestra (1900)
Pittsburgh Symphony Orchestra (1935)
Rochester Philharmonic Orchestra (1920)
St. Louis Symphony Orchestra (1910)
San Francisco Symphony Orchestra (1910)
Seattle Symphony Orchestra (1930)
Utah Symphony Orchestra (1940)
National Symphony Orchestra (1930)

NOTE:
Date in parentheses indicates the beginning of the half decade in which the orchestra was first covered. In the case of the New York Symphony Orchestra, the dates are those of its actual operations.
Source: Mueller Repertory Survey.

Appendix N

Publications of the American
Symphony Orchestra League

Analysis of Major Orchestra Contracts, by Carol Kniebusch, 1972.
Analysis of Metropolitan Orchestra Contracts, by Carol Kniebusch, 1972.
Community Projects Involving Symphony Women's Associations, 1970–71 Season, compiled by
    June M. Wainwright, 1971.
*The Community Symphony Orchestra, by Helen M. Thompson, 1952.
*Economic Conditions of Symphony Orchestras and Their Musicians, by Helen M. Thompson,
    1961.
Fund-raising Projects Involving Symphony Women's Associations, 1970–71 Season, compiled by
    June M. Wainwright, 1971.
Governing Boards of Symphony Orchestras, by Helen M. Thompson, 1958.
A Guide to Accounting Procedures and Record Keeping for Community Symphony Orchestras,
    by William C. Nelms, 1965.
Handbook for Symphony Orchestra Women's Associations, by Helen M. Thompson, 1963, 1971.
Legal Documents of Symphony Orchestras, 1958.
Survey of Arts Councils, edited by Leslie C. White and Helen M. Thompson, 1959.
*Survey of Opinions of Governing Boards of Symphony Orchestras on the Role of the Federal
    Government in the Arts,* edited by Helen M. Thompson, 1962.
Symphony News, published six times a year; previously *Inter-orchestra Bulletin* and *Newsletter
    of the American Symphony Orchestra League,* 1948–71.
*Symphony News Is Good News, A Publicity Handbook for Symphony Orchestras and Symphony
    Women's Associations,* 1971.
The Symphony Orchestra Abroad, by Howard Taubman, 1970.

* Indicates publications out of print, 1972.

Notes

In the following notes will be found general acknowledgments and specific citations, as indicated by number in the text of each chapter. References to published material—books, magazines, and pamphlets—are in brief form; a full description of each will be found in the Bibliography.

Chapter I—*Before Thomas*

I am indebted to the Music Division of the New York Public Library, at the Library and Museum of the Performing Arts, part of Lincoln Center for the Performing Arts, for the extensive use of its collection and for the assistance of its staff. There I was able to review thoroughly such basic sources as *Dwight's Journal of Music* and Odell's *Annals of the New York Stage,* which give a detailed account of the musical and theatrical life of the mid 19th-century.

1. Lorenzo da Ponte, *Memoirs,* pp. 446–49.
2. The "official" history of the Philharmonic Society of New York and of its successors, the New York Philharmonic-Symphony Society and the New York Philharmonic, has been published in several volumes by Henry Edward Krehbiel (1892), James Gibbons Huneker (1917), and Charles Erskine (1943). A new and comprehensive history of this orchestra by Howard Shanet is now in preparation.
3. Krehbiel, p. 62.
4. *Dwight's Journal of Music,* November 3, 1855.
5. Krehbiel, p. 44.
6. For a good account of the Germania Musical Society, see H. Earle Johnson's article, *The Germania Musical Society,* in *Musical Quarterly,* XXXIX, p. 75. *Dwight's Journal of Music,* which began publication only toward the end of Germania activity, has notices of its appearances in Boston and elsewhere; the issue of September 16, 1854, includes a comprehensive review of the Germania's six years in America on the occasion of its disbanding.
7. Theodore Thomas, *A Musical Autobiography,* p. 26.
8. See Berlioz, *Evenings with the Orchestra,* p. 112 ff.; Berlioz, *Memoirs,* pp. 448–50 and 483–84; Adam Carse, *The Orchestra from Beethoven to Berlioz* (numerous citations); and Harold C. Schonberg, *The Great Conductors,* pp. 149–55. Max Maratzek, *Sharps and Flats* (published together with *Crochets and Quavers* as *Revelations of an Opera Manager in 19th Century America*), makes numerous references to Jullien in the course of his highly entertaining life abroad and in this country.
9. Harold C. Schonberg, *The Great Conductors,* p. 155.
10. Odell, *Annals of the New York Theater,* includes many references to these operatic and concert productions in its year-to-year coverage of this era.

Chapter II—*Theodore Thomas, Conductor*

Shortly before his death, Thomas responded to a request from a friend, the *Chicago Tribune* critic George P. Upton, with an extended autobiographical memoir. To this, Upton added his own *Reminiscences and Appreciation* and a second volume listing a substantial representation of Thomas's programs, preceded by the conductor's introductory note on program making. These two volumes were published in 1905 as *Theodore Thomas, a Musical Autobiography.* In 1964, a new edition of Upton's book was issued, edited by Leon Stein, with new material and appendices, but omitting the listing of programs in Upton's second volume. This basic authority on Thomas's career was generously used by Rose Fay Thomas in her *Memoirs of Theodore Thomas* and by Charles Edward Russell in his *The American Orchestra and Theodore Thomas.*

After her husband's death, Mrs. Thomas entrusted to the Newberry Library in Chicago a considerable collection of Thomas's papers. These included voluminous scrapbooks containing most of the programs he conducted, the books and some scores from his personal library, and some very interesting correspondence with such notable figures as von Bülow, Liszt, Saint-Saëns, Wagner and other composers. I am indebted to the Newberry Library and to its staff for the opportunity to study this collection and to base some of the data in this chapter on it. Specific acknowledgment of previously unpublished material will be found below.

Secondary material on Thomas appears in John Mueller's *The American Symphony Orchestra,* the histories of the New York Philharmonic cited in the previous chapter, and in the books by William Mason, Henry Finck, Amy Fay, Walter Damrosch, Max Maratzek, Margaret Grant and Herman S. Hettinger, and Milton Goldin, listed in the Bibliography.

Philo Otis's *The Chicago Symphony Orchestra* is a prime source, not only on the formation of that organization and Thomas's role there but also on the history of the orchestra to 1924. I am indebted to the Orchestral Association and to the orchestra's librarian, Lionel Sayers, for making a copy of this rare book available to me. On the occasion of its seventy-fifth anniversary in 1966, the Orchestral Association published an extensive historical brochure, which, while not as thorough as Otis's book, is nevertheless an important source for the orchestra's more recent history.

Finally, my own association with the Chicago Symphony Orchestra from 1956 to 1961 provided me with my first impression of Thomas's importance and with a great deal of atmospheric background on him, the orchestra, and Orchestra Hall.

1. Rose Fay Thomas, *Memoirs of Theodore Thomas* (hereafter RFT), p. 543.
2. I am indebted to Mrs. Jeannann Celli for tabulating Thomas's touring activities from the program scrapbooks in the Newberry Library at Chicago.
3. RFT, p. 3.
4. Theodore Thomas, *A Musical Autobiography,* ed. Upton (hereafter Thomas-Upton), p. 21.
5. Thomas-Upton, p. 29.
6. Thomas-Upton, p. 32.
7. William Mason, *Memories of a Musical Life,* p. 200.
8. For this program, like others cited here, see Volume II of the first edition of Thomas-Upton.
9. RFT, p. 31.
10. RFT, p. 50.
11. Edwin T. Rice, *Thomas and Central Park Garden,* in *Musical Quarterly,* XXVI (April, 1940), p. 21.
12. RFT, p. 36 ff. Thomas does not describe this trip in his *Autobiography,* but Mrs. Thomas quotes in some detail from a diary which he kept in German. This diary is not among the Thomas papers in the Newberry Library.
13. Harold C. Schonberg, *New York Times,* May 9, 1971.
14. Among the Thomas papers in the Newberry Library are a few letters and contracts with soloists such as August Wilhelmi concerning the terms of their engagement.
15. Amy Fay's book *Music Study in Germany* contains interesting information on her studies abroad, but it does not mention her American debut.
16. All three books on Thomas have accounts of this tour, but Milton Goldin's *The Music Merchants* recounts the Rubinstein-Wieniawski tour more thoroughly from the point of view of the artists and Steinway.
17. RFT, p. 86.
18. Philo Adams Otis, *The Chicago Symphony Orchestra—Its Organization, Growth, and Development, 1891–1924* (hereafter Otis), p. 97. This is a comprehensive, year-by-year account. For Thomas's Chicago career and for subsequent events until 1924, this book has been my primary source. Both Mrs. Thomas and Russell recount much the same story, and where they offer data not in Otis, they are important sources; otherwise, Otis's book is a basic authority. Otis was born at Berlin Heights, Ohio, in 1846, and died in 1930 in Chicago. A member of a socially prominent family in Chicago, he was also a trained musician, especially in choral work. He attended Thomas's first concert in Chicago in 1870, heard him conduct there frequently, and became a close and admiring friend. He was, in 1872, one of the organizers of the Apollo Musical Club chorus, which appeared frequently with the Thomas orchestra and the Chicago Symphony. Though close to Thomas from the beginning of the Orchestral Association, Otis did not become a trustee until 1894; he served in that post until his death.
19. RFT, p. 16.
20. RFT, pp. 179–87.
21. RFT, pp. 271–72.
22. A pencil draft of this letter in Thomas's handwriting is in the Newberry Library collection. I am indebted to the Newberry Library for permission to quote this previously unpublished letter.
23. RFT, p. 233.
24. *Musical America,* February 14, 1906.
25. RFT, p. 258.

26. RFT, p. 214. The invitation was extended in a letter dated January 18, 1882, from the composer John Knowles Paine, music professor at Harvard (the first to hold such a position in the United States). It probably reflects the discontent of local Boston musicians with the stringent requirements imposed by Higginson on his players.

27. Russell, *The American Orchestra and Theodore Thomas,* p. 156, reports an incident in Cincinnati when Thomas himself physically ejected a persistent newspaperman from the office of the Music Hall.

28. Frances Dillon, in her introduction to Amy Fay's *Music Study in Germany,* gives a brief account of the Fay family.

29. Fay's account of this meeting was told by him in an article in *Outlook Magazine* (February, 1910) and is reported in its entirety by Otis, pp. 25–26. Mrs. Thomas does not mention this episode in her *Memoirs.*

30. Otis, pp. 27–29.

31. Otis, p. 106.

32. Thomas-Upton, p. 104.

33. Unpublished letter from Thomas to Fay, September 14, 1900, in the Newberry Library collection.

34. RFT, p. 503. Mrs. Thomas here and elsewhere includes extensive correspondence between Strauss and Thomas.

35. Otis, p. 130.

36. The clipping, in the New York Public Library, carries no identification as to date or source, but from the context, the interview took place shortly after Thomas's death. Russell, p. 268, has a slightly different version of the story, including previous efforts by Thomas to keep his head warm by wearing a cap during rehearsal.

37. The story of Thomas's participation in the Columbian Exposition is told in detail by Otis, Russell, and Mrs. Thomas. In addition to the Steinway-piano problem, there were similar difficulties with harps from the Chicago firm of Lyon and Healy. Thomas himself makes no mention of the Exposition in his *Autobiography.*

38. Otis, p. 119 and elsewhere.

39. Otis reports the Boston refusal on p. 54, the New York refusal on p. 58.

40. Otis, pp. 114–15.

41. RFT, pp. 510–11.

42. Otis, pp. 130, 134 ff.

43. RFT, p. 539. Both Mrs. Thomas and Otis report on the planning and first tests of Orchestra Hall in considerable detail. However, there is no basis for Frank Lloyd Wright's oft-quoted assertion that the disappointment of Thomas in Orchestra Hall "killed" him.

44. RFT, p. 530.

45. RFT, pp. 531–32.

46. RFT, pp. 542–43.

47. For data on the Chicago Symphony Orchestra after Thomas's death, see Otis and the 1966 historical brochure.

48. Bernard Asbell's article *Claudia Cassidy, the Queen of Culture and Her Reign of Terror* (*Chicago Magazine,* June, 1956) reviews the more lurid aspects of Miss Cassidy's contribution to the performance arts in Chicago.

49. The Orchestral Association usually published financial summaries in the first concert program of each season.

Chapter III—*Henry Lee Higginson, Patron*

Though Bliss Perry's *Life and Letters of Henry L. Higginson* is the authoritative work on the subject, I have relied heavily on Mark DeWolfe Howe's 1914 history of the Boston Symphony for much of his account of Higginson's role as founder and patron of the orchestra. Howe's book, written under the eagle eye of Higginson himself, was later brought up to 1931 by its author and John H. Burk in anticipation of the orchestra's fiftieth anniversary. More objective is H. Earle Johnson's *Symphony Hall, Boston,* though it deals only tangentially with the orchestra and Higginson, and again relies upon Howe for much of its information. Moses Smith, *Koussevitzky,* also contains valuable historical data on the orchestra, based to a great extent on these other sources but occasionally offering a less adulatory approach.

I am indebted to the Boston Symphony Orchestra and to its manager Thomas D. Perry, Jr., for the opportunity to go through the few Higginson papers carefully preserved in his safe.

1. Bliss Perry, *The Life and Letters of Henry Lee Higginson* (hereafter Perry), pp. 291–96.

2. For early music activity in Boston, see Howard and Bellows, *A Short History of Music in America,* in addition to Mark DeWolfe Howe, *The Boston Symphony Orchestra,* and H. Earle Johnson, *Symphony Hall* (hereafter Howe and Johnson respectively).

3. Perry, p. 2. Higginson's youth, up to his founding of the Boston Symphony Orchestra, is covered in detail, with copious quotations from letters and diaries, in the first nine chapters of Perry's biography.

4. Perry's account of the founding of the Boston Symphony Orchestra, written after the first edition of Howe's history of the orchestra had been published in 1914, is largely based on Howe, though he often quotes in detail from Higginson's letters and diaries, which may not have been available to Howe. The latter, of course, wrote while Higginson was alive and worked under his close scrutiny.

5. Howe, pp. 16–20.

6. Howe, pp. 32–33, gives the full text.

7. Howe, pp. 38–42, gives excerpts from newspaper accounts of this matter; Higginson's players' contract is given on p. 39.

8. Howe, pp. 70, 71.

9. This contract is in the archives of the Boston Symphony Orchestra, and I am indebted to the orchestra and its manager for permission to quote from it. The Nikisch contract has penciled notations indicating that it was used in drafting subsequent agreements with conductors.

10. In the archives of the Boston Symphony Orchestra there is a small notebook in which Higginson entered the contributions of various Bostonians to the American Opera Company; his is the largest gift recorded there.

11. Perry, Chapters XI, XII, and XIII, has a detailed account of Higginson's nonsymphonic service, from which the summary here is drawn to round out the full activities of Higginson.

12. Howe, Perry, and Johnson give few details about the design of the hall, but with the help of an architect friend, Helge Westermann of New York, I was able to locate the files of McKim, Mead, and White at the New-York Historical Society. I am indebted to the Society, and to Mr. Dupre, the curator of its Map and Print Room, for an opportunity to study this file, on which this account is based to a large degree. The Society's permission to cite this material, and to quote from letters from Higginson to McKim, is gratefully acknowledged.

13. Previously unpublished letter in New-York Historical Society.

14. Perry, pp. 469–70. Howe's history of the orchestra contains less documentation of Higginson's wartime problems than does Perry, who quotes extensively from Higginson's numerous letters to President Eliot and others. See also Irving Lowens, *L'Affaire Muck,* in *Musicology,* Vol. I, No. 3 (1947). Moses Smith, *Koussevitzky,* also has an account of this affair, and Schonberg has a chapter on Muck containing a good evaluation of his ability, as well as a summary of his problems in Boston.

15. Perry, pp. 480–81.

16. Perry, p. 482.

17. Perry, p. 481.

18. Perry, p. 484.

19. Perry, p. 487.

20. Perry, p. 487.

21. Perry, p. 494.

22. Perry, pp. 499–500.

23. Louise Hall Tharp, *Mrs. Jack* (hereafter Tharp), pp. 295–300, has a full account of the Muck affair from the point of view of Mrs. Gardner.

24. Tharp, p. 299.

25. Perry, p. 501.

26. Perry, pp. 503–05.

27. Howe recounts the story of the 1920 strike in some detail, but basically from the trustees' point of view. Robert D. Leiter, *The Musicians and Petrillo,* pp. 122–24, gives a more balanced account. Moses Smith, *Koussevitzky,* also covers this strike.

28. Leiter, p. 123, citing an article by John T. Morse, *Henry Lee Higginson,* in the *Harvard Graduates' Magazine,* March, 1920, p. 391.

29. Perry, pp. 519–20.

Chapter IV—*Arthur Judson, Manager*

No single comprehensive documentation of the career of Arthur Judson has been published. Thanks to the hereditary longevity of the Judson stock, the subject of this chapter is, at an age of over ninety, still very much a prime source of information. I am deeply indebted to Arthur Judson for several long and frank interviews that he gave me in 1970 at his home in Rye, New York. In addition to those occasions when I talked to Judson specifically about this book, I have known him professionally since 1942 and have had a number of occasions to discuss symphonic affairs and the music business in general with him.

Every concert artist, conductor, or manager who has come in contact with Judson in his long career has vivid memories of him and equally strong opinions; I am especially indebted to Frederick C. Schang, Jr., Ruth O'Neill, Reginald Allen, Boris Sokoloff, Rudolf Serkin, Samuel R. Rosenbaum, David M. Keiser, Eugene Ormandy, and Maurice Abravanel, among many others, both for specific information on Judson and for the general background they supplied. (Much to my regret, circumstances beyond my control have prevented me from including Leopold Stokowski among these colleagues of Judson with firsthand recollections.) In some cases, they gave me information on an "off the record" basis, information that I have been able to confirm by cross-checking but for which I cannot always cite sources.

Dorle Jarmel Soria, who served as publicist for the New York Philharmonic and Columbia Artist Management for many years, has not only recalled for me her recollections of Judson but also allowed me to Xerox press releases and newspaper clippings from her files.

For specific documentation on many events in Judson's career, I have referred to a number of books and new articles cited below.

1. Unless specifically stated otherwise, all opinions attributed to Arthur Judson in this chapter were expressed by him in the course of interviews at his home between January and November, 1970.

2. Interview with Helen M. Thompson, April 30, 1971, in New York.

3. *The Making of a Name,* by Arthur Judson; an article in *The Etude,* January, 1940.

4. Nicolas Slonimsky in *Baker's Biographical Dictionary of Musicians;* Herbert Kupferberg in *Those Fabulous Philadelphians* (hereafter Kupferberg), p. 31. Kupferberg cites Stokowski's birth certificate.

5. Kupferberg is my main source for much detailed data on the Stokowski era in Philadelphia, except when other sources are specifically identified.

6. Edward Arian's *Bach, Beethoven, and Bureaucracy,* in Tables III–1 through III–4, lists the founding incorporators (p. 53), directors from 1900 through 1969 (pp. 54–56), presidents and board chairmen (p. 57), and directors in 1969 with professional or business associations (pp. 60–61), with indications of those included in the Social Register. From 1900 to 1969, the total service of directors in the Social Register was 1175 years; for those not so listed is was 390 years.

7. Kupferberg's interview with Stokowski, p. 106.

8. Frances A. Wister, *Twenty-Five Years of the Philadelphia Orchestra* reviews in some detail the year-to-year concert activity in Appendix E, pp. 193–200.

9. Judson made a tape recording of his account of the founding of the Columbia Broadcasting System for the Oral History collection at Columbia University, on which an article in *American Heritage* (VI: 77–81; August, 1955), *How CBS Got Its Start* is based. Additional information on this topic is contained in an article by Ralph F. Colin in *Variety* (January 9, 1971): *Arthur Judson at 90: Sparked CBS Opposition to Sarnoff "Red" and "Blue."* Colin has represented the Paley interests in their investment in CBS and was legal counsel for CBS until 1970; he was also legal counsel for Columbia Concerts Corporation and its successor, Columbia Artist Management.

10. There are numerous accounts of the formation of Columbia Concerts Corporation and Community Concerts, both printed and through the reminiscences of the original participants. In addition to Judson himself, I am especially indebted to Frederick C. Schang, Jr. (interview October 27, 1971) for his inimitable anecdotes and to Dorle Jarmel Soria for press material from her files.

11. Because of legal hazards, it has always been difficult to document specific instances of close cooperation between the two giant booking agencies, but, from personal experience as a concert manager in the Pacific Northwest from 1942 to 1956, I can testify that I was myself

involved in such "gentlemen's agreements" and was well aware of their operation in other situations.

12. John Erskine, *The Philharmonic-Symphony Society of New York, First Hundred Years*, contains much specific documentation of the New York Philharmonic between 1891 and 1941. James Gibbons Huneker, *The Philharmonic Society of New York, A Retrospect*, also covers New York Philharmonic history until 1917.

13. Walter Damrosch, *My Musical Life*, contains an account of the history of the New York Symphony until the early 1920s; it does not cover the merger with the Philharmonic or his later career at NBC.

14. *Time*, XLIX (February 17, 1947), pp. 73–74, *Master Builder;* and *Newsweek*, XXIX (February 17, 1947), p. 90, *Row over Rodzinski.*

15. Judson learned of the Chicago contract afterward from the management there. When I joined the Chicago Symphony Orchestra staff several years later, the entire Rodzinski episode was still fresh in the minds of all concerned.

Chapter V—*James Caesar Petrillo and the Militant Musician*

The history of musicians' unionism, the American Federation of Musicians, and James C. Petrillo is well covered in Leiter's *The Musicians and Petrillo* up to 1951. Other information is available in such union publications as the *International Musician;* however, data there are fragmentary and often mystifying since they often do not tell the whole story, even from the union's point of view. Much of the history of the International Conference of Symphony and Opera Musicians can be reconstructed from the files of its publication *Senza Sordino.*

On many matters concerning the role of the Chicago Symphony Orchestra players in the removal of Petrillo and in the organization of ICSOM, I have relied on my own memory of events of which I had firsthand or authoritative knowledge. But I have also gone to considerable effort to check personally with many of the actual participants in these events to verify and expand my own recollection. Many of these participants remain reluctant to be cited directly by name and I must honor their reticence. I am, however, deeply indebted to ICSOM chairman Ralph Mendelson for a long and most enlightening interview at his home in New York.

Ted Dreher of the AFM New York office has supplied me with considerable data on Federation activities and history, from union publications and press releases. Kenneth E. Raine and his assistant, Frank Olin, of the Music Performance Trust Funds, have made available to me not only the published reports of the trustee but also information from their files. Samuel R. Rosenbaum, in an interview in Philadelphia, reviewed the early history and objectives of the MPTF.

For many years, while I was active in music in Portland, Oregon, and Herman D. Kenin was president of Local 99, we were close friends and worked together on a number of projects, including the revival of the Portland (later Oregon) Symphony Orchestra. I owe to him some essential insight into union attitudes and problems.

1. This account of the anti-Petrillo campaign is based on my personal recollection, confirmed more recently by checking back with several participants.

2. Robert D. Leiter's *Petrillo and the Musicians* (hereafter Leiter) is my basic source for data on the history of music unionism, except where another authority is specifically cited.

3. The figures given here represent my own estimate based on conversations with both local and national union officials and with others acquainted with the music profession.

4. Leiter has a full account of the New York problems of the AFM on pp. 28–32.

5. See Leiter, p. 34.

6. Leiter, p. 66.

7. Leiter is a basic source on Petrillo's career.

8. Leiter, pp. 47–48.

9. Leiter, pp. 49–50.

10. Leiter, p. 80, has a table showing this data for selected years from 1896 to 1951; the 1971 figures are from official AFM data.

11. Leiter, p. 114.

12. My account of the unionization of the Boston Symphony Orchestra relies both on Leiter (pp. 119–31) for a general summary and on Moses Smith, *Koussevitzky* (pp. 308–23, here-

after Smith), for a great deal of specific information about trustees' attitude and especially for the part that Koussevitzky played in this matter.

13. Leiter, p. 126.
14. Both Leiter (p. 128) and Smith (p. 218) report this visit and Petrillo's later comment.
15. Leiter, p. 127.
16. *The © Quagmire,* by Dan Lacy (*Saturday Review,* November 27, 1971, pp. 24–28), reviews the status of copyright legislation as of late 1971.
17. Leiter, pp. 132–41, for the 1942–43 ban; pp. 164–69 for the 1948 ban and formation of the MPTF.
18. Coincident with the completion of periodic trade agreements between the Federation and industry, a trust agreement is also drawn up, covering the operation of the MPTF for the period of the trade agreement. The most recent trust agreement for the record industry was signed in April, 1972, when the latest trade agreement was made. Data on present royalties and operations are from the 1969 agreement and from recent reports of the trustee, which are published in comprehensive form semiannually.
19. 44th Semi-Annual Report, July 1–December 31, 1970, Music Performance Trust Funds.
20. Much of the information regarding the development of players' militancy in symphony orchestras given here is based on my own experience in orchestra management, with personal recollection checked with a number of participants—managers, players, board members—of my own acquaintance.
21. William J. Baumol and William G. Bowen, *Performing Arts—The Economic Dilemma* (hereafter Baumol and Bowen), pages 102–03.
22. Baumol and Bowen, pp. 222–23, for trends in professions, and p. 216 for trends in eleven orchestras.
23. Work stoppages between 1922 and 1960 are listed in Michael H. Moskow, *Labor Relations in the Performing Arts,* p. 115; data for subsequent years have been assembled from the files of *Senza Sordino.*
24. See Note 1 to this chapter.
25. In addition to the files of *Senza Sordino,* many musicians involved in ICSOM affairs have supplied information in interviews. Among these I am especially indebted to Ralph Mendelson, present chairman of ICSOM.
26. *Senza Sordino,* Vol. IX, No. 6 (August, 1971), p. 3.
27. *New York Times,* October 12, 1971. This episode received extensive coverage in the national press and continuing coverage in the local Cleveland press.
28. *Senza Sordino,* Vol. IX, No. 3 (February, 1971), p. 4.

Chapter VI—*Helen M. Thompson and the ASOL*

Richard H. Wangerin and the staff of the American Symphony Orchestra League have been extremely helpful in supplying me with material from their files on the history and activity of the League. Mrs. Thompson, both during and after her service with the League, has given me an account of her own career and the development of her philosophy. I am especially indebted to her and to present League personnel for their courtesy and help. My own files of League *Newsletters,* publications, and other materials have provided me with additional factual data cited here.

1. Some biographical information on Mrs. Thompson is in publicity material from the ASOL and in a press release announcing her appointment as manager of the New York Philharmonic on March 4, 1970. Other information given here is from an interview with her in New York on April 30, 1971.
2. There is no single up-to-date history of the ASOL, though the twentieth-anniversary issue of the *Newsletter of the American Symphony Orchestra League* for April–May, 1962, contains a comprehensive review of League activities to that time, as well as Mrs. Snow's own account of its founding. The *Newsletter* and other releases by the ASOL are the sources for data here unless otherwise stated.
3. Arthur Judson clearly recalls Mrs. Snow's visit and the reasons for his advice to her.
4. I was present at managers' meetings when the problem of the admissions tax was discussed and learned then for the first time of the existence of the League, with whom cooperation on this matter was decided upon.
5. Interview with Mrs. Thompson, April 30, 1971.

6. Helen M. Thompson, *The Community Orchestra, How to Organize and Develop It*, p. 11.
7. Ibid., p. 12.
8. Mrs. Hampton S. Lynch, of the New York Philharmonic board of directors and secretary of the League board, provided me with a summary history of WASO. I am indebted to her also, and to Mrs. Joe Henry Roberts of Dallas, for additional materials, including those distributed at the 1971 conference in Dallas.
9. President Wangerin of the League and his staff have supplied data on membership and nonmembership files used here.
10. The list of orchestras originally included in the 1966 Ford Foundation grants was first announced in a press release on October 22, 1965, subsequently revised slightly in a press release on July 6, 1966. On September 30, 1970, the Foundation issued a fourteen-year summary, *Activities in the Creative and Performing Arts, Support in the Musical Arts (1957–1970)*, which includes a list of these orchestras on pp. 2–5. See Appendix H for a full list.
11. Personal communications from executives of Hurok Attractions and Columbia Artist Management.
12. Margaret Grant and Herman S. Hettinger, *America's Symphony Orchestras*, pp. 13, 23.
13. John H. Mueller, *The American Symphony Orchestra*, p. 37.
14. See League Memo No. 597 (December 2, 1970) advising League members of efforts on this issue and attaching a copy of Wangerin's letter of the previous day to the Commissioner of Internal Revenue.

Chapter VII—*Philadelphia Orchestra*

Herbert Kupferberg's *Those Fabulous Philadelphians* contains much factual information about this orchestra—its history and present activities; as its title indicates, it tends toward glamorization of its subject. Two earlier books, Frances A. Wister's *Twenty-Five Years of the Philadelphia Orchestra, 1900–1925* and R. L. F. McCombs' *The Philadelphia Orchestra* contain little of importance not covered by Kupferberg. Edward Arian's *Bach, Beethoven, and Bureaucracy* offers information and a point of view of exceptional importance; though I cannot accept all of his premises, his book has a thoughtful approach to the modern American symphony orchestra found nowhere else.

Personal interviews, press clippings, and publicity materials have provided a major source of information, and I have had superb cooperation from everyone at the Philadelphia Orchestra. My interviews included:

Eugene Ormandy
C. Wanton Balis, Jr., chairman of the board
Henry W. Sawyer III, trustee
Anthony A. Tomei, union official
Mason Jones, personnel manager
Ernest L. Goldstein, James Fawcett, Charles Griffin, Irving Segall, and Wilfrid Batchelder, musicians
Samuel R. Rosenbaum, former trustee
Arthur Judson and Reginald Allen, former managers

Joseph Santarlasci, Wayne Shilkret, and John D. Healy of the management staff rendered major assistance and gave me much information, orally and in documents. Last and by no means least, I owe a deep debt of gratitude to Boris Sokoloff for the information he provided himself and for his help in arranging my interviews with others.

1. Herbert Kupferberg *Those Fabulous Philadelphians* (hereafter Kupferberg), pp. 112–21, has a good report of the oft-told story of Ormandy's arrival in this country and his early career. Both Ormandy and Arthur Judson have given me essentially the same account in interviews.
2. The Philadelphia Orchestra *Press Book*, October, 1970.
3. This summary of activity is based on work schedules and information received in interviews with Boris Sokoloff and assistant manager Joseph H. Santarlasci.
4. See Kupferberg, pp. 151–54, for further details on the Academy of Music. The building project which he mentions was modified and postponed during the recent business recession, but some development will undoubtedly materialize eventually.
5. Boris Sokoloff himself was one of several who made this observation to me.
6. Schwann Catalog, 1970 Artist Issue, pp. 77–80.
7. American Federation of Musicians, Phonograph Labor Agreement, April, 1969, p. 19.

8. Philadelphia Orchestra Association, *Annual Report 1960–61, Annual Report 1970–71.*

9. Neither party to this agreement will confirm or deny this figure, which was widely quoted in musical and recording circles at the time. See Kupferberg, p. 181.

10. Both Balis and Sokoloff discussed these relationships in some detail at various separate interviews in Philadelphia.

11. See Edward Arian *Bach, Beethoven, and Bureaucracy* (hereafter Arian), pp. 53–57, for Social Register listing of directors from 1900 to 1969, and pp. 60–61 for business or professional affiliations of directors in 1968–69.

12. Arian, pp. 17–50.

13. Kupferberg, pp. 169–71, gives a brief review of labor strikes in the Philadelphia Orchestra. Arian contains more details, especially from the players' point of view. I personally encountered the intense and often vitriolic feelings of some of the players in an interview in November, 1970, with Messrs. Goldstein, Fawcett, Griffin, Segall, and Batchelder.

14. Arian, p. 136.

15. Arian, p. 33, here slightly modified.

16. Kupferberg, pp. 195–218, reflects much of the pride and *esprit de corps,* but he failed either to encounter or to report the bitterness that is the opposite side of this coin.

17. Kupferberg, p. 171.

18. From *Annual Reports,* Philadelphia Orchestra Association, for 1962–63 and 1965–66.

19. Arian, pp. 74–108, gives a detailed account of actual events and player psychology; this unique report is the most valuable contribution of his study.

20. Willard Randall, *The Oboe Jungle,* a review of Arian's book in *Philadelphia Magazine,* Vol. LXII, No. 11 (November, 1971), p. 44.

21. Arian, pp. 98–99.

22. Data on 1966 negotiations are based on my own study of the press-clipping files in the Association office and verification of some questions with management and players. Kupferberg's account, pp. 174–76, is very superficial and Arian deals only with background preliminary to the stoppage.

23. This possibility was recounted to me both by players and by an Association director.

24. Kupferberg, p. 170.

25. This account of the 1969 negotiations is based on interviews with Sokoloff and players.

26. Attitudes as of 1971 and looking forward to bargaining in 1972 were explicitly expressed to me in interviews with players.

27. Arian, pp. 136–37.

28. Kupferberg, p. 183, covers this matter rather cursorily. Arian apparently had access to the text of the Brakeley report, for he quotes it. This report as such was not available to me, but both Sokoloff and Healy gave me comprehensive reviews of its major recommendations.

29. Interview in April, 1971, with Balis.

30. Kupferberg, pp. 193–94.

Chapter VIII—*Utah Symphony Orchestra*

Material for this chapter was assembled from interviews, October 28–30, 1970, in Salt Lake City, and various printed materials from the files of the Utah Symphony Orchestra. Herold L. Gregory, its executive director, gave indispensable assistance to me, in providing documentary materials, answering innumerable queries, and arranging interviews with:

Maurice Abravanel
Wendell J. Ashton, president
Glen R. Swenson, chairman of the Utah State Institute of Fine Arts
Dr. Lowell Durham, professor of music, University of Utah
Harold Lundstrom, music critic, *Deseret News*
Shirl H. Swenson, manager
Robert G. Bradford, director of public affairs
Sheldon F. Hyde, personnel manager

To all of these, and especially to Mr. Gregory, I give very grateful acknowledgment for their most friendly cooperation.

1. Maurice Abravanel gave me his account of this meeting, and AFM executive Ted Dreher's report in an interview with me covered the same episode from a different point of view.

2. 1970 U.S. Census, for Standard Metropolitan Statistical Area as defined by the Bureau of the Budget.

3. The Utah Symphony Orchestra concert program, April 10, 1971, carries a complete list of the season's concerts; a few final corrections on the Latin-American tour schedule were subsequently supplied by Gregory.

4. Virtually everyone I talked with in Utah, Mormon and non-Mormon alike, readily volunteered a more or less standard dissertation on Mormonism and its influence on the orchestra.

5. In addition to hearing Abravanel's own vivid account of his career, I have consulted the official press material of the orchestra and Conrad B. Harrison's *The Utah Symphony Story,* a series of historical articles which appeared in the orchestra concert program books during the 1960–61 season.

6. Information on Gregory personally and on administration generally were supplied by him and his staff in interviews—October, 1970, and subsequently.

7. Adapted from 1970–71 annual financial report issued by the Utah Symphony Orchestra. Other information used in my commentary on this financial report was supplied in interviews with Gregory.

8. This was reported not only by Abravanel and Gregory but also by the players with whom I talked at some length in October, 1970.

9. Ashton's views were communicated at an interview over breakfast at the Utah Club in October, 1970. Comments on his role in leadership and concerning long-range problems were voiced in interviews with a number of people.

Chapter IX—*Louisville Orchestra*

The friendly and ready cooperation of manager James D. Hicks made my task of research on the Louisville Orchestra a rewarding pleasure. In addition to answering my inquiries with extensive materials, he arranged interviews for me with the following:

Jorge Mester
Robert Whitney
Charles P. Farnsley
Barry Bingham, Jr., president of the board
James Livingston, assistant conductor; Paul Kling, concertmaster; Francis Fuge, flutist; and Peter McHugh, personnel manager
Bill Woolsey, music critic, *Louisville Times*
Jerry W. Ball, University of Louisville

This comprehensive coverage made it possible for me to cross-check certain off-the-record information, especially regarding the Louisville Fund, which I cannot attribute directly in the notes that follow.

1. Whitney's own vivid account of his early days in Louisville was supplemented by the colorful recollections of Farnsley.

2. In addition to Whitney's and Farnsley's account of the recording project, I have consulted various press materials giving its history.

3. Catalogs of records currently available list most of the music recorded.

4. The variety of professional life was described for me, from various points of view, by the above-mentioned musicians in several interviews. Hicks also explained the complexities of schedule coordination.

5. As a former orchestra player, Ball could give me a comprehensive and sympathetic account of the advantages and disadvantages of the symphony-university relationship and of its future problems.

6. This admittedly personal conclusion is based on explicit statements of musicians, conductor, and manager and was implicit in everything they had to say about the players.

7. Based on official financial report of the Louisville Philharmonic Society, Inc.

8. Interview with Barry Bingham, Jr.

9. Information on Mester has been provided in press material prepared by the orchestra, from an interview, and from my own personal acquaintance with him during our years together at Juilliard.

Chapter X—*Buffalo Philharmonic*

Howard A. Bradley, then general manager and executive vice-president and now president of the Buffalo Philharmonic Society, gave me complete cooperation in arranging interviews on June 1–2, 1971, in Buffalo with key individuals involved with the orchestra, and has supplied me with copious documentary material. Among the people I saw there were:

Leon Lowenthal, president of the board of directors and president of WGR, the radio and television stations owned by the Taft Broadcasting Company of Cincinnati

Robert I. Millonzi, long-time member and former president of the board, and member of its musical committee

The Reverend James M. Demske, S.J., a member of the council of trustees, and president of Canisius College

Robert G. Webber, treasurer of the Philharmonic Society

George L. Wessel, a member of the board, and president of the Buffalo AFL-CIO

James H. Righter, member of the Philharmonic board and publisher of the *Buffalo News*

Mrs. Ralph Jones, Jr., member of the board and president of the women's committee board

Dr. Allan D. Sapp, former member of the Philharmonic board and its music committee, and on leave as head of the music department at the State University of New York at Buffalo, with whom I talked at greater length at my home in Santa Fe, New Mexico, on August 13, 1971

Jesse Levine, principal violist and member of the orchestra committee of the Philharmonic

Rodney Pierce, principal oboist and member of the orchestra committee, who graciously provided me with an extensive file of newspaper clippings on the 1969 Save-the-Philharmonic campaign

In addition I had frank and informative talks with Michael Tilson Thomas at Tanglewood on August 16, 1971; with former manager Seymour L. Rosen (now general manager of the Pittsburgh Symphony) at the annual conference of the American Symphony Orchestra League in Seattle on June 11, 1971; and with Carl W. Shaver at his office in New York on June 7, 1971.

To all of these individuals, and especially to Howard A. Bradley for his great help, I express my grateful acknowledgment and sincere thanks.

1. Though many gave me various accounts of this activity, the most vivid and detailed came from Rodney Pierce and Jesse Levine; the former placed at my disposal a large file of press clippings covering the event and illustrating the extensive press coverage it received.

2. U.S. Census 1970 for Standard Metropolitan Statistical Area as defined by the Bureau of Budget.

3. Data on historical background of the Buffalo Philharmonic are based on press material from the Society's files, plus recollections of various people interviewed.

4. Specific additional information on Cameron Baird was obtained from Allan D. Sapp and from Mischa Schneider, cellist in the Budapest String Quartet and now on the faculty of the University.

5. Though most allusions to the "Philharmonic family" imply criticism of its exclusivity, some in Philharmonic circles today still recall its period of domination with considerable nostalgia.

6. Sapp's own account of his relations with the Philharmonic and his role in engaging Foss confirms the information I had received from Millonzi and others on the board.

7. Interview with Sapp, August 13, 1971.

8. *Which Runs an Orchestra: the Conductor? the Men? the Dollar?*, interview by Donal Henahan with Lukas Foss, *New York Times*, May 18, 1969.

9. Subscription data from files of Buffalo Philharmonic. Comments on Foss's activities, and reactions to them, are based on interviews with a variety of people in Buffalo.

10. Interviews with Sapp. For additional information on the Center I am indebted to Mrs. Jesse (Renée) Levine, coordinator of the program and wife of the principal violist of the Philharmonic.

11. Comments on Foss's relations with the orchestra musicians are based on interviews with both present players and past members of the orchestra, some of whom requested anonymity in our discussions.

12. Security posted for bank loans is specifically noted in the Society's financial statements and auditor's reports.

13. This question was discussed in some detail in my interview with Robert G. Webber, the Society's treasurer, on June 2, 1971.

14. In addition to local interviewees in Buffalo, Carl W. Shaver himself discussed his experiences in Buffalo with me at an interview. Shaver also discussed the Buffalo-Rochester merger in a wider context, since his firm had made a report for the Rochester Civic Music Association in the spring and summer of 1969.

15. Data supplied by Bradley in phone conversation, February 28, 1972.

16. Interviews with Rodney Pierce and Jesse Levine.

17. See Donal Henahan, *4 Orchestras Play Merger Tune, New York Times,* May 14, 1969,

18. Bradley outlined his ideas to me in great detail in interviews and has given me later reports on the results of his negotiations with the orchestra players by phone. I have also discussed the musical-resource concept with Arthur Kerr, Bradley G. Morison, and Roberta G. Jachim on various occasions.

19. The burgeoning career of Michael Tilson Thomas has been widely reported in the national press. My account of his career and thoughts has been based on press material supplied by the Buffalo and Boston orchestras, my interview with Thomas at Tanglewood on August 16, 1971, and Donal Henahan, *"He Reminds Me of Me at that Age," Says Leonard Bernstein,* in *New York Times Magazine,* October 24, 1971.

20. Henahan, *New York Times Magazine,* October 24, 1971.

21. Interview with Thomas at Tanglewood, August 16, 1971.

22. Henahan, *New York Times Magazine,* October 24, 1971.

23. *New York Council on the Arts Aid to Cultural Arts Funding 1970–71,* Associated Councils of the Arts, Special Report, March, 1971.

24. *Report on the Feasibility of an Endowment Fund for the Rochester Philharmonic Orchestra,* C. W. Shaver and Company, Inc., August 6, 1969.

Chapter XI—*Albuquerque Symphony Orchestra*

As in my investigations of other orchestras, my major sources of information have been the people actually involved in the operation of the Albuquerque Symphony, and I am deeply indebted to Mrs. Raymond H. Dietrich, manager of the orchestra, both for supplying a great deal of operating data and for arranging interviews with the following:

Yoshimi Takeda, conductor of the orchestra

Gordon W. Paul, president of the board

Mrs. Alec Grossetete, president of the Albuquerque Symphony Women's Association

Kurt Frederick, former conductor and on the faculty of the University of New Mexico

Kenneth Anderson, first trumpet and personnel manager, and Don Robertson, cellist and member of the orchestra committee

In addition, I have interviewed several others on musical life in Albuquerque:

William Martin, manager of Popejoy Hall at the university

Martha Buddecke, arts editor of the *Albuquerque Journal*

Dale Kempter, former cellist in the orchestra and supervisor of music in the Albuquerque public schools

Miss Josephine Cudney, secretary of the New Mexico Arts Commission

To all of these, and especially to Mrs. Dietrich for her information and help, I render most grateful acknowledgment.

1. 1970 U.S. Census. Other data concerning Albuquerque, its history and environment, are from local Chamber of Commerce and newspaper sources.

2. 1972 *World Almanac,* p. 96.

3. Historical data from the files of the Albuquerque Symphony Orchestra, from interview with Kurt Frederick, December 15, 1971, and from program book for January 26, 1972.

4. Interview with Kurt Frederick.

5. Interview with Kenneth Anderson, personnel manager, and with others, including Dale Kempter, on February 7, 1972.

6. Interviews with Yoshimi Takeda, December 15, 1971, and February 24, 1972.

7. Musicians' salary data from office files and interviews with Mrs. Dietrich and Kenneth Anderson, personnel manager.

8. *Albuquerque Journal* report of board meeting, January 15, 1972.

9. All financial data are from the files of the Albuquerque Symphony Orchestra; annual financial reports and monthly statements of financial status are distributed at board meetings and are available to the press.

10. Interview with Gordon W. Paul, December 15, 1971.

11. Data from symphony files and interview with Mrs. Alec Grossetete, February 24, 1972.

12. Interview with Gordon W. Paul, December 15, 1971.

13. *Albuquerque Journal*, January 30, 1972, has an account of legislative attitude toward the arts; other newspapers carried similar accounts during the 1972 legislative session in Santa Fe.

14. Jim Gilbert, *A Survey of the Arts in New Mexico; A Report on the Cultural and Arts Survey of New Mexico, conducted by the New Mexico Arts Commission.*

15. Compiled from the annual reports of the New Mexico Arts Commission, 1966 to 1971, checked with Josephine Cudney, secretary of the Commission, and with the *Directory of State Arts Council 1970–71*, compiled by Associated Councils of the Arts.

16. New Mexico Arts Commission, *Fourth Annual Report*, p. 8.

Chapter XII—*Cincinnati Symphony Orchestra*

Most of the research for this chapter was done in Cincinnati during a visit on January 16–19, 1972. General manager Albert K. Webster, whom I had known earlier in New York, arranged for me to attend a subscription concert and Young People's concert in the Music Hall, an Area Artist Series concert in Wilmington, and a program for schoolchildren in Fairborn. He also arranged interviews with the following in Cincinnati:

Edgar J. Mack, Jr., chairman of the board of trustees
Thomas J. Klinedinst, president
Lucien Wulsin, Jr., trustee
Frank T. Hamilton, chairman of the Cincinnati Institute of Fine Arts
Mrs. Fred T. Lazarus III, a trustee and member of the executive board of the American
    Symphony Orchestra League
Mrs. Maurice D. Marsh, president of the women's committee
Lloyd Haldeman, former general manager
Erich Kunzel, resident conductor
Mrs. Judith Arron, director of regional and educational programs
Mrs. William R. Stilz, director of public relations and sales promotion
Paul Elbert, controller
Eugene Frey, president of Local 1, AFM
Elinor Bell, music critic of the *Cincinnati Enquirer*

In addition, Webster arranged for me to interview Thomas Schippers in New York on January 24, 1972, and supplied me with copious material from the files. To all those interviewed, and especially to Albert K. Webster for his friendly cooperation, I offer sincere thanks and acknowledgment.

1. I attended a concert by a chamber orchestra from the Cincinnati Symphony in Wilmington on January 17, 1972, with Webster and Mrs. Arron; on this trip, and in other interviews with them, I received a full account of the Area Artist Series.

2. Historical information from the orchestra files and from Thomas materials cited in Chapter II.

3. Orchestra files and *Baker's Biographical Dictionary of Musicians.*

4. Kupferberg, *Those Fabulous Philadelphians*, p. 32.

5. Orchestra files and my own recollection of Reiner's reminiscences before his death in 1963.

6. Orchestra files, interview with Elinor Bell, and recollections of Arthur Judson in my interviews with him.

7. Interviews with Wulsin, Mack, Haldeman, and Schippers all produced essentially the same account of the Milan meeting.

8. Orchestra files and interview with Schippers provided information on his career.

9. Interview with Schippers.

10. Information on Kunzel and DeLeone from orchestra files; also interview with Kunzel.

11. Orchestra files; notations of estimate by author.

12. The following description of activities is from orchestra files.

13. Orchestra files and interview with Kunzel.
14. I personally attended this concert in the Music Hall on January 19, 1972.
15. Various interviews with Mrs. Arron.
16. Interview with Elbert.
17. From orchestra and Institute files, and from interviews with Mack, Hamilton, Webster, and others.
18. Interview with Hamilton.
19. Mack was one of these, in my interview with him.
20. Interviews with Mrs. Lazarus and Mrs. Marsh.
21. Interview with Webster.
22. Interviews with Frye and Webster, and subsequent telephone reports from Webster on the outcome of negotiations, which were actually in progress when I was in Cincinnati.
23. Interviews with Schippers and Kunzel.

Chapter XIII—*Symphony Economics*

Performing Arts—The Economic Dilemma, the 1966 Twentieth Century Fund study by William J. Baumol and William G. Bowen, remains a basic source in the field it covers, even though it is now no longer up to date and was compiled before such major developments as the Ford Foundation grants and increase in government funding. Nevertheless, its definition of the income gap, rebuttal of superficial talk of a "cultural explosion," and assembly of historical data make this book a landmark in the study of the performance arts. Similar treatment of the symphony orchestras alone would be highly desirable, but it would require expert staffing and financial support beyond my resources; I have therefore confined myself to updating some of their data with information available to me. I gratefully acknowledge the permission of the Twentieth Century Fund to use and adapt data and analyses in that book.

As the repository of annual statistical reports by orchestras, the American Symphony Orchestra League has vast quantities of information in its files, but these were supplied by orchestras on a confidential basis and thus are barred from direct study. For this study I devised a "blind" system of category averages that would protect the confidentiality of the material in the League files. Without these my discussion here would have been meaningless, and I am deeply indebted to Richard M. Wangerin, to the League officials, and especially to William C. Nelms, who actually prepared this information for me.

The June, 1972, issue of *Symphony News* included an eight-page supplement, *How to Resolve the Growing Financial Crisis of Our Symphony Orchestras,* by John Macomber and John T. Wooster, who were associated with McKinsey and Company. Basically an appeal for increased government funding substantiated by statistics from the American Symphony Orchestra League, it includes extremely important data on 28 Major orchestras for the crucial 1961–71 decade. With the help of Mr. Nelms, I assembled similar data, though by no means as complete, from the ASOL files for the Metropolitan orchestras. These have been reproduced, with additional computations by me, in Appendix G. Permission by the League to use these data is gratefully acknowledged.

Ralph Rizzolo, formerly in charge of research for the League and now on the staff of the National Endowment for the Arts, has been especially helpful in interpreting statistical data. The NEA report on *Economic Aspects of the Performing Arts* has also been an indispensable source. W. Granville Meader of the Business Committee for the Arts, Joseph Farrell of the National Research Center of the Arts, and Bradley G. Morison have also given me important information and suggested where I might find more. While this book was being written, the Ford Foundation began its comprehensive data bank on the arts; though no policy had been determined about its eventual use for studies such as this, its establishment came too late even to raise the question. However, in the future, such a resource, as well as that of the newly organized National Research Center of the Arts, should eventually provide students of the symphony orchestra with easier access to more accurate and comprehensive information than I had to work with.

Having outlined my general sources, I must also warn that many of them are of variable reliability; the orchestra world simply has never had funds or personnel to gather, analyze, and interpret its statistical data. However, it has made conscientious attempts in this respect, especially through the League, and there one finds far more and better information on orchestras than on other arts activities. Since most of the material used by Baumol and Bowen in their study came from the ASOL, it must be regarded with the same qualifications. I am, therefore, by no means satisfied with some of the information available: wherever I have such doubts, I have expressed them frankly, not as a criticism of conscientious and cooperative sources, but rather to make sure that the reader knows just how reliable these data are.

1. William J. Baumol and William G. Bowen, *Performing Arts—The Economic Dilemma* (hereafter Baumol and Bowen), pp. 161–72, present a comprehensive explanation of the basic economics of the income gap in the performance arts.

2. Baumol and Bowen, p. 169.

3. *Wage Scales and Conditions in the Symphony Orchestra*, ICSOM reports for 1963–64, 1964–65; *Senza Sordino*, February, 1967, April, 1968, January, 1969, and May, 1970; American Federation of Musicians, 1971 (hereafter ICSOM-AFM Reports).

4. John Macomber and John T. Wooster, *How to Resolve the Growing Finincial Crisis of Our Symphony Orchestra*, in *Symphony News*, June, 1972 (hereafter Macomber and Wooster). The percentages are my own based on figures given there. See Appendix G for the complete data.

5. Macomber and Wooster.

6. Baumol and Bowen, p. 172.

7. National Endowment for the Arts, *Economic Aspects of the Performing Arts, A Portrait in Figures*, May 1971 (hereafter *NEA, Economic Aspects*).

8. Actual 1970–71 figures are given by Macomber and Wooster; compare NEA estimates in Appendix F with the actual figures in Appendix G.

9. Broadway, "road," and motion-picture data from *Variety*, June 9, 1971; symphony, theater, opera, and dance from *NEA, Economic Aspects*.

10. Baumol and Bowen, p. 95.

11. Compare Appendices E and F.

12. The average data for the five categories were prepared, in accordance with my outline, by William C. Nelms directly from the 1970–71 reports supplied the ASOL by orchestras. Because of the confidential nature of these reports, it was impossible for me to see these sources.

13. *Symphony News*, Vol. XXIII, No. 1 (February, 1972), p. 27.

14. My computation from data in Appendix E.

15. I can only make "educated guesses," based on my own experience and off-the-record discussions with managers, as to many of the salary estimates suggested here.

16. Based on ICSOM-AFM Reports.

17. Macomber and Wooster.

18. Baumol and Bowen, especially pp. 161–80, 291–304.

19. Baumol and Bowen, p. 440.

20. Adapted from *Figure XII-1, The Income Gap: Basic Eleven Major Orchestras, Metropolitan Opera and Covent Garden, 1948–1964* (Baumol and Bowen, p. 299), with omission of Covent Garden and extended to 1970–71 from data supplied by the ASOL and from the Metropolitan Opera annual report for 1970–71.

21. Adapted from *Figure VIII-3, Expenditures Per Performance and the Wholesale Price Index, 1947–64* (Baumol and Bowen, p. 198) and *Figure X-1, Earned Income of Major Orchestras, Broadway, and All Live Performing Arts, 1929–1964* (Baumol and Bowen, p. 242). In my adaptation, which shows symphony orchestras only, I have adjusted the 1937 index base for the income chart to 1947 to conform with the expense graph and have extended the figures (dotted lines) to 1971 with data from the ASOL. Wholesale price index is from U.S. Department of Commerce, Bureau of the Census, *Statistical Abstract of the United States—1971*, p. 333.

22. Baumol and Bowen, p. 295, *Figure XII-3, Total Expenditure, Earned Income, and Income Gap as Percent of Expenditure, Average of Basic Eleven Orchestras, 1936–64*. Extension to 1970–71 is based on ASOL figures.

23. My own computation of percentages in Appendix G.

24. Baumol and Bowen, p. 295.

25. These and other projections here are based on computations shown in Appendix G.

26. My calculations of percentages from data in American Association of Fund-Raising Counsel, Inc., *Giving U.S.A.*, p. 15.

Chapter XIV—*Private Philanthropy and the Foundations*

There are considerable documentary materials on American philanthropy, and I have used three major sources: publications by the American Association of Fund-Raising Counsel, Inc., the Business Committee for the Arts, and the Foundation Center. Some of their data are based on information from the Internal Revenue Service, others on special surveys, and still others on a canvass of their membership. Unfortunately, when they work down from total national philanthropy to the relatively small areas of the performance arts and symphony orchestras, they rely much on conjecture and estimate. In evaluating these data, I am grateful for the help of W. Granville Meader, Director of Programs, Business Committee for the Arts, who also suggested other sources of information. Alvin H. Reiss, *Culture and Company*, published too recently for citation here, is an important account of the role of business in arts philanthropy.

For my discussion of the Ford Foundation, I make special acknowledgment to Marcia Thompson of the foundation staff, who has supplied me with the documents I needed and whose discussions of the symphony program helped me interpret them. In my own comments and evaluation of this important program, I am indebted to innumerable managers, conductors, and board members for their views and suggestions; not surprisingly, the Ford Foundation is a favored topic of conversation, pro and con, in the symphony world.

1. *Giving USA, A compilation of facts and trends on American philanthropy for the year 1970,* published by the American Association of Fund-Raising Counsel, Inc. (hereafter *Giving USA*). The figures there were largely based on information from the Internal Revenue Service.

2. *Giving USA*, pp. 48–51.

3. See National Endowment for the Arts, *Economic Aspects of the Performing Arts*, p. 7, for figures on which my percentages are based.

4. Gideon Chagy, ed., *Business in the Arts '70* (hereafter Chagy), p. 18, "A survey of corporate support of the visual and performing arts in the United States," conducted by the Business Committee for the Arts. The percentages here are based on responses from 260 corporations.

5. Chagy, p. 16.

6. Chagy, p. 32.

7. Chagy, p. 30.

8. *Giving USA*, p. 49.

9. Joseph C. Goulden, *The Money Givers*, a not always friendly but generally accurate and comprehensive discussion of foundations, draws heavily on various Congressional documents and hearings, most of them involving Representative Wright Patman of Texas. *Foundations, Private Giving, and Public Policy, Report and Recommendations of the Commission of Foundations and Private Philanthropy* (the so-called Peterson Commission), is a less polemical, but in many ways equally critical, study of the same subject. Since this book was written, the Twentieth Century Fund has published another important study of foundations, Waldemar A. Nielsen, *The Big Foundations.*

10. *The Foundation Directory, Edition 4*, p. viii.

11. *The Foundation Directory, Edition 4*, p. xvi.

12. The background and history of the Ford Foundation symphony program are covered in press releases (notably that of July 6, 1966, updating a previous announcement of October 22, 1965) and other bulletins issued by the foundation. I am also grateful to Edward d'Arms for giving me his recollections of his part in the early days of the program, in an interview at his home in Princeton, New Jersey, April 23, 1971.

13. Ford Foundation, *Activities in the Creative and Performing Arts, Support in the Musical Arts (1957–70)* (hereafter Ford Foundation, *Activities 1957–1970*).

14. The following description of the terms of the endowment trust and agreements between the foundation and orchestras is based on copies of the trust agreement with the Bank of New York, April 25, 1966, and of letters of agreement with the orchestras, June 24, 1966, which were supplied me by the foundation.

15. Compiled from trust agreement and press release July 6, 1966, and subsequently checked with foundation staff.

16. Interview, June 7, 1971, at his office in New York.

17. Information on orchestras failing to meet the matching requirement by June 30, 1971, was reported to me by Mrs. Thompson in a letter, December 29, 1972. See Appendix H for a full summary of orchestras involved in this program.
18. Ford Foundation, *Activities 1957–1970.*
19. Press release, April 26, 1971.
20. See Joseph C. Goulden, *The Money Givers,* and the Peterson Commission report cited in Note 9 above.
21. The ASOL's data service to managers and board presidents gave a running account of its efforts in 1970 and 1971 on this front.

Chapter XV—*The Government*

The problem of government subsidy has long concerned me: more than a decade ago, I undertook extensive research on it for a magazine article that never reached print, and many of the materials assembled then have provided considerable background. However, this present discussion centers on government aid as a *fait accompli* in the 1970s, and I have drawn on a wide variety of interviews and documentary sources, for it is difficult to discuss symphony matters with anyone without readily getting involved in questions of public funding of the arts.

In addition to the specific references cited in these notes, I am especially grateful to Donald L. Engle for many enlightening and stimulating discussions both of the mechanics of government aid and its broader implications. The staffs of both the National Endowment (Nancy Hanks, Douglas Richards, Dr. Walter Anderson, and Ralph Rizzolo) and the New York State Council on the Arts (Arthur J. Kerr, Bradley G. Morison, and Rudolph Nashan among others) have been most helpful in supplying information and in verifying many of the data I have used here. At the Associated Councils of the Arts, Suzanne Fogelson was extremely helpful in providing me with materials and in suggesting other sources of information. Amyas Ames was especially generous with his time and in supplying me with materials on the Partnership for the Arts. Isaac Stern took time during a busy concert tour to give me a brief account of his recollections of the early development of the National Council on the Arts and Humanities. Helen M. Thompson and Richard H. Wangerin of the American Symphony Orchestra League gave me much help, both in reviewing their past activities and in locating important documents in the League files.

More than in other areas of my research, I encountered some reluctance of symphony and arts leaders to express their views "on the record"; in such sensitive and still fluid relations as those now developing between orchestras and public agencies, I can appreciate this reluctance, though I have sought to verify information given in this manner from other sources wherever possible.

1. Howard Taubman, *The Symphony Orchestra Abroad,* summarizes the European scene (including Israel) rather cursorily, in a report commissioned in 1970 by the American Symphony Orchestra League. However, in limiting himself to thirteen orchestras in England, Holland, Germany, Austria, and Israel, he says little about the radio orchestras, the symphonic activities of important opera orchestras, or about other countries—notably Scandinavia, France, Italy, and Spain. Nevertheless, his general comments are perceptive and his specific descriptions of thirteen important orchestras contain information not available elsewhere.
2. William J. Baumol and William G. Bowen, *Performing Arts—The Economic Dilemma* (hereafter Baumol and Bowen), p. 371. See pp. 347–86 for their comprehensive discussion of government funding of the arts.
3. John H. Mueller, *The American Symphony Orchestra,* p. 176, makes brief mention of the Baltimore city subsidy as beginning in 1914 as support of a municipal band.
4. Baumol and Bowen, p. 348.
5. American Symphony Orchestra League, *Survey of Opinions of Governing Boards of Symphony Orchestras on the Role of the Federal Government in the Arts,* June 21, 1962 (hereafter ASOL Survey).
6. ASOL Survey, p. 15, includes the full statement.
7. Arthur J. Goldberg, *Arbitrator's Award, In the Matter of Arbitration between Metropolitan Opera Association and Local 802, American Federation of Musicians,* December 14, 1961 (hereafter Goldberg Arbitration), p. 47.
8. Goldberg Arbitration, pp. 50–54.
9. These and other fiscal data are from the various reports and press releases of the National Endowment for the Arts, subsequently verified by its staff.

10. Interview with Isaac Stern, April 7, 1972.
11. This and other grants during this period are listed in detail in *The First Five Years: Fiscal 1966 through Fiscal 1970,* issued by the Council and Endowment.
12. Interview with Isaac Stern, above.
13. McKinsey and Company, *The Need for Concerted Action, Memorandum to the Presidents of The Boston Symphony Orchestra, The Chicago Symphony Orchestra, The Cleveland Orchestra, The New York Philharmonic, The Philadelphia Orchestra,* May 8, 1969.
14. Information on Endowment procedures has been supplied in interviews with various officials and members of the advisory panel.
15. The following comments are based on a great deal of discussion that I have shared with a variety of symphony and Endowment personnel, much of it off the record and speculative; here I try to summarize its major points of argument.
16. Associated Councils of the Arts, *Directory of State Arts Councils 1970–71* (hereafter ACA Directory), p. 67.
17. ACA Directory, p. 3, together with data from the National Endowment for the Arts.
18. Survey conducted by Frances T. Poteet, executive director of the Missouri State Council on the Arts, to whom I acknowledge her permission to use this information. I am also grateful to Josephine Cudney of the New Mexico Arts Commission for bringing this survey to my attention. I have added data for Massachusetts and New York to Mrs. Poteet's survey in incorporating it in Appendix K.
19. During the summer and fall of 1971, I addressed questionnaires to all Major and Metropolitan orchestras on the ASOL list, including queries concerning government funds they might have received. The following figures were tabulated from the 46 replies received, somewhat less than half the orchestras originally queried.
20. For information on the history and operations of the New York State Council on the Arts I am indebted to interviews with Arthur J. Kerr of the Council staff, to Bradley G. Morison, and to others active in its work; I have also received considerable documentary information from the Council and from the Associated Councils of the Arts.
21. New York State Commission on Cultural Resources, *State Financial Assistance to Cultural Resources,* March, 1971, p. 20.
22. Ibid., p. 20.
23. Associated Councils of the Arts, *New York State Council on the Arts Aid to Cultural Institutions' Funding 1970–71,* March, 1971, for FY 1971 data; press release from NYSCA, April, 1972, for FY 1972.
24. My extracts from listing of funded organizations reported in the above.
25. Interview with Bradley G. Morison, January 12, 1972, in Minneapolis.
26. These impressions were gained in a number of off-the-record interviews in Buffalo and elsewhere in New York State.
27. Interview with Amyas Ames, May 6, 1971, in New York.
28. Letter from Senator Charles M. C. Mathias of Maryland, to presidents of Major and Metropolitan orchestras, March 1972.
29. Letter from Amyas Ames to me, March 23, 1972; I thank Mr. Ames for allowing me to quote his statement.
30. Observation based more on casual conversation with arts leaders across the nation than on any precise survey of sentiment or actual support.
31. Goldberg Arbitration, p. 49.

Chapter XVI—*The Audience*

Except where specific quantitative and qualitative data can be cited, especially from the comprehensive Baumol and Bowen Twentieth Century Fund report, the comments in this chapter are based on my own years of activity in the symphony field, many conversations with managers, trustees, and others interested in the audience problem, and my own reflection upon years of thinking and talking about it. In this, I owe a special but general debt to Bradley G. Morison, Joseph Farrell of the National Research Center for the Arts, and to Donald L. Engle. Specific citations below are mostly to Baumol and Bowen's study, to which I owe a debt for general understanding of the economics of the performance arts far greater than page references can indicate.

1. My estimate based on extrapolation of ASOL averages for Major and Metropolitan orches-

tras listed in Appendix E, totaling nearly 18 million, plus another 1 million for other types of orchestras.

2. William J. Baumol and William G. Bowen, *Performing Arts—The Economic Dilemma;* most of the following data are from Chapter IV, pp. 71–99.

3. Baumol and Bowen, pp. 67 and 95, for performance arts not in parentheses. I have made estimates for other arts: the "road" from *Variety* data cited in Chapter XIII, concert recitals from rough estimates by national artist managements. To these I have applied comparable attendance ratios given by Baumol and Bowen.

4. Baumol and Bowen, p. 96.

5. My own estimate based on questionnaires prepared by me and returned by 70 out of 100 Major and Metropolitan orchestras.

6. Baumol and Bowen, p. 60.

7. Baumol and Bowen, p. 62. Table III-K in the appendix to their book, pp. 439–40, gives considerable data on orchestra operations from 1936 to 1964.

8. Baumol and Bowen, pp. 75–84.

9. As quoted by Martin Mayer, *Managing Orchestras Is a Fine Art, Too,* in *Fortune,* September 1, 1968.

10. I am indebted to Lanham Deal, general manager of the Seattle Symphony Orchestra, for making several students' reports available for my study; for my purposes here, the tabulation of results in these reports was most valuable.

Chapter XVII—*Repertory*

This chapter would have been impossible without the cooperation of Kate Hevner Mueller and Oliver Daniel. Mrs. Mueller welcomed me to her home in Bloomington, showed me the extraordinary files that she and her husband have assembled in the course of three decades, and made Xerox copies of every document I requested. Though I have drawn my own conclusions from these data, she has been kind enough to review my use of them. Her generosity with these materials, which she now plans to publish herself, is deeply appreciated. Mr. Daniel, in the midst of moving his office files, went to great trouble to assemble the BMI Surveys for me to study when I was unable to locate a complete set elsewhere, and I sincerely appreciate his interest and assistance. Because the source of data is generally indicated in the text, specific citations are necessary only in a few cases.

1. *The Symphony: Is It Alive? or Just Embalmed?,* symposium of Paul Hume, Elliott Carter, Leon Kirchner, and Lukas Foss; *New York Times,* September 22, 1968, Section II, p. 25.

2. Leonard Bernstein, *The Infinite Variety of Music,* p. 139; this section is a reprint of an article originally published in the *New York Times,* October 24, 1965, entitled *Bernstein: What I Thought.* This is the source of some confusing opinions attributed to Bernstein on the demise of the symphony orchestra and should be read in its entirety by those seeking to cite him as an authority on this question.

3. As this book goes to press, the Mueller survey is about to be published by Indiana University Press as *Twenty-seven Major Symphony Orchestras: A History and Analysis of Their Repertoires, Seasons 1842–43 through 1969–70.* However, since I worked from loose unnumbered Xerox copies of working papers, graciously supplied me by Mrs. Mueller, I cannot give specific citations to this source.

4. Broadcast Music, Inc., in cooperation with the American Symphony Orchestra League, *Orchestral Program Surveys, 1959–60 to 1969–70.* The surveys for 1959–60, 1962–63, and 1964–65 were issued in mimeograph form; that for 1961–62 was published in the ASOL *Newsletter,* December, 1962; the remaining surveys were printed as bound pamphlets. A full file of back issues was loaned to me by Oliver Daniel for my study.

5. *BMI Orchestral Program Survey, 1969–70.*

6. *BMI Orchestral Program Survey, 1969–70.*

7. Leonard Bernstein, *The Infinite Variety of Music,* p. 140. See Note 2 above.

8. Schuller interview, August 16, 1971, at Tanglewood.

9. I personally made the suggestion as a query during a symposium on programming at this conference, and received the same reply from both representatives.

10. See John Ardoin, *The Performing Arts Are in Hot Water,* in *Musical America,* March, 1972, p. 23.

11. *The Symphony: Is It Alive or Just Embalmed?* See Note 1 above.

12. *The Symphony: Is It Alive or Just Embalmed?*

Chapter XVIII—*Education and the Musical Experience*

Though I have relied upon some documentary material in this chapter, its thrust and argument would never have come from my symphony experience alone. My association with the Juilliard School from 1961 to 1969 gave me invaluable insights into intensive practical musical training that required a rethinking of my symphonic background. Most important of all, my work on the Lincoln Center Student Program—as much from directing the Juilliard artists' participation as from membership in the Lincoln Center Council on Educational Programs—has been of crucial importance. No less so has been my personal association with Mark Schubart, a unique arts administrator, instigator of so much of the Lincoln Center Student Program, and author of *The Hunting of the Squiggle*. That report said little about our joint experience that I did not already know, but I cannot resist extensive quotation of its lucid and provocative prose as a far better statement of these ideas than my own could be. Though not specifically cited here, I am also indebted to a number of conductors, administrators, teachers, and musicians for the stimulation of their ideas in our many discussions of the education question, among them June Dunbar at Juilliard and Lincoln Center; Gerry J. Watson, Warren H. Yost, Mrs. Edgar M. Leventritt, Mrs. T. Roland Berner, and Mrs. John W. Straus of Young Audiences; Stephen Sell of the St. Paul Philharmonic; Mrs. Judith Arron of the Cincinnati Symphony; conductors Maurice Abravanel and Milton Katims; and many Juilliard students and alumni with whom I worked in the Lincoln Center Student Program.

1. Herbert Kupferberg, *Those Fabulous Philadelphians*, p. 91.
2. Thomas H. Hill and Helen M. Thompson, *The Organization, Administration and Presentation of Symphony Orchestra Youth Concert Activities for Music Educational Purposes in Selected Cities* (hereafter Hill and Thompson), p. 10. Although this study covered only twenty cities, it contains copious information on how these programs are administered and financed. Published by the U.S. Office of Education, it exists in two forms: a full account of all data for each city, and a shorter summary.
3. Hill and Thompson, p. 13.
4. Information on Young Audiences, Inc., was supplied by Gerry J. Martin, national executive director, and from data in their files.
5. Hill and Thompson, p. 22.
6. Hill and Thompson, p. 37.
7. My own extraction of data from National Endowment for the Arts press releases, August 25 and November 23, 1970, announcing grants for 1970–71 to symphony orchestras, together with the purposes of these grants.
8. Hill and Thompson, p. 13.
9. Hill and Thompson, p. 16.
10. Hill and Thompson, p. 59.
11. These and other data reported here are from interviews with Young Audiences personnel and from reports and publications supplied me from their files; I am especially grateful to Mrs. Berner, Mrs. Straus, Mr. Martin, and Mr. Yost for their generous time and interest.
12. Mr. Yost, the national music coordinator of Young Audiences, gave me a copy of his extremely interesting proposal, *Young Audiences Research-Development Project*, which outlines these ideas in some detail.
13. Though the following account of the Lincoln Center Student Program is based on my participation in it from 1961 to 1969, I have checked my own recollection with the Lincoln Center staff and with Mark Schubart, *Performing Arts Institutions and Young People— Lincoln Center Study: "The Hunting of the Squiggle."*
14. Schubart, p. 17.
15. The Center for Field Research and School Services, School of Education, New York University, *Lincoln Center High School Program, Lincoln Center Elementary Program*, August, 1971.
16. Schubart, pp. 15–16.
17. Schubart, pp. 27–28, develops these in greater detail.
18. Schubart, pp. 34–36.
19. Schubart, pp. 39–41, on programs in St. Louis; New York City; Mineola, New York; Rhode Island; Columbus, Ohio; Eugene, Oregon; Glendale, California; Philadelphia; Troy, Ala-

bama; and Minneapolis. See also pages 61–62 for an account of a school-originated program at Ballston Spa, New York.

20. Schubart, pp. 64–87, describes the need and specific proposals for such an institution.
21. Schubart, p. 68.
22. Schubart, p. 77.
23. Sir Herbert Read, *Art and Society* (hereafter Read), pp. 82–95.
24. See, for instance, Ernst Kris, *Psychoanalytic Explorations in Art;* Lawrence J. Hatterer, *The Artist in Society;* and William Phillips, ed., *Art and Psychoanalysis.*
25. Read, pp. 96–111.
26. The Juilliard Repertory Library, Cincinnati, Canyon Press, Inc.
27. Sir Herbert Read, *Art and Society,* in UNESCO, *The Arts and Man,* pp. 27–46. Despite the identity of titles, this essay is not to be confused with the book cited above in Note 23, though both cover some of the same material.

Chapter XIX—*Toward a Responsible Institution*

For obvious reasons, this chapter requires little detailed citation of sources. In the course of these personal conclusions, I have mentioned information given earlier in this book, for which I have given sources and authority in the proper place; only when new material is offered has it been necessary to substantiate it with these notes.

1. This report, known unofficially as the "Kansas City Study," received wide dissemination in distorted and fragmentary summaries carried by the national press services. Of all sources from whom I have sought information for this book, the publishers of this report were the only ones to fail even to acknowledge my request; I therefore obtained a copy on loan elsewhere.
2. Rosenbaum's misgivings about the state of the symphony orchestra, stemming from his long experience as a trustee of the Philadelphia Orchestra Association and the Music Performance Trust Fund, have been widely cited in symphonic circles. In my interview with him in Philadelphia on November 14, 1970, he reviewed these for me, with greater emphasis on his "unless" qualification than is usually attributed to him.
3. Harry Ellis Dickson, *Gentlemen, More Dolce, Please!*, p. 45.
4. Leonard Bernstein, *The Infinite Variety of Music, An Open Letter,* pp. 9–14; and *A Sabbatical Report,* pp. 137–46, a reprint of an article in the *New York Times,* October 25, 1965.
5. A paraphrase, condensed and with libelous comments deleted, of fervent expostulation by a violin player in a large orchestra. I have heard similar statements from players in other orchestras, large and small.
6. See Howard Taubman, *The Symphony Orchestra Abroad,* p. 50.
7. I am indebted to Lanham Deal, general manager of the Seattle Symphony Orchestra, for providing me with copies of the 1971–72 trade agreement and for his most enlightening explanation and reports on progress.
8. *New York Times,* February 24, 1971, *Musicians' Stress Likened to Pilots'.*
9. My questionnaire, distributed in 1971, covered a wide variety of requests for information not readily available. Over half of the Major and Metropolitan orchestras responded, though by no means all of them answered all my questions. More than 40 orchestras supplied information on board membership.
10. Sir Herbert Read, *Art and Society,* an essay in UNESCO, *The Arts and Man,* p. 41.

Bibliography

In addition to listing all published sources cited in the text and notes, this bibliography includes other publications relating to symphony orchestras and the music scene in general. It does not include such unpublished materials as publicity releases, financial statements, letters, program books, and other matter issued by orchestras internally or to the public.

American Association of Fund-Raising Counsel, *Giving USA, a Compilation of Facts and Trends on American Philanthropy for the Year 1970*, New York, 1971.
American Federation of Musicians, *Phonograph Labor Agreement, April 1969*, New York, 1969.
———,*Wage Scales and Conditions in the Symphony Orchestras, 1970–71 Season*, New York, 1971.
———, *Wage Scales and Conditions in the Symphony Orchestras, 1971–72 Season*, New York, 1972.
American Symphony Orchestra League, *Legal Documents of Symphony Orchestras*, Charleston, West Virginia, 1958.
———, *Survey of Opinions of Governing Boards of Symphony Orchestras on the Role of the Federal Government in the Arts*, Charleston, West Virginia, 1962.
———, *Symphony News Is Good News, A Publicity Handbook for Symphony Orchestras and Symphony Women's Associations*, Vienna, Virginia, 1971.
Other ASOL publications are listed according to author; see Appendix N.
Ardoin, John, *The Performing Arts Are in Hot Water*, in *Musical America*, March, 1972.
Arian, Edward, *Bach, Beethoven, and Bureaucracy*, University, Alabama, 1971.
Asbell, Bernard, *Claudia Cassidy, the Queen of Culture and Her Reign of Terror*, in *Chicago Magazine*, June, 1956.
Associated Councils of the Arts, *Directory of Community Arts Councils*, New York, 1972.
———, *Directory of National Arts Organizations*, New York, 1972.
———, *Directory of State Arts Councils, 1970–71*, New York, 1971.
———, *New York State Council on the Arts Aid to Cultural Institutions' Funding 1970–71*, New York, 1971.
———, *State Arts Councils*, New York, 1972.
———, *Washington and the Arts*, New York, 1971.
Barzun, Jacques, *Pleasures of Music*, New York, 1951.
———, *Music in American Life*, Bloomington, Indiana, 1962.
Baumol, William J., and Bowen, William G., *Performing Arts—The Economic Dilemma*, New York, 1966.
Bekker, Paul, *The Orchestra*, New York, 1963.
Beranek, Leo, *Music Acoustics, and Architecture*, New York, 1962.
Berlioz, Hector, *Evenings with the Orchestra*, translated and edited by Jacques Barzun, New York, 1956.
———, *Memoirs*, translated and edited by David Cairns, New York, 1969.
Bernstein, Leonard, *The Infinite Variety of Music*, New York, 1970.
Blume, Friedrich, *Classic and Romantic Music*, New York, 1970.
Broadcast Music Incorporated (in cooperation with the American Symphony Orchestra League), *Orchestral Program Surveys, 1959–70*, New York, 1960–71.
Buddecke, Martha, *Legislative Attitude toward the Arts*, in *Albuquerque Journal*, January 30, 1972.
———, News report of Albuquerque Symphony Orchestra Board of Directors' Meeting, in *Albuquerque Journal*, January 16, 1972.
Carpenter, Paul S., *Music, an Art and a Business*, Norman, Oklahoma, 1950.
Carse, Adam, *The Orchestra from Beethoven to Berlioz*, New York, 1949.
———, *The Orchestra in the XVIIIth Century*, New York, 1940.
Chagy, Gideon, ed., *Business in the Arts '70*, New York, 1970.
———, *The State of the Arts and Corporate Support*, New York, 1971.
Colin, Ralph F., *Arthur Judson at 90: Sparked CBS Opposition to Sarnoff "Red" and "Blue,"* in *Variety*, January 9, 1971.
Commission on Foundations and Private Philanthropy, *Foundations, Private Giving, and Public Policy*, Chicago, 1970.
Copland, Aaron, *Music and Imagination*, Cambridge, Mass. 1952.
———, *What to Listen for in Music*, New York, 1939.
Damrosch, Walter, *My Musical Life*, New York, 1923.
Da Ponte, Lorenzo, *Memoirs*, New York, 1929.
Dickson, Harry Ellis, *Gentlemen, More Dolce, Please!*, Boston, 1969.
Dorian, Frederick, *Commitment to Culture*, Pittsburgh, 1964.
Dwight, John Sullivan, *Dwight's Journal of Music*, Boston, 1852–81.
Edwards, Allen, *Flawed Words and Stubborn Sounds, a Conversation with Elliott Carter*, New York, 1971.
Erskine, John, *The Philharmonic Symphony Society of New York, First Hundred Years*, New York, 1943.

Fay, Amy, *Music Study in Germany,* New York, 1965.

Finck, Henry, *My Adventures in the Golden Age of Music,* New York, 1926.

Flanagan, Hallie, *Arena,* New York, 1940.

Ford Foundation, *Activities in the Creative and Performing Arts, Support in the Musical Arts (1957–70),* New York, 1971.

————, *Annual Reports,* New York.

Foundation (Library) Center, *Annual Reports,* New York.

————, *The Foundation Directory, Edition 4,* New York, 1971.

Gaisberg, W. F., *The Music Goes Round,* New York, 1942.

Gerson, Robert A., *Music in Philadelphia,* Philadelphia, 1940.

Gilbert, Jim, *A Survey of the Arts in New Mexico,* Santa Fe, 1966.

Goldberg, Arthur J., *Arbitrator's Award, in the Matter of Arbitration between Metropolitan Opera Association and Local 802, AFM,* New York, 1961.

Goldin, Milton, *The Music Merchants,* New York, 1969.

Gottschalk, Louis Moreau, *Notes of an American Pianist,* New York, 1964.

Goulden, Joseph C., *The Money Givers,* New York, 1971.

Grant, Margaret S., and Hettinger, Herman S., *America's Symphony Orchestras,* New York, 1940.

Green, Donle L., and Randell L., *Meet the Mormons,* Salt Lake City, 1967.

Harrison, Conrad B., *The Utah Symphony Story* (Utah Symphony Orchestra program books), Salt Lake City, 1960–61.

Hatterer, Lawrence J., *The Artist in Society,* New York, 1965.

Heckscher, August, *The Arts and National Government, Report to the President,* Washington, 1963.

Henahan, Donal, *Four Orchestras Play Merger Tune,* in *New York Times,* May 14, 1969.

————, *"He Reminds Me of Me at That Age," Says Leonard Bernstein,* in *New York Times Magazine,* October 24, 1971.

————, *Which Runs an Orchestra: the Conductor? the Men? the Dollar?* (Interview with Lukas Foss), *New York Times,* May 18, 1969.

Hill, Thomas H., and Thompson, Helen M., *The Organization, Administration, and Presentation of Symphony Orchestra Youth Concert Activities for Music Educational Purposes in Selected Cities,* Washington, 1968.

Hodeir, André, *Since Debussy: A View of Contemporary Music,* New York, 1961.

Houseman, John, *Runthrough,* New York, 1972.

Howard, John Tasker, and Bellows, George Kent, *A Short History of Music in America,* New York, 1967.

Howe, Mark A. DeWolfe, *The Boston Symphony Orchestra, 1881–1931,* Boston and New York, 1931.

Hume, Paul; Carter, Elliott; Kirchner, Leon; and Foss, Lukas, *The Symphony: Is It Alive? or Just Embalmed?* in *New York Times,* September 22, 1968.

Huneker, James Gibbons, *The Philharmonic Society of New York, A Retrospect,* New York, 1917.

Johnson, H. Earle, *The Germania Musical Society,* in *Musical Quarterly,* Vol. 39.

————, *Musical Interludes in Boston,* New York, 1943.

————, *Symphony Hall, Boston;* Boston, 1950.

Judson, Arthur, *How CBS Got Its Start,* in *American Heritage,* August, 1955.

Julliard Repertory Library, Cincinnati, 1970.

Kniebusch, Carol, *Analysis of Major Orchestra Master Contracts,* Vienna, Virginia, 1972.

————, *Analysis of Metropolitan Orchestra Contracts,* Vienna, Virginia, 1972.

Kolodin, Irving, *The Metropolitan Opera, 1883–1966,* New York, 1967.

Krehbiel, Henry Edward, *Philharmonic Society of New York,* New York, 1892.

Krenek, Ernst, *Music Here and Now,* New York, 1939.

Kris, Ernst, *Psychoanalytic Explorations in Art,* New York, 1964.

Kupferberg, Herbert, *Those Fabulous Philadelphians,* New York, 1969.

Lacy, Dan, *The © Quagmire,* in *Saturday Review,* November 27, 1971.

Langer, Susanne K., *Philosophy in a New Key,* Cambridge, Mass., 1942.

Leichtentritt, Hugo, *Serge Koussevitzky, the Boston Symphony, and the New American Music,* Cambridge, Mass., 1940.

Leiter, Robert D., *The Musicians and Petrillo,* New York, 1953.

Lourie, A., *S. A. Koussevitzky and His Epoch,* New York, 1931.

Lowens, Irving, *L'Affaire Muck,* in *Musicology,* Vol. I, No. 3 (1947).

Majeda, Stanley S., *All the Arts for Every Child,* New York (JDR 3rd Fund, Inc.), 1973.

Mapleson, J. H., *The Mapleson Memoirs,* edited by Harold Rosenthal, New York, 1966.

Maratzek, Max, *Revelations of an Opera Manager in 19th Century America* (contains *Crochets and Quavers,* 1855, and *Sharps and Flats,* 1890), New York, 1968.

Mason, William, *Memories of a Musical Life,* New York, 1901.

Mayer, Martin, *Bricks, Mortar, and the Performing Arts, Background Paper of Report of the Twentieth Century Fund Task Force on Performing Arts Centers,* New York, 1970.

————, *Managing Orchestras Is a Fine Art, Too,* in *Fortune,* September, 1969.

McCombs, R. L. F., *The Philadelphia Orchestra*, Philadelphia, 1947.

McKinsey and Company, *The Need for Concerted Action, Memorandum to the Presidents of the Boston Symphony Orchestra, the Chicago Symphony Orchestra, the Cleveland Orchestra, the New York Philharmonic, the Philadelphia Orchestra*, Cleveland, 1969.

Metropolitan Opera Association, *Annual Reports 1969–72*, New York, 1970–73.

Midwest Research Institute, *An Evaluation of the Performing Arts: I, The Symphony*, Kansas City, 1969.

Mitchell, Arnold, *Marketing the Arts*, Menlo Park, 1962.

——, and Anderson, Marylou, *The Arts and Business*, Menlo Park, 1962.

Mitchell, Donald, *The Language of Modern Music*, London, 1963.

Monteux, Doris, *It's All in the Music*, New York, 1965.

Morison, Bradley G., and Fliehr, Kay, *In Search of an Audience*, New York, 1968.

Moskow, Michael H., *Labor Relations in the Performing Arts, a Preliminary Survey*, New York, 1969.

Mueller, John H., *The American Symphony Orchestra: A Social History of Musical Taste*, Bloomington, Indiana, 1951.

Mueller, Kate Hevner, *Twenty-seven Major Symphony Orchestras: A History and Analysis of Their Repertoires, Seasons 1842–43 through 1969–70*, Bloomington, Indiana, 1973.

Music Performance Trust Funds, *44th Semi-Annual Report, July 1–December 31, 1970*, New York, 1971.

National Education Association (Association for Supervision and Curriculum Development), *Cable TV—Protecting Its Future in Education*, Washington, 1971.

National Endowment for the Arts, *Annual Report, 1969*, Washington, 1970.

——, *Economic Aspects of the Performing Arts, A Portrait in Figures*, Washington, 1971.

——, *The First Five Years: Fiscal 1966 through Fiscal 1970*, Washington, 1970.

——, *New Dimensions for the Arts 1971–72*, Washington, 1973.

Nelms, William C., *A Guide to Accounting Procedures and Record Keeping for Community Symphony Orchestras*, Vienna, Virginia, 1965.

New Mexico Arts Commission, *Annual Reports*, Santa Fe, 1966–71.

New York State Commission on Cultural Resources, *State Financial Assistance to Cultural Resources*, New York, 1971.

New York University Center for Field Research and School Services, *Lincoln Center High School Program, Lincoln Center Elementary Program*, New York, 1971.

Newsweek Magazine: Row over Rodzinski, February 17, 1947.

Nielsen, Waldemar A., *The Big Foundations*, New York, 1972.

Odell, William C., *Annals of the New York Stage*, New York, 1927–45.

Orcutt, William Dana, *Wallace Clement Sabine, a Study in Achievement*, Boston, n.d.

Otis, Philo Adams, *The Chicago Symphony Orchestra—Its Organization, Growth, and Development, 1891–1924*, Evanston, 1925.

Perry, Bliss, *Life and Letters of Henry Lee Higginson*, Boston, 1921.

Phillips, William, ed., *Art and Psychoanalysis, Studies in the Application of Psychoanalytic Theory to the Creative Process*, Cleveland and New York, 1957.

Pleasants, Henry, *The Agony of Modern Music*, New York, 1955.

Randall, Willard, *The Oboe Jungle*, in *Philadelphia Magazine*, November, 1971.

Read, Herbert, *Art and Society*, New York, 1945.

Reeves, C. Thomas, ed., *Foundations under Fire*, Ithaca, 1971.

Reiss, Alvin H., *Culture and Company*, New York, 1972.

Rice, Edwin T., *Thomas and Central Park Garden*, in *Musical Quarterly*, April, 1940.

Ritter, Frederic Louis, *Music in America*, New York, 1883.

Robbins, (Lord) Lionel C. R., *Art and the State*, New York, 1963.

Rockefeller Panel Report, *The Performing Arts, Problems and Prospects*, New York, 1965.

Russell, Charles Edward, *The American Orchestra and Theodore Thomas*, Garden City and New York, 1927.

Salzman, Eric, *Twentieth-Century Music: An Introduction*, Englewood Cliffs, New Jersey, 1967.

Sargeant, Winthrop, *Geniuses, Goddesses, and People*, New York, 1949.

Schlesinger, Janet, *Challenge to the Urban Orchestra: The Case of the Pittsburgh Symphony*, Pittsburgh, 1971.

Schnabel, Artur, *Music and the Line of Most Resistance*, Princeton, 1942.

Schonberg, Harold C., *The Great Conductors*, New York, 1967.

——, *Troy Music Hall*, in *New York Times*, May 9, 1971.

Schubart, Mark, *Performing Arts Institutions and Young People—Lincoln Center's Study: "The Hunting of the Squiggle,"* New York, 1972. (Originally issued by Lincoln Center for the Performing Arts as *The Hunting of the Squiggle: A Study of a Performing Arts Institution and Young People*, New York, 1972.)

Schwann Catalog, *Artist Issue 1970*, Boston, 1970.

Senza Sordino, published four or five times a year, from 1963, by the International Conference of Symphony and Opera Musicians.

Senza Sordino: Wage Scales and Conditions in the Symphony Orchestras 1963–70 (reported annually in tabular form in various issues).

Sessions, Roger, *The Musical Experience,* Princeton, 1950.
————, *Questions about Music,* New York, 1971.
Shaver, C. W., and Company, *Report on the Feasibility of an Endowment Fund for the Rochester Philharmonic Orchestra,* New York, 1969.
Shemel, Sidney, and Krasilovsky, M. William, *This Business of Music,* New York, 1971.
Slonimsky, Nicolas, *Baker's Biographical Dictionary of Music,* 5th ed. with 1965 and 1971 Supplements, New York, 1958, 1965, 1971.
————, *Music Since 1900,* 4th ed., New York, 1971.
Smith, Cecil, *Worlds of Music,* Philadelphia and New York, 1952.
Smith, Moses, *Koussevitzky,* New York, 1947.
Sonneck, E. G., *Early Concert Life in America,* Leipzig, 1907.
Stoddard, Hope, *Subsidy Makes Sense,* Newark, n.d.
————, *Symphony Conductors in the U.S.A.,* New York, 1957.
Storr, Anthony, *The Dynamics of Creation,* New York, 1972.
Swoboda, Henry, ed., *The American Symphony Orchestra,* New York, 1967.
Szigeti, Joseph, *With Strings Attached,* New York, 1947.
Taper, Bernard, *The Arts in Boston,* Cambridge, Mass., 1970.
Taubman, Howard, *The Symphony Orchestra Abroad,* Vienna, Virginia, 1970.
Tharp, Louise Hall, *Mrs. Jack,* Boston, 1965.
Thomas, Rose Fay, *Memoirs of Theodore Thomas,* New York, 1911.
Thomas, Theodore, *A Musical Autobiography* (2 volumes), edited by George P. Upton, Chicago, 1905. (First volume only reissued New York, 1964.)
Thompson, Helen M., *The Community Symphony Orchestra, How to Organize and Develop It,* Charleston, West Virginia, 1952.
————, *Economic Conditions of Symphony Orchestras and Their Musicians,* Charleston, West Virginia, 1961.
————, *Governing Boards of Symphony Orchestras,* Charleston, West Virginia, 1958.
————, *Handbook for Symphony Orchestra Women's Associations,* Vienna, Virginia, 1971.
————, *Survey of Opinions of Governing Boards of Symphony Orchestras on the Role of the Federal Government in the Arts,* Vienna, Virginia, 1962.
————, *Symphony Orchestra Women's Associations,* Vienna, Virginia, 1963.
————, and White, Leslie C., *Survey of Arts Councils,* Charleston, West Virginia, 1959.
Thomson, Virgil, *The Musical Scene,* New York, 1945.
————, *The State of Music,* New York, 1962.
————, *Virgil Thomson,* New York, 1966.
Time Magazine: Master Builder, February 17, 1947.
Toffler, Alvin, *The Culture Consumers,* New York, 1964.
UNESCO, *The Arts and Man,* Englewood Cliffs, New Jersey, 1969.
U.S. Department of Commerce, Bureau of the Census, *Statistical Abstract of the United States, 1971,* Washington, 1971.
Wainwright, June M., ed., *Community Projects Involving Symphony Women's Associations, 1970–71 Season,* Vienna, Virginia, 1971.
————, *Fund-Raising Projects of Women's Associations, 1970–71 Season,* Vienna, Virginia, 1971.
Wister, Frances Anne, *Twenty-Five Years of the Philadelphia Orchestra, 1900–1925,* Philadelphia, 1925.
Woolridge, David, *Conductor's World,* London, 1970.
Yates, Peter, *Twentieth-Century Music,* New York, 1967.

Index